D0959726

Croatia

Jeanne Oliver

Contents

Hrvatsko Zagorje p71

Zagreb p48

Slavonia p81

Istra p127

Kvarner Region p91

Zadar Region p154

Šibenik-Knin Region p178

Central Dalmatia p188

Southern Dalmatia p227

Destination Croatia

Don't tell anyone, but Croatia is Europe's hottest new destination. After slumbering in the shadows of former Yugoslavia for decades, the country burst onto the map in 1991, billing itself as 'the Mediterranean as it used to be'.

Along its 1778km coastline, a glistening sea winds around rocky coves, lapping at pine-fringed beaches. Istrian ports bustle with fishermen while children dive into the sparkling water. Dalmatian cities throb with nightlife amid ancient Roman ruins. Then there's the magical city of Dubrovnik, adorned with Renaissance carving and marble-paved streets.

Croatia's 1185 islands make it a yachter's paradise. There's one for every taste – from stark, empty outposts baking in the Adriatic sun, to lushly wooded Shangri-las, replete with mountains, lakes, vineyards and olive trees.

The interior landscape is no less beguiling. Soak in a thermal spa in the rolling hills of the north. Hike through pristine forests watered by mountain streams in the west. Let the waterfalls of Plitvice moisten your face.

Yet Croatia is more than just pretty scenery. The country that endured Roman, Venetian, Italian and Austro-Hungarian rule has a complex and unique cultural identity. You'll find a strong central European flavour in the baroque architecture of Zagreb, and Italian devotion to the good life percolates up from the coast, permeating Croatian food and style. During holidays and festivals the country's Slavic soul emerges, as colourfully costumed dancers whirl about to traditional folk melodies.

It all adds up to a relaxed, easy-going country that offers an unparalleled wealth of holiday opportunities. But, please, try to keep it a secret.

MARTIN MOOS

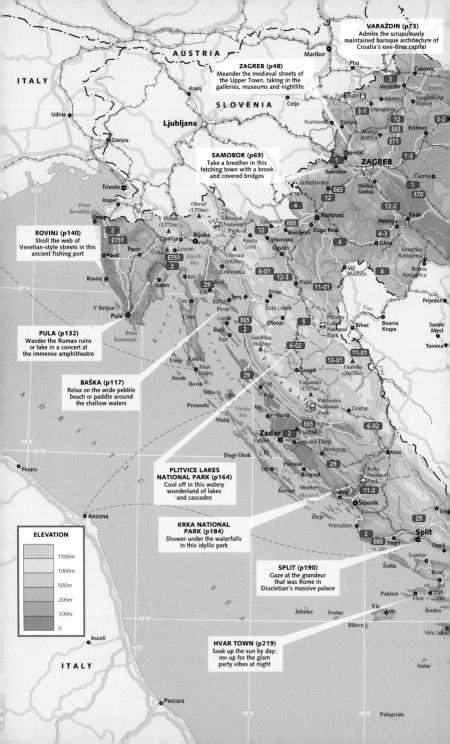

VARAŽDIN (p73)
Admire the scrupulously maintained baroque architecture of Croatia's one-time capital

ZAGREB (p48)
Meander the medieval streets of the Upper Town, taking in the galleries, museums and nightlife

SAMOBOR (p69)
Take a breather in this fetching town with a brook and covered bridges

ROVINJ (p140)
Stroll the web of Venetian-style streets in this ancient fishing port

PULA (p132)
Wander the Roman ruins or take in a concert at the immense amphitheatre

BAŠKA (p117)
Relax on the wide pebble beach or paddle around the shallow waters

PLITVICE LAKES NATIONAL PARK (p164)
Cool off in this watery wonderland of lakes and cascades

KRKA NATIONAL PARK (p184)
Shower under the waterfalls in this idyllic park

SPLIT (p190)
Gaze at the grandeur that was Rome in Diocletian's massive palace

HVAR TOWN (p219)
Soak up the sun by day; rev up for the glam party vibes at night

ELEVATION

1500m
1000m
500m
200m
100m
0

BRELA (p207)
Promenade amid the pines lining a string of pearly beaches

KORČULA TOWN (p247)
Experience a moreška sword dance in this fortified peninsula town, adorned with fine stone carving

MLJET (p242)
Bike, boat, hike or dream the day away on the isle that enchanted Odysseus

DUBROVNIK (p229)
Explore the jewel of the Adriatic with its Renaissance architecture, massive walls and sparkling sea

From the scrupulously maintained baroque architecture of Croatia's one-time capital, **Varaždin** (p73) to the grandeur that was Rome in **Diocletian's palace** (p192) in Split, Croatia offers an astounding array of natural and historic wonders. Take a breather in the fetching town of **Samobor** (p69) with a brook and covered bridges, or paddle around the shallow waters of **Baška** (p117). Bike, boat, hike or dream the day away on **Mljet** (p242). Get the adrenalin pumping at a **moreška sword dance** (p252) in Korčula Town or meander the medieval streets of **Zagreb's Upper Town** (p53), taking in the galleries, museums and nightlife.

DAMIEN SIMONIS

Hire a fishing boat at Rovinj,
Istria (p140)

Promenade on the Opatija waterfront (p100)

MARTIN MOOS

Wander through a medieval hilltop town, Motovun (p152)

WAYNE WALTON

MARTIN MOOS

Take in the awe-inspiring sights and sounds of waterfalls, Plitvice Lakes National Park (p164)

Revisit history at the Roman Amphitheatre, Pula (p133)

WAYNE WALTON

MARTIN MOOS

Leap off one of the Skradinski Buk waterfalls, Krka National Park (p184)

JAN STROMME

Wander the old city, Dubrovnik (p229)

Enjoy the sunshine on a pebbly beach, Brela (p207)

MARTIN MOOS

Pause and relect at the Vrboska waterfront, Hvar (p219)

WAYNE WALTC

Getting Started

Croatia has decades of experience in welcoming travellers, whether in luxurious hotels, modest family-owned *pensions* or beachfront camping grounds. Advance planning is a good idea in peak season (mid-July through August) especially if you'll be staying on one of the islands. Car ferries to and from Italy and among the islands can also fill up. At any time of year, pay close attention to the ferry schedules to the islands as they change with the seasons. You may have more flexibility than you think in July and August but a lot less from September to June.

WHEN TO GO

Most people visit Croatia between April and September. Although the coast is too cool for swimming in April, you'll enjoy warm, clear skies south of Split and rock-bottom accommodation prices. Zagreb is likely to be comfortable and the cultural season is in full swing at this time. May and June are great months for all outdoor activities (except skiing). In these months, Italian and German tourists have yet to arrive, accommodation prices are still reasonable and you'll enjoy long, sunny days. Watch out for battalions of school students on class field trips at the end of May and beginning of June. Hotels and transport around cultural highlights can suddenly fill up with boisterous youths and their harried chaperones.

See p261 for Climate Charts

July and August are the most expensive months to visit Croatia as the tourist season swings into gear. Accommodation prices are highest in summer and popular places can become uncomfortably crowded. The advantages of high-season travel are the extra boat lines to whisk you to the islands, and organised excursions to take you to out-of-the-way highlights.

September is perhaps the best month to visit since it's not as hot as summer, though the sea remains warm, the crowds will have thinned out as children return to school, off-season accommodation rates will be in place, and fruit such as figs and grapes will be abundant. In October it may be too cool for camping, but the weather should still be fine along the coast, and private rooms will be plentiful and inexpensive. See p256 for more on Croatia's tourist seasons.

COSTS & MONEY

Croatia is reasonably inexpensive as a Mediterranean destination from September to May. The summers are another story. Accommodation, boat fares, car rental and anything else relating to tourism skyrockets in summer, reaching a peak in July and August. In the low season, you

---

DON'T LEAVE HOME WITHOUT...

▪ Rubber shoes to wade into the water along Croatia's rocky coast.

▪ Maximum-protection sunscreen.

▪ Valid travel insurance (p265).

▪ Your ID card or passport and visa if required (p269).

▪ Instant coffee, to replace the foul brew poured in hotels.

can find a simple private room for as little as 90KN but you'll pay double that in the high season. Accommodation prices are a lot higher in Zagreb and stay high all year-round. Your daily expenses will come way down if you can find a private room to use as a base for exploring nearby areas. Coastal towns that lend themselves to this include Dubrovnik, Korčula, Hvar, Pula, Split and Zadar. You will also escape the 30% to 50% surcharge on private rooms rented for under four nights.

Concert and theatre tickets and museums are cheap (concert and theatre tickets run from about 60KN to 200KN and museums are about 10KN, except in Zagreb where they are slightly more expensive); boat transport is also cheap unless you take a car on board in which case you'll pay around 120KN for a short ride. The average intercity bus fare ranges from 30KN to 60KN. You can easily get a pizza for 25KN, and a plate of pasta costs about 50KN even in the more expensive restaurants. Because of the high percentage of imported food, self-catering is not much cheaper than carefully selected restaurant meals unless you can live on sandwiches and yogurt. Taking half board in a hotel or *pension* can also save money. If you take half board in a hotel the industrialised food is likely to be disappointing, but in a private *pension* you'll probably eat better and more cheaply than at a local restaurant. Backpackers who stay in one place can plan on spending about 200KN a day. Staying in nicely appointed private rooms, eating in moderate restaurants and travelling along the coast costs about 400KN per day and at least double that amount to stay in the best hotels and eat at the best restaurants. Families are always better off renting an apartment than staying in a hotel. A one-bedroom apartment sleeping three costs 375KN to 600KN per night along the coast, but at least you can save on meals.

In a good, moderate restaurant expect to pay about 35KN to 55KN for a starter and 70KN to 100KN for a meat or fish main course. Bread usually costs extra and a few restaurants tack on a service charge, which is supposed to be indicated on the menu. Fish and shellfish are more expensive and usually charged by the kilogram. An average portion is about 250g but sometimes you'll be expected to choose a whole fish from a selection, making it more difficult to estimate the final cost. Squid runs at about 280KN per kilogram but for fish and shrimp you'll pay from 300KN to 320KN per kilogram.

TRAVEL LITERATURE

As Croatia emerges from the shadow of former Yugoslavia, several writers of Croatian origin have taken the opportunity to rediscover their roots. *Plum Brandy: Croatian Journeys* by Josip Novakovich is a sensitive exploration of his family's Croatian background. *Croatia: Travels in Undiscovered Country* by Tony Fabijancic recounts the life of rural folks in a new Croatia. The classic travel book on Yugoslavia, indeed one of the all-time great travel books, is Rebecca West's *Black Lamb and Grey Falcon*. Written in 1941 as the world was becoming enmeshed in WWII, this massive volume recounts several trips that the writer took through Croatia, Serbia, Bosnia, Macedonia and Montenegro, weaving her observations into a seamless narrative. Passionate, forthright and wise, West's encyclopedic knowledge of Balkan history and culture illuminates many of the region's current difficulties.

Robert Kaplan is a contemporary journalist who travelled through the Balkans in the 1980s and early 1990s as Yugoslavia began to fall apart. His book *Balkan Ghosts* vividly presents the people and places that form the tangled web of Balkan culture.

TOP TENS

ISLAND GETAWAYS

With 1100 islands to choose from, it's a tough call to have to pick the best of the lot. There are the big ones that get all the press – Hvar, Mljet, Korčula – and then there are the simple small, pine-covered rocks pushing up out of the deep blue sea. Clothing is optional; bliss is mandatory.

- Crveni Otok (p144), near Rovinj
- Jerolim & Stipanska (p222), near Hvar
- Susak (p108), near Mali Lošinj
- Drvenik Mali (p204), near Trogir
- Lokrum (p237), near Dubrovnik
- Koločep (p241), near Dubrovnik
- Badija (p250), near Korčula
- Sveti Nikola (p146), near Poreč
- Šolta (p200), near Split
- Ugljan (p163), near Zadar

OUR FAVOURITE FESTIVALS

It's a new country and they just love to show off their culture. Whether they are dressing up in elaborate traditional costumes or showing off their fine musicians, Croats honour their culture and traditions with verve and style. For an overview of national and major regional festivals see p264.

- International Folklore Festival (Zagreb), July (p58)
- Rijeka Carnival (Rijeka), eve of Lent (p98)
- Varaždin Baroque Evenings (Varaždin), September (p76)
- Đakovo Embroidery (Đakovo), July (p89)
- Sveti Kristofor Day (Rab), 27 July (p123)
- Days of Jules Verne (Pazin), June (p150)
- Motovun Film Festival (Motovun), July (p152)
- Pag Carnival (Pag), 31 July (p175)
- Dubrovnik Summer Festival (Dubrovnik), July–August (p237)
- Holy Week (Korčula), week before Easter (p250)

AND THE WINNER IS. . .

Obscure sights, unexpected views, detours and strange flavours always make a trip highly unique and personal. Follow the list we've provided below and jar your senses with one of these 'winners'.

- Most macabre sight: The mummies of Vodnjan (p139)
- Most original museum: Town Museum of Labin (p131)
- Most underappreciated town: Varaždin (p73)
- Most undervisited national park: Risnjak (p103)
- Best spa: Krapinske Toplice (p78)
- Most evocative castle: Trakošćan Castle (p78)
- Best new museum: War Photos Limited, Dubrovnik (p236)
- Best taste sensation: Pag cheese (p173)
- Best photo opportunity: Korčula town from a ferry (p247)
- Tiniest Town: Hum (p151)

Zoë Brân's perceptive *After Yugoslavia*, part of the Lonely Planet *Journeys* series, recounts the author's 1999 trip across the former Yugoslavia, comparing it with a journey she made in 1978.

INTERNET RESOURCES

Croatia Homepage (www.hr) Hundreds of links to everything you want to know about Croatia.
Crotraveler (www.crotraveler.com) Travel forums, articles, transport and hotel links.
Dalmatia Travel Guide (www.dalmacija.net) About Dalmatia, including reservations for private accommodation.
Find Croatia (www.findcroatia.com) More Croatia links with an emphasis on tourism and outdoor activities.
Visit Croatia (www.visit-croatia.co.uk) Easy to navigate with updated travel and tourist information.

Itineraries
CLASSIC ROUTES

ESSENTIAL CROATIA

Two Weeks / Zagreb to Dubrovnik

Two-tiered **Zagreb** (p48) is your starting point, with its simmering nightlife, fine restaurants and choice museums divided between the medieval Upper Town and Austrian-influenced Lower Town.

From Zagreb, head north to the stunning baroque city of **Varaždin** (p73). This one-time capital of Croatia retains a strong sense of its glory. Spend a night, then head south to World Heritage site **Plitvice Lakes National Park** (p164), a watery wonderland of lakes and waterfalls. After a day soaking up the spray move on to historic **Zadar** (p156). Take a day trip to **Pag** (p173) for its unique culture and then move on to **Šibenik** (p180), home of the finest cathedral in Croatia, the Cathedral of St Jacob. Don't miss out on a swim under the falls at the **Krka National Park** (p184). Next is a stroll through lovely **Trogir** (p202) and then a meander around the Roman ruins of **Solin** (p200). By then you'll be ready for Diocletian's Palace in **Split** (p190). This exuberant city on the sea makes a fascinating contrast to busy Zagreb. Take the coastal road down to **Dubrovnik** (p229). Its pride and cultural identity are still intact from centuries as an independent city-state.

From major cities to natural wonders, this 750km itinerary brings you all that makes Croatia Croatian. You'll experience the Central European flavour of the interior and the Latin-inspired coast.

THE COASTAL ROUTE

Two Weeks / Poreč to Dubrovnik

Think you've already seen the Mediterranean? Think again. This 645km route takes you through the Mediterranean the way it used to be. Unspoiled fishing villages and ancient towns dot a rugged coastline, and a smattering of offshore islands rises out of the sparkling water.

Start your journey at the Unesco World Heritage site of **Poreč** (p144). You'll need a day to admire the marvellous Byzantine frescoes and straight Roman streets before heading south to the charming fishing port of **Rovinj** (p140) and its outstanding Venetian-inspired architecture.

Wander Rovinj's cobblestone streets for a day, then go on to **Pula** (p132). Tour the evocative Roman ruins and amphitheatre, before heading to the beach for some R and R. Don't forget to sample one of the fine restaurants in the evening. After two days in Pula, head north. Stop for a night in the old Austrian resort of **Opatija** (p100) for a healthy stroll along the seaside promenade and gorgeous views of the Kvarner coast. From nearby **Rijeka** (p93), you can catch coastal boats for the rest of your journey. Sail down to **Zadar** (p156). There's a wealth of museums and churches to explore, promenade strolls, café life and a bar scene. Settle in for a few days, resting up at Borik beach before heading down to energetic **Split** (p190), a fascinating blend of ancient architecture and up-to-the-minute nightlife. From there, it's a short boat hop to **Hvar** (p219) for the exquisite Renaissance architecture, and then on to unique **Korčula** (p247), birthplace of Marco Polo. Cap off the coastal journey with a leisurely stay in **Dubrovnik** (p229), 'the pearl of the Adriatic'. The gleaming marble streets nestled within a curtain of stone walls contain a profusion of fine sculpture and a vibrant cultural life.

ROADS LESS TRAVELLED

INTERIOR CROATIA

Two Weeks / Zagreb to Osijek

Start off in Croatia's dynamic capital, **Zagreb** (p48). Enjoy the museums, art and nightlife, then head to charming little **Samobor** (p69) for small-town pleasures and good regional food. Now its time to explore the relatively untouristed **Zagorje region** (p71), a bucolic landscape of forests, pastures and farms. Head north to **Klanjec** (p80) and admire the work of sculptor Antun Augustinčić in the town's fine little museum. Of course, you'll want to see Tito's birthplace at **Kumrovec** (p79), a fascinating examination of traditional village life. The castle of **Trakošćan** (p78) has all the mysterious aroma of times past that you could want. From there, it's on to another beautifully restored castle at **Varaždin** (p73). Soak up the Baroque architecture and then take to the waters at the **Varaždinske Toplice spa** (p77). On the way south, stop at the pilgrimage site of **Marija Bistrica** (p80) for heady views of the surrounding region. The green rolling hills of Zagorje flatten out as you head east to Slavonia. On the edge of Croatia is the Hungarian-influenced town of **Osijek** (p83) on the Drava river. Enjoy Osijek's unique architecture and take day trips to the **Kopački Rit Nature Park** (p87), with its profusion of bird life; to war-torn **Vukovar** (p89); and to see the majestic Lipizzaner horses of **Đakovo** (p88). All through the region, you can feast on its spicy food, washed down with fine local wine.

Allergic to sun, sea and crowds? This 660km itinerary takes you through Croatia's unspoiled interior, from the gentle hills of Zagorje to the wide-open landscape of Slavonia. Along the way, there are castles, spas, villages, an unusual park and a refreshing absence of crowds.

TAILORED TRIPS

ISLAND HOPPING

From the teeming port of **Rijeka** (p93), head to nearby **Krk Island** (p113), famous for the walled Krk town and fine white wines. Take a swim at sandy Baška beach and then catch the ferry over to the savagely beautiful **Cres Island** (p110). Check out the griffon vultures in **Beli** (p111) before moving south to the picturesque fishing port of **Mali Lošinj** (p105). Enjoy rocky Čikat bay but try to squeeze in a trip to nearby **Susak** (p108), famous for maintaining its traditional village ways. Next, hop a boat to **Rab Island** (p119), a European holiday spot for over a century. If you're not

beached-out, take a dip around **Lopar** (p125) before heading over to pretty Rab town and its four bell towers. Take a boat to Novalja on **Pag Island** (p173). Its dry, flat landscape has a stark beauty that contrasts sharply with green Rab. From Pag town, where lady lacemakers still exercise their skills on the straight, narrow streets, it's a short drive to Zadar and a boat to **Dugi Otok** (p170), well away from noise and crowds. Go back to Zadar and catch a coastal ferry to **Stari Grad** (p224) on **Hvar Island** (p218), perhaps the most beautiful island in the Adriatic, replete with pine, lavendar fields and idyllic offshore islets. Move on to lushly wooded **Korčula** (p247). From Korčula, cross the waters to **Mljet National Park** (p242), a magical isle that is said to have bewitched Odysseus.

OUTDOOR ADVENTURES

Hikers, bikers, windsurfers and divers have no shortage of options in Croatia. The hills around **Samobor** (p69) are favourite weekend hiking spots for Zagreb's urbanites, but real nature-lovers head down to the less-visited **Risnjak National Park** (p103) for gentle walks and more demanding hikes. **Rovinj** (p140) is known for its many dives, especially

the wreck of the Baron Gautsch, one of the Adriatic's most fascinating shipwrecks. Hiking up **Mt Učka** (p101) from Lovran provides unforgettable views of the Kvarner coast. **Mali Lošinj** (p105) is crisscrossed with bike paths, and nearby **Susak Island** (p108) is known for its reef, accessible even for beginning divers. **Paklenica National Park** (p167) is popular for its rock climbing and provides a good base for hikes along the Velebit range. **Dugi Otok** (p170) has a spectacular underwater landscape for experienced cave divers and the **Pakleni Islands** (p222) off Hvar have an underwater reef and canyon to explore. **Bol** (p215) on Brač island is the windsurfing capital of Croatia, while **Mljet National Park** (p242) is best explored by bike.

The Author

JEANNE OLIVER

Jeanne is a freelance journalist who lives in the south of France. She first visited Croatia for Lonely Planet in 1996, just as peace was settling over the country. In 1998 she researched and wrote the first edition of *Croatia*, the first guidebook in English to the country, and has returned almost every year since. Travelling the country by bus, boat, train and car, she's swum in its waters, hiked its trails and stuffed her backpack full of Pag cheese, *travarića* (local brandy) and a fistful of recipes to keep her going until the next trip.

My Favourite Trip

I usually start or finish in Zagreb (p48), a city I find strangely relaxing for a major European capital with a charm not easily captured in photos. Opatija (p100) is an essential stop for me because I can just trot down to the sea from any hotel in town. Zadar (p156) has undergone an astonishing transformation since my first visit, from morose and war-damaged to ebullient and dynamic. After checking on its progress I move down the coast, stopping in Korčula (p247) for swimming and a boat trip, and finishing in Dubrovnik (p229), whose beauty remains undimmed no matter how often I visit.

Snapshot

Europe, Europe, Europe. No question more preoccupies Croatians than the issue of EU membership. Ever since the Dayton Accord secured Croatia's borders in 1995, Croatia's foreign policy has been focused on gaining admission to the exclusive club. The fervour for admission intensified when neighbouring Slovenia started accession talks in 1998. Yet now that Slovenia has been admitted to the hallowed halls and Croatia is beginning its own accession talks, Croatians have become ever more dubious about the benefits of EU membership.

FAST FACTS

Area: 56,538 sq km

Population: 4.4 million

GDP growth rate: 4.2%

Head of State: President Stipe Mešić

Unemployment rate: 22.1%

Average net monthly salary: 4226KN

Inflation: 2.5%

Life expectancy: male 70.2, female 78.2

Primary trading partner: Italy

Population growth rate: -0.02%

While the government, led by Prime Minister Ivo Sanader, is rolling ahead with plans to join the EU in 2007 (although 2008 or 2009 seems more realistic), Croatians are asking themselves, 'What's in it for me?' Although a bare majority still support Croatia's EU membership, eurosceptics worry that membership would bring high prices, low salaries, a loss of Croatia's traditional way of life and foreign domination of the economy. Europhiles point to the benefits from foreign investment; eurosceptics see the sale of the country. Few Croatians believe that EU membership will do much to solve the country's most pressing problems: unemployment, declining living standards and corruption.

For now, Croatians respectfully disagree on EU matters but other issues provoke vein-popping passion. In order to even be considered for EU membership, Croatia had to prove it was serious about either prosecuting war criminals at home or turning them over for trial at the Hague. Croats are delighted to see former Yugoslav strongman Slobodan Milošević in the dock in the Hague. Most felt a sense of vindication when those responsible for the massacre at Vukovar and the shelling of Dubrovnik were convicted. Yet, Croatian culpability in the ethnic cleansing in Bosnia and the expulsion of the Serbs from the Krajina region during the 1991–95 Homeland War remains a highly contentious subject. Despite the ferocious opposition of Croat nationalists, several generals have been convicted of war crimes or extradited, but the prize remains fugitive General Ante Gotovina. When the Hague indicted the general for ordering the ethnic cleansing of the Krajina region, Croats across the political spectrum reacted with anger. The popular general was regarded as a war hero for delivering the rebellious region to Croatia. Rather than turning himself in, the general disappeared – or so the government claims. Prosecutors at the Hague accuse the government of protecting him rather than face domestic opposition to his arrest.

With a weak parliamentary majority, Prime Minister Sanador has little room for manoeuvre. Although elected on a crowd-pleasing platform of tax reduction, benefit increases to mothers and veterans, and jobs for all, the campaign promises have had to confront hard economic realities. Maintaining an economic climate favourable to investment involves fiscal discipline and further privatisation of state-owned companies. With exploding receipts from tourism and a heavy investment in infrastructure, namely motorways and rail links, the macroeconomic outlook for Croatia remains positive.

History

EARLY INHABITANTS

Excavations in Krapina have revealed that the area has been inhabited since the Paleolithic Age. The population grew during the Bronze Age and crafts multiplied. Eastern Slavonia was the base for what became known as the Vucedol culture, which reached Slovakia, Slovenia, Austria, Germany, Hungary and the Czech Republic before moving southward to the Adriatic islands.

The Illyrians, an Indo-European people, began migrating into the region around 1000 BC. Although Greeks set up trading posts on the eastern Adriatic coast in the 6th century BC, their influence was kept in check by the war-like Illyrians. Invading Celts pushed the Illyrians further south in the 4th century, towards what is today Albania. Later, the Romans pushed their way into the region and, in 168 BC, they finally conquered Genthius, the last Illyrian king.

DID YOU KNOW?

The Adriatic is derived from the name of the ancient Illyrian tribe, Ardeioi.

THE ROMANS

The initial Roman province of Illyricum was gradually enlarged during a series of wars which brought much of the Dalmatian coast within their control. By 11 BC Rome conquered much of the interior which was inhabited by the Pannonian tribe, extending the empire's reach to the middle and lower Danube. The realm was reorganised into Dalmatia (the former Illyricum), and Upper and Lower Pannonia which covered much of the interior of modern Croatia.

The Romans ruled the area for five centuries, making Salona (now Solin) their administrative headquarters. Their network of roads, linking the coast with the Aegean and Black Seas and with the Danube, facilitated trade, making the region a nice money-maker for the Romans. In addition to Salona, other important Roman towns included Jadera (Zadar), Parentium (Poreč), Polensium (Pula) and, later, Spalato (Split).

When the Roman Empire began to crack in the late 3rd century AD, two strong Dalmatian emperors emerged. Emperor Diocletian was born in Salona in AD 236 and became emperor in 285. While establishing strong central control, he divided Dalmatia into Dalmatia Salonitana, with its capital at Salona and Dalmatia Praevalitana, with its capital at Scodra (Schkoder in modern Albania). By placing the two regions in separate dioceses, he sowed the seeds for the later division into the Eastern and Western Roman Empire. In AD 305 Diocletian retired to his palace in Split, today the greatest Roman ruin in Eastern Europe.

The last Roman leader to rule a united empire was Theodosius (the Great), who adeptly managed to stave off serious threats from the northern Visigoths. On Theodosius' death in AD 395, the empire was formally divided into eastern and western realms. What is now Slovenia, Croatia and Bosnia and Hercegovina were assigned to the Western Roman Empire, while present-day Serbia, Kosovo and Macedonia went to what was to become the Byzantine Empire. Visigoth, Hun and Lombard invasions marked the fall of the Western Roman Empire in the 5th century.

TIMELINE	**9 BC**	**7th century**
	End of the Roman conquest of the Croatian coast and interior	Beginning of the Slav migration into the Balkans

MIGRATION

While the Roman Empire was disintegrating, the Croats and other Slavic tribes were tending fields and raising livestock in a swampy terrain that roughly covered the area of modern Ukraine, Poland and Belarus. It appears that early in the 7th century they moved south across the Danube and joined the Avars in their attacks on Byzantine Dalmatia. Salona and Epidaurus were ravaged, their inhabitants taking refuge in Spalato (Split) and Ragusa (Dubrovnik) respectively. Sometimes the Croat and Slavic tribes joined Avars in their attacks on Byzantium and other times they were persuaded by Byzantium to attack the Avars.

By the middle of the 7th century the Croatian tribe had begun to settle in Pannonia and Dalmatia, mingling with earlier Slav settlers on the Pannonian plains and forming communities around the Dalmatian towns of Jadera (Zadar), Aeona (Nin) and Tragurium (Trogir). During the course of the 8th century the Dalmatian and Pannonian Croats organised themselves around powerful clans, one of which was called Hrvat (Croat), a name that the clan gave to its territory in central Dalmatia, Bijela Hrvatska (White Croatia).

DID YOU KNOW?

Dalmatian dogs probably did not originate in Dalmatia. The origins of the breed are uncertain but some experts believe the dogs may have been brought into Dalmatia by the Roma and used to guard the Dalmatian border.

CROATIAN KINGS

Charlemagne's Frankish army seized Dalmatia in AD 800, which led to the Christianisation of the Croat rulers in a series of mass baptisms. After Charlemagne's death in AD 814, the Pannonian Croats revolted unsuccessfully against Frankish rule without the support of the Dalmatian Croats, whose major coastal cities remained under the influence of the Byzantine Empire throughout the 9th century. Even as Dalmatia accepted the political domination of Byzantium, the spread of Christianity encouraged cultural ties with Rome which proved to be the unifying factor in forging a national identity.

The first ruler to unite Pannonia and Dalmatia was Tomislav, who was crowned in AD 925 and recognised by the pope as king. His territory included virtually all of modern Croatia as well as part of Bosnia and the coast of Montenegro.

By the mid-10th century, the country's fragile unity was threatened by power struggles in its ruling class. Venice took advantage of the disarray to launch an invasion of Dalmatia at the turn of the 11th century that established its first foothold on the coast.

Krešimir IV (1058–74) regained control over Dalmatia with the help of the papacy, but the kingdom once again descended into anarchy upon his death. The next king, Zvonimir (1075–89), also cemented his authority with the help of the pope but the independent land he forged did not survive his death.

Marcus Tanner's *Croatia: A Nation Forged in War* is the most comprehensive recent account of Croatian history. From the Roman era to President Tudjman, the complicated struggles of Croatia are presented in a lively, readable style.

HUNGARY VERSUS VENICE

Hungary's King Ladislav invaded northern Croatia in 1091 but his plans to conquer Dalmatia were thwarted by a Byzantine attack on Hungary which kept Dalmatia under Byzantine control. Although Ladislav's successor, King Koloman, managed to persuade the Dalmatian nobility to accept his rule in exchange for self-government, his victory was somewhat limited by the increasing control that Venice was exerting over the Dalmatian coast.

925	1091
Croatia becomes a kingdom under King Tomislav	Hungary launches first invasion of Croatia

Upon Koloman's death in 1116 Venice launched new assaults on Biograd, Zadar, and the islands of Lošinj, Pag, Rab and Krk. Venice laid siege to Zadar for 10 years but managed to capture it only after the doge of Venice paid 13th-century Crusaders handsomely to attack and sack the town before proceeding on to Constantinople.

The 13th century also brought new troubles in the form of a Mongol invasion that pushed the Hungarian King Bela IV down to Trogir. Dalmatian cities warred with each other and Venice again took advantage of the confusion to consolidate its hold on Zadar. The death of King Bela in 1270 led to another power struggle among the Croatian nobility which allowed Venice to add Šibenik and Trogir to its possessions.

King Ludovik I of Hungary (1342–82) re-established control over the country and even persuaded Venice to relinquish Dalmatia. The Hungarian victory was short-lived. New conflicts emerged upon Ludovik's death and the Croatian nobility rallied around Ladislas of Naples who was crowned King in Zadar in 1403. Short of funds, Ladislas then sold Zadar to Venice in 1409 for a paltry 100,000 ducats and renounced his rights to Dalmatia. In the early 15th century Venice solidified its grip on the Dalmatian coastline from Zadar to Dubrovnik and remained in control until the Napoleonic invasion of 1797.

DID YOU KNOW?

Šibenik-born Faust Vrančić (1551–1617) made the first working parachute.

HABSBURGS 1 OTTOMANS 0

The rise of the Ottoman Empire brought new threats to 16th-century Croatia. The defeat of the Serbs in 1389 at Kosovo opened the door to Bosnia, which did not last long after the fall of Constantinople in 1453. Sensing nasty weather from the east, the Croatian nobility desperately appealed to foreign powers for help but to no avail. The Ottomans continued their relentless advance, virtually wiping out the cream of Croatian leadership at the 1493 Battle of Krbavsko Polje. Despite the sudden unity of the remaining noble families, one city after another fell to the Ottoman sultans. The important bishopric at Zagreb heavily fortified the cathedral in Kaptol which remained untouched, but the gateway town of Knin fell in 1521. Towns were burned, churches and monasteries sacked, and tens of thousands of citizens were either killed or dragged off into slavery.

Neither Hungary nor Austria was able to protect Croatia against the Ottoman onslaught and the Croats continued to lose territory. By the end of the century only a narrow strip of territory around Zagreb, Karlovac and Varaždin was under Habsburg control. The Adriatic coast was threatened by the Turks but never captured and Ragusa (Dubrovnik) maintained its independence throughout the turmoil.

To form a buffer against the Turks the Austrians maintained a string of forts south of Zagreb called the Vojna Krajina (Military Frontier). Initially open to anyone who wanted to live on the marshy land, the Habsburgs invited Vlachs to settle the land in the 16th century. At the time, most Vlachs belonged to the Serbian Orthodox Church, which irritated the Croatian Sabor; however, they were much more irritated by the arrangement allowing the settlers to escape the harsh feudal system that the Hungarians had instituted in the country. Despite repeated efforts by the Croatian nobility to either turn them into serfs or get rid

1409	**1493**
Venice buys all rights to Dalmatia	The Battle of Krbavsko Polje

of them completely, the free peasants stayed on their land until they were expelled in 1995.

It wasn't until the Ottoman rout at the siege of Vienna in 1683 that Croatia and much of Europe finally freed themselves from the Turkish threat. In the Treaty of Sremski Karlovci (1699) the Turks renounced all claims to Hungary and Croatia. During the 18th century, Croat and Serb immigrants flooded into Slavonia joined by Hungarians, Slovaks, Albanian Catholics and Jews. Under the rule of Maria Theresa of Austria, the region returned to stability.

VENETIAN EMPIRE

Venetian rule in Dalmatia and Istria was a ruthless record of nearly unbroken economic exploitation. Early in their rule, the Venetians ordered the destruction of Dalmatian mulberry trees in order to kill the silk trade for no other apparent reason than to keep the region poor and dependent. Other trees also suffered as the Venetians systematically denuded the landscape in order to provide wood for their ships. Olive oil, figs, wine, fish and salt were in effect confiscated, since merchants were forced to sell only to Venetians and only at the price the Venetians were willing to pay. Dalmatian fisherman were unable to salt their fish for preservation because salt was kept unreasonably expensive by a state monopoly. Shipbuilding was effectively banned since Venice tolerated no competition with its own ships. No roads or schools were built, no investment made in local industry. All manufactured articles had to be imported and, by the latter half of the 18th century, even agricultural products had to be imported to keep the population – barely surviving on roots and grass – from starving to death. In addition to Venice's iron fisted economic policies, the population was also subject to malaria and plague epidemics that ravaged the region.

ENTER NAPOLEON

Habsburg support for the restoration of the French monarchy led to Napoleon's invasion of Austria's Italian states in 1796. After conquering Venice in 1797 he agreed to transfer Dalmatia to Austria in the Treaty of Campo Formio in exchange for other concessions. Croatian hopes that Dalmatia would be united with Slavonia were soon dashed as the Habsburgs made it clear that the two territories would retain separate administrations.

Austrian control of Dalmatia only lasted until Napoleon's 1805 victory over Austrian and Prussian forces at Austerlitz forced Austria to cede the Dalmatian coast to France. Ragusa (Dubrovnik) quickly surrendered to French forces. Napoleon renamed his conquest the 'Illyrian provinces' and moved with characteristic swiftness to reform the crumbling territory. A tree-planting programme was established to reforest the barren hills. Since almost the entire population was illiterate, the new government set up primary schools, high schools and a college at Zadar. Roads and hospitals were built and new crops introduced. A programme was instituted to drain the marshes that were breeding malarial mosquitoes. Yet the French regime remained unpopular, partly because the anticlerical French were staunchly opposed by the clergy and partly because the population was heavily taxed to pay for the reforms.

DID YOU KNOW?

The neck tie is a descendant of the 'cravat', which originated in Croatia as part of military attire and was adopted by the French in the 17th century. The name 'cravat' is a corruption of Croat and Hrvat.

Misha Glenny's *The Balkans: Nationalism, War & the Great Powers, 1804–1999* is a passionately argued book that explores the destructive history of outside interference in the Balkans.

1699	1805–15
Ottoman Turks renounce all claims to Croatia	French control Dalmatian coast

The fall of the Napoleonic empire after his disastrous Russian campaign led to the 1815 Congress of Vienna which recognised Austria's claims to Dalmatia and placed the rest of Croatia under the jurisdiction of Austria's Hungarian province. For the Dalmatians, the new regime meant a return to the status quo since the Austrians restored the former Italian elite to power. For the northern Croats the agreement meant submission to Hungary's insistent desire to impose the Hungarian language and culture on the population.

THE 1848 REVOLUTION

One of the effects of Hungarian heavy-handedness was to create the first stirrings of a national identity among the southern Slavic people. The sense of a shared identity first found expression in an 'Illyrian' movement in the 1830s which centred on the revival of the Croatian language. Traditionally, upper-class Dalmatians spoke Italian, and northern Croats spoke German or Hungarian. The establishment of the first 'Illyrian' newspaper in 1834, written in Zagreb dialect, prompted the Croatian Sabor to call for the teaching of the Slavic language in schools and even for the unification of Dalmatia with Slavonia. Despite Hungarian threats, in 1847 the Sabor voted to make 'Illyrian' the national language.

The increasing desire for more autonomy and the eventual unification of Dalmatia and Slavonia led the Croats to intervene on the side of the Habsburgs against a Hungarian revolutionary movement that sought to free the country from Austrian rule. The Croatian Sabor informed Austria that it would send the Croatian commander Josip Jelačić to fight the Hungarian rebels in return for the cancellation of Hungary's jurisdiction over Croatia, among other demands. Unfortunately, Jelačić's military campaign was unsuccessful. Russian intervention quelled the Hungarian rebellion and Austria firmly rejected any further demands for autonomy from its Slavic subjects.

DID YOU KNOW?

Nikola Tesla (1856–1943), the father of the radio and alternating electric current technology, was born in Croatia. The Tesla unit for magnetic induction was named after him.

DREAMS OF YUGOSLAVIA

Disillusionment spread after 1848, and was amplified by the birth of the Austro-Hungarian Dual Monarchy in 1867. The monarchy placed Croatia and Slavonia within the Hungarian administration, while Dalmatia remained within Austria. Whatever limited form of self-government the Croats enjoyed under the Habsburgs disappeared along with 55% of their revenues earmarked for the imperial treasury.

The river of discontent running through late-19th century Croatia forked into two streams that dominated the political landscape for the next century. The old 'Illyrian' movement became the National Party, dominated by the brilliant Bishop Josif Juraf Strossmayer. Strossmayer believed that the differences between Serbs and Croats were magnified by the manipulations of the Habsburgs and the Hungarians, and that only through Jugoslavenstvo (south-Slavic unity) could the aspirations of both peoples be realised. Strossmayer supported the Serbian independence struggle in Serbia but favoured a Yugoslav entity within the Austro-Hungarian empire rather than complete independence.

By contrast, the Party of Rights, led by the militantly anti-Serb Ante Starčević, envisioned an independent Croatia made up of Slavonia,

1815	**1848**
Austria awarded control of Dalmatian coast; Hungary controls the interior	Croatian Sabor demands greater autonomy and the attachment of Dalmatia to Slavonia

Dalmatia, the Krajina, Slovenia, Istria, and part of Bosnia and Herce-govina. At the time, the Eastern Orthodox Church was encouraging the Serbs to form a national identity based upon their religion. Until the 19th century, Orthodox inhabitants of Croatia identified themselves as Vlachs, Morlachs, Serbs, Orthodox or even Greeks but, with the help of Starčević's attacks, the sense of a separate Serbian, Orthodox identity within Croatia developed.

Under the theory of 'divide and rule', the Hungarian-appointed Ban (viceroy) of Croatia blatantly favoured the Serbs and the Orthodox Church, but his strategy backfired. The first organised resistance formed in Dalmatia. Croat representatives in Rijeka and Serb representatives in Zadar joined together in 1905 to demand the unification of Dalmatia and Slavonia with a formal guarantee of Serbian equality as a nation. The spirit of unity mushroomed, and by 1906 Croat-Serb coalitions had taken over local government in Dalmatia and Slavonia, forming a serious threat to the Hungarian power structure.

THE KINGDOM OF SERBS, CROATS & SLOVENES

With the outbreak of WWI, Croatia's future was again up for grabs. Sens-ing that they would once again be pawns to the Great Powers, a Croatian delegation, the 'Yugoslav Committee', convinced the Serbian government to agree to the establishment of a parliamentary monarchy that would rule over the two countries. The Yugoslav Committee became the National Council of Slovenes, Croats and Serbs after the collapse of the Austro-Hungarian empire in 1918 and they quickly negotiated the establishment of the Kingdom of Serbs, Croats and Slovenes to be based in Belgrade. Although many Croatians were unsure about Serbian intentions, they were very sure about Italian intentions since Italy lost no time in seizing Pula, Rijeka and Zadar in November 1918.

Given, in effect, a choice between throwing in their lot with Italy or Serbia, the Croats chose Serbia.

Problems with the kingdom began almost immediately. Currency re-forms benefited Serbs at the expense of the Croats. A treaty between Yugoslavia and Italy gave Istria, Zadar and a number of islands to Italy. The new constitution abolished Croatia's Sabor and centralised power in Belgrade while new electoral districts under-represented the Croats.

Opposition to the new regime was led by the Croat Stjepan Radić, who remained favourable to the idea of Yugoslavia but wished to transform it into a federal democracy. His alliance with the Serb Svetpzar Pribićevic proved profoundly threatening to the regime and Radić was assassi-nated. Exploiting fears of civil war, on 6 January 1929 King Aleksandar in Belgrade proclaimed a royal dictatorship, abolished political parties and suspended parliamentary government, thus ending any hope of democratic change.

WWII & THE RISE OF USTAŠE

One day after the proclamation, a Bosnian Croat, Ante Pavelić, set up the Ustaše Croatian Liberation Movement in Zagreb with the stated aim of establishing an independent state by force if necessary. Fearing arrest, he fled to Sofia in Bulgaria and made contact with anti-Serbian

1867	1918
Austria and Hungary agree to divide Croatia between the Austrian coast and Hungarian interior	Foundation of the Kingdom of Serbs, Croats and Slovenes

Macedonian revolutionaries before fleeing to Italy. There, he established training camps for his organisation under Mussolini's benevolent eye. After organising various disturbances, in 1934 he and the Macedonians succeeded in assassinating King Aleksandar in Marseilles while he was on a state visit. Italy responded by closing down the training camps and imprisoning Pavelić and many of his followers. When Germany invaded Yugoslavia on 6 April 1941 the exiled Ustaše were quickly installed by the Germans, with the support of the Italians who hoped to see their own territorial aims in Dalmatia realised.

Within days the Independent State of Croatia (NDH) headed by Pavelić issued a range of decrees designed to persecute and eliminate the regime's 'enemies' who were mainly Jews, Roma and Serbs. Over 80% of the Jewish population was rounded up and packed off to extermination camps between 1941 and 1945. Serbs fared no better. The Ustaše programme called for 'one-third of Serbs killed, one-third expelled and one-third converted to Catholicism', a programme that was carried out with a brutality that appalled even the Nazis. Villages conducted their own personal pogroms against Serbs and extermination camps were set up, most notoriously at Jasenovac (south of Zagreb), which also liquidated Jews, Roma and political prisoners. The exact number of Serb victims is uncertain and controversial, with Croatian historians tending to minimise the figures and Serbian historians tending to maximise them. The number of Serb deaths range from 60,000 to 600,000, but the most reliable estimates settle somewhere between 80,000 to 120,000, including victims of village pogroms. Whatever the number, it's clear that the NDH and its supporters made a diligent effort to eliminate the entire Serb population.

Richard West's *Tito and the Rise and Fall of Yugoslavia* is a knowledgeable biography of the former Yugoslav leader and an incisive analysis of the troubles besetting postwar Yugoslavia that spearheaded its descent into war.

TITO & THE PARTISANS

Not all Croats supported these policies. The Ustaše regime drew most of its support from the Lika region southwest of Zagreb and western Hercegovina, but Pavelić's agreement to cede a good part of Dalmatia to Italy was highly unpopular to say the least and the Ustaše had almost no support in that region.

Armed resistance to the regime took the form of Serbian 'Chetnik' formations led by General Draza Mihailovic, which began as an antifascist rebellion but soon degenerated into massacres of Croats in eastern Croatia and Bosnia.

The most effective antifascist struggle was conducted by National Liberation Partisan units and their leader, Josip Broz, known as Tito. With their roots in the outlawed Yugoslavian Communist party, the Partisans attracted long-suffering Yugoslav intellectuals, Croats disgusted with Chetnik massacres, Serbs disgusted with Ustaše massacres, and antifascists of all kinds. The Partisans gained wide popular support with their early programme which, although vague, appeared to envision a postwar Yugoslavia that would be based on a loose federation.

Can't get enough of Tito? Neither can tens of thousands of ex-Yugoslavs who visit his 'home page', www.titoville.com.

Although the Allies initially backed the Serbian Chetniks, it became apparent that the Partisans were waging a far more focused and determined fight against the Nazis. With the diplomatic and military support of Churchill and other Allied powers the Partisans controlled much of Croatia by 1943. The Partisans established functioning local governments

1928	**1941**
Croat leader Stjepan Radić assassinated	Ante Pavelić proclaims the Independent State of Croatia (NDH) a Nazi puppet state

in the territory they seized, which later eased their transition to power. On 20 October 1944 Tito entered Belgrade with the Red Army and was made prime minister. When Germany surrendered in 1945, Pavelić and the Ustaše fled and the Partisans entered Zagreb.

The remnants of the NDH army, desperate to avoid falling into the hands of the Partisans, attempted to cross into Austria at Bleiburg. A small British contingent met the 50,000 troops, and promised to intern them outside Yugoslavia in exchange for their surrender. It was a trick. The troops were forced into trains that headed back into Yugoslavia where the Partisans awaited them. The ensuing massacre claimed the lives of at least 30,000 men (although the exact number is in doubt) and left a permanent stain on the Yugoslav government.

YUGOSLAVIA

Tito's attempt to retain control of the Italian city of Trieste and parts of southern Austria faltered in the face of Allied opposition, but Dalmatia and most of Istria were made a permanent part of postwar Yugoslavia. The good news was that Tito was determined to create a state in which no ethnic group dominated the political landscape. Croatia became one of six republics – Macedonia, Serbia, Montenegro, Bosnia and Hercegovina, and Slovenia – in a tightly configured federation. The bad news was that Tito effected this delicate balance by creating a one-party state and rigorously stamping out all opposition whether nationalist, royalist or religious. The government's hostility to organised religion, particularly the Catholic Church, stemmed from its perception that the Church was complicit in the murderous nationalism that surfaced during WWII.

The Death of Yugoslavia by Laura Silber and Allan Little, based on the 1995 BBC television series of the same name, is a riveting, if depressing, account of ineffectual Western peace initiatives trying to rein in power-driven regional despots.

During the 1960s, the concentration of power in Belgrade became an increasingly testy issue as it became apparent that money from the more prosperous republics of Slovenia and Croatia was being distributed to the poorer republics Montenegro and Bosnia and Hercegovina. The problem seemed particularly blatant in Croatia, which saw money from its prosperous tourist business on the Adriatic coast flow into Belgrade. At the same time Serbs in Croatia were over-represented in the government, armed forces and the police, partly because state-service offered an opportunity for a chronically disadvantaged population.

In Croatia the unrest reached a crescendo in the 'Croatian Spring' of 1971. Led by reformers within the Communist Party of Croatia, intellectuals and students first called for greater economic autonomy and then constitutional reform to loosen Croatia's ties to Yugoslavia. Tito's eventual crackdown was ferocious. Leaders of the movement were 'purged' – either jailed or expelled from the Party. Careers were abruptly terminated; some dissidents chose exile and emigrated to the USA. Serbs viewed the movement as the Ustaše reborn, and jailed reformers blamed the Serbs for their troubles. The stage was set for the later rise of nationalism and war that followed Tito's death in 1980, even though his 1974 constitution afforded the republics more autonomy.

INDEPENDENCE

Tito's habit of borrowing from abroad to flood the country with cheap consumer goods produced an economic crisis after his death. The country

1945	**1980**
Tito founds Yugoslavia	Death of President Tito

was unable to service the interest on its loans and inflation soared. The authority of the central government sank along with the economy and long-suppressed mistrust among Yugoslavia's ethnic groups resurfaced.

In 1989 severe repression of the Albanian majority in Serbia's Kosovo province sparked renewed fears of Serbian hegemony and heralded the end of the Yugoslav Federation. With political changes sweeping Eastern Europe, many Croats felt the time had come to end more than four decades of Communist rule and attain complete autonomy into the bargain. In the free elections of April 1990 Franjo Tudjman's Croatian Democratic Union (HDZ; Hrvatska Demokratska Zajednica) secured 40% of the vote, to the 30% won by the Communist Party which retained the loyalty of the Serbian community as well as voters in Istria and Rijeka. On 22 December 1990 a new Croatian constitution was promulgated, changing the status of Serbs in Croatia from that of a 'constituent nation' to a national minority.

The constitution's failure to guarantee minority rights, and mass dismissals of Serbs from the public service, stimulated the 600,000-strong ethnic Serb community within Croatia to demand autonomy. In early 1991 Serb extremists within Croatia staged provocations designed to force federal military intervention. A May 1991 referendum (boycotted by the Serbs) produced a 93% vote in favour of independence, but when Croatia declared independence on 25 June 1991, the Serbian enclave of Krajina proclaimed its independence from Croatia.

WAR & PEACE

Under pressure from the EC (now EU), Croatia declared a three-month moratorium on its independence but heavy fighting broke out in Krajina, Baranja (the area north of the Drava River opposite Osijek) and Slavonia. The 180,000-member, 2000-tank Yugoslav People's Army, dominated by Serbian Communists, began to intervene on its own authority in support of Serbian irregulars under the pretext of halting ethnic violence.

When the Croatian government ordered a blockade of 32 federal military installations in the republic, the Yugoslav navy blockaded the Adriatic coast and laid siege to the strategic town of Vukovar on the Danube. During the summer of 1991, a quarter of Croatia fell to Serbian militias and the Serb-led Yugoslav People's Army.

In early October 1991 the federal army and Montenegrin militia moved against Dubrovnik to protest the ongoing blockade of their garrisons in Croatia, and on 7 October the presidential palace in Zagreb was hit by rockets fired by Yugoslav air-force jets in an unsuccessful assassination attempt on President Tudjman. When the three-month moratorium on independence ended Croatia declared full independence.

On 19 November, heroic Vukovar finally fell when the army culminated a bloody three-month siege by concentrating 600 tanks and 30,000 soldiers there. During six months of fighting in Croatia 10,000 people died, hundreds of thousands fled and tens of thousands of homes were destroyed.

To fulfil a condition for EC recognition, in December the Croatian Sabor belatedly amended its constitution to protect minority groups and human rights.

John Macphee's *The Silent Cry: One Man's Fight for Croatia in the Bosnian War* is a remarkable account of the fighting in former Yugoslavia by a soldier who remains haunted by the brutality he witnessed and participated in.

The BBC traces the history of Yugoslavia from 1918 to 2003 at www.bbc.co .uk/history/state/nations /yugoslavia_01.shtml.

1990	1991
Collapse of the Communist system in Eastern Europe	Croatian Sabor proclaims the independence of Croatia; war breaks out

Beginning on 3 January 1992, a UN-brokered ceasefire generally held. The federal army was allowed to withdraw from its bases inside Croatia and tensions diminished.

In January 1992 the EC, succumbing to strong pressure from Germany, recognised Croatia. This was followed three months later by US recognition and in May 1992 Croatia was admitted to the UN.

The UN peace plan in Krajina was supposed to have led to the disarming of local Serb paramilitary formations, the repatriation of refugees and the return of the region to Croatia. Instead, it only froze the existing situation and offered no permanent solution.

In January 1993 the Croatian army suddenly launched an offensive in southern Krajina, pushing the Serbs back as much as 24km in some areas and recapturing strategic points such as the site of the destroyed Maslenica bridge, Zemunik airport near Zadar and the Peručac hydroelectric dam in the hills between Split and Bosnia and Hercegovina. The Krajina Serbs vowed never to accept rule from Zagreb and in June 1993 they voted overwhelmingly to join the Bosnian Serbs (and eventually Greater Serbia).

The self-proclaimed 'Republic of Serbian Krajina' held elections in December 1993, which no international body recognised as legitimate or fair. Meanwhile, continued 'ethnic cleansing' left only about 900 Croats in Krajina out of an original population of 44,000. In March 1994, the Krajina Serbs signed a comprehensive ceasefire which substantially reduced the violence in the region and established demilitarised 'zones of separation' between the parties.

Richard Holbrooke's *To End a War* recounts the events surrounding the Dayton Accords. As the American official who prodded the warring parties to the negotiating table to hammer out a peace accord, Holbrooke was in a unique position to evaluate the personalities and politics of the region.

While world attention turned to the grim events unfolding in Bosnia and Hercegovina, the Croatian government quietly began procuring arms from abroad. On 1 May 1995, the Croatian army and police entered occupied western Slavonia, east of Zagreb, and seized control of the region within days. The Krajina Serbs responded by shelling Zagreb in an attack that left seven people dead and 130 wounded. As the Croatian military consolidated its hold in western Slavonia, some 15,000 Serbs fled the region despite assurances from the Croatian government that they were safe from retribution.

Belgrade's silence throughout this campaign showed that the Krajina Serbs had lost the support of their Serbian sponsors, encouraging Croats to forge ahead. On 4 August the military launched a massive assault on the rebel Serb capital of Knin, pummelling it with shells, mortars and bombs. Outnumbered by two to one, the Serb army fled towards northern Bosnia, along with 150,000 civilians whose roots in the Krajina stretched back centuries. The military operation ended in days, but was followed by months of terror. Widespread looting and burning of Serb villages, and attacks upon the few remaining elderly Serbs, seemed designed to ensure the permanence of this huge population shift. Allegations of atrocities caught the attention of the International Criminal Tribunal for the former Yugoslavia at the Hague. Of the two Croatian generals charged with committing crimes against the Serb population, General Gotovina remains at large and General Norac has turned himself in for trial.

The Dayton Accord signed in Paris in December 1995 recognised Croatia's traditional borders and provided for the return of eastern

1992	1995
UN-brokered ceasefire takes effect; EU recognises Croatian independence; Croatia admitted into the UN	Dayton Accords establish the borders of Croatia

Slavonia, which was effected in January 1998. The transition proceeded relatively smoothly with less violence than was expected, but the two populations still regard each other over a chasm of suspicion and hostility. The Serbs and Croats associate with each other as little as possible and clever political manoeuvering has largely barred Serbs from assuming a meaningful role in municipal government.

Although stability has returned to the country, a key provision of the agreement was the promise by the Croatian government to facilitate the return of Serbian refugees, a promise that is far from being fulfilled. Although the central government in Zagreb has made the return of refugees a priority in accordance with the demands of the international community, its efforts have often been subverted by local authorities intent on maintaining the ethnic purity of their regions. In many cases, Croat refugees from Hercegovina have occupied houses abandoned by their Serb owners. Serbs intending to reclaim their property face a forbidding array of legal impediments in establishing a claim to their former dwellings.

Human Rights Watch has its eye on Croatia. See its reports on refugee returns and other matters at www.hrw.org.

1999	2001
Death of Croatia's first president, Franjo Tudjman	Stabilization and Association agreement signed with the EU

The Culture

THE NATIONAL PSYCHE

Despite a recent softening of support for Croatia's bid to join the EU, the vast majority of Croats have a strong cultural identification with Western Europe. In fact, if you ask a Croat what distinguishes Croatian culture from Bosnian or Serbian culture, the answer is likely to be a variant of 'We are Western and they are Eastern'. The idea that Croatia is the last stop before the Ottoman East is very much alive in all segments of the population. Liberal, cosmopolitan Croats, who bear no particular ill will against other ethnicities, will nonetheless note that their former compatriots in Bosnia and Hercegovina, Macedonia, Serbia and Montenegro eat different food, listen to different music, have different customs and, of course, go to different churches. Most Croats do not believe that the former Yugoslavia was driven by 'ancient hatreds' before the 1991–95 war but admit that there was an unease among the various ethnicities.

The word 'normal' pops up frequently in Croatian conversations about themselves. 'We want to be a normal country,' they might say. Croats will frequently make a distinction between rabid, flag-waving, nationalists and 'normal people' who only wish to live in peace. For Croats, 'normal' is equated with the Western European values of democracy and tolerance. International isolation is exceedingly painful for most Croats, which is why Croatia reluctantly bowed to international pressure to turn over its war criminals.

Croats are united by a common religion, Catholicism, but their eventful history has left varying imprints across the country. Austrian influence is strongest in the orderly interior where German is likely to be the second language; business hours are longer and more reliable and people tend to focus on personal advancement rather than personal pleasure. The opposite is true along the relaxed coast, where Italian is likely to be the second language. Many offices empty out at 3pm, allowing people to enjoy the long hours of sunlight on a beach or in an outdoor café. Hungary has had the weakest impact, apparent mainly in the Eastern Slavonian taste for spicy food.

Attitudes towards the 1990s 'Homeland War' or 'Patriotic War' vary by region. The destruction of Vukovar, the shelling of Dubrovnik and Osijek, and the ethnic cleansing of and by the Krajina Serbs has left an ugly feeling in the surrounding regions. Comments questioning the assumption that Croats were wholly right and Serbs were wholly wrong are not likely to be appreciated. In other parts of the country, Croats are more open to a forthright discussion of the last decade's events.

Café Europa is a series of essays by a Croatian journalist, Slavenka Drakulić, which provides an inside look at life in the country since independence.

LIFESTYLE

Croats like the good life and take a lot of pride in keeping up appearances. Streets are tidy, clothes are stylish and money can usually be found to brighten up the façades of their homes. Even with a tight economy, people will cut out restaurants and films in order to afford a shopping trip to Italy for some new clothes.

Given high unemployment and stagnant wages, visitors often wonder how Croatians manage and why there is not more visible evidence of poverty. In many ways, Croatians are still living out the remnants of the Tito era. Adults of that generation were encouraged to buy their own homes and many did. Unfortunately, their children usually don't have the means to live on their own now and many stay with their parents until (and sometimes after) marriage. Many families were also able to accumulate a nest egg under Tito that they use to help out their unemployed kids.

Although attitudes are slowly changing towards homosexuality, Croatia is an overwhelmingly Catholic country with highly traditional views of sexuality. In a recent survey only 58% of those surveyed said they regarded gays as 'normal people with a different sexual orientation'. The rest consider it a perversion. Most homosexuals are highly closeted, fearing harassment if their sexual orientation were revealed.

POPULATION

According to the most recent census Croatia had a population of roughly 4.5 million people, a decline from the pre-war population of nearly five million. Some 59% live in urban areas. About 280,000 Serbs (50% of the population) departed in the early 1990s; an estimated 110,000 have returned. In the post-independence economic crunch, 120,000 to 130,000 Croatians emigrated abroad but a roughly equal number of ethnic Croat refugees arrived from Bosnia and Hercegovina and another 30,000 or so came from the Vojvodina region of Serbia. The current break-down after the 2001 census is Croat 89.6%, Serb 4.5%, Bosniak 0.5%, Hungarian 0.4%, Slovene 0.3%, Czech 0.2%, Roma 0.2%, Albanian 0.1%, Montenegrin 0.1%, others 4.1%. The Serb population is highest in eastern Slavonia, which also includes a significant number of Hungarians and Czechs. Italians, Albanians and Muslims are concentrated in Istria.

War and a discouraging economic outlook is responsible for a steady decline in Croatia's population as educated, young people leave in search of greater opportunities abroad. Some experts predict that in 50 years only 13% of the population will be children under 14 and adults be-tween 25 and 64 will drop to only 54%. There are no easy solutions, but the government is hoping to encourage the children of expats working abroad to return to Croatia.

About one million Croats live in the other states of former Yugoslavia, mainly Bosnia and Hercegovina, northern Vojvodina and around the Bay of Kotor in Montenegro. Some 2.3 million ethnic Croats live abroad, including almost 1.5 million in the USA, 270,000 in Germany, 240,000 in Australia, 150,000 in Canada and 150,000 in Argentina. Pittsburgh and Buenos Aires have the largest Croatian communities outside Europe. Croatians outside of the country retain the right to vote in national elec-tions and many do. These voting expatriates take a hard nationalistic line and tend to vote for right-wing parties.

DID YOU KNOW?

In Croatia 32% of women and 34% of adult men are smokers.

SPORT

Football, tennis and skiing are enormously popular and sporty Croatia has contributed a disproportionate number of world-class players in each sport.

Tennis

'I don't know what's in the water in Croatia, but it seems like every player is over seven feet tall' – Andy Roddick.

Not quite. Yet, Croatia is producing some mighty big players, in every sense of the word.

The 2001 victory of 6ft 4in Goran Ivanišević at Wimbledon provoked wild celebrations throughout the country, especially in his home town of Split. The charismatic serve-and-volley player was much loved for his engaging personality and on-court antics and dominated the top 10 rankings during much of the 1990s. Unfortunately he was plagued by injuries and, after slipping precipitously in the world rankings, announced his retirement in 2004. Up-and-coming players on the Croatian men's circuit include young Mario Ančić, also a six-foot plus player from Split and a semi-finalist at Wimbledon in 2004. At 6ft 10in, Ivo Karlović from Zagreb is another giant to be reckoned with, although his stunning first-round Wimbledon 2003 victory over defending champion Lleyton Hewitt was followed by a disappointing year.

The women's side is less stellar. Zagreb-born Iva Majoli won the French Open in 1997 with an aggressive baseline game but failed to follow up with other Grand Slam victories. Varaždin-born Karolina Sprem had a good year in 2004, finishing 18th in the World Tennis Association (WTA) rankings, but Jelena Kostanic from Split failed to crack the top 20.

Tennis is more than a spectator sport in Croatia. The coast is amply endowed with clay courts and they are rarely empty. The biggest tournament in Croatia is the Umag Open in Istria, held in July.

Football

By far the most popular spectator sport in Croatia is football (soccer) which frequently serves as an outlet for Croatian patriotism and, occasionally, as a means to express political opposition. When Franjo Tudjman came to power, he decided that the name of Zagreb's football club, 'Dinamo', was 'too communist', so he changed it to 'Croatia'. Waves of outrage followed the decision led by angry young football fans who used the controversy to express their opposition to the regime. Even though the following government restored the original name, you will occasionally see *Dinamo volim te* (Dinamo I love you) graffiti in Zagreb. Dinamo's frequent rival is Hajduk of Split, named after ancient resisters to Roman rule.

The national team performed outstandingly to finish third in the 1998 World Cup in France, following stunning victories over teams of the calibre of Germany and Holland. In addition, Davor Šuker won the prestigious 'Golden Boot' award for being the tournament's leading goal scorer with six goals. By career end Šuker scored 46 international goals, 45 of them for Croatia; he is the Croatian national team's all-time goal-scoring leader. Football great Pelé named him one of the top 125 greatest living footballers in March 2004.

The team continues to do well, although less outstandingly than in the past. In 2002, it made it to Round One of the World Cup in Japan and South Korea and in 2004 to Round One of Euro 2004 in Portugal.

Skiing

If Croatia had a national goddess, it would be Janica Kostelić. Born in Zagreb to a family of winter-sports nuts, Kostelić is the most accomplished skier to have emerged from Croatia. After winning the Alpine Skiing World Cup in 2001, Kostelić won three gold medals and a silver in the 2002 Winter Olympics – the first Winter Olympic medals ever for an athlete from Croatia. At the age of 20, she became the first female skier ever to win three gold medals in one Olympics.

Maybe it's in the genes. Brother Ivica Kostelić took the men's slalom World Cup title in 2002.

MEDIA

The Croatian constitution guarantees freedom of press and, by and large, this ideal has been implemented. It wasn't always that way. Former president Tudjman came down with a heavy hand on media outlets. Government-owned radio and TV became propaganda organs, spouting politically correct nationalism to deflect attention from a corrupt and incompetent regime. Newspapers that wouldn't play along found themselves the target of relentless harassment. The satirical newspaper, *Feral Tribune*, skewered the political class with its sly graphics and fulminating editorials. In response, the government tried to tax it out of existence by la-belling it a 'pornographic' journal. Lengthy legal procedures ensued but the journal was finally saved by the arrival of a new government in 2000.

Another battle centered on Radio 101, an independent station based in Zagreb that was also critical of Tudjman's government. In 1996 the government tried to expel the station from its frequency in favour of a pro-government station. Mass protests, including tens of thousands of people in the centre of Zagreb, forced the government to back down.

In 2004, Croatia's first private TV station began broadcasting. TV Nova promises a more diverse offering than those on Croatia's three government stations. There are also three national radio stations.

DID YOU KNOW?

About 27% of Croatians are Internet users.

RELIGION

According to the 2001 census, 87.8% of the population identified itself as Catholic, 4.4% Orthodox, 1.3% Muslim, 0.3% Protestant, 6.2% others and unknown. Croats are overwhelmingly Roman Catholic, while virtually all Serbs belong to the Eastern Orthodox Church, a division that has its roots in the fall of the Roman Empire. In fact, religion is the only factor separating the ethnically identical populations. In addition to various doctrinal differences, Orthodox Christians venerate icons, allow priests to marry and do not accept the authority of the pope.

It would be difficult to overstate the extent to which Catholicism shapes the Croatian national identity. The Croats pledged allegiance to Roman Catholicism as early as the 9th century and were rewarded with the right to conduct Mass and issue religious writings in the local language, which eventually became the Glagolitic script. The popes supported the early Croatian kings who in turn built monasteries and churches to further promote Catholicism. Throughout the long centuries of domination by foreign powers, Catholicism was the unifying element in forging a sense of nationhood.

Tragically, the profound faith that had animated Croatian nationalism was perverted into a murderous intolerance under the wartime Ustaše regime. The complicity of local parishes in 'cleansing' the population of Jews and Serbs prompted Tito to suppress religion – and, he hoped, nationalism – when he took power. Although religion was not officially forbidden, it was seen as 'politically incorrect' for ambitious Croats to at-tend Mass. Small wonder that the Vatican was the first entity to recognise an independent Croatia in 1991.

The Church enjoys a respected position in Croatia's cultural and politi-cal life and Croatia is the subject of particular attention from the Vatican. Nearly 76% of Croatian Catholics answering a poll said they considered themselves religious and about 30% attend services weekly. The Church is also the most trusted institution in Croatia, rivalled only by the mili-tary. Also, Croats both within Croatia and abroad provide a stream of priests and nuns to replenish the ranks of Catholic clergy.

Former president Tudjman cultivated a close relationship with the Church, signing a series of treaties with the Vatican that codified the relationship between the Church and state in Croatia. The most im-portant provisions deal with the equivalency of a church marriage and a civil wedding, the introduction of obligatory religious instruction in the state school system, and restitution of Church property nationalised under Tito's Communists. The state also agreed to give financial support to Church activities.

Croatia's special relationship with the Vatican is a mutual one. In 2003 Pope John Paul II made his third trip to Croatia since independence. As the Catholic Church loses ground in much of secular Europe, Croatia's strong identity as a Catholic country has become increasingly important to the Vatican. Religious holidays are celebrated with fervour and Sunday Mass is strongly attended. The Pope clearly hopes that Croatia will be carrying the Catholic banner as it marches into Europe but the question remains open: will Croatia Christianise Europe or will Europe secularise Croatia?

WOMEN IN CROATIA

Women face special hurdles in Croatia. Under Tito's brand of socialism, women were encouraged to become politically active and their representation in the Croatian Sabor increased to 18%. Since independence, it has fallen to a mere 8%. Because of the overwhelming 'maleness' of politics, some 80% of men and women find it highly unlikely that a woman would be head of state. More and more wives and mothers must work outside the home to make ends meet (48% of women are in the workforce, the same level as New Zealand) but they still perform most household duties and are under-represented on the executive levels. Only 66% of women and 42% of men unequivocally accept the idea of a female boss.

To get a head of steam worked up on women's issues, turn to the feminist e-zine www .crowmagazine.com.

Women fare worse in traditional villages than in urban areas and were hit harder economically than men after the homeland war. Many of the factories that closed, especially in Eastern Slavonia, had a high proportion of women workers. Both physical abuse at home and sexual harassment at work are common in Croatia and the legal system is not yet adequate for women to seek redress.

ARTS
Music

Although Croatia has produced many fine classical musicians and composers, its most original musical contribution lies in its rich tradition of folk music. Croatian folk music itself bears many influences, much dating back to the middle ages when the Hungarians and the Venetians vied for control of the country. Franz Joseph Haydn (1732–1809) was born near a Croat enclave in Austria and was strongly influenced by Croatian airs. Traditional Croatian music has also influenced modern musicians, most notably the Croatian-American jazz singer Helen Merrill, who recorded Croatian melodies on her album, *Jelena Ana Milcetic a.k.a. Helen Merrill.*

The instrument most often used in Croatian folk music is the *tamburitza*, a three- or five-string mandolin that is plucked or strummed. Introduced by the Turks in the 17th century, the instrument rapidly gained a following in Eastern Slavonia and came to be closely identified with Croatian national aspirations.

Tamburitza music survived the Yugoslav period, when it remained the dominant music played at weddings and local festivals. In the 1980s it modernised and many groups began to include electric bass and guitar. First was Zlatni Dukati, who became known for their patriotic music before and during the 1990s war. They were quickly followed by the rock-and-roll influenced Gazde, who are still turning out top-selling CDs.

RECOMMENDED RECORDINGS

- *Croatie; musiques d'autrefois* is a good starting point as it covers the whole gamut of Croatian music.
- *Lijepa naša tamburaša* is a selection of Slavonian chants accompanied by *tamburitza* (a three- or five-string mandolin).
- *Omiš 1967–75* is an overview of *klapa* (outgrowth of church-choir singing) music.
- *Pripovid O Dalmaciji* is an excellent selection of *klapa* in which the influence of church choral singing is especially clear.
- *Mirakul* joins young star Gibboni with luminaries from world music such as the drummer Manu Katche and the singer Geoffrey Oriema.

Vocal music followed the *klapa* tradition. Translated as 'group of people', *klapa* is an outgrowth of church-choir singing. The form is most popular in rural Dalmatia and can involve up to 10 voices singing in harmony about love, tragedy and loss. Traditionally the choirs were all-male but now women have been getting into the act, although there are very few mixed choirs.

Yet another popular strain of folk music emanates from the region of Međimurje in northeastern Croatia. Strongly influenced by music in neighbouring Hungary, the predominant instrument is a *citura* (zither). The tunes are slow and melancholic, frequently revolving around love-lost themes. New artists have breathed life into this traditional genre. Vještice (The Witches) updates traditional Međimurje folk songs with rock rhythms. Lidija Bajuk and Dunja Knebl are female singers who have also done much to resuscitate the music and have gained large followings.

Keep abreast of the latest in *tamburitza* music at www.tamburaland.com.

Not everyone is listening to folk music of course. Croatian pop is alive and well and you'll hear plenty of it on the radio. Ivo Robić was one of the few Croatian singer-songwriters to gain a following abroad. Doris Dragović has been on the scene for nearly 20 years, while younger stars Severina and Gibonni have wildly enthusiastic fans.

If anything unifies the fractious former republics of Yugoslavia, it's music. Bosnian Goran Bregović teamed up with film maker Emir Kusturica for some remarkable scores and his music remains loved throughout the region. *Turbofolk*, a super-charged version of Serbian music, is widely listened to in Croatia and most Croatian stars regularly perform in Serbia and Montenegro, Bosnia and Macedonia.

Like the music, Croatian traditional dances are kept alive at local and national festivals. Look for the *drmeš*, a kind of accelerated polka danced by couples in small groups. The *kolo*, a lively Slavic round dance in which men and women alternate in the circle, is accompanied by Gypsy-style violinists. In Dalmatia, the *poskočica* is also danced by couples creating various patterns.

Literature

The Croatian language developed in the centuries following the great migration into Slavonia and Dalmatia. Originally influenced by Latin, Greek and the language of Franciscan and Benedictine monks, the oldest Slavic influence was the Church-Slavonic language, which became influential around the 10th century. In order to convert the Slavs to Christianity, Greek missionaries Cyril and Methodius learned the language. It was Cyril who first put the language into writing which became known as Glagolitic script. The earliest known example of Glagolitic script was an 11th-century inscription in a Benedictine abbey on Krk Island, and ecclesiastical works in Glagolitic continued to appear until the Middle Ages.

The first literary flowering in Croatia, however, took place in Dalmatia, which was strongly influenced by the Italian Renaissance. The works of the scholar and poet Marko Marulić (1450–1524), from Split, are still venerated in Croatia. His play *Judita* was the first work produced by a Croatian writer in his native tongue. Ivan Gundulić (1589–1638) from Ragusa (Dubrovnik) is widely considered to be the greatest Croatian poet. His epic poem *Osman* celebrated the Polish victory over the Turks in 1621 – a victory that the author saw as heralding the destruction of the detested Ottoman rule. The plays of Marin Držić (1508–67), especially *Dundo Maroje*, express humanistic Renaissance ideals and are still performed, especially in Dubrovnik.

Croatia's towering literary figure is 20th-century novelist and playwright Miroslav Krleža. Always politically active, Krleža broke with Tito in 1967 over the writer's campaign for equality between the Serbian and Croatian literary languages. Depicting the concerns of a changing Yugoslavia, his most popular novels include *The Return of Philip Latinovicz* (1932), which has been translated into English, and *Banners* (1963–65), a multi-volume saga about middle-class Croatian life at the turn of the 20th century.

Mention should also be made of Ivo Andrić (1892–1975), who won the Nobel Prize for literature in 1961 for his Bosnian historical trilogy *The Bridge on the Drina*, *Bosnian Story*, and *Young Miss*. Born as a Catholic Croat in Bosnia, the writer used the Serbian dialect and lived in Belgrade, but identified himself as a Yugoslav.

In poetry, the most towering postwar figure was the lyrical and sometimes satirical Vesna Parun. Although often harassed by the government for her 'decadent and bourgeois' poetry, her *Collected Poems* have reached a new generation who find solace in her vision of wartime folly.

Contemporary writers have been strongly marked by the implications of Croatian independence. Alenka Mirković is a journalist who wrote a powerful memoir of the siege of Vukovar. Goran Tribuson uses the thriller genre to explore the changes in Croatian society after the war. In *Oblivion* Pavao Pavličić uses a detective story to explore the problems of collective historical memory.

Architecture, Painting & Sculpture

Examples of Roman architecture are abundant in Dalmatia, and the Euphrasian Basilica in Poreč is an outstanding example of Byzantine art; however, the first distinctively Croatian design also appeared along the coast. *Pleter* (plaited ornamentation) first appeared around AD 800 on the baptismal font of Duke Višeslav of Nin in the Church of the Holy Cross (Nin). This ornamentation appears frequently on church entrances and church furniture from the early medieval period. Around the end of the 10th century, the lattice-work began to acquire leaves and tendrils. The design is so linked with the country's culture that President Franjo Tudjman used it in a campaign poster in his first election to signal a return to traditional Croatian culture.

The best example of pre-Romanesque architecture is found on the Dalmatian coast, beginning with the 11th-century Church of the Holy Cross in Nin, built in the shape of a cross with two apses and a dome above the centre point. There are remains of circular pre-Romanesque churches in

Split, Trogir and Ošalj, but the most impressive is the Church of St Donat in Zadar, dating from the 9th century. Its round central structure and three semicircular apses make it most unusual. Other smaller churches in Šipan and Lopud from the 10th and 11th centuries are built with a cross-shaped ground plan indicating the growing influence of Byzantine culture at that time.

The Romanesque tradition persisted along the coast long after the Gothic style had swept the rest of Europe. In the 13th century the earliest examples of Gothic style usually appeared still mixed with Romanesque forms. The most stunning work from this period is the portal on the Cathedral of St Lovro carved by the master-artisan Radovan. Depicting human figures performing everyday chores was a definite break with traditional Byzantine reliefs of saints and apostles. The unusual wooden portal on Split's Cathedral of St Domnius (1240), made up of 28 square reliefs by Andrija Buvina, is another masterpiece from the Gothic period. The Cathedral of the Assumption of the Blessed Virgin Mary (formerly St Stephen's) in Zagreb was the first venture into the Gothic style in northern Croatia. Although reconstructed several times, the sacristy has remnants of 13th-century murals.

Art Treasures of Croatia by Radovan Ivančević is a great summary of the history of Croatian art.

Late-Gothic building was dominated by the builder and sculptor Juraj Dalmatinac, born in Zadar in the 15th century. His most outstanding work was Šibenik's Cathedral of St Jacob, which marks a transition from the Gothic to the Renaissance period. In addition to constructing the church entirely of stone, without timber, Dalmatinac adorned the apses with a wreath of realistically carved local people. At the same time, the painter Vincent of Kastav was producing lovely church frescoes in Istria. The small church of St Maria near Beram contains his frescoes, most notably the *Dance of Death*. Another notable Istrian painter of the 15th century is Ivan of Kastav, who has left frescoes throughout Istria, mostly in the Slovenian part.

Many artists born in Dalmatia were influenced by, and in turn influenced, Italian Renaissance style. The sculptors Lucijano Vranjanin and Frano Laurana, the minituarist Julije Klović and the painter Andrija Medulić left Dalmatia while the region was under threat from the Turks, and worked in Italy. Museums in London, Paris and Florence contain examples of their work, but few of their creations are in Croatia.

In independent Ragusa (Dubrovnik), however, the Renaissance flourished. By the second half of the 15th century, Renaissance influences were appearing on late-Gothic structures. The Sponza Palace, formerly the Customs House, is a fine example of this mixed style. By the mid-16th century, Renaissance features began to supplant the Gothic style in the palaces and summer residences built in and around Ragusa by the wealthy nobility. Unfortunately, much was destroyed in the 1667 earthquake and now Dubrovnik is more notable for the mixed Gothic-Romanesque Franciscan monastery, the 15th-century Orlando column and the Onofrio fountain, and the baroque St Blaise's Church, the Jesuit St Ignatius Church and Dubrovnik's cathedral.

Northern Croatia is well-known for the baroque style introduced by Jesuit monks in the 17th century. The city of Varaždin was a regional capital in the 17th and 18th centuries and, because of its location, enjoyed a steady interchange of artists, artisans and architects with northern Europe. The combination of wealth and a creatively fertile environment led to it becoming Croatia's foremost city of baroque art. You'll notice the style in the elaborately restored houses, churches and especially the impressive castle.

In Zagreb good examples of the baroque style are found in the Upper Town (Gornji Grad). Notice the Church of St Catherine and the Church of St Xavier and the restored baroque mansions that are now the Croatian Historical Museum and the Croation Museum of Naive Art. Wealthy families built baroque mansions around Zagreb, including mansions at Brezovica, Milyana, Lobor and Bistra.

In the 19th century, Dalmatian style stagnated as the region fell prey to political problems, but Zagreb underwent a revival. Vlaho Bukovac (1855–1922) was the most notable painter in the late 19th century. After working in London and Paris, he came to Zagreb in 1892 and produced portraits and paintings on historical themes in a lively style. Early-20th-century painters of note include Miroslav Kraljević (1885–1913) and Josip Račić (1885–1908), but the most internationally recognised artist was the sculptor Ivan Meštrović (1883–1962), who created many masterpieces on Croatian themes. Antun Augustinčić (1900–79) was another internationally recognised sculptor whose *Monument to Peace* is outside New York's UN building. A small museum of his work can be visited in the the town of Klanjec, north of Zagreb.

Postwar artists experimented with abstract expressionism but this period is best remembered for the naive art that began with the 1931 *Zemlja* (Soil) exhibition in Zagreb, which introduced the public to works by Ivan Generalić (1914–92) and other peasant painters. Committed to producing art that could be easily understood and appreciated by ordinary people, Generalić was joined by painters Franjo Mraz and Mirko Virius and sculptor Petar Smajic in a campaign to gain acceptance and recognition for naive art.

Abstract art also infiltrated the postwar scene. The most celebrated modern Croatian painter is Edo Murtić (1921–), who drew inspiration from the countryside of Dalmatia and Istria. In 1959, a group of artists – Marijan Jevsovar, Julije Knifer and Ivan Kožarić – created the Gorgona group, which pushed the envelope of abstract art.

Recent trends have included postmodern installation art, minimalism, conceptualism and video art. Contemporary artists who are attracting notice include Jasna Barišić of Zadar, Andrea Musa of Split, Višeslav Aralica and Ivana Ožetski of Zagreb.

The Art Pavilion in Zagreb, designed by Vlaho Bukovac, is a good place to keep up with the latest developments in Croatian art. Built as a space for large exhibitions, this elaborate structure presents the finest contemporary local artists.

DID YOU KNOW?

Travel and tourism accounts for 10.6% of Croatia's GDP, generating 139,000 jobs and representing 13% of total employment.

Environment

THE LAND

Croatia is half the size of present-day Serbia and Montenegro in area and population. The republic swings around like a boomerang from the Pannonian plains of Slavonia between the Sava, Drava and Danube Rivers, across hilly central Croatia to the Istrian Peninsula, then south through Dalmatia along the rugged Adriatic coast. The unusual geography makes it tricky to circle the country. Touring the country from Zagreb to Dubrovnik means either flying back to Zagreb from Dubrovnik, or driving up through Bosnia and Hercegovina to enter Croatia from the east.

The narrow Croatian coastal belt at the foot of the Dinaric Alps is only about 600km long as the crow flies, but it's so indented that the actual length is 1778km. If the 4012km of coastline around the offshore islands is added to the total, the length becomes 5790km. Most of the 'beaches' along this jagged coast consist of slabs of rock sprinkled with naturists. Don't come expecting to find sand, but the waters are sparkling clean, even around large towns.

Croatia's offshore islands are every bit as beautiful as those off the coast of Greece. There are 1185 islands and islets along the tectonically submerged Adriatic coastline, 66 of them inhabited. The largest are Cres, Krk, Mali Lošinj, Pag and Rab in the north; Dugi Otok in the middle; and Brač, Hvar, Korčula, Mljet and Vis in the south. Most are barren and elongated from northwest to southeast, with high mountains that drop right into the sea.

WILDLIFE
Animals

Deer are plentiful in the dense forests of Risnjak, as well as brown bears, wild cats and *ris* (lynx) from which the national park gets its name. Occasionally a wolf or wild boar may appear but only rarely. Plitvice Lakes National Park, however, is an important refuge for wolves. A rare sea otter is also protected in Plitvice as well as in Krka National Park.

The griffon vulture, with a wing span of 2.6m, has a permanent colony on Cres Island, and Paklenica National Park is rich in peregrine falcons, goshwaks, sparrow hawks, buzzards and owls. Krka National Park is an important migration route and winter habitat for marsh birds such as herons, wild duck, geese, cranes and rare golden eagles, and short-toed eagles. Kopački Rit swamp near Osijek in eastern Croatia is an extremely important bird refuge.

Two venomous snakes are endemic in Paklenica – the nose-horned viper and the European adder – and the nonvenomous leopard snake, four-lined snake, grass snake and snake lizard species can also be found in Krka National Park.

Plants

The richest plant life is found in the Velebit Range, part of the Dinaric Range. Botanists have counted 2700 species and 78 endemic plants there, including the increasingly threatened edelweiss. Risnjak National Park is another good place to find edelweiss along with black-vanilla orchids, lilies and hairy alpenroses, which look a lot better than they sound. The dry Mediterranean climate along the coast is perfect for *maquis*, a low brush that flourishes all along the coast but especially on the island of

Mljet. You'll also find oleander, jasmine and juniper trees along the coast, and lavender is cultivated on the island of Hvar. Typically, Mediterranean olive and fig trees are also abundant.

NATIONAL PARKS

When the Yugoslav Federation collapsed, eight of its finest national parks ended up in Croatia covering 7.5% of the country and with a total area of 994 sq km of which 235 sq km is water. Risnjak National Park south of Zagreb is the most untouched forested park, partly because the climate at its higher altitudes is somewhat inhospitable – an average temperature of 12.6°C in July. The winters are long and snowy but when spring finally comes in late May or early June, everything blooms at once. The park has been kept deliberately free of tourist facilities, with the idea that only mountain lovers need apply.

DID YOU KNOW?

The Croatian kuna is named for the pelt of the stone marten (kuna), which was used as currency under the Venetians.

The dramatically formed karstic gorges and cliffs make Paklenica National Park along the coast a rock climbing favourite and the scene of a European rock-climbing competition held each year in early May. Large grottoes and caves filled with stalactites and stalagmites make it an interesting park for cave explorers and there are many kilometres of trails for hiking. Tourist facilities are well developed here. More rugged is the mountainous Northern Velebit National Park, a stunning patchwork of forests, peaks, ravines and ridges.

The waterfalls of Plitvice Lakes National Park were formed by mosses that retain calcium carbonate as river water rushes through the karst. Travertine, or tufa, builds up sprouting plants which grow on top of each other to create barriers to the river. The park has been named a Unesco World Heritage site and is easily accessible from either Zagreb or Zadar. The falls are at their watery best in the spring.

DID YOU KNOW?

Sea-water temperature ranges from a low of 7°C in December to 25°C in August.

Krka National Park is an even more extensive series of lakes and water-falls than Plitvice. The Zrmanja, Krka, Cetina and Neretva Rivers form waterfalls, but Manojlovac's power plant upstream can interfere with the flow, which can slow considerably in July or August. The main access point is in Skradinski Buk, with the largest cascade covering 800m.

The Kornati Islands consist of 140 islands, islets and reefs scattered over 300 sq km. They are sparsely inhabited and sparsely vegetated but the great indented form of the islands and extraordinary rock forma-tions make them an Adriatic highlight. Unless you have your own boat, however, you'll need to join an organised tour from Zadar.

Only the western third of Mljet Island has been named a national park due to the two highly indented salt-water lakes surrounded by lush vegetation. Maquis is thicker and taller on Mljet than nearly anywhere else in the Mediterranean, which makes it a natural refuge for many animals. Snakes nearly overran the island until the Indian mongoose

WORLD HERITAGE SITES

- Old City of Dubrovnik (p229)
- Historical Complex of Split with Diocletian's Palace (p192)
- Plitvice Lakes National Park (p164)
- Episcopal Complex of the Euphrasian Basilica in the Historic Centre of Poreč (p145)
- Historic City of Trogir (p202)
- Cathedral of St Jacob in Šibenik (p181)

was introduced in 1909. This idyllic island is accessible by regular boats from Dubrovnik.

The Brijuni (Brioni) Islands are the most cultivated national park since they were developed as a tourist resort in late 19th century. They were the getaway paradise for Tito and now attract glitterati, their helpers and their yachts. Most of the exotic animals and plants were introduced (elephants are not normally found in the Adriatic) but the islands are lovely. An organised tour is required.

ENVIRONMENTAL ISSUES

The lack of heavy industry in Croatia has had the happy effect of leaving its forests, coasts, rivers and air fresh and unpolluted. Nevertheless, there are some problems. Although 23% of Croatia is covered by forests, they are under serious threat. It's estimated that about 50% of the forests are imperilled as a result of acid rain, mostly from neighbouring countries. Logging and building projects are cutting into forested land at the rate of about 1000 hectares a year.

The website of the Ministry of Environmental Protection, www.mzopu .hr, is the place for the latest news on Croatia's environment.

Coastal and island forests face particular problems. First logged by Venetians to build ships, then by local people desperate for fuel, centuries of neglect have left many island and coastal mountains barren. The dry summers and brisk *maestrals* (strong, steady westerly wind) also pose substantial fire hazards along the coast. In the last 20 years, fires have destroyed 7% of Croatia's forests.

Although the sea along the Adriatic coast is among the cleanest in the world, overfishing has greatly reduced the fish population. With a tourist boom, the demand for fresh fish and shellfish has risen exponentially. As it's becoming increasingly difficult to fish their way out of the problem, the only alternative for Croatians is to grow their own seafood. The production of farmed sea bass, sea bream and tuna (for export) is projected to rise substantially with all the resulting environmental pressure along the coast.

Food & Drink

Croatian cuisine is a savoury smorgasboard of taste, reflecting the cultures that have influenced the country over the course of its history. You'll find a sharp divide between the Italian-style cuisine on the coast and the Hungarian, Viennese and even Turkish-style cuisine in the interior. Each region has its own speciality, but wherever you go you'll be surprised by the generally good-quality food, made from fresh, seasonal ingredients.

The price and quality of meals varies little as there is an upper limit to what the local crowd can afford to pay, and a bottom line to what they'll find acceptable. Croatians have little money for dining out, but when they do they expect the food to be worth it, which it usually is. Restaurants cluster in the middle of the range – very few are unbelievably cheap and even fewer are exorbitantly expensive. Whatever your budget, it's hard to get a truly bad meal anywhere in Croatia.

STAPLES & SPECIALITIES

Zagreb and northwestern Croatia favour the kind of hearty meat dishes you might find in Vienna. Juicy *pečenje* (spit-roasted meat), *janje* (lamb), *svinjetina* (pork) and *patka* (duck) are real favourites, often accompanied by *mlinci* (baked noodles) or *prženi krumpir* (roast potatoes). *Puran* (turkey) with *mlinci* is practically an institution on Zagreb menus along with steak *a la Zagreb* (veal stuffed with ham and cheese, then fried in breadcrumbs) – another calorie-ridden speciality. Hungarian influence is found in the *gulaš* (goulash) and *palačinka* (thin pancakes filled with jam and topped with chocolate) that you'll find on many menus.

Cuisine in Eastern Slavonia, which uses liberal amounts of paprika and garlic, is spicier than in other regions. The nearby Drava River provides fresh fish such as carp and pike, which is stewed in a paprika sauce and served with *riblji paprikaš* (fish stew with paprika). The region's sausages are also renowned, especially *kulen,* a paprika-flavoured sausage served with cottage cheese, peppers, tomatoes and *turšija* (pickled vegetables). Cakes stuffed with walnuts, poppyseeds and plum jam make a delicious dessert.

Coastal cuisine is typically Mediterranean, using a lot of olive oil, garlic, fish and herbs. Meals often begin with a first course of pasta such as spaghetti or *rizot* (risotto) topped with *prstaci* (seafood). In Istria you may see *menestra*, which is a vegetable-and-bean soup similar to Italian minestrone soup. If you see risotto or pasta with *tartufe*, grab it – these wild truffles are a real delicacy in Istria. Thin slices of smoked Istrian or Dalmatian ham are often on the appetiser list. It's expensive because of the long hours and personal attention involved in smoking the meat, but it does acquire a unique flavour. For a special nonmeat appetiser, try Pag cheese, a pungent hard cheese from Pag Island which is served with olives. Dalmatian *brodet* (mixed fish stewed with polenta) is another regional treat but it's often only available in two-person portions. Dalmatian *pašticada* (beef stuffed with lard and roasted in wine and spices) appears more on menus in the interior than it does along the coast and makes a hearty winter dish.

DRINKS

It's customary to have a small glass of brandy before a meal. Croatia is famous for its *šljivovica* (plum brandies), *travarica* (herbal brandies), *vinjak* (cognacs) and liqueurs such as maraschino, a cherry liqueur made in Zadar, *prosecco*, a sweet dessert wine, and *pelinkovac*, a herbal liqueur.

Zagreb's Ožujsko *pivo* (beer) is very good, but Karlovačko beer from Karlovac is better. You'll want to practise saying the word *živjeli!* (cheers!).

Wine is an important part of Croatian meals but oenophiles will be dismayed to see Croats diluting their wine with water. It's hardly necessary. Although not on a world-class level, Croatian wines are eminently drinkable and occasionally distinguished. Virtually every region produces its own wine. The Istria and Kvarner regions are known for Žlahtina of Vrbnik on Krk Island, cabernet from Poreč and Terrano from Buzet. Dalmatia has the oldest wine-producing tradition – look for Pošip and Grk on Korčula, Dingač and Postup from the Pelješac Peninsula, Plavac from Brač Island and Malmsy from Dubrovnik. Eastern Slavonia produces excellent white wines such as Kutjevačka Graševina, Kutjevo chardonnay, Rhine riesling and Krauthaker Graševina.

Strongly brewed espresso served in tiny cups is popular throughout Croatia. You can have it diluted with milk or order cappuccino, regular or decaf. Herbal teas are widely available but regular tea is apt to be too weak for aficionados.

WHERE TO EAT & DRINK

A *restauracija* or *restoran* (restaurant) is at the top of the food chain, generally presenting a more formal dining experience and an elaborate wine list. A *gostionica* or *konoba* is usually a simple and family-run establishment. The produce may come from the family garden. A *pivnica* is more like a pub, with a wide choice of beer. Sometimes there's a hot dish or sandwiches available. A *kavana* is a café. The only food you're able to order in a *kavana* is cake and ice cream, but you can nurse your coffee for hours. A *slastičarna* serves ice cream, cakes, strudels and sometimes coffee but you usually have to gobble your food standing up, or take it away.

It's in Croatian, but www .gastronaut.hr has a constantly updated list of the 10 best Croatian eateries.

For inexpensive, quick meals, you'll find that pizza is often astonishingly good wherever you go and costs about half of what you'd pay in Western Europe. The spaghetti and risotto listed as an appetiser can make a filling meal, especially if you soak up the sauce with heaps of bread. For fast food, you can usually snack on *ćevapčići* (spicy beef or pork meatballs), *ražnjiči* (shish kebab) or *burek* (a heavy pastry stuffed with meat or cheese). Along the coast, look for lightly breaded and fried *lignje* (squid) as a main course.

Self-service *samoposluživanje* (cafeterias) are quick, easy and inexpensive, though the quality of the food varies. If the samples behind glass look cold or dried out, ask for a fresh plate to be dished out. Better restaurants aren't that much more expensive if you choose carefully, and pizzerias are often cheaper.

MYSTERIOUS FLAVOURS

No Croatian cook could do without it yet it is rarely used outside former Yugoslavia. It's the secret ingredient in nearly every fish, vegetable or meat dish yet it's hard to describe what it actually contains. What is it? It's *vegeta*, sold by the kilo in nearly every grocery store. We know that there's salt, sugar, corn starch and various dehydrated vegetables plus 'flavour enhancers' that end in -ate. There are also 'spices' of indeterminate composition. We don't know how it works its magic in Croatian dishes, but even the simplest sauces are imbued with subtle flavours. Pick up a package and add a tablespoon or so to your favourite tomato sauce. *Dobar tek!*

If you're on your own, breakfast is difficult as all you can get easily is coffee. Otherwise, you can buy some bread, cheese and milk at a supermarket and have a picnic somewhere. If you're staying in a hotel, you'll be served a buffet breakfast that includes cornflakes, bread, yoghurt and a selection of cold meat, powdered 'juice' and cheese. More upmarket hotels have better buffets that include eggs, sausages and home-made pastries.

Fruit and vegetables from the market can make a healthy, cheap picnic lunch. There are plenty of supermarkets in Croatia – cheese, bread, ham and milk are readily available and fairly cheap. The person behind the meat counter at supermarkets will make a big cheese or bologna sandwich for you upon request and you only pay the regular price of the ingredients.

VEGETARIANS & VEGANS

The Best of Croatian Cooking by Liliana Pavicic and Gordana Pirker-Mosher has 200 recipes gathered from all over Croatia and adapted to ingredients commonly found in North America.

Vegetarians have a tough time of it in northern Croatia and vegans have an extremely limited selection, but you can begin with a hearty soup such as *manistra od bobića* (bean and fresh maize soup) or *juha od krumpira na zagorski način* (Zagorje potato soup), followed by *štrukli* (baked cheese dumplings) or *blitva* (Swiss chard boiled and often served with potatoes, olive oil and garlic). Along the coast, you'll find plenty of spaghetti and pasta with various vegetable toppings and delicious cheese. If fish and seafood are part of your diet, you'll eat royally nearly everywhere.

WHINING & DINING

Croatians are kid-friendly and you shouldn't hear too much whining while you're dining. Children's portions are easily arranged but you won't often find high chairs for the tinier tots. Dining facilities are rarely equipped with nappy-changing facilities. Baby food and powdered baby milk formulas are easily found at most supermarkets and pharmacies and sold according to age group.

HABITS & CUSTOMS

Croatian Cuisine the Modern Way by Ivanka Biluš et al has simple but authentic Croatian recipes that work well, but you'll need *vegeta* (Croatian flavouring added to dishes) to execute them.

Throughout the former Yugoslavia the breakfast of the people was *burek*, a greasy multi-level cheese or meat pastry. Unless they work on fishing boats, modern Croatians have opted for a lighter start to their day, usually just coffee and pastry with yoghurt and fresh fruit.

Restaurants open for lunch around noon and usually serve well into the afternoon. Croatians tend to eat a large, late lunch and a light dinner but most restaurants have adapted their schedules to the needs of tourists who tend to load up at night. Also, few Croatians can afford to eat out regularly; when they do, it's likely to be a large family outing Saturday night or Sunday afternoon.

Croatians are proud of their cuisine and vastly prefer it to all others (except Italian). Outside of Zagreb, there are few exotic restaurants and few variations on the basic Croatian themes.

EAT YOUR WORDS
Useful Phrases

I'm hungry.	*Ja sam gladan.*
Ya sam *gla*·dan	
I'm a vegetarian.	*Ja sam vegetarijanac/vegetarijanka. (m/f)*
Ya sam ve·ge·ta·ree·*ya*·nats/ve·ge·ta·ree·*yan*·ka	
I don't eat meat.	*Ja ne jedem meso.*
Ya ne *ye*·dem *me*·saw	
Waiter!	*Konobar!*
Kaw·naw·bar!	

The menu, please.   *Molim vas jelovnik.*
    Maw·leem vas ye·*lawv*·neek
What's the speciality of the house?   *Što je vaš specijalitet kuće.*
    Shtaw ye vash spe·tsee·ya·*lee*·tet *koo*·che
What would you recommend?   *Što biste nam preporučili?*
    Shtaw *bee*·ste nam pre·paw·*roo*·chee·lee
Please bring the bill.   *Molim vas donesite račun.*
    Maw·leem vas daw·*ne*·see·te *ra*·choon
Enjoy your meal!   *Dobar Tek!*
    Daw·bar tek!

Menu Decoder

STARTERS

bouzara – a sauce of tomatoes, onions, herbs, white wine and breadcrumbs
buzara – a sauce of tomatoes, white wine, onions and breadcrumbs
brodet – mixed fish stewed with polenta, also called *brodetto*
burek – a heavy pastry stuffed with meat or cheese
čevapčiči – spicy beef or pork meatballs
dalmatinski pršut – lightly smoked ham
formaggio pecorino – Istrian sheep cheese
janjeća juha – lamb soup
juha od krumpira na zagorski način – Zagorje potato soup
klipići – Varaždin's special finger-shaped bread
kulen – a paprika-flavoured sausage served with cottage cheese, peppers, tomatoes
manistra od bobića – bean and fresh maize soup
maneštra – vegetable-and-bean soup similar to Italian minestrone soup
miješana salata – mixed salad
paški sir – sheep's milk cheese from the island of Pag
ražnjiči – shish kebab
riblji paprikaš – fish stew with paprika
štrukli – baked cheese dumplings
turšija – pickled vegetables

MAIN COURSES

baccala – cod with potatoes
bakalar – codfish stew
blitva – Swiss chard boiled and often served with potatoes, olive oil and garlic
crni rižoto – 'black risotto' usually with cuttlefish, squid, olive oil, onion, garlic, parsley, red wine and is given its black colour by the addition of squid ink
djuveč – stew of rice, carrots, tomatoes, peppers and onions and fine local cheese
fuši – special home-made egg pasta twisted into a unique shape
gulaš – goulash
hrvatska pisanica – beef steak in a spicy mushroom, onion, tomato and red wine sauce
husarska pečenka – steak with onions and bacon
lignje na žaru – grilled squid
mlinci – baked noodles
mučkalica – stewed chicken and vegetables in a spicy sauce
pašticada – beef stuffed with lard and roasted in wine and spices
pečenje – spit-roasted meat
pileći ujušak – chicken stew
pljeskavice – minced pork, beef or lamb shaped as a hamburger
prženi krumpir – roast potatoes
punjene paprike – peppers stuffed with minced beef or port and rice in tomato sauce
purica s mlincima – turkey with *mlinci*
ražnjiči – small chunks of pork grilled on a skewer

riblji paprikaš – fish stew
riblji rižoto – fish risotto usually with tomato sauce
rižot – risotto
štruklova juha – soup with *štrukli*
šurlice – home-made noodles topped with goulash

DESSERTS
amareta – round, rich cake with almonds
cukarini – sweet biscuit
klajun – pastry stuffed with walnuts
kremšnite – custard pie
palačinka – thin pancakes filled with jam and topped with chocolate
palačinka sa sirom – pancakes filled with cottage cheese, sugar, raisins, egg and sour cream and then oven baked
torta od oraha – walnut layer cake
sladoled sa šlagom – ice cream with whipped cream

Glossary
BASICS

čaša	glass
doručak	breakfast
kavana	café
luk	onion
med	honey
nož	knife
papar	pepper
pivnica	pub
račun	bill/cheque
restoran or restauracija	restaurant
ručak	lunch
samoposluživanje	cafeteria
šećer	sugar
sol	salt
tanjur	plate
večera	supper
Vegeta	flavouring
viljuška	fork
žlica	spoon

MEAT

govedina	beef
guska	goose
hladni pladanj	cold cuts
janje	lamb
patka	duck
piletina	chicken
puran	turkey
ražnjići	shish kebab
šunka	ham
svinjetina	pork

VEGETABLES & FRUIT

artičoka	artichokes
breskva	peach
krumpira	potato

TOP FIVE RESTAURANTS

It was a tough job but somebody had to do it. After poking into all the corners of the Croatian culinary scene, the following (highly personal) list is the final chow-down:

■ **Boban** (p63) Never one to rest on its trendiness, this Zagreb kitchen is ever-inventive.

■ **Vela Nera** (p137) It's not just the fish or the airy terrace, but the attention to detail that makes this Pula eatery special.

■ **Bevanda** (p102) Right on the Opatijan sea, the fish is cooked to divine perfection.

■ **Zigante** (p152) Truffles, that rare delicacy, are coaxed into imaginative new dishes here in Livade.

■ **Slavonska Kuća** (p86) If you are absolutely besotted with *riblji paprikaš* (fish stew with paprika), as we are, and you must have the best, as we must, then you will drive to this place in Osijek for it, as we do.

kukuruz	corn
kupus	cabbage
naranča	orange
rajčica	tomato
riža	rice
tartufe	wild truffles

FISH

brancin lubin	sea bass
dagnja	mussels
lignje	squid
losos	salmon
oslić	hake
pastrva	trout
prstaci	seafood
rak	crab
riba	fish
škamp	prawns

DRINKS

biska	a strong, sweet local brandy made from mistletoe
Krauthaker Graševina	white wine from Eastern Slavonia
Kutjevačka Graševin	white wine from Eastern Slavonia
Kutjevo	chardonnay
prosecco	sweet dessert wine
pelinkovac	herbal liqueur
pivo	beer
šljivovica	plum brandies
travarica	herbal brandies
vinjak	cognacs

ZAGREB

Zagreb

Zagreb may not dazzle with its charms at first glance, but it doesn't take long to fall under its spell. As the political, economic and cultural capital of Croatia, the city throbs with energy but has retained a good deal of old-world graciousness. Architecturally sober Zagreb is Croatia's largest city, the seat of government, and headquarters for most of Croatia's international companies. Cutting-edge restaurants and fashionable boutiques outfit it in smart European style. Yet the city honours its past by preserving the stately 19th-century buildings in the commercial centre and the intimate streets of the city's old quarter. The beautifully crafted façades may remind you of Vienna or Budapest, while the landscaped park promenade that extends from the train station to the town centre freshens the city with an expanse of greenery. If you linger in a sidewalk café on bohemian Tkalčićeva ulica or Trg Preradovića a pleasure-loving side of the city emerges. Take in one of the many fine museums or galleries and you'll see that Zagreb is not all business but is a lively cultural centre as well.

Although the architecture dwindles into monotonous apartment blocks beyond the central core, several large parks provide a welcome escape from the bustling city. Maksimir Park, northeast of the city centre, is a romantic oasis of shady walks and placid ponds. Jarun Lake in the southwest is less alluring but there's swimming and boating in the summer. When Zagreb residents head for the hills, they don't have far to go: Mt Medvednica is only a tram ride away and offers hiking, skiing and great views over the city.

HIGHLIGHTS

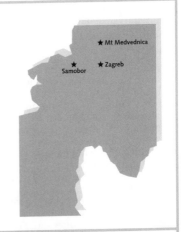

- Enjoying the paintings at the **Museum Mimara** (p55)
- Exploring the hilly streets of Zagreb's **Gradec** (p51) and **Kaptol** (p51) neighbourhoods
- Marvelling at Meštrović's masterful sculpture, **The Well of Life** (p65), in front of the Croatian National Theatre
- Wandering amid the trees and tombs in **Mirogoj cemetery** (p56)
- Bar-hopping on trendy **Tkalčićeva** (p64)
- Sipping a *bermet* (liquor) and munching on a slice of *kremšnite* (custard pie) in **Samobor** (p69)
- Taking in the view from the **Medvedgrad monument** (p57) at Mt Medvednica

| ■ TELEPHONE CODE: 01 | ■ POSTCODE 10000 |

HISTORY

Little is known about Zagreb's history prior to the development of a canonical settlement on Kaptol hill, now the site of Zagreb's towering cathedral, in the 11th century. Another small settlement was developing on Gradec hill, but both were devastated by the Mongol invasion of 1242.

In order to attract foreign artisans to the devastated region, King Bela walled Gradec and turned it into a sort of royally controlled 'fiscal paradise' (tax haven) with numerous privileges. Kaptol remained unprivileged, unwalled and under the church's jurisdiction. As the centuries rolled on, a ruinous rivalry developed between the two towns that frequently descended into violence and near-warfare.

On a number of occasions, the bishops of Kaptol excommunicated the entire town of Gradec, which responded by looting and burning Kaptol. The two communities put aside their quarrels only when their commercial interests united them, such as during the annual fairs that brought merchants and money to the neighbourhood. Unfortunately, there were only three big fairs a year.

In the middle of the 15th century the Turks got as far as the Sava river, prompting the bishop to finally fortify Kaptol. By the mid 16th century the Turks had taken much surrounding territory, but not the two hill towns. Both towns lost their economic importance by the beginning of the 17th century and, out of self-preservation, merged into one town which was called Zagreb.

Zagreb emerged as the capital of the tiny Croatian state largely because there were few towns left standing after the Turkish onslaught. The commercial life of the city stagnated during the ensuing two centuries of warfare, compounded by fires and plague. In 1756 the seat of Croatian government fled from Zagreb to Varaždin, where it remained until 1776. By the end of the 18th century there were a mere 2800 residents of Zagreb, of whom the majority were German or Hungarian.

Meanwhile, the plain below the fortified hill towns became a commercial centre when the space now known as Trg Josip Jelačića was chosen as the site of Zagreb's lucrative trade fairs. The new marketplace spurred construction around its edges that increased as the Turkish threat receded in the 18th century. The straight streets running south of Trg Josip Jelačića provided an important link between Zagreb and other villages on and beyond the Sava River.

In the 19th century, Zagreb finally came into its own. The economy expanded with the development of a prosperous clothing trade, a steam mill and a tannery. A rail link to Vienna and Budapest connected Zagreb to important markets. The city's cultural and educational life also blossomed with the opening of the Music Institute, a theatre, the Academy of Arts and Sciences and the University of Zagreb. Zagreb also became the centre for the Pan-Slavic Illyrian movement that was pressing for south-Slavic unification, greater autonomy within the Austro-Hungarian Empire and recognition of the Slavic language. Count Janko Drašković, lord of Trakošćan castle, published a manifesto in Illyrian in 1832 and his call for national revival resounded throughout Croatia.

Drašković's call came to fruition when Croatia and its capital joined the Kingdom of Serbs, Croats and Slovenes after WWI. Between the two world wars, working-class neighbourhoods emerged in Zagreb between the railway and the Sava River and new residential quarters were built on the southern slopes of Mt Medvednica. In April 1941, the Germans invaded Yugoslavia and entered Zagreb without resistance. Ante Pavelić and the Ustaše moved quickly to proclaim the establishment of the Independent State of Croatia (Nezavisna Dršava Hrvatska) with Zagreb as its capital (see p24 for more on Pavelić and the Ustaše). Although Pavelić ran his fascist state from Zagreb until 1944, he never enjoyed a great deal of support within the capital, which consistently maintained support for Tito's Partisans.

In postwar Yugoslavia, Zagreb (to its chagrin) clearly took second place to Belgrade but the city continued to expand. The area south of the Sava River developed into a new district, Novi Zagreb, with residential blocks, Pleso airport and the Zagreb fairgrounds.

Zagreb was made the capital of Croatia in 1991, the same year that the country became independent.

ORIENTATION

Lying between the southern slopes of Mt Medvednica and the Sava River, Zagreb covers 631 sq km, but most of the city's highlights lie within the Upper Town (Gornji Grad) which includes Gradec and Kaptol and the Lower Town (Donji Grad), which runs between the Upper Town and the train station. The majestic central square of the Lower Town is Trg Josip Jelačića, which is the hub for most of Zagreb's trams. Radiating west from Trg Josip Jelačića is Ilica, the main commercial street lined with offices, shops and a department store. North of the square is the Cathedral of the Assumption of the Blessed Virgin Mary and the medieval Gradec and Kaptol neighbourhoods. Many streets in the Upper and Lower Towns are closed to cars, which makes driving a nightmare but brings a measure of peace to the city's centre.

The train station is in the southern part of the city just a few blocks north of the Sava River. Novi Zagreb is south of the train station, across the Sava River, and is the only substantial development on the southern side of the river. As you come out of the train station, you'll see a series of parks and pavilions directly in front of you which lead into the centre of town.

From the airport, you can take the Croatia Airlines bus to the bus station.

The bus station is 1km east of the train station. Tram Nos 2, 3 and 6 run from the bus station to the train station, with No 6 continuing to Trg Josip Jelačića.

See p266 for more information on the use of street names in Zagreb.

INFORMATION
Bookshops

Algoritam (Gajeva; Hotel Dubrovnik) This shop off Trg Josip Jelačića has a wide selection of books and magazines in English, French, German, Italian and Croatian to choose from.

Knjižara Ljevak (Ilica 1) Has an excellent selection of maps as well as English translations of destination guides and Croatian cookbooks.

Emergency

Police station (☎ 45 63 311; Petrinjska 30) Assists foreigners with visa problems.

Internet Access

In addition to the two listed here, there are a number of smaller Internet cafés along Preradovićeva.

Art Net Club (☎ 45 58 471; Preradovićeva 25; per hr 20KN; 9am-11pm) Zagreb's flashiest cybercafé, it hosts frequent concerts and performances.

ZAGREB IN...

Two Days

Start your day with a stroll through **Strossmayerov trg** (p68), Zagreb's oasis of greenery. While you're there, take a look at the **Strossmayer Gallery of Old Masters** (p55) and then walk on to the town centre, Trg Josip Jelačića. Avoiding being hit by a tram as you cross the square, head up to Kaptol for a look at the centre of Zagreb's (and Croatia's) religious life, the **Cathedral of the Assumption of the Blessed Virgin Mary** (p54). As long as you're 'uptown', pick up some fruit at the **Dolac** (p53) fruit and vegetable market or have lunch at **Kaptolska Klet** (p62) and head over to Gradec for a church and museum tour. Don't miss **Meštrović's studio** (p53). Try the nightlife along **Tkalčićeva** (p64) and sup at **Baltazar** (p63).

On the second day, make a tour of the Lower Town museums, reserving a good two hours for the **Museum Mimara** (p55). Take tea at **Kazališna Kavana** (p64) and an afternoon break in the **Botanical Gardens** (p53). Early evening is best at Trg Preradovića before dining at one of the many scrumptious Lower Town restaurants and sampling some of Zagreb's nightlife.

Four Days

Your third day should take in lovely **Mirogoj cemetery** (p56) with maybe a stop at **Medvedgrad** (p57) or **Maksimir Park** (p57).

On your last day, make a trip out to **Samobor** (p69) for a heavy dose of small-town kitschy charm. Eat, drink and then take a nice walk to digest it all.

Sublink (☎ 48 11 329; Teslina 12; per hr 20KN; ☻ 9am-10pm Mon-Sat, 3-10pm Sun) It was the city's first cybercafé and has a comfortable setup.

Laundry

If you're staying in private accommodation, you can usually arrange with the owner to do your laundry, which would be cheaper than the two options listed below. Both charge about 60KN for 5kg of laundry.

Petecin (Kaptol 11; ☻ 8am-8pm Mon-Fri)

Predom (Draškovićeva 31; ☻ 7am-7pm Mon-Fri)

Left Luggage

Garderoba Train station (per day 10KN; ☻ 24hr);
Bus station (per hr 1.20KN; ☻ 5am-10pm Mon-Sat, 6am-10pm Sun)

Libraries

British Council (☎ 48 13 700; Ilica 12; ☻ 10am-4.30pm Mon, Tue, Thu, Fri &1.30-6.30pm Wed) Has a library where you can read British and American newspapers, books and periodicals, watch BBC news and borrow books and videotapes. It also sponsors occasional plays, concerts and exhibitions.

French Cultural Institute (☎ 48 10 745;
Preradovićeva 40) Has a reading room and media centre. Enter at No 5 to listen to French tapes or watch French news in the **Mediateque** (☻ 10am-5pm Mon-Thu, to 4pm Fri). The institute's **library** (☻ 10am-5pm Mon-Fri) has a selection of French books, magazines and newspapers. Both libraries are closed for five or six weeks in the summer.

Medical Services

Dental Emergency (☎ 48 28 488; Perkovčeva 3; ☻ 24hr)

KBC Rebro (☎ 23 88 888; Kišpatićeva 12; ☻ 24hr) East of the city, it provides emergency aid.

Pharmacy (☎ 48 48 450; Ilica 43; ☻ 24hr)

Money

ATMs can be found at the bus and train stations and the airport, as well as at numerous locations around town. There are banks in the train and bus stations that accept travellers cheques and exchange offices can be found in the Importanne Centar.

Atlas Travel Agency (☎ 48 13 933; Zrinjevac 17) The Amex representative in Zagreb.

Post

Main Post Office (☎ 48 11 090; Jurišićeva 13) Has a telephone centre.

Post Office (Branimirova 4; ☻ 24hr Mon-Sat,

1pm-midnight Sun) Holds poste restante mail. This post office is also the best place to make long-distance telephone calls and send packages.

Telephone

VIP (☎ 46 91 091; Iblerov trg) Rents mobile phones (per day 40KN). Bring a credit card and passport. Also sells SIM cards (305KN).

Tourist Information

Main Tourist Office (☎ 48 14 051; www.zagreb -touristinfo.hr; Trg Josip Jelačića 11; ☻ 8.30am-8pm Mon-Fri, 9am-5pm Sat, 10am-4pm Sun) Distributes city maps and free leaflets. It also sells the Zagreb Card, which costs 60KN and includes 72 hours of free travel on public transport and a 50% discount on museum entry.

Plitvice National Park Office (☎ 46 13 586; Trg Krajla Tomislava19) Has details on Croatia's national parks.

Tourist Office Annexe (☎ 49 21 645; Trg N Šubića Zrinjskog 14; ☻ Mon-Fri 9am-6pm) Same services as the Main Tourist Office but less documentation.

Tourist Office of the Zagreb County Tourist Board (☎ 48 73 665; www.tzzz.hr; Preradovićeva 42; ☻ 8am-4pm Mon-Fri) Has information about attractions in the region outside Zagreb.

Travel Agencies

Croatia Express (☎ 48 11 842; www.zug.hr; Branimirova 1) This office opposite the train station changes money, makes train reservations, rents cars, sells air tickets and books hotels around the country.

Dali Travel (☎ 48 47 472; hfhs-cms@zg.htnet.hr; Dežmanova 9; ☻ 9am-5pm Mon-Fri) The travel branch of the Croatian YHA can provide information on HI hostels throughout Croatia and make advance bookings.

Dalmacijaturist (☎ 48 73 073; Zrinjevac 16) Next to the tourist office; specialises in the Dalmatian coast, also books excursions and air tickets and is a good source of information on boat and ferry routes along the coast.

Generalturist (☎ 48 10 033; www.generalturist.com in Croatian; Petriceva 5) Has branches throughout Croatia and books excursions to the coast, cruises and plane tickets.

Marko Polo (☎ 48 15 216; Masarykova 24) Handles information and ticketing for Jadrolinija's coastal ferries.

SIGHTS

You can pick up a copy of *City Walks* free from any tourist office. It suggests two walking tours around the town centre exploring both the Upper and Lower Town. As the oldest part of Zagreb, the Upper Town offers landmark buildings and churches from the earlier centuries of Zagreb's history. The Lower Town has the city's most interesting art museums and fine examples of

19th- and 20th-century architecture. For a change from museums and galleries, relax in the lovely **Botanical Gardens** (Mihanovićeva ulica; admission free; 7am-9pm Apr-Oct), laid out in 1890. In addition to 10,000 species of plant, including 1800 tropical flora specimens, the landscaping has created restful corners and paths that seem a world away from bustling Zagreb.

Zagreb's main orientation point and the spiritual if not the geographic heart of the city is **Trg Josip Jelačića**. Ban Jelačić was the 19th-century *ban* (viceroy or governor) who led Croatian troops into an unsuccessful battle with Hungary in the hope of winning more autonomy for his people (see Ban Josip Jelačić, p56). The statue of Jelačić in the centre stood in the square from 1866 until 1947, when Tito ordered its removal because it was too closely linked with Croat nationalism. One of the first acts of the new government in 1990 was to dig the statue out of storage and return it to the square. Most of the buildings date from the 19th century but note the reliefs by sculptor Ivan Meštrović at No 4.

Upper Town Monuments

The lovely medieval Upper Town centres on **Kaptol square**, with most buildings dating from the 17th century. At the lower end is the **Dolac quarter** containing Zagreb's colourful fruit and vegetable market. Don't miss the **Stone Gate** – the eastern gate to medieval **Gradec town** (Gornji Gradec), now a shrine. According to legend, a great fire in 1731 destroyed every part of the wooden gate except for the painting of the Virgin and Child by an unknown 17th-century artist. People believe that the painting possesses magical powers and come regularly to pray before it and leave flowers. On the western façade of the Stone Gate you'll see a **statue** of Dora, the heroine of an 18th-century historical novel who lived with her father next to the Stone Gate.

The eastern side of Markov trg is taken up by the Croatian **Sabor** (Parliament; Markov trg), built in 1910 on the site of baroque 17th- and 18th-century townhouses. The neoclassical style seems incongruous here but the secession of Croatia from the Austro-Hungarian Empire was proclaimed from its balcony in 1918 and it is still the centre of Croatian politics. On the opposite side of the square

is the **Ban's Palace** (Banski dvori), once the seat of Croatian viceroys and now the presidential palace. The building is composed of two baroque mansions and houses courts, archives and other government offices. In October 1991 the palace was bombed by the federal army, in what some believe to have been an assassination attempt on President Franjo Tudjman. From April to September there is a guard-changing ceremony every Friday, Saturday and Sunday at noon. Leaving the square by Ćirilometodska ulica, named after the Slav apostles Cyril and Methodius, you'll come across a **sculpted stone head** representing Matija Gubec, the leader of a celebrated peasant rebellion who was allegedly beheaded in Markov trg. At No 5 is the Old City Hall, where municipal assembly meetings are held.

The **Lotrščak Tower** (Kula Lotrščak; ☎ 48 51 926; Strossmayerovo šetalište; admission 5KN; 11am-7pm Tue-Sun) was built in the middle of the 13th century in order to protect the southern city gate. For the last hundred years a cannon has been fired every day at noon commemorating an event from Zagreb's history. According to the legend, a cannon was fired at noon one day at the Turks camped across the Sava River. On its way across the river, the cannonball happened to hit a rooster. The rooster was blown to bits and, the story goes, that's why the Turks became so demoralised they failed to attack the city. A less fanciful explanation is that the cannon shot allows churches to synchronise their clocks. The tower may be climbed for a sweeping 360-degree view of the city.

Upper Town Museums

Don't miss the **City Museum** (Muzej Grada Zagreba; ☎ 48 51 364; www.mdc.hr; Opatička 20; adult/concession 20/10KN; 10am-6pm Tue-Fri, 10am-1pm Sat & Sun) housed in the 17th-century Convent of St Clair, which is built along the eastern wall of the town. Since 1907 it has housed a historical museum presenting the history of Zagreb in documents, artwork and crafts plus interactive exhibits that fascinate kids. Most interesting is a scale model of old Gradec. Summaries of the exhibits are posted in English and German in each room and evocative music accompanies your visit.

Also highly interesting for its insights into Croatia's most recognised artist is **Ivan Meštrović's Studio** (☎ 48 51 123; Mletačka 8;

adult/concession 20/10KN; 10am-6pm Tue-Fri, to 2pm Sat). From 1922 to 1942, Meštrović lived and worked in this 17th-century house, which now presents an excellent collection of some 100 sculptures, drawings, lithographs and furniture from the first four decades of his artistic life. The museum reflects the artist's preoccupations with philosophical and religious themes as well as nudes, portraits and self-portraits.

There are over 1000 works, mainly paintings and drawings, at the **Croatian Museum of Naïve Art** (Hrvatski Muzej Naivne Umjetnosti; ☎ 48 51 911; www.hmnu.org; 3 Ćirilometodska ulica; adult/student 10/5KN; 10am-6pm Tue-Fri to 1pm Sat). The most important artists in Croatia's long tradition of naive art, including Generalić, Mraz, Virius and Smaljić are represented here, as well as international artists working in the same style.

The **Galerija Klovićevi Dvori** (☎ 48 51 926; Jezuitski trg 4; adult/student 20/10KN; 11am-7pm Tue-Sun) is housed in a former Jesuit monastery and is the city's most prestigious space for exhibiting modern Croatian and international art, which is presented in a series of changing exhibitions. Some of the more noted exhibitions have included *Treasure of the Zagreb Cathedral, Ivan Meštrović, The Ancient Chinese Culture* and *The Golden Era of Dubrovnik*. Opposite the Galerija Klovićevi Dvori is the 18th-century **Dverce mansion**, which was restored in the 19th century and is now used for official receptions. Before leaving the square, note the **fountain** with the statue *Fisherman with Snake* which was created by Simeon Roksandić in 1908.

As long as you're in the neighbourhood, try to fit in a visit to the **Croatian Natural History Museum** (Hrvatski Prirodoslovni Muzej; ☎ 48 51 700; Demetrova 1; adult/concession 15/7KN; 10am-5pm Tue-Fri, to 1pm Sat & Sun), which houses a collection of prehistoric tools and bones excavated from the Krapina Cave as well as exhibits showing the evolution of animal and plant life in Croatia. Temporary exhibits often focus on specific regions, such as the island of Mljet.

If you have time, stop in at the **Croatian Historical Museum** (Hrvatski Povijesni Muzej; ☎ 48 51 900; www.hismus.hr; Matoševa 9; admission 10KN; 10am-5pm Mon-Fri, 10am-1pm Sat & Sun), which currently only presents temporary exhibitions on Croatian history.

Upper Town Churches

Kaptol is dominated by the **Cathedral of the Assumption of the Blessed Virgin Mary** (Katedrala Marijina Uznesenja; ☎ 48 14 727; Kaptol; 7am-7.30pm), formerly known as St Stephen's, whose twin spires soar over the city. Built on the site of an earlier Romanesque cathedral, which had been destroyed by the Tartar invasion in 1242, construction of this cathedral began in the second half of the 13th century following the prototype of the church of St Urban in Troyes, France. Although the cathedral's original Gothic structure has been transformed many times over, the sacristy still contains a cycle of frescoes that date from the second half of the 13th century. As the furthest outpost of Christianity in the 15th century, the cathedral was surrounded by walls with towers, one of which is still visible on the eastern side. An earthquake in 1880 badly damaged the cathedral and reconstruction in a neogothic style began around the turn of the 20th century. Despite the scars inflicted on the structure, there is much to admire on the inside. Notice the triptych by Albrecht Dürer on the side altar; baroque marble altars; statues and pulpit; and the tomb of Cardinal Alojzije Stepinac by Ivan Meštrović.

To the north of the cathedral an **Archbishop's Palace** was built in the 18th century in a baroque style, but little remains. Under the northeastern wing of the cathedral is a 19th-century park with a sculpture of a female nude by Antun Augustinčić.

One of Zagreb's most emblematic buildings is the colourful **St Mark's Church** (Crkva Svetog Marka; ☎ 48 51 611; Markov trg; 11am-4pm & 5.30-7pm), with its unique tiled roof constructed in 1880. The tiles on the left side depict the medieval coat of arms of Croatia, Dalmatia and Slavonia, while the emblem of Zagreb is on the right side. The 13th-century church was named for the annual St Mark's fair, which was held in Gradec at the time, and it retains a 13th-century Romanesque window on the southern side. The Gothic portal composed of 15 figures in shallow niches was sculpted in the 14th century. The present bell tower replaces an earlier one that was destroyed by an earthquake in 1502. The interior contains sculptures by Meštrović.

The fine baroque **Jesuit Church of St Catherine** (Crkva Svete Katarine; ☎ 48 51 959; Katarina trg; ⊙ 7am-noon) was built between 1620 and 1632. Although battered by fire and earthquake, the façade still gleams and the interior contains a fine altar dating from 1762. The interior stucco work dates from 1720 and there are 18th-century medallions depicting the life of St Catherine on the ceiling of the nave.

Lower Town Museums

Housed in a neo-Renaissance former school building (1883), the **Museum Mimara** (Muzej Mimara; ☎ 48 28 100; Roosveltov trg 5; adult/concession 20/15KN; ⊙ 10am-5pm Tue, Wed, Fri & Sat, to 7pm Thu & to 2pm Sun) displays a diverse collection showing the loving hand of Ante Topić Mimara, a private collector who donated over 3750 priceless objects to his native Zagreb, even though he spent much of his life in Salzburg, Austria. The collection spans a wide range of periods and regions. There is an archaeological collection with 200 items from Egypt, Mesopotamia, Persia, Greece, Rome and early-medieval Europe; exhibits of ancient Far Eastern artworks; a glass, textile and furniture collection that spans centuries; and 1000 European art objects. In painting, Italian artists Raphael, Veronese, Caravaggio and Canaletto are represented. Dutch artists Rembrandt and Ruisdael are

also present, and there are Flemish paintings from Bosch, Rubens and Van Dyck. Spanish painters Velázquez, Murillo and Goya; German and English painters; and French masters de la Tour, Boucher, Delacroix, Corot, Manet, Renoir and Degas are also in the collection.

The **Strossmayer Gallery of Old Masters** (Strossmayerova Galerija Starih Majstora; ☎ 48 95 115; www.mdc .hr/strossmayer; Zrinjevac 11; adult/concession 20/15KN; ⊙ 10am-1pm Tue-Sun & 5-7pm Tue) is another fine art museum exhibiting the collection donated to the city by the illustrious Bishop Strossmayer in 1884. The original collection was extended by subsequent donations from private collectors. Housed on the 2nd floor of the 19th-century neo-Renaissance Croatian Academy of Arts and Sciences, the museum includes Italian masters from the 14th to 18th centuries such as G Bellini, Veronese and Tiepolo; Dutch and Flemish painters such as J Brueghel the Younger; and French artists Proudhon and Carpeaux; as well as classic Croatian artists Medulić and Benković. The interior courtyard contains the **Baška Slab** (Bašćanska Ploča), a stone tablet from Krk Island which contains the oldest example of Glagolitic script, dating from 1102. Note the statue of Bishop Strossmayer by Ivan Meštrović.

The **Archaeological Museum** (Arheološki Muzej; ☎ 48 73 101; www.amz.hr; Trg N Šubića Zrinjskog; adult/concession 20/10KN; ⊙ 10am-5pm Tue-Fri, to 1pm Sat & Sun) displays artefacts from prehistoric to medieval times including Egyptian mummies. The coin collection is one of the most important in Europe, containing some 260,000 coins, medals, medallions and decorations. The courtyard has a collection of Roman monuments dating from the 5th to 4th century BC and functions as an open-air café in summer.

The **Ethnographic Museum** (Etnografski Muzej; ☎ 48 26 220; www.ethnografski-muzej.hr; Mažuranićev trg 14; adult/concession 15/10KN; ⊙ 10am-6pm Tue-Thu, to 1pm Fri-Sun) is also worth a visit. Housed in a domed building dating from 1903, the museum contains some 70,000 items, cataloguing the ethnographic heritage of Croatia. Only about 2750 exhibits are on display, including ceramics, jewellery, musical instruments, tools and weapons; as well as Croatian folk costumes, gold-embroidered scarves from Slavonia and lace from Pag Island. Thanks to donations from the

---

ZAGREB ARCHITECTURE

Most of the grand old houses you'll see in the Lower Town were built in the last decades of the 19th century in a historicist style, that is, neoclassic, neogothic and neo-Renaissance. Vienna was the final arbiter of style at the time, and historicism had taken the city by storm. Among the outstanding public buildings, note the **Croatian Academy of Arts and Sciences** by the Viennese architect F Schmidt (1884) in a Tuscan Renaissance style; the **Arts and Crafts Museum** designed by Herman Bollé (1891) in German Renaissance style; and the **Art Pavilion** (1898) and **Croatian National Theatre** (1895), both designed by the Viennese architectural team of Helmer and Fellner in Art Nouveau style. The 'green horseshoe' of squares and parks that runs from the train station to the town centre was designed by Milan Lenuci and laid out from 1865 to 1887 as a public promenade.

Croatian explorers Mirko and Stevo Seljan, there are also exhibits from South America, the Congo, Ethiopia, China, Japan, New Guinea and Australia.

Nearby is the **Arts and Crafts Museum** (Muzej Za Umjetnost i Obrt; ☎ 48 26 922; www.muo.hr in Croatian; Trg Maršala Tita 10; adult/student 20/10KN; ⊗ 10am-6pm Tue-Fri, to 1pm Sat & Sun), built between 1882 and 1892. The museum exhibits furniture, textiles, metal, ceramic and glass dating from the Middle Ages to contemporary times. You can see Gothic and baroque sculptures from northern Croatia as well as paintings, prints, bells, stoves, rings, clocks, bound books, toys, photos and industrial designs. The museum also contains an important library and there are frequent temporary exhibitions.

The yellow **Art Pavilion** (Umjetnički Paviljon; ☎ 48 41 070; www.umjetnicki-pavilion.hr; Trg Kralja Tomislava 22; adult/concession 20/10KN; ⊗ 11am-7pm Mon-Sat & 10am-1pm Sun), presents changing exhibitions of contemporary art. Constructed in 1897 in stunning Art Nouveau style, the pavilion is the only space in Zagreb that was specifically designed to host large exhibitions.

West of the Strossmayer Gallery is the **Gallery of Modern Art** (Moderna Galerija; ☎ 49 22 368; Andrije Hebranga 1; adult/concession 20/10KN), which at the time of writing was only open for temporary exhibitions, although the permanent collection includes works by 19th- and 20th-century Croatian artists such as Bukovac, Mihanović, Račić and others.

The **Croatian Artists' Centre** (Dom Hrvatskih Likovnih Umjetnika; ☎ 46 11 818; Trg Zrtava Fašizma; admission free; ⊗ 11am-7pm Tue-Sat, 2-7pm Sun) is one of the few architectural works by Ivan Meštrović. The centre was built as an exhibition pavilion, and then transformed into a mosque before finally becoming a showplace for contemporary Croatian artists. It may be slightly out of the way but the unusual architecture makes it worth the walk.

North of the Centre

A 20-minute ride north of the city centre on bus No 106 from the cathedral takes you to **Mirogoj** (Medvednica; ⊗ 6am-10pm), one of the most beautiful cemeteries in Europe. One wag commented that the people here are better housed in death than they ever

---

BAN JOSIP JELAČIĆ

When you're a new country with almost no independent history, you have to take your heroes how you find them. The stirring **monument** (p53) to Ban Josip Jelačić on the main square testifies to the reverence in which Josip Jelačić was and is held. Yet, in some ways he was an unlikely Croatian hero. First, he was born in Serbia in 1801. Educated in Vienna, the young Jelačić made a name for himself in a daring raid against the Turks in the Serb-dominated Krajina region.

The Illyrian party drafted the popular officer into becoming a *ban* (viceroy) of Croatia in 1848, intending to implement their goal of south-Slavic unity, the unity that Croatia so firmly rejected in 1990. He was able to finally fold Dalmatia and the Krajina region into Croatia, a goal that had long eluded the country. Under Jelačić's leadership, the Sabor (Parliament) allowed the participation of elected, as well as hereditary, representatives. Feudalism was finally abolished although the peasants remained grindingly poor for many more years.

Far from leading the charge for independence, Jelačić fought for the Habsburgs against revolutionary movements in Hungary and Vienna. Having successfully quelled the uprising, Jelačić and the Croatians expected that their demands for greater self-rule would be met by a grateful Austria. It was not the case. A new reactionary government in Vienna clamped down viciously on Croatia, closing the Sabor and suspending the constitution.

Jelačić was embittered by the realisation that he had achieved nothing for Croatia, although he continued as *ban* with greatly diminished influence in Vienna. The disappointments in his professional life were compounded by the tragic loss of his only child. His health broke under the strain and he died in 1859.

Plans to erect a monument in his honour began almost immediately after his death but it was several years before the money was raised and the statue was cast. Finally, in November 1866 his statue was placed on Trg Josip Jelačića in a splendid ceremony. Tens of thousands of people crowded the square. As the cannons boomed, the crowd shouted over and over 'Slava mu!' – hail him! The first death knell for Habsburg rule had sounded.

were in life. The cemetery was designed in 1876 by one of Croatia's finest architects, Herman Bollé, who also created numerous buildings around Zagreb (see Zagreb Architecture, p55). In Mirogoj he built a majestic arcade topped by a string of cupolas, which looks like a fortress from the outside but is calm and graceful on the inside. The cemetery is lush and green and the paths are interspersed with sculpture and artfully designed tombs. Highlights include the graves of poet Petar Preradović, the political leader Stjepan Radić, the bust of Vladimir Becić by Ivan Meštrović and the sculpture by Mihanović for the Mayer family. The newest addition is the grandiose marble memorial to Croatia's first president, Franjo Tudjman, which is found right inside the main entrance.

The medieval fortress of **Medvedgrad** (Medvednica; admission free; ⏰ 7am-10pm), on the southern side of Mt Medvednica just above Zagreb, is the most important medieval monument in Zagreb. Built from 1249 to 1254, it was erected to protect the city from Tartar invasions and is itself well protected by high rocks. The fortress was owned by a succession of aristocratic families but fell into ruin as a result of an earthquake and general neglect. Restoration began in 1979, but was pursued with greater enthusiasm in 1993 and 1994, when the country was looking to honour monuments from its past. Today you can see the rebuilt thick walls and towers, a small chapel with frescoes and the Shrine of the Homeland, which pays homage to those who have died for a free Croatia. On a clear day, it also offers a beautiful view of Zagreb and surrounds.

East of the Centre

Maksimir Park (Maksimirska cesta; ⏰ 9am-dusk) is a peaceful wooded enclave covering 18 hectares; it is easily accessible by tram Nos 4, 7, 11 and 12. Opened to the public in 1794, it was the first public promenade in southeastern Europe and is landscaped like an English garden-style park with alleys, lawns and artificial lakes. The most photographed structure in the park is the exquisite Bellevue Pavilion, which was constructed in 1843, but there is also the Echo Pavilion and a house built to resemble a rustic Swiss cottage. There's also a modest **zoo** (adult/children under 8 20/10KN; ⏰ 9am-8pm).

ACTIVITIES

The **Sports Park Mladost** (☎ 36 58 541; Jarunska cesta 5; family day ticket 60KN; ⏰ 11am-3pm Mon-Fri, 6-8pm Mon, Tue, Thu, Fri, 1-5pm Sat, 10am-2pm Sun) has outdoor and indoor Olympic-sized swimming pools, as well as smaller pools for children, and a gym.

The **Sports and Recreational Centre Šalata** (☎ 46 16 300; Schlosserove stube 2; admission 25KN; ⏰ 1.30-6pm Mon-Fri, 11am-7pm Sat & Sun) offers outdoor and indoor tennis courts, a gym, a winter ice-skating rink and two outdoor swimming pools. There's also an indoor ice-skating rink which rents skates.

Although Zagreb is not normally associated with winter sports, if the snow lasts long enough you can ski right outside town at Sljeme, the main peak of Mt Medvednica. It has four ski-runs, three ski-lifts and a triple chairlift; call the **ski centre** (☎ 45 55 827) for information on snow conditions.

Jarun Lake in south Zagreb is a popular getaway for residents any time of year but especially in the summer when the clear waters are ideal for swimming. Although part of the lake is marked off for boating competitions, there is more than enough space to enjoy a leisurely swim. Take tram No 5 or 17 to Rudeska. Walk back two streets and follow signs to the *jezero* (lake). When you come to the lake you can head left to Malo Jezero for swimming and canoe or pedal-boat rental, or right to Veliko Jezero, where there's a pebble beach and windsurfing.

Mt Medvednica to the north of Zagreb offers excellent hiking opportunities. There are two popular routes: you can take tram No 14 to the last stop and then change to tram No 15 and take it to the last stop. Here you'll be near the funicular that goes to the top of the mountain and next to the funicular there is a clearly marked footpath that also takes you to the top. Or you can take bus No 102 from Britanski trg, west of the centre on Ilica, to the church in Šestine and take the hiking route from there. Allow about three hours for each of these hikes and remember that this is a heavily wooded mountain with ample opportunities to become completely lost. Take warm clothes and water, and make sure to return before sundown. There is also a danger of disease-carrying ticks in the summer, so wear trousers and long sleeves, and examine your body carefully after the hike for ticks (for more information on tick-borne infections, see p281).

ZAGREB FOR CHILDREN

Zagreb has some wonderful attractions for kids but getting around with small children can be a challenge. Between the tram tracks, high kerbs and cars, manoeuvring a stroller on the streets is not easy. Buses and trams are usually too crowded to accommodate strollers even though buses have a designated stroller spot. Up to the age of seven, children travel free on public transport. If you choose taxis, be aware that few have working seat belts for either you or Junior. The only English-speaking nanny service is **Uspinjača** (☎ 48 13 726; Tkalčićeva 27). It is used to dealing with English-speaking residents and generally requires an annual membership fee but you may be able to work something out for a shorter period.

After checking out the bug collection at the Croatian Natural History Museum (p54), take your kids to the **Technical Museum** (Tehnički Muzej; ☎ 48 44 050; Savska cesta 18; admission 10KN; ⊙ 9am-5pm Tue-Fri, to 1pm Sat & Sun), which has a planetarium, steam-engine locomotives, scale models of satellites and space ships, and a replica of a mine within the building, as well as departments of agriculture, geology, energy and transport.

For a little open-air activity, the best place for tots to work off steam is **Bočarski Dom** (☎ 619 57 13; Prisavlje 2). The park has the best in playground equipment, playing fields and a roller-blading ramp. There's also a relaxing path along the Sava river for parents to enjoy. To get there take the No 17 tram west to the Prisavlje stop.

There are two playgrounds (as well as a zoo) inside Maksimir Park (p57), but these are smaller than Bočarski Dom and usually more crowded. Aquatically minded kids will like the pools in the Sports Park Mladost (p57) or the lake at Jarun (p57).

TOURS

The tourist office sells tickets for two-hour walking tours (95KN), which operate on Monday afternoon and Tuesday and Thursday mornings, leaving from in front of the tourist office on Trg Josip Jelačića. It also sells tickets for three-hour bus tours (150KN) that operate on Wednesday and Friday afternoons and weekend mornings.

Tours are conducted by noted journalists and novelists.

FESTIVALS & EVENTS

During odd-numbered years in April there's the Zagreb Biennial of Contemporary Music, Croatia's most important music event. Zagreb also hosts a **festival of animated films** (www .animafest.hr) during even-numbered years in June and a **film festival** (www.zagrebfilmfestival.com) in October. Croatia's largest international fairs are the Zagreb spring (mid-April) and autumn (mid-September) grand trade fairs. In July and August, the **Zagreb Summer Festival** presents a cycle of concerts and theatre performances on open stages in the upper town. The atrium of MGC Klovićevi dvori on Jezuiti trg, the Jesuit Church of St Catherine, St Mark's Church and the Zagreb cathedral are often used, and sometimes the concerts are held in squares in the Upper Town.

The **International Folklore Festival** has been taking place in Zagreb for over 30 years, usually for six days in July. As one of the city's more colourful events, the programme includes folk dancers and singers from Croatia and other European countries dressed in traditional costumes. There are processions and performances from Trg Josip Jelačića to the Upper Town and you are free to join workshops in dance, music and art that are designed to introduce you to Croatian folk culture.

For a complete listing of Zagreb events, see www.zagreb-convention.hr. Open-air events are free but admission is usually charged for the indoor concerts. Prices depend upon the concert, but tickets for most musical events can be purchased from **Koncertna Direkcija Zagreb** (☎ 46 11 808; www.kdz .hr; Kneza Mislava 18).

SLEEPING

As Croatia reaches out to embrace international trade, Zagreb finds itself hosting a wealth of visitors who come for professional conferences, government affairs or business deals. It is not yet a major destination on the tourist circuit, which has left the hotel scene lopsidedly favouring expense-account travellers. Budget and even moderately priced hotels offering good value for money are in extremely short supply.

Other budget accommodation is lacking in Zagreb. Hostels and dorms are one option and several are well located. Private accommodation is another good option but it is usually out of the town centre. Hotels tend to be geared towards business travellers and are now offering a good level of comfort, though at a price. Prices stay the same in all seasons, but be prepared for a 20% surcharge if you arrive during a festival, especially the autumn fair. The rates of the budget and mid-range hotels listed here include breakfast.

Budget

Ravnice Hostel (☎ /fax 23 32 325; www.ravniceyouth -hostel.hr; Ravnice 38d; dm 99KN; 💻) This is really a delightful option, designed and run by an Australian woman. Comfortable, clean rooms have two, four or 10 beds. Solo female travellers would be most comfortable. Tram Nos 4, 7, 11 and 12 will get you here.

Studenthotel Cvjetno Naselje (☎ 61 91 239; per person 210KN) Off Slavonska avenija in the south of the city, this dormitory has good rooms, each with a private bathroom. Cvjetno Naselje is available to visitors only from mid-July to the end of September. Take tram No 4, 5, 14 or 17 southwest on Savska cesta to 'Vjesnik'.

Studentski dom Stjepan Radić (☎ 36 34 255; Jarunska ulica 3; dm 125KN) This student dorm is near Jarun Lake and its nightlife in the southwest of the city. Take tram No 5 or 17. This is also a decent place to stay with old but tidy rooms.

Omladinski Hotel (☎ 48 41 261; fax 48 41 269; Petrinjska 77; per person 6-/3-/d r 73/83/211KN) Some say it's a dump. We prefer to call it an auditory and visual challenge with maintenance issues and a 9am check-out. The only reason to stay here is if you really must be close to the train station.

Mid-Range

Hotel Ilica (☎ 37 77 522; www.hotel-ilica.hr in Croatian; Ilica 102; s/d/tr/apt 349/549/549/749KN; Ⓟ 🌣) For a small hotel, you can't do better than this stylish joint with comfortable rooms and friendly service. The vaguely classical decorative motifs in the common areas create a warm and inviting ambience. Highly successful since it opened eight years ago, the hotel has recently added an annexe with newer and somewhat larger rooms. Even though it's on a main street, both buildings are set back slightly, ensuring a good night's

sleep. Trams 6, 11 and 12 stop right outside the entrance.

Hotel Fala (☎ /fax 61 94 498; www.hotel-fala-zg.hr; Trnjanska 18; s/d 350/470KN; Ⓟ 🌣) The small rooms have no frills but the price is right and you're not too terribly far from the town centre. Take the No 5 or 13 tram to Lisinski.

Hotel Dora (☎ 63 11 900; dora@zug.hr; Trnjanska 11E; s/d 360/650KN) Located in the same neighbourhood as the Hotel Fala, it has also successfully avoided the horrors of over-decoration; the staff are friendly enough, rooms are comfortable in an efficient way and there's a restaurant on site.

Hotel Sliško (☎ 61 84 477; www.slisko.hr; Bunićeva 7; s/d 380/510KN; 🌣 💻) Right next to the main bus station, this hotel couldn't be more convenient for a late-night arrival or early-morning departure. The friendly staff takes good care of the rooms, which have some surprising amenities for the price such as satellite TV, air-conditioning and modem plugs. Guests can even use the computer in the lobby to check their email.

Pansion Jägerhorn (☎ 48 33 877; fax 48 33 573; Ilica 14; s/d/apt 550/750/900KN; 🌣) The downstairs restaurant is known for serving wild game but there's no wildness in the civilised rooms here. Everything is up to date, quiet and well maintained.

Central Hotel (☎ 48 41 122; www.hotel-central.hr in Croatian; Branimirova 3; s/d 520/680KN; 🌣) Entirely renovated with modern, plush rooms, this hotel represents good value for money, especially given its location across from the train station. The service is coldly efficient.

Hotel Jadran (☎ 45 53 777; fax 46 12 151; www .hum.zagreb.hr; Vlaška 50; s/d 490/860KN; 🌣) This six-storey hotel has a superb location only minutes from Trg Josip Jelačića. The 48 rooms could use a facelift but will do at a pinch. Try for a room on the courtyard since the hotel is on a noisy street.

Top End

Palace Hotel (☎ 48 14 611; www.palace.hr; Strossmajerov trg 10; s/d from 770/980KN; Ⓟ ✖ 🌣 💻) This hotel oozes European charm and is the oldest in Zagreb. Built in 1891, it's both aristocratic and outfitted with the latest modern comforts. Try to get a front room for the luscious views over the park.

Arcotel Allegra (☎ 46 96 000; www.arcotel.at /allegra; Branimirova 29; r 680-2410KN; Ⓟ ✖ 🌣 💻)

ZAGREB

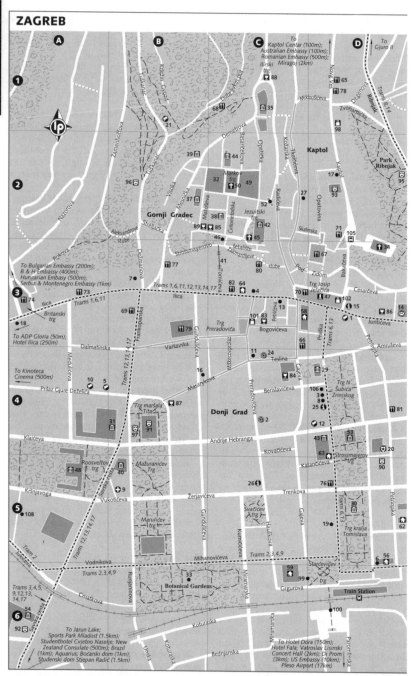

0 ——————— 200 m
0 ——————— 0.1 miles

INFORMATION
Albanian Embassy	**1** D3
Algoritam	(see 58)
Art Net Club	**2** C4
Atlas Travel Agency	**3** D4
British Council	**4** C3
Canadian Embassy	**5** A4
Croatia Express	**6** D5
Dali Travel/Croatian YHA	**7** B3
Dalmacijaturist	**8** D4
Dental Emergency	**9** B5
Embassy of Slovakia	**10** A4
French Cultural Institute	**11** C4
French Embassy	**12** D4
Generalturist	**13** C3
Knjižara Ljevak	(see 13)
Main Post Office/Telephone Centre	**14** D3
Main Tourist Office	**15** D3
Marko Polo	**16** B4
Petecin Laundry	**17** D2
Pharmacy	**18** A3
Plitvice National Park Office	**19** D5
Police Station	**20** D4
Polish Embassy	**21** B1
Post Office	**22** E6
Predom	**23** E4
Sublink	**24** C4
Tourist Office Annexe	**25** D4
Tourist Office of the Zagreb County Tourist Board	**26** C5
Uspinjača	**27** C2
VIP	**28** E3

SIGHTS & ACTIVITIES (pp52–8)
Archaeological Museum	**29** D4
Art Pavilion	**30** D5
Arts and Crafts Museum	**31** B4
Ban's Palace	**32** C2
Botanical Gardens	**33** B6
Cathedral of the Assumption of the Blessed Virgin Mary - formerly St Stephen's	**34** D3
City Museum	**35** C1
Croatian Academy of Arts & Science	(see 53)
Croatian Artists' Centre	**36** F4
Croatian Historical Museum	**37** B2
Croatian Museum of Naive Art	**38** C2
Croatian Natural History Museum	**39** B2
Ethnographic Museum	**40** B5
Funicular Railway	**41** C3
Galerija Klovićevi Dvori	**42** C2
Gallery of Modern Art	**43** D4
Ivan Meštrović's Studio	**44** C2
Jesuit Church of St Catherine	**45** C2
Lotršćak Tower	**46** C2
Monument to Ban Josip Jelačić	**47** D3
Museum Mimara	**48** A5
Sabor	**49** C2
St Mark's Church	**50** C2
Sports & Recreational Centre Šalata	**51** E2
Stone Gate	**52** C2
Strossmayer Gallery of Old Masters	**53** D4
Technical Museum	**54** A6

SLEEPING (pp58–62)
Arcotel Allegra	**55** E5
Central Hotel	**56** D5
Evistas	**57** E5
Hotel Dubrovnik	**58** C3
Hotel Esplanade	**59** C6
Hotel Jadran	**60** E3
Hotel Sliško	**61** H6
Omladinski Hotel	**62** D5
Palace Hotel	**63** D4
Pansion Jägerhorn	**64** C3

EATING (pp62–4)
Baltazar	**65** D1
Boban	**66** C3
Din Don	(see 28)
Dolac Fruit & Vegetable Market	**67** D3
Dubravkin Put	**68** C1
Frankopan	**69** B3
Gavrilović	**70** C3
Kaptolska Klet	**71** D2
Konoba Čiho	**72** E5
Makronova	**73** A3
Market	**74** A3
Mimiće	**75** E3
Murano 2000	(see 59)
Paviljon	(see 30)
Pekarnica Dora	**76** D5
Pivnica Stari Fijaker 900	**77** B3
Pizzeria 2	**78** D1
Pizzicato	**79** B3
Pod Gričkom Topom	**80** C3
Purger	**81** D4
Vincek	**82** C3

DRINKING (p64)
BP Club	(see 84)
Bulldog Cafe	**83** C3
Hard Rock Cafe	**84** C4
Indy's	**85** C2
K & K	**86** D3
Kazališna Kavana	**87** B4
Palainovka	**88** C1
Tolkien's House	**89** B3

ENTERTAINMENT (pp64–6)
Bijoux	**90** D5
Croatian Music Institute	(see 79)
Croatian National Theatre	**91** B4
Dražen Petrović Basketball Centre	**92** A6
Kazalište Komedija Office	(see 101)
Komedija Theatre	**93** D2
Koncertna Direkcija Zagreb	**94** F4
Purgeraj	**95** D2
Saloon	**96** B2
Sokol Klub	**97** B4

SHOPPING (p66)
Bornstein	**98** D1
Importanne Shopping Centre Entrance 1	**99** C6
Importanne Shopping Centre Entrance 2	**100** D6
Kroata Cravata	(see 101)
Oktogon	**101** C3
Rokotvorine	**102** D3
Vartek's	(see 102)

TRANSPORT (pp66–7)
Budget	**103** E5
Bus Station	**104** G6
Bus to Mirogoj	**105** D2
Croatia Airlines	**106** D4
Croatian Auto Club	**107** E4
Hertz	**108** A5

AUTHOR'S CHOICE

Hotel Esplanade (☎ 45 66 666; esplanade@ esplanade.hr; Mihanovićeva 1; s/d 1875/2025KN; P ☒ ☐) This six-storey, 215-room hotel was built next to the train station in 1924 to welcome the Orient Express crowd in grand style. It's an Art Deco masterpiece replete with walls of swirling marble, immense-ly wide staircases and wood-panelled el-evators. Even if you're not staying at the hotel, take a peek at the magnificent Em-erald Ballroom or eat at Murano 2000, the hotel restaurant and one of the finest dining experiences in Croatia.

Rooms vary greatly in size, but all are high-ceilinged and plushly decorated in period upholstery. The best rooms look out at the esplanade in front of the train sta-tion. The double-glazed windows mean that you won't be bothered by noise while you contemplate the street scene.

Throughout its history, the hotel has wel-comed kings, journalists, artists and politi-cians with a coolly professional attention to service. The slightly formal, courtly attitude of the staff blends perfectly with the hotel's style – traditional, classic, unswayed by fads, a bulwark of stability in a frivolous world.

Billing itself as Zagreb's first 'lifestyle hotel', it's clear that the style of life is quite high here. Your lifestyle, should you choose to accept it, will include ultra-contemporary Mediterranean-inspired décor and a fitness centre, plus rooms and accoutrements for your business meetings. The hotel is gay friendly.

Hotel Dubrovnik (☎ 48 73 555; www.hotel-dub rovnik.htnet.hr; Gajeva 1; s/d from 650/850KN; ☒) Busi-ness travellers love this modern hotel right in the centre of town. There are 262 well-maintained rooms in this glass-fronted tower. The double windows in front keep out most noise from the square below, un-less there is a special event. Service, rooms and facilities are all first rate.

Private Rooms

Try not to arrive on Sunday if you intend to stay in a private house or apartment, since most of the agencies are closed. Prices run from about 170/220KN per single/double

and apartments cost at least 300KN per night. There's usually a surcharge for stay-ing only one night. There are almost no rooms or apartments whatsoever in the Upper Town and only a limited number available in the town centre. A wider choice is available in Novi Zagreb, south of the Sava River. Although most are in uninspir-ing 1970s apartment blocks, there is a real neighbourhood life, with businesses, cafés and markets. Some of these agencies are listed here:

ADP Gloria (☎ 48 23 567; www.adp-glorija.com; Britanski trg 5) An option for private rooms.

Di Prom (☎ 65 50 039; fax 65 50 233; Trnsko 25a) South of the town centre with rooms in Novi Zagreb.

Evistas (☎ 48 39 554; evistas@zg.htnet.hr; August Šenoe 28; s 172-227KN, d 234-314KN, apt 364-835KN; ✆ 9am-1.30pm & 3-8pm Mon-Fri, 9.30am-5pm Sat) This agency is closest to the train station and finds private accommodation.

EATING
Budget

Pizzicato (☎ 48 31 555; Gundulićeva 4; pizzas from 20KN) Pizza is a popular dish for budget-minded Croatians (which includes just about the entire country) and the pies at Pizzicato in the Academy of Music are excellent. The copious toppings and the freshly made dough are in perfect balance, making a hearty and delicious meal. The menu has English translations.

Mimiće (Jurišićeva 21; mains 12-30KN; ✆ closed Sun) It's a local favourite and deservedly so. The fish is sure to be fresh because turnover is high, especially at around noon when work-ers in the offices around Trg Josip Jelačića turn out in droves for their lunch.

Pizzeria 2 (☎ 48 17 462; Nova Ves 2; pizzas 25-35KN) Slightly more upmarket than Pizzi-cato, this restaurant, in Upper Kaptol, is another contender for the 'best pizza in Zagreb' title. It also turns out a variety of pasta dishes.

Din Don (☎ 46 19 135; Iblerov trg bb; mains 18-42KN) Although not strictly vegetarian, there is a wide array of vegetarian pizzas, pastas, risottos and sandwiches on offer, as well as a fresh and tasty salad bar.

Mid-Range

Kaptolska Klet (☎ 48 14 838; Kaptol 5; mains 55-70KN) This huge and inviting space is comfortable for everyone from solo diners to groups of noisy backpackers. There's a huge outdoor terrace for romantic dining and a brightly lit beer-hall-style interior for reading a newspaper or celebrating a birthday. Although famous for its Zagreb specialities such as grilled meats and spit-roasted lamb, duck, pork and veal, as well as home-made sausages, it also turns out a nice platter of grilled vegetables and a vegetable loaf.

Frankopan (☎ 48 48 547; Frankopanska 8; mains 35-85KN; ☷ closed Sun) It's a gilt trip here with chubby cherubs frolicking on the ceiling while you munch on relatively adventurous dishes which the bright lighting allows you to examine carefully. The prices are good because meals are prepared by a hostelry school.

Pod Gričkom Topom (☎ 48 33 607; Zakmardijeve stube 5; mains from 70KN) Tucked away by a leafy path below the Upper Town, this restaurant has a somewhat self-conscious charm but it has an outdoor terrace and good Croatian meat-based specialities. Holing up here on a snowy winter evening is one of the great Zagrebian pleasures.

Baltazar (Nova Ves 4; mains from 70KN; ☷ closed Sun) Duck, lamb, pork, beef and turkey are cooked to perfection here, served with a good choice of local wines. It's where Zagreb professionals take their parents for their anniversary.

Konoba Čiho (☎ 48 17 060; Pavla Hatza 15; mains from 55KN; ☷ closed Sun) Tucked away downstairs, this cosy restaurant turns out a startling assortment of fish and seafood that is grilled, fried and combined in delicious stews. There is a great number of photos, knick-knacks and what-nots on the walls to look at while waiting for your meal. The wait can be long.

Purger (☎ 48 73 394; Petrinjska 33; mains 40-50KN) This restaurant serves up a good assortment of meat and fish dishes at reasonable prices. It has an open-air terrace at the

back. Recent graduates are inclined to blow their first pay cheque here.

Pivnica Stari Fijaker 900 (☎ 48 33 829; Mesnička 6; mains from 40KN) It was once the height of dining out in Zagreb and still has a certain staid sobriety in the décor, which is composed of banquettes, wood and white linen. Tradition reigns in the kitchen, which turns out hearty Zagreb meat and bean dishes.

Makronova (☎ 48 47 115; Ilica 72; mains around 70KN; ☷ closed Sun) All very Zen and purely macrobiotic and more than welcome for those of the vegan persuasion. There's also shiatsu treatment, yoga classes and feng-shui courses.

Top End

Dubravkin Put (☎ 48 34 975; Dubravkin put 2; mains from 90KN) In a woodsy area northwest of the town centre, this upscale refurbished restaurant is Zagreb's trendiest spot. The décor is light, pleasant and modern, with pine floors and ceiling lights, but it is the outstanding fish specialities that attract Zagreb's fashionable crowd. The owner is from Dubrovnik and the cuisine is inspired by his native Dalmatia, with risottos as starters and main courses of perfectly grilled fish. The restaurant is not cheap but it makes a fine evening out.

Murano 2000 (☎ 456 66 66; Hotel Esplanade, Mihanovićeva 1; mains 90-200KN; ☷ closed Sun) Here are the tastiest, most creative dishes in town served with polish in the dining room of a world-class hotel. The cutlery is heavy silver and the clientele tends to wear a lot of heavy gold. No matter. It's not stuffy and there's no dress code.

Paviljon (☎ 48 13 066; Trg Tomislava 22; mains from 80KN) In the yellow Art Pavilion across the park from the train station, this is undoubtedly one of the most elegant places in town. The spacious, glossy dining room is a favourite of local business people trying to impress their clients. The food has an Italian accent and is beautifully presented. There's an outdoor terrace.

Okrugljak (☎ 46 74 112; Mlinovi 28; mains from 75KN) This is a popular spot on Mt Medvednica for city people celebrating a special occasion. Dining is casual; you can sit at wooden tables in carved-out wine barrels or on the terrace. There is usually music on weekends, and the occasional wedding reception can make the ambience more than lively. The spit-roasted meat, especially lamb or duck, is unusually juicy and served with delicious *mlinci* (baked noodles).

Quick Eats

The town's main shopping street, Ilica, is lined with fast-food joints and inexpensive snack bars.

Pekarnica Dora (Strossmajerov trg 7) Close to the train station, this bakery is open 24 hours for those late-night pastry needs.

Vincek (☎ 48 33 612; Ilica 18) This *slastičarna* (pastry shop) is reputed to serve the best ice cream in town. The long lines as soon as summer starts attest to its popularity.

Self-Catering

Right in the centre of town, there's **Gavrilović** (closed Sun) for excellent local cheese, smoked meat and cold cuts. On Ilica, there's a daily fruit and vegetable **market** (Britanski trg) which sells farm-fresh produce and is open every day until 3pm. There's also the fruit and vegetable market at Dolac. Don't hesitate to bargain.

DRINKING

The narrow streets in the Upper Town are lined with outdoor cafés and bars that attract crowds of strollers and sightseers, especially on summer evenings. The liveliest scene is along Tkalčićeva, to the north of Trg Josip Jelačića, where crowds spill out of cafés onto the street, drinks in hand. Further up on Kožarska, the city's young people cluster shoulder to shoulder.

Trg Preradovića is the most popular spot in the Lower Town. Zagreb's flower-market square attracts street performers and occasional bands in mild weather. With a half-dozen bars and sidewalk cafés between Trg Preradovića and Bogovićeva, the scene on some summer nights resembles a vast outdoor party.

Cafés provide long sipping hours, usually from 10am until about midnight.

Bulldog Cafe (☎ 49 17 393; Bogovićeva 6) It's easy to sit for hours outside, watching the activity on this busy pedestrian street. At night, it's a good place to meet your evening playmates.

Kazališna Kavana (☎ 48 55 851; Trg Maršala Tita) Opposite the Croatian National Theatre, 'Kavkaz', as it's called, is a tad pretentious but has some loyal habitués who can usually

be found puffing thoughtfully on a cigarette with a copy of *Vjesnik* in front of them.

K & K (☎ 48 13 558; Jurišićeva 5) The name is short for *kniza* and *kava* (books and coffee). The literary atmosphere is enhanced by photos and drawings of Zagreb scenes and the coffee is excellent.

Palainovka (☎ 48 51 357; Ilirski trg 1) Claiming to be the oldest café in Zagreb (dating from 1846) this Viennese-style café serves delicious coffee, tea and cakes under pretty, frescoed ceilings.

The places below all open around noon and serve drinks all day but the action heats up at night.

Tolkien's House (☎ 48 52 050; Vranicanijeva 8) This most unusual bar is just up the street from Lotrščak Tower. It's decorated in the style of Tolkien's famous books and has a cosy enclosed terrace where you can drink the best hot chocolate in Zagreb.

Indy's (☎ 48 52 053; Vranicanijeva 6) Just next door to Tolkien's is this trendy cocktail bar decorated Mexican-style. Zagreb's yuppies feel right at home.

Hard Rock Cafe (☎ 48 72 548; Gajeva 10) Although not part of the famous international chain, it's full of similar 1950s and 1960s memorabilia. In summer the café extends across the street to the garden of the Archaeological Museum, and becomes the Rock Forum Cafe.

Brazil (☎ 091 200 24 81; Veslačka bb) Latin-American style is big in Zagreb now. Parked on the Sava River, this bar on a boat refreshes a throng of thirsty revellers and offers occasional live music.

A couple of other cafés and music shops share the lively complex at the corner of Teslina and Gajeva streets, including **BP Club** (☎ 48 14 444; Teslina 7; 10pm-2am). Check out this club in the complex basement for jazz, blues and rock bands.

ENTERTAINMENT

Zagreb is a happening city. Its theatres and concert halls present a great variety of programmes throughout the year. Many (but not all) are listed in the monthly brochure *Zagreb Events & Performances*, which is available from the Main Tourist Office. The daily newspapers *Jutarnji list* and *Večernji list* show the current offerings on the concert, gallery, museum, theatre and cinema circuit on the back page.

Theatre tickets are usually available, even for the most in-demand shows. A small office marked **Kazalište Komedija** (☎ 48 12 657; ◷ 8am-5.30pm Mon-Fri, 8am-1pm Sat) – look for the posters – in the Oktogon also sells theatre tickets; it's in a passage connecting Trg Preradovića to Ilica near Trg Josip Jelačića.

Theatre

Croatian National Theatre (☎ 48 28 532; Trg Maršala Tita 15) This neobaroque theatre, established in 1895, stages opera and ballet performances. You have a choice of *parket* (orchestra), *lože* (lodge) or *balkon* (balcony) seats. Check out Ivan Meštrović's sculpture *The Well of Life* (1905) standing in front. The theatre was designed in 1894 by Herman Helmer and Ferdinand Fellner, the same team that designed the Art Pavilion.

Komedija Theatre (☎ 48 14 566; Kaptol 9) Close to the Zagreb cathedral, this theatre stages a good range of operettas and musicals.

Vatroslav Lisinski Concert Hall (☎ 61 21 166; www.lisinski.hr in Croatian; Trg Stjepana Radića 4) This is the city's most prestigious venue in which to hear symphony concerts and attend theatrical presentations.

Croatian Music Institute (☎ 48 30 822; Gundulićeva 6a) This is another good venue for concerts.

Discos & Clubs

Entry ranges from 40KN to 80KN, depending upon the evening and the event. Clubs open around 10pm but most people show up around midnight.

Sokol Klub (☎ 48 28 510; Trg Maršala Tita 6) Across the street from the Ethnographic Museum, this club admits women free before midnight (40KN after). The music is standard commercial disco.

Saloon (☎ 48 34 903; Tuškanac 1a) This fashionable watering hole tries to attract a slightly older crowd by devoting at least one night a week to classic rock. Other nights, the emphasis is on Croatian techno.

Purgeraj (☎ 48 14 734; Park Ribnjak) It's a funky, relaxed space to listen to live rock, blues, rock-blues, blues-rock, country rock...you get the idea.

Aquarius (☎ 36 40 231; Jarun Lake) A truly fab place to party, this enormously popular spot has a series of rooms that open onto a huge terrace on the lake. House and techno are the standard fare here.

Gay & Lesbian Venues

The gay and lesbian scene in Zagreb is finally becoming more open than it had previously been, although 'freewheeling' it isn't. Many gays discreetly cruise the south beach around Jarun Lake and are welcome in many discos, especially Gjuro II.

Gjuro II (☎ 46 83 381; Medveščak 2) A mixture of gays and straights patronise this club from Wednesday through to Sunday for a programme that includes dance music and occasional live concerts.

Glob@l (☎ 48 76 146; Hatza 14; Ⓟ) Gays and lesbians are more than welcome to take in the friendly, tolerant vibes at this mixed place.

Bijoux (☎ 091 533 7757; Mrazovićeva 9) This is strictly men only, especially cyber-studs hitting the bank of computers.

Cinemas

There are 18 cinemas in Zagreb that show foreign movies in their original language with subtitles. Ticket prices differ for each show but they are slightly cheaper on Monday. Tickets are sold for numbered seats. Look for posters around town advertising the programmes.

Kinoteca (☎ 37 71 753; Kordunska 1) This cinema, to the west of the town centre, shows classic foreign arthouse movies.

Spectator Sports

Jarun Lake hosts competitions in rowing, kayaking and canoeing in the summer. There's a racetrack in south Zagreb, across the Sava River.

BASKETBALL

Dražen Petrović Basketball Centre (☎ 48 43 333; Savska cesta 30; tickets from 35KN) Basketball is popular in Zagreb, and from September to April Zagreb's basketball team, Cibona, plays here next to the Technical Museum, usually on Saturdays at 7.30pm. Tickets are available at the door.

FOOTBALL

Stadion Maksimir (☎ 48 43 769; Maksimirska 128; tickets from 30KN) Take tram No 4, 7, 11 or 12 to Bukovačka. Dinamo Zagreb is the town's most popular football (soccer) team and they play their matches here, on the eastern side of Zagreb, on Sunday afternoons between August and May. If you arrive too early for the game, Zagreb's zoo is across the street.

SHOPPING

Ilica is Zagreb's main shopping street with fashionable international brands peeking out from the staid buildings. Residents who used to travel to Austria to shop now find everything they need – clothes, accessories, homewares, computer supplies – here or at **Kaptol Centar** (Nova Ves 17).

Pricier leather and accessories can be found at shops in the Oktogon complex, just south of Ilica. For general shops, fast-food outlets and grocery stores, head for the Importanne Shopping Centre, a mall under the tracks beside the train station; shops there have long opening hours.

Vartek's (Trg Josip Jelačića) The latest addition to the shopping scene, Vartek's has an excellent selection of music discs on the top floor along with a cybercafé.

Kroata Cravata (☎ 48 12 726; Oktogon) Since the necktie originated in Croatia, nothing could make a more authentic gift and this is the place to get one. The locally made silk neckties here are priced from 175KN to 380KN.

Rokotvorine (☎ 48 31 303; Trg Josip Jelačića 7) Sells traditional Croatian handicrafts such as dolls, pottery and red-and-white embroidered tablecloths.

Bornstein (☎ 48 12 361; Kaptol 19) If Croatia's wine and spirits have gone to your head, get your fix here. It presents an astonishing collection of brandy, wine and gourmet products.

GETTING THERE & AWAY
Air

Zagreb's Pleso airport is one of the country's major airports offering a range of international and domestic services. See p271 and p276 for details.

Bus

Zagreb's big, modern **bus station** (☎ 61 57 983; www.akz.hr in Croatian; Avenija M Držića) has a large, enclosed waiting room where you can stretch out while waiting for your bus (but be warned – there's no heating in winter).

Buy most international tickets at window Nos 11 and 12. Buses depart from Zagreb bound for most of Croatia, Slovenia and places beyond. You'll need to purchase an advance ticket at the station if you're planning on travelling far.

The following domestic buses depart from Zagreb:

Destination	Cost	Duration	Frequency
Dubrovnik	205-401KN	11hr	7 daily
Koprivinica	52KN	2hr	6 daily
Krk	136KN	4-5hr	4 daily
Ljubljana	115KN	2½hr	2 daily
Makarska	127-138KN	8hr	10 daily
Mali Lošinj	201KN	6hr	3 daily
Osijek	88KN	4hr	8 daily
Plitvice	50KN	2½hr	19 daily
Poreč	123KN	5hr	6 daily
Pula	114-161KN	4-6hr	13 daily
Rab	144KN	4½-5hr	2 daily
Rijeka	75-129KN	2½-3hr	21 daily
Rovinj	132KN	5-8hr	8 daily
Split	112-143KN	6-9hr	27 daily
Varaždin	51KN	1¾hr	20 daily
Zadar	97-157KN	4-5hr	20 daily

Train

The following domestic trains depart from the Zagreb **train station** (☎ 060 33 34 44; www.hznet.hr/):

Destination	Cost	Duration	Frequency
Koprivnica	55KN	2hr	6 daily
Ljubljana	70KN	3hr	7 daily
Osijek	117KN	4½hr	4 daily
Pula	123KN	5½hr	2 daily
Rijeka	102KN	5hr	4 daily
Split	168KN	6-8½hr	4 daily
Varaždin	47KN	3hr	13 daily
Zadar	134KN	6½hr	2 daily

Trains to Zadar stop at Knin. Reservations are required on some trains. For train information call ☎ 9830.

For information on international train connections see p274.

GETTING AROUND

Zagreb is a fairly easy city to navigate, whether by car or public transport. Traffic isn't bad, there's sufficient parking and the efficient tram system should be a model for more polluted, traffic-clogged European capitals.

To/From the Airport

The Croatia Airlines bus to Pleso airport, 17km southeast of Zagreb, leaves from the bus station every half-hour or hour from about 4am to 8.30pm depending on flights, and returns from the airport on about the same schedule (25KN). A taxi would cost about 250KN.

Car

Budget Rent-a-Car (☎ 45 54 936), in the Hotel Sheraton; **Avis Autotehna** (☎ 48 36 006), at the Hotel Opera; and **Hertz** (☎ 48 46 777; Vukotinovićeva 1) are all represented. Bear in mind that local companies usually have lower rates. Zagreb is a fairly easy city to navigate by car; boulevards are wide, traffic isn't too dense and parking is relatively abundant. Watch out for trams buzzing around. The **Croatian Auto Club (HAK) Information Centre** (☎ 46 40 800; Draskoviceva 25) helps motorists in need.

Taxi

Zagreb's taxis all have meters, which begin at a whopping 25KN and then ring up 7KN per kilometre. On Sunday and at night from 10pm to 5am there's a 20% surcharge. Waiting time is 40KN per hour. The baggage surcharge is 2KN per suitcase. At these rates, you'll have no trouble finding idle taxis, usually at blue-marked taxi signs, or you can call ☎ 970 to reserve one.

Tram

Public transport is based on an efficient but overcrowded network of trams, although the city centre is compact enough to make them unnecessary.

Zagreb has installed tram maps at most stations, making the system easier to navigate. Tram Nos 3 and 8 don't run on weekends. Buy tickets (6.50KN) at newspaper kiosks or on the bus for 8KN. You can use your ticket for transfers within 90 minutes, but only in one direction.

A *dnevna karta* (day ticket), valid on all public transport until 4am the next morning, is available for 18KN at most *Vjesnik* or *Tisak* news outlets.

AROUND ZAGREB

BANIJA-KORDUN REGION

South of Zagreb and bound by the Sava River basin in the north, the Una and Kupa Rivers in the east and west, and Mala Kapela Mountain in the south, the Banija-Kordun region is trying to recapture some of the tourism it had before the war. Until 1991 the region's many rivers were popular with local anglers, and hunters combed the woods for prey. The large Serbian majority made it a tempting target for Serbian expansion in the early days of the war and large parts of the region remained under Serbian control until 1995. The many mines laid in the countryside have curtailed the hunting and fishing that made the area famous but as de-mining proceeds, anglers and hunters are returning.

KARLOVAC

☎ 047 / pop 49,000

Lying at the confluence of four rivers – the Kupa, the Korana, the Mrežnica and the Dobra – it's not surprising that Karlovac and its surrounds have become a haven for city folk looking for waterside relaxation. The town itself is unique in that its historical centre is shaped in the form of a six-point star, divided into 24 almost rectangular blocks. It lies on the main road that links Zagreb with Rijeka and was constructed in 1579 as a military stronghold against the Turks. Although only the moats remain from the original fortifications, the town centre retains its tidy geometrical streets of baroque buildings.

Orientation & Information

The Kupa River divides the town along an east–west axis. The main road through town is Prilaz Vece Holjevca, which runs north-south. The old town is east of Prilaz Vece Holjevca and lies on the southern bank of the Kupa River. The main square in the old town is Trg Jelačića. The bus station is on Prilaz Vece Holjevca, about 500m south of the town centre, and the train station is 1.5km north of the town centre also along Prilaz Vece Holjevca.

The **Tourist Office** (☎ /fax 615 115; www.karlovac -touristinfo.hr; Šetalište F Tuđmana 10; 8am-8pm Mon-Fri, to 1pm Sat & Sun) has a limited amount of documentation available.

Sights & Activities

The main attraction of Karlovac is the **Zvijezda** (Star, or old town). The 17th-century **Church of the Holy Trinity**, with its altar of black marble, and the adjacent **Franciscan monastery**, are the highlights of Trg Jelačića.

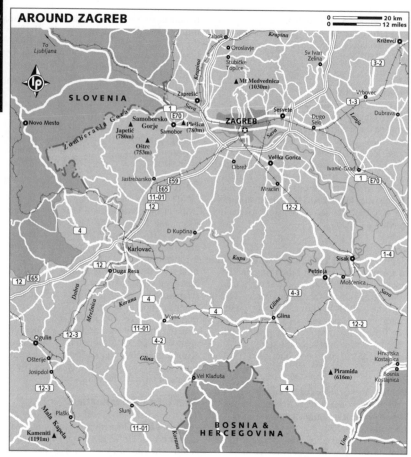

AROUND ZAGREB

The 17th- and 18th-century merchant and military residences on the surrounding streets are being restored to emphasise their fine features. Merchants' houses are recognisable by their inscriptions showing the year of construction and the owner's initials. Military houses are often distinguished by stone carvings and wrought-iron work. Particularly attractive is a stroll down Radićeva, which features the house of Count Janko Draxć.

One block north of Trg Jelačića is Strossmayerov trg, a semicircular baroque-style square that contains the **Town Museum** (Gradski Muzej; ☎ 615 980; Strossmayerov trg; adult/student 10/7KN; ☼ 7am-3pm Mon-Fri, 10am-noon Sat & Sun). The museum is in a Frankopan palace

and features scale models of old Karlovac among its displays of local handicrafts and historical exhibits.

A 30-minute walk north along the banks of the Kupa River and then uphill takes you to **Dubovac** (Zagrad 10), a medieval fortress that now contains a restaurant and affords an excellent view of Karlovac.

Sleeping & Eating
The tourist office can help you find private accommodation (about 80KN per person) and there is one hotel in the town centre.

Carlstadt Hotel (☎ /fax 611 111; www.carlstadt .hr; Vranicanijeva 1; s/d 310/455KN; Ⓟ Ⓧ) This hotel serves the needs of visiting business people who, it would appear, could be distracted by an excess of decorative flourishes. Rooms have TV and phone, and the location is excellent.

Mirna (☎ 65 41 72; Rakovačko Šetlište bb; mains from 70KN) After a drink in the aperitif bar, head here for fresh- and saltwater fish served up on a pretty terrace overlooking the Korana river.

Getting There & Away

Karlovac is well connected to Zagreb by bus (28KN, 50 minutes, 20 daily) with good onward connections to Pag Rab, Rijeka and Split. There are also frequent trains to Zagreb (26KN, 50 minutes, 18 daily) and to Rijeka (67KN, three hours, six daily).

SAMOBOR
pop 14,000

It's almost too little-village-cute, but after a week of crowded trams in Zagreb, Samobor provides a perfect breather for stressed-out Zagrebians. A shallow stream stocked with trout curves through a town centre that is composed of trim pastel houses and several old churches. The town has conserved its culture as well as its architecture. The small family businesses involved in handicrafts, restaurants and the production of mustard and spirits have survived well, seemingly untouched by the political fads sweeping through the rest of the country. The town's literary and musical traditions, which produced the poet Stanko Vraz and the composer Ferdo Livadić, are reflected in a number of annual festivals, most famously the **Fašnik** (Samobor Carnival) on the eve of Lent, which attracts some 300,000 visitors.

Orientation & Information

The bus stop (no left-luggage office) is on Šmidheva, about 100m uphill from the town, which centres around Trg Kralja Tomislava.

In the town centre, the **Tourist Office** (☎ 33 60 044; www.samobor.hr in Croatian; Trg Kralja Tomislava 5; ☽ 8am-3.30pm & 4.30-7.30pm Mon-Fri, 9am-noon & 2-7.30pm Sat & Sun) has limited documentation but you can get hiking maps.

Sights & Activities

The **Town Museum** (Gradski Muzej; ☎ 33 61 014; Livadićeva 7; adult/student 8/5KN; ☽ 9am-3pm Tue-Sat, to 1pm Sun) has moderately interesting exhibits on regional culture. It's housed in

Livadićev Dvor Villa, which once belonged to composer Ferdinand Livadić and was an important centre for the 19th-century nationalist cause.

Samobor is a good jumping-off point for **hikes** into the Samoborsko Gorje, a mountain system (part of the Žumberak Range) which links the high peaks of the alps with the karstic caves and abysses of the Dinaric Range. Carpeted with meadows and forests, the range is the most popular hiking destination in the region. Most of the hikes are easy and there are several mountain huts that make pleasant rest stops. Many are open weekends only except in the high season.

The range has three groups: the Oštrc group in the centre, the Japetić group to the west, and the Plešica group to the east. Both the Oštrc and the Japetić groups are accessible from Šoićeva Kuća, a mountain hut 10km west of Samobor only reachable by foot. From there, it's an easy 30-minute climb to the hill fort of Lipovac and an hour's climb to the peak of Oštrc (753m). Another popular hike is the 1½-hour climb from Šoićeva Kuća to Japetić (780m). You can also follow a path from Oštrc to Japetić which will take about two hours. If you want to explore the Plešica group, head east to the hunting cabin Srndać on Poljanice (12km) from which it's a 40-minute climb to Plešivica peak (780m). The tourist office in town has maps and information on hikes in the region.

Sleeping & Eating

Most people come to Samobor on a day trip from Zagreb but you can also stay here and commute into Zagreb. The one hotel in town offers better value for money than any of the Zagreb hotels.

Hotel Livadić (☎ 33 65 850; www.hotel-livadic.hr; Trg Kralja Tomislava 1; s/d 410/465KN) This atmospheric place is decorated in 19th-century style and provides spacious, comfortable rooms with TV and phone. Since cuisine is a major draw for Samobor, you can count on the quality of the restaurant and café. Prices stay the same year-round.

Meals tend to be more expensive than in Zagreb but are well worth it.

Pri Staroj Vuri (☎ 33 60 548; Giznik 2; 2-course meal 90-110KN) Sitting about 50m uphill from Trg Kralja Tomislava, this restaurant serves traditional dishes in a homy cottage, and sometimes hosts poetry readings.

The specialities of the house are *Hrvatska pisanica* (beef steak in a spicy mushroom, onion, tomato and red wine sauce) and *struklova juha* (soup with *štrukli*).

Samoborska Pivnica (☎ 33 61 623; Šmidhena 3; mains 35-65KN) This restaurant, on the edge of the car park, serves less expensive but well-prepared meals. Try the steak stuffed with ham, mushrooms and cheese.

U Prolazu (☎ 83 66 420; Trg Kralja Tomislava 5) This eatery, on the main square, serves the best *kremšnite* (custard slice) in town.

Shopping

The local aperitif is a delicious, woody red drink called Bermet, which Samobor has been producing for centuries according to a top-secret recipe. It's not for every taste so try it in town first with lemon and ice before deciding to buy a bottle, which will cost about 120KN.

Samoborska Muštarda, or Samobor mustard, is from another age-old recipe. The 60KN price tag may seem expensive for mustard, but it comes in attractive (and re-usable) clay pots.

Getting There & Away

Samobor is easy to reach by public transport. Local buses leave from the bus station in Zagreb every 30 minutes or so for the price of a local ride.

STUBIČKE TOPLICE

As the spa closest to Zagreb, Stubičke Toplice steams away the stress for a devoted band of Zagreb habitués. The hot-spring water (69°C) rising from the subterranean rock layers has spurred tourism since the 18th century. The pools – eight outdoor and one indoor – have a temperature of between 32°C and 36°C and are used to treat a variety of muscular and rheumatic conditions.

The bus drops you off in the centre of town near the **Tourist Office** (☎ 282 727; tz.stubaki@kr.htnet.hr; Šipeka 24; ☯ 9am-5pm Mon-Fri, to 1pm Sat), which can help you find private accommodation.

Hotel Matija Gubec (☎ 282 630; hmg@kr.htnet .hr; Šipeka 27; s/d 295/465KN) offers modest rooms with TVs and phones, plus you get to use all the swimming pools, sauna and gym.

If you don't stay in the hotel, it costs 25KN to use its outdoor pools and 45KN to use the hotel's pool, sauna and massage facilities.

This spa is connected to Zagreb by bus (32KN, one hour, 13 daily) and, less conveniently, by train (22KN, 1½ hours, one daily).

Hrvatsko Zagorje

CONTENTS

The green, rolling hills of Hrvatsko Zagorje, dotted with bucolic villages, medieval castles and thermal springs, deserve to be better known by travellers making a beeline for the coast. Over 40% of the surface is covered with forests – mostly beech, oak, chestnut and fir trees. Even though the sandy soil is generally unreceptive to cultivation, you'll see vineyards, orchards and an occasional corn or wheat field. Besides the landscape, the main attractions of the region are castles, museums and a taste of small-town life in the Croatian interior. The Zagorje region receives relatively few tourists even at the height of the summer season. Its cool hills and spas make a good escape from the summer heat and the Austrian-influenced food and architecture contrast well with the Mediterranean-inspired south.

Northwest of Zagreb, this region begins north of Mt Medvednica outside of Zagreb, and extends west to the Slovenian border, east to the E71 highway and as far north as Varaždin, its largest city and one-time capital of Croatia.

Many of the region's inhabitants speak a local dialect called Kajkavski, named after their word for 'what?' *(kaj?)*. After Croatian or Kajkavski, the second language is likely to be German; few speak English. Although the cities and attractions are well linked to Zagreb by bus and train, it helps to have your own wheels to fully appreciate the landscape.

HIGHLIGHTS

- Admiring the baroque glory of **Varaždin** (p73)
- Wandering the castle of **Trakošćan** (p78)
- Paying homage to Tito at **Kumrovec** (p79)
- Watering yourself at the **Krapinske Toplice** (p78) spa
- Gawking at the bugs of the **Entomological Collection** (p74) in Varaždin

★ Varaždin
★ Trakošćan
★ Krapinske Toplice
★ Kumrovec

- TELEPHONE CODE: 049
- POSTCODE: 49000

VARAŽDIN

☎ 042 / pop 43,000

Varaždin, 81km north of Zagreb, is often ill-used as a mere transit point on the way to or from Hungary, but in fact it's well worth a visit in its own right. The town centre is a marvel of baroque architecture, scrupulously restored and well tended. It was once Croatia's capital and most prosperous city, which explains the extraordinary refinement of the architecture. In many ways, it's a mini-Prague without the crowds or the prices. Topping off the baroque symphony is the gleaming white and turreted Stari Grad (Old City), which now contains a museum.

History

As the centre of Varaždin county, the city played an important role in Croatia's history. The town of Garestine (now Varaždin) became a local administrative centre in 1181 under King Bela III. It was later raised to the status of a free royal borough and given its own seal and coat of arms.

When Croatia was under siege by the Turks, Varaždin was the most powerful stronghold on the Slavonian frontier and the residence of choice for generals. As the threat receded, Varaždin prospered as the cultural, political and commercial centre of Croatia and was made the capital in 1756, a position it held until 1776.

The town's prosperity and proximity to northern Europe facilitated the development of baroque architecture which was flourishing in Europe during this period. Top artisans and builders gravitated to the town, designing mansions, churches and public buildings in the new style. After a disastrous fire of 1776, the Croatian *ban* (viceroy or governor) moved his administration to Zagreb and the town was left to rebuild.

Today the town is a centre for textiles, shoes, furniture and agricultural products. It also has an army base that once belonged to the former Yugoslav army. Apart from that, the town was left unscathed by the war and remains relatively prosperous.

Orientation

The bus and train stations are at opposite ends of town, about 2km apart, and are not linked by public transportation. The town centre lies between them and to the north. The main commercial street is Gundulića; it leads to the main square, Trg Kralja Tomislava, surrounded by Varaždin's famous baroque buildings.

Information

INTERNET ACCESS

Internet caffe Sakcinski (9 I Kukuljević; per hr 10KN; ⏲ 7.30am-10pm) Large and modern, the connections are good here.

LEFT LUGGAGE

Garderoba Bus station (per day 5KN; ⏲ 6am-10pm); Train station (per day 10KN; ⏲ 24hr)

MONEY

Varaždinska Banka (Kapucinski trg 5) This branch is opposite the bus station, but all branches have ATMs.

POST

Post office (Trg Slobode 9)

TOURIST INFORMATION

Turistička Zajednica (☎ /fax 210 987; www.varazdin .hr; Padovčeva 3; ⏲ 8am-6pm Mon-Fri, 9am-1pm Sat Apr-Oct, 8am-4pm Mon-Fri Nov-Mar) The tourist office has plenty of colourful brochures and is a wealth of information.

TRAVEL AGENCIES

Atlas Travel Agency (☎ 313 618; B Radić 20) Represents American Express.
T-Tours Agency (☎ 210 989; t-tours@vz.htnet.hr; Gundulićeva 2) Finds private accommodation and is a good source of information on town events.

Sights

In addition to several excellent museums, Varaždin offers a fine ensemble of baroque buildings in its centre, a number of which have been turned into museums. Many of the aristocratic mansions and elegant churches are being restored as part of the town's bid to be included in Unesco's list of World Heritage sites. Conveniently, most buildings have plaques out the front with architectural and historical explanations in English.

MUSEUMS

The **Town Museum** (Gradski Muzej; ☎ 210 339; Strossmayera 7; adult/student 15/12KN; ⏲ 10am-5pm Tue-Fri, 10am-3pm Sat & Sun Jun-Aug, 10am-3pm Tue-Fri, 10am-1pm Sat & Sun Sep-May) is part of the **Stari Grad** (Old City), which is a beautifully preserved example of medieval defensive architecture. Construction of this fortress began in the 14th century, but it was the Earl of Celje

HRVATSKO ZAGORJE

SLOVENIA   HUNGARY

WHAT'S FREE

The best free sight in Varaždin is the town centre, composed of baroque buildings ornamented with pastel stucco. Trg Kralja Tomislava is the central square, dominated by the town hall which has a tower that makes it resemble a church. The old streets radiate from the square in a large pedestrian zone of attractive 18th-century buildings. There's a guard-changing ceremony in front of the town hall every Saturday from 11am to noon.

---

who turned it into a strong fortress in the 15th century, adding the rounded towers that typify Gothic architecture in northern Croatia. By the early 16th century, it was the chief regional fortification against the encroaching Ottoman Turks, but the two large courtyards and massive corridors made it look more like a castle. It remained in private hands until 1925 when it was turned into a museum. Today, it houses furniture, paintings, decorative objects and

weapons amassed during the course of Varaždin's history. The exhibits are divided into eight different rooms, each one reflecting a different historic period. The architecture alone is worth paying the admission; the exhibits are interesting enough.

Varaždin's other major museum is the fascinating **Entomological Collection** (Entomološka Zbirka; ☎ 210 474; Franjevački trg 6; adult/student 15/12KN; ✆ 10am-3pm Tue-Fri, 10am-1pm Sat & Sun). Housed in the baroque **Herczer Palace**, the collection comprises nearly 4500 exhibits of the bug world, including 1000 different insect species. The examples of insect nests, habitats and reproductive habits are informative and displayed with flair. The collection was amassed and mounted by a local entomologist, Franjo Košćec, who also created the tools to mount the tiny creatures.

Just south of the palace is the **Gallery of Old and Modern Masters** (Galerija Starih i Novih Majstora; ☎ 214 172; Trg Stančića 3; adult/student 15/12KN; ✆ 10am-2pm Tue-Fri, 10am-1pm Sat & Sun), housed in the rococo-style **Sermage Palace**, which was built in 1759. Note the carved medallions on the façade and then enjoy the museum, which exhibits portraits and landscapes from Croatian, Italian, Dutch, German and Flemish schools.

Nearby is **Lisak's Tower** (Kula Lisak; Trg Jelačića 2) the only remaining part of the city's medieval walls.

CHURCHES
The **cathedral** (Katedrala; ☎ 210 688; Pavlinska 5), formerly a Jesuit church, was built in 1646. The façade is distinguished by an early baroque portal bearing the coat of arms of the noble Drašković family. Inside, the highlight is the 18th-century altar with the altarpiece of the Assumption of the Virgin Mary. Also impressive are the choir stalls and 18th-century paintings in the sanctuary.

The **Franciscan Church of St John the Baptist** (Crkva Svetog Ivana Krstitelja; Franjevački trg 4) contains an ancient pharmacy ornamented with a series of 18th-century frescoes depicting the continents and natural elements. Next to the church is a copy of the **statue of Bishop Grgur Ninski** that Ivan Meštrović created for Split. Touching the statue's big toe is supposed to bring good luck.

Walk south on Draškovića and look out for the **Church of St Nicholas** (Crvka Svetog Nikole; Draškovića 7) on the left, with its medieval Gothic tower.

OTHER SIGHTS
One of the town's most striking buildings is the **town hall** (Gradska Vijećnica; Trg Kralja Tomislava), a handsome Romanesque-Gothic structure that has served as the town hall since the 16th century. Notice the town's coat of arms at the foot of the tower and the carved portal dating from 1792 (see What's Free, p74). From 10am to 1pm on Saturday from April to October, a colourfully dressed 'Notary' issues 'passports' to visit the town's beer halls while the Town Blacksmith forges 'Varaždin Medallions' out the front of the town hall.

Other baroque highlights include the **Patačić Palace** (Palača Patačić), an exquisitely restored rococo palace dating from 1764 with a finely carved stone portal; and the **Patačić-Puttar Palace** (Palača Patačić-Puttar; Zagrebačka 2), a striking mixture of baroque and classicist styles with a richly decorated stone portal featuring the coat of arms of

HRVATSKO ZAGORJE

VARAŽDIN

0 ————— 300 m
0 ————— 0.2 miles

To Drava River (1km); Čakovec

INFORMATION	
Atlas Travel Agency	1 A3
Garderoba	(see 27)
Internet caffe Sakcinski	2 B2
Post Office	3 B3
T-Tours	4 B2
Varaždinska Banka	5 B3

SIGHTS & ACTIVITIES	(p73–6)
Cathedral	6 B2
Church of St Nicholas	7 B2

Croatian National Theatre	8 B3
Entomological Collection	9 B2
Franciscan Church of St John the Baptist	10 B2
Gallery of Old and Modern Masters	11 B2
Lisak's Tower	12 B2
Patačić Palace	13 B2
Patačić-Puttar Palace	14 B3
Stari Grad (Old City)	(see 17)
Statue of Bishop Grgur Ninski	15 B2
Town Hall	16 B2
Town Museum	17 B2

SLEEPING	🛏 (p76)
Garestin Hotel	18 B3
Hotel Turist	19 B3
Pansion Maltar	20 B3

EATING	🍴 (p76)
Korzo	21 B2
Market	22 B2
Park	23 B2
Pivnica Raj	24 B2
Tempio	25 B3
Zlatna Guska	26 B2

TRANSPORT	(pp76–7)
Bus Station	27 B3

To Train Station (25m); Garderoba (25m)

To Zagreb

the Patačic family. The **Croatian National Theatre** (Hrvatsko Narodno Kazalište; A Cesarca 1) was built in 1873 in a neo-Renaissance style, following the designs of Viennese architect Hermann Helmer.

For a more bucolic stroll, walk down to the Drava river. This wide, tranquil river is bordered by footpaths, and there are a few outdoor cafés in which to relax.

Festivals & Events

Varaždin is famous for its baroque music festival, **Varaždin Baroque Evenings**, which takes place over three to four weeks each September. Local and international orchestras play baroque music in churches and theatres around the city for prices ranging from 30KN to 100KN, depending on the programme. Tickets are available about two hours before the beginning of the concert at travel agencies, the **Varaždin Concert Bureau** (☎ /fax 212 907) at the Croatian National Theatre, or at the cathedral. In July and August there's also a **Summer Cultural Festival** of music, dance and theatre; it's often held in the city's squares and parks.

Sleeping

Accommodation is less expensive than in Zagreb and offers better value. Most hotels in Varaždin are clean, well maintained and offer good value for money. Their clientele is mostly visiting business people from Zagreb and neighbouring countries – this means they are likely to be full on Monday to Friday and empty on weekends.

Pansion Maltar (☎ 311 100; fax 211 190; F Prešerna 1; s/d 200/375KN) This cheerful little *pension*, not far from the bus station, is the cheapest place in town but has only 10 rooms. Booking in advance is advised, but a challenge if your Croatian isn't up to par. Rooms are in excellent condition and have satellite TV but no phones.

Garestin Hotel (☎ /fax 214 314; Zagrebačka 34; s/d 250/360KN) This establishment has a glossy, modern décor that usually indicates high prices. Yet rooms with phone, TV and minibar are reasonably priced. The hotel is only a short walk from the bus station.

Hotel Turist (☎ 395 395; turist@vz.htnet.hr; Kralja Zvonimira 1; s/d from 300/415KN; P ✕ ☐) This is a higher-end hotel which is well located and offers excellent service. The more expensive 'business class' rooms are slightly larger than the 'simple' ones and are equipped with a minibar.

PRIVATE ROOMS

T-Tours Agency has single/double private rooms from about 85/150KN. There is generally no supplement for a single night's stay and prices stay the same year-round. There aren't many rooms available, but then there aren't many people asking for them either.

Eating & Drinking

Tempio (☎ 210 136; Prešlerna 3; mains from 50KN) Many restaurants in Varaždin are located within pleasant, renovated courtyards of old buildings, and this is one of the best. It offers fine local specialities such as *husarska pečenka* (steak with onions and bacon) and an interesting selection of fried or baked vegetable platters.

Pivnica Raj (☎ 213 146; Gundulića 11; mains from 35KN) The brew flows freely in this enormously popular local beer hall where the food is old-fashioned and hearty but with a nod to vegetarians. On weekends there's traditional *tamburitza* (three- or five-string mandolin) music but it's a good time here any time, whether on the terrace or in the cosy interior.

Zlatna Guska (☎ 213 393; Habdelića 4; mains around 70KN) The interior is designed to resemble a knights' dining hall with plenty of armour and equipment and dishes called 'the last meal of a victim of an execution' among other evocative names. It's fun and the dishes are cooked to perfection. The portions would make a knight burst his tin suit.

Park (☎ 211 498; Habdelića 6; mains 45-65KN) This restaurant overlooks a leafy park and offers delicious grilled meat or chicken and a copious salad buffet.

Korzo (☎ 320 914; Trg Kralja Tomislava 2) Tables extend far out onto the square in nice weather, making this an excellent café for sipping a cocktail and people-watching.

There is a daily **market** (Trg Bana Jelačića), open until 2pm, and there are many bakeries that sell Varaždin's special finger-shaped bread, *klipići*.

Getting There & Away

Varaždin is a major transportation hub in north Croatia, with bus and train lines running in all directions. For information on long-haul buses to Germany and northern Europe, see the Bus section in the Transport chapter (p274). Remember that northbound buses originate in Zagreb, stop at Varaždin and cost the same whether you buy the ticket in Zagreb or Varaždin.

All buses to the coast go through Zagreb. There's a daily bus to Nagykanizsa, Hungary (52KN, three hours) and a daily bus to Graz, Austria (78KN, three hours). There are buses to Trakošćan castle about every hour (22KN, one hour), to Varaždinske Toplice (15KN, 30 minutes, eight daily) and buses to Zagreb every 30 minutes to an hour (51KN, two hours).

There's a daily train to Rijeka (112KN, seven hours) and Zadar in the summer (164KN, 11 hours). There's one direct train day to Budapest (179KN, five hours) and three unreserved trains to Nagykanizsa (39KN, 1½ hours).

VARAŽDINSKE TOPLICE

Sulphurous springs at a temperature of 58°C have been attracting weary visitors to Varaždinske Toplice since the Romans first established a health settlement here at the beginning of the 1st century AD. Gentle, wooded hills surround this spa, which offers various fitness and anti-stress programmes as well as three indoor and two outdoor pools. In addition to relaxing water therapies, you can explore the surrounding town which contains an appealing assortment of 16th- to 19th-century buildings. There is also the remains of the Roman settlement.

The **Tourist Office** (☎ 633 133; www.varazdin sketoplice.tk; Trg Slobode 4; ⏲ 8am-3pm Mon-Fri) is located in the centre of town not far from the bus stop on Trg Republike Hrvatske. Staff will help you find private accommodation.

At the **Hotel Minerva** (☎ 630 000; fax 630 826; Trg Slobode 1; s/d 220/376KN; 🏊), the town's only hotel, you'll have access to a sauna, fitness room and all outdoor and indoor pools.

The spa is 12km southeast of Varaždin and 69km northeast of Zagreb. There are numerous buses from Varaždin (17KN, 30 minutes, eight daily).

KRAPINA

pop 4481

The Zagorje region has been inhabited since the Paleolithic Age. On Hušn Đakovo hill, near Krapina, archaeological excavations

revealed human and animal bones from a Neanderthal tribe that lived in the cave from 100,000 BC to 35,000 BC. Some 650 bones belonging to 80 Neanderthals were found along with tools and weapons, making the site one of the most significant in Europe.

Krapina is a busy commercial town in the midst of a lovely region, but there is little of interest to keep visitors occupied for more than half a day.

Orientation & Information

The main road that runs through town is Zagrebačka cesta, which becomes Ljudevita Gaja in the town centre and Magistratska at the northern end. The centre of town is Trg Stjepana Radića, with the bus station about 100m further south and the train station another 200m.

There's a **Tourist Office** (☎ 371 330; tzg-krapina@ kr.htnet.hr; Magistratska 11; ⏲ 8am-3pm Mon-Fri) but it generally doesn't keep its regular hours.

Sights & Activities

Although the bones and artefacts are now displayed in the Croatian Natural History Museum (p54) in Zagreb, there's a park on the hill in Krapina with sculpted life-sized models of Neanderthals engaged in everyday activities such as wielding clubs and throwing stones. The nearby **Museum of Evolution** (☎ 371 491; Šetalište V Sluge bb; adult/ student 15/10KN; ⏲ 9am-5pm Tue-Sun Apr-Oct, 8am-3pm Tue-Sun Nov-Mar) has a few prehistoric artefacts and other exhibits tracing the history and geology of the region.

The town of Krapina is unremarkable but take a look at the baroque **Franciscan monastery and church**, with a 17th-century altar and 18th-century paintings. Next to the church is an 18th-century column dedicated to the Virgin Mary. There's also the **City Art Gallery** (☎ 214 172; Magistratska 25; admission free; ⏲ 10am-1pm Mon-Sat).

Festivals & Events

If you're around at the beginning of September, check out the **Festival of Kajkavian Songs**, which includes regional folklore concerts, poetry readings and a lot of delicious Zagorje food at street stalls.

Sleeping

There's no private accommodation but one pleasant *pension*, **Pansion Pod Starim Krovovima**

(☎ 370 536; Trg L. Gaja 15; r 310KN), a few kilometres north of town.

Getting There & Away

There are nine buses a day from Zagreb to Krapina (29KN, one hour) on Monday to Friday, and four on weekends. There are up to 14 trains daily from Zagreb, changing at Zabok (29KN, 1½ hours).

KRAPINSKE TOPLICE

This spa, about 17km southwest of Krapina and 46km northwest of Zagreb, is beautifully located in the Zagorje countryside. The complex has four outdoor thermal pools rich in minerals and never below 39°C. There are also six indoor pools and a sports complex, which makes the centre attractive to those looking for relaxation as well as medical treatments and rehabilitation.

The bus station is in the centre of town, a short walk from most facilities and the **Tourist Office** (☎ 232 106; tzo-krapinske.toplice@kr.htnet.hr; Zagrebačka 2; ☯ 7am-3pm Mon-Fri, 8am-noon Sat).

The **Hotel Aquae Vivae** (☎ 202 202; www.aquae -vivae.hr; Antuna Mihanovića 2; s/d 270/420KN) has a section for patients and one for visitors but all rooms are comfortable. The room rates include bathroom, balcony and breakfast, but there are also more expensive rooms that also have TV and phone. Half and full board are also available.

The spa is well connected to Zagreb by bus (24KN, 1¼ hours, 10 daily).

VELIKI TABOR CASTLE

The drive from Zagreb or Varaždin to Veliki Tabor, 57km northwest of Zagreb, is a beautiful one, with an unfolding panorama of hills, pastures and forests. The area also offers good dining and lodging, making a trip to the castle well worth while. The Croatian aristocracy began building fortified castles in the region to stave off the Turkish threat at the end of the 16th century. **Veliki Tabor castle** (☎ 343 052; Desinić; adult/student 20/15KN; ☯ 10am-6pm Apr-Oct, 9am-5pm Nov-Mar) was built in the early 16th century and restored several times. Strategically perched on top of a hill, the fortress-mansion has everything a medieval master could want – towers, turrets and holes in the walls for pouring tar and hot oil on the enemy. It later belonged to the venerable Ratkaj family, then to the painter Iveković, and is now devoted to an unexciting exhibition of medieval weaponry. Plans are afoot to install other exhibits in the hope that one day the interior will be as fascinating as the exterior.

Sleeping & Eating

Dvorec Bežanec (☎ 376 800; www.bezanec.hr; Bežanec; r from 615KN) This is a beautifully restored 18th-century castle surrounded by a landscaped park, 12km east of Veliki Tabor castle. The rooms are immaculately decorated and there is an excellent selection of contemporary art on display throughout. The rate includes breakfast, and it's worthwhile eating lunch or dinner at the hotel; three-course menus start at 110KN and the wine list is excellent. Horse riding, tennis, bike riding and hot-air ballooning can be arranged. You'll never want to leave.

Grešna Gorica (☎ 049-343 001; Taborgradska klet; Desinić; mains from 55KN) This rustic eatery is a favourite with families. Kids love running around the garden and grown-ups love the selection of superbly prepared Croatian specialties. The restaurant is on a side road about 1km east of Veliki Tabor and has refreshing countryside views.

Getting There & Away

There are nine daily buses from Zagreb to Desinić (69KN, 2½ hours) but you'll have to walk 3km northwest to Veliki Tabor.

TRAKOŠĆAN CASTLE

The most impressive castle in Croatia is **Trakošćan Castle** (☎ 042-796 281; Trakošćan; adult/student 20/10KN; ☯ 9am-6pm Apr-Oct, 9am-4pm Nov-Mar), 83km northwest of Zagreb. Although the exact date of its construction is unknown, it retains classical 12th- and 13th-century features and was occupied by the aristocratic Drašković family from the end of the 16th century. Unlike Veliki Tabor castle, the interior is furnished with original pieces from the Draškovićs, who occupied the castle until the early 20th century. When the castle was restored in 1860 the surrounding grounds were landscaped and turned into an attractive park with exotic trees and an artificial lake. If you wonder what the Draškovićs looked like, there are plenty of family portraits throughout the castle as well as an armaments collection, cavalry flats, a kitchen and library. Note the unusual exterior heating system that

JOSIP BROZ TITO

Josip Broz was born in Kumrovec in 1892, to a Croat father and Slovene mother. When WWI broke out, Tito was drafted into the Austro-Hungarian army and was taken prisoner by the Russians. He escaped just before the 1917 revolution, became a Communist and joined the Red Army, where he served with distinction. He returned to Croatia in 1920 and became a union organiser while working as a metalworker.

As secretary of the Zagreb committee of the outlawed Communist Party, he worked hard to unify the party and managed to dramatically increase its membership by the end of the 1930s. When the Nazis invaded Yugoslavia in 1941 he adopted the name Tito, after the 18th-century Croat writer Tito Brezovački, and organised small bands of guerrillas called Partisans. His successful campaign against the Germans, Italians and Chetniks attracted military support from the British and Americans but Russia repeatedly rebuffed his requests for aid, perhaps setting the stage for the later rift between Yugoslavia and the Soviet Union.

In 1945, he became premier of a reconstituted Yugoslavia. Although loyal to Moscow, Tito had a pronounced streak of independence that led him to clash sharply with Stalin. In 1948 he was effectively banished from the Cominform (the Communist Information Bureau, established in 1947 to exchange information between European Communist parties) and thereafter adopted a conciliatory policy towards the West which nevertheless continued to consider Yugoslavia as a Soviet satellite state.

Yugoslavia's rival nationalities were Tito's biggest headache, which he dealt with by suppressing all dissent and trying to ensure a rough equality of representation at the upper echelons of government. Although he was half-Croat, he manifested no particular favouritism towards Croat interests and resided in Belgrade. None of his wives or mistresses were Croat (in fact two were Serb) and Tito never publicly referred to himself as a Croat. As a committed Communist, he viewed ethnic disputes as unwelcome deviations from the pursuit of the common good.

Yet Tito was well aware of the ethnic tensions that simmered just below the surface of Yugoslavia. Preparations for his succession began in the early 1970s as he aimed to create a balance of power among the ethnic groups of Yugoslavia. He set up a collective presidency that was to rotate annually among representatives of each of the six republics plus Serbia's two autonomous provinces of Kosovo and Vojvodina. The system proved unworkable. Later events revealed how dependent Yugoslavia was on their wily, charismatic leader.

When Tito died in May 1980, his body was carried from Ljubljana to Belgrade in a blue train. Thousands of mourners flocked the streets to pay respects to the man who had united a difficult country for 35 years. It was the last common outpouring of emotion that all Yugoslavia's fractious nationalities were able to share.

In the nationalistic fervor that followed Croatia's independence, Tito's name was anathema. Fondness for the Tito era was derided as Yugo-nostalgia, a sort of mental disease. Now that Croatia is confronting an era of economic belt-tightening, young Croatians are impressed with the ease and prosperity of their parents' lives. Tito is back in style as a countercultural hero. Interest in the Tito era has never been higher; don't be surprised to see Tito T-shirts and posters in the trendiest bars.

allowed servants to stoke the fires without entering the family rooms.

There are no buses operating between Zagreb and Trakošćan, but there are buses from Varaždin (24KN, 50 minutes, 11 daily).

KUMROVEC

The Zagorje region was the birthplace of several celebrated Croats, most notably Tito, born as Josip Broz in Kumrovec. The entire village has been transformed into a re-creation of a **19th-century village** (☎ 553 107; adult/student 10/5KN; ☻ 9am-4pm Nov-Mar, 9am-6pm Apr-Oct). About 40 houses and barns made of pressed earth and wood have been preserved and filled with tools, furniture and mannequins in order to evoke their original function. There are toys in the toymaker's hut, a wine press in the winemaker's hut, a blacksmith's hut with tools and so forth. Lying on a slope beside the

Sutla River with a stream bubbling through the rustic setting, this open-air museum presents an idyllic view of village life (if villages were this pleasant, no-one would ever have left), but the thoughtful exhibits with captions in English give a vivid glimpse of traditional peasant life. On weekends from May to September there are demonstrations of traditional blacksmithing, pottery and weaving.

There are three daily buses running between Zagreb and Kumrovec (27KN, one hour, three daily) and one extremely early train (22KN, one hour).

KLANJEC

The sculptor Antun Augustinčić (1900–79), who created the *Monument to Peace* in front of the UN building in New York, was another notable Croat from Zagorje. His hometown, Klanjec, has a **museum** (☎ 550 343; Trg Antuna Mihanovića; adult/student 20/10KN; ⊙ 9am-3pm Tue-Sun Oct-Mar, 9am-5pm Apr-Sep) devoted to his work, including his memorial to fallen Partisans. It's pleasant to stroll around the small town, which also has a 17th-century baroque church.

The three daily buses running from Zagreb to Kumrovec stop in Klanjec (28KN, 50 minutes).

MARIJA BISTRICA

The largest pilgrimage centre in Croatia is in Zagorje at Marija Bistrica, a village 37km north of Zagreb on the northern slopes of Mt Medvednica. The focus of attention is the **Marija Bistrica Church** (Hodočasnička Crkva Marije Bistricvke), which contains a wooden Gothic statue of the Madonna created in the 16th century. The statue's alleged miraculous power dates back to the 16th-century Turkish invasions when the statue was saved from destruction. Behind the church is the 'Way of the Cross', a path leading up the Calvary Hill on which the 14 stations of the cross are marked with works by Croatian sculptors. The church attracts 600,000 visitors a year, but there were even more in 1998 when Pope John Paul II arrived to beatify Archbishop Stepinac.

There are 15 buses a day from Zagreb to Marija Bistrica (35KN, 40 minutes) from Monday to Saturday, and eight on Sunday.

Slavonia

SLAVONIA

For a visitor, Slavonia provides a landscape nearly untouched by tourism yet with some unique wonders. The park of Kopački Rit is one of Europe's finest ornithological reserves and most of the time it's just you and the birds. The region's largest town is Osijek, well worth a visit for its remarkable fortress and Secession architecture. Throughout the region are peaceful farming villages and an extraordinarily tasty cuisine.

Slavonia is Croatia's breadbasket, a fertile region that yields wheat, corn, sugar beets, sunflowers, alfalfa and clover in addition to some of Croatia's finest wines. In contrast to the rugged Croatian coastline, the terrain is pancake-flat; as locals say, 'the highest mountain is a cabbage'. Stretching from the Ilova River in the west, over the Sava and Drava basins to the Hungarian border in the north, to the border of Bosnia and Hercegovina in the south and the Yugoslav border in the east, it's a region of cultural, if not geographic, diversity.

There is a small Hungarian minority in Slavonia, recalling the days when its powerful neighbour to the north ruled the region. Other traces of Hungarian influence include a scattering of baroque architecture in the cities. Few Serbs remain after the bitter war of the early 1990s, but their presence is a powerful and tragic reminder of the ethnic diversity that once characterised Slavonia.

HIGHLIGHTS

- Touring the birdland of **Kopački Rit Nature Park** (p87)
- Enjoying spicy treats such as *kulen*, a paprika-flavoured sausage, or *riblji paprikaš*, fish stew (p42)
- Guzzling local beer on Radićeva in **Osijek** (p86)
- Getting down with the crowd at **Đakovački Vezovi** festival (p89)
- Admiring the fine **Lipizzaner horses** (p89) in Đakovo

- TELEPHONE CODE: 031
- POSTCODE: 31000

History

Before the 1991 war displaced tens of thousands of inhabitants, Slavonia contained one of the most ethnically diverse populations in Europe. Settled by Slavic tribes in the 7th century, the region was conquered by the Turks in the 16th century. Catholic residents fled and Serbian Orthodox settlers, who were better received by the Turks, arrived en masse.

In 1690, Serb supporters of Vienna, in their battles with the Turks, left Kosovo and settled in the Srijem region around Vukovar. The Turks ceded the land to Austria in 1699 and the Habsburgs turned a large part of the region into a Military Frontier (Vojna Krajina).

The Muslim population fled but more Serbs arrived, joined by German merchants, Hungarian, Slovak and Ukrainian peasants, Catholic Albanians and Jews. Much land was sold to German and Hungarian aristocrats who built huge baroque and classical mansions around Osijek, Vukovar, Ilok and other towns.

Many Germans were killed or expelled after WWI and WWII and their homesteads occupied by Serbs and Montenegrins from southern Yugoslavia.

The large Serbian community prompted Serbian president Slobodan Milošević's attempt to incorporate the region into 'Greater Serbia'. This assault began with the destruction of Vukovar and the shelling of Osijek in 1991. A ceasefire prevailed in 1992, but it wasn't until January 1998 that the region was returned to Croatia as part of the Dayton peace agreement. The scars of war remain unhealed, however. The region's economy was destroyed and has not yet been rebuilt. Few towns remain unmarked by traces of the war and ethnic tensions remain high.

Dangers & Annoyances

Osijek and the surrounding region was heavily laid with land mines during the 1990s war. Although the city and its outskirts along the main road have been demined and are completely safe, it would be unwise to wander through the swampland north of the Drava River which leads to Kopački Rit.

In summer, the mosquitoes are bloodthirsty little devils, chewing through every bit of flesh they can find. Wear long sleeves and trousers or slather on a lot of insect repellent after dark.

OSIJEK

pop 91,000

Photographs of Osijek before the 1990s reveal a relaxed river city of wide avenues, leafy parks and stately 19th-century Viennese architecture. The avenues and parks are still there, but the fine old mansions were badly scarred by the shells that fell on the town as part of the 1991 Yugoslav offensive.

Although many major buildings along the avenues were patched up and restored to their former lustre, the pits and pockmarks on other buildings are grim reminders of the war that ravaged eastern Slavonia in the early 1990s.

Nevertheless, through the general aura of decay, you can still perceive the resilient spirit of the city. A shortage of decent accommodation makes a visit here problematic and expensive, but if you're willing to put up with the hassle there's a pleasant waterfront promenade and an imposing 18th-century fortress on the hill, and you can swim in the Drava River.

History

Osijek's excellent location on the Drava River, near its junction with the Danube (Dunav) has made it strategically important for more than two millennia. After the Illyrians, the Romans arrived in the 1st century and built a military colony; these buildings were destroyed in the Barbarian invasions of the 6th century.

It was the Slav settlers that gave Osijek its name, and by the 12th century it was a thriving market town owned by the Cistercian abbey. When the Turks conquered Osijek in 1529, they made it an important administrative centre and the town became predominantly Muslim.

The Austrians finally chased the Turks out in 1687, the Muslims fled into Bosnia and the city was repopulated with Serbs, Croats, Germans and Hungarians. The new settlers erased all remnants of Turkish rule and demolished the mosques, erecting churches on the ruins.

Still wary of Turkish attacks, the Austrians made Osijek the capital of the Slavonian Military Frontier and in the early 18th

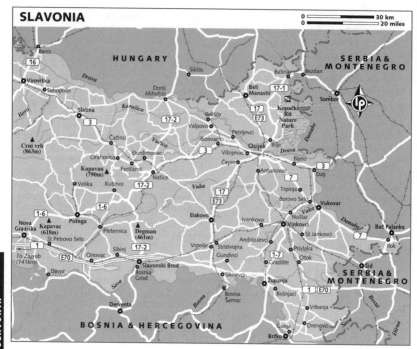

SLAVONIA

0 ————— 30 km
0 ————— 20 miles

century, built the fortress, Tvrđa, which still dominates the town.

Osijek prospered during the 18th and 19th centuries and remained part of the Austro-Hungarian empire until 1918 when it joined the Kingdom of Serbs, Croats and Slovenes. Until the recent 1991 war, Osijek was a powerful industrial centre producing matches, beer, refined sugar, chemicals, textiles, shoes and agricultural machinery.

When war broke out in 1991 following Croatia's declaration of independence, the federal Yugoslav army and Serbian paramilitary units overran the Baranja region north of Osijek. The first shells began falling in July 1991 from Serbian positions across the Drava River and continued into the autumn. When Vukovar fell in November of that year, federal and Serbian forces made Osijek the object of their undivided attention, pounding the city with artillery as thousands of terrified residents poured out of the city. By that time, Serbian President Milošević was committing Yugoslavia to a peace-keeping operation, and the

expected destruction of Osijek never materialised, although the devastating shelling continued until May 1992.

The city is still struggling to recover – the economy has been badly hurt by the costs of reconstruction and of housing refugees, as well as the loss of markets for its products.

Orientation

Stretching along the southern bank of the Drava River, Osijek is composed of three settlements: the Upper Town (Gornji Grad) the Lower Town (Donji Grad) and the 18th-century fortress, Tvrđa. The bus station and train station are adjacent in the southern part of the Upper Town, and you'll find most of the sights, hotels, cafés and shopping between the train and bus station and the river.

The main shopping street is Kapucinska, which becomes Europska Avenija in the east, bordered by three parks planted with chestnut and linden trees. A promenade stretches along the riverbanks until the city's outskirts.

Information

INTERNET ACCESS
Internet caffe (☎ 204 250; Sunčana 18; per hr 20KN)

LEFT LUGGAGE
Garderoba (Bus station; ☥ 7am-8pm Mon-Sat,
7am-4pm Sun)

MONEY
Croatia Express (In the train station) Changes money.
Privredna Banka (Kapucinska 25) Has an ATM.
Zagrebačka Banka (Strossmayera 1) In town; you can
change money here.

POST
Main Post Office (Kardinala Alojzja Stepinca 17) Here
you can change money, make phone calls and get cash
advances on MasterCard.

TOURIST INFORMATION
Tourist Office (☎ /fax 203 755; www.tzosijek.hr;
Županijska 2) Has brochures and maps. Ask for the helpful
Gradski Vodič, which lists each month's events and has
dozens of useful phone numbers.

TRAVEL AGENCIES
Generalturist (☎ 211 500; Kapucinska 39) Sells air
tickets and package tours to European destinations.
OK Tours (☎ 212 815; www.ok-tours.hr; Slobode trg 8)
Good local information and some private accommodation.
Panturist (☎ 214 388; Kapucinska 19) The largest
travel agency in Slavonia; runs buses to the coast as well as
Germany, Switzerland and Bosnia and Hercegovina. It sells
bus and air tickets and arranges accommodation along the
Adriatic coast.

Sights

TVRĐA
Built under Habsburg rule as a defence
against Turkish attacks, the 18th-century
fortress was relatively undamaged during
the recent war, leaving its baroque architecture intact. Because most of it was designed solely by the Austrian architect
Maximilian de Gosseau between 1712 and
1721, the buildings present a remarkable
architectural unity.

The main square, Trg Svetog Trojstva, is
marked by the elaborate **Holy Trinity Monument**, erected in 1729 to commemorate the
victims of the 15th-century plague that
swept through the city.

The **Museum of Slavonia** (Muzej Slavonije Osijek;
☎ 208 501; Trg Svetog Trojstva 6; adult/student 12/6KN;
☥ 10am-1pm Tue-Sun, 6-9pm Sat), on the eastern

side of the square, is housed in the former
1702 Magistrate Building. It traces Slavonia's long history, beginning with implements from the Bronze Age and displays of
coins, pottery, sculpture and utensils from
the Roman occupation.

UPPER TOWN
The towering **Church of St Peter and St Paul**
(☎ 369 626; ☥ 7am-noon & 3-8pm) looms over Trg
Ante Starčevića. The 90m-high tower is the
second highest in Croatia, surpassed only
by the cathedral in Zagreb (p54). Although
often referred to as the 'Cathedral' because
of its size and majesty, in fact this brick neo-
gothic structure is a parish church which
was built at the end of the 19th century. The
style is Viennese, from the overall design
to the 40 stained-glass windows inside, as
well as the stone-work from the Viennese
sculptor, Eduard Hauser. The wall paintings have long been attributed to Croatian
painter Mirko Rački, but recent scholarship
indicates that they were in fact executed by
one of his disciples.

The **Gallery of Fine Arts** (☎ 213 587; Europska
Avenija 9; adult/student 10/5KN; ☥ 9am-1pm & 5-8pm
Tue-Fri) is housed in an elegant 19th-century
mansion and contains a collection of paintings by Slavonian artists, and some contemporary Croatian works.

Sleeping
There are no camping grounds or hostels
and limited private accommodation in
Osijek. Ask at OK Tours.

Hotel Central (☎ 283 399; hotel-central@os.htnet
.hr; Trg Ante Starčevića 6; s/d 272/420KN) This has the
most character of any of the hotels, with its
stunning Art Deco lobby and café. Rooms
are comfortable but could use a facelift.

Waldinger (☎ 250 450; www.waldinger.hr; Županijska 8; s/d 390/440KN) Osijek's most elegant
tearoom-art gallery (where the pastries are
outstanding) has recently expanded into a
smart little guesthouse. The rooms don't
quite equal the lavishness of the tearoom
but they'll do nicely.

Hotel Osijek (☎ 201 333; Šamačka 4; s/d from
400/500KN) This hotel could use a makeover
but at least some rooms overlook the Drava.
Other than that, there's nothing that special
here.

Hotel Ritam (☎ 310 310; www.hotel-ritam.hr;
Kozjačka 76; s/d 450/700KN) This new place offers

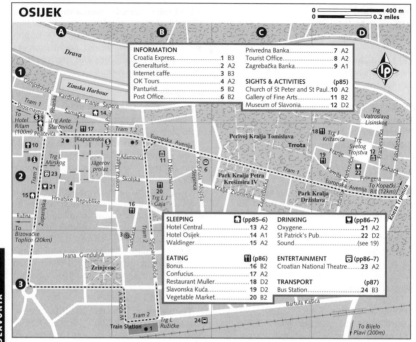

OSIJEK

0 — 400 m
0 — 0.2 miles

INFORMATION
Croatia Express................1 B3
Generalturist.................2 A2
Internet caffe................3 B3
OK Tours.....................4 A2
Panturist....................5 B2
Post Office..................6 B2
Privredna Banka..............7 A2
Tourist Office...............8 A2
Zagrebačka Banka.............9 A1

SIGHTS & ACTIVITIES (p85)
Church of St Peter and St Paul..10 A2
Gallery of Fine Arts.........11 B2
Museum of Slavonia..........12 D2

SLEEPING (pp85–6)
Hotel Central...............13 A2
Hotel Osijek................14 A1
Waldinger..................15 A2

EATING (p86)
Bonus.....................16 B2
Confucius..................17 A2
Restaurant Muller...........18 D2
Slavonska Kuća..............19 D2
Vegetable Market............20 B2

DRINKING (pp86–7)
Oxygene...................21 A2
St Patrick's Pub............22 D2
Sound....................(see 19)

ENTERTAINMENT (pp86–7)
Croatian National Theatre.....23 A2

TRANSPORT (p87)
Bus Station................24 B3

large, bright rooms with modern furnishings and satellite TV. Some rooms have balconies.

Eating

Food is the strong point of Osijek and it offers much better value for money than the accommodation available here. The cuisine is spicy and strongly influenced by neighbouring Hungary, although Slavonia does produce its own brand of hot paprika. As elsewhere in Croatia, there is a strong emphasis on meat but you can also find freshwater fish, which is often served in a delicious stew called *riblji paprikaš*, with noodles.

Bonus (☎ 202 0300; Hrvatske Republike 1; mains from 30KN) The Art Deco/tropical ambience here is relaxing and the standard Croatian dishes are well prepared.

Confucius (☎ 210 104; Kapucinska 34; mains from 45KN) The people of Osijek are probably the only Croats with enough of a taste for spicy food to support a Szechuan Chinese restaurant. The décor is Chinese-red and the dishes are authentic.

Bijelo Plavi (☎ 571 000; Divaltova 8; mains from 45KN) Visiting businesspeople come here for a meaty meal in a slightly formal atmosphere. It's about 2km southeast of the train station.

Slavonska Kuća (☎ 208 277; Kamila Firingera 26, Tvrđa; mains from 50KN) One of the best places to try *riblji paprikaš* as well as other regional specialities, it is in an appealingly rustic old house, with wooden booths and lace curtains. Wash your meal down with Krauthaker, a fruity white *graševina* wine.

Restaurant Muller (☎ 204 270; Trg Križanića 9; mains from 50KN) The culinary concept is 'international' with good old standards like roast turkey plus a smattering of local specialities.

There's a daily **vegetable market** (Trg LJ Gaja) open until mid-afternoon.

Drinking & Entertainment
BARS & DISCOS

Nightlife in Osijek is pretty dynamic. In summer, everyone heads to the outdoor cafés, usually near the river around Hotel Osijek. Radičeva has a cluster of cafés and bars catering to the local student population. In winter, the Art Deco café in the Hotel Central is popular. Most nightlife is in Tvrđa where nobody minds the noise. Opening hours run from about 10pm Thursday through Sunday.

St Patrick's Pub (Kuhačeva 15) Right on Tvrđa main square is where laddies and lassies chug their brews. Thursday night is rock and blues.

Sound (☎ 201 057; Firingera 24) Next door to Slavonska Kuća (p86), this spot is also popular.

Oxygene (☎ 128 224; Županijska 7) After catching an opera next door at the Croatian National Theatre, this is the place to come for techno.

THEATRE

Croatian National Theatre (Hrvatsko Narodno Kazalište; ☎ 220 700; Županijska 9) This theatre was designed in 1866 and is a fine example of historicist style. In a strange paradox, local pride prompted a painstaking restoration of the building after it had been damaged by shells in the war, only to then see a McDonald's open up on the ground floor. The theatre features a regular programme of drama and opera performances from September to May.

Getting There & Away

Osijek is a major transport centre, with buses and trains arriving and departing in all directions.

BUS

Following are some of the international buses that depart from Osijek. Many more buses leave for Germany than can be listed here. To get to Sarajevo, take the bus to Tuzla and get a connecting bus (€7, 3½ hours); from Vukovar you can catch another bus to Belgrade.

Destination	Cost	Duration	Frequency
Mohaćs	67KN	1½hr	daily
Pećs	83KN	2½hr	3 daily
Tuzla	86KN	3½hr	2 weekly
Vienna	260KN	10hr	2 weekly
Zürich	670KN	19½hr	weekly

The following domestic buses depart from Osijek.

Destination	Cost	Duration	Frequency
Bizovačke Toplice	19KN	25min	19 daily
Đakovo	27KN	40min	17 daily
Dubrovnik	282KN	13hr	1 daily
Požega	54KN	2hr	5 daily
Rijeka	135KN	8¾hr	1 daily
Slavonski Brod	49KN	1¾hr	20 daily
Split	250KN	11hr	1 daily
Vukovar	26KN	40min	14 daily
Zagreb	88KN	4hr	8 daily

TRAIN

There are two trains per day in either direction between Pećs and Osijek (454KN, three hours). The trains from Osijek connect to Budapest (162KN, 7½ hours).

The following domestic trains depart from Osijek.

Destination	Cost	Duration	Frequency
Bizovačke Toplice	11KN	15min	13 daily
Đakovo	19KN	40min	6 daily
Požega	44KN	2½hr	3 daily
Rijeka	162KN	8hr	2 daily
Šibenik	199KN	12hr	1 daily
Slavonski Brod	53KN	1½hr	15 daily
Zagreb	117KN	4hr	5 daily

Getting Around

Osijek has a tram line that dates from 1884 and makes transportation within the city easy. The fare is 6.50KN each way if you buy from the driver, but you get two trips for 11KN if you buy at a *tisak* (kiosk).

For visitors, the most useful tram lines are the No 2, which connects the train and bus station with Trg Ante Starčevića in the town centre and the No 1, which connects the town centre with Tvrđa.

AROUND OSIJEK
Kopački Rit Nature Park

Only 12km northeast of Osijek, **Kopački Rit Nature Park** (Park Prirode Kopački Rit; adult/child 20/10KN) is one of the largest wetlands in Europe, home to 141 bird species nesting throughout its 23,000 hectares. This vast nature park was formed by the confluence of the Drava and Danube Rivers. The fast-flowing Drava forces the Danube to back up and flood the flatlands, which change shape each year according to the force of the flood. The two main lakes, Sakadaško and Kopačevo, are surrounded by a remarkable variety of vegetation: marshes and grassland as well as willow, poplar and oak forests. Depending on the time of year, you can find water lilies, irises and various sorts of duckweeds, reeds and senegrass.

Beneath the waters lie 44 species of fish, including carp, pike, catfish and perch. Mammals include red deer, boars, hares and red foxes. And then there are the birds. Look for herons, terns, cormorants, sea eagles, black storks, falcons, egrets, ducks and wild geese. The best time to come is during the spring and autumn migrations, when hundreds of thousands of birds rest in the park before continuing their flight. There's not much to see in winter. If you come in the summer, bring a tonne of mosquito repellent.

At the northern end of the park is a villa, Dvorac Tikveš, which was once used by Tito as a hunting lodge. At the time of writing, the structure was undergoing renovation and may eventually serve as a hotel-ecocentre.

The park was closed for many years following the war because it was heavily mined. Most mines have been cleared and safe trails have been clearly marked but it would be unwise to wander off on your own. Although the park is open to visitors, it is still in the process of developing its tourist facilities. You can drive or walk through the park but you see a lot more if you go by boat. Currently a 15-person boat makes a two-hour tour of the lake for 75KN per person. The boat embarkation point is on Kopačevo Lake.

The **park administrative office** (☎ 750 855; pp-kopacki-rit@os.htnet.hr; Petefi Šandora 33, Bilje) is about 9km north of Osijek. Here you can get information on the park and the boat excursions.

Although there is currently no accommodation in or around the park, there is a good, typical local restaurant in Kopačevo, **Zelena Žaba** (☎ 752 212; Ribarska 3; mains 30-80KN). Its name means 'green frog' after the thousands of squatters bellowing in the backyard swamp. In addition to *riblji paprikaš* stewed in big pots, the restaurant specialises in *fiš perkelt*, a fish stew with home-made noodles, soft cheese and bacon.

There is no public transport to the park but you can take a local Osijek bus to Bilje and walk the 3km to the park.

Bizovačke Toplice

The **Bizovačke Toplice spa** (☎ 685 100; www.bizovacke-toplice.hr; Sunčana 39) is about 20km west of Osijek, in the town of Bizovac. Opened in 1974, this vast complex offers 10 pools of which six are fed by thermal springs. There are pools with caves, slides and water jets, an Olympic-sized pool, a children's pool and several interconnected indoor and outdoor pools. It's an impressive water park and makes a relaxing break from Osijek or a good alternative place to stay. If you don't stay in the hotel, it costs 20/10KN per adult/child to use the pools.

The rooms at **Hotel Termia** (☎ 685 100; www.bizovacke-toplice.hr; Sunčana 39; s/d 279/454KN) could use freshening up, but all is clean and correct. You'll be in the pools all day, anyway. A nearby annexe, Hotel Toplice, offers singles/doubles with no bathroom for 114/119KN.

The spa is well connected to Osijek by train (11KN, 15 minutes, 13 daily) and the train station is about 1km from the spa. There are also buses from Osijek, which run every half-hour (19KN, 25 minutes, 19 daily).

ĐAKOVO
pop 20,300

Đakovo is an easy day trip from Osijek and a peaceful provincial town. There's not a lot to do but it's known for its impressive cathedral, the Lipizzaner horses, a wonderful folk festival and fine Slavonian cuisine. The town emerged relatively unscathed from war and attracts few tourists.

Orientation & Information

The train station lies right outside the town centre across from a market which operates Wednesday and Saturday mornings. The **Tourist Office** (☎ /fax 812 319; tz-grada-djakova@os.htnet.hr; Kralja Tomislava 3) contains limited information.

Sights & Activities

The town's pride and glory is the **cathedral** (katedrala; ☎ 811 784; Trg Strossmayera; ☉ 8am-noon & 3-6pm). Commissioned by Bishop Strossmayer in 1862, this magnificent brick structure dominates the town centre with its two 84m-high belfries. It's built in a neo-Romanesque style and the three-nave interior is colourfully painted with biblical scenes. The large crypt holds Strossmayer's tomb.

Just north of the cathedral is the **Strossmayer Museum** (Spomen-muzej Biskupa Josipa Jurja Strossmayera; ☎ 813 254; L Botića 2; admission 7KN; ⏱ 9.30am-2.30pm & 4-7pm Mon-Fri, 9am-1pm Sat). Strossmayer fans will find the small displays about his life interesting; others may not.

Đakovo is also famous for its Lipizzaner horses, which are bred in a farm outside town. This noble horse traces its lineage back to the 16th century and is the world's most popular riding horse. The **Lipizzaner training stables** (Lipicanac; ☎ 813 286; Auga Šenoe 45) are in town, only a short walk from the cathedral. About 50 horses are stabled there and undergo daily training for their eventual work as high-class carriage horses. It's usually not a problem to stop by and watch their morning workouts.

Festivals & Events

Đakovo's main event is the yearly **Đakovački Vezovi** (Đakovo Embroidery) festival which takes place at the beginning of July. In addition to a display by the Lipizzaner horses, there's a folklore show that includes folk costumes, folklore dancing and traditional songs from the entire region.

Sleeping & Eating

There's no camping or private accommodation but the one family-run *pension* in town is excellent.

Croatia-Turist Restaurant-Pension (☎ 813 391; fax 814 063; Preradovića 25; d with half board 300KN; mains 28-68KN) The restaurant is famous throughout the region for its Slavonian cuisine, especially the spicy *kulen* sausages. The atmospheric interior manages to be at once vast and cosy. There are 13 rooms over the restaurant, all with TV, modern bathrooms and (a welcome touch) fans. The décor and the service are warm and inviting. If you intend to stay during the Đakovački Vezovi, reserve long in advance.

Getting There & Away

Đakovo is connected to Osijek by bus and train.

VUKOVAR

☎ 032 / pop 32,000

Until 1991, Vukovar was a bustling town of elegant baroque mansions, art galleries and museums. It was one of the prettiest towns on the Danube, with historical roots that stretched back to the 10th century. Now most of it lies in ruins. The museums, galleries and library have been plundered and the town centre reduced to jagged, pockmarked buildings filled with heaps of rubble. The once-prosperous economy that centred around the Borovo tyre-producing plant has virtually disappeared, leaving its workers to eke out a living smuggling cigarettes and tampons from the Serbian side of the river.

Before the war Vukovar had a multiethnic population of about 44,000, of which Croats constituted 44% and Serbs 37%. As Croatia edged away from former Yugoslavia in early 1991, tensions mounted between the two groups. The town had never been a hotbed of nationalism but many of its outlying suburbs were populated by Serbs sympathetic to the cause of the Krajina rebels. Barricades sprouted around Borovo Selo, a Serbian suburb 2km north of the town centre. Croat extremists saw an opportunity to jump-start the independence drive and, in April of that year, future Croatian defence minister Gojko Šušak and others fired a rocket into Borovo. Its desired effect was to promote ethnic conflict and it worked well. Within weeks, two Croatian policemen were attacked and captured in the town and a rescue party of other Croatian policemen was massacred. Public opinion was inflamed and the Yugoslav army moved in to 'separate the warring factions'. When war broke out later that summer the army was in an advantageous position to set about securing Slobodon Milošević's territorial ambitions. Vukovar suffered a brutal siege before finally capitulating on 18 November.

Since the return of Vukovar to Croatia, there has been some progress in repairing the destruction. Certain public buildings – the museum, a church, a school – were the first to be repaired and there are some buildings in the town centre that have been lovingly restored, but by and large the town centre remains in ruins. Of the pre-war population of 45,000, only about 32,000 are still living in the town. The pre-war economy has completely disappeared and the local Serbs and Croats live in parallel and hostile universes. Visiting the town can be a painful but sobering experience. No war museum filled with mementoes, photos, arms and uniforms could more eloquently capture the horror and futility of war than the ruined buildings of downtown Vukovar.

Orientation & Information

The bus station is at the northern end of town. Opposite is the market from which the town's main street, Strossmayera, leads south into the town centre. When you cross over the Vuka River, this street becomes Ulica Dr. Franje Tuđman. (That a majority Serb town should have a street named after former president Tudjman says a lot about twisted local politics.) Some buildings on this street have been restored, giving a taste of what the entire town must have been like.

ATM (Strossmayera 11)

Left-luggage Office (☾ 5am-9pm) At the bus station.

Post Office (Strossmayera 4)

Tourist Office (☎ /fax 442 889; JJ Strossmayera 15) Has limited documentation but much information.

Sights

The 18th-century **Franciscan monastery** (Franjevački Samostan; ☎ 441 381) is strikingly placed on top of the hill.

The **Town Museum** (Gradski Muzej; ☎ 441 270) is lodged in the former Eltz Palace at the top of Strossmayera, to the left of the bus station. The museum functions as a sort of arts centre, with prestigious art exhibits and occasional concerts.

Sleeping & Eating

Hotel Dunav (☎ 441 285; fax 441 762; Trg Republike 1; s/d 220/320KN) This is the only hotel in town and it has been renovated. Rooms are simple but functional and some have views of the river. The hotel also has a restaurant but even better is **Pleter** (Žrtava Fašizma 9; mains from 40KN), next to the courthouse. With paintings, crystal and lovingly prepared regional dishes, it's a testament to hope as well as fine dining.

Getting There & Away

Vukovar has good bus connections to Osijek and Slavonski Brod (55KN, three hours, four daily). There's also a daily bus that runs from Vukovar to Belgrade (60KN, 2½ hours).

Kvarner Region

CONTENTS

The holiday experiences on offer in the Kvarner (Quarnero in Italian) region are incredibly diverse. Rijeka makes a good base from which to connect to the 19th-century elegance of Opatija or Baška's sandy beach on Krk Island.

You can explore the colourful old towns of Krk, Rab, Mali Lošinj and Cres, or take a boat to the remote coves of these large islands. The clear sea is ideal for swimming or scuba diving and inland there are plenty of trails for hiking or biking.

The mild weather explains the region's rich variety of vegetation: Cres, Lošinj and Krk number some 1300 plant species; Rab is known for its evergreen forests; and the luxuriant greenery around Opatija helped establish its reputation as a health resort.

Although the islands are well connected to Rijeka, transportation between them can be inconvenient. Unless you have your own car, you may have to backtrack to Rijeka to get from one island to another. Krk is the largest island, but it's overrun with tourists in July and August. Mali Lošinj also gets loads of visitors, however, you're within easy reach of unspoiled Cres. Rab has the most picturesque old town and enough coves and bays for you to easily escape the shoulder-to-shoulder crowds at summertime.

The Kvarner coast and its offshore islands are a microcosm of the many influences that have formed Croatian culture. Rijeka, Croatia's third-largest city, owes its architecture to Hungary, which ruled the city in the late 19th century. The opening of a rail link to Vienna in 1857 made Opatija the resort of choice for the Austrian aristocracy. Venetian influence pervades the islands of Cres, Lošinj and Rab, while Krk was the seat of Croatia's native nobility, the Frankopan dukes.

KVARNER REGION

HIGHLIGHTS

- Taking dips in the sea from the **Lungomare promenade** (p101) in Opatija
- Enjoying the view from Rijeka's **Trsat Castle** (p98) on a clear day
- Walking the Leska Path in **Risnjak National Park** (p103)
- Wine tasting in **Vrbnik** (p117)
- Watching the crossbow competition on **Sveti Kristofor day** (p123) in Rab

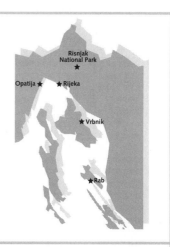

- TELEPHONE CODE: 051
- POSTCODE: 51000

Climate

The region's mild climate has played an important part in the growth of tourism. The Gulf of Kvarner is protected from harsh weather by the mountain range running from Mt Učka in the northwest to Gorski Kotor in the east and the Velebit Range in the southeast. Summers are long and cooled by the *maestral* (strong, steady westerly wind) and although the *bura* (cold northeasterly wind) brings sudden rushes of cold air in winter, temperatures rarely drop below freezing.

RIJEKA

pop 147,700

Although Rijeka (Fiume in Italian) is hardly a 'must-see' destination, it does have some real assets, such as Korzo (the pedestrian mall), a tree-lined promenade along the harbour, and the imposing hilltop fortress of Trsat. Despite some unfortunate postwar architectural ventures in the outskirts, much of the cityscape contains the sort of ornate, imposing public buildings you would expect to find in Vienna or Budapest, evidence of the strong Austro-Hungarian influence exerted on the city's cultural and economic life in the 19th century. It's such an important transport hub that it's almost impossible to avoid. The network of buses, trains and ferries connecting Istria and Dalmatia with Zagreb and points beyond, all seem to pass through the city. As Croatia's largest port, Rijeka is full of boats, cargo, fumes, cranes and the kind of seedy energy that characterises most port cities. However, because there's no beach, resources for visitors are scarce. The assumption seems to be that everyone will either leave the area as fast as possible or base themselves in Opatija.

History

Following their successful conquest of the indigenous Illyrian Liburnian tribe, the Romans built a settlement here called Tarsaticae. Excavations have revealed the foundations of ancient walls under Korzo, a gate and a necropolis.

The Slavic tribes that migrated to the region in the 7th century built a new settlement within the old Roman walls, attracted by the port and the abundance of drinking water from the nearby Rječina River.

TOP FIVE BEACHES

- **Baška** (p117) – a rare sweep of sandy beach with a glorious mountain backdrop
- **Valun** (p112) – this cosy cove has calm, crystal water
- **Lopar** (p125) – sandy beaches bordered by pine groves
- **Čikat Bay** (p106) – plenty of rocky and pebbly coves with pine tree shade
- **Lungomare** (p101) – the rock formations create dozens of private beaches along the promenade

---

Although initially under the jurisdiction of the bishop in Pula, Rijeka developed more autonomy in the 13th century under the feudal authority of German nobility. After briefly passing into the hands of the Frankopan dukes of Krk, the town changed feudal masters a few times before becoming part of the Austrian empire at the end of the 15th century.

Rijeka was an important outlet to the sea for the Austrians and a new road was built in 1725 connecting Vienna with the Kvarner coast at Kraljevica, south of the city. The new road spurred economic development, especially shipbuilding. The first modern shipyard in the region opened in Kraljevica in 1729 and the industry has remained the centrepiece of Rijeka's economy ever since. In the 19th century, Rijeka modernised its harbour and successfully managed the transition to the building of steamships.

With the birth of the Austro-Hungarian dual monarchy in 1867, Rijeka was given over to the jurisdiction of the Hungarian government, with the support of a pro-Hungarian faction in Rijeka.

The urban landscape acquired a new look as Hungarian architects descended upon the city to erect municipal buildings. A new railway was built linking the city to Zagreb, Budapest and Vienna, further assisting shipbuilding and bringing the first tourists to the Gulf of Kvarner.

In 1918, Italian troops seized Rijeka and Istria, and in the 1920 Treaty of Rapallo between Yugoslavia and Italy, Rijeka became an independent state under the trusteeship

KVARNER REGION

KVARNER REGION

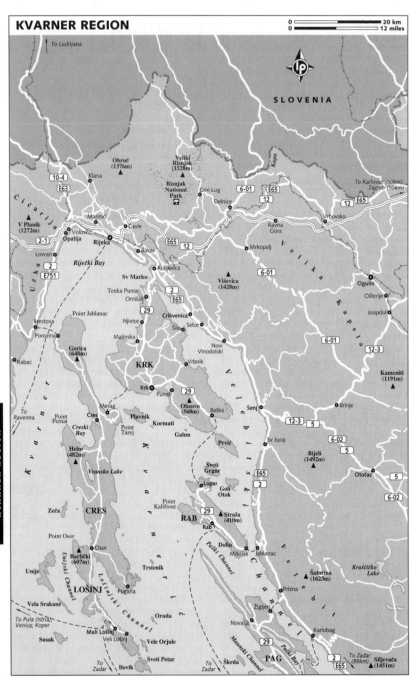

0   20 km
0   12 miles

To Ljubljana

SLOVENIA

Obruč (1376m)
Veliki Risnjak (1528m)
Klana
10-4
E63
Risnjak National Park
Crni Lug
6-01
E65
Delnice
12
To Karlovac (50km); Zagreb (95km)
12
E65
Vrbovsko

Mannici
V Planik (1272m)
Ravna Gora
Čičarija
Vološko
Opatija
Rijeka
Čavle
2-1
Bakar
E65
12
Mrkopalj
Velika Kapela
Ogulin
Ošterije
Josipdol

Lovran
2
Riječki Bay
Kraljevica
E751
Sv Marko
Višević (1428m)
6-01

Učka
Tenka Punta
Omišalj
2
E65
29
6-01
12-3
Brestova
Point Jablanac
Njivice
Crikvenica
Selce
Porozina
Malinska
Šilo
Novi Vinodolski
Kameniti (1191m)
Rabac

Gorica (648m)
KRK
Vrbnik
Velebit
Kvarner
Krk
Punat
29
Senj
12-3
5
Brinje

To Ravenna
Merag
Cres
Obzovo (568m)
Baška
6-02
5
Point Pernat
Plavnik
Point Tarej
Kormati
Galun
Prvić
Sv Juraj
Bijeli (1492m)

Creski Bay
Kvarnerić
Helm (482m)
Vransko Lake
Sveti Grgur
E65
2
Otočac
5

Zeča
CRES
Lopar
Goli Otok
6-02

Point Kalifront
RAB
29
Straža (410m)
Šatorina (1623m)
Point Osor
Rab
Kruščićko Lake
Unije
Barlički (607m)
Osor
Trstenik
Dolin
Mišnjak
Jablanac
Velebit
Channel

Lošinjski Channel
Pašku Channel
Prizna
Vela Srakane
LOŠINJ
Pogana
Žigljen

To Pula (Istria); Venica; Koper
Oruda
Novalja
Karlobag

Susak
Mali Lošinj
Veli Lošinj
Vele Orjule
Maunski Channel
29
PAG
Pašku Bay
2
To Zadar (89km)
E65
Siljevača (1451m)
To Zadar
Ilovik
Sveti Petar
Škrda
To Zadar

of the League of Nations. Independence didn't last long. As part of the 1924 Treaty of Rome, Rijeka west of the Rječina River became part of Italy, while the Susak region east of the river became part of the Kingdom of Serbs, Croats and Slovenes. The Italian part of Rijeka was freed from Fascist control in 1942 by the Partisans and became part of postwar Yugoslavia. Rijeka retains a sizable, well-organised Italian minority who have their own newspaper, *La Voce del Popolo*.

Orientation

Korzo runs in an easterly direction through the city centre towards the fast-moving Rječina River.

The bus station is south of the Capuchin Church in the centre of town. The train station is a five-minute walk west of the bus station.

The Jadrolinija ferry wharf (Adamićev Wharf) is a few minutes east of the bus station. There's no left-luggage section.

Information

There's an ATM at the train station and the exchange offices adjacent to the train and bus stations keep long hours. There are a number of ATMs along Korzo and an exchange counter in the main post office.

Blitz (Krešimirova 3a; small load 60KN; ☺ 7am-8pm Mon-Fri, 7am-1pm Sat) This laundry is between the bus and train stations.

Garderoba Bus station (per day 10KN; ☺ 5.30am-10.30pm); Train station (per day 10KN; ☺ 24hr)

Hotel Continental (☎ 372 008; www.jadran-hoteli.hr; Andrije Kašića Miočica; per hr 10-15KN) Has a full bank of modern computers to check your email.

Main Post Office (Korzo) Opposite the old city tower; has a telephone centre.

Tourist Information Centre (☎ 335 882; www .tz-rijeka.hr; Korzo 33) Distributes *Rijeka Tourist Route*, a walking-tour guide that is so well produced it makes you actually want to stay and look around.

Sights
MONUMENTS

Rijeka was struck by a devastating earthquake in 1750 and the city was almost entirely rebuilt. The pedestrian street **Korzo** was built as a wide commercial avenue on the site of the demolished town walls. The **City Tower** was originally one of the main gates to the city and one of the few monuments

---

MORČIĆI

The *morčići* (or, historically, *moretto*) is a traditional symbol of Rijeka. The image of a black person topped with a colourful turban is made into ceramic brooches and earrings, and is a popular disguise at the Rijeka Carnival (p98). In 1991 it was proclaimed the official mascot of Rijeka.

Two legends explain its emergence as Rijeka's most recognisable symbol. One story places its origin in the 16th-century Turkish invasions. According to this version, the men were waging a losing battle against the Turks, while the women and children were praying for a rain of stones to bury their enemy. Finally one of their arrows struck the Turkish Pasha in the temple, killing him. The Turks scattered and – lo and behold! – the skies opened and a hail of stones buried the Turks. The men were so grateful for their wives' assistance that they presented them with not a pot or a broom, but colourful *moretto* earrings.

Another version has it that an Italian baroness was so fond of her black slave that she granted the woman her freedom and had earrings made in her image.

More mundanely, it appears that the *morčići* was a spin-off from the Venetian *moretto* design that was part of a 17th- and 18th-century fad for the Orient. The gem-encrusted Venetian moor was simplified by Rijekan jewellers and sold to poorer women as simple black-and-white ceramic earrings. Men picked up on the fashion. A single earring was worn by only sons, sailors and fishermen for good luck. There was a male *morčići* with a turban and a female one with a straw hat, although today's *morčići* is fairly androgynous.

In the second half of the 19th century, Rijekan jewellers improved the quality of the artisanship and branched out into rings, brooches and necklaces. Upper-class women snatched up the pieces and, with a display at the Vienna International Exhibition of 1873, *morčići* became popular throughout Europe. After WWII, many of the jewellers emigrated and the *morčići* dropped out of sight, but in the recent back-to-basics trend in Croatian culture, this endearing figure has regained the prominence it deserves.

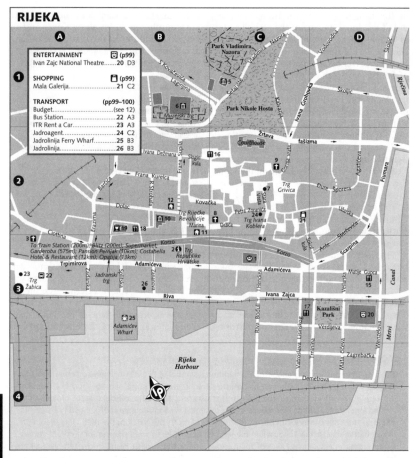

RIJEKA

ENTERTAINMENT	🎭 (p99)
Ivan Zajc National Theatre	20 D3

SHOPPING	🛍 (p99)
Mala Galerija	21 C2

TRANSPORT	(pp99–100)
Budget	(see 12)
Bus Station	22 A3
ITR Rent a Car	23 A3
Jadroagent	24 C2
Jadrolinija Ferry Wharf	25 B3
Jadrolinija	26 B3

to have survived the earthquake. The portal with reliefs of emperors was added soon after the disaster and in 1873 a clock was mounted on the tower, which is still functioning. The tower was reconstructed again in 1890 and a new dome added.

Passing under the City Tower and continuing through Trg Ivana Koblera, you'll find the oldest architectural monument in Rijeka, the **Roman Gate** (Stara Vrata). The lack of decoration indicates that it was probably the entrance to a Roman fortification.

CHURCHES

Rijeka's churches are open Sunday morning and Monday to Friday from early-morning Mass until noon. It would be hard to miss the **Capuchin Church of Our Lady of Lourdes** (Gospe Lurdske; ☎ 335 233; Trg Žabica) with its ornate neo-gothic façade looming over the bus station. The Capuchin sponsors of the project ran into financing problems midway through the construction and enlisted the aid of a 'St Johanca', who allegedly sweated blood in front of the credulous masses. Gifts and money poured into the coffers and the building was finally completed in 1929. ('St Johanca' was arrested for fraud in 1913.) The ceiling was decorated with frescoes of angels by a prominent local artist, Romulo Venucci.

Another prominent church is **St Vito** (Sv Vida; ☎ 330 879; Trg Grivica 11). St Vito is the patron saint of Rijeka and construction of

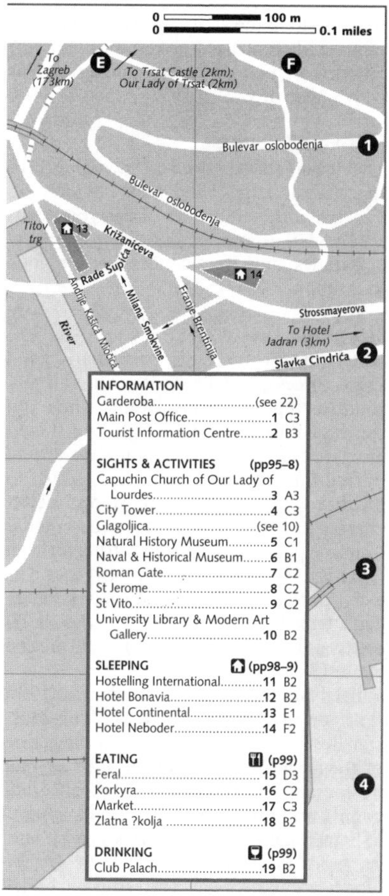

this building was begun in 1638 on the site of an older church dedicated to the saint. The Jesuit order supervised the project, which lasted several hundred years. Massive pillars support the central dome and surround chapels with multicoloured baroque marble altars. The main altar has a 13th-century Gothic crucifix that belonged to the older church. According to the legend, someone threw a stone at the crucifix in 1296 and blood began to flow from Christ's body – the blood is still held in an ampoule.

Also of note is **St Jerome** (Sv Jeronima; ☎ 332 181; Trg Riječke Rezolucije). The church was part of a 14th-century Augustinian monastery complex that once dominated this square and was financed by the Counts of Duino, the feudal lords of Rijeka at the time. Construction lasted from 1315 to 1408 and the church sanctuary houses the tombs of the financing families. Little of the original Gothic structure remains due to the 1750 earthquake. The church was rebuilt in a baroque style in 1768 and contains tombs of captains, noblemen and patricians from Rijeka.

The most renowned church in Rijeka is **Our Lady of Trsat** (Gospe Trsatske; ☎ 217 018; Trsat Hill), a centuries-old magnet for believers. According to legend the angels carrying the house in which the Annunciation took place rested in Trsat before depositing the building in Italy. A chapel erected on the site attracted some pilgrims, but numbers were increased in the 14th century when the local nobility petitioned the pope for the donation of a 'miraculous' icon of Mary thought to have been painted by St Luke. A bigger church was soon needed, and in 1453 the Frankopan prince Martin built a single-nave church to house the painting and a Franciscan monastery next door. The monastery was rebuilt in 1691 after a fire and a new nave was added to the church in 1644.

The famous painting is on the main altar and the church also contains tombs of the Frankopans and other notables. There is a magnificent wrought-iron gate separating the sanctuary from the nave, and the treasury of the Franciscan monastery contains a valuable art collection, open by appointment only.

MUSEUMS

The **Naval & Historical Museum** (Pomorski i Povijesni Muzej Hrvatskog Primorja; ☎ 335 772; Muzejski trg 1; adult/student 10/1KN; 9am-1pm Tue-Sat) was founded in 1876 at the height of Rijeka's shipbuilding years. Part of the museum traces the development of sailing, with models and paintings of ships and portraits of captains. There are also various archaeological finds, weapons and documents, as well as furniture from the 17th to 20th centuries.

The museum is housed in the imposing Governor's palace and some of the rooms are decorated in period style. The Governor's palace was the residence of the Hungarian governor after a Hungarian provisional government was established here in 1869. The building was intended to show off the best of Hungarian architecture and to impress the populace with the power of Hungarian rule. The Budapest architect, Alayos Hauszmann, took full advantage of his prestigious assignment to create a glittering showpiece of white stone.

The **Natural History Museum** (Prirodoslovni Muzej; ☎ 334 988; Lorenzov prolaz 1; admission free; ✆ 9am-7pm Mon-Fri, 9am-2pm Sat), just above Muzejski trg, is devoted to the geology and botany of the region. There are also exhibits on the sea life and vertebrates of the region.

If you have time to kill in Rijeka, stop by the **University Library** (Dolac 1), which houses two exhibition spaces. Most interesting is the **Modern Art Gallery** (Moderna Galerija; ☎ 334 280), which hosts occasional art exhibits. Prices and opening hours vary according to the exhibit. There's also the permanent **Glagoljica** (☎ 336 129; admission 10KN; ✆ 8am-3pm Mon-Fri), a display of manuscripts written in Glagolitic script.

TRSAT CASTLE

High on a hill overlooking Rijeka and the Rječina River, this 13th-century **fort** (☎ 217 714; admission 15KN; ✆ 9am-11pm Tue-Sun Apr-Nov, 9am-3pm Tue-Sun Dec-Mar) occupies a position of immense strategic importance. There may have been a Liburnian hill fort here, but it was the Frankopan dukes of Krk who built the present castle to protect their holdings in Vinodol, further east. The **Konak**, an enclosed yard with a cistern, is the best-preserved part of the original structure. From the 13th to the 15th century, Trsat belonged to the Frankopans or their relatives, but it was seized by the Habsburgs at the end of the 15th century.

As threats from Venice and the Ottoman Empire receded in the 17th century, the castle fell into decay and its decline was accelerated by the earthquake of 1750. In 1826, the fortress was purchased by the Austrian vice-marshal Laval Nugent, who had it restored in a neogothic style and built a mausoleum adorned with the coat of arms of the Nugent family.

The fortress houses concerts and plays during the summer, and **art galleries** (✆ 9am-1pm & 6-9pm).

Bus No 1 takes you to Trsat Castle or you can climb the **Petar Kružić stairway** from Križanićeva ulica. Captain Petar Kružić built the lower part of the stairway in 1531 and it was expanded later to 538 steps. The chapels along the staircase are dedicated to saints and were used as rest stops for the pilgrims on their way to pay homage to Our Lady of Trsat.

Festivals & Events

The **Rijeka Carnival** (www.ri-karnival.com) in February is the largest and most elaborate in Croatia, with seven days of partying. Balls are by invitation only, but there are plenty of parades and street dances that are open to everyone.

Sleeping

Hotels in Rijeka are not particularly good value. Prices generally stay the same all year round except at Carnival time, when you can expect to pay a surcharge. You should also book far in advance if you want a room during this time. It's just as easy to get to Opatija where there are more and better choices for hotels and private accommodation (see p103 for details on getting to/from Opatija). The closest camping ground is listed in the Opatija section (p102). **Hostelling International** (☎ 264 176; Korzo 22) sells HI cards and is a good source of information about Croatian hostels.

Hotel Bonavia (☎ 333 744; www.bonavia.hr; Dolac 4; s/d from 830/980KN; Ⓟ ☒ ☒ ☒) The four-star Bonavia is the only hotel in the centre of town and it has all of the niceties that businesspeople on generous expense accounts find indispensable.

Hotel Continental (☎ 372 008; www.jadran-hoteli .hr; Andrije Kašića Miočića; s/d 376/425KN; Ⓟ ☒) Northeast of the town centre, this old building has spacious rooms that could use an overhaul. At least you're close to Internet access.

Hotel Neboder (☎ 373 538; fax 373 515; Strossmayerova 1; s/d without shower 140/170KN, with shower 260/330KN) If a tight budget is what you've got, this one-star hotel is your kind of place. A certain dreariness seeps from the neighbourhood into the hotel; rooms are tattered but clean.

Hotel Jadran (☎ 216 230; www.jadran-hoteli .hr; Šetalište XIII divizije 46; s/d 290/395KN; Ⓟ) The Jadran is 3km east of the city centre on the coastal road. Although the rooms are unexceptional, there is a restaurant and private beach.

There are two small hotels west of the city centre on the road to Opatija.

Pansion Pernjak (☎ 622 069; Pionirska 64; r per person 104KN; **P**) This small, family-run *pension* offers appealing rooms with simple bathrooms in a friendly environment. It is about 10km west of Rijeka in the suburb of Kantrida.

Costabella Hotel & Restaurant (☎ 623 010; vior@vior.hr; Opatijska cesta 17; s/d 295/460; **P**) A little more elaborate than Pansion Pernjak, this small hotel is a few kilometres further on the road to Opatija. Airy rooms with polished wooden floors are well appointed and the hotel is just a short walk from the beach.

PRIVATE ROOMS

There are no agencies in town that find private rooms. If you are determined to stay in Rijeka, you could check out the tourist office website or try the agencies in Opatija.

Eating

If you must eat on Sunday, you'll be relegated to either fast food or a hotel restaurant as nearly every other place in Rijeka is closed. There are a number of cafés on Korzo that serve light meals. For self-caterers, there's a large **supermarket** (ulica Krešimirova) between the bus and train station, and a **market** (Vatroslava Lisinkog).

Korkyra (☎ 339 528; Slogin kula 5; mains from 40KN) This cosy restaurant has an appealingly casual ambience and serves up risotto, grilled calamari and an assortment of specialities such as *brodetto* (fish stew), *bakalar* (codfish stew) and various pastas. Prices are cheaper if you come before 1pm. The restaurant is closed on Sunday.

Feral (☎ 212 274; Matije Gupca 6; mains from 65KN) This fine restaurant has a subdued marine-theme décor that complements the many fish specialities on offer. Try the cold *baccala* (cod with potatoes) with parsley, olive oil and wine. Occasionally, there are piano players on weekends and the ambience is romantic.

Zlatna Školja (☎ 213 782; Kružna 12; mains around 100KN) The fetching maritime décor puts you in the mood to savour the astonishingly creative seafood dishes. The wine list is also notable.

Drinking

Croatia's recent zero-tolerance approach to drunk driving has been good for Rijeka's nightlife. Everyone used to go to Opatija to drink, but now no-one wants to take the chance of getting stopped on the route back. Bar-hoppers cruise along Riva or Korzo for the liveliest bars and cafés.

In the back alley, accessible through a small passageway off Jadranski trg, **Club Palach** (☎ 215 063; Kružna 6) caters to students who find it a good, low-key place to drink and dance.

Entertainment

Ivan Zajc National Theatre (☎ 211 268; Ivana Zajca bb) Performances at this theatre, built in 1885, are mostly dramas in Croatian, though opera and ballet are sometimes offered.

Shopping

Look for the traditional Rijeka design known as *morčići*, a ceramic jewellery piece of a Moor wearing a turban (see Morčići, p95). This jewellery, made from specially prepared enamel, has traditionally been manufactured on Užarska.

You can buy pieces of *morčići* jewellery at **Mala Galerija** (☎ 335 483; Užarska 25).

Getting There & Away

BOAT

Jadroagent (☎ 211 276; Trg Ivana Koblera 2) has information on all boats to Croatia.

Jadrolinija (☎ 211 444; www.jadrolinija.hr; Riva 16) sells tickets for the large coastal ferries that run all year between Rijeka and Dubrovnik. Southbound ferries depart from Rijeka's **ferry wharf** (Adamićev Wharf) at 6pm twice weekly in winter, four times weekly in June and late September, and at 8pm daily from July to early September.

Fares for a reclining seat are 200KN to Split (13 hours), 254KN to Korčula (18 hours) and 277KN to Dubrovnik (17 to 24 hours). Fares are lower in winter and higher on summer weekends. Prices are higher for couchettes, inside and outside berths and cabins with private bathrooms.

Since the Jadrolinija ferries travel between Rijeka and Split at night you don't get to see a lot, so it's probably better to go from Rijeka to Split by bus and enjoy excellent views of the Adriatic coast. In contrast, the ferry trip from Split to Dubrovnik is highly recommended.

BUS

The **bus station** (☎ 060 333 444; Trg Žabica) is in the town centre.

For international connections see p271. Following are some of the more popular domestic routes:

Destination	Cost	Duration	Frequency
Baška (Krk Island)	42KN	2hr	1 daily
Dubrovnik	205-309KN	13hr	2 daily
Krk Town	35KN	1½hr	13 daily
Poreč	55KN	4½hr	5 daily
Pula	48KN	2½hr	17 daily
Rab	87KN	3½hr	2 daily
Rovinj	73KN	3½hr	10 daily
Split	161-231KN	8½hr	11 daily
Trieste	62KN	2-3hr	3 daily
Zadar	115KN	5hr	12 daily
Zagreb	90-98KN	3½hr	24 daily

CAR

ITR Rent a Car (☎ 337 544; Riva 20), near the bus station, has rental cars from around 595KN per day with unlimited kilometres. On a weekly basis it's 3560KN with unlimited kilometres. You can also try **Budget** (☎ 214 742) in the Hotel Bonavia (p98).

TRAIN

From the **train station** (ulica Krešimirova) four trains daily run to Zagreb (102KN, five hours). There's also a daily direct train to Osijek (164KN, eight hours) and a daily train to Split (142KN, 10 hours) that changes at Ogulin where you wait for two hours. Several of the seven daily services to Ljubljana (86KN, three hours) require a change of trains at the Slovenian border and again at Bifka or Bistrica in Slovenia, but there are also two direct trains. Reservations are compulsory on some *poslovni* (express) trains.

OPATIJA

pop 9073 / postcode 51410

Just 13km west of Rijeka, Opatija (Abbazia in Italian) has the most stunning coastal views in Croatia. The forested hills sloping down to the sparkling sea can be appreciated from the Lungomare, a waterfront promenade that stretches for 12km along the Gulf of Kvarner. The vista is enhanced by Mt Učka (1401m), west of Opatija and the highest point on the Istrian Peninsula. Small surprise that Opatija was *the* fashionable seaside resort of the Austro-Hungarian empire until WWI. The grand residences of the wealthy are now hotels that offer a healthy dose of the elegance and sophistication of a bygone age. This is a good place to splurge on a hotel as you have virtually no chance of landing in one of the concrete boxes that litter so many coastal resorts. The façades are painted in fresh pastels and the interiors offer spacious halls and chandeliers.

History

The town sprung up around St Jacob's church, which was built on the foundations of a Benedictine abbey. (The word 'abbey' translates as *opatija* in Croatian.) Until 1844, the town was a humble fishing village with 35 houses and a church, but the arrival of wealthy Iginio Scarpa from Rijeka turned the town around. He built the villa Angiolina (named after his wife) on the shore and surrounded it with species of exotic plants from Japan, China, South America and Australia. The villa hosted some of the European aristocracy's finest, including the Austrian queen Maria Anna, wife of Ferdinand. The town's reputation as a retreat for the elite was born.

Opatija's development was also assisted by the construction of a rail link on the Vienna–Trieste line from Pivka in Slovenia to Rijeka in 1873. Construction of Opatija's first hotel, the Quarnero (today the Hotel Kvarner), began and wealthy visitors arrived en masse. Between 1884 and 1895 they tried to outdo each other in building elaborate mansions, hiring the finest architects they could find – or afford. Doctors were quick to proclaim the climate healthy, thus providing a perfect excuse for a long vacation for those who could afford it.

It seemed everyone who was anyone was compelled to visit Opatija, including kings from Romania and Sweden, Russian tsars and the celebrities of the day such as Isadora Duncan, Gustav Mahler, Puccini, Mascagni, Chekov, Franz Lehar and Beniamino Gigli, who came to rehabilitate his vocal cords.

The outbreak of WWI put an end to the Austro-Hungarian empire and an aristocracy that could frolic by the sea, but Opatija has never really lost its popularity.

Although Opatija has never acquired the glitter of the French Riviera, it has become a favoured vacation spot for sleek, bronzed

Italians in the summer, while the mild winters attract a sizable number of elderly Austrians who come to nibble on cakes in the Hotel Kvarner and take a healthy promenade by the sea. The stunning coastal scenery, clear waters and many parks have kept a steady flow of tourists, even during the dark days of war.

Orientation

Opatija sits on a narrow strip of land sandwiched between the sea and the foothills of Mt Učka. Obala Maršala Tita is the main road that runs through the town and is also where you'll find travel agencies, restaurants, shops and hotels. The bus from Rijeka stops first at the Hotel Belvedere, then near the market and finally at the bus station at the foot of the town on Trg Vladimira Gortana. If you're looking for private accommodation, it's better to get off at the second stop and walk downhill to the travel agencies, rather than walking uphill from the bus station.

Information

INTERNET ACCESS
Grand Hotel Adriatic (☎ 719 000; M Tita 200; per 20 min 10KN; ☼ 24hr)

LEFT LUGGAGE
Autotrans Agency (Trg Vladimira Gortana) There's no left-luggage facility, but this agency at the bus station will usually watch luggage.

MONEY
Maršala Tita has numerous ATMs and travel agencies eager to change money.

POST
Main Post Office (Eugena Kumičića 2; ☼ 8am-7pm Mon-Sat) Behind the market.

TOURIST INFORMATION
Tourist Office (☎ 271 310; www.opatija-tourism.hr; Maršala Tita 101; ☼ 8am-7pm Mon-Sat & 2-6pm Sun Jun-Sep, 9am-noon & 2-4.30pm Mon-Sat Oct-May) Has some information on local events.

TRAVEL AGENCIES
Atlas Travel Agency (☎ 271 032; Maršala Tita 116) Books accommodation and excursions.
Da Riva (☎ 272 482; www.da-riva.hr; Maršala Tita 162) Finds private accommodation and organises group transfers to regional airports.

GIT Travel Agency (☎ /fax 271 967; gi-trade@ri.htnet.hr; Maršala Tita 65) Finds private accommododation, books excursions and changes money.

Sights & Activities

The exquisite **Villa Angiolina** (Park Angiolina; ☼ 10am-9pm Jun-Sep) has been restored to its former neoclassical splendour. The interior is a marvel of trompe l'oeil frescoes, Corinthian capitals, and geometric floor mosaics. The exterior and interior were designed in accordance with strict classical rules of harmony and proportion, which is extraordinarily pleasing to the eye. Currently it is being used to exhibit contemporary artists and artisans, with plans to stage various concerts – classical of course.

The **Lungomare** is the highlight of the region. This shady coastal promenade winds along the sea for 12km from Volosko to Lovran. Along the way there are innumerable rocky outgrowths to throw down a towel and jump into the sea. It's a better option than the town's concrete 'beach'.

Opatija and the surrounding region offer some wonderful opportunities for hiking through the **Učka mountain range**. The highest point is Vojak (1401m) which can be reached most directly from **Lovran**, a 5km walk south from Opatija along the Lungomare. There's a natural halfway mark at 700m where the chestnut and oak trees stop and the beech forests begin. The ascent takes about 3½ hours but the view makes it worth it. You can then descend via Poklon (922m) to Opatija, landing in front of Hotel Palace. You can also do the hike in reverse or take a bus to Poklon from Opatija if time is short. There are a number of other hikes. Pick up the free hiking map at Opatija's tourist office for more suggestions.

Sleeping

There are no real budget hotels in Opatija, but the mid-range and top-end places offer surprisingly good value for money, considering Opatija's overall aura of chic. In high season (which only runs from mid-July to mid-August) you may be required to take half board, which will add about another 40KN per person. The prices listed in this section are all high-season rates and breakfast is included in the price. Most hotels are handled by **Liburnia Hotels** (☎ 710 300; www.liburnia.hr).

BUDGET

Camping Opatija (☎ 704 387; fax 704 112; Liburnjska 46, Ičići; per adult/site 30/50KN; 🌄 May-Sep) It's right on the sea and only 5km south of town.

Medveja (☎ /fax 291 191; ac-medveja@lrh.htnet.hr; per adult/site 35/35KN; 🌄 May-Sep) The Medveja is on a pretty cove 7km south of Opatija.

MID-RANGE

Hotel Residenz (☎ 271 399; residenz@liburnia.hr; Maršala Tita 133; s/d from 325/550KN) It has stodgy, but decent rooms in a classic building. You can use the swimming pool at the neighbouring Hotel Kristol and the hotel is right on the sea. More expensive rooms are available with balconies.

Hotel Opatija (☎ 271 388; fax 271 317; Gortanov trg 2/1; s/d 330/500KN; P 🛓) At the top of a hill, this old-style hotel is getting frayed around the edges but retains a strong taste of its former grandeur. The high-ceiling halls and overstuffed chairs are most comforting.

Hotel Kvarner (☎ 271 233; kvarner@liburnia.hr; s/d from 410/580KN; P 🛓) Stay here and you'll feel like European royalty – paddling in an indoor swimming pool, walking through plush hallways, reclining on antique furniture in high-ceilinged rooms. Rooms vary considerably in size and are more expensive when they face the sea of course. The hotel's proudest feature is the eye-popping Crystal Ballroom, now used for conventions and banquets. They don't build them like that any more. The indoor swimming pool leading to the outdoor swimming pool that leads down to the sea is another large part of its appeal.

Hotel-Restaurant Ika (☎ 291 777; www.hotel-ika .hr; Obala Maršala Tita 16; r with/without sea view per person 295/225KN; P) This hotel is 3km south of Opatija in Ika, but it's on a rocky beach and offers a good deal in a small, family-run environment. Rooms have a telephone and TV.

TOP END

Villa Ariston (☎ 271 379; www.villa-ariston.com; s/d from 480/600KN; P 🗶) This gorgeous villa was built by the Viennese architect Carl Seidl in 1924 and designed in a lush, Mediterranean style. Any wedding in Opatija is sure to be celebrated here where the décor oozes romance. The hotel **restaurant** (mains from 60KN) is also excellent whether you order fish, meat or a special vegetarian dish.

Hotel Millennium (☎ 202 000; fax 202 020; Maršala Tita 9; s/d 625/895KN; P 🗶 🛓) After a long and expensive renovation, the Millennium has achieved five-star status for its plush, aircon rooms with minibars and glistening bathrooms. The enthusiastic, somewhat scattered service is not as impressive as the facilities, but the hotel overlooks the water.

Hotel Mozart (☎ 718 260; www.hotel-mozart.hr; s/d 625/910KN; P 🗶 🛓) The beautifully decorated classic rooms harmonise perfectly with the Secession-style halls, dining room and rosy façade. It's in the centre of town and provides a high standard of comfort. Rates are the same all year.

PRIVATE ROOMS

Private rooms are abundant and reasonably priced. The travel agencies listed on p101 all find private accommodation. Rooms start at 150KN to 210KN, depending on the amenities. There are few apartments available and you may have difficulty renting for under a week in high season.

Eating

Obala Maršala Tita is lined with serviceable restaurants offering pizza, grilled meat and fish, but the better restaurants are out of town.

Restaurant Bevanda (☎ 701 411; Obala Maršala Tita 62; mains from 70KN) At this excellent fish restaurant on the eastern edge of town, you can get the usual specialities such as scampi, grilled calamari and the freshest fish available. The setting is equally as wonderful, especially if you get a table on the terrace next to the sea.

Madonnina Pizzeria (☎ 272 579; Pava Tomašića 3; mains from 35KN) Hidden away near the Hotel Kvarner, the Madonnina has a long menu of delicious pizza and pasta dishes at reasonable prices.

Pomodoro (Obala Maršala Tita 136; snacks 14-18KN) This is a good place to grab small pizzas and sandwiches.

For self-caterers there's a **supermarket/ deli** (Obala Maršala Tita 80), and a *burek* (a heavy pastry stuffed with meat or cheese) stand down the stairs next to No 55 on Stubište Tomaševac.

Drinking

Opatija's nightlife took a hit when the police started cracking down on drunk drivers, ending the practice of driving from Rijeka to Opatija to drink along the harbour. All is not lost however. In the summer, a bar scene populated by locals and tourists is still centred around the harbour and the ever-popular Caffé Harbour or Hemingways.

Getting There & Away

Bus No 32 stops in front of the train station in Rijeka (11KN, 11km) and runs right along the Opatija Riviera west from Rijeka to Lovran every 20 minutes until late in the evening.

AROUND OPATIJA
Volosko

Two kilometres east of the town of Opatija, Volosko is a little fishing village with appealing Mediterranean features such as narrow alleyways, stone cottages and balconies dripping with flowers. Its small harbour recalls the days when tuna fishing was the main source of income in the bay. The town's quiet allure makes it irresistible to tourists, but it is still a relatively quiet retreat from Opatija when the summer crowds descend in force. The coastal promenade from Opatija ends in Volosko, making it an easy walk past bay trees, palms, figs and oaks, behind which you can glimpse a number of villas dating from the end of the 19th century.

While in Volosko try **Restaurant Amfora** (☎ 701 222; Crinkovica bb; mains from 50KN), which serves fish and Croatian dishes in a great location overlooking the sea.

RISNJAK NATIONAL PARK

Relatively isolated, undervisited and certainly underappreciated by foreign tourists, this majestic 2560-acre (6400-hectare) park 43km northeast of Rijeka deserves to be much better known. The park is part of the Gorski Kotar region and is often visited by groups of schoolkids in spring and autumn and skiers in the winter, but is nearly empty all summer. Thickly forested with pines and carpeted with meadows and wildflowers, the landscape is defined by its karstic formations: sinkholes, cracks caves and abysses. The highest peak is Veliki Risnjak which rises to 1528m; even Delnice at the foot of the mountain is at 696m. The bracing alpine breezes make the park the perfect escape when the coastal heat and crowds become overpowering.

Orientation & Information

Most of the park is unspoiled virgin forest with only a few settlements. The largest is Crni Lug at the park's edge where you'll find the **Park Information Office** (☎ 836 133), a desultory operation in the park's only hotel, the **Motel Risnjak** (☎ 836 133; Bijela Vodica; d 200KN; P). The **park entrance** (adult/concession 30/15KN) is a few hundred metres behind the motel.

Sights & Activities

The best way to discover the park is to walk the **Leska Path**, a delightful 4.5km path that begins at the park's entrance. It's an easy and shady walk, punctuated by several dozen explanatory panels (in English) telling you all about the park's history, topography, geology, flora and fauna. You'll pass streams disappearing into the karst, a feeding station for the deer, boar and bears that frequent the park and a typical mountain hut with a picnic table.

Getting There & Away

There's no public transport to the park. To get there by car, exit the main Zagreb–Rijeka motorway at Delnice and follow signs to Crni Lug.

LOŠINJ & CRES ISLANDS

These two serpentine islands in the Kvarner archipelago are separated by only an 11m-wide canal, and are thus often treated as a single entity. Although their topography is different, the islands' identities are blurred by a shared history and close transportation links. On Lošinj (Lussino in Italian) the fishing villages of Mali Lošinj and Veli Lošinj attract hordes of tourists in summer, especially from Italy, which is linked to Mali Lošinj from Venice. Cres (Crepsa in Italian) is more deserted, especially outside Cres town, and you can still find many remote camping grounds and pristine beaches. Both islands are crisscrossed by hiking and biking trails.

Cres is the longer island, stretching 68km from tip to tip. About half the island is covered with fields and rocks, with large pine and oak forests in the north. The western coast is more settled than the eastern coast, which is home to the griffon vulture (see The Threatened Griffon Vulture, p109). Lošinj is 31km long and has a more indented coastline than Cres, especially in the south. The towns of Mali Lošinj and Veli Lošinj are ringed by natural pine forests interspersed with tall Aleppo pines, which were planted in the 19th century.

History

Excavations indicate that a prehistoric culture spread out over both islands from the Stone Age to the Bronze Age. The first recorded settlements sprang up on Cres, where the Liburnian tribe used the natural harbours of Cres town and Osor, and built hilltop fortresses at Merag, Porozina and Lubenice. The ancient Greeks called both islands the Apsirtides, and they were conquered by the Romans in the 1st century BC. After the division of the Roman Empire, the islands spent a few centuries under Byzantine rule and were settled by Slavic tribes in the 6th and 7th centuries. In the 6th century a bishopric was established in Osor, on the southern tip of Cres, which controlled both Cres and the largely unpopulated Lošinj throughout the early Middle Ages. From 1000 to 1358, the islands were under Venetian rule, followed by that of the Croatian-Hungarian kings, and returning to Venice from 1409 to 1797.

The islands stagnated under Venetian rule. All maritime activity was suppressed as the Venetians were fearful of rivalry from the substantial fleet at Osor. Male residents were pressed into service as galley slaves on Venetian ships. The final blow to Osor's importance came in the 15th century when a malaria epidemic chased people out of the town to the safer settlements at Cres, Mali Lošinj and Veli Lošinj.

By the time Venice fell in 1797, Veli Lošinj and Mali Lošinj had become important maritime centres while Cres devoted its attention to vineyards and olive production. During the 19th century, shipbuilding flourished in Lošinj, but the advent of steam ships at the end of the century caused an irreversible decline in the maritime business. Meanwhile, Cres had its own problems in the form of a phylloxera epidemic that wiped out its vineyards. Both islands were poor when they were annexed to Italy as part of the 1920 Treaty of Rapallo. They became part of Yugoslavia in 1945.

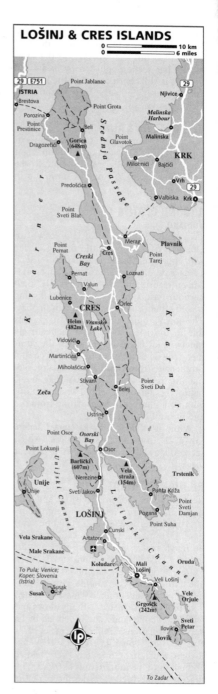

MARTIN MOOS

Trams on Trg Josip Jelačića, Zagreb (p48)

GUY MOBERLY

Zagreb's medieval quarter (p51)

MARTIN MOOS

Arches and pillars of the Mirogoj Cemetery (p56)

Flowers in front of the Museum Mimara (p55)

MARTIN MOOS

Holiday-makers in Opatija (p100)

Elegant villas surrounding Čikat Bay,
Mali Lošinj (p105)

Boats on Osor harbour (p111)

Pine-fringed beach, Cres Island (p110)

Today, there's a small shipyard in Ne-rezine in north Lošinj and olive cultivation in Cres. There's some sheep farming on Cres, and fishermen regularly ply the waters, but the main activity on both islands is now tourism.

Getting There & Away
BOAT
The main maritime port of entry for the islands is Mali Lošinj, which is connected to Pula, Zadar, Venice and Koper in the summer. **Jadrolinija** (☎ 231 765; Riva Lošinjskih Kapetana 20) runs a weekly ferry between Zadar and Mali Lošinj (32KN, four hours). From June to September there is the car ferry, *Marina*, operated four times a week by Lošinjska Plovidba (p108) and running from Zadar and Pula to Mali Lošinj (73KN, four hours), going on to Koper (136KN, nine hours). From April to October **Venezia Lines** (☎ 041 52 22 568; www.venezialines.com) runs a weekly catamaran from Venice to Poreč, Rovinj, Pula and Mali Lošinj (€60, four hours). In July and August, Jadrolinija runs a daily catamaran from Mali Lošinj to Cres (21KN, 2½ hours) and Rijeka (34KN, 3¾ hours).

There is also a car ferry that runs from Brestova in Istria to Porozine at the tip of Cres (13KN, 30 minutes, hourly).

BUS
All buses travelling to and from the islands originate in Veli Lošinj and stop in Mali Lošinj before continuing to Cres and the mainland. There are six daily buses from Veli Lošinj to Cres town (30KN, 1½ hours), two daily buses to Merag (44KN, two hours), two buses a day to Valbiska on Krk Island (59KN, 2½ hours), two daily buses to Porozina (61KN, 2½ hours), two daily buses to Brestova in Istria (78KN, three hours), four buses a day to Rijeka (91KN, 3½ hours), two buses a day to Zagreb (193KN to 204KN, 6½ hours) and one daily bus to Ljubljana (218KN, six hours).

LOŠINJ ISLAND
Mali Lošinj
pop 6500 / postcode 51550
Mali Lošinj sits at the foot of a protected harbour on the southeast coast of Lošinj Island. Its 19th-century prosperity is evident in the stately sea captain's houses lined up along the northeastern harbour, but its

20th-century affluence rests upon the large hotels leading up from the southwest harbour to Čikat Bay. In the late 19th century, as shipbuilding was dying out, the wealthy citizens of Vienna and Budapest gravitated to the 'healthy air' of Mali Lošinj, building villas and luxurious hotels on Čikat Bay. Some old villas remain, but even though most of the current hotels are modern developments, they blend in fairly well with the dense pine forests that blanket the cove. During the summer, Mali Lošinj may not be the most relaxed place, but it's a good base for excursions around Lošinj and Cres or to the small islands of Susak and Ilovik.

ORIENTATION
The Jadrolinija dock for all the large boats is at the northeastern part of town, a 500m walk along the harbour from the town centre. The bus station is on the edge of Riva Lošinjskih Kapetana, the road that runs along the harbour.

Most stores, travel agencies and cafés are along the stretch of Riva Lošinjskih Kapetana that runs from the tourist office to the Trg Republike Hrvatske and its new fountain. When you cross over to the other end of the harbour, roads take you to the hotels and beaches of Čikat Bay.

INFORMATION
With the town's long history of tourism there is no shortage of travel agencies to arrange private accommodation, handle air tickets, change money and book excursions.

Garderoba (Riva Lošinjskih Kapetana; ☼ 6am-midnight) At the bus station.

Jadranka agency (www.jadranka.hr) Handles bookings for camping grounds.

Kvarner Express (☎ 231 831; Vladimira Gortana 20) Travel agency.

Manora Lošinj (☎ 520 101; Velopin Priko 29) This travel agency is friendly and keeps long hours.

Post Office (Riva Lošinjskih Kapetana 9)

Riječka Banka (Riva Lošinjskih Kapetana 4) There's an ATM outside and you can change money here.

Tourist Office (☎ /fax 231 884; www.tz-malilosinj.hr; Riva Lošinjskih Kapetana 29; ☼ 8am-8pm daily Jun-Sep, 8am-1pm Mon-Fri Oct-May) Has useful information.

SIGHTS
The main attraction of Mali Lošinj is the attractive port and the greenery of the surrounding hills dipping into the sea, but

there are a few sights that recall the island's history. In the graveyard around the **Church of St Martin** are the tombs of earlier inhabitants of Mali Lošinj – sailors, fortune-seekers from Italy and Austria, Italian royalty and 19th-century Austrian children sent here in the hopes that the mild climate would cure their tuberculosis or respiratory problems.

In the town centre, peek into the **Church of the Nativity of the Virgin** (Župna Crkva Male Gospe; Ulica Sveta Marija) either before or after Sunday Mass. Built from 1696 to 1757, the baroque façade overlooks a paved square that used to be the central meeting place for the town. Inside there are some notable artworks, including a painting of the *Nativity of the Blessed Virgin* by an 18th-century Venetian artist, a marble *Crucifixion* by the sculptor Bartolomeo Ferrari and a painting of the saints on the northern altar that shows the church neighbourhood in the 18th century.

Mali Lošinj's fine-arts scene centres on the **Art Collections** (Umjetničke Zbirke; ☎ 231 173; Vladimira Gortana 35; admission 8KN; ☺ 10am-noon Mon-Fri) of the Mihičić and Piperata families. The highlight of the Mihičić collection of contemporary Croatian works is the paintings of Emanuel Vidović. The Piperata collection concentrates on the old master with emphasis on Italian, French and Dutch painting from the 17th and 18th centuries. Opening hours are unreliable.

ACTIVITIES

Čikat Bay offers the best swimming, with its long, narrow pebble beach and tiny sandy beach.

The gentle hills and many paths on the island are great for cycling. You can rent a mountain bike at **Sunbird** (☎ 097 228 676; mountain bike hire 1hr/8hr 18/75KN) on Čikat Bay near the Hotel Bellevue.

Čikat Bay is a great spot for windsurfing and the best months are April to May and mid-August to September. Sunbird rents boards and also offers windsurfing courses.

The waters surrounding Lošinj Island offer good opportunities for scuba diving. There's a wreck dating from 1917, a large, relatively shallow cave suitable for beginners and the wonderful Margarita Reef off the island of Susak. Although it can't be guaranteed that you'll see one, the waters off Lošinj and Cres host a protected colony of 150 dolphins. The two leading dive

operations on Čikat Bay are **Adriatic Divers** (☎ /fax 232 918; www.adriaticdivers.de) and **Divers Sport Center** (☎ 219 111; www.diver.hr). The price of the boat dives depends upon the distance, but generally ranges from 180KN to 240KN. Both operations offer courses and dive packages that include accommodation.

SLEEPING

Mali Lošinj offers a range of accommodation options.

Most hotels are in the pine forest on the hill over Čikat Bay. The hotel resorts around Čikat Bay are the usual tourist developments and nearly indistinguishable, at least from the outside.

Budget

Camping Čikat (☎ 232 125; fax 231 708; Čikat Bay; per adult/site 50/25KN) This large camping ground is close to the beach.

Poljana (☎ /fax 231 728; Polijana; per adult/site 45/15KN) Poljana, on the road to Rijeka, is a smaller, quieter and more remote camping ground about 5km north of town. Although there is no local bus, you can take any Rijeka-bound bus and ask to be dropped off at the camping ground.

Hotel Helios (☎ 232 124; jadranka@ri.htnet.hr; Čikat Bay; s/d from 215/430KN; **P**) This is the cheapest hotel on the bay, its bland modernity softened by the surrounding greenery.

Mid-Range

Hotel Alhambra (☎ 232 022; alhambra@jadranka.htnet .hr; Čikat Bay; d 445KN; **P**) A vaguely Moorish-style lobby ushers in spare but attractive rooms.

Hotel Bellevue (☎ 231 222; hotel.bellevue@jadranka .htnet.hr; Čikat Bay; s/d 340/610KN; **P** ☒ ☙) It was once the best and most expensive hotel on the island, but has faded a bit. It's still comfortable enough, only steps from the bay and with an indoor swimming pool. There are more expensive rooms available with views.

Top End

Villa Favorita (☎ 520 640; www.villafavorita.hr; Sunčana uvala; r per person 580KN; **P** ☒ ☙) This small four-star hotel is in a lovely, 19th-century mansion. The completely updated rooms are furnished with charm and personality; many have sea views. Plus, you can de-stress with a sauna, massage or a nap by the garden swimming pool.

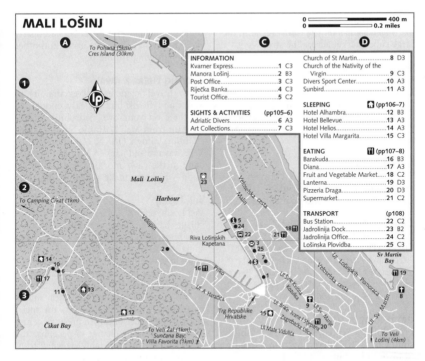

MALI LOŠINJ

Hotel Villa Margarita (☎ 233 837; www.vud.hr; Bočac 64; s/d 410/590KN) If you're more interested in staying near the town centre for the excursions or restaurants, this is the place. Everything is tidily correct.

Private Rooms

Jadranka Agency, Kvarner Express and Manora Lošinj are three of many agencies that find rooms and apartments around Mali Lošinj, but there is little available in the town itself. Prices are more or less the same. Expect to pay about 110KN per person for a room. There are also studios available for 325KN daily and two-room apartments for 430KN daily. In summer, you may pay a penalty for a stay under seven nights.

EATING

Catering to the tremendous influx of Italian tourists in the summer has lent the island's cuisine a decidedly Italian flavour. As on many islands, there is not a wide variety in price or quality and the menus tend to be more or less the same, with an accent on seafood, grilled fish, pasta and risotto.

You'll generally eat better at places away from the main harbour area. Most restaurants close for a month or two in winter.

Diana (☎ 232 055; Čikat Bay; mains from 60KN) Diana is beautifully located on the sea and offers delicious grilled fish.

Veli Žal (☎ 231 530; Sunčana Bay; meals from 50KN) Cooled by the sea breezes of Sunčana Bay, Veli Žal, near the Hotel Aurora, is a wonderful terrace restaurant specialising in fish, but also offering a full menu of other Croatian dishes.

Lanterna (☎ 233 625; Sveti Marije bb; mains from 40KN) On a small boat harbour near the Church of St Martin, this restaurant serves up a tangy octopus salad for 35KN, as well as the usual fish, pasta and grilled-meat main courses. It's off the tourist track and apt to attract boating and fishing types.

Pizzeria Draga (☎ 231 132; Braće Vidulića 77; pizza from 30KN) There are plenty of pizza places, but this one seems to make a special effort.

Barakuda (☎ 233 309; Priko 3; mains from 60KN) It's usually crowded with plenty of tourists, but for a harbourside restaurant, it offers good quality and good value.

Self-caterers can head to the daily **fruit and vegetable market** (Trg Zagazinjine) and the large supermarket across the street.

ENTERTAINMENT

On summer evenings many of the large hotels in Čikat have 'terrace dancing'; that is, a couple of musicians with an electronic keyboard playing an assortment of local or international tunes, according to their mood.

GETTING THERE & AWAY

There are nine buses a day between Mali Lošinj and Veli Lošinj (9.50KN, 10 minutes). For other bus and boat connections, see p105.

Jadrolinija Office (☎ 231 765; Riva Lošinjskih Kapetana 20) Has ferry information and tickets.

Lošinjska Plovidba (☎ 231 077; www.losinplov.hr; Riva Lošinjskih Kapetana 8) Sells tickets for its boats connecting Mali Lošinj to Koper and other islands. There's a small Lošinska Plovidba ticket office near the marina, open half an hour before each sailing.

GETTING AROUND

From June to September there is an hourly shuttle bus (7KN) that runs from the centre of town to the hotels in Čikat.

You can also zip around the island on a motorcycle for 250KN a day, which is available at Manora Lošinj travel agency.

Around Mali Lošinj

The nearby islands of Susak and Ilovik are the most popular day trips from Mali Lošinj. Tiny **Susak** (population 188, 3.8 sq km) is unique for the thick layer of fine sand that blankets the underlying limestone and creates delightful beaches. The island culture is also unusual. You can still see the local women outfitted in traditional multi-coloured skirts and red leggings on feast days or wedding days. Islanders speak their own dialect, which is nearly incomprehensible to other Croats. When you see the old stone houses on the island, consider that each stone had to be brought over from Mali Lošinj and hand carried to its destination. No wonder the island has steadily lost its population, with many of its citizens heading to the USA – Hoboken, New Jersey, to be precise.

In contrast to flat Susak, **Ilovik** (population 145, 5.8 sq km) is a hilly island which is a popular destination for boaters. There are some secluded swimming coves and nearly every house has oleanders, roses and other flowers growing around it.

GETTING THERE & AWAY

Many travel agencies sell excursions to Susak and Ilovik but it's easy enough to get there on your own. Jadrolinija makes a circuit from Mali Lošinj to Susak (34KN, 2½ hours), Ilovik (18KN, one hour), Unije, Vela Srakane and back to Mali Lošinj twice daily in the early morning and late afternoon, which can make a pleasant day trip.

Veli Lošinj

Veli Lošinj retains much more of its fishing-village character than busy Mali Lošinj, only 4km northwest, and it's smaller, quieter and somewhat less crowded. Pastel-coloured baroque houses cluster around a narrow bay that protrudes like a thumb into the southeastern coastline of Lošinj. Hilly, cobblestoned streets lead from the central square past cottages buried in foliage to the rocky coast. The absence of cars in the town centre is also a refreshing change of pace, but the town can be uncomfortably crowded from mid-July to the end of August.

Like Mali Lošinj, Veli Lošinj had its share of rich sea captains who built villas and surrounded them with gardens of exotic plants they brought back from their travels. You can glimpse these villas on a walk up the steep, narrow streets. Sea captains also furnished the churches in town, most notably Sveti Antun on the harbour.

ORIENTATION

The bus station (without left-luggage office) is on a hill over the harbour. Ulica Vladimira Nazora takes you down to the harbour, which is the town centre. The bank, post offices, tourist agencies and a number of cafés are on Obala Maršala Tita, which wraps around the bay. A coastal route leads north up to the Hotel Punta beach and east to the Rovenska Bay beach.

INFORMATION

There's an ATM outside the ASL Travel Agency.

ASL Travel Agency (☎ 236 256; Obala Maršala Tita 17) Small but finds private accommodation, changes money and rents bikes.

THE THREATENED GRIFFON VULTURE

Of all Croatia's birds, the griffon vulture is the most majestic. With a wing span of almost 3m, measuring about 1m from end to end, and weighing 7kg to 9kg, the bird looks big enough to take on passengers. They're speedy as well, cruising comfortably at 40km/h to 50km/h and reaching speeds of up to 120km/h. The vulture's powerful beak and long neck are ideally suited for rummaging around the entrails of its prey, which is most likely to be a dead sheep.

Finding precious sheep carcasses is a team effort for griffon vultures. Usually a colony of birds will set out and fly in a comb formation of up to a kilometre apart. When one of the vultures spots a carcass, it circles as a signal for its neighbours to join in the feast. Shepherds don't mind griffons, reasoning that the birds prevent whatever disease or infection killed the sheep from spreading to other livestock.

The total known number of griffon vultures in Croatia is 150, with 140 of them living on the coastal cliffs of Cres and small colonies on Krk and Prvić Islands. The bird's dietary preferences mean that griffons tend to follow the sheep although they will eat other dead mammals, to their peril. The last remaining birds in Paklenica National Park recently died after eating poisoned foxes. Shepherding is still active on Cres, encouraged and supported by the Eco-Centre Caput Insulae in Beli. Krk Island used to host a larger griffon colony but the lack of sheep plus over-development has eliminated the population. On Cres, the best area to spot a griffon vulture is on the sea crags from Orlec south to Belej, Plat and Verin.

Their breeding habits discourage a large population, as a griffon couple produces only one fledgling a year and it takes five years for the young bird to reach maturity. During that time, the growing griffons travel widely: one griffon tagged in Paklenica National Park was found in Chad, 4000km away.

The griffon population enjoys legal protection as an endangered species in Croatia. Killing a bird or disturbing them while nesting carries a €5000 fine. Intentional murder is rare now but, because the young birds cannot fly more than 500m on a windless day, tourists on speedboats who provoke them into flight often end up killing them. The exhausted birds drop into the water and drown. The eco-centre in Beli on Cres Island serves as a kind of hospital and rest home for injured or exhausted vultures and is urging that even stronger measures be taken to protect the griffon.

Post Office (Obala Maršala Tita 33)

Riječka Banka (Obala Maršala Tita) Has a foreign-exchange counter.

Val Tourist Agency (☎ /fax 236 352; val@cres-losinj .com; Obala Maršala Tita 34; ☀ 9am-8pm Apr-Oct, 9am-noon Mon-Fri Nov-May) Finds private accommodation and changes money.

SIGHTS & ACTIVITIES

You can't miss the hulking **St Anthony's Church** (Crkva Sveti Antun; Trg Sveti Antun) on the harbour with its tall bell tower. Built in 1774 on the site of an older church, St Anthony's contains an impressive collection of Italian paintings thanks to generous sea captains. The captains also saw that the church's old wooden altars were replaced by seven baroque marble altars, which were bought second-hand in Italy. The church is only open for Mass on Sunday, but you can catch a glimpse of the interior through a metal gate.

The striking **Venetian Tower**, behind the town, was built in 1455 to defend the town from the notorious *uskok* (a community of pirates that lived in Senj in the 16th century; see Uskoks: The Pirates of Senj, p163). With the decline of piracy, it fell into ruin but has recently been restored. It now contains a small **museum** (☎ 231 173; admission 8KN; ☀ 10am-noon & 7-9pm Mon-Sat Jun-Sep), which centres on the development of Mali Lošinj.

SLEEPING

Both Val and ASL travel agencies will find you private accommodation for about the same price as in Mali Lošinj.

Hotel Saturn (☎ 236 102; fax 236 652; Obala Maršala Tita; d from 470KN) This pretty pink-and-white renovated villa, across from the church, has minibars in its rooms. The front rooms on the harbour are more expensive, but apt to be noisy on summer evenings, when crowds fill the downstairs terrace restaurant.

Hotel Punta (☎ 662 000; hotel-punta@jadranka.ht net.hr; s/d 290/535KN; P ⊠) The Punta offers a standard resort experience on a hill overlooking the harbour with easy access to a swimming cove. Rooms have sea views and balconies, but some of the singles are ridiculously small.

EATING

There are a couple of places here worth sampling.

Bistro Sirius (☎ 236 399; Rovenska 4; mains from 50KN) This is a good escape from the open-air restaurants that sprawl around the harbour in the summer. On quiet Rovenska Bay east of the town centre, the exceptionally fresh fish makes the restaurant popular with a local crowd.

Ribarska Konoba (☎ 236 235; Obala Maršala Tita 1; mains from 40KN) Just around the corner from St Anthony's Church, this pleasant place serves good seafood on a shady, open-air terrace.

CRES ISLAND
Cres Town
pop 2234 / postcode 51557

Cres town so resembles an Italian fishing village you might wonder if you have strayed across a border somewhere. Pastel terrace houses crowd around the harbour-within-a-harbour (Mandrać) glinting in the afternoon sun. Even at the height of the tourist season, when the harbour is crowded with boats, it's a lazy, sun-drenched town.

The Italian influence dates from the 15th-century Venetians who relocated their headquarters to Cres town after Osor fell victim to plague and pestilence. Public buildings and patricians' palaces were built along the harbour and in the 16th century the Venetian administration built a town wall. As you stroll the streets you'll notice reminders of Venetian rule, including coats of arms of powerful Venetian families. You may hear as much Italian spoken as Croatian since the port is a popular destination for Italian boaters.

ORIENTATION

The bus stop (there is no left-luggage office) is on the southeastern side of Mandrać harbour next to the tourist office and bank. The old town stretches from the harbour promenade, Riva Creskih Kapetana, inland to Aprila XX Šetalište. You'll find most of the monuments and churches within this area. If you continue around the harbour to Lungomare Sveti Mikula, you will come to the rocky beaches around the Hotel Kimen and Autocamp Kovačine after about 1km.

INFORMATION

Cresanka (☎ 571 133; www.cresanka. hr; Cons 11; 8am-8pm Jul-Aug, 8am-4pm Mon-Fri Sep-Jun) The staff can arrange private accommodation and change money.
Post Office (Cons 4)
Riječka Banka (Cons 8) Changes money.
Tourist Agency Croatia (☎ 573 053; valdarke@ri.htnet .hr; Cons 10) In addition to finding accommodation, there is a computer available to check your email.

SIGHTS

At the end of Riva Creskih Kapetana is Trg F Petrica and the graceful 16th-century **loggia**, scene of public announcements and judgments, financial transactions and festivals under Venetian rule. On the central pillar in front of the loggia you can see signs of the chain that used to bind lawbreakers to the column for public ridicule. Now the loggia is the scene of a morning fruit and vegetable market.

Behind the loggia is the 16th-century **Main Gate**. The niche above the gate used to hold the Venetian lion but after the fall of Venice in 1797 the lion was removed and thrown into the sea while the townspeople cheered.

The church on Pod Urom inside the gate is **St Mary of the Snow** (Sveta Marija Snježne; Pod Urom; ☽ Mass only). The façade is notable for the Renaissance portal with a relief of the Virgin and Child, and above the double-sided pilasters are statues of the archangel Gabriel and the Virgin. Although the church is only open for Mass, it's worth arriving half an hour before or after the Mass to see the serene interior. The bottom part of the altarpiece on the right altar shows a panorama of Cres town in the 18th century and the left altar has a lovely carved wooden Pietà from the 15th century (now under protective glass).

ACTIVITIES

The best swimming is around the Hotel Kimen. **Diving Cres** (☎ /fax 571 706; www.divingcres .de) is in the Autocamp Kovačine and offers scuba diving.

FESTIVALS & EVENTS

The patron saint of the town is St Mary of the Snow and on her feast day, 5 August, there's an outdoor bazaar on the main square where stalls sell a selection of the island's offerings – olive oil, honey, herbs, fruits and vegetables.

SLEEPING

Tourist Agency Croatia can find private rooms for around 135KN per person. You can also rent a studio for 250KN.

Autocamp Kovačine (☎ 571 423; www.campingcres .com; Glavni Put; per person 50KN; ☯ Apr-Oct) There's no tent charge at this huge camping ground about 1km out of town.

Kimen (☎ 571 161; fax 571 163; Melin; r per person 325KN; P) The only hotel in town, this is a large development on the road to Autocamp Kovačine, but right near beaches for swimming. Rooms are simple but large with phones and balconies. A pretty seaside promenade leads from the hotel 1km to the town centre.

Kovačine Rooms (☎ 571 423; fax 571 163; Glavni Put; r per person 354KN; ☯) Part of the Autocamp Kovačine, this small building has efficient new rooms with phones and TV. Some have balconies with views over Valun Bay.

EATING

Restaurant Riva (☎ 571 107; Obala Creskih Kapetana 13; mains from 40KN) It has an attractive terrace on the harbour and serves good fish and pasta.

Belona Gostionica (☎ 571 203; Šetalište XX Apra 24; mains from 50KN) This is a favourite when the locals want to enjoy a night out. Fish is the speciality, but you can also get meat and pasta dishes.

Supermarket (☯ 6.30am-9pm Mon-Sat, 7am-noon Sun) It's across from the loggia.

GETTING THERE & AWAY

There are four buses a day to Opatija (52KN, two hours) and five to Rijeka (57KN, 2½ hours). **Autotrans** (☎ 571 810) at the bus station sells tickets.

For more information on buses between Cres and Mali Lošinj, see p105.

Around Cres Town

Eco-Centre Caput Insulae (☎ /fax 840 525; www.caput -insulae.com; Beli 4; adult/concession 20/10KN; ☯ 8am-9pm) is part nature park, part sanctuary for the endangered griffon (see The Threatened Griffon Vulture, p109). Located in Beli near the island's northern tip, the eco-centre is devoted to caring for and maintaining the habitat of these majestic birds. There are now about 70 nesting couples inhabiting the coastal cliffs, but their situation is precarious. Fewer local farmers are raising the sheep that the vultures need to survive and the summer influx of tourists unnerves the young vultures. The centre works with local farmers to ensure a sheep supply and with local fishermen to rescue drowning vultures.

A visit to the centre starts with exhibits explaining the biology and habits of the vulture but the highlight is the vultures themselves. There are usually about four or five birds in residence flapping around in a caged-in area behind the centre. With their powerful beak and 3m wing span, the creatures look far more terrifying than they are. It is comforting to know that they only eat carrion.

Admission to the centre also includes access to the well-maintained nature trails around the centre. There are three trails of 5km, 6km and 7km, and a helpful booklet published by the centre explains the history, culture, flora and fauna of the region.

GETTING THERE & AWAY

From Cres town, there's an early-morning bus on Monday and Thursday which goes to Beli (15KN, 30 minutes) and returns in the late afternoon. Buses to Porozine drop you on the main road from where it's a 7km walk down to the village and eco-centre.

Osor
pop 80

When crossing from Lošinj to Osor, you may have to wait at the drawbridge spanning the canal, as the bridge is raised twice a day to allow boats to move from the Lošinski Channel to the Gulf of Kvarner and back. It's a treat to watch the yachts, sailboats and motorboats file through the narrow canal that separates the two islands. Usually the bridge opens at 9am and then again in the evening.

The channel is thought to have been dug by the Romans, and because of it Osor was able to control a key navigational route throughout the Middle Ages. Until the 15th-century, Osor was a strong

KVARNER REGION

commercial, religious and political presence in the region, but a combination of plague, malaria and new sea routes devastated the town's economy and it slowly decayed. Now it's gaining a new life as a museum-town of churches and country lanes that meander off from a traditional 15th-century town centre.

There's been an obvious investment in bringing the village back to life, even though practically no-one lives here and there's no tourist office. The town square and a few other smaller squares display modern sculpture of an astonishingly high quality. The Musical Evenings of Osor in July and August draw fine musicians from around the country to perform in the churches. Osor is an easy day trip from Mali Lošinj and Cres town, and is worth a stop. Bring a bathing suit, as there are swimming coves outside of town past the Franciscan monastery.

SIGHTS
Entering through the gate on the canal, you walk right into the centre of the village. First you'll pass the remains of an old castle and then on your right, the **Archaeological Museum** (☎ 237 173; adult/student 8/4KN; ♥ 10am-noon & 7-9pm Jun-Sep) on the main square in the old town hall, which contains a collection of stone fragments and reliefs from the Roman and early Christian periods.

Next door is the **Church of the Assumption** (Crkva Uznesenja; ♥ 10am-noon & 7-9pm Jun-Sep). Built in the late 15th century, the façade has a rich Renaissance portal and inside there's a baroque altar from the 17th century, as well as paintings by Venetian artists from the 16th to 18th centuries. On the western side of the cathedral, notice the altar picture of St Gaudencius with a snake at his feet. According to local legend, Gaudencius was born in the 11th century in nearby Tršic and became a bishop. As a bishop, he took it upon himself to castigate the townspeople for their sins and corruption for which he was expelled from town. The bitter bishop became a hermit in a cave and put a curse upon all the poisonous snakes on the island.

Before leaving the square, notice the Meštrović statue *Daleki Akordi* (Distant Chords), one of many sculptures on a musical theme scattered throughout the town.

Take the road between the town hall and the bell tower heading away from the canal, and on the remains of the eastern town gate you'll notice **St Mark's lion**, the Venetian reminder of who built the 15th-century walls. Continue past the walls and follow the laneway down to the cove, where you'll find the remains of a **Franciscan monastery**, with Glagolitic inscriptions on the stone jamb of the monastery and on the bell tower of the church. The monastery was taken over by the Franciscans in 1460 and abandoned in 1841.

FESTIVALS & EVENTS
The **Musical Evenings of Osor** take place from mid-July to mid-August and attract a range of high-calibre classical artists from around the country. Information about the concerts is posted around town or you can inquire at the tourist offices in Mali Lošinj and Cres town.

SLEEPING
There are no hotels in Osor, but there are two delightful camping grounds nearby.

Preko Mosta (☎ 237 350; Osor; per person/site 45/45KN) This is the closest camping ground to Osor, overlooking the bridge to Mali Lošinj.

Bijar (☎ 237 027; near Nerezine; per person/site 45/45KN) Bijar is twice the size of Preko Mosta, but its location on a remote cove makes it a tranquil hideaway.

EATING
You can grab a snack at one of the stalls outside town as there's not much inside town.

Konoba Bonifačić (☎ 237 413; mains from 35KN) is one of the town's few restaurants. It's a homy family-run place, which serves up fresh fish dishes on an outdoor terrace surrounded by greenery.

GETTING THERE & AWAY
All buses travelling between Cres and Mali Lošinj stop at Osor (20KN, one hour).

Valun
pop 68
In a country with numerous idyllic coves, Valun is a standout. The little hamlet, 15km southwest of Cres town, is buried at the foot of steep cliffs and surrounded by shingle beaches. It's a long descent by car, and then you leave the car on top of the hill and go down steep steps to the old town that

drops to the cove. The relative inaccessibility means that the narrow cove is rarely crowded and there are no souvenir stalls blocking your view of the old stone town clinging to the hills. There are a few restaurants along the harbour that serve seafood and pasta dishes on wooden tables as you gaze out at the tranquil cove.

The town was founded by villagers from Bućevo, further up the hill above the car park, who gradually moved down to the coast. The main sight is the 11th-century **Glagolitic tablet** in Valun's parish church. The tablet is a tombstone that was originally found in St Mark's church in Bućevo. It's inscribed in both Glagolitic and Latin, reflecting the ethnic composition of the island, which was inhabited by Roman descendants and newcomers who spoke Croatian.

Valun's main attraction is the **beaches**. To the right of the harbour a path leads to a beach and camping ground. West of the hamlet, about 700m further on, there's another lovely pebble beach bordered by pines.

The **Tourist Office** (☎ 525 050, 525 084; cresanka@ri.htnet.hr; ☽ 8am-10pm Jul & Aug) is in the town centre up a few steps from the harbour and will book private accommodation by fax or email. Private accommodation is scarce in Valun (it's a tiny town) and usually reserved long in advance. Expect to pay the same price as for private accommodation in Cres town.

Zdovice (☎ 535 050; fax 535 085; per person 60KN; ☽ Apr-Sep) is a small camping ground on the eastern cove. Reservations should be made in advance.

GETTING THERE & AWAY
The long, steep hill leading down to the cove would make hiking or biking back from Valun a long, exhausting struggle. It's best to have your own wheels but, if not, there are a few buses a week from Cres town.

KRK ISLAND

pop 16,402 / postcode 51500
Croatia's largest island, 409-sq-km Krk (Veglia in Italian) is also one of the busiest in the summer as Germans and Austrians stream over the Krk bridge to its holiday houses, autocamps and hotels. Krk's booming tourist industry managed to weather the

storm in the former Yugoslavia, helped by its proximity to the mainland and distance from the fighting. It may not be the lushest or most beautiful island in Croatia, but its decades of experience in tourism make it an easy place to visit, with good transport connections and a well-organised tourism infrastructure.

The northwestern coast of the island is rocky and steep with few settlements, probably because of the fierce *bura* wind that whips the coast in winter. The climate is milder in the south, with more vegetation and beaches, coves and inlets. The forests that account for 31% of the island are mainly found on the southwestern coast, along with the major towns – Krk, Punat and Baška.

Krk town is centrally located and makes a good base for exploring the island. From Punat, you're within easy reach of the unique Košljun Island and monastery, and Baška is on a wide sandy bay at the foot of a scenic mountain range. On the southeast coast, the main town is Vrbnik, a cliff-top medieval village known for its fine Žlahtina wine.

History
The oldest-known inhabitants of Krk were the Illyrian Liburnian tribe, followed by the Romans. Taking advantage of the island's position on an important maritime route through the Adriatic, the Romans settled near Omišalj on the northern coast. In 49 BC a naval battle between Octavian and Mark Antony was waged near the island. With the decline of the Roman Empire, Krk was incorporated into the Byzantine Empire, then passed between Venice and the Croatian-Hungarian kings.

In the 11th century, Krk became the centre of the Glagolitic language – the old Slavic language put into writing by the Greek missionaries Cyril and Methodius. The oldest preserved example of the script was found in a former Benedictine abbey in Krk town. A later tablet with the script was found near Baška and is now exhibited in Zagreb. The script was used on the island up to the first decades of the 19th century.

In 1358, Venice granted rule over the island to the Dukes of Krk, later known as the Frankopans, who became one of the richest and most powerful families in Croatia. Although vassals of Venice, they ruled with a measure of independence until

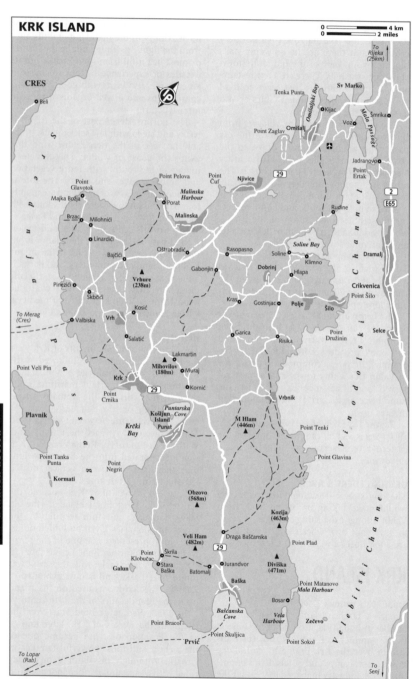

KRK ISLAND

0 — 4 km
0 — 2 miles

CRES

Beli

S

To
Rijeka
(25km)

Tenka Punta

Sv Marko

Kijac

Smrika

Omišaljski Bay

Voz

Point Zaglav

Omišalj

Mala Passage

Jadranovo

Point
Ertak

Point Pelova

Point
Čuf

Njivice

29

2

E65

Rudine

Point
Glavotok

*Malinska
Harbour*

Majka Božja

Porat

Malinska

S

Brzac

Milohnići

Linardići

Oštrobradić

Rasopasno

Soline

Soline Bay

Dramalj

Bajčić

Gabonjin

Dobrinj

Klimno

Hlapa

Vrhure
(238m)

Crikvenica

Pirieziči

Kras

Gostinjac

Polje

Point Šilo

Šilo

To Merag
(Cres)

Skbčiči

Kosić

Garica

Selce

Valbiska

Vrh

Salatić

Point
Družinin

Risika

P

Point Veli Pin

Lakmartin

Mihovilov
(180m)

Muraj

Vrbnik

Plavnik

Krk

29

Point
Crnika

Kornić

*Puntarska
Cove*

Košljun
Island
Punat

M Hlam
(446m)

Point Tenki

Point Glavina

a

s

s

a

g

e

Point Tanka
Punta

Kormati

Point
Negrit

*Krčki
Bay*

Obzovo
(568m)

Kozija
(463m)

Point Plad

Point Veli Pin

Veli Ham
(482m)

Draga Baščanska

29

Diviška
(471m)

Point Matanovo

Mala Harbour

Point
Klobučac

Škrila

Galun

Stara
Baška

Batomalj

Jurandvor

Baška

Bosar

Zečevo

*Baščanska
Cove*

*Vela
Harbour*

To Lopar
(Rab)

Point Bracol

Point Škuljica

Prvić

Point Sokol

To
Senj

Vinodolski Channel

Velebitski Channel

Mala Passage

KVARNER REGION

1480, when the last member of the line put the island under the protection of Venice. Venetian rule was painful for the island, its male residents forced into service as oarsmen on Venetian galleys and its oak trees felled to build Venetian ships.

Although tourism is the dominant activity on the island, there are two shipyards in Punat and Krk for small-ship repairs and some agriculture and fishing. Vineyards surround Vrbnik and lamb from the island's sheep is especially tasty. Fishermen still ply the sea and olive oil production remains strong, exploiting the groves around Punat, Krk, Malinska and Njivice.

Getting There & Away

The ferry between Baška and Lopar (31KN) on Rab Island operates from June to September two to five times daily, but between October and May there is no service.

About 14 buses a day travel between Rijeka and Krk town, stopping at Omišalj, Njivice, Malinska and Punat. Eleven continue on to Baška and two to Vrbnik (15 minutes). There are four daily buses from Zagreb which make most of the same stops as the Rijeka bus. To go from Krk to the islands of Cres and Lošinj, change buses at Malinska for the Lošinj-bound bus that comes from Rijeka, but check the times carefully as the connection only works once or twice a day.

The Krk bridge links the northern part of the island with the mainland and a regular car ferry links Valbiska with Merag on Cres Island (10KN).

Getting Around

Bus connections between towns are frequent because the many buses to and from Rijeka pick up passengers in all the island's main towns.

KRK TOWN

On the southwestern coast of the island is the town of Krk on Krčki Bay. The medieval walled town has expanded to include a port, beaches, camping grounds and hotels dotted around the surrounding coves and hills. The harbour can get crowded in the summer, but the real attraction is the narrow streets that weave around the Romanesque cathedral and a 15th-century castle.

Krk was already settled by the time of the Roman occupation; the Romans built walls around the town and baths with an underground heating system called a hypocaust. Some walls are still visible but the baths were later covered with the cathedral and are inaccessible.

You won't need more than a couple of hours to see the sights in town but, from a base in Krk town, it's easy to hop on a bus to other island towns or take a boat trip around the island.

Orientation

The bus station (no left-luggage office) is on the harbour, only a few minutes' walk north to the historic town centre, which is the nucleus of a modern residential district. Most hotels are east of the town centre past Drašica Cove's small sandy beach and pine forest.

For information on getting to and from Krk town, see left.

Information

You can change money at any travel agency or at the post office.

Aurea (☎ 222 277; www.aurea-krk.hr; Pupačića 1) This travel agency finds private accommodation and books excursions.

Autotrans (☎ 222 661; krk@autotrans.hr) The best and most conveniently placed travel agency is in the bus station. It finds private accommodation, changes money, sells international bus tickets and is a good source of information.

Post Office (Ognjana Price) You can change money and get cash advances on your credit cards.

Riječka Banka (Trg Josip Jelačića) It has an ATM.

Tourist Office (Turistička Zajednica; ☎ /fax 221 414; tz@tz-krk.hr; Vela Placa 1; ☺ 8am-3pm Mon-Fri) It is in the city wall's Guard Tower and has some brochures, but the travel agencies will have more specific practical information about accommodation, excursions etc.

Sights

On the site of a 6th-century early-Christian basilica, the present **Krk Cathedral** (Katedrala; A Mahnića; ☺ 9.30am-1pm) began being built in the 13th century and finished with a 16th-century bell tower. The cathedral's early-Christian origins are apparent in a carving of two birds eating a fish on the first column next to the apse (the fish is an early-Christian symbol of Christ and Christians were often represented as birds). The left nave features the Frankopan Chapel dating from the 15th century, with the coats of arms of the Frankopan princes. In the chapel at the end of the right nave, notice *The Entombment* by Pordenone.

Although the cathedral is only open for Mass, you can enter the adjoining **St Quirinus** (Sveti Kvirin) from a side entrance that looks out over the cathedral. The **church museum** (A Mahnića; admission 5KN; ⏱ 9.30am-1pm) has a collection of Italian paintings from the 16th and 17th centuries and a silver altarpiece of the Madonna from 1477.

The fortified **Kaštel** on the edge of town, with a round tower and three gates, is a Venetian structure from around the 15th or 16th century. The castle is now used as an open-air theatre for summer concerts. The **Franciscan monastery** northwest of the harbour is closed to the public, but nearby you can see remains of the Roman walls. Other interesting sites include the **Galeria Fortis** (☎ 221 695; Vitezića 1; admission free; ⏱ 9.30am-1pm & 6-10pm Mon-Sat, 6-11pm Sun) with its small collection of objects from the Roman era including amphorae, pottery, tools and tablets.

Activities

A number of outfits organise scuba-diving trips around the island and especially to the nearby island of Plavnik. Try **Diving Centre Krk** (☎ 222 563; www.fundivingkrk.de; Braće Juras 3). Popular dive sites include a sunken Greek cargo vessel, an underwater cave near Vrbnik and, in particular, the red coral on the vertical walls around Plavnik Island.

Festivals & Events

In July and August the **Krk Summer Festival** presents concerts, plays and dances in the Kaštel. The town celebrates its patron saint, Sveti Kvirin, on 4 July, with music and processions.

Sleeping

There are three camping grounds and a range of hotel options in and around Krk, but many places only open for the summer. Most hotels are handled by the agency **Hoteli Krk** (www.hotelikrk.com) and are located in a large complex east of the town centre. There's a 30% single supplement.

Veli Jože (☎/fax 220 212; damir.dugandzija@sb.ht net.hr; Vitezića 32; dm 145KN) This comfortable hostel is in a spruced-up older building and has a restaurant that turns out pizza, pasta, fish and an array of vegetarian dishes.

Autocamp Ježevac (☎ 221081; jezevac@zlatni-oto .hr; Plavnića bb; per adult/site 35/45KN; ⏱ mid-Apr–mid-Oct) Situated on the coast, this is the closest camping ground to Krk town (a 10-minute walk southwest). The rocky soil makes it nearly impossible to use tent pegs, but there are lots of stones to anchor your lines. The ground offers good, shady sites and places to swim.

Camping Bor (☎ 221 581; fax 222 429; Crikvenička bb; per adult/site 30/40KN) This ground is on a hill inland from Ježevac and is about 600m from the sea.

Politin FKK (☎ 221 351; fax 221 246; per adult/site 35/45KN; ⏱ Apr-Sep) This is a naturist camping ground southeast of Krk, just beyond the large resort hotels.

Marina (☎ 221 357; fax 221 128; Obala Hrvatske Mornarice 6; d 600KN) This is the most centrally located hotel with views over the harbour, but the rooms don't amount to much, especially given the price.

Hotel Lovorka (☎ 665 755; fax 221 022; Ružmarinska 6; d 790KN; Ⓟ Ⓧ Ⓡ) It has recently been completely refurbished and is comfortable if not particularly charming.

Dražica (☎ 655 755; fax 221 022; Ružmarinska 6; d 880 KN; Ⓟ Ⓧ Ⓡ) Nearby and in the same development as Hotel Lovorka, the Dražica has a café and restaurant and somewhat more lavish rooms.

Koralj (☎/fax 221 044; www.zlatni-otok.hr; Vlade Tomašića bb; d 550KN; Ⓟ) If you can do without air-con, this is the nicest option and it's located on a peaceful cove about 500m northeast of the town centre.

PRIVATE ROOMS

Krk-Info (☎ 222 222; www.multilink/hr/quanarius; Nikolića 34) and the agencies listed on p115 will find private accommodation. Prices are fixed by the tourist association and range from 270KN to 300KN for a double room with a private bathroom.

Eating

Konobo Nono (☎ 222 221; Krčkih iseljenika 8; mains 35-50KN) This is a delightful place with a spacious, rustic interior and an outdoor terrace. It offers a range of local specialities such as *šurlice*, which is home-made noodles topped with goulash (45KN), as well as grilled fish and meat dishes.

Galeb (☎ 221 261; Obala Hrvatske Mornarice 3; mains from 35KN) This is a popular, inexpensive

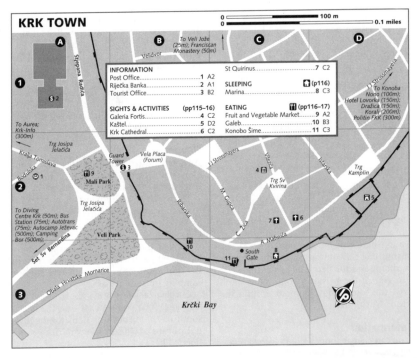

KRK TOWN

INFORMATION	
Post Office.............................1 A2	
Riječka Banka........................2 A1	
Tourist Office........................3 B2	

SIGHTS & ACTIVITIES	(pp115–16)
Galeria Fortis........................4 C2	
Kaštel...................................5 D2	
Krk Cathedral.......................6 C2	

St Quirinus...........................7 C2	

SLEEPING	(p116)
Marina..................................8 C3	

EATING	(pp116–17)
Fruit and Vegetable Market....9 A2	
Galeb....................................10 B3	
Konobo Šime.........................11 C3	

To Veli Jože (25m); Franciscan Monastery (50m)

To Konoba Nono (100m); Hotel Lovorka (150m); Dražica (150m); Korali (200m); Politin FKK (300m)

To Aurea; Krk-Info (300m)

To Diving Centre Krk (50m); Bus Station (75m); Autotrans (75m); Autocamp Ježevac (500m); Camping Bor (500m)

Krčki Bay

pizzeria with a large open-air terrace on the harbour. It's a great place to linger and people-watch.

Konoba Šime (☎ 221 426; Obala Hrvatske Mornarice; mains from 40KN) For a quick bite, head to this popular restaurant by the harbour. It has a medieval, cave-like interior and serves a good selection of drinks and snacks.

There's a daily fruit and vegetable market outside the western walls, which also sells bread, pastry, pizza, fast food and roast chicken. You can pick up picnic supplies at the large, modern supermarket across from the bus station, or at the supermarket on JJ Strossmayera in the old town.

VRBNIK

This enchanting medieval village of steep, arched streets is perched on a cliff overlooking the sea. It was once the centre of the Glagolitic language and repository for many Glagolitic manuscripts. The language was kept alive by priests, who were always plentiful in the town since many young men entered the priesthood to avoid serving on Venetian galleys.

Now the town is a good place to sample the Žlahtina wine produced in the surrounding region. After strolling the streets and admiring the view you can descend to the town beach for some swimming.

Restaurant Nada (☎ 857 065; Glavača 22; mains from 55KN) has a bar for wine tasting, as well as a cosy cave-like restaurant to sample excellent seafood specialities. It's worth a trip to Vrbnik just to eat here.

Only two buses a day travel the 12km to Vrbnik, making it tricky to organiseas a day trip unless you have your own wheels.

BAŠKA

pop 816 / postcode 51523

At the southern end of Krk Island, Baška is a popular resort with a 2km-long pebbly beach set below a high ridge. The swimming and scenery are better here than at Krk town, and there are a number of hiking trails leading up to the surrounding mountains.

Dating back to the Roman era, the original settlement was erected on a hill overlooking the northeastern corner of town,

KVARNER REGION

now the site of the Sveti Ivan church. The old settlement was burned in 1380 by the Venetians in the course of a battle. In 1525 a new settlement was begun closer to the sea, marked today by rows of houses with interconnected façades. These 16th-century houses are well preserved, despite the shops and small businesses installed in many of the ground floors. Although crowded in summer, the old town and harbour make a pleasant stroll and there's always that splendid beach.

Orientation

The town lies at the northern end of Baška Draga Bay, encircled by a dramatic, barren range of mountains. The bus from Krk stops at the top of a hill on the edge of the old town, between the beach and the harbour (there's no left-luggage office). The main street is Zvonimirova, overlooking the harbour, and the beach begins at the western end of the harbour, continuing south past the tourist development around the Hotel Corinthia.

Information

You can change money at any travel agency.
PDM Guliver (☎ 856 004; www.pdm-guliver.hr; Zvonimirova 98) Finds private accommodation and changes money.
Post Office (cnr Prilaz Kupalistu & Zdenke Čermakove) You can withdraw cash on MasterCard and Diners Club.
Primaturist (☎ 856 132; www.primaturist.hr; Zvonimirova 98) Finds accommodation and is a good source of information.
Riječka Banka (Zvonimirova) Next to the tourist office; there's an ATM.
Tourist Office (☎ 856 544; www.tz-baska.hr; Zvonimirova 114; ☯ 8am-8pm daily mid-Jun–Sep & 8am-3pm Mon-Fri Oct-May) It is just down the street from the bus stop.

Sights & Activities

The tourist office provides a good free map of marked hiking trails throughout the southern tip of the island. Several popular trails begin around Camping Zablaće, including an 8km walk to **Stara Baška**, a restful little village on a bay surrounded by stark, salt-washed limestone hills.

Another short 2.5km route leads to **St Lucy church** (Sveti Lucija; Jurandvor; admission 10KN; ☯ 8am-noon & 2-8pm), where the 11th-century Baška tablet was found. You can see a replica as the original is now in the Archaeological

Museum in Zagreb. The church was built at the end of the 9th century by Benedictine monks on the site of a Roman villa. In addition to a great view, you'll see ruins of the former monastery, which was abandoned at the end of the 15th century.

A trail from the naturist camp leads east to the remains of the ancient Illyrian settlement of **Bosar** (Corinthia) between the Vela Luka and Mala Luka Bays.

Sleeping

All hotels are in the 'tourist settlement', about 1km southwest of town, and are managed by **Hoteli Baška** (☎ 656 801; www.hotelibaska.hr).

During July and August, it is essential to arrange accommodation well in advance as the town is swarming with Austrian, German and Czech tourists. Hotel space is booked solid for the summer season by late spring, and accommodation is tight in the shoulder season as well. There are two camping options at Baška.

Camping Zablaće (☎ 856 909; fax 856 604; per adult/site 40/50KN; ☯ May-Sep) It's on the beach southwest of the bus stop (look for the rows of caravans). In heavy rain you risk getting flooded here.

FKK Camp Bunculuka (☎ 856 806; fax 856 595; per adult/site 40/50KN; ☯ May-Sep) This quiet, shady naturist camping ground is a 15-minute walk over the hill east of the harbour.

Hotel Zvonimir (☎ 656 111; fax 856 584; Emilia Geistlicha 34; s/d 625/985KN; P ☒) This four-star hotel on the beach has recently been renovated. The rooms are soothingly furnished and modern, even if the exterior is a charmless arrangement of angles and concrete.

Hotel Corinthia (☎ 656 111; fax 856 584; Emilia Geistlicha 34; s 450-535KN, d 670-790KN; P ☒) Another vast tourist complex offering rooms at a variety of price and comfort levels. For the extra money you get sea views, plus slightly more décor.

Villas Corinthia (☎ 656 111; fax 856 584; Emilia Geistlicha 34; apt from 1060KN; P) Near the hotel is this 10-unit complex offering two comfortable apartments per building. The apartments are spacious and well outfitted with TVs and modern bathrooms.

PRIVATE ROOMS

PDM Guliver and Primaturist arrange for private accommodation at about the same rate as in Krk town.

If you come in July or August, you may find it impossible to rent a room for less than four nights, a single room or a room near town. Plan ahead.

PUNAT

pop 1696 / postcode 51521
Eight kilometres southeast of Krk town, Punat has replaced its traditional shipbuilding industry with the task of tending to the many yachts that descend upon the port each summer. Although the town is not as attractive as Krk or Baška, the presence of several camping grounds and a youth hostel makes it a good alternative place to stay.

Orientation

The bus drops you off at the southern end of town close to several hotels.

Information

Marina Tours Travel Agency (☎ 854 375; marina-tours@marina-punat.hr; Obala 81) Changes money and finds private accommodation.
Post Office (Obala 81)
Punat Tours Travel Agency (☎ 854 104; punattours@ri.htnet.hr; Obala 94) Changes money and finds private accommodation.
Riječka Banka (Obala 85) There's an ATM here.
Turistička Zajednica (☎ /fax 854 970; www.tzpunat .hr; Obala 72; 8am-noon & 2-6pm Mon-Sat, 8am-3pm Sun Jul & Aug, 8am-3pm Mon- Fri & 8am-1pm Sat) A good source of free town maps and brochures.

Sleeping

Punat has a couple of camping grounds, a youth hostel and rather uninteresting hotels. The travel agencies above find private accommodation for about the same price as in Krk town.
Camping Pila (☎ 854 122; fax 854 020; per adult/site 38/70KN; Apr–mid-Oct) This camping ground occupies a large area just south of the town centre, only a few minutes' walk from the bus stop.
FKK Konobe (☎ 854 036; per adult/site 38/70KN; Apr–mid-Oct) The FKK Konobe is a naturist camping ground in the same direction as Camping Pila, about 3km down the coast.
Youth Hostel (☎ 854 037; fax 434 962; Novi Put 8; dm 110KN; mid-Jun–mid-Sep) Although it offers breakfast you're close enough to town to grab some coffee and a pastry in a local café. Its rooms are clean and neat and it has a bouncy, international ambience. The

90-bed hostel is often booked by groups so it's wise to reserve ahead.
Park (☎ 854 024; fax 854 101; Obala 102; d 815KN) Within the white, box-like buildings are tidy, modern rooms with TVs and phones. The hotel complex includes two buildings and is at the southern end of town near the bus stop and the beach.

AROUND PUNAT
Košljun Island Monastery

Perhaps the best reason to pay a visit to Punat is the monastery on Košljun Island. Only a 20-minute boat ride from Punat, the tiny island contains a 16th-century **Franciscan monastery** (☎ 854 017; admission 15KN; 9.30am-6.30pm Mon-Sat) built on the site of a 12th-century Benedictine abbey. The monastery church contains a large, appropriately chilling *Last Judgment*, painted in 1653, as well as several other religious paintings.

The monastery also contains a museum displaying other paintings, an ethnographic collection and a rare copy of Ptolemy's *Atlas* printed in Venice in the late 16th century. Concerts are sometimes held in the summer. After visiting the monastery, take time to stroll around the forested island.

Although agencies in Krk town organise excursions to Košljun, it's cheaper to take one of the frequent buses to Punat and then one of the taxi boats from the harbour (20KN return, six per day).

RAB ISLAND

Rab (Arbe in Italian), near the centre of the Kvarner island group, is the most enticing island in the northern Adriatic. The more densely populated southwest is green with pine forests and dotted with sandy beaches and coves. High mountains protect Rab's interior from cold northeast winds, allowing olives, grapes and vegetables to be cultivated. The Lopar Peninsula in the northeast corner is a fertile oasis offering the island's best beaches along its two wide bays. The northwest peninsula, which emerges from Supetarska Draga, is fringed with coves and lagoons that continue on to the Kalifront Peninsula and the Suha Punta resort.

The cultural and historical centre of the island is Rab town, characterised by four elegant bell towers rising from the ancient stone streets. The island has a strong tourist business, but outside of July and August you'll find it lively without being overrun with visitors.

History

Like much of the Adriatic, Rab was first inhabited by the Illyrian Liburnian tribe before it was occupied by the Romans in the 2nd century BC. Defensive towers and walls protected the settlement and the Romans built country villas and naval bases. With the division of the Roman Empire, Rab came under Byzantine rule in the 9th century.

In the 10th century, Byzantium and the Croatian king Tomislav made a deal which acknowledged Croatian sovereignty over the island, but the rising power of Venice forced Byzantium and then the Croatian-Hungarian kings to gradually allow increasing Venetian influence in Rab.

In 1409, Rab was sold to Venice along with Dalmatia and remained under Venetian rule until 1797. Farming, fishing, vineyards and salt production were the economic mainstays, but most income from these activities ended up in Venice. The inhabitants succeeded in wresting some political autonomy from Venice, but class divisions prevented the islanders from fighting their way out of poverty. Two plague epidemics in the 15th century nearly wiped out the population and brought the economy to a standstill. The Turkish penetration of Bosnia in the 15th century forced many Slavs to migrate to Rab, which placed further economic pressure on the island and increased the division between the Italianised elite and Slav commoners.

When Venice fell, there was a short period of Austrian rule until the French arrived in 1805. After the fall of Napoleon in 1813, Rab became part of the Austrian territories. The Austrians favoured the Italianised elite and it was not until 1897 that Croatian was made an 'official' language. After the fall of Austria in 1918, Rab eventually became part of the Kingdom of Yugoslavia. The island was occupied by Italian troops in 1941 and by the Germans in 1944, and it was liberated in 1945.

The tourism industry that began gearing up at the turn of the 20th century was a godsend for the impoverished island. Even during the 1990s war, Rab managed to hold on to its German tourists, which is not surprising considering the hospitality of the people and the beauty of the island. Rab would be the perfect stepping stone between Krk Island and Zadar, if only the boat transport connections were more convenient.

Getting There & Away

The ferry between Baška on Krk Island and Lopar (31KN, one hour) operates between June and September from two to five times daily, but between October and May there's no service. There's a daily catamaran service between Rijeka and Rab from June to September (40KN, two hours) and a car ferry three times a week between October and May running from Rijeka to Rab (40KN, two hours) and on to Mali Lošinj from where you can get a boat to Zadar.

The most reliable way to come and go is on one of the two daily buses between Rab and Rijeka (87KN, 2½ hours). In the high season there are two direct buses from Zagreb to Rab (143KN, five hours). These services can fill up, so book ahead if possible. There's no direct bus from Rab to Zadar, but there are two daily buses that connect at Senj with Rijeka buses travelling to Zadar (114KN, five hours). In order to avoid backtracking from Senj to Jablanac, and also to save some kuna, you can take the bus to the highway at Jablanac, wait for about 1½ hours and catch the Rijeka bus as it heads to Zadar (83KN).

If you have your own car, there are nonstop ferries in July and August from Jablanac on the mainland to Mišnjak on the southeastern corner of Rab, and frequent ferries throughout the year.

Getting Around

In addition to island tours operated from Rab town (see p123), there's a water-taxi service between Rab town and Suha Punta resort that operates four times a day in July and August (25KN), leaving from the front of the Hotel Istra and the Hotel Padova.

From Lopar to Rab town (12km) there are nine buses daily in either direction (11KN); some are timed to meet the Baška–Lopar ferry. There are eight daily buses from Rab town to Kampor (15 minutes), eight to Barbat (20 minutes) and five to Suha Punta (25 minutes).

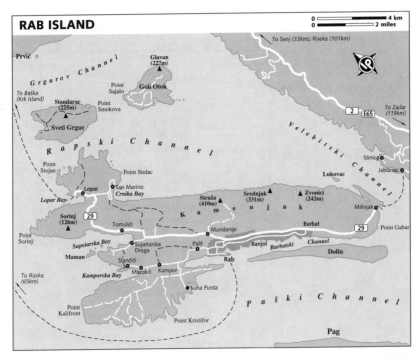

RAB ISLAND

0 _____ 4 km
0 _____ 2 miles

To Senj (33km); Rijeka (101km)

Prvić

Grgurov Channel

Glavan (227m) ▲

Goli Otok

Point Sajalo

To Baška (Krk Island)

Standarac (225m) ▲

Point Smokova

Point Stojan

Sveti Grgur

Rapski Channel

Velebitski Channel

Stinica

Lukovac

Jablanac

To Zadar (119km)

2 E65

Point Stolac

Lopar

San Marino

Crnika Bay

Lopar Bay

Straža (410m) ▲

Srednjak (331m) ▲

Zvonici (242m) ▲

Mišnjak

Sorinj (126m) ▲

29

Tomulići

Kamenjak

Mundanije

Barbat

29 Point Gabar

Point Sorinj

Supetarska Bay

Supetarska Draga

Palit

Banjol

Barbatski Channel

Dolin

Maman

Stančići

Macolići

Kampor

Rab

Kamporska Bay

To Rijeka (65km)

Suha Punta

Point Kalifront

Point Kristifor

Paški Channel

Pag

RAB TOWN

pop 592 / postcode 51280

Medieval Rab town has a unique and instantly recognisable look. Crowded onto a narrow peninsula, four bell towers rise like exclamation points over the red-roofed stone buildings. The steep streets that climb up from the harbour cross a series of richly endowed churches to reach lovely lookout points. Wandering the narrow old roads interspersed with shady parks is a pure joy and the churches often host concerts and art exhibitions. When you get 'churched out', there are excursion boats to whisk you off to beaches and coves around the island.

History

The oldest part of town is Kaldanac on the southeastern tip of the peninsula, which was settled before the Roman conquest. In the 14th and 15th centuries the town expanded to include the Varoš section, further north, and, as an important military outpost for the Venetians, it became surrounded by defensive walls, some of which are still visible today. Trg Municipium Arba divides the two sections and you'll notice a difference in architectural styles.

Orientation

The old town lies directly across the bay from the marina. Narrow side streets climb up from the main north–south streets – Donja, Srednja and Gornja ulica, literally, lower, middle and upper roads.

A five-minute walk north of the old town is the new commercial centre with Merkur department store, some travel agencies and the bus station. Despite a sign at the bus station advertising a left-luggage office, it's not operational because the station is only open limited hours. The northwestern portion of the peninsula is given over to the 100-year-old Komrčar Park, bordered by the town's beaches. There are also beaches around the hotel and Autocamp Padova, but you'll find better swimming further from town.

Information

INTERNET ACCESS

Digital X (☎ 777 010; Donja ulica bb; per hour 20KN; ⏰ 10am-2pm & 6pm-1am Mon-Fri, 6pm-1am Sat)

RAB TOWN

0 ————————— 100 m
0 ————————— 0.1 miles

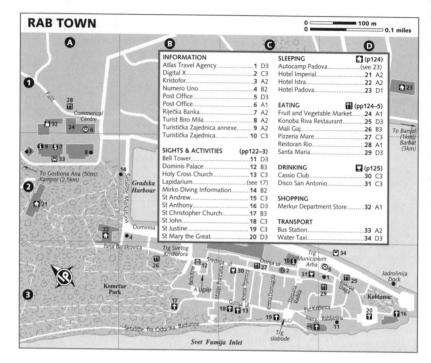

MONEY

Rijecka Banka (Commercial Centre) Changes money and has an ATM.

POST

Post Office (Commercial Centre; Trg Municipium Arba) You can get cash advances on your MasterCard or Diners Club card at either branch.

TOURIST INFORMATION

Turisticka Zajednica (☎ 771 111; www.tzg-rab.hr; Donja Ulica 2; ☒ 8am-noon & 7-9pm Oct-May, 8am-10pm Jun-Sep) It's the head office of the tourist association and there's an annexe around the corner from the bus station, opposite Merkur department store.

TRAVEL AGENCIES

Atlas Travel Agency (☎ 724 585; www.atlas-rab.com; Trg Municipium Arba; ☒ 8am-1pm Mon-Sat Oct-May, 8am-10pm Jun-Sep)

Kristofor (☎ 725 543; www.kristofor.hr; Palit bb) Next to the bus station, this friendly and efficient agency finds private accommodation, changes money, rents boats and scooters and is a good source of information.

Numero Uno (☎ /fax 724 688; numero-uno@ri.htnet .hr; Dominisa 5) Opposite Hotel Istra.

Turist Biro Mila (☎ 725 499; www.mila.hr; Palit 68) At the southeastern corner of the bus station, this is a helpful agency.

Sights

Most of Rab's famous churches and towers are along Gornja ulica, the upper road that continues on as Ivana Rablianina in the Kaldanac section. Unless otherwise indicated the churches are open only for Mass but, even when churches are closed, most have metal grates over the front door, through which you can glimpse the interior.

Start your walk from Trg Svetog Kristofora near the harbour. In the centre of the square is a **fountain** with sculptures of the two legendary figures Kalifront and Draga. According to the story, the passionate Kalifront attempted to seduce the shepherdess Draga, who had taken a vow of chastity. The goddess to whom Draga had pledged chastity turned her into stone to save her from the seducer.

Go up Bobotine and pause at the corner of Srednja ulica to admire the **Dominis Palace** on the left. Built at the end of the 15th century for a prominent patrician family, the façade has decorated Renaissance windows and a striking portal decorated with the family coat of arms. Continue to the top and the **St Christopher Church** (Crkva Sveti Kristofor; 7.30-9pm Jun & Sep, 9am-noon & 7.30-10pm Jul & Aug) was part of the highest tower of the ramparts. Next to it is a **lapidarium** (admission 5KN; 9am-1pm & 6-8pm). From the tower a passage leads to Komrčar Park.

Continuing south along Gornja ulica, you'll come to the ruins of the church of **St John** (Sveti Ivan), which probably dates to the beginning of the 7th century. Little survives but the 13th-century bell tower next to it, which can be climbed. The church was part of a monastery that was occupied by Benedictine nuns in the 11th century, Franciscans from 1298 to 1783, and was later converted into a bishop's residence. Next to the bell tower is the 16th-century **Holy Cross church** (Sveti Križa; 7.30-9pm Jun & Sep, 9am-noon & 7.30-10pm Jul & Aug), which was briefly called the Church of the Weeping Cross after a legend circulated that Christ wept on the church's cross because of the immorality of the town's residents.

Further along Gornja ulica is **St Justine church** (Sveti Justina; 7.30-9pm Jun & Sep, 9am-noon & 7.30-10pm Jul & Aug) with a bell tower dating from 1572. Today the church hosts a collection of religious artefacts including a portable altar donated to the town by King Koloman, fragments of the illuminated evangelism from the 11th century and the silver-plated reliquary for the head of St Christopher. There's also a polyptych by Paolo Veneziano and a Renaissance terracotta of the Madonna from the 15th century.

Pass Trg Slobode bearing right and on your right you'll see the Romanesque **bell tower** of the church of **St Andrew** (Sveti Andrije), which dates from 1181. The biggest tower is coming up on the right. The cathedral of **St Mary the Great** (Sveta Marija Velika; 724 195; 10am-1pm & 7.30-10pm) and its bell tower were built in the 12th century. The 25m-tall tower stands on the remains of Roman buildings and is divided into four floors, terminating in an octagonal pyramid surrounded by a Romanesque balustrade. The pyramid is topped by a cross with five small globes and reliquaries of several saints were placed in the highest globe. The symmetrical arrangement of windows and

arches creates a wonderful sense of lightness and harmony that makes the tower one of the most beautiful on the Croatian coast. You can climb it for a small fee.

The extreme end of the cape accommodates a monastery of Franciscan nuns and the baroque church of **St Anthony** (Sveti Antun; Gornja ulica) built in 1675. The altar is decorated with 17th-century inlaid marble and a painting of St Anthony.

Activities

From behind the Hotel Istra, there's a marked hiking trail that leads northeast to the top of Sveti Ilija (100m). It only takes about 30 minutes and the view is great.

Kristofor travel agency (p122) rents motorboats, starting at about 400KN a day depending on size, as well as scooters for 220KN per day. You can rent bicycles at the Hotel Padova. You can arrange to scuba dive for about 120KN per dive from the **Mirko Diving Information office** (098 903 8060; Šetalište Markatuma) in town but the company's boats leave from its **main office** (/fax 721 154; Barbat).

Tours

Atlas and other travel agencies offer day tours of the island by boat, which include plenty of swim stops around the island and at nearby Sveti Grgur Island. In summer, tourist agencies offer day excursions to Lošinj or Pag Island once or twice a week.

Festivals & Events

Rab has revived the crossbow competitions that date from its early history. Residents are becoming increasingly practised at the skill and are proud to demonstrate it on several national and local holidays – they don't even seem to mind dressing up in tunics, plumed hats and tights for the occasion. **Sveti Kristofor Day** is 27 July, when the town's patron saint is celebrated with crossbow competitions and local dances.

The **Assumption** celebration on 15 August is another good opportunity to see the crossbow competitors, and they make another appearance on the **Croatian National Day** of 29 May. Rab's **Musical Evenings** take place from June to September and revolve around the Thursday-night concerts (9pm) in the Holy Cross church. Tickets costs between 25KN and 50KN depending on the artist.

NAKED ON THE BEACH

Naturism in Croatia enjoys a long and venerable history, beginning on Rab Island around the turn of the 20th century. Its reputation as a health centre in the Austro-Hungarian empire coincided with the rise of the German physical culture (körperkultur) movement which held that frolicking naked in the outdoors was a sign of physical and mental health. Hotels that were treating Europeans for heart and respiratory ailments soon began setting aside beds for naturists.

Austrian Richard Ehrmann opened the first naturist camp on Paradise Beach, near Lopar, in 1934 but the real founders of Adriatic naturism were Edward VIII and Wallis Simpson, who were allowed to skinny dip in Kandalora Bay in 1934. Near the Suha Punta resort complex, the bay is now nicknamed 'English Bay'.

The naturist business in Croatia took off in the 1960s with the transformation of Koversada, near Vrsar, into a totally nude islet in 1961. The naturist colony spread to the nearby coast and soon nude resorts began opening up all along the coast. There are now 20 officially naturist camping grounds that also offer some 5300 beds in apartments or on-site hotels. In addition to the sprawling naturist camps (marked 'FKK'), there are innumerable coves and inlets given over to clusters of naturists. Partly because of the influence of the Catholic Church, Croats make up only a minuscule percentage of nude bathers but they remain remarkably tolerant of the naked guests. Still, there are a few rules you should respect:

■ Nudism is generally frowned upon when within view of a town or village.

■ Some naturist swimming areas are 'clothing optional'; others do not encourage clothing at all.

■ Families are accepted at all naturist centres but single men are usually required to show the International Naturist Federation members card.

For more details, see www.cronatur.com.

Sleeping

Everything from camping to expensive hotels can be found in and around Rab town. Hotels are all in the mid-range level with nothing too basic and nothing that could be called luxurious. Most hotels and camping grounds are managed by **Imperial** (www.imperial.hr).

Autocamp Padova (☎ 724 355; Banjol; per adult/tent 67/45KN; ☻ Apr-Oct) To sleep cheap, carry your tent around the bay and walk south along the waterfront for about 25 minutes to this camping ground.

Hotel Imperial (☎ 724 522; imperial@imperial.hr; Palit bb; s/d 330/470KN; ℗) Set back from the town in a wooded park, the lush green surroundings do a lot to mitigate the white, charmless exterior.

Hotel Istra (☎ 724 134; fax 724 050; M de Dominisa bb; s/d 370/660KN; ℗) It's a cheery yellow building right on the edge of town with sweetly decorated rooms.

Hotel Padova (☎ 724 444; padova@imperial.hr; Banjol bb; s/d 625/890KN; ℗ ☒ ☒) Lying across the bay, this is an oversized concrete hotel but the facilities are good. You can even sweat it out in a sauna if you wish.

PRIVATE ROOMS

The travel agencies (p122) can organise private rooms, with prices beginning at 60KN per person in a double room. There are plenty of them to go around although the selection in the town centre is limited. You can also rent a studio for 250KN a night and some agencies forgo the surcharges when things are slow.

Eating

Rab cuisine revolves around fresh fish, seafood and pasta. The quality and prices are generally uniform – you'll pay 80KN to 100KN for a complete meal.

Pizzeria Mare (☎ 771 315; Srednja Ulica 8; mains from 25KN) It's reputed to be the best pizza place in town, which would explain why it's often crowded.

Restoran Rio (☎ 725 645; Palit 57; mains from 35KN) There is a fish theme in the décor and the menu, but the meat is good and there's a pleasant terrace.

Konoba Riva Restaurant (☎ 725 887; Biskupa Draga 3; mains 45-60KN) The Riva has a particularly atmospheric stone interior and a terrace with a sea view.

Mali Gaj (☎ 724 279; Jurja Barakovića 3; mains from 60KN) This is another popular seafood/pasta place situated on the edge of Komrčar Park.

Gostiona Ana (☎ 724 376, Krstinić 6; mains from 55KN) A little away from the tourist trail, this classy place serves up an array of dishes from simple pizza (from 33KN) to excellent seafood platters.

Santa Maria (☎ 724 196; Dinka Dakulo 6; mains from 50KN) The unusual interior of Santa Maria is decked out with wooden tables and benches and there's an upstairs terrace with a sea view. The speciality here is meat although there are also some fish dishes.

There's a good supermarket in the basement of the Merkur department store for picnic supplies, and a fruit and vegetable market in the Commercial Centre on Trg Municipium Arba.

Drinking

Disco San Antonio (☎ 724 145; Trg Municipium Arba) Situated behind Trg Municipium Arba, this is the most popular disco in town.

Cassio Club (☎ 098 369 087; Srednja ul bb) This is a much more intimate club than Disco San Antonio, with cosy banquettes and a small dance floor.

AROUND RAB TOWN

The **Franciscan Monastery of St Euphemia** (Samostan svete Fumije; ☎ 724 951; Kampor; admission 5KN; ꙮ 9am-noon & 3-5pm Jun & Sep, 10am-noon & 4-6pm Jul & Aug) is about 3km southwest of town in Kampor. It's a peaceful spot, usually deserted, but worth the walk for the Gothic church of St Bernardin. The painted ceiling is ethereal, a stark contrast to the agony depicted on the late-Gothic wooden crucifix. Note also the 15th-century polyptych by the Vivarini brothers.

LOPAR

The ferry from Baška lands at Lopar, but the ferry stop is the least attractive part of the peninsula, which is marked by beautiful coves, bays and hamlets. There are 22 sandy beaches bordered by pine groves around Lopar, and the shallow sea makes them perfect for small children. Lopar Bay is on one side of the peninsula and Crnika Bay is on the other. The northeastern part of the peninsula is steep and barren, with many naturist beaches.

Orientation & Information

The 1500m-long **Paradise Beach** (Rajska Plaša) lies 3km south of the ferry landing on Crnika Bay. The road between the ferry landing and the San Marino Hotel and autocamp on Crnika Bay passes a small commercial centre and several restaurants.

There is a **tourist office** (Turistička Zajednica; ☎ 775 508; www.lopar.com; Commercial Centre; ꙮ 8am-8pm Mon-Sat & 8am-1pm Sun Jul & Aug, 8am-5pm Mon-Fri Sep-Jun).

Sleeping

For private accommodation, go to **Dedan Tours** (☎ 775 105; fax 775 185; Commercial Centre), which has rooms for about the same price as you would pay in Rab town. There are also some houses with *sobe* (rooms available) signs along the road.

Camping San Marino (☎ 775 133; fax 775 290; adults/tent 40/50KN; ꙮ Apr-Oct) San Marino is among pine groves on the wide swath of sandy beach, called Paradise Beach. It's large (3600 places) and can get crowded in the summer, but the setting is unbeatable.

San Marino Hotel (☎ 775 149; san-marino@imperial .hr; Paradise Beach; s/d 400/685KN; ℗) This has the usual package-tour ambience but the location makes up for the dreary architecture.

BARBAT

Barbat is the southernmost village on Rab Island, sprawling along the Barbatski Channel that separates Rab from Dolin Island. It's 3km southeast of Rab town on a coastal plateau covered with vineyards and vegetable gardens. Although the tiny town centre is nowhere near as interesting as Rab town, it has a 3km coast lined with houses offering private accommodation. Boating facilities have taken over a good part of the coast but there are several attractive gravel beaches close to town.

From the main road about 1km northwest of the bus stop, marked trails lead to the ruins of **Sveti Damjana** church and the remains of what may have been a Greek military fortress. You'll also have a great view of the coast down to Mali Lošinj on a clear day.

The **Der Barbat tourist agency** (☎ 721 500; fax 721 321) is a few metres from the bus stop and finds rooms for about 80KN per person.

There are 15 buses a day between Rab town and Barbat, which drop you off on the main road overlooking the coast.

SUHA PUNTA

The Suha Punta resort is on the southeastern side of the forested Kalifront Peninsula overlooking a spectacular bay. The hotel complex is integrated into the surrounding pine forest, leaving the natural beauty of the setting more or less intact. The beaches are rocky, but a shady coastal path leads east through the pines to other coves and naturist beaches. Another pleasant walk leads northwest to the village of Kampor and the sandy Bay of Kampor. There's a supermarket and a couple of restaurants as well as tennis and miniature golf at the resort. As far as tourist developments go, this is one of the least objectionable and it makes an easy day trip from Rab town.

Sleeping

There is no camping or private accommodation.

Suha Punta Tourist Village (☎724 060; suhapunta@ imperial.hr; Kampor bb; apt 340KN; ℗) The simple bungalows here are the cheapest places to stay in the area. They are short on niceties but provide good value for money.

Hotel Eva (☎ 668 200; eva@imperial.hr; Kampor bb; s/d 360/555KN; ℗) For a package-tour hotel it could be worse. Rooms face either the sea or the surrounding park, and all have balconies.

Hotel Carolina (☎ 724 133; eva@imperial.hr; Kampor bb; s/d 410/650KN; ℗ ✖ ✉) Carolina is in a great location overlooking the cove. The modern rooms have recently been renovated.

Istria

CONTENTS

The Adriatic's largest peninsula (3160 sq km), Istria (Istra in Italian) is blessed with a 430km indented shoreline and green rolling hills, drowned valleys and fertile plains. The scenic interior is less visited by tourists but contains fetching medieval hill towns with panoramic views. The coast offers a smorgasbord of water sports and rocky coves dotted by vibrant historic towns.

Pazin, in the interior, is the administrative capital of the region while Pula, with its thriving shipyard, is the economic centre. The northern part of the peninsula belongs to Slovenia, while the Dinaric Range in the northeastern corner separates Istria from the continental mainland. Most of the resorts are on the highly developed west coast.

Flat and over-endowed with bland tourist complexes, the Istrian coast isn't the most beautiful but its culture is unique. With borders that have changed five times in the last century, it's unsurprising that Istria is the most tolerant and cosmopolitan Croatian region. In a 1991 census, nearly 20% of the inhabitants declared their nationality as Istrian rather than Croatian, and although only 8% of the population is ethnic Italian, many Istrians have Italian passports.

There's a heavy Italian influence in the language and food of Istria, and if you visit in July and August, the streets will be thronged with Italian tourists. Outside the high season you are free to enjoy the Roman ruins, old Venetian ports, beaches, forests, vineyards and hill towns of this fascinating region.

HIGHLIGHTS

- Admiring the mosaics in **Poreč's Euphrasian Basilica** (p145)
- Listening to music under the stars at **Pula's Roman amphitheatre** (p133)
- Examining the morning catch at **Rovinj's harbour** (p140)
- Snorkelling in **Crveni Otok** (p144)
- Taking in the views from **Motovun** (p152)

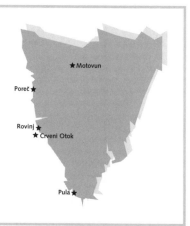

★ Motovun

Poreč ★

Rovinj ★
★ Crveni Otok

Pula ★

- TELEPHONE CODE: 052
- POSTCODE: 52000

ISTRIA

History

Towards the end of the 2nd millennium BC, the Illyrian Histrian tribe settled the region and built fortified villages on top of the region's coastal and interior hills. Ancient Greek chroniclers indicated that the region was on an important trade route – the Amber Route – through which Greek ships passed on trading missions from the Aegean.

The Romans swept into Istria in the 3rd century BC and, after fierce resistance, managed to subdue the region in the 2nd century BC. After the conquest, the Romans began building roads and fortified towns. Pola (Pula) and Parentium (Poreč) were Illyrian hill forts that the Romans chose as highly fortified strongholds because of their well-sheltered bays and strategic positions overlooking the lowlands. The best preserved Roman ruins are in Pula and date from the reign of Augustus (63 BC to AD 14).

In the 4th and 5th centuries, Rome and Istria came under assault from Huns and Visigoths and the empire began to crumble. The Byzantine Empire crushed the Ostrogoths in the 6th century and Istria remained under Byzantine rule from 539 to 751. The most impressive remnant of Byzantine culture is the Euphrasian Basilica in Poreč, with its stunning mosaics.

Slavic tribes moved into the region in the 6th and 7th centuries and enjoyed some autonomy before Charlemagne's conquest of Istria in 788. The ensuing centuries brought more turbulence as the Franks were supplanted by a succession of German rulers that lasted until the death of Friedrich II in 1250.

An increasingly powerful Venice wrested control of the Istrian coast from German rulers in the early 13th century, forcing the rulers of continental Istria to turn to the Habsburgs for protection. Treaties signed in 1374 and 1466 gave continental Istria to the Habsburgs. Istrian coastal cities, under threat from Southern Dalmatian pirates, were willing to become vassals of Venice in exchange for Venetian protection of their trade routes.

Istrian coastal towns became important way stations for the repair and maintenance of Venetian ships, but the Venetian embrace brought other problems in the form of devastating attacks by Venice's rival, the Genoans.

Misery, famine and warfare haunted the peninsula. Bubonic plague first broke out in 1371 and regularly ravaged Istrian cities until the 17th century. Malaria was endemic. Although the Turks never reached Istria, the peninsula lay in the path of the fearsome Uskoks from Senj who repeatedly attacked Venice's Istrian cities throughout the 16th and 17th centuries.

With the fall of Venice in 1797, Istria fell under Austrian rule, followed by the French (1809–13), and again the Austrians. During the 19th and early 20th century most of Istria was little more than a neglected outpost of the Austro-Hungarian empire, which concentrated on developing the port of Trieste. The economy of the coastal cities was badly affected by the decline in sailing ships although the construction of a naval port and shipyard in Pula in the late 19th century gave the region a boost. The Slavic farmers in the interior of the peninsula continued to cultivate the land and raise cattle.

When the Austro-Hungarian empire disintegrated at the end of WWI, Italy moved quickly to secure Istria. Italian troops occupied Pula in November 1918, and, in the 1920 Treaty of Rapallo, the Kingdom of Serbs, Croats and Slovenes ceded Istria along with Zadar and several islands to Italy as a reward for joining the Allied powers in WWI. A massive population shift followed as 30,000 to 40,000 Italians arrived from Mussolini's Italy and many Croats left, fearing fascism. Their fears were not misplaced as Istria's Italian masters attempted to consolidate their hold by banning Slavic speech, printing, education and cultural activities.

Italy retained the region until its defeat in WWII when Istria became part of Yugoslavia, causing another mass exodus as Italians and many Croats fled Tito's Communists. Trieste and the northwestern tip of the peninsula was a point of contention between Italy and Yugoslavia until 1954 when it was finally awarded to Italy. As a result of Tito's reorganisation of Yugoslavia, the northern part of the peninsula was incorporated into Slovenia, where it has remained.

LABIN

pop 9000

Labin is the undisputed highlight of Istria's eastern coast. On top of one of the hills

ISTRIA

0 _____ 10 km
0 _____ 6 miles

To Trieste (Italy) (19km)
To Trieste (Italy) (72km)
To Ljubljana

Koprski Bay

Koper

SLOVENIA

Point Savudrija

Portorož

Piranski Bay

SLOVENIA

Čičarija

10-4

Umag

Pt Umaški

Buje

2

Krasica

Grožnjan

E751

Brest

Buzet

Roč

Mirna

To Rijeka (11km); Zagreb (171km)

Point Dajla

Mirna

Under Construction

Motovun

Hum

V Planik (1272m)

Opatija

Novigrad

Mirna Harbour

Kaštelir

Baredine Cave

Gedići

Karojba

Boljun

Lovran

Point Basuja

Nova Vas

Višnjan

Cerovlje

2-1

Učka

2

Riječki Bay

E751

Poreč

Pazin

Sušnjevica

Mošćenice

Plava Laguna

2-1

Pićan

Zelena Laguna

Brseč

Funtana

Medaki

Sv Petar u Šumi

Raša

Vozilići

Brestova

Vrsar

Žminj

Porozina Point Prestinice

Cres

Limska Draga Fjord

Valalta

Kanfanar

Dragozetići

Rovinj

Point Kurenf

Svet Vinčenat

Labin

Bale

Barban

Rabac

2

Point Gustinja

2

Trget

E751

E751

Barbariga

Vodnjan

Koromačno

Crna Punta

Point Pernat

Fažanski Channel

Marčana

Raški Bay

Cres

Mali Brijun

Fažana

Brijuni National Park

Veli Brijun

Kavran

Point Kumpar

Pula

Stoja

Verudela Peninsula

Banjole

Medulin

Point Marlera

Premantura

Medulinski Bay

Zeča

Point Kamenjak

Lošinj

Unije

To Mali Lošinj (Lošinj Island)

ADRIATIC SEA

Kvarner

that undulate westward from Opatija, Labin's old town is a beguiling conglomeration of stepped streets, cobblestone alleys and pastel houses festooned with stone ornamentation. It looks much too pretty for an industry as grubby as coal mining, but it was the mining capital of Istria until the 1970s. Labin's hill was mined so extensively that the town began to collapse about 30 years ago. Mining stopped, the necessary repairs were undertaken and the town emerged with a new sense of itself as a tourist destination. It has a lot to offer. There's an unusual museum, a wealth of Venetian-inspired churches and palaces, a sprinkling of arts and craft shops and an overdeveloped coastal resort at Rabac, a few kilometres away.

Orientation

Labin is divided into two parts: the hill-top old town with the most travel agencies; and a much newer section at the bottom of the hill, with most of the town's shops, restaurants and services. Buses stop at Trg 2 Marta in the new town, from which it's a short walk uphill to Titov trg, the centre of the old town.

Information

Main Tourist Office (☎ /fax 852 399; tzg.labin@pu .htnet.hr; Trg M Tita 10; 8am-9pm Mon-Sat, 10am-1pm & 6-9pm Sun Jun-Sep, 8am-3pm Mon-Fri Oct-May) In the upper old town.

Post Office (Titov trg 2) In the old town.

Riadria Banka (Trg 2 Marta bb) At the bus stop, it has an ATM.

Tourist Office Annexe (☎ /fax 855 560; A Negri 20; 8am-9pm Mon-Sat, 10am-1pm & 6-9pm Sun Jun-Sep, 8am-3pm Mon-Fri Oct-May) In the new town.

Sights & Activities

The **Town Museum** (Gradski Muzej; ☎ 852 477; Ulica 1 Maja 6; adult/concession 12/6KN; 🕙 10am-1pm & 5-7pm Mon-Fri, 10am-1pm Sat Jul-Aug, 10am-1pm Mon-Sat Sep-Jun) is one of the most interesting regional museums. Lodged in an 18th-century palace, the ground floor is devoted to an archaeological collection, traditional costumes, musical instruments and implements from daily farm life. Upstairs is a photo

---

MAGIC MUSHROOMS?

The truffle trade is less like a business than a highly profitable cult. It revolves around an expensive, malodorous fungus endowed with semimagical powers which is collected by shadowy characters who deal in cash and smuggle their booty across borders. Devotees claim that once you've tasted this small, nut-shaped delicacy, all other flavours seem insipid.

Although France, Spain and Italy are the traditional truffle-producing countries, Istrian truffles are rapidly gaining a foothold in the marketplace. Even at 14KN per gram, the price is significantly lower than other European truffles and the taste is said to be at least as good as their more expensive counterparts. In fact, there have been unconfirmed reports that certain nefarious parties are collecting Istrian truffles and packaging them as Italian truffles.

The Istrian truffle business is relatively young. In 1932, when Istria was occupied by Italy, an Italian soldier from the truffle capital of Albi allegedly noticed vegetational similarities between his region and Istria. He returned after his military service with specially trained dogs who, after enough sniffing and digging, eventually uncovered the precious commodity.

Dogs are still the key to a successful truffle hunt. Istrian truffle-hunting dogs (called *breks*) may be mongrels but they are highly educated. Puppies begin their training at two months old but only about 20% of them go on to fully fledged careers as truffle trackers. Their lives are short. For reasons that remain unclear, breks are peculiarly subject to a variety of cancers.

The truffle-hunting season lasts from October to January, during which time at least 3000 people and 9000 to 12,000 dogs are wandering around Istrian forests. The Motovun region is especially rich in truffles, but they are also found on the slopes of Mt Učka and in the Labin region. Truffle hunters are so determined to remain underground (for obvious tax reasons) that they will never admit to truffle hunting, no matter how unmistakable the evidence.

Some people believe truffles are an aphrodisiac, though scientific research has failed to uncover any basis for this claim. Conduct your own experiment: get a truffle and mix a few shavings into scrambled eggs or sprinkle them on top of a risotto. Turn the lights way down low, put on some nice music and see what happens.

gallery with a changing selection of exhibits and the top floor is a contemporary art gallery. The museum is over a coal pit that has been turned into a realistic re-creation of an actual coalmine. As you make your way through the claustrophobic tunnels, you'll understand why people have tended to prefer other employment.

Wandering the streets of Labin is fascinating. Take a look at the **Church of the Birth of the Blessed Virgin Mary** (Ulica 1 Maja), which is a mixture of the Venetian Gothic and Renaissance styles featuring a finely carved Venetian lion over the portal. Notice also the 15th-century Renaissance **Scampicchio Palace** (Ulica Pina Budicina) with its inner courtyard; and the graceful **loggia** (Titov trg) which was the community centre of Labin in the 16th century. Important events were announced under its roof and in front there was once a pillory to punish the wayward.

The highest point in Labin is the **fortress** (fortica) at the western edge of town. You can walk along Ulica 1 Maja or take the long way around by following Šetalište San Marco along the town walls. From the top there is a sweeping view of the coast and the island of Cres.

Sleeping & Eating

There are no hotels right in Labin, but there are big resort hotels in nearby Rabac, the coastal resort 5km southwest of Labin. **Rabac Hotels** (www.rabac-hotels.com) manages the resorts and also finds private accommodation. Prices run from 210KN to 550KN per person depending upon the presence of air-con, swimming pools, minibars and sports equipment. Little is available in the old town. The **Veritas Agency** (☎ 854 428; www.istra-veritas.hr; Svete Katarine 8) near Titov trg finds double rooms/apartments for 150/280KN.

Labin is known for its truffles cooked with pasta or eggs, which are generally priced well.

Camping Oliva (☎ 872 258; fax 872 258; Rabac bb; per adult/site 37/60KN) This is the closest camping ground located right on Rabac beach, in the middle of the action and in front of the big hotels.

Gostiona Kvarner (☎ 851 337; S Marco bb; mains from 50KN) Just steps from Titov trg, looks touristy because of its terrace overlooking the sea but the food is good and it attracts plenty of locals. The tagliatelle with truffles

is a measly 70KN which is a bargain considering the expense of truffle-hunting.

Getting There & Away

Labin is well connected with Pula by bus (27KN, one hour, 15 daily).

PULA

pop 58,340

Pula (ancient Polensium) is a large regional centre with a wealth of Roman ruins to explore. The highlight is a remarkably well-preserved Roman amphitheatre that dominates the town centre and is often the scene of concerts and shows. Despite the busy commercial life, Pula retains an easy-going small-town appeal. The nightlife, restaurants and cultural activity are the best in Istria. Although there are no beaches within the city, a short bus ride takes you south to the resorts on the Verudela Peninsula. The scenery around Pula is undramatic, as the region is relatively flat and its original oak forests have been replaced with shrubs and pine groves. The landscape is also marred by a crush of residential and holiday developments, but the indented coastline south of the city that extends to the Premantura Peninsula is studded with rocky bays and coves.

History

In the 1st century BC, the Illyrian Pola (now Pula) was conquered by the Romans and used as their administrative headquarters for the region that stretched from the Limska Draga Fjord to the Raša River. The Romans cleverly exploited Pula's terrain, using Kaštel Hill, which now contains the citadel, as a vantage point to protect the bay. The ancient town developed in concentric circles around Kaštel Hill, with the amphitheatre placed outside the fortified city centre. Pula joined the powerful Venetian empire in 1150 to protect itself against piracy, but the city suffered badly under Venetian rule. First subjected to ruinous assaults by Genoa, the city was then repeatedly invaded by Venice's rivals – the Patriarch of Aquilea, the Croatian-Hungarian kings and the Habsburgs. Plague and malaria had nearly wiped out the population by the 17th century.

The fall of Venice in 1797 brought in the Habsburgs as the new rulers. Pula continued to stagnate until the Austro-Hungarian monarchy chose Pula as the empire's main naval port in 1853. The construction of its naval port and the 1886 opening of its large shipyard unleashed a demographic and economic expansion that transformed Pula into a military and industrial powerhouse. The city fell into decline once again under Italian fascist rule, which lasted from 1918 to 1943, when the city was occupied by the Germans. At the end of WWII, Pula was administered by Anglo-American forces until it became part of postwar Yugoslavia in 1947. Pula's industrial base weathered the recent war relatively well and the city remains an important centre for shipbuilding, textiles, metals and glass.

Orientation

The oldest part of the city follows the ancient Roman plan of streets circling the central citadel, while the city's newer portions follow a rectangular grid pattern. Most shops, agencies and businesses are clustered in and around the old town as well as on Giardini, Ulica Carrarina, Istarska ulica and Riva, which runs along the harbour. Most hotels, restaurants and beaches are 3km south of the city on the Verudela Peninsula and can be reached by walking south on Arsenalska ulica and then Ulica Veruda. The bus station is 500m northeast of the town centre. The centre of town is Giardini, while the harbour is west of the bus station. The train station is near the water just less than a kilometre north of town.

Information

INTERNET ACCESS

Cyber@cafe (☎ 215 345; Flanatička 14; per hr 20KN)
Enigma (☎ 381 615; Kandlerova 19; per hr 20KN)

LEFT LUGGAGE

Garderoba Bus station (per day 10KN; ☺ 5am-10pm);
Train station (per day 10KN; ☺ 9am-4pm Mon-Sat)

MONEY

You can exchange money in travel agencies or at the post office, where there is an ATM.
Zagrebačka Banka (M Laginje 1) Has an ATM.

POST

Main Post Office (Danteov trg 4; ☺ 7am-8pm) You can make long-distance calls here.

TOURIST INFORMATION

Tourist Information Centre (☎ 219 197; www.pula info.hr; Forum 2; ☺ 9am-8pm Mon-Sat, 10am-6pm Sun) Knowledgeable and friendly, it provides maps, brochures and schedules of upcoming events in Pula and around Istria.

TRAVEL AGENCIES

Arena Turist (☎ 529 400; www.arenaturist.hr; Splitska 1a) In the Hotel Riviera, it finds private accommodation and books rooms in the network of hotels it manages.
Atlas Travel Agency (☎ 393 040; atlas.pula@atlas.hr; Starih Statuta 1) Finds private accommodation and organises tours.
Globtour (☎ 211 255; globtour-pula@pu.htnet.hr; Giardini 10) Finds private accommodation.
Jadroagent (☎ 210 431; jadroagent-pula@pu.htnet .hr; Riva 14) Has schedules and tickets for boats connecting Istria with Italy and the islands.

Sights

ROMAN RUINS

Pula's most imposing sight is the 1st-century Roman amphitheatre (☎ 219 028; Flavijevska; adult/concession 16/8KN; ☺ 8am-9pm Jun-Sep, 8.30am-4.30pm Oct-May) overlooking the harbour northeast of the old town. Built entirely from local limestone, the amphitheatre was designed to host gladiatorial contests and could accommodate up to 20,000 spectators. The 30m-high outer wall is almost intact and contains two rows of 72 arches but the stone spectator seats were removed for building materials in the Middle Ages. On the top of the walls is a gutter that collected rain water and you can still see the slabs used to secure the fabric canopy, which protected spectators from the sun. Around the end of July a Croatian film festival is held in the amphitheatre, and there are also pop and classical concerts all summer.

Along the street facing the bus station are Roman walls, which mark the eastern boundary of old Pula. Follow these walls south and continue down Giardini to the Triumphal Arch of Sergius. This majestic arch was erected in 27 BC to commemorate three members of the Sergius family who achieved distinction in Pula. The outer side of the arch is lavishly ornamented with columns and friezes while the inner side that led to the old town is simpler. Until the 19th century the arch was backed by the city gate and was surrounded by walls that were pulled down to allow the city to expand beyond the old town.

ISTRIA

The pedestrian street beyond the arch, Ulica Sergijevaca, winds right around old Pula. Follow it to where you'll find the ancient **Forum**, the town's central meeting place from antiquity through the Middle Ages. It used to contain temples and public buildings, but today the only visible remnant from the Roman era is the **Temple of Augustus**, erected from 2 BC to AD 14. When the Romans left, the temple became a church and then a grain warehouse. The building suffered a direct hit when Pula was bombed in 1944, and it was almost totally destroyed. It was reconstructed in 1947. Also in the Forum, notice the **old town hall**, which was built in 1296 as the seat of Pula's municipal authorities. The building underwent a number of reconstructions over the centuries, which is apparent in the mixture of architectural styles – from Romanesque to Renaissance. It's still the seat of Pula's mayor.

Just off Sergijevaca is a **Roman floor mosaic** dating from the 3rd century. In the midst of remarkably well-preserved geometric motifs is the central panel, which depicts bad-girl Dirce from Greek mythology being punished for the attempted murder of her cousin.

CHURCHES

The **cathedral** (Katedrala; Kandlerova ulica; ☙ 7am-noon & 4-6pm) traces its origins back to the 5th century. The main altar is even older, being a Roman sarcophagus from the 3rd century, and the floor reveals fragments of 5th- and 6th-century mosaics. The church was reconstructed following a fire in 1242 and again in the 15th century when the Renaissance southern portal was added. The Late-Renaissance façade was added in the early 16th century and the 17th-century bell tower was made of stones from the amphitheatre.

The **Chapel of St Mary of Formosa** (Kapela Marije Formoze; Ulica Flaciusova) is all that remains of the 6th-century Benedictine abbey that once stood here. This Byzantine structure was adorned with mosaics, which are now in the city's Archaeological Museum. The chapel is only open for occasional art exhibitions in the summer.

MUSEUMS

The **Archaeological Museum** (Arheološki Muzej; ☎ 218 603; Cararina 3; adult/concession 12/6KN; ☙ 9am-7pm Mon-Sat, 10am-3pm Sun Jun-Sep, 9am-3pm Mon-Fri Oct-May) opposite the bus station presents archaeological finds from all over Istria. The permanent exhibits cover prehistory to the Middle Ages, but the accent is on the period from the 2nd century BC to the 6th century AD. Even if you don't visit the museum be sure to visit the large sculpture garden around it, and the **Roman theatre** behind. The garden is entered through 2nd-century twin gates and is often the site of concerts in the summer.

The **Museum of History** (Povijesni Muzej Istre; ☎ 211 740; Kaštel; admission 7KN; ☙ 8am-7pm daily Jun-Sep, 9am-5pm Mon-Fri Oct-May) is in a 17th-century Venetian citadel. The museum is on a hill in the centre of the old town. The meagre exhibits deal mostly with the maritime history of Pula but the views of Pula from the citadel walls are good.

BEACHES

Pula is surrounded by a half-circle of beaches (actually coastal-rock formations) and each one has its own fans. Like bars or nightclubs, beaches go in and out of style. The most touristy beaches are undoubtedly the ones surrounding the hotel complex on **Verudela** although some locals will dare to be seen at **Hawaii Beach** near the Hotel Park. Southwest of the town centre on the way to Autocamp Stoja is the ever-popular **Valkana Beach**, which attracts a young, lively set of loud-music lovers. If you have your own wheels, head out to the **Nature Park** (admission 10KN; ☙ 7am-9pm) on the Premantura Peninsula 10km south of town. **Kolumbarica Beach**, on the peninsula, is especially popular with daring young men who dive from the high cliffs and swim through the shallow caves at the waters' edge. There is also a delightful little bar-grill, Safari, half-hidden in the bushes near the beach. Nearby is **Debeljak**, one of the region's rare sandy beaches.

Activities

At **Sports Center Verudela** (☎ 529 400) on the Verudela Peninsula near Hotel Brioni there's water-skiing and parasailing, and rowboats, canoes and jet skis. Scuba diving is handled by **Gratsch** (☎ 210 033, 098 335 763) at the Hotel Histria, with boat dives for 200KN.

Tours

Most excursions are operated by Atlas Travel Agency, which offers trips to the

PULA

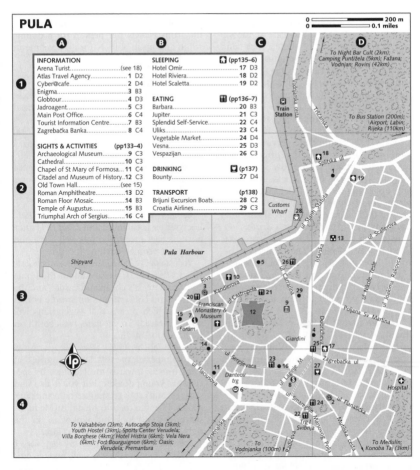

INFORMATION	
Arena Turist.............................(see 18)	
Atlas Travel Agency.........................1	D2
Cyber@cafe....................................2	D4
Enigma...3	B3
Globtour......................................4	D3
Jadroagent....................................5	C3
Main Post Office.............................6	C4
Tourist Information Centre.................7	B3
Zagrebačka Banka...........................8	C4

SIGHTS & ACTIVITIES	(pp133–4)
Archaeological Museum....................9	C3
Cathedral....................................10	C3
Chapel of St Mary of Formosa........11	C4
Citadel and Museum of History....12	C3
Old Town Hall...........................(see 15)	
Roman Amphitheatre....................13	D2
Roman Floor Mosaic.....................14	B3
Temple of Augustus......................15	B3
Triumphal Arch of Sergius............16	C4

SLEEPING	(pp135–6)
Hotel Omir..................................17	D3
Hotel Riviera...............................18	D2
Hotel Scaletta.............................19	D2

EATING	(pp136–7)
Barbara.....................................20	B3
Jupiter......................................21	C3
Splendid Self-Service...................22	C4
Uliks...23	C4
Vegetable Market........................24	D4
Vesna..25	D3
Vespazijan..................................26	C3

DRINKING	(p137)
Bounty......................................27	D4

TRANSPORT	(p138)
Brijuni Excursion Boats..................28	C2
Croatia Airlines...........................29	C3

Pula Harbour

Shipyard

To Valsabbion (2km); Autocamp Stoja (3km);
Youth Hostel (3km); Sports Center Verudela;
Villa Borghese (4km); Hotel Histria (6km); Vela Nera
(6km); Fort Bourguignon (6km); Oasis;
Verudela; Premantura

To Night Bar Cult (2km);
Camping Puntižela (5km); Fažana;
Vodnjan; Rovinj (42km)

Train
Station

To Bus Station (200m);
Airport; Labin;
Rijeka (110km)

Customs
Wharf

Hospital

To Medulin;
Konoba Taj (3km)

Brijuni Islands, the Limska Draga Fjord, Rovinj and Crveni Otok.

Sleeping

Pula's high season runs from the second week of July to the end of August. During this period, it's wise to make advance reservations. There are a couple of camping grounds near Pula and a few hotels in Pula but most are out of town in Verudela. The tip of the Verudela Peninsula, 6km southwest of the city centre, has been turned into a vast tourist complex replete with hotels and apartments. It's not especially attractive but there are beaches, restaurants and water sports. Any travel agency can give you information and book you into one of the

hotels, or you can contact **Arena Turist** (☎ 529 400; www.arenaturist.hr).

Autocamp Stoja (☎ 387 144; fax 387 748; per person/tent & car 50/110KN; ☼ Apr-Oct) The closest camping ground to Pula, it's 3km southwest of the centre in Verudela, and has lots of space on the shady promontory, with two good restaurants and swimming possible off the rocks. Take bus No 1 to the terminus at Stoja.

Camping Puntižela (☎ 517 433; fax 517 399; Puntižela; per adult/tent 40/55KN; ☼ Apr-Oct) This is a lovely camping ground on a bay 5km north of central Pula.

Youth Hostel (☎ 391 133; pula@hfhs.hr; per tent site/tent rental 72KN/10.50KN, B&B/half board 110/142KN) Only 3km south of central Pula, this hostel overlooks a beach and is near one of the region's largest discos. You can sit and sip cold beer on the terrace, where a rock band plays on some summer evenings. Take the No 2 or 7 Verudela bus to the 'Piramida' stop, walk back to the first street, then turn left and look for the sign. The rate for camping includes breakfast. The hostel and camping grounds are open all year.

Hotel Riviera (☎ 211 166; fax 211 166; Splitska ul 1; s/d 437/715KN) Neither the service nor the comfort quite justifies the price (which eases substantially in the low season) in this one-star hotel, but there is an undeniably appealing old-world elegance and the rooms are spacious. The front rooms have a view of the water and the wide, shady hotel terrace is a relaxing place for a drink.

Hotel Omir (☎ 210 614; fax 213 944; Dobricheva 6; s/d incl breakfast 424/550KN) The Omir is a 14-room hotel just off Zagrebačka ulica near Giardini. Rooms are on the small side but the staff are friendly and service is good. All rooms have private bathroom and the rates stay the same all year.

Hotel Scaletta (☎ 541 599; www.hotel-scaletta.com; Flavijeska 26; s/d 410/535KN; P ✕) This family-owned hotel has been beautifully restored offering tastefully decorated rooms with breakfast, phones, TVs and private bathrooms. The restaurant is also excellent, making it worthwhile to take half board.

Valsabbion (☎ 218 033; www.valsabbion.hr; Pješčana Uvala IX/26; d from 665KN; P ✕) Situated 6km south of the city (take bus No 6) in a villa by the sea, this small, family-owned hotel offers a more personal experience than the other hotels and is a welcome addition to Pula's accommodation scene, with 15 attractively decorated rooms. There's a rooftop fitness centre with a pool, and the restaurant is considered the finest in Croatia. Half board is expensive but the food is worth it. The rates are 10% lower in off-season; breakfast costs 60KN.

Hotel Histria (☎ 590 000; fax 214 175; Verudela; s/d from 685/1135KN; P ✕ ▣) This is the best and most expensive of the five hotels on the peninsula with indoor and outdoor swimming pools, casino, disco and sauna. The well-appointed rooms have satellite TV.

PRIVATE ROOMS
The travel agencies listed on p133 find private accommodation but there is little available in the town centre. Count on paying from 110KN per person for a double room and up to 430KN for an apartment.

Eating
CITY CENTRE
There are a number of good eating places in the city centre, although most locals head out of town.

Jupiter (☎ 214 333; Castropola 38; mains from 25KN) This popular place serves up the best pizza in town and the pasta is good too.

Vespazijan (☎ 210 016; Amfiteatarska 11; mains from 30KN) This unpretentious spot conjures up yummy risottos and a variety of seafood dishes.

Barbara (☎ 219 317; Kandlerova 5; mains from 25KN) It's your basic calamari and čevapčići (spicy pork or beef meatballs) but well done and in a great people-watching location.

Vodnjanka (☎ 210 655; Vitešića 4; mains from 25KN; ☿ lunch Mon-Fri) Locals rave about the home cooking here. It's cheap and casual, and the small menu concentrates on simple Istrian dishes, which means that vegetarians will not be pleased. To get here, walk south on Radićeva to Vitežića.

Konoba Taj (☎ 505 557; Škokovica 3; 2-course meal 80KN) Another inexpensive local favourite that leans heavily towards meat dishes, its speciality is young donkey, but you'll also find sausages and cabbage, smoked ham and pork chops. Take the road to Medulin (Medulinska cesta) and look for Škokovica on the right, about 3km from the city centre.

Splendid Self-Service (☎ 223 284; Trg I Svibnja 5; meals 20KN) Opposite the vegetable market, dining at this place is easy since you see what you're getting and pay at the end of the line.

Vesna (Giardini; sandwiches 10KN) The people at the cheese counter in Vesna, next to Kino Istra, prepare healthy sandwiches while you wait.

Uliks (☎ 219 158; Trg Portarata 1) Located in the apartment building where James Joyce once taught, this café is a popular meeting place and a good spot to linger over coffee or a drink.

SOUTH OF THE CITY
The best dining is out of town on and around the Verudela Peninsula.

Villa Borghese (☎ 392 111; Monte Paradiso 25; 2-course meal 120-150KN) The restaurant, in a freshly renovated country villa with an elegant, upmarket ambience, has a devoted

WAYNE WALTON

Byzantine mosaics in the
Euphrasian Basilica, Poreč (p145)

WAYNE WALTON

Café life in Rovinj (p143)

Medieval hilltops and vineyards, Motovun (p152)

WAYNE WALTON

Karst cliffs, Paklenica National Park (p167)

Hiking to Manita Peć
cave (p169)

Wooden walkways over azure pools,
Plitvice Lakes National Park (p164)

Scuba diving from Sali (p171)

AN ISTRIAN FEAST

Istrian cuisine closely resembles that of its Italian neighbour but with a few distinctive touches. The recipes below use typically Istrian ingredients or combine flavours in a way that Italians normally would not, such as wrapping shellfish in meat. Risotto and polenta are Istrian staples that are becoming widely available either in original or instant versions. Here are some simple recipes that serve four people.

Antipasto

On a large platter arrange eight slices of Istrian prosciutto and eight thinly sliced wedges of Istrian sheep cheese or *formaggio pecorino* around a pile of black olives. Your guests must be strictly limited to two each or they'll lose their appetite for the rest of the meal.

Involtini di Prosciutto Agli Scampi (Shrimp Wrapped in Prosciutto)

Take 12 prawns and drop them into boiling water. Cook for up to five minutes, depending on the size of the prawn. Remove, peel and cut off the heads and tails. Wrap each prawn in a slice of prosciutto. Heat a third of a cup of good olive oil in a skillet. Brown the prawns quickly over medium-high heat until the prosciutto colours slightly, turning frequently. Add ½ cup of wine and reduce the heat to low. Sprinkle with freshly ground pepper and salt to taste. Simmer for eight minutes and serve on top of risotto.

Brodetto All'istriana (Istrian-Style Fish Stew)

Choose about a kilogram of mixed shellfish such as shrimps, crabs, mussels and clams and one whole white fish such as snapper, sea bass, halibut or groper. Cut 150g of squid into small bite-sized rounds. (Unless the squid is young it may need to be beaten with a hammer first to tenderise it.) Clean and wash the fish. Heat ¼ cup of olive oil in a large pot and sauté the fish until brown. Add the shellfish and squid, 250g of sliced onion, four peeled garlic cloves, 300g fresh tomatoes cut into quarters, two tablespoons of chopped parsley, two bay leaves and salt and pepper to taste. Add water to cover and bring to a boil. When it reaches a boil add ½ cup of wine. Cook for 30 minutes, stirring from time to time. Serve with polenta or large chunks of bread.

Frittelle Istriane (Istrian Pancakes)

Beat three egg yolks with ¼ cup (120g) sugar until thick. Add ¼ teaspoon each of grated orange and lemon peel and one tablespoon of grappa. Beat egg whites until stiff and fold into the yolk mixture along with 400g cream cheese or ricotta. Mix until thick and creamy. In another bowl blend three eggs with a pinch of salt. Add 250g flour, one cup milk and one cup mineral water. Ladle onto a hot skillet and fry the pancakes. Add the filling to the fried pancakes on one end only and roll them. Place on a buttered, ovenproof dish and top with a dollop of sour cream. Place under a hot grill until piping hot and serve immediately.

following of Italian residents and tourists who appreciate the fine pasta starters and fresh fish.

Valsabbion (☎ /fax 218 033; Pješčana uvala IX/26; 2-course meals from 120KN; ☼ noon-midnight) Generally considered one of the best restaurants in Croatia, the menu has a variety of international dishes and the culinary style reflects the imaginative flavours of nouvelle cuisine. It's not cheap, but the quality is outstanding.

Vela Nera (☎ 219 209; Pješčana uvala bb; 2-course meals from 100KN) Nearby is this delightful place, a rival of Valsabbion for renowned dining, with a terrace overlooking the sea and excellent seafood specialities.

Drinking

Bounty (☎ 218 088; Veronska 8) If Irish beer and cheer is your thing, head here for 23 different brews and a wide selection of sandwiches and salads.

Night Bar Cult (☎ 573 430; Pomer 286) In the suburb of Pomer, 2km north of town, this popular nightclub has a restaurant and disco.

ISTRIA

Entertainment

Posters around Pula advertise live performances and you should definitely try to catch
a concert in the spectacular amphitheatre;
the tourist office will have the details. Although most of the nightlife is out of town
in Verudela, in mild weather the cafés on
the Forum and along the pedestrian streets,
Kandlerova, Flanatička and Sergijevaca, are
lively people-watching spots.

Fort Bourguignon (Verudela; ☾ weekends only Nov-
Apr) This multi-level disco at Verudela organises techno and rave parties that attract
huge crowds.

Oasis (Verudela; ☾ weekends only Nov-Apr) This is
another popular disco within walking (and
hearing) distance from the youth hostel.

Getting There & Away
AIR

There are weekday early-morning flights to
Zagreb (475KN, 45 minutes). **Croatia Airlines**
(☎ 218 909; Carrarina 8) has an office here.

BOAT

For information on connections to Italy and
Slovenia, see p275. The line that connects
Pula with Koper goes on to Mali Lošinj
(73KN, 4½ hours) and Zadar (112KN, 8½
hours).

BUS

From the **bus station** (☎ 502 997; Istarske Brigade bb) there are 17 daily buses to Rijeka
(two hours, 110km). They are sometimes
crowded, especially the eight that continue
on to Zagreb, so reserve a seat a day in
advance if you can. Going from Pula to
Rijeka, be sure to sit on the right-hand side
of the bus for a stunning view of the Gulf
of Kvarner.

Other buses departing from Pula:

Destination	Cost	Duration	Frequency
Dubrovnik	366KN	15hr	1 daily
Koper	85KN	4hr	1 daily
Labin	27KN	1hr	12 daily
Poreč	32KN	1hr	12 daily
Portorož	59KN	1½hr	1 daily
Rovinj	23KN	40min	18 daily
Split	215-278KN	10hr	2 daily
Trieste	80-100KN	3hr	3 daily
Zadar	161KN	7hr	3 daily
Zagreb	121-130KN	5-7hr	11 daily

TRAIN

Ever since Pula was the main port of the
Austro-Hungarian empire, the railway line
in Istria has run north towards Italy and
Austria instead of east into Croatia, but there
are two daily trains to Ljubljana (115KN,
four hours) and two to Zagreb (123KN,
6½ hours). You must board a bus for part
of the trip.

Getting Around

There's no public transport from the airport to town. Taxis are available and cost
about 100KN.

The only city buses of use to visitors
are the No 1, which runs to the Autocamp
Stoja, and bus Nos 2 and 7 to Verudela,
which pass the youth hostel. Frequency
varies from every 15 minutes to every half
hour, with services from 5am to 11.30pm
daily. Tickets are sold at *tisak* (newsstands)
for 10KN and are valid for two trips.

BRIJUNI ISLANDS

The Brijuni (Brioni in Italian) island group
consists of two main pine-covered islands
and 12 islets off the coast of Istria, just
northwest of Pula. Only the two larger
islands, Veli Brijun and Mali Brijun, can be
visited. The islands are a national park, but
one with a decidedly artificial cast. As the
second residence of Maršal Tito, the flora
and fauna of the island were mostly placed
there to create a comfort zone for the former Yugoslav leader. Elephants, zebra and
antelope do not generally run wild in the
Adriatic but Tito liked them and so they
are there. Of the 680 species of plant on
the islands, many subtropical, most were
brought there at Tito's request. Each year
from 1949 until his death in 1980, Maršal
Tito spent six months at his Brijuni 'hide-
aways'. He had three palaces on Veli Brijun – Vila Jadranka, Bijela Vila and Vila
Brionka – in which he received 90 heads
of state and a bevy of movie stars in lavish
style. Bijela Vila was Tito's 'White House';
the place for issuing edicts and declarations
as well as entertaining. The islands have
tremendous natural beauty which emerges
despite their strange inhabitants and they
have become a favourite spot on the international yachting circuit. Crowned heads
and dot-com billionaires love the place, re-
viving its bygone aura of glamour.

The islands are still used for official state visits but Croatian president Stipe Mešić spends less time there than his predecessor. Access is still restricted, however, and you must visit on an organised tour unless you stay at one of the hotels on Veli Brijun. Even staying at a hotel doesn't bring unrestricted freedom. For certain sights on the island, you must hire a guide and jeep.

As you arrive on Veli Brijun, after a half-hour boat ride from Fažana on the mainland, you'll dock in front of the Hotel Istra-Neptun where Tito's illustrious guests once stayed. An English-speaking guide and a miniature tourist train take you on a three-hour tour of the island beginning with a visit to the **safari park**. The fenced area was Tito's private hunting ground, and the exotic animals held there were given to Tito by world leaders.

Other stops on the tour include the ruins of a **Byzantine fortress** inhabited from the 2nd century BC, a **Roman country house** dating from the 1st century AD, and **Sveti Germana Church**, now a gallery displaying copies of medieval frescoes in Istrian churches. Most interesting is the **Tito on Brijuni exhibit** in a building near the hotels. Downstairs is a collection of stuffed animals. Many of the animals sent to Tito as presents failed to survive the long voyage and were dead on arrival. Upstairs are large photos of Tito with film stars such as Gina Lollobrigida, Sophia Loren, Elizabeth Taylor and Richard Burton, all of whom visited Tito here.

Sleeping

There are three hotels on Veli Brijun which are excessively expensive for what they offer, but you do get to look around the island. Boat transport back and forth to the mainland is included in the prices.

Hotel Jurina (☎ 525 806; fax 521 367; d from 985KN) Located near the remains of a Roman castle, rooms are nice enough but hardly luxurious. More expensive rooms overlook the bay.

Hotel Istra-Neptun (☎ 525 806; fax 521 367; s/d 815/1425KN) Rooms are spacious with large, modern bathrooms, TVs, phones, minibars and balconies. The hotel has a large terrace overlooking the port.

Hotel Karmen (☎ 525 806; fax 521 367; s/d 765/1300KN) It is also on the port and only slightly less luxurious than the Hotel Istra-Neptun.

Getting There & Away

You may only visit Brijuni National Park with a group. Instead of booking an excursion with one of the travel agencies in Pula, Rovinj or Poreč, which costs 340KN, you could take a public bus from Pula to Fažana (8km), then sign up for a tour (180KN) at the **Brijuni Tourist Service** (☎ 525 883) office near the wharf. It's best to book in advance, especially in summer.

Also check along the Pula waterfront for excursion boats to Brijuni. The five-hour boat trips from Pula to Brijuni (60KN) may not actually visit the islands but only sail around them. Still, it makes a nice day out.

VODNJAN

pop 3700

Connoisseurs of the macabre won't want to miss Vodnjan (Dignano in Italian) located 10km north of Pula. Lying inside a sober church in this sleepy town are the 'mummies' that constitute Vodnjan's primary tourist attraction. The mummies are the desiccated remains of centuries-old saints whose bodies mysteriously failed to decompose and are considered to have magical powers.

There's not much going on in the rest of the town but the medieval centre is largely intact. Narodni trg, composed of several neo-gothic palaces in varying stages of decay and restoration, contains the **tourist office** (☎ 511 672; tz-vodnjan-dignano@pu.htnet.hr; Narodni trg 3; ☼ 8.30am-3pm Mon-Fri) and is the centre of town.

The mummies' resting place is just a few steps away from Narodni trg in **St Blaise's Church** (Crkva Svetog Blaša; ☎ 511 420; Trg Sveti Blaz; ☼ 9am-7pm Jul-Sep). This handsome, neo-Baroque church was built at the turn of the 19th century when Venice was the stylesetter for the Istrian coast. Modelled after the Venetian Church of San Pietro in Castello designed by Andrea Palladio, its 60m-high bell tower is as high as St Mark's tower in Venice. It's the largest parish church in Istria and would be worth a visit for its magnificent altars even without its eerie exhibits. The mummies are in a curtained-off area behind the **main altar** (adult/concession 30/18KN). In the dim lighting, the complete bodies of St Nikolosa Bursa, St Giovanni Olini of Venice and St Leon Bembo resemble wooden dolls in their glass cases. Assorted body parts of three other saints complete the display. As you examine the skin, hair and finger nails of these long-dead people, a cassette in English narrates their life stories.

If the mummies have whetted your appetite for saintly relics, head to the **Collection of Sacral Art** (Zbirka Sakralne Umjetnosti; adult/concession 30/18KN) in the sacristy where there are over 200 relics belonging to 150 different saints, including the undecayed tongue of St Mary of Egypt. Less grisly exhibits include a masterful polyptych of Leon Bembo by Paolo Veneziano painted in 1321 to serve as the lid of Bembo's coffin.

Vodnjan's other attraction is an excellent regional restaurant. **Gostiona-Trattoria Vodnjanka** (☎ 511 435; Istarska bb; mains from 30KN) resembles a sprawling country manor with several rustic rooms and warm, personal service. The Istrian specialities are delicious, especially the *fuši* (special home-made egg pasta twisted into a unique shape) topped with truffles, boneless pork loin and Istrian prosciutto.

Vodnjan is well connected with Pula by bus (11KN, 20 minutes, 18 daily).

ROVINJ
pop 12,910

Rovinj (Rovigno in Italian) is Istria's star attraction. Yes, it's touristy and residents are developing a sharp eye for maximising their profits, but Rovinj is one of the last of the true Mediterranean fishing ports. Fishermen haul their catch into the harbour in the early morning, followed by a horde of squawking gulls, and mend their nets before lunch. Prayers for a good catch are sent forth at the massive Cathedral of St Euphemia whose 60m-high tower punctuates the peninsula. Wooded hills and low-rise luxury hotels surround a town webbed by steep, cobbled streets. The 13 green, offshore islands of the Rovinj archipelago make for pleasant, varied views and you can swim from the rocks in the sparkling water below Hotel Rovinj.

History

Originally an island, Rovinj was first mentioned in the 7th century as Ruvignio, but it's believed that the town emerged at least several centuries earlier – possibly between the 3rd and 5th centuries. It was settled by Slavs in the 7th century and began to develop a strong fishing and maritime industry.

In 1199, Rovinj signed an important pact with Dubrovnik to protect its maritime

trade, but in the 13th century the threat of piracy forced it to turn to Venice for protection. The town was fortified under the Venetians but was still subject to attacks from Genoa and the Uskoks.

From the 16th to the 18th centuries its population expanded dramatically with an influx of immigrants fleeing Turkish invasions of Bosnia and continental Croatia. The town began to develop outside the walls and, in 1763, the islet was connected to the mainland and Rovinj became a peninsula. Perhaps because of its location, Rovinj was spared the epidemics that ravaged the rest of the Istrian peninsula and enjoyed greater economic development.

Although its maritime industry thrived in the 17th century, Austria's 1719 decision to make Trieste and Rijeka free ports dealt the town a blow. The rise of sailing ships further damaged Rovinj's shipbuilding industry and in the middle of the 19th century it was supplanted by the shipyard in Pula. Like the rest of Istria, Rovinj bounced from Austrian to French to Austrian to Italian rule before finally becoming part of postwar Yugoslavia. There's still an Italian community here.

Orientation

The old town of Rovinj is contained within an egg-shaped peninsula, with the bus station just to the southeast. There are two harbours – the northern open harbour and small, protected Rovinj Harbour to the south. About 1.5km south of the old town is the Punta Corrente Forest Park and the wooded cape of Zlatni Rat (Golden Cape), which has several large hotels. A small archipelago of islands lies just offshore, the most popular being Crveni Otok (Red Island) Sveti Katarina (St Catherine's Island) and Sveti Andrija.

Information
INTERNET ACCESS

Planet Tourist Agency (☎ 840 494; Sv Križ 1; per hr 30KN) The most convenient Internet access; it has a couple of computers.

LAUNDRY

Galax Lavonderia (☎ 814 059; M Benussi; per 5kg 50KN; ⏲ 7am-8pm Mon-Fri, to 3pm Sat)

LEFT LUGGAGE

Garderoba (per day 10KN; ⏲ 5.15am-8.30pm) At the bus station.

MONEY

There's an ATM next to the bus station entrance, and Autotrans Travel Agency will change money.

POST

Main Post Office (M Benussi 4) Across from the bus station, you can make phone calls here.

TOURIST INFORMATION

Tourist Office (☎ 811 566; www.tzgrovinj.hr; Obala Pina Budicina 12; ☻ 8am-9pm Mon-Sat, 9am-1pm Sun Jul & Aug, 8am-3pm Mon-Fri & to 2pm Sat Sep-Jun) Just off Trg Maršala Tita, it has limited information.

TRAVEL AGENCIES

Atlas Travel Agency (☎ 813 463; V Nazora bb) Next to the Hotel Park.

Autotrans Travel Agency (☎ 811 453)

Delfin Travel Agency (☎ 813 266; ferry dock) Runs excursions, and rents cars, scooters and bicycles.

Eurostar Travel (☎ 813 144; Obala Pina Budicina 1) Has schedules and tickets for boats to Italy.

Futura Travel (☎ 817 281; futura-travel@pu.htnet.hr; M Benussi 2)

Planet Tourist Agency (☎ 840 494; Sv Križ 1)

Sights

The massive **Cathedral of St Euphemia** (Katedrala Sveti Eufenija; ☎ 815 615; Petro Stankovića; ☻ 10am-2pm & 3-6pm daily Jul-Aug) completely dominates the town from its hill-top location in the middle of the peninsula. Built in 1736, it's the largest baroque building in Istria, reflecting the period during the 18th century when Rovinj was its most populous town, an important fishing centre and the bulwark of the Venetian fleet. Next to the side door of the church is a 14th-century marble relief of St Euphemia. Inside the cathedral, don't miss the tomb of St Euphemia behind the right-hand altar. The saint was born around 290, became a Christian and was tortured mercilessly by Emperor Diocletian before being thrown to the lions in 304. Her body was later taken to Constantinople where it remained until 800. According to legend, the body disappeared one dark and stormy night only to appear off the coast of Rovinj in a spectral boat. The townspeople were unable to budge the heavy sarcophagus until a small boy appeared with two cows, also spectral, and claimed that the saint had appeared to him. The sarcophagus was dragged to the top of the hill and

placed in the small Church of St George that preceded the present-day cathedral. On the anniversary of her martyrdom (16 September) devotees congregate here.

The 60m bell tower was constructed by Italian architects who modelled it after St Mark's bell tower in Venice. The tower is topped by a copper statue of St Euphemia, which was created in 1758 and acts as a weather vane.

The **Regional Museum** (☎ 816 720; Trg Maršala Tita; adult/concession 10/8KN; ☻ 9am-12.30pm & 6-9pm Mon-Sat mid-Jun–mid-Sep, 10am-1pm Tue-Sat rest of year) contains a collection of 15th- to 19th-century paintings and works by contemporary artists in Rovinj, as well as several Etruscan pieces. Its opening hours are irregular in the low season.

Nearby is the elaborate **Balbi Arch**, built in 1679 on the location of the town gate. The top of the arch is ornamented with a Turkish head on the outside and a Venetian head on the inside. To the right and left over the arch are the coats of arms of the Balbi family and above it there's a relief of the Venetian lion.

The baroque **Franciscan monastery** (☎ 815 615; Ulica deamicis 36; ☻ for Mass) was built at the beginning of the 18th century and contains a valuable library as well as a small museum of 18th- and 19th-century paintings and sculptures.

Established in 1891, the best museum is the **Rovinj Aquarium** (☎ 804 700; Obala Giordano Paliaga 5; admission 10KN; ☻ 10am-5pm mid-Apr–Jun & Sep–mid-Oct, 9am-9pm Jul-Aug). It exhibits a good collection of local marine life, from poisonous scorpion fish to colourful anemones.

The winding narrow **backstreets** that lie behind the Balbi Arch are Rovinj's finest attraction. Windows, balconies, portals and squares are a pleasant confusion of styles – Gothic, Renaissance, baroque and neoclassical. Notice the unique *fumaioli* (exterior chimneys), built when the town's population was exploding and entire families were housed in a single room with a fireplace. Ulica Grisia is the 'artists' street' where local artists sell their work, especially in mid-August during the open-air art show. There's also a fairly dense assortment of souvenir shops.

When you've seen enough of the town, follow the waterfront south past Hotel Park to the **Punta Corrente Forest Park**, which was established in 1890 by Baron Hütterodt,

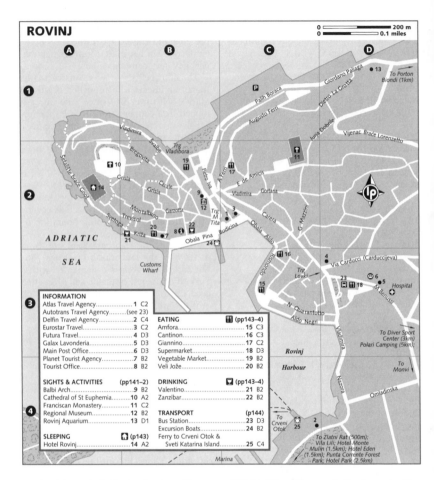

ROVINJ

INFORMATION	
Atlas Travel Agency	1 C2
Autotrans Travel Agency	(see 23)
Delfin Travel Agency	2 C4
Eurostar Travel	3 C2
Futura Travel	4 D3
Galax Lavonderia	5 D3
Main Post Office	6 D3
Planet Tourist Agency	7 B2
Tourist Office	8 B2

SIGHTS & ACTIVITIES	(pp141–2)
Balbi Arch	9 B2
Cathedral of St Euphemia	10 A2
Franciscan Monastery	11 C2
Regional Museum	12 B2
Rovinj Aquarium	13 D1

SLEEPING	(p143)
Hotel Rovinj	14 A2

EATING	(pp143–4)
Amfora	15 C3
Cantinon	16 C3
Giannino	17 C2
Supermarket	18 D3
Vegetable Market	19 B2
Veli Jože	20 B2

DRINKING	(pp143–4)
Valentino	21 B2
Zanzibar	22 B2

TRANSPORT	(p144)
Bus Station	23 D3
Excursion Boats	24 B2
Ferry to Crveni Otok &	
Sveti Katarina Island	25 C4

an Austrian admiral who kept a villa on Crveni Otok. Here you can swim off the rocks, climb a cliff or just sit and admire the offshore islands.

Activities

Most people hop aboard a boat for serious swimming, snorkelling and sunbathing. A trip to Crveni Otok or Sveti Katarina is easily arranged (see p144). **Diver Sport Center** (☎ 816 648, 099 519 230; www.diver.hr; Villas Rubin) is the largest operation in Rovinj offering boat dives that start at about 200KN. Equipment rental is an extra 225KN. The main scuba attraction here is the wreck of the *Baron Gautsch*, an Austrian passenger-steamer sunk in 1914 by an Austrian mine, causing

177 fatalities. The wreck lies in up to 40m of water and offers plenty of marine life. For more information, see p259.

There are also 80 rock-climbing routes in a former Venetian stone quarry in Zlatni Rat, many suitable for beginners. **Pro Montana** (☎ 384 184) at the entrance to Zlatni Rat will provide a guide and equipment for 180KN. They also offer a climbing excursion to Vranjska Draga on the western slopes of the Učka range for 600KN.

Tours

Delfin Agency runs half-day scenic cruises to the Limska Draga Fjord (130KN) or you could try one of the independent operators at the end of Alzo Rismondo which run half- and full-day boat trips there and elsewhere around the region.

Festivals & Events

The city's annual events include the **Rovinj-Pesaro Regata** (early May) the **Rovinj Summer concert series** (July and August), the **Rovinj Fair** (August), and a series of **sailing regattas** from August to October. On the second Sunday in August Ulica Grisia becomes an **open-air art-fest** where anyone from children to professional painters can display their work. The narrow street is packed with tourists and Istrians as the event is renowned throughout the region.

Sleeping

Rovinj has become Istria's destination of choice for hordes of summertime tourists. Prices have been rising steadily and probably will continue to do so. It is strongly recommended to reserve in advance. There are a few camping grounds near Rovinj plus a few hotels in the old town. Most hotels are on the Zlatni Rat Cape.

Hotel Rovinj (☎ 811 288; fax 840 757; Svetoga Križa; s/d from 380/640KN; ☒) With a splendid location overlooking the sea, this hotel was undergoing renovation when we visited, which may make it more expensive. If prices stay the same, it's a great deal.

Vila Lili (☎ 840 940; www.cel.hr/vilalili; Mohorovicica 16; s/d 410/750KN; ☒) This small hotel provides an excellent level of comfort that includes satellite TV, a sauna and bright, modern rooms. It's just a short walk out of town past the marina.

Hotel Monte Mulin (☎ 811 512; fax 815 882; s/d 241/410KN; ℙ) On the wooded hillside overlooking the bay just beyond Hotel Park, it's about a 15-minute walk heading south of the bus station. Rooms are bland but perfectly serviceable.

Hotel Villa Angelo D'Oro (☎ 840 502; www.rovinj .at; Via Svalba 38-42; s/d 823/1455KN; ☒) This new luxury hotel in a renovated Venetian building has plush, lavishly decorated rooms with satellite TV, minibar and a free sauna and Jacuzzi room.

Hotel Adriatic (☎ 815 088; fax 813 573; P Budicina bb; s/d 480/770KN; ☒) The Adriatic is in a 1912 building right in the town centre. The rooms are large and in good shape but there are only a few dozen so it is wise to reserve.

Hotel Eden (☎ 800 400; fax 811 349; L Adamovića, Zlatni Rat Cape; s/d 735/1275KN; ℙ ☒ ☒) With sports grounds, a gym, a sauna and indoor and outdoor pools there's plenty to do in all weather. You'll have plenty of company since the complex holds 733 beds.

Hotel Park (☎ 811 077; fax 816 977; IM Ronjigova; s/d 585/1015KN; ℙ ☒ ☒) Somewhat smaller than the Eden, this hotel also offers such pleasing amenities as indoor and outdoor pools and a sauna. Plus, it's conveniently close to the ferry dock for Crveni Otok.

If you want to camp, **Porton Biondi** (☎ 813 557; per person/site 55/35KN) is less than 1km from the town (on the Monsena bus route) and **Polari Camping** (☎ 800 376; per person/site 55/30KN) is about 5km southeast from town; it is much larger but has more facilities.

PRIVATE ROOMS

There are few rooms available in the old town. Rooms with two beds cost 200KN in high season with a small discount for single occupancy. The surcharge for a stay of less than three nights is 50% and guests who stay only one night are punished with a 100% surcharge, but you should be able to bargain the surcharge away outside of July and August. You can book directly from www.inforovinj.com or consult one of the travel agencies listed on p141.

Eating & Drinking

Picnickers can get supplies at the supermarket next to the bus station, or pick up a *burek* (a heavy pastry stuffed with meat or cheese) from one of the kiosks near the vegetable market.

Most of the fish and spaghetti restaurants that line the harbour cater to well-heeled tourists.

Cantinon (☎ 811 970; 18 Obala Alzo Rismondo; mains from 25KN) You won't mind the paper tablecloths and napkins when you taste the fresh grilled fish at this large, informal canteen.

Veli Jože (☎ 816 337; Svetoga Kriša 1; mains 35KN) Though somewhat more expensive than Cantinon, this is a good place to try Istrian dishes, either in an interior crammed with knick-knacks or on outdoor tables. Try the *bakalar* (cod) in a white sauce, or baked lamb with potatoes.

Amfora (☎ 815 525; Rismondo 23; mains from 50KN) One of the best restaurants in town, it's expensive and packed in high season but you will eat well.

Giannino (☎ 813 402; A Ferri 38; mains from 70KN) If you like Italian food, it doesn't get much better than this. Everything from the olive oil to the grilled seafood is first rate.

Valentino (☎ 830 683; Santa Croce 28) The best show in town is watching the sunset from this place. Cocktails are pricey but sitting on the rocks next to the sea with a view of Katarina Island is definitely worth the splurge.

Zanzibar (☎ 813 206; P Budicina bb) Indonesian wood, palms, subdued lighting and various imaginative decorative touches create a vaguely tropical and definitely upscale ambience in this cocktail bar.

Getting There & Away
There are buses from Rovinj to Pula (23KN, 40 minutes, 18 daily), Dubrovnik (355KN, 17½ hours), Labin (42KN, 2½ hours, six daily), Ljubljana (165KN, 5½ hours), Poreč (23KN, one hour, seven daily), Trieste (75KN, six hours, one daily), Venice (180KN, eight hours) and Zagreb (132KN, five to eight hours, eight daily). For more information on connections to Italy, see p274.

The closest train station is Kanfanar, 19km away on the Pula–Divača line.

Getting Around
You can rent bicycles at Delfin Travel Agency for 45KN per half-day.

AROUND ROVINJ
A popular day trip from Rovinj is a boat ride to the lovely **Crveni Otok** (Red Island). Only 1900m long, the island includes two islets, Sveti Andrija and Maškin, which are connected by a causeway. From the 6th century, Sveti Andrija had a Benedictine monastery, later kept by the Franciscans. In the 19th century the island became the property of Baron Hütterodt who transformed it into a luxuriantly wooded park. The Hotel Istra complex now dominates Sveti Andrija but its small gravel beaches and playground make it popular with families. Maškin is quieter and more wooded. Half of the island is naturist but there are plenty of secluded coves for everyone. Bring a mask for snorkelling around the rocks.

There's an hourly ferry to Crveni Otok (20KN return, 15 minutes) and frequent ferries (10KN return, five minutes) to nearby **Sveti Katarina**, which was forested by a Polish count in 1905 and now houses Hotel Katarina. You board the boat in Rovinj without a ticket, then pay for the return ticket onboard as you leave Crveni Otok.

The **Limska Draga Fjord** is the most dramatic sight in Istria. About 9km long and 600m wide, the inlet was formed when the Istrian coastline sank during the last ice age, allowing the sea to rush in and fill the Draga Valley. The walls of the valley become steeper the further inland you go, rising to a height of 100m. There are hills on both sides of the inlet and two caves that have revealed traces of prehistoric settlements. Fishing, oyster farming and excursion boats are the only activities in the fjord. You can take an excursion from Rovinj, Pula or Poreč or follow signs to the fjord past Krunčići. At **Sveti Lovrec**, you'll find several waterside restaurants that serve up the freshest seafood in all Istria. At **Viking** (☎ 448 223) or **Fjord** (☎ 448 222) you can get a seafood meal on a terrace overlooking the fjord for less than 100KN. In addition to the restaurants, there's a picnic area, a swimming cove and a cluster of souvenir stands. Small excursion boats will take you on a one-hour boat ride for €10 (negotiable). They leave every half hour in July and August but less frequently in June and September.

POREČ
pop 17,000
Poreč (Parenzo in Italian; Parentium in Roman times) and the surrounding region is like a country unto itself, one that is devoted to tourism. Year after year the town wins a national award for tourism in recognition of its efficiency and imagination in developing the only real industry in the region. Poreč is the centrepiece of a vast system of tourist resorts that stretch north and south along the Istrian coast. The most scenic are south of the city and the largest is Zelena Laguna, with a full range of facilities and accommodation.

These holiday villages and tourist camps offer a somewhat industrialised holiday experience with too much concrete and too many tour buses for some tastes. The hotels, restaurants, tourist offices and travel agencies, however, are almost universally staffed by friendly, multilingual people who make a real effort to welcome visitors. Tourism is all they've got and they know it, and they're not ashamed of it. This is not the place for a quiet little getaway (unless you come in January), but there's a World Heritage–site basilica and the Istrian interior is within easy reach.

History

The coast of Poreč measures 37km, islands included, but the ancient town is confined to a peninsula 400m long and 200m wide. The Romans conquered the region in the 2nd century BC and made Poreč an important administrative centre from which they were able to control a sweep of land from the Limska Draga Fjord to the Mirna River. Poreč's street plan was laid out by the Romans, who divided the town into rectangular parcels marked by the longitudinal Dekumanus and the latitudinal Cardo.

On the collapse of the Western Roman Empire, Poreč came under Byzantine rule, which lasted from the 6th to 8th centuries. It was under the influence of Byzantine culture that the Euphrasian Basilica, with its magnificent frescoes, was erected. The Aquilean patriarchs ruled the city in the early Middle Ages but Poreč was forced to submit to Venetian rule in 1267.

Poreč was particularly hard hit by the Istrian plague epidemics, with the town's population declining to about 100 in the 17th century. The town was repopulated with refugees fleeing the Turks in the second half of the 17th century.

With the decline of Venice, the town fell under Austrian, French and then Austrian rule before the Italian occupation that lasted from 1918 to 1943. Upon the capitulation of Italy, Poreč was occupied by the Germans and damaged by Allied bombing in 1944 before becoming part of postwar Yugoslavia.

Orientation

The compact old town is squeezed into the peninsula and packed with thousands of shops. The ancient Roman Dekumanus, with its polished stones, is still the main street. Hotels, travel agencies and excursion boats are on the quay, Obala Maršala Tita which runs from the small-boat harbour to the tip of the peninsula. The bus station is directly opposite the small-boat harbour just outside the old town.

Information

INTERNET ACCESS
Internet Center Cyberm@c (☎ 427 075; Grahalića 1; per hr 42KN) A full-service Internet and computer centre.

LEFT LUGGAGE
Garderoba (Bus station; ☒ 6am-8pm Mon-Sat, 6am-5pm Sun)

MONEY
You can change your money at any travel agency.
Istarska Banka (A Negrija 6) Has an ATM.

POST
Main Post Office (Trg Slobode 14) Has a telephone centre.

TOURIST INFORMATION
Tourist Office (☎ 451 293; www.istra.com/porec; Zagrebačka 11; ☒ 8am-10pm Mon-Sat year-round, 9am-1pm & 6-10pm Sun Jul & Aug)

TRAVEL AGENCIES
Atlas Travel Agency (☎ 434 983; Eufrazijeva 63) Represents Amex.
Di Tours (☎ 432 100, 452 018; www.di-tours.hr; Prvomajska 2) Finds private accommodation.
Fiore Tours (☎ /fax 431 397; fiore@pu.htnet.hr; Mate Vašića 6) Also handles private accommodation.
Istra-Line (☎ 451 067; P Setaliste 2) If you follow Nikole Tesle until it becomes Kalčića you'll come to Mate Vašića, where you'll find this agency in a pink building.
Sunny Way Agency (☎ 452 021; Alda Negrija 1) Has information about boat connections to Italy.

Sights

The main reason to visit Poreč is to see the 6th-century **Euphrasian Basilica** (☎ 431 635; Sv Eleuterija; admission free, to climb belfry 10KN; ☒ 7am-8pm Apr-Sep, 7am-7pm Oct-Mar) a World Heritage site and one of the finest intact examples of Byzantine art. Built on the site of a 4th-century basilica and 5th-century church, the complex includes a church, atrium and baptistry. Mosaics from the earlier structures are still visible on the floor of the northern nave but it is the glittering wall mosaics in the apse that packs in the crowds. These 6th-century masterpieces feature Biblical scenes, archangels and Istrian martyrs.

Notice the group to the left, which shows Bishop Euphrasius, who commissioned the basilica, with a model of the church in his hand. The ciborium over the main altar

ISTRIA

was erected in 1277, modelled after the one in St Mark's in Venice. The southern wall has three chapels. The western chapel (Chapel of the Holy Cross) is decorated with a large polyptych created in 1440 by Antonio Vivarini and Jacobo Palma Junior's oil painting *The Last Supper*. In the central chapel (Chapel of the Crucifixion) there are choir pews that were carved in 1452. The belfry affords an invigorating view of the region. The adjacent **Bishop's Palace** (admission 10KN) was also built in the 6th century and contains a display of ancient stone monuments as well as many 4th-century mosaics. It's well worth a visit.

Trg Marafor is where the Roman Forum used to stand; the original pavement has been preserved along the northern row of houses on the square. West of the square are the ruins of the 2nd-century **Temple of Neptune** and another large temple from the beginning of the 1st century.

Southeast of Trg Marafor on Dekumanus there is an interesting 13th-century **Romanesque house** with a wooden balcony, and further east there's a **Gothic house** from the 15th century with a Renaissance portal. The baroque Sinčić Palace houses the **Regional Museum** (☎ 431 585; Dekumanus 9; adult/concession 10/5KN; ☽ 10am-1pm & 5-9pm Jul-Aug, 10am-1pm Sep-Jun) which opened in 1884. It contains over 2000 exhibits spanning Poreč's tumultuous history from the Palaeolithic Age until the 20th century. In addition to furniture, paintings and artefacts, there are mosaic fragments from the 3rd century, crosses, choir stalls and altar paintings.

The few remaining parts of the ramparts are visible from the north side of the city and there are three 15th-century towers that date from the Venetian rule: the **Pentagonal Tower** (the only preserved part of the former town gates); the **Round Tower** on Trg Narodni; and the **North-East Tower** on Peškera Bay.

Activities

Nearly every activity you might want to enjoy is outside the town in either Plava Laguna or Zelena Laguna. Most of the sports centres in Plava Laguna are affiliated with hotels and have tennis courts with basketball and volleyball, windsurfing, rowing, bungee jumping, water-skiing, parasailing, boat rentals and canoeing. If the weather turns bad, you can always work out in the fitness

centre. For further information, call the tourist office or the **City of Poreč Sports Association** (☎ 431 132).

The gently rolling hills of the interior and the well-marked bike paths make **cycling** an excellent way to experience the region. The tourist office issues a free map of roads and trails stemming from Poreč, along with suggested routes. You can rent a bike from **Ivona** (☎ 434 037; Prvomajska 2) next to Di Tours, for 20/50/80KN per hour/half/full day.

Hotel Galijot in Plava Laguna has the largest and best equipped diving centre in the region. At **Plava Laguna Diving Center** (☎ 451 549; www.plava-laguna-diving.hr) boat dives start at 90KN (more for caves or wrecks) plus 225KN for full-equipment rental.

From May to mid-October there are a number of passenger boats (20KN return) travelling to **Sveti Nikola**, the small island opposite Poreč harbour. The boats depart every 30 minutes from the wharf on Obala Maršala Tita.

Tours

Most travel agencies offer boat tours along the Istrian coast for about 200KN, and Atlas Travel Agency offers a full-day tour of the Istrian interior that includes stops at Grošnjan and Motovun for 325KN, with lunch included.

Festivals & Events

On 30 April, Poreč celebrates two major events – the city's liberation during WWII and the opening of the tourist season. The mayor presents various awards and honours to 'good citizens', which generally means people who have made an effort to further tourism by sweeping the streets or opening a new service. During July and August there's **Annale**, one of the oldest Croatian art exhibitions, which usually has a theme. It's a great opportunity to catch up on the latest Croatian and international artists. Other annual events include the **Musical Summer** (May to September). There are also **summer concerts** in Trg Slobode each Thursday at 9pm – ask about these and other concerts at the tourist office.

Sleeping

Accommodation in Poreč is not cheap and if you come in July or August advance bookings are essential.

ISTRIA

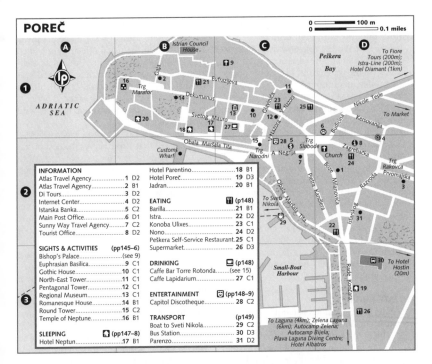

POREČ

Camping grounds are usually large, well-organised little cities with plenty of activities. There are two camping grounds at Zelena Laguna, 6km south of Poreč. Take the 'Zelena Laguna' resort tourist train (20KN) that runs half-hourly or hourly from the town centre between April and October, or catch the boat shuttle.

Hotels in and around Poreč are not particularly cheap but generally in good condition. The major hotel complexes are in Brulo, 2km south of town, Plava Laguna, 4km south of the old town, and Zelena Laguna, 2km further. Some 20 hotels are planted in these three wooded areas, as well as another dozen or so apartment complexes. The hotels are mostly in the three-star category and generally include air-con, TVs, phones and beach access. A number are half-board arrangements.

Most hotels are managed by **Riviera** (☎ 408 000; www.riviera.hr) or **Plava Laguna** (☎ 410 101; www.plavalaguna.hr). All hotels are open from April to October but there is only one hotel in town open in winter and it changes every year.

Hotel Hostin (☎ 432 112; www.hostin.hr; Rade Končara 4; per person 556KN; P ⊠ ⚄ 🖥 🏊) One of the newer entries on the hotel scene, this sparkling place is in verdant parkland just behind the bus station. An indoor swimming pool, fitness room and sauna are nice little extras, plus the hotel is only 70m from a pebble beach. The price includes obligatory half board.

Hotel Poreč (☎ 451 811; www.hotelporec.com; Rade Končara 1; s/d 445/678KN; ⚄) Near the bus station and an easy walk from the old town, you'll find freshly renovated and comfortable rooms at this hotel. The views over the bus station and shopping centre are less than inspiring.

Hotel Neptun (☎ 400 800; riviera@riviera.hr; Obala Maršala Tita 15; s/d 436/685KN; P ⚄) It's the best hotel in the town centre which is an advantage if you want to be in the action but it also means being in the middle of a traffic snarl in peak season. The front rooms with harbour views are unbeatable.

Hotel Parentino (☎ 431 925; riviera@riviera .hr; Obala M Tita 17; d from 530KN) Nearby and affiliated to the Neptun, Hotel Parentino has no-frills doubles in a very elegant 19th-century building with high ceilings.

Jadran (☎ 431 236; riviera@riviera.hr; Obala M Tita; s/d 340/490KN) The hotel is in a solid old building on the waterfront. The front rooms can be noisy in summer.

Autocamp Zelena Laguna (☎ 410 541; per adult/site 50/70KN) Well equipped for sports, it can house up to 2700 people.

Autocamp Bijela Uvala (☎ 410 5511; per adult/site 50/70KN) Houses up to 6000, so it can be crowded.

There are family-orientated hotels that are designed to be self-contained, with restaurants, bars, nearby mini-markets and plenty of activities, especially for the kids. These range in price from the **Hotel Albatros** (☎ 410 561; albatros@plavalaguna.hr; s/d 240/460KN) to the **Hotel Diamant** (☎ 400 000; riviera@riviera.hr; Brulo; s/d 570/1125KN). For a family holiday they offer a good deal – quiet and romantic they are not.

PRIVATE ROOMS

All of the travel agencies listed on p145 find private accommodation. Expect to pay from 165/240KN for a room with shared/private facilities in the high season plus a 30% surcharge for stays less than three nights. There are a limited number of rooms available in the old town and it's wise to reserve far in advance for the July-August period.

FARMHOUSES

'Agritourism' is an increasingly popular accommodation option in and around Poreč. Some of the residences are actual farms engaged in producing wine, vegetables and poultry; some are country houses with a few rooms to let; others are modern villas with swimming pools and opportunities for hiking and bike riding. The tourist office has issued a brochure with photos and information about rural holidays throughout Istria offering visits and stays, or you can consult www.istra.com/agroturizam. You'll need your own car and prices run from 145KN to 600KN per person for a double room with half board, depending upon the location and facilities.

Eating

A large supermarket and department store are situated next to Hotel Poreč, near the bus station.

Istra (☎ 434 636; Milanovića 30; mains from 50KN) This is where locals go for a special meal. In addition to the usual offerings of grilled fish, spaghetti and calamari there are delicious local specialities such as a mixed seafood starter and *mućkalica*, stewed chicken and vegetables in a spicy sauce. There's a cosy interior and a covered terrace with wooden booths.

Nono (☎ 435 088; Zagrebačka 4; pizzas 25-30KN) You can tell that Nono serves the best pizzas in town because it's always crowded. With their soft, puffy crust and fresh toppings, these pizzas are actually memorable.

Barilla (☎ 452 742; Eufrazijana 26; mains 50-90KN) This authentic Italian restaurant serves delicious pasta and pizza as well as more sophisticated Italian dishes on two outdoor terraces.

Konoba Ulixes (☎ 451 132; Dekumanus 2; mains 40-100KN) Truffles are one of Istria's most precious products and you can taste them here in pasta, with beef or fresh tuna. The fish and shellfish is also excellent, and be sure to look for the special asparagus dishes in season.

Peškera Self-Service Restaurant (Nikole Tesle bb; mains 28-40KN; ☷ 9am-10pm) Situated just outside the northwestern corner of the old city wall, this is one of the best of its kind in Croatia. You can get a cheap but good main course such as fried chicken, grilled calamari or rump steak and eat it on a terrace facing the sea.

Drinking

Caffe Lapidarium (Svetog Mauro 10) The sound of Croatian crooners sails forth from the sound system while you relax in a large courtyard or antique-filled inner rooms. Wednesday night is jazz night in the summer when all sorts of groups turn up to play.

Caffe Bar Torre Rotonda (Narodni trg 3a) In the historic Round Tower, this upstairs café is a good spot to watch the action on the quays in a soft, jazzy atmosphere.

Entertainment

Most nightlife is out of town at Zelena Laguna where the big hotels host discos and various party nights, but the old town has its attractions a well.

Capitol Discotheque (V Nazora 9) This is the oldest disco in town, playing a mix of commercial music.

Getting There & Away

For information on connections to Italy and Slovenia inquire at Sunny Way travel agency and see pp274-5.

There are buses from the **bus station** (☎ 432 153; Rade Končara 1) to Rovinj (23KN, one hour, seven daily), Zagreb and Rijeka (55KN, 5½ hours, eight daily), and Pula (33KN, 1¼ hours, 12 daily). Between Poreč and Rovinj the bus runs along the Limska Draga Fjord (Lim Channel), a drowned valley. To see it clearly, sit on the right-hand side if you're southbound, or the left if you're northbound.

The nearest train station is at Pazin, 30km to the east (five buses daily from Poreč).

Getting Around

From June to mid-September a tourist train operates hourly or half-hourly from Trg Slobode to Zelena Laguna (20KN) and there's also a passenger boat that makes the same run. There are hourly buses to Vrsar that stop at Plava Laguna, Zelena Laguna and the other resorts south of the city.

Parenzo (☎ 427 103; Istarskog razvoda 11) offers reasonable prices for car rental.

THE ISTRIAN INTERIOR

As you head inland from the coast you'll notice less crowds, less hotel complexes and a magnificent countryside dotted with stone villages. The rhythm of daily life slows down considerably, defined less by the needs of tourists and more by the demands of harvesting grapes, hunting for truffles and cultivating orchards. Still, changes are afoot. Farmhouses are opening their doors to tourists looking for a more authentic holiday experience. Remote hill-top villages that once seemed doomed to ruin are attracting colonies of artists and artisans. Foreigners are buying second residences in a bucolic region some are calling 'the new Tuscany'.

PAZIN

pop 5200

No fashionable foreigners are crowding Pazin's streets and that's part of its appeal. This workaday town in central Istria deserves a stop, not only for its famous Chasm that so inspired Jules Verne or the stolid medieval castle that dominates the western portion of town, but also for its neighbourly small-town feel. The rolling Istrian countryside creeps right up to the town's outskirts while most of the centre is given over to pedestrian-only areas. Not only is Pazin the geographic heart of Istria, it's the county's administrative seat as well. As transport connections by road or rail put you within an hour's reach of virtually every other destination in Istria, Pazin makes an excellent, relaxed, inexpensive base to explore the region.

Orientation

From east to west, the town is relatively compact, stretching little more than a kilometre from the train station on the eastern end to the Kaštel on the western end which is at the edge of the Pazin Cave. The bus station is 200m west of the train station and the old part of town comprises the 200m leading up to the Kaštel.

Information

Futura Travel (☎ 621 045; 25 Rujna 42) Changes money, books excursions and provides regional information.
Post Office (MB Rašana 7A)
Tourist Office (☎ /fax 622 460; www.tzpazin.hr; Franinei Jurine 14; 🕑 8.30am-6pm daily Jul-Aug, 8am-3pm Mon-Fri Sep-Jun) It finds private accommodation.

Sights

Pazin's most renowned site is undoubtedly the **Pazin Chasm**, an abyss of about 100m through which the Pazinčica river sinks into subterranean passages forming three underground lakes. Its shadowy depths inspired the imagination of Jules Verne (see Mathias Sandorf and the Pazin Chasm, p150) as well as numerous Croatian writers. There's a viewing point just outside the castle and a footbridge that spans the abyss about 30m further on.

Pazin's **Kaštel** (☎ 625 040; Istarskog Razvoda 1; 🕑 10am-6pm Tue-Sun mid-Apr–mid-Oct, 10am-3pm Tue-Thu, noon-5pm Fri, 11am-5pm Sat-Sun mid-Oct–mid-Apr; adult/concession 15/8KN) is the largest and best preserved medieval structure in Istria. Overlooking the Pazin Cave, it was first mentioned in 983 but the current structure dates from about 1537. Within the castle, there's an **Ethnographic Museum** with a collection of medieval Istrian church bells as well as Istrian implements, garments and musical instruments.

ISTRIA

MATHIAS SANDORF & THE PAZIN CHASM

The writer best known for going around the world in 80 days, into the centre of the earth, and 20,000 leagues under the sea, found inspiration in the centre of Istria. The French futurist-fantasist Jules Verne (1828–1905), set *Mathias Sandorf* (1885), one of his 27 books in the series *Voyages Extraordinaires,* in the castle and chasm of Pazin.

In the novel, later made into a movie, Count Mathias Sandorf and two cohorts are arrested by the Austrian police for revolutionary activity and are imprisoned in the Pazin castle. Sandorf escapes by climbing down a lightening rod but, (wouldn't you know it?) lightning hits the rod and he tumbles down, down into the roaring Pazinčica river. He's carried along into the murky depths of the Chasm but our plucky hero holds on fast to a tree trunk and, (phew !), six hours later the churning river deposits him at the tranquil entrance to the Limska Draga Fjord. He walks to Rovinj and is last seen jumping from a cliff into the sea amid a hail of bullets. Hold on for the sequel!

What an imagination. Verne spun Sandorf's excellent and utterly impossible adventure from photos and travellers' acounts but that hasn't stopped Pazin from celebrating it at every opportunity. There's a street named after Jules Verne, special Jules Verne days and a website (www .ice.hr/davors/jvclub.htm) for the Pazin-based Jules Verne club.

Near the tourist office is the **Church of St Nickolas** (Svetog Nikola; Muntriljska; ☺ Mass only) notable for its late-Gothic polygonal presbytery and 15th-century frescoes of the Creation in the vault.

Festivals & Events

The first Tuesday of the month is **Town Fair Day**, featuring products from all over Istria. **The Days of Jules Verne** in the third week of June is Pazin's way of honouring the writer that put Pazin on the cultural map. There are races, re-enactments from his novel, and journeys retracing the footsteps of Verne's hero Mathias Sandorf.

Sleeping & Eating

The tourist office helps arrange private accommodation, which is generally reasonably priced. Count on spending about 125KN per person for a room.

Hotel Lovac (☎ 624 324; tisadoo@inet.hr; Kurelića bb; s/d 240/345KN; P) The only hotel in town is a not-especially-characterful place on the western edge of town.

Poli Luce (☎ 687 081; Grašišće; per person 125KN; P) If you don't mind being out of town, try with beautifully restored rooms in an old farmhouse. It's at Grašišće, a sleepy rustic village about 7km south of Pazin.

Konoba Marino (☎ 687 081; mains from 40KN; ☺ closed Wed) The same owners of Poli Luce run Konoba, which is a good place to sample home-made Istrian sausage and other home-smoked meat in copious portions.

Getting There & Away

From the **bus station** (☎ 624 437; Šetalište Pazinske Gimnazije) there are services to Buzet (25KN, 50 minutes, three daily), Motovun (18KN, 35 minutes, five daily), Poreč (23KN, 40 minutes, 10 daily), Pula (29KN, 50 minutes, nine daily), Rijeka (34KN, one hour, five daily) and Rovinj (27KN, one hour, five daily). Service is reduced on weekends. For information on connections to Italy see p274. Pazin **train station** (☎ 622 710; Stareh Kostanje 1) has services to Buzet (18KN, 45 minutes, three daily), Ljubljana (81KN, four hours, one daily), Pula (26KN, one hour, eight daily) and Zagreb (99KN, eight hours, seven daily). There is reduced service on weekends.

BUZET

pop 500

It may not be the most fascinating town around, but in sleepy Buzet you get a whiff of the timeless grace of old Istria. Lying only 39km northeast of Poreč over the Mirna River and first settled by the Romans, Buzet achieved real prominence under the Venetians who endowed it with walls, gates and several churches. The greystone buildings are crumbling now; most have been boarded up. The cobblestone streets are nearly deserted, the old town's residents having long ago resettled in Fontana at the foot of the hill. The only excitement in town is generated by the glorious truffle. Buzet is the centre of the truffle-growing region and celebrates its presence

ISTRIA

on the second Saturday in September with a truffle festival.

Orientation

Most commerce is in the new Fontana section of town at the foot of the hill-top old town. The bus stops in Trg Fontana, a small square in the centre of town, which is where you'll find a few cafés and shops. The train station is 5km east of the town centre and there's no public transport.

Information

Bus Information (☎ 622 811; Fontana bb)
Riječka Banka (Trg Fontana 4) Has an ATM.
Tourist Office (Turistička Zajednica; ☎ /fax 662 343; www.istra.com/buzet; II Istarska Brigade 2; ☒ 8am-3pm Mon-Fri) Has maps and information on wine and truffle roads throughout the region.
Train Information (☎ 622 899)

Sights

The main sight in Buzet is the **Regional Museum** (Zavičajni Muzej Buzet; ☎ 662 792; Trg Rašporskih Kapetana 1; admission 7KN; ☒ 12.30-3.30pm Mon-Fri). The museum displays a collection of prehistoric and Roman artefacts as well as a re-creation of a traditional kitchen. On a square a few metres north of the museum is an exquisite baroque **municipal well**, which was restored in 1789 and sports a Venetian lion relief.

Sleeping & Eating

Surrounding Buzet are a number of farmhouses with rooms to rent. The tourist office should be able to help. There are two hotels in the new town.

Hotel Fontana (☎ 662 466; fax 663 423; Trg Fontana 1; s/d 280/460KN; ℗) Rooms are spacious but worn, but they all have balconies and the staff can offer helpful information on the town and the region. The hotel's restaurant serves up decent food, including truffle-based dishes.

Motel Sunsport (☎ /fax 663 140; cnr Sportska & Riječka; s/d 300/480KN; ℗) Built over a local bar 500m northeast of Trg Fontana, the rooms are in good shape but minuscule. The staff speak only Croatian and German.

Getting There & Away

Buzet is connected by bus with Poreč (29KN, one hour, one daily) and by train with Pula (41KN, two hours, four daily).

AROUND BUZET

The rolling hills, woods, pastures and vineyards southeast of Buzet make for a memorably scenic drive. Off the main road lie two rustic villages of picture-perfect prettiness. **Roč**, 8km southeast of Buzet, is so small that it would seem crowded if its entire population of 17 were outdoors at once.

Snug within its 15th-century walls, the town slumbers most of the year, roused only by the annual Trieština Accordion Festival, which takes place on the second weekend in May. The rest of the year Roč's delights are mainly visual: the view of wooded hills rising in the distance; the Romanesque **Church of St Anthony** (Crkva Svetog Antuna); a 15th-century **Renaissance house** in a square next to the church; and **Roman monuments** inside the town gate. One of the low, stone buildings houses an excellent regional restaurant, **Ročka Konoba** (☎ 666 451; mains from 35KN). Whether you are warmed by the interior fireplace or enjoying the view from the outdoor tables, you will have a chance to discover first-rate Istrian specialities such as *fuši* pasta, home-made sausages and *maneštra* (minestrone or vegetable and bean soup).

Outside Roč is the **Glagolitic Lane**, a series of 11 sculptures commemorating the town's importance as a centre of Glagolitic literature. The lane ends in **Hum**, another 7km to the southeast, which bills itself as the world's smallest town with a population of eight or 23, depending on who's counting. Legend has it that the giants that built Istria had only a few stones left over and used them to build Hum. Once Istria's best-kept secret, the tiny village is developing a following.

Although Hum has roughly the same population as Roč, it seems more active, possibly because it has a museum/souvenir shop. The **Town Museum** (Gradski Muzej; ☎ 660 054; admission free; ☒ 11am-7pm Mar-Oct) displays a few Glagolitic writings and also sells *biska*, a strong, sweet local brandy made from mistletoe. It takes just a few minutes to walk around the narrow village lanes, but don't miss the 12th-century frescoes in the **Chapel of St Jerome** (Crkvica Svetog Jerolim). The paintings depict the life of Jesus with unusually vivid colours. The chapel is locked but you can get the key at the town inn, Humska Konoba.

ISTRIA

Humska Konoba (☎ 660 005; Hum 2; mains from 25KN; 🕒 closed Mon) is another fine regional restaurant, with an outdoor terrace offering panoramic views. Start with a shot of *biska* then go on to the *fuši* with truffles (70KN) or the *bobići* corn soup (14KN).

Getting There & Away

You really need your own wheels to visit this region. Roč is on the Pula–Buzet rail line but the train station is 1500m east of the village. Hum is on the same line but the train station is 5km from the village.

MOTOVUN

pop 590

Motovun is a captivating little town perched on a hill in Mirna River Valley, about 20km northeast of Poreč. It was the Venetians who decided to fortify the town in the 14th century, building two sets of thick walls. A Venetian lion scowls down from the outer gate and a cheerier lion adorns the inner gate. Venetian coats of arms on many buildings recall the noble families that once lived here. Once crumbling into ruin, the town is attracting artists who have set up studios in the tumble of Romanesque and Gothic houses, while newer houses have sprung up on the slopes leading up to the old town.

Orientation & Information

If you come in a car, leave it at the foot of the village. There's a 10KN charge in season which includes a little 'tourist train' to take you up the steep hill through the city gates. It also makes a nice walk.

The **Tourist Office** (☎ 681 758; opcina-motovun@pu.htnet.hr; Zadrugarska 20B) has a limited amount of information. There's an ATM just after the entrance on the right.

Sights & Activities

The highlight of the town is the Renaissance church of **St Stephen** (Sveti Stjepan; Trg Andrea Antico; 🕒 10am-1pm & 4-8pm Apr-Oct) designed by Venetian artist Andrea Palladio. Venetian Francesco Bonazzo contributed the marble altar statues of St Stephen and St Laurence and an unknown 17th-century Venetian produced the painting of the Last Supper behind the altar. Along the inner wall that encloses the old town rises a 16th-century **bell tower**, which you can climb (5KN) for a magnificent view. You can also walk around the outer walls that connect the more recent suburbs at the southeastern end of the old town. The view over vineyards, fields and woods is memorable. There are a number of galleries and crafts shops throughout the town, including an **art gallery** (admission free) just after the entrance gate that exhibits contemporary paintings and old weaponry.

Festivals & Events

Motovun's **International Film Festival** (www.motovunfilmfestival.com) takes place in the last week in July and presents independent and avant-garde films from the USA and Europe. For information see the festival website.

Sleeping & Eating

Hotel Kaštel (☎ 681 607; www.hotel-kastel-motovun.hr; Trg Andrea Antico 7; s/d 330/550KN; **P**) The town's only hotel is in a restored stone building with 28 simply furnished rooms. It has a good restaurant offering truffles and the local *teran* wine.

Restaurant Zigante (☎ 664 302; Livade 7, Livade; meals from 142KN) Just outside Motovun in Livade, this restaurant dominates the town centre. In fact, it *is* the town centre. The all-inclusive menu for 142KN is a truffle-taster's treat and the wine list is superb. There's no better place to sample the best of Istrian wine and cuisine in a refined, low-key atmosphere.

Getting There & Away

It's not easy to visit Motovun without your own car but there are connections from Pazin (18KN, 35 minutes, five daily).

AROUND MOTOVUN

Istarske Toplice

Dating from the Roman era, **Istarske Toplice** (www.istarske-toplice.hr) is one of Croatia's oldest and most scenic thermal spas. Beneath a 100m-high cliff and surrounded by greenery, the spa complex boasts a large outdoor pool that reaches 36°C. The high sulphur and radioactive content is alleged to help rheumatism, skin disease, respiratory tract disorders and gynaecological problems. Healthy but stressed-out folks can take advantage of the aromatherapy, massage, mud and beauty treatments, or just paddle around in the pool (25KN). The **Hotel Terme**

Mirna (☎ 664 300; ljeciliste-istarske-toplice@pu.htnet .hr; s/d 255/430KN) has been renovated and offers a variety of all-inclusive packages. There are also hiking, biking and climbing opportunities in the surrounding forest and excursions to Motovun.

There's no public transport but the spa is easily accessible by road, only 10km north of Motovun and 11km south of Buzet on the main road that connects the two towns.

GROŽNJAN

pop 193

Until the mid-1960s, Grožnjan, 26km northeast of Poreč, was slipping towards oblivion. For the 14th-century Venetians, this strategic hill-top town was an important fortress in their Istrian defensive system. They created a system of ramparts and gates, built a loggia, a granary and several fine churches. With the collapse of the Venetian empire in the 18th century, Grožnjan suffered a decline in its importance and its population.

In 1965 sculptor Aleksandar Rukavina and a small group of other sculptors and painters 'discovered' the crumbling medieval appeal of Grožnjan and began setting up studios in the abandoned buildings. As the town crawled back to life, it attracted the attention of Jeunesses Musicales International, an international training programme for young musicians. In 1969 a summer school for musicians, Jeunesses Musicales Croatia, was established in Grožnjan and it has been going strong ever since. Each year there are music, orchestra and ballet courses and recitals. In July, August and the beginning of September, concerts and musical events are held almost daily, and you can often overhear the musicians practising while you browse the many crafts shops and galleries.

Orientation & Information

The tiny town is a jumble of crooked lanes and leafy squares. Near the centre is the

Tourist Office (Turistička Zajednica; ☎ /fax 776 131; www.groznjan-grisignana.hr; Gorjan 3; ☼ 9am-noon & 5-8pm Mon-Sat May-Sep). Its staff can help find private accommodation in and around town and provide a small map with a list of galleries.

Sights & Activities

There are nearly 20 galleries and studios scattered around town and most are open daily from May to September. The Renaissance **loggia** is immediately to the right of the town gate and on top of the loggia is the **granary**. Keep going and on your right you'll see the baroque **Spinotti Morteani Palace** and then the **Kaštel** where many concerts are held. The town is dominated by the bell tower of the **Church of St Vitus, St Modest and St Crecsentius**, which was built in the late 18th century and contains striking baroque choir stalls.

Summer music concerts are organised by the **International Cultural Centre of Jeunesses Musicales Croatia** (ICCJMC; ☎ 01-611 600; www.hgm .hr in Croatian; Trg Stjepana Radića 4, Zagreb). The concerts are free and no reservations are necessary. They are usually held in the church, main square, loggia or the Kaštel at 9pm (8pm in September).

Sleeping & Eating

The tourist office can put you in touch with private rooms. Count on about 100KN per person.

Ladonja (☎ 776 125; s/d 250/300KN) This small hotel has 28 beds in simply furnished rooms over its restaurant. You can get a decent dish of pasta with truffles for 70KN.

Getting There & Away

If you don't have your own wheels, you can take the morning bus that runs from Pula to Poreč and Trieste (22KN), and get off at the town of Krasica, before Buje. It's a 3.5km-walk to Grožnjan, but the road winds along a scenic ridge with great views.

ISTRIA

Zadar Region

CONTENTS

Whether your interests are poking around in old churches, trekking through unspoiled wilderness or getting away from it all in a sleepy fishing village, you're sure to find it in the Zadar region. Paklenica National Park offers the best hiking and rock-climbing opportunities in Croatia; the waterfalls of Plitvice Lakes National Park are a green and watery wonderland; and the islands of Pag and Dugi Otok are good off-the-beaten-track destinations for resort-weary travellers. Ancient Zadar, the region's capital, is a fascinating coastal city with good national and international bus and boat connections to take in one of the national parks or hopscotch among the islands.

The area around Zadar is heavily urbanised with a sprawl of new construction. The coastal terrain is flat, whether you head northwest to Pag or southeast to Šibenik, but the low-lying coastal region allows the *maestral* (strong, steady westerly wind) to bring refreshing breezes. The Velebit Range in the northeast containing Paklenica National Park protects the coast from the *bura* (cold northeasterly wind) in the winter, lending it a mild climate.

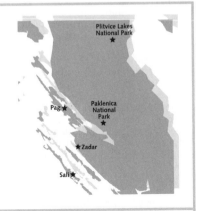

HIGHLIGHTS

- Shopping for lace and cheese in **Pag** (p174)
- Scuba diving from **Sali** (p171)
- Rock climbing in **Paklenica National Park** (p167)
- Strolling the quays of **Zadar** (p156)
- Getting sprayed by the waterfalls in **Plitvice Lakes National Park** (p164)

■ TELEPHONE CODE: 023   ■ POSTCODE: 23000

ZADAR

pop 69,200

Zadar (ancient Zara), the main city of northern Dalmatia, is one of Croatia's more underrated destinations. The old town has been rebuilt several times but retains the look and feel of an ancient Mediterranean city. The marble, traffic-free streets are replete with Roman ruins, medieval churches and several fascinating museums. Massive 16th-century fortifications still shield the city on the landward side, with high walls running along the harbour. The tree-lined promenade along Obala Kralja Petra Krešimira IV is perfect for a lazy stroll or a picnic and there are several small beaches east of the old town. More beaches lie to the west at Borik as well as on the islands of Ugljan and Dugi Otok, within easy reach of the town.

History

Zadar was inhabited by the Illyrian Liburnian tribe as early as the 9th century BC. At the end of the 3rd century BC, the Romans began their 200-year-long struggle with the Illyrians and by the 1st century BC, Zadar had become a Roman municipality and later a colony. It acquired the characteristics of a typical Roman town, with a rectangular street plan, a forum and baths. Water came from the nearby Lake Vrana. Zadar does not appear to have been a particularly important town for the Romans but when the Roman Empire was divided, it became the capital of Byzantine Dalmatia. In the 6th and 7th centuries, the city was settled by Slav migrants and Zadar eventually fell under the authority of Croatian-Hungarian kings.

All was well until the rise of the Venetian empire in the mid-12th century. For the next 200 years Zadar was subjected to relentless assault by Venetians seeking to expand their hold on Adriatic trading interests. There were four unsuccessful citizens' uprisings in the 12th century, but in 1202 the Venetians managed to sack the city and expel its citizens with the help of French Crusaders. The people of Zadar continued to rebel throughout the 13th and 14th centuries, with the help of Croatian-Hungarian kings, but finally it was sold to Venice in 1409 along with the rest of Dalmatia.

Zadar's economic growth declined under Venetian rule because of Turkish attacks and frequent Veneto-Turkish wars. The city walls were built in the 16th century and it was not until the end of the 17th century that the Turkish threat finally receded. With the fall of Venice in 1797, the city passed to Austrian, French, then again Austrian rule. The Austrians took a city that had an Italianised aristocracy and imported more Italians from their provinces in Italy to administer the city. Italian influence endured well into the 20th century, Zadar being excluded from the Kingdom of Serbs, Croats and Slovenes and remaining an Italian province. When Italy capitulated to the Allies in 1943, the city was occupied by the Germans and then bombed to smithereens by the Allies; almost 60% of the old town was destroyed.

The city was rebuilt following the original street plan and an effort was made to harmonise the new with what remained of old Zadar. As though the city had some magnetic power to attract trouble, history repeated itself in November 1991 when Yugoslav rockets launched an attack, keeping it under siege for three months. Bombs sailed overhead and the city's residents were virtually imprisoned in their homes with insufficient food or water. Although the Serb gunners were pushed back by the Croatian army during its January 1993 offensive, this experience has embittered many residents and made them more receptive to nationalists and flag-wavers.

Few war wounds are visible, however, and Zadar's narrow, traffic-free stone streets are again full of life. Tremendous 16th-century fortifications still shield the city on the landward side and high walls run along the harbour. Zadar can be a fascinating place in which to wander and, at the end of the day, you can sample its famous maraschino cherry liqueur.

Orientation

Zadar occupies a long peninsula (4km long and only 500m wide), which separates the harbour on the east from the Zadarski Channel on the west. The old town lies on the northwestern part of the peninsula and encompasses the port and Jazine Bay. It's neatly contained between two roads that

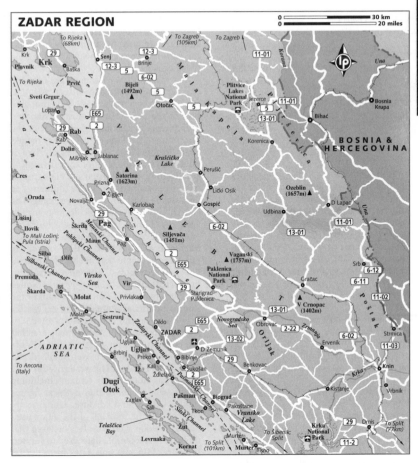

ZADAR REGION

run along the quays. Within the old town, you'll find all of the city's museums, churches and monuments. Most travel agencies are along the town's main commercial street, Široka ulica. The new suburbs of Voštarnica and Brodarica are along the northeastern coast outside the peninsula, and the northwestern coast is given over to the 'tourist zone' of Borik. The Jadrolinija boats are lined up on the northeastern harbour, which is connected by a footbridge across Jazine Bay to Obala Kneza Branimira. Continuing northwest you'll come to the marina and then to Borik, about 3km from the old town. The train and bus stations are a 15-minute walk southeast of the harbour and old town. From the train and bus stations, Zrinsko-Frankopanska ulica leads northwest past the main post office to the harbour.

Information
INTERNET ACCESS
Multi-net (☎ 302 207; Stomorica 8; per hr 30KN)

LEFT LUGGAGE
Garderoba Bus station (per hour 1.2KN; ☯ 6am-10pm Mon-Fri); Jadrolinija dock (☯ 7am-8pm Mon-Fri, 7am-3pm Sat); Train station (☯ 24hr)

MONEY
Travel agencies also change money and there's an exchange office and an ATM at the bus station.

Zagrebačka Banka (Knezova Šubića Bribirskih 4) Change money or withdraw cash at the ATM.

POST
Post Office (Poljana Pape Aleksandra III) You can make phone calls here.

TOURIST INFORMATION
Tourist Office (☎ 316 166; tzg-zadar@zd.htnet.hr; Mihe Klaića 5; 8am-8pm Mon-Sat & 8am-1pm Sun Jun-Sep, 8am-6pm Mon-Sat, closed Sun Oct-May) It's the main information centre.

TRAVEL AGENCIES
Aquarius Travel Agency (☎ /fax 212 919; juresko@zd .htnet.hr; Nova Vrata bb) Accommodation and excursions.
Atlas Travel Agency (☎ 235 850; atlas@zadar.net; Obala Branimirova 12) Across the footbridge over the harbour and just northeast of Narodni trg, it finds private accommodation and runs excursions.
Miatours (☎ /fax 212 788; miatrade@zd.htnet.hr; Vrata Sveti Krševana) Arranges accommodation and excursions.

Sights
CITY WALLS
A tour of the city walls gives an insight into Zadar's history. If you tour the walls chronologically, you'll begin with the eastern walls near the footbridge. These walls are the only remains of the ancient Roman and early Medieval fortifications, as most of the walls were built under the Venetians. Opposite the footbridge there are four old **city gates**. Heading northwest you'll pass first the **Gate of St Rok**, then the **Port Gate** built in 1573, which still sports the Venetian lion, the symbol of Venice. The gate contains part of a Roman triumphal arch and has a memorial inscription of the 1571 Battle of Lepanto in which the Austrians delivered a decisive blow to the Turkish navy.

Heading back in the opposite direction along the quays, you'll come to the **Square of the Five Wells** (Trg 5 Bunara), behind St Simeon's Church, built on the site of a former moat in 1574 and containing a cistern with five wells that furnished Zadar with water until 1838.

Continuing southwest you'll come to the **Town Gate**, the most elaborate of all the gates. Built under the Venetian administration in 1543, the gate's Renaissance-styled decorations include St Krževan on horseback, the Venetian lion, inscriptions and coats of arms.

CHURCHES
Unless otherwise stated the following churches are only open for daily Mass but the schedule varies – check at one of the travel agencies.

The main places of interest are near the circular **Church of St Donat** (Sveti Donat; ☎ 250 516; Šimuna Kožičića Benje; admission 5KN; 9.30am-2pm & 4-6pm daily Mar-Oct) one of the most outstanding monuments in Dalmatia. Dating from the beginning of the 9th century, it was named after Bishop Donat who allegedly had it built following the style of early Byzantine architecture. The unusual circular ground plan is especially visible on the southern side because the southern annexe is missing. The church was built over the Roman forum, which was built between the 1st century BC and the 3rd century AD. A few architectural fragments are preserved and two complete pillars are built into the church. The original floors were removed, and now slabs from the ancient forum are clearly visible. Notice the Latin inscriptions on the remains of the Roman sacrificial altars.

Outside the church on the northwestern side is a pillar from the Roman era that served as a 'shame post' in the Middle Ages, where wrongdoers were chained and publicly humiliated. The western side of the church has more Roman remains, including pillars with reliefs of the mythical figures Jupiter, Amon and Medusa. Underneath, you can see the remains of the altars used in pagan blood sacrifices. It is believed that this area was a temple dedicated to Jupiter, Juno and Minerva, and dates from the 1st century BC.

The Romanesque **Cathedral of St Anastasia** (Katedrala Svete Stošije; ☎ 251 708; Trg Svete Stos), near the Church of St Donat, was built in the 12th and 13th centuries on the site of an older church. Behind the richly decorated façade is an impressive three-nave interior marked by 13th-century wall paintings in the side apses. Notice particularly the fresco of a gateway in the southern apse, which was used as a model for the door frame of the main portal. On the altar in the left apse is a marble sarcophagus containing the relics of St Anastasia, commissioned by Bishop Donat in the 9th century. The presbytery contains choir stalls lavishly carved by the Venetian artist Matej Morozon in the 15th century. The cathedral was badly

ZADAR

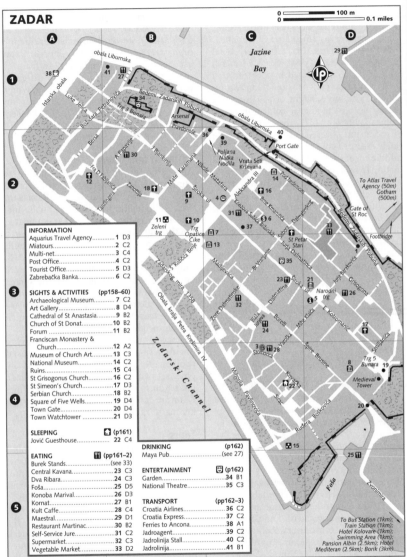

0 ─────── 100 m
0 ─────── 0.1 miles

Jazine
Bay

To Atlas Travel
Agency (50m);
Gotham
(500m)

To Bus Station (1km);
Train Station (1km);
Hotel Kolovare (1km);
Swimming Area (1km);
Pansion Albin (2.5km); Hotel
Mediteran (2.5km); Borik (3km)

---

bombed during WWII and has since been
reconstructed.

The **Franciscan monastery and church** (Samostan
Svetog Frane; ☎ 250 468; Zadarskog mira 1358; admission
free; ⏰ 7.30am–noon & 4.30-6pm) a few blocks
away is in better shape. Although it's the
oldest Gothic church in Dalmatia – it was
consecrated in 1280 – the interior has a

number of Renaissance features such as a
lovely chapel of St Anthony, which contains
a 15th-century wooden crucifix. In the
sacristy a memorial tablet commemorates
the seminal event in Zadar's history – the
1358 treaty under which Venice relinquished
its rights to Dalmatia in favour of the
Croatian-Hungarian king, Ludovic. The

large Romanesque painted crucifix in the treasury behind the sacristy is worth seeing. The monastery is named after St Donat.

St Simeon's Church (Crkva Svetog Šime; ☎ 211 705; Trg Šime Budinica; ☽ 8am-noon & 6-8pm daily Jun-Sep) was reconstructed in the 16th and 17th centuries on the site of an earlier church. The sarcophagus of St Šimun is a masterpiece of medieval goldsmith work. Commissioned in 1377, the coffin is made of cedar and covered inside and out with finely executed gold-plated silver reliefs. The middle relief showing Christ's presentation in the Temple is a copy of Giotto's fresco from *Capella dell'Arena* in Padua, Italy. Other reliefs depict scenes from the lives of the saints and King Ludovic's visit to Zadar. The lid shows a reclining St Šimun.

Another notable church is **St Grisogonus Church** (Crkva Sveti Krš* evan; Brne Krnarutića), which was part of a 12th-century Benedictine monastery that was destroyed by Allied bombs in 1944. The church has a baroque altar constructed in 1701 and Byzantine frescoes on the northern wall and in the northern apse. Frescoes on the southern apse are poorly preserved.

MUSEUMS

The captions in all Zadar's museums are in Croatian only.

The outstanding **Museum of Church Art** (☎ 211 545; Poljana Opatice Čike bb; adult/student 20/10KN; ☽ 10am-12.30pm 6-8pm Mon-Sat, closed Sun) in the Benedictine monastery opposite the Church of St Donat offers an impressive display of reliquaries and religious paintings. Along with the goldsmiths' works in the first hall, notice the 14th-century painting of the Madonna. She features again in the second hall, where the most notable works of her are a marble sculpture and Paolo Veneziani's painting. On the 2nd floor you'll find 15th- and 16th-century sculptures and embroidery, and six pictures by the 15th-century Venetian painter Vittore Carpaccio.

Nearby is the modern **Archaeological Museum** (☎ 250 516; Trg Opatice Čike 1; adult/student 10/5KN; ☽ 9am-1pm & 6-9pm Mon-Fri, 9am-1pm Sat, closed Sun), with pottery fragments dating back to the Neolithic Age. From the Liburnian era, there are bronze swords, jewellery and pottery. Also interesting is a model of Zadar as it existed in Roman times, and statues of emperors Tiberius and Augustus.

The **National Museum** (Narodni Muzej; ☎ 251 851; Poljana Pape Aleksandra III; admission 5KN; ☽ 9am-noon & 5-8pm Mon-Fri, 9am-noon Sun), in the Benedictine monastery of St Krževan's Church, is an excellent historical museum. It features scale models of Zadar from different periods, and old paintings and engravings of many coastal cities. The same admission ticket will get you into the local **Art Gallery** (☎ 211 174; Šmiljanića; admission 5KN; ☽ 9am-noon & 5-8pm Mon-Fri, 9am-1pm Sat, closed Sun).

OTHER ATTRACTIONS

Apart from the museums and churches, a number of other sights scattered around town add distinction to the city. **Narodni trg** was traditionally the centre of public life. The western side of the square is dominated by the late-Renaissance **Town Watchtower**, dating from 1562. The clock tower was built under the Austrian administration in 1798. Public proclamations and judgments were announced from the **loggia** across the square, which is now an exhibition space. Several hundred metres northwest of Narodni trg is the **Serbian Church**, behind which is a small Serbian neighbourhood.

There's a **swimming area** with diving boards, a small park and café on the coastal promenade off Zvonimira. Bordered by pine trees and small parks, the promenade takes you to a beach in front of the Hotel Kolovare and then winds on for about a kilometre along the coast.

Tours

Any of the many travel agencies around town can supply information on the tourist cruises to Telaščica Bay and the beautiful Kornati Islands, which include lunch and a swim in the sea or a salt lake. As this is about the only way to see these 101 barren, uninhabited islands, islets and cliffs, it's worthwhile if you can spare the cash. Check with Aquarius Travel Agency or Miatours, or go down to Obala Liburnska where the excursion boats leave.

You can also take an excursion to Paklenica National Park, the Krka waterfalls or Plitvice Lakes National Park.

Festivals & Events

Mid-July to mid-August is a good time to be in Zadar. The **Zadar Dreams** (Zadar Snova) theatrical festival takes over Zadar's parks and squares with offbeat theatrical happenings. Major annual events include the **Musical Evenings** in the Church of St Donat (July) and the **Choral Festival** (October).

Sleeping

There is one small hotel in town and a few private rooms available but most visitors head out to the 'tourist settlement' at Borik on the Puntamika bus (every 20 minutes from the bus station), where there are hotels, a hostel, a camping ground and many *sobe* (room available) signs. Several hotels have been transformed into upscale establishments and there's an all-inclusive family resort, Funimation, complete with an aquapark, tennis courts and more. Most are managed by the Austria-based **Falkensteiner group** (www.falkensteiner.com).

BUDGET

Borik Youth Hostel (☎ 331 145; zadar@hfhs.hr; Obala Kneza Trpimira 76; B&B/half board 90/120KN) Friendly and well kept, it's near the beach at Borik.

Čazmatrans Youth Hotel (☎ 213 816; fax 224 503; Kralja S Držislava 10; B&B 136KN) Conveniently located near the bus station, these three-bed rooms are oldish but clean.

Zaton (☎ 280 280; fax 264 225; Nin; per adult/site 50/30KN; ☺ May-Sep) A huge development on a sandy beach 16km northwest of Zadar in Nin, with a 5000-person capacity. It's not attractively landscaped – the terrain is flat and uninteresting – but there is a long stretch of beach and enough sports facilities to keep you busy. There are eight buses daily marked 'Zaton' from the bus station (fewer on weekends), which drop you off in Zaton village, about 1km from the camp.

Autocamp Borik (☎ 332 074; per adult/site 30/60KN; ☺ Apr-Oct) This site is somewhat smaller than Zaton and only steps away from Borik beach.

MID-RANGE

Jović Guest House (☎ 214 098, 098 330 958; Šime Ljubića 4a; d 300KN) If you want to stay in the town, the best choice is this 12-room guesthouse right in the heart, with smallish but cool and attractive rooms with private bathroom. The price does not include breakfast but there are plenty of cafés around. If you can't reach the owner, the rooms can be reserved through Aquarius Travel Agency (p158).

Hotel Mediteran (☎ 337 500; www.hotelmediteran-zd.hr; M Gupca 19; s/d 380/495KN; P ☒ ☐) Friendly and relaxed, it has comfortable rooms and is fairly close to the beach.

Pansion Albin (☎ 331 137; www.albin.hr; Put Dikla 47; s/d 345/460KN; P ☒ ☎) In this friendly, family-run *pension* you'll find more warmth and hospitality than at the big hotels. There's a small swimming pool surrounded by a garden, a good local restaurant, and the beach is just a 15-minute walk away.

TOP END

Hotel Adriana Select (☎ 206 637; adriana.select@ falkensteiner.com; Majstora Radovana 7; per person incl half board 600KN; P ☒ ☒) All the rooms in this 'lifestyle hotel' are termed 'junior suites'. They are up-to-the-minute modern with hairdryers, sparkling bathrooms, balconies and lots of other little niceties. Plus, you have access to all of the facilities offered at nearby Funimation, including the aquapark. The hotel is housed in a skilfully restored 19th-century villa.

Hotel President (☎ 333 464; www.hotel-president .hr; Vladana Desnice 16; s/d 800/1200KN; P ☒ ☐) This is for the full first-class treatment, also near the beach. Notwithstanding its location, the décor is sophisticated and plush rather than Mediterranean in style. The hotel restaurant, Vivaldi, is also a first-rate address for a classy meal.

Hotel Kolovare (☎ 203 200; fax 203 300; Bože Peričića 14; s/d 550/850KN; P ☎) Neither friendly nor particularly good value, at least it's close to the train and bus stations and only a 20-minute walk to town.

PRIVATE ROOMS

The travel agencies listed on p158 find private accommodation. Expect to pay about 140KN per person for a room with a private bathroom. Very little is available in the old town but you can find some decent deals in Puntamika.

Eating

Self-Service Jure (☎ 211 714; Knezova Šubića Bribirskih 11; mains from 25KN) This renovated self-service restaurant doesn't have much ambience, but it does have the advantage of letting you point to the dishes you want rather than try to pronounce them.

Dva Ribara (Blaža Jurjeva 1; mains from 40KN) With a wide range of food and an outdoor terrace, it's justifiably popular with the local crowd.

Restaurant Martinac (Papavije 7; mains from 55KN) The secluded backyard terrace behind the restaurant provides a relaxed ambience to sample delicious risotto and fish.

Konoba Marival (☎ 213 239; Don Ive Prodana 3; mains from 45KN) If your mama married a fisherman, she'd probably dream up the kinds of dishes that are served here. The ambience is also homy and intimate.

Foša (☎ 314 421; Kralja Dmitra Zvonimira 2; mains from 50KN) If the funky '70s décor gets to you, concentrate on the view over the marina. An oldish crowd of regulars keeps coming back for the attentively prepared fish.

Maestral (☎ 430 455; Ivana Mažuranića 2; mains from 40KN) On the 1st floor of a waterfront building, the meat is tender, the variety of fish excellent and the panoramic view of the harbour most relaxing. There's no better place to view the sunset while you dine.

Kornat (☎ 254 501; Obala Liburnska 6; mains from 45KN) This place has an imaginative chef who's bringing a whiff of exoticism to traditional Croatian staples.

Local people usually head out to Borik to find something to eat. **Restaurant Albin** (☎ 331 137; mains 40-100KN), on the road to Borik, is one of the most popular establishments because the fish is extremely well prepared and it has a spacious outdoor terrace.

Back in town, there's a **supermarket** (cnr Široka & Dalmatinske) that keeps long hours, and you'll find a number of *burek* (a heavy pastry stuffed with meat or cheese) stands around the vegetable market.

Drinking

In summer the many cafés along Varoška and Klaića place their tables on the street, which is great for people-watching.

Central Kavana (Široka ulica) This spacious café is a popular hang-out and has live music on Saturday and Sunday (an otherwise dead day). Ice cream and a full cocktail menu keeps it packed.

Kult Caffe (Stomarica 4) The Kult Caffe draws a young crowd to listen to rap music indoors or to relax on the large shady terrace outside.

Maya Pub (☎ 251 716; Obala Liburnska 6) The Buddha Bar becomes the Shiva Bar in Zadar. The smooth-electro sounds swirl around an imposing sculpture of Shiva and there are

occasional live concerts. It's the latest place to go.

Bounty (Mate Gupca 2, Borik; ☒ closed Sun & Mon) Staying in Borik doesn't mean being out of the action. This new spot with a pirate theme is where Borikians hang out.

Entertainment

THEATRE

National Theatre (☎ 314 552; Široka ulica) The box office sells tickets to the cultural programmes advertised on posters outside.

CLUBS

Garden (☎ 450 907; Bedemi Zadarskih Pobuna) The newest and hottest nightlife in Zadar enlivens this traditional walled garden. A top-of-the-line sound system and celebrated DJs have made this the primary spot to see and be seen.

Gotham (☎ 200 289; Marka Oreškovića 1; ☒ closed Mon) Go-go dancers, tropical fantasy nights and '70s nights liven up this club north of the old town.

Getting There & Away

AIR

Croatia Airlines (☎ 250 101; Poljana Natka Nodila 7) has all flight and ticket information.

Zadar's airport is about 10km east of the town centre. There are daily flights to Zagreb and the Croatia Airlines bus meets all arrivals (15KN). A taxi costs about 175KN.

BOAT

On the harbour, **Jadrolinija** (☎ 254 800; Obala Liburnska 7) has tickets for all local ferries, or you can buy ferry tickets from the Jadrolinija stall on Obala Liburnska. The Jadrolinija ferry from Rijeka to Dubrovnik calls at Zadar twice weekly (138/168KN low/high season, six hours). It arrives around midnight.

From mid-June to the beginning of September Lošinjska Plovidba (p275) runs a ferry five times a week connecting Zadar with Pula (112KN, eight hours), Mali Lošinj (73KN, four hours) and Koper (175KN, eleven hours, once weekly). Buy tickets from **Jadroagent** (☎ 211 447; jadroagent-zadar@zd .htnet.hr; Poljana Natka Nodila 4), just inside the city walls.

For information on the boat connections to Italy see p275.

BUS

Croatia Express (☎ 250 502; croatiae@zd.htnet.hr; Široka ulica) sells bus tickets to Zagreb, Split and Trieste plus many German cities. See p271 for details. From the **bus station** (☎ 211 035) there are also buses from Zadar to Rijeka (117KN to 127KN, 4½ hours), Split (120KN, three hours) and Dubrovnik (160KN to 190KN, 6½ hours).

TRAIN

There are four daily trains to Zagreb (134KN, 6½ hours) that change at Knin, but the bus to Zagreb is quicker and passes by Plitvice Lakes National Park (three hours).

Getting Around

Buses run frequently from the bus station to the harbour and to Borik. Buses marked 'Poluotok' run to the harbour and buses marked 'Puntamika' run to Borik. Tickets are 6KN (10KN for two trips) and you can buy them at a *tisak* (newsstand) or from the driver.

AROUND ZADAR
Ugljan

The island of Ugljan is easily accessible by boat from Zadar, making it a popular getaway for the locals and a kind of residential suburb for people who work in Zadar. The 50-sq-km island is densely populated, housing about 7500 people, and it can get crowded on summer weekends. There are few forests but much *macchia* (shrubs), some pines and a good deal of farmland with vegetable gardens, olive groves and vineyards. The eastern coast is the most indented and most developed part of the island, while the west is relatively deserted.

The port of entry is **Preko**, directly across from Zadar, with two small harbours and a ferry port. Although there's a town beach,

---

USKOKS: THE PIRATES OF SENJ

As a tale of adventure on the high seas, derring-do and murderous rebellion, the history of the Uskoks surpasses anything that could be dreamt up by a novelist. This remarkable tribe appeared in Dalmatia in the middle of the 16th century when the Ottoman Turks were laying waste to Serbia, Bulgaria and Bosnia. Many Catholic residents of the afflicted region fled westward in the face of the Turkish advance, eventually arriving at the fortress of Klis, near Split. They called themselves Uskoci, or Fugitives, and battled the Turks for five years before Venice signed a pact with the invaders and directed the Uskoks to abandon the position in 1537.

They settled in Senj, north of Zadar, and were confronted with the perennial refugee problem – how to make a living in their new home. Unfazed by their total lack of naval experience, the Uskoks learned how to make light, fast boats that were uniquely adapted to the Dalmatian coast. Reasoning that they had every right to punish the Turks who had driven them from their homes, the Uskoks pursued Turkish ships up and down the coast, stripping and sinking every one they could get their hands on.

For nearly 30 years they attacked only Turkish ships, receiving blessings and subsidies from the Catholic Church. Then Venice changed its policy and decided to make peace with the Turks. Suddenly the Uskoks were outcasts. Since the two Adriatic powers, Venice and Austria, refused their requests to resettle them in the interior where they could farm, nothing was left for them but piracy.

In 1566, the Uskoks began to attack Venetian ships and brought new ferocity to their exploits. The Austrians were unmoved by the problems of their naval rival but the Venetians were greatly perturbed. Captured Uskoks were treated with merciless cruelty and the Venetians eventually launched a blockade of Senj to starve out the inhabitants. The Uskoks continued to harass the Venetians, their numbers enhanced by adventure-seekers, bored noblemen and thugs from all over Europe.

In 1615, Venice and Austria used the Uskoks as a pretext for a short war. As part of the peace treaty Austria agreed to liquidate the pirates' nest. A number of the pirates were hanged or beheaded while the rest were transported to the interior as they had wanted all along. Although they were allegedly deported to villages in the Krajina, no certain trace of them has ever been found.

the best beach is on the little island of **Galovac**, only 80m from the town centre. Small, pretty and wooded, Galovac has a Franciscan monastery dating from the 15th century. If you have your own car you could visit Ugljan village, positioned on an indented bay with a sandy beach, the fishermen's village of Kali and the nearby islet of Ošljak, which is covered with pine and cypress trees.

There are hourly ferries that make the 30-minute run between Zadar and Preko year-round.

PLITVICE LAKES NATIONAL PARK
☎ 053

Plitvice Lakes National Park lies midway between Zagreb and Zadar. The 19.5 hectares of wooded hills enclose 16 turquoise lakes, which are linked by a series of waterfalls and cascades. Wooden footbridges follow the lakes and streams over, under and across the rumbling water for an exhilaratingly damp 18km. In 1979, Unesco proclaimed the Plitvice Lakes a World Heritage site, and the lakes and forests are carefully regulated to ensure their continuing preservation.

The extraordinary natural beauty of the site merits at least a three-day visit but you can experience a lot simply on a day trip from Zadar or Zagreb. There's no bad time to visit – in the spring the falls are flush with water, in summer the surrounding hills are greener and in autumn there are fewer visitors and you'll be treated to the changing colours of leaves.

The lake system is divided into the upper and lower lakes. The upper lakes lying in a dolomite valley are the most impressive, surrounded by dense forests and interlinked by several gushing waterfalls. The lower lakes are smaller and shallower, surrounded only by sparse underbrush. Most of the water comes from the Bijela and Crna Rijeka (White and Black Rivers), which join south of Prošćansko Lake, but the lakes are also fed by underground springs. In turn, water disappears into the porous limestone at some points only to re-emerge in other places. All the water empties into the Korana River near Sastavci.

The upper lakes are separated by dolomite barriers, which expand with the mosses and algae that absorb calcium carbonate as river water rushes through the karst. The encrusted plants grow on top of each other, forming travertine barriers and creating waterfalls. The lower lakes were formed by cavities created by the water of the upper lakes. They undergo a similar process, as travertine is constantly forming and reforming itself into new combinations so that the landscape is ever changing. This unique interaction of water, rock and plant life has continued more or less undisturbed since the last ice age.

The colours of the lakes also change constantly. From azure to bright green, deep blue or grey, the colours depend upon the quantity of minerals or organisms in the water, whether rain has deposited mud, and the angle of sunlight.

The luxuriant vegetation of the national park is another delight. The northeastern section of the park is covered with beech forests while the rest of it is covered with beech, fir spruce and white pine dotted with patches of whitebeam, hornbeam and flowering ash, which change colour in autumn.

History
After prehistoric settlements, the first recorded inhabitants in the region were the Thracians who arrived in the 1st millennium BC, followed by the Illyrians and then the ubiquitous Romans who visited in 59 BC and stayed for 600 years. Slavs migrated to the area in the 7th century and were eventually organised into the feudal system that dominated the early middle ages. The Turks seized power in 1528 and when they were driven out 150 years later, the Austrians tried to attract new settlers by making it a feudal-free zone. The area became part of the Krajina military frontier and was settled by Vlachs and Morlachs who followed the Serbian Orthodox faith.

Even as early as 1896 when the first hotel was built, the tourism potential of the lakes was apparent. A preservation society founded in 1893 ensured the protection of the lake environment well into the 20th century. The boundaries of the national park were set in 1951 with a view towards minimising degradation and maximising tourism. Before the recent 1991 war, the lakes were a major tourist attraction but their presence within the Serb-dominated Krajina region meant

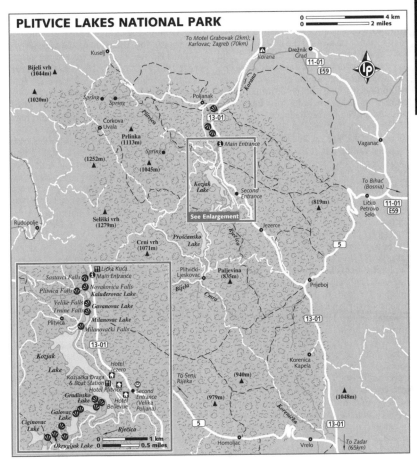

PLITVICE LAKES NATIONAL PARK

trouble was inevitable when the former Yugoslavia began to crack up.

The civil war in former Yugoslavia actually began in Plitvice on 31 March 1991, when rebel Serbs from Krajina region took control of the park headquarters. The murdered Croatian police officer Josip Jović became the first casualty of the ruthless war that Easter Sunday. Rebel Serbs held the area for the war's duration, turning hotels into barracks and plundering park property. When the Croatian army finally retook the park in August 1995, they found the natural beauty intact but the hotels and facilities completely gutted. All has been repaired since and tourists are flocking to one of Croatia's most wondrous sights.

Wildlife

Animal life flourishes in the unspoiled conditions. The stars of the park are bears and wolves but there are also deer, boar, rabbits, foxes and badgers. There are over 120 different species of bird such as hawks, owls, cuckoos, thrushes, starlings, kingfishers, wild ducks and herons. You might occasionally see black storks and ospreys and flocks of butterflies flutter throughout the park.

Orientation & Information

The **tourist office** (☎ 751 015; www.np-plitvicka -jezera.hr; adult/student 75/45KN Oct-May, 95/55KN Jun-Sep; ⏱ 7am-8pm) has its main entrance on Plitvička jezera, and a secondary entrance at

Velika Poljana, near the hotels. At the main entrance you can pick up brochures and a map to walk you around the lakes. There are well-marked trails throughout the park and a system of wooden walkways that allow you to appreciate the beauty of the landscape without disturbing the environment. The admission ticket includes the boats and buses you need to see the lakes.

The post office is near the hotels and there's an ATM near the Hotel Bellevue. Luggage can be left at the tourist information centre at the main entrance to the park or at one of the hotels.

Sights

The lower lakes string out from the main entrance and are rich in forests, grottoes and steep cliffs. **Novakovića Falls** is nearest the entrance and is followed by **Kaluđerovac Lake**, near two caves – the Blue Cave and Šupljara. Next is **Gavanovac Lake** with towering waterfalls and last is **Milanovac Lake**, notable for colours that are variously sky-blue, azure or emerald green.

Kozjak is the largest lake and forms a boundary between the upper and lower lakes. Three kilometres long, the lake is surrounded by steep, forested slopes and contains a small oval island, composed of travertine. Past the hotels, you'll see **Gradinsko Lake** bordered by reeds that often harbour nesting wild ducks. A series of cascades links Gradinsko to **Galovac Lake**, considered the most beautiful lake of all. An abundance of water has formed a series of ponds and falls. A set of concrete stairs over the falls, constructed long ago, have eventually been covered by travertine, forming even more falls in a spectacular panorama. Several smaller lakes are topped by the larger **Okrugljak Lake**, supplied by two powerful waterfalls. Continuing upward you'll come to **Ciginovac Lake** and finally **Prošćansko Lake**, surrounded by thick forests.

Sleeping

The Zagreb buses drop you off just outside the camping ground while the hotels are clustered on Velika Poljana overlooking Kozjak Lake.

Korana (☎ 751 015; per adult/site 35/50KN; ☼ May-Oct) This is a large, well-equipped autocamp about 6km north of the main entrance on the main road to Zagreb.

Hotel Bellevue (☎ 751 700; Velika Poljana; s/d 380/515KN) It's the cheapest hotel around but the rooms and atmosphere are dreary.

Hotel Plitvice (☎ 751 100; Velika Poljana; s/d from 403/547KN; Ⓟ) Completely renovated into a comfortable modern hotel, you'll find spacious, well-equipped rooms, each with TV, phone and minibar. There are more expensive rooms which are larger and have views.

Hotel Jezero (☎ 751 400; jezero@np-plitvicka -jezera.hr; Velika Poljana; s/d 578/790KN; Ⓟ ☎) This is by far the most comfortable and best-appointed hotel in the park. There's even a sauna and swimming pool.

Motel Grabovac (☎ 751 999; s/d 320/441KN) About 10km north of the entrance on the road to Zagreb this large, modern motel offers bland but functional rooms.

PRIVATE ROOMS

There are many *sobe* signs along the road from Korana village to the national park. The tourist office in the park or its branch in Zagreb can refer you to rooms in the neighbouring villages, the closest of which is about 400m from the entrance. Expect to pay about 225KN for a double room.

Eating

There's an inexpensive self-service cafeteria next to the tourist office, at the second entrance, as well as a café, which sells sandwiches, pastries and roast chicken, and a minimarket for picnic supplies.

Lička Kuća (☎ 751 024; mains from 50KN) Just across from the main entrance, this sprawling place is usually crowded with tourists who come for the local sausages and roasted-meat dishes. Vegetarians will appreciate the *djuveč*, a stew of rice, carrots, tomatoes, peppers and onions, as well as the fine local cheese.

Getting There & Away

All the Zagreb–Zadar buses stop at Plitvice – it takes three hours from Zadar (55KN) and 2½ hours from Zagreb (50KN). It's possible to visit here for the day on the way to or from the coast, but be aware that buses will not pick up passengers if they are full. On summer weekends you could spend a good part of the day stuck in traffic since the road to Plitvice is the main artery to the coast for holidaying city folk.

PAKLENICA NATIONAL PARK

Rising high above the Adriatic, the stark peaks of the Velebit Massif stretch for 145km in a dramatic landscape of rock and sea. Paklenica National Park covers 3657 hectares of the Velebit Range, extending in a rough circle from the park entrance in the village of Marasovići. For everyone from Sunday strollers to rock climbers and serious hikers, the park offers a wealth of opportunities to trek across steep gorges, crawl up slabs of stone, or meander along shady paths next to a rushing stream. The panorama inside the park is ever changing and much greener than you would think when looking at the chalky mountains from the sea.

The national park circles around two deep gorges, Velika Paklenica (Great Paklenica) and Mala Paklenica (Small Paklenica), which scar the mountain range like hatchet marks, with cliffs over 400m high. The dry limestone karst that forms the Velebit Range is highly absorbent, but several springs in the park's upper reaches provide a continuous source of water, which explains the unusually lush vegetation. About half the park is covered with forests, mostly beech and pine followed by white oak and varieties of hornbeam. The vegetation changes as you ascend, as does the climate, which progresses from Mediterranean to continental to subalpine. The lower regions, especially those with a southern exposure, can be fiercely hot in the summer and the cold *bura* that whips through the range in winter brings rain and sudden storms.

Animal life is scarce but you may see Egyptian vultures, golden eagles, striped eagles and peregrine falcons, which nest on the cliffs of the two gorges. If you've forgotten what they look like, there's an illustrated sign at the park's entrance. Rumour has it that bears and wolves live in the park's upper regions, but your chances of actually seeing one are minuscule.

The best time to visit the park is in May, June or September. In late spring the park is greenest, the streams become torrents and there are few other visitors. In July and August you'll still find the trails uncrowded, since most people come to the region for

KARST

The most outstanding geological feature of Croatia is the prevalence of the highly porous limestone and dolomitic rock called karst. Stretching from Istria to Montenegro and covering large parts of the interior, karst is formed by the absorption of water into the surface limestone, which then corrodes and allows the water to seep into the harder layer underneath. Eventually the water forms underground streams, carving out fissures and caves before resurfacing, disappearing into another cave and finally emptying into the sea. Caves and springs are common interior features of karstic landscapes, which explains the Pazin Chasm, Plitvice Lakes and the Krka waterfalls as well as the Manita Peć cave in Paklenica. The jagged, sparsely vegetated exterior landscape is dramatic, but deforestation, wind and erosion in Croatia has made the land unsuitable for agriculture. When the limestone collapses, a kind of basin is formed known as *polje*, which is then cultivated despite the fact that this kind of field drains poorly and can easily turn into a temporary lake.

the sun and sea, but it might be too hot to hike comfortably. In September the weather is mild during the day and cool at night, making it perfect hiking weather, plus you can still finish off a day on the trails with a refreshing swim.

Orientation

The best base for exploring the park is Starigrad (sometimes also referred to as Starigrad-Paklenica, to differentiate it from another Starigrad near Senj, which has nothing to do with Paklenica National Park).

Starigrad is the site of the national park office and has the most possibilities for restaurants and accommodation. It's also near the entrance to Velika Paklenica, which offers the most varied walks and climbs. The entrance to the national park is in the village of Marasovići, which is about 2km north of the town of Starigrad. The road to the entrance is not particularly interesting, so a lot of people drive to the car park past the reception area. The entrance to Mala

Paklenica is on the far side of Seline village, about 2.5km southeast of Starigrad on the road to Zadar. Follow the road opposite St Mark's (Sveti Marko) church towards the canyon. Trails throughout the park are marked by small white and red posts.

Information

The **Paklenica National Park office** (☎ /fax 369 202; www.paklenica.hr; Starigrad; adult/student 30/15KN; ☺ 8am-3pm Mon-Fri Apr-Oct, park 6am-8.30pm daily) sells booklets and maps, and is in charge of maintaining the park. The *Paklenica National Park* guide gives an excellent overview of the park and suggests various walks. Rock climbers should talk to one of the guides employed by the park administration who can provide detailed advice on climbing routes and their difficulty levels.

The **Croatian Mountaineering Association** (☎ /fax 01-48 23 624; http://hps.inet.hr in Croatian; Kozarićeva 22, 10000 Zagreb) also has up-to-date information and publishes a useful map of the park with clearly marked routes. It's on sale at larger bookstores in Zagreb.

Activities
HIKING

Most hikes are one-day affairs either from 'base camp' at Starigrad or Seline, or from one of the mountain huts.

Mala Paklenica to Velika Paklenica

Mala Paklenica is smaller and less visited than Velika Paklenica, which is why you stand a better chance of glimpsing a griffon vulture. The karst formations are outstanding in **Mala Paklenica** but the trail can get slippery in spring and autumn, and you may have to cross Mala Paklenica stream a few times. You'll be following the stream through rocks and boulders for the first four hours or so and then zigzagging uphill to about 680m. Take the left-hand path marked Starigrad and Jivile. You'll pass through fields and pastures before descending to a rocky gully that leads to the valley floor. You'll arrive at **Velika Paklenica**, enjoy a marvellous view and then follow the path through the gorge with Anića Kuk on your left down to the valley floor.

Starigrad to Planinarski Dom

Immediately after the park's entrance you'll reach the floor of **Velika Paklenica Gorge**, with grey-stone massifs looming on either side. In July and August, you're sure to find rock climbers making their way up the cliffs. About 200m up from the car park on the left you'll enter **tunnels** (admission free; Sun Jul-Aug) that contain well-lit, neat halls and rooms carved out of the rock by the federal Yugoslav army before the 1990s war.

When you pass a rock fall with a stream on your right you'll be at **Anića Luka**, a green, semicircular plateau. In another kilometre or so there's a turn-off to the cave of **Manita Peć** (admission 10KN; 10am-1pm daily Jul & Aug, 10am-1pm Wed & Sat Jun & Sep). Take the steps down from the antehall to the centre of the cave, with a wealth of stalagmites and stalactites enhanced by strategically placed lighting. The area is 40m long and reaches a height of 32m. It's about a two-hour walk from the car park and must be visited with a guide.

From the cave you can follow the trail to **Vidakov Kuk**, which takes 1½ hours. The ascent up the 866m peak is fairly rugged, but on a clear day you'll be rewarded with an unforgettable view over the sea to Pag. You can continue on an easy trail to **Ramići** and then head east to the main trail up to the shelter, **Planinarski Dom Paklenica**.

You can also bypass the Manita Peć detour and continue up to the Game Warden's hut in the **Lugarnica** area (about two hours' walk from the car park), open daily June to September. You can buy snacks and drinks in the hut before continuing on up to Planinarski Dom Paklenica. You'll pass beech and pine forests before coming to the shelter.

In another route to the hut, take the right path after Anića Luka past the little farmhouse at Jurline. The left fork leads to the black-pine forests of Mala Močilo but you can also continue straight ahead to **Veliko Močilo** and rest beside a spring of drinkable water (three hours from the car park). From here you can take the right fork to the Ivine Vodice hut (p170), or at Martinovo Marilo you can take the left path along the southern slope of the upper Velika Paklenica valley, following the Velika Paklenica River to Planinarski Dom Paklenica (about 1½ hours from Veliko Močilo; see right).

Upper Velebit

From Planinarski Dom you'll easily reach any of the Velebit peaks in a day, but you'd need about a week to explore all of them. The highest point in the Velebit Range is **Vaganski vrh** (1757m). From the flat, grassy top you have a view of up to 150km inland over the Velebit peaks on a clear day. It may be a long, hard day (depending on your fitness level) but it can be reached with enough time to return to the shelter by nightfall.

Another popular destination is **Babin vrh** (Grandmother's Peak; 1741m). Follow the trail with the Brezimenjača stream on the left to the pass of Buljma (1394m) and then continue to Marasova gora through deciduous forest. There's a small lake at the foot of Babin vrh that never dries up (but the water has been polluted by sheep).

It's also possible to reach all the peaks along the Velebit ridge from Mala Paklenica, but make sure you have survival equipment, a map and the assurance that both huts are open. Past Sveti Jakov in Mala Paklenica take the right path to the Ivine Vodice hut. Marked trails lead past Sveto brdo (1751m), Malovan (1709m), Vaganski vrh and Babin vrh before descending the Planinarski Dom shelter.

ROCK CLIMBING

The national park offers a tremendous variety of rock-climbing routes from beginners' level to borderline suicidal. The firm, occasionally sharp limestone offers graded climbs, including 72 short sports routes and 250 longer routes. You'll see the beginners' routes at the beginning of the park with cliffs reaching about 40m, but the best and most advanced climbing is on Anića Kuk, which offers over 100 routes up to a maximum of 350m. Nearly all routes are well equipped with spits and pitons, except for the appropriately named Psycho Killer route.

The most popular climbs here are Mosoraški (350m), Velebitaški (350m) and Klin (300m). Spring is the best climbing season as summers can be quite warm and winters too windy. A rescue service is also available. For more information and a few pictures, check the 'Free Climbing in Croatia' website at http://public.srce.hr (in Croatian).

Sleeping

Planinarski Dom Paklenica (Mountain Lodge Paklenica; 213 792; dm 65KN; Jun-Sep, Sat & Sun Oct-May) This is the most convenient mountain hut.

There's no hot water or electricity but you can reach the highest peaks of Velebit from here. It has 45 beds in four rooms but a sleeping bag is advisable since the lodge provides blankets but no sheets. Reservations are advisable for weekends from June to September.

Ivine Vodice (Sklonište; ☽ Jun-Sep, Sat & Sun Oct-May) East of Planinarski Dom, this hut has no beds or running water but can host 10 people with sleeping bags. It's free and it's not necessary to reserve in advance.

Getting There & Away
The entrance to the national park is in the village of Marasovići, which is about 2km north of the town of Starigrad.

STARIGRAD
pop 1160
Starigrad is on either side of the main coastal road from Rijeka to Zadar. All buses from Rijeka or Zadar stop in front of the Hotel Alan, and 2km north in the centre of town.

The **Tourist Office** (☎ /fax 369 255; tz-starigrad@zd .htnet.hr; ☽ 8am-9pm Jul-Aug, 8am-2pm Mon-Sat, closed Sun Sep-Jun) is in the centre of town on the main road across from the small harbour.

Splitskabanka (☽ 8am-noon & 6-8pm Mon-Fri, 8am-noon Sat) is between the tourist office and the Hotel Alan. It has an ATM.

Sleeping & Eating
Although camping is not permitted in the national park, there are numerous camping grounds in and around Starigrad. In addition to the larger camping grounds listed here, there are small, private camping grounds stationed along the main road leading into and out of town. The tourist office can put you in touch with them. Starigrad offers a few hotels.

Camping Paklenica (☎ 369 236; fax 369 203; Dr Franje Tuđman bb; per adult/site 25/50KN; ☽ Apr-Oct) Next to the Hotel Alan, this is one of the largest camping grounds, overlooking a pebble beach only 50m from the road leading to the entrance of the national park. Reservations are highly recommended during the summer season.

National Park Camping (☎ 369 202; Dr Franje Tuđman bb; per adult/site 25/50KN; ☽ Apr-Oct) This camping ground is similarly located to Camping Paklenica.

Rajna (☎ 369 130; www.hotel-rajna.com; Dr Franje Tuđman 105; per person d 150KN; ☒ ☐) As the closest hotel to the park entrance, this is a popular meeting place for climbers and the food is good as well. Its recent upgrades have added comfort to its warm and homy atmosphere.

Hotel Vicko (☎ /fax 369 304; www.hotel-vicko .hr; Jose Dokoze bb; s/d from 385/500KN; ☐ ☒ ☐) Though not quite as stylish as the Hotel Alan, it's only 50m from the beach and it has a comfortable, intimate ambience. Prices drop by about a third outside July and August.

Hotel Alan (☎ 369 236; fax 369 203; Dr Franje Tuđman 14; s/d 430/655KN; ☐ ☒ ☒) The hotel has been renovated and now sports modern rooms with views over the seaside or the mountains.

PRIVATE ROOMS
Private accommodation is abundant in and around Starigrad. Although no agency 'officially' finds accommodation, the tourist office makes it its business to connect people looking for rooms or apartments with the many residents offering them. Prices range from 95KN to 150KN for a double depending on the amenities and 150KN to 200KN for a studio. Breakfast is another 18KN to 30KN. Full board and larger apartments are also available. You can find accommodation for yourself by walking along the main road and checking out the many *sobe* signs.

Getting There & Away
Starigrad is 45km from Zadar and 200km from Rijeka, and all buses between these cities stop at Starigrad. However, if the buses are full they won't stop to pick up passengers. To get to Zagreb you can backtrack to Zadar or take a bus to Maslenica and pick up the Zagreb-bound bus there.

DUGI OTOK

pop 1800
Dugi Otok may not be the place to find artfully designed villages or historic old towns, but the natural, unspoiled beauty of the island makes it a perfect getaway for those seeking a peaceful, relaxing holiday. The island has a brief high season around

the first three weeks of August when Italian vacationers boat over on the ferry from Ancona or on private vessels, and then all is quiet for another year. Among the highlights of the island are the Telašćica Bay nature park with its cluster of small islands, the nearby saltwater Mir Lake, sandy Sakarun Bay and a panoramic drive along the rocky, indented coast. There isn't much to do here besides swim, scuba dive and enjoy the spectacular scenery, but you'll certainly be free of package tourists, cruise lines and souvenir sellers.

The name Dugi Otok means long island. Stretching northeast to southwest, the island is 43km long and 4km wide. The southwestern coast is marked by steep hills and cliffs, while the northern half is cultivated with vineyards, orchards and sheep pastures. In between is a series of karstic hills rising to 338m at Vela Straža, its highest point.

Ruins on the island reveal early settlement by Illyrians, Romans and then early Christians but the island was first documented in the mid-10th century. It later became the property of the monasteries of Zadar. Settlement expanded with the 16th-century Turkish invasions, which prompted residents of Zadar and neighbouring towns to flee to the island.

Dugi Otok's fortunes have largely been linked with Zadar as it changed hands between Venetians, Austrians and the French, but when northern Dalmatia was handed over to Mussolini, the island stayed within Croatia. Old-timers still recall the hardships they endured when the nearest medical and administrative centre was in Šibenik, a long, hard boat ride up the coast.

Economic development of the island has always been hampered by the lack of any freshwater supply – drinking water must be collected from rainwater or, in the dry summers, brought over by boat from Zadar. Like many Dalmatian islands, the population has drifted away over the last few decades, leaving a few hardy souls to brave the dry summers and *bura*-chilled winters.

Most people base themselves in either Sali on the southeastern coast or Božava on the northeastern coast. Sali has more opportunities for private accommodation while Božava offers more of a resort experience. Roughly in the middle is Brbinj, which is the main ferry stop.

Getting There & Away
There are daily ferries all year from Zadar to Brbinj, Zaglav and Sali, which cost 17KN and take about 1½ hours. Miatours in Zadar runs a fast passenger boat from Zadar to Zaglav and Sali from June to September (18KN, 45 minutes). Miatours also connects Božava to Ancona (€60, 3½ hours) and Pesaro (€60, four hours) by hydrofoil once a day from mid-June to early September.

Getting Around
There is little public bus transport throughout the island, only a weekly bus taking Božavo villagers to Sali and back. On days when the ferry stops at Zaglav and not Sali, there is a bus that connects Sali with the ferry stop.

If you're entering the island at Brbinj without your own transport, you may have little choice but to head to Božava. There are no buses between Brbinj and Sali but buses to Božava from Brbinj (14km) meet all ferries except the one from Ancona that lands at 6am on Sunday.

SALI
pop 1190
As the island's largest town and port, Sali is a metropolis compared to the other small towns and villages scattered along Dugi Otok's coast. Named after the saltworks that employed villagers during the medieval period, the town has a rumpled, lived-in look that is comfortable and unpretentious.

Sali's low-key appeal is undisturbed by the yachts and small passenger boats that dock there during the summer on the way to and from Telašćica Bay and the Kornati Islands. Although the town is tantalisingly close to these natural wonders, you'll need to come with a boat, rent a boat or take a boat tour to visit them.

Orientation & Information
The town centres around the port on Porat Bay, where you'll find restaurants, cafés and offices. West of the town centre is sparkling Šašćica Bay, tucked between two hills with swimming coves. From the foot of the port, a path and stairs lead to the upper town, surrounded by small vineyards and fields.

The **Tourist Office** (Turistička Zajednica; ☎ /fax 377 094; tz-sali@zd.htnet.hr; Obala Kralja Tomislava; ✆ 8am-10pm daily Jul & Aug, 8am-noon Mon-Fri Sep-Jun) is the source of all information about Sali. It finds private accommodation, books excursions and distributes the few brochures and maps available.

There is no bank but you can change money or get cash on your MasterCard or Diners Club card at the **post office** (Obala Petra Lorinija; ✆ 8am-2pm & 5-8pm Mon-Sat).

Sights & Activities

Sightseeing within the town is limited but there is the interesting **St Mary's Church** (Crkva Sveti Marije; ☎ 377 041; ulica Sveti Marije; ✆ Mass only), built in the 15th century on the site of an earlier church. It is especially notable for the wooden altar and several Renaissance paintings.

The town's proximity to the underwater marine park at the Kornati Islands makes it an excellent base for scuba diving. Hotel Sali (see right) has a **dive shop** (☎ 377 079; www.dive-kroatien.de) that runs courses and dive trips around Dugi Otok and to the Kornati Islands. Diving in the Kornati Islands is marked by steep drop-offs and numerous caves because of its position facing the open sea. There are also possibilities for cave diving on the northern side of Dugi Otok where the caves are relatively shallow and large, making them suitable for beginners.

The tourist office can book you on **boat trips** that include a leisurely tour of Telašćica Bay and a stop on one of the Kornati Islands for about 250KN.

Festivals & Events

The weekend before the Assumption (15 August), the island hosts the **Saljske Užance Festival**, which draws visitors from the entire region. Highlights are the donkey races and the candlelight procession of boats around the harbour. Men and women don traditional costumes, play instruments devised from cow horns and perform traditional village dances.

Sleeping

There are no camping grounds on the island although it would seem that there are some splendid sites. Camping in the wild is inadvisable as there is a large population of rats on the island.

If you prefer the comforts of a hotel, you're in luck. **Hotel Sali** (☎ 377 049; www.hotel-sali.hr; s/d 280/535KN; ☒) is well located, in excellent condition and offers good value for money. It overlooks swimming coves and is freshly painted in white and marine-blue. All rooms have modern bathrooms, satellite TV and balconies, many with views over the sea. The price falls 25% in early July and late August, and 50% in June and September. The hotel restaurant is also very good.

PRIVATE ROOMS

Private accommodation is reasonable in Sali, especially out of the high season, and the tourist office can connect you with some wonderful, out-of-the-way places, including a house on its own little island. In high season you can find a room for 180KN to 220KN, usually with a shared bathroom. The price is based on double occupancy, so if you're travelling solo you may have to pay the price of a double. Off-season you have a lot more bargaining power to push the price down 20% to 30%. Try www.sali-dugiotok.com for apartment referrals.

A fully equipped studio runs from 280KN to 300KN and a two-room apartment is priced at 385KN. All prices are based upon a three-night minimum stay with a 30% surcharge for fewer nights. The surcharge is usually waived in off season.

If you come in the summer, it would be a good idea to ask the proprietor if there are any restrictions on the use of water. Even if nothing is spelled out, chances are that long, luxurious showers will not be appreciated.

Eating

There are a few restaurants along Obala Kralja Tomislava.

Grill Tamaris (☎ 377 236; mains from 30KN; ✆ closed Nov-Mar) This is the best restaurant on the street. It offers dishes such as spaghetti with mixed seafood and freshly grilled shrimp and fish at reasonable prices. The restaurant is closed for several months in winter.

Grill Toni (mains from 30KN) Offering a similar menu to Grill Tamaris, the food here is not bad either.

There's also a supermarket near Jadrolinija dock.

TELAŠĆICA BAY

The southeastern tip of Dugi Otok is split in two by the deeply indented Telašćica Bay, dotted with five small islands and five more even tinier islets. In fact, the 8200m bay contains five smaller bays, which form an indented coastline of 28km and one of the largest and most beautiful natural harbours in the Adriatic.

The Kornati Islands extend nearly to the edge of Telašćica Bay and the topography of the two island groups is identical – stark white limestone with patches of brush. The tip of the western side of the island faces the sea where the wind and waves have carved out sheer cliffs dropping 166m. There are no towns, settlements or roads on this part of the island, only a couple of restaurants on Mir Bay catering to the boaters who spend days or even weeks cruising the islands.

Next to Mir Bay is the saltwater Mir Lake, fed by underground channels that run through the limestone to the sea. The lake is surrounded by pine forests and the water is much warmer than the sea. The lake is clear but has a muddy bottom. Like most mud in unusual places it's supposed to be very good for you – rumour has it that it cure ailments and keeps you young.

BOŽAVA

pop 115

For visitors who think even Sali is too urban, there's always Božava, which is smaller still and quieter, greener and more remote. The town is overgrown with lush, flowering trees and there are lovely shady paths along the coast. It is on a harbour with many opportunities for swimming and strolling on pine-shaded paths.

If you arrive by bus, walk downhill from the bus stop to the tiny town centre where you'll find the **Tourist Office** (Turistička Zajednica; ☎ /fax 377 607; ☽ 8am-noon & 6-8pm daily Jun-Sep). It can arrange bike, scooter and car rental and can find you private accommodation (130/90KN with/without private facilities).

Veli Rat is a village on the northwestern point of the island on the scenic Čuna Bay, about 6km northwest of Božava. Although the area is lovely, there's no transport. Unless you come with your own wheels, you'll be relegated to hitching, walking or paying a resident to drive you out there.

Sleeping

Božava Hotel complex (☎ 291 291; www.hoteli -bozava.hr) This refurbished complex includes Hotel Lavanda and Hotel Kadulja. Room comforts vary, but you'll have access to a sauna, gym and massage services. Taking half board adds another 40KN per person to the charge.

Hotel Lavanda (☎ 291 291; www.jadera.com/boza va; s/d 435/715KN; P ✕ ⬚) This has always enjoyed an idyllic location on a cove, and has been stunningly refurbished and offers comfortable modern rooms with satellite TV as well as balconies with views.

Hotel Kadulja (☎ 291 291; www.jadera.com /bozava; s/d 345/535KN; P ⬚) Rooms are much simpler but you also get great views from most of them and access to Hotel Lavanda facilities.

PAG ISLAND

A barren, rocky island with no trees, little vegetation and no rivers or streams, Pag nonetheless has a stark, ethereal beauty enhanced by a highly original culture. The sharp-flavoured cheese and intricate lace from Pag is renowned throughout Croatia, while the 15th-century Pag town reflects Croatia's great builder, Juraj Dalmatinac, who designed the neat, orderly streets.

The 63km karstic island is a strange moonscape defined by two mountain ridges, patches of shrubs and a dozen or so villages and hamlets. There are peaceful coves and bays for swimming in around the main towns of Pag and Novalja, as well as the smaller settlements of Šimuni, Mandre and Straško on the southwestern coast, but the island is never overrun by tourists. Pag town is roughly in the centre of the island on the southeastern coast of the large Pag Bay (Paški Zaljev), while Novalja is 20km northwest on a small cove. The island is linked to the mainland by Pag Bridge in the southeast.

Today the primary occupations are agricultural as islanders attempt to wring a living from their unforgiving land. The sandy soil yields a decent domestic white wine, *Šutica*, and the hardy sheep graze on herbs and salty grass, lending their meat and milk a distinctive flavour. *Paški sir* (Pag-sheep cheese soaked in olive oil and aged in stone) is a prized speciality of Croatian cuisine. The marvellous lace from the island is a slim underpinning for economic viability but it does help bring in tourists.

History

The island was inhabited by the Illyrians before falling to the Romans in the 1st century BC. The Romans constructed forts and aqueducts. The Slavs settled around Novalja in the 7th century AD and began building churches and basilicas. In the 11th century a new settlement called Stari Grad emerged in the south of the island, 2km south of today's Pag, near the saltworks that became the foundation of the island's economy. The next centuries were turbulent for the island as it competed fiercely with Zadar and Rab over the salt trade. Zadar launched brutal attacks on the island in the 13th and 14th centuries but in 1409 it was sold to Venice along with Zadar and the rest of Dalmatia.

Getting There & Away
BOAT

In July and August, there's a regular catamaran service running from Rijeka to Novalja (34KN, three hours, three weekly) that passes through Rab (18KN, 50 minutes). If you're travelling up the coast by car, note that there are regular car ferries (12KN) from Žigljen on the northeast coast to Prizna on the mainland, which run roughly hourly in winter and nonstop from June to September.

BUS

There are two buses a day from Pag town to Zadar (29KN, one hour), two buses a day to Rijeka from Monday to Saturday and one on Sunday (89KN, four hours) and five buses a day to Zagreb (116KN, six hours). Nine buses a day make the 30-minute trip between Pag town and Novalja (17KN).

PAG TOWN
pop 2420

The appeal of Pag town is the straight, narrow streets and low, stone houses with living rooms that are practically on the street. There's a sense of intimacy and involvement with the town residents who socialise, repair appliances and make lace on stools outside their houses. The small-town ambience is captivating and there are pebble beaches to relax upon after a morning of lace-shopping.

In the early 15th century, the increasingly prosperous salt business prompted the construction of Pag town when nearby Stari Grad could no longer meet the demands of its burgeoning population. The Venetians engaged the finest builder of the time, Juraj Dalmatinac, to design a new city and the first cornerstone was laid in 1443. In accordance with what were then the latest ideas in town planning, the main streets and the cross streets intersect at right angles and lead to four city gates. In the centre, there's a square with a cathedral, St Mary's Church (Crka Sveta Marija), a ducal palace and a bishop's palace, which remained unfinished because Pag never succeeded in having its own bishop. In 1499, Dalmatinac began working on the city walls but only the northern corner, with parts of a castle, remains.

Orientation

The old town, bordered by Vangrada and Podmir streets, is a pedestrian zone that retains the original simplicity of its architecture. Everyone congregates around the cafés and benches on the main square, Trg Kralja Krešimira IV. Outside the old town there's a newer section with a couple of hotels, narrow beaches on the bay, travel agencies and restaurants. The bus station (no left-luggage office) is next to the Hotel Jadran, just outside the old town. A bridge across the bay to the southwest leads to a residential quarter, which contains the large hotels, bigger beaches and most private accommodation.

Information
MONEY

ATM (Trg Kralja Krešimira IV)
Riječka Banka (Vela ulica 18) Changes money.

POST

Post Office (Antuna Šimića) You can change money and access cash using MasterCard or Diners Club.

TOURIST INFORMATION

Tourist Office (Turistička Zajednica; ☎ /fax 611 301; www.pag-tourism.hr; Katine; ☻ 7am-midnight mid-Jun–mid-Sep, 7am-noon & 6pm-midnight May–mid-Jun & mid-Sep–Oct) A limited amount of documentation is available.

DELICATE & DURABLE: PAG LACE

The exact origins of the lace-making tradition in Pag are unknown but it probably began in the Renaissance as ornamentation for the traditional white linen shirts and neckerchiefs worn on Pag Island. As traditional dress began to die out in the 20th century, lace edging decorated tablecloths, altar cloths, bedspreads and handkerchiefs. In 1906 a School for Lace Making was established in Pag and the lace began to assume the geometrical shapes you see today. In 1911, Pag's lace received wider attention as a result of the efforts of an Austrian writer, Natalie Bruck-Auffenberg, who presented a lace blouse to the Archduchess Maria Josephine. The archduchess travelled to Pag to place an order and more noble ladies followed suit. The lace-making school was closed for a time but re-opened three years ago to keep the craft alive.

Lace-making requires a needle, thread, clean hands, good eyesight and a lot of time. The needle is an ordinary mending needle and the work is done on a backing, which is usually a hard stuffed pillow. Lace-makers work without drawings, based on designs handed down from generation to gener-ation to which each lace-maker adds their own personal touch. Within the many variations, there is a solid geometric structure called the *reticela* that is the skeleton of each design. At the centre is a circle that is traversed by eight thread sticks that radiate outward through an intricate web of circles and triangles. The result is a piece of handiwork that is as delicate as a snowflake but stiff and durable enough to withstand laundering.

TRAVEL AGENCIES

Travel agencies are open daily May to September, and Monday to Saturday only for the rest of the year.

Maricom (☎/fax 611 331; Stepjana Radića 8)
Mediteran (☎/fax 611 238; V Nazora 12)
Meridian 15 (☎ 612 162; fax 612 161; Starčevića 1) Near the Hotel Pagus.
Sunturist (☎ 612 040; fax 612 659; V Nazora bb)

Sights & Activities

The simple, Gothic **St Mary's Church** (Crkva Sveta Marija; ☎ 611 576; Trg Kralja Krešimira IV; ⏰ 9am-noon & 5-7pm May-Sep, Mass only Oct-Apr), built by Juraj Dalmatinac, is in perfect harmony with the modest structures surrounding it. The lunette over the portal shows the Virgin with women of Pag in medieval blouses and headdresses, and there are two rows of unfinished sculptures of saints. Completed in the 16th century, the interior was renovated with baroque ceiling decorations in the 18th century. The Gothic wooden crucifix on the altar dates from the 12th century and there are a variety of gold and silver liturgical objects housed in the church's treasury. Other notable churches include **St Margaret's** (Sveta Margarita; ☎ 611 069; Felicinovića 1; ⏰ Mass only), with a Renaissance-baroque façade and a treasury with paintings and reliquaries, and **St George's** (Sveti Juraj; Trg Sveti Jurja; ⏰ 8-10pm for exhibits), which houses changing art exhibits. Notice also the elaborate portal over the

Ducal Palace (Kneževa Palaća) attributed to a disciple of Dalmatinac.

No visit to Pag would be complete without a look at the small **Lace Museum** (Kralja Zvonimira; admission free; ⏰ 8-11pm daily mid-Jun–mid-Sep), off the main square, which gives a good overview of the island's most famous craft.

Festivals & Events

The last day of July is the **Pag Carnival**, which is a good opportunity to see the traditional *kolo* (a lively Slavic round dance) and appreciate the elaborate traditional dresses of Pag. The main square is filled with dancers and musicians, and a theatre troupe presents the traditional folk play *Paška Robinja* (The Slave Girl of Pag).

Sleeping

Pag has a few hotel options and an out-of-town camping ground.

Camping Šimuni (☎ 697 44; uzorit@zg.htnet.hr; Šimuni; per adult/site 60/80KN; ⏰ Apr-Sep) This is on a rocky beach on the southwestern coast, about halfway between Pag town and Novalja, near the port of Šimuni. All buses from Pag to Novalja stop here.

Hotel Pagus (☎ 611 310; zeljka.stosic@zg.htnet .hr; A Starčevića 1; s/d 275/400KN; P ☒) The Pagus, on a narrow beach in the bay, is in excellent condition, with renovated and relatively spacious rooms furnished in a light Mediterranean style. Rooms have a phone but no TV.

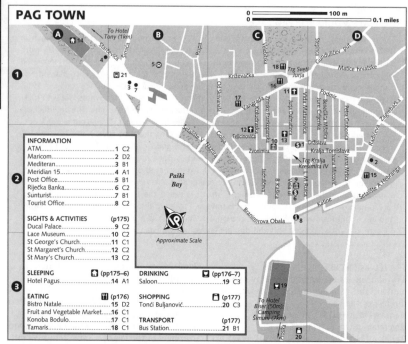

PAG TOWN

0 _____ 100 m
0 _____ 0.1 miles

Paški Bay

Approximate Scale

Hotel Tony (☎ /fax 611 370; www.hotel-toni.com; Dubrovačka 39; s/d 245/370KN; P ⊠ ▯) A casual place along the shore about 1km east of Hotel Pagus, it's quiet and relaxing but somewhat isolated in the bushes and reeds. Some of the large and well-fitted rooms have balconies and there are a few studios available. It's only about another 40KN per person to take half board and the food is well worth it.

Hotel Biser (☎ 611 333; www.hotel-biser.com; Matoša 8; s/d 275/375KN; P ⊠ ▯) This 24-room hotel has comfortable enough rooms even though the outside has the boxy look that is all too prevalent in Croatia. It's across the water from the old town but close to the beach.

PRIVATE ROOMS

If there are no ladies waiting at the bus station to offer *sobe*, you will find a lot of signs advertising *sobe* on Ulica Prosika across the bridge. Any of the travel agencies listed on p175 will find you private accommodation for about 130/200KN for a single/double.

Eating

Most restaurants offer a little bit of everything – pizza, pasta, fish, meat and salads. Curiously, the price of a starter of Pag cheese isn't much cheaper than anywhere else on the coast, but the quality is apt to be better.

Self-caterers can pick up fruit, vegetables and local cheese at the daily morning fruit and vegetable market.

Tamaris (☎ 612 277; Križevačka bb; mains from 27KN) Pizza, fresh pasta and fried calamari are prepared for a local crowd at a reasonable price.

Bistro Natale (☎ 611 194; Radićeva 2; pizza from 25KN) This restaurant serves up pizza and pasta in a narrow courtyard and is popular with kuna-counting locals.

Konoba Bodulo (☎ 611 989; Vangrada 19; mains from 30KN) At this family-run spot you can dine on country-fresh ingredients under a grapevine.

Drinking

In a former salt warehouse just over the bridge, **Saloon** (☾ from 11pm nightly Jul-Aug, weekends only Sep-Jun) is the only disco on the island

and a good place to research Pagian party habits.

Shopping

Pag offers the most distinctive products in all Croatia. It would be a shame to leave the island without buying lace, since the prices are relatively cheap and buying a piece helps keep the tradition alive. A small circle or star about 10cm in diameter costs about 80KN, but it takes a good 24 hours to make. Larger pieces cost from 150KN to 300KN. The best way to buy lace is to walk down Kralja Tomislava or Zvonimira in the morning while the women are lace-making and buy from them directly. Prices are marked on a card and bargaining is usually futile.

Unlike lace, Pag cheese is not sold in town and requires some effort to find. Often there's just a home-made sign, *Pakši Sir*, posted outside a house on a remote road somewhere. The asking price for a kilogram is usually 100KN but you can often bargain down to 70KN or 80KN a kilogram. It can get you through a lot of dreary hotel breakfasts.

Try also the pungent Pag cheese made at **Tonči Buljanović** (☎ 611 228; Prosika 6), close to town. The price is 100KN to 110KN a kilogram.

Getting Around

Pag's flat landscape makes bike riding a breeze. You can rent bikes at the Mediteran travel agency for 20/80KN per hour/day.

NOVALJA

pop 1900

Although lacking the unique charm of Pag town, the beaches of Novalja have sparked a thriving tourist business. On the southwestern coast of the island, the town, port and bay are protected from the winds that can buffet Pag town. The surrounding beaches of Zrće, Caska, Straško and Trinčel are on lovely, wide shallow coves, ideal for frolicking kids.

Just before the entrance to Novalja is **Uvala Zrće**, a long stretch of white-sand beach, the most beautiful and popular on the island. Between Pag and Novalja is **Uvala Caska**, a shingle beach with shallow water.

Orientation & Information

The town centre is compact with the tourist office, post office and all shops and services within few blocks of each other. The bus stop is on the eastern edge of town. Follow the harbour road straight ahead to find travel agencies and shops.

The **Tourist Board** (☎ 663 570; www.tz-novalja .hr; Šetalište hrvatskih mornara 1; ☯ 8am-8pm daily Jul & Aug, 8am-3pm Mon-Fri Sep-Jun) will find private accommodation. **Chery** (☎ 662 174; B Radić) finds private accommodation and has boat information.

Sleeping & Eating

The tourist office or any travel agency can help find private accommodation. You'll pay from 70KN to 100KN per person.

Hotel Loža (☎ 663 381; www.turistdd.hr; Trg Loža; s/d 470/625KN; Ⓟ) The rooms and design are pretty much standard issue but you won't be uncomfortable. Some rooms have balconies and views over the sea and the hotel is in the centre of town.

Hotel Liburnija (☎ 661 328; www.turistdd.hr; Šetalište hrvatskih mornara bb; s/d 460/610KN; Ⓟ) A few hundred metres southeast of the town centre, this hotel is right next to a beach.

Starac i More (☎ 662 423; Braće Radić; mains from 40KN) Right on the quay, this seafood restaurant serves up the right stuff without fuss or pretension.

Šibenik-Knin Region

CONTENTS

Šibenik-Knin county contains two of Croatia's most beautiful national parks: the Krka National Park and the Kornati Islands. The relatively flat coast contains a string of resorts, private accommodation and tourist settlements, and the sea is dotted by several small islands. Without a direct boat connection to Italy, the tourist business is slower here than elsewhere along the coast, making it a good region to consider when the rest of the coast is jam-packed.

Stony, dry and carpeted with maquis, the karstic interior is divided by the Krka River which connects the coastal bay with the splendid Krka waterfalls. Along the coast, the major town is Šibenik, which has extraordinary Renaissance architecture. Spreading over several hills at the centre of a 10km bay that spreads from Zaton in the northwest to Mandalina in the southeast, Šibenik makes an excellent base to explore the region.

The interior of the region includes part of the Vojna Krajina (Military Frontier) established by the Austrians in the 16th century as protection from the Turks. It was settled by Vlachs and Morlachs belonging to the Orthodox Church and thus developed a large Serbian population. Upon the Croatian declaration of independence in 1990, the Krajina Serbs, with the help of arms from Belgrade, established their own state and made Knin its capital. When Croatia retook the territory in 1995, virtually the entire Serbian population fled, leaving a landscape of smashed buildings and ruined villages. Most of the physical damage has now been repaired, but the economy is in tatters and the interior villages have remained underpopulated.

Knin is still a vital transit point between the coast and the Croatian heartland but its remoteness and lack of an economic base has made it hard for the government to attract residents or visitors.

HIGHLIGHTS

- Boating the **Kornati Islands** (p186)
- Counting the faces on Šibenik's **Cathedral of St Jacob** (p181)
- Strolling the village and beaches of **Primošten** (p184)
- Showering under a waterfall in **Krka National Park** (p184)

- TELEPHONE CODE: 022
- POSTCODE: 22000

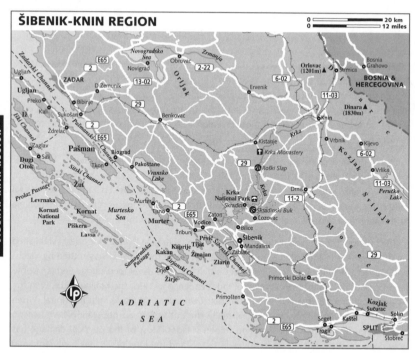

ŠIBENIK

pop 41,012

Although Šibenik is not often promoted as a tourist destination, the town centre does have a remarkable cathedral and a network of streets and squares that were laid out in the 15th and 16th centuries. Restaurants, hotels and entertainment venues are scattered among the tourist complexes along the coast, but if you find a place to stay in town, you can take some interesting strolls along the harbour and through the steep back streets and alleys. The city also makes an excellent base for exploring two beautiful national parks, especially the waterfalls at the Krka National Park, which can be visited without booking an organised tour.

History

Unlike many other Dalmatian coastal towns, Šibenik was settled first by Croat tribes, not Illyrians or Romans. First mentioned in the 11th century by the Croatian king Krešimir IV, the city was conquered by Venice in 1116 but was tossed back and forth among Venice, Hungary, Byzantium and the Kingdom of Bosnia until Venice seized control in 1412 after a three-year fight. At the end of the 15th century Ottoman Turks burst into the region as part of their struggle against Venice. Over the course of the succeeding two centuries, Turks periodically attacked the town, disrupting trade and agriculture. The fortresses which were built by the Venetians in defence of the town are still visible, most notably the fortress of St Nikola at the entrance to the Šibenski Channel. The Turkish threat receded with the 1699 Treaty of Karlowitz but the city continued to suffer from Venetian rule until it passed into the hands of Austria in 1797, where it remained until 1918.

Šibenik fell under attack in 1991 from the Yugoslav federal army, and was subject to shelling until its liberation as part of 'Operation Storm' by the Croatian army in 1995. Little physical damage is visible, but the city's aluminium industry, which was an important part of the regional economy, was shattered by the war. The city is trying to make a comeback but the struggle to survive leaves people with little money for cafés, restaurants or other luxuries.

Orientation

The city spreads like an amphitheatre from the harbour uphill to the surrounding hills. The main road is Kralje Zvonimira and the old town lies between it and the harbour, which is in a large bay. The entire old town is a pedestrian area and contains the cathedral and several notable churches. The oldest part of the town is on Zagrebačka ulica and the streets running north. The bus station is in a modern jumble of concrete blocks in the city's southern corner. The main commercial street is Ante Starčevića and Ante Šupuka east of the old town, with the train station lying southeast.

Information

LEFT LUGGAGE
Garderoba Bus station (🕑 6am-10pm); Train station (🕑 24hr)

MONEY
The post office, travel agencies and Croatia Express change money. There's an ATM on Kralja Zvonimira and a Zagrebačka banka with an ATM on Ante Šupuka.

POST
Post Office (Vladimira Nazora 51) You can make calls and change money here.

TOURIST INFORMATION
Croatia Express (☎ 333 669; Train Station) It changes money and sells train tickets.
Jadrolinija (☎ 213 468; Obala Franje Tuđmana 8) It's a good source of information for ferry sailings.
Tourist Office (Turistička Ured; ☎ 212 075; www .summernet.hr/sibenik; Fausta Vrančića 18; 🕑 8am-9pm Mon-Sat, 8am-2pm Sun mid-Jun–mid-Sep, and 8am-3pm Mon-Fri mid-Jun–mid-Sep)

TRAVEL AGENCIES
Atlas Travel Agency (☎ 330 232; Trg Republike Hrvatske 2) It changes money, and books excursions.
NIK Travel Agency (☎ /fax 338 540; www.nik.hr; Ante Šupuka 5) The largest travel agency in town. It finds private accommodation and sells international bus and air tickets.

Sights & Activities

Juraj Dalmatinac was the sculptor and the **Cathedral of St Jacob** (Katedrala Sveti Jakova; Trg Republike Hrvatske; 🕑 8am-noon & 6-8pm daily May-Oct, Mass only Nov-Apr) is his masterpiece. Unquestionably the crowning glory of the Dalmatian coast, the cathedral is worth a considerable

detour to see. Its most unusual feature is the frieze of 71 heads on the exterior walls of the apses. These portraits in stone are vivid character studies of ordinary 15th-century citizens. Placid, annoyed, proud or fearful, their expressions convey the timelessness of human emotion through the centuries.

Dalmatinac was not the first or the last sculptor to work on the cathedral. Construction began in 1431 but after 10 years of toying around with various Venetian builders, the city appointed the Zadar native, Dalmatinac, who increased the size and transformed the conception of the church into a transitional Gothic-Renaissance style.

In addition to the exterior frieze, other examples of Dalmatinac's style include the two aisle staircases descending into the sacristy on one side and exquisite baptistry on the other, in which three angels support the baptismal font. The latter was carved by Andrija Aleši after Dalmatinac's designs. Other interior artwork worth noting are the crypt of bishop Šižigorić (by Dalmatinac), who supported the building of the cathedral; the altar painting of St Fabijan and St Sebastijan (by Zaniberti); the painting *The Gift of the Wise Men* (by Ricciardi); and, next to it, two marble reliefs of angels (by Firentinac). Note also the *Lion's Portal* on the northern side, created by Dalmatinac and Bonino da Milano, on which two lions support columns containing the figures of Adam and Eve, who appear to be excruciatingly embarrassed by their nakedness.

The cathedral was constructed entirely of stone quarried from the islands of Brač, Korčula, Rab and Krk, and is reputed to be the world's largest church built completely of stone without brick or wood supports. The unusual domed-roof complex was completed after Dalmatinac's death by Nikola Firentinac, who continued the façade in a pure Renaissance style. The church was finally completed in 1536.

Across the square from the cathedral is the **town hall**, a harmonious Renaissance arrangement of columns and a balustrade, which was constructed between 1533 and 1546. Destroyed during an Allied air attack in 1943, the building was completely rebuilt to its original form, which explains its shiny, new appearance.

On the southern side of the cathedral is the **Town Museum** (Gradski Muzej; ☎ 213 880;

ŠIBENIK

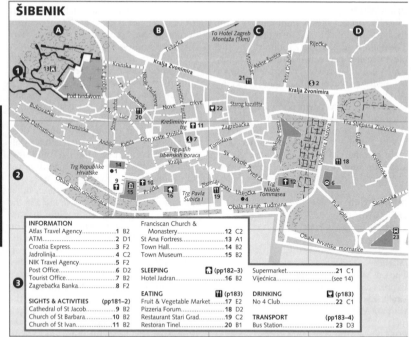

INFORMATION			Franciscan Church &		
Atlas Travel Agency	1	B2	Monastery	12	C2
ATM	2	D1	St Ana Fortress	13	A1
Croatia Express	3	F2	Town Hall	14	B2
Jadrolinija	4	C2	Town Museum	15	B2
NIK Travel Agency	5	F2			
Post Office	6	D2	**SLEEPING**		(pp182–3)
Tourist Office	7	B2	Hotel Jadran	16	B2
Zagrebačka Banka	8	F2			
			EATING		(p183)
SIGHTS & ACTIVITIES		(pp181–2)	Fruit & Vegetable Market	17	E2
Cathedral of St Jacob	9	B2	Pizzeria Forum	18	D2
Church of St Barbara	10	B2	Restaurant Stari Grad	19	C2
Church of St Ivan	11	B2	Restoran Tinel	20	B1

Supermarket	21	C1
Viječnica	(see 14)	
DRINKING		(p183)
No 4 Club	22	C1
TRANSPORT		(pp183–4)
Bus Station	23	D3

Gradska Vrata 3; admission free; ☺ 10am-1pm & 7-10pm daily Apr-Sep, 5-7pm Oct-Mar), which has no permanent collection but presents a series of temporary exhibits that change every two months. Often the exhibits are Šibenik specific and are captioned in English.

The town has a wealth of beautiful churches but they are only open for Mass, and nonworshipping visitors are not appreciated. The **Church of St Ivan** (Crkva Svetog Ivana; Trg Ivana Paula II) is a fine example of Gothic-Renaissance architecture dating from the end of the 15th century. The **Franciscan Church and Monastery** (Franjevački Samostan; Ćulinoviča), which dates from the end of the 14th century, has 14th- and 15th-century frescoes and an array of Venetian baroque paintings. There is a **Museum of Church Art** (admission 10KN; ☺ 9am-1pm Mon-Fri) at the **Church of St Barbara** (Crkva Svete Barbare; Kralja Tomislava) on the side of the cathedral. The museum exhibits paintings, engravings and sculptures from the 14th to the 18th centuries.

You can climb to the top of **St Ana fortress** in the northeast for a magnificent view over Šibenik and the surrounding region.

Tours
Atlas Travel Agency (p181) organises full-day trips to the Kornati Islands for 300KN, with a lunch stop at Piškera and a few swim stops; a half-day trip to the Krka waterfalls for 175KN; and a full-day trip that includes Skradinski Buk and Visovać for 300KN. All admission fees are included in the prices.

Festivals & Events
Šibenik hosts a renowned **International Children's Festival** during the last week of June and the first week of July. There are workshops in crafts, music and dance, children's film and theatre, puppets and parades.

Sleeping
Commercial accommodation possibilities are largely confined to the resort centre **Solaris** (☎ 363 951; www.solaris.hr), 6km southwest of town. It's an enormous complex with six hotels, two highly populous camping grounds and a sprinkling of self-contained apartments. It's on the beach.

Hotel Zagreb Montaža (☎ /fax 331 750; Bana Josipa Jelačića 21; d 200KN) This hostel for visiting

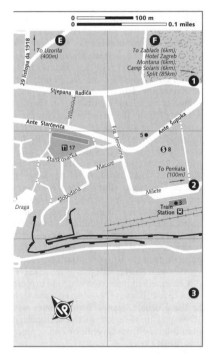

workers is also open to tourists and fills the gap left by Šibenik's now-closed youth hostel. Rooms are impersonal but clean.

Hotel Jadran (☎ 212 644; www.rivijera.hr; Obala Oslobođenja 52; s/d 385/625KN) This modern hotel conveniently located along the harbour is the only one in town. It's somewhat impersonal but in excellent condition and rooms are equipped with satellite TV. The hotel can be warm in the summer, so try to get a room overlooking the harbour to get some breezes.

Camp Solaris (☎ 364 450; www.solaris.hr; Solaris; per adult/site 35/55KN; ✷ mid-Mar–Oct) is an elaborate camping ground complete with a seawater pool, sports facilities and restaurants. Smaller and cheaper, **Zablaće** (☎ /fax 354 015; Solaris; per adult/site 25/50KN) is another camping alternative.

PRIVATE ROOMS

Most private accommodation is in neighbouring villages such as Primošten, Tribunj and Vodice along the coast, easily reached by bus from Šibenik. In July and August, you may be met by women at the bus or train station offering *sobe* (rooms available) at much lower prices. NIK Travel Agency (p181) has private rooms from about 200KN and studios from about 340KN.

Eating & Drinking

Like the rest of the Dalmatian coast, the menus in Šibenik restaurants lean heavily towards fish and are influenced by the pastas and risottos of Italy. Fish can be expensive but there are plenty of pizzerias.

Penkala (☎ 219 869; Jeronima Milete 17; mains from 25KN; ✷ closed Sun) Popular with the locals and very good, this neighbourhood spot serves up homespun cooking with a tendency to hearty meat stews.

Uzorita (☎ 213 660; Bana Josip Jelačića 50; mains from 50KN) This old standby with a shady terrace has a menu featuring fish and meat dishes with a nod to bean-eating vegetarians.

Pizzeria Forum (☎ 218 646; Vladimira Nazora 7; mains from 27KN) Near the post office, feast on good pies at good prices here.

Restaurant Stari Grad (☎ 219 330; Obala Oslobođenja 12; mains from 35KN) On the port, its speciality is seafood, of course.

Vijećnica (☎ 213 605; Trg Republike Hrvatske; mains from 60KN) On the ground floor of the town hall and across from the cathedral, the terrace and stunning interior offer a fine setting and there are many cosmopolitan dishes on the menu.

Restoran Tinel (☎ 331 815; Trg Puckih kapetana 1; mains from 50KN) This two-floor restaurant offers the finest dining in town with an excellent wine list. Try the wonderful *brodet* (mixed fish stewed with polenta) and wash it down with an Istrian *malvazija* (type of wine).

No 4 Club (☎ 217 57; Dinka Zavorovića trg 4) Young trendies down cocktails on the ground floor and snack upstairs.

Self-caterers can stock up at the **supermarket** (Zvonimira) or the **fruit and vegetable market** (btwn Starčevića and Stankovačka).

Getting There & Away

There are two overnight trains daily between Zagreb and Šibenik, a fast train that leaves in the morning (135KN, six hours) and an overnight train (129KN, 10 hours); from Monday to Saturday there are six trains a day between Šibenik and Split (33KN, two hours) which drops to four trains on Sunday.

Šibenik is well connected by bus to local and international destinations.

Destination	Cost	Duration	Frequency
Dubrovnik	125KN	6hr	8 daily
Murter	17KN	45min	9 daily
Osijek	249KN	8½hr	1 daily
Primošten	14KN	25min	6 daily
Pula	189KN	8hr	3 daily
Rijeka	153KN	6hr	13 daily
Split	36-50KN	1¾hr	hourly
Zadar	47KN	1½hr	½ hourly
Zagreb	139KN	6½hr	15 daily

AROUND ŠIBENIK

The city is surrounded by villages by the sea, which become major tourist resorts in summer. The largest resort is **Vodice**, located 11km northwest of Šibenik on the Adriatic Highway. This small fishing village on the harbour has been amplified by the construction of several large hotels and apartment complexes. It has a baroque church and a 16th-century tower, but most people head to one of the beaches and coves around the town centre. From Monday to Saturday there are three ferries a day between Šibenik and Vodice and two on Sunday.

Tribunj, on a small peninsula 4km west of Vodice, claims to have the largest fishing fleet in Central Dalmatia, making it a good place to sample fresh fish, mussels and crabs. The local speciality is fish ragout with polenta.

By far the most attractive town within reach of Šibenik is **Primošten**, about 20km southeast of the town centre. The small village of medieval streets dominated by a large belfry is neatly contained within a peninsula, making it resemble the Istrian town of Rovinj. Across the bay is another peninsula thickly wooded with pines and bordered by pebbly beaches. The hotels are discrete enough not to spoil the landscape.

Šibenik is easily connected by ferry to several small islands that can be explored in a day trip. **Zlarin** is only 30 minutes by boat and is known for the coral that used to be abundant before it was torn from the sea and sold for jewellery. Because there are no cars allowed on the island, it makes a tranquil retreat from Šibenik and boasts a sand beach, pine woods and a spacious port.

Prvić is only 15 minutes further than Zlarin and contains two villages, Prvić Luka and Šepurine (10 minutes further on the ferry), which retain the flavour of simple fishing settlements; this is probably because there are no large hotels on the island, only private accommodation.

Murter is 29km northwest of Šibenik, separated from the mainland by a narrow channel. The steep southwestern coast is indented by small coves, most notably the cove of Slanica, which is the best for swimming. Murter village is in the northwest and has a good harbour and not-so-good beach. The **tourist office** (☎ /fax 434 995; www .murter.com; Rudina 2; ☺ 7.30am-9.30pm mid-Jun—mid-Sep, 8am-noon mid-Sep–mid-Jun) will direct you to all accommodation possibilities. **KornatTurist** (☎ 435 855; www.kornatturist.hr; Hrvatskih Vladara 2) is one of several agencies that run full-day excursions to the Kornati Islands (215KN).

Although Murter village is unremarkable, it is an excellent base from which to explore the Kornati Islands. Booking an excursion to the Kornati Islands from Murter will allow you to see more of the archipelago than booking from Šibenik or Zadar, since it is much closer.

If you'd like to splurge and stay on an island, KornatTurist arranges private accommodation. It will cost about 3700KN per week for a two-person cottage including the boat transfer, a twice-weekly food delivery, gas for lighting and the admission fee for the Kornati National Park. You can also rent a motorboat for 700KN per week.

Keep in mind that Murter inhabitants are the owners of the Kornati Islands and visit it occasionally by private boat to tend their land. Asking around town may put you in touch with someone who will run you out there and arrange for you to stay overnight in their cottage on one of the islands for less money.

KRKA NATIONAL PARK

From the western foot of the Dinaric Range into the sea near Šibenik, the 72.5km Krka River and its wonderful waterfalls define the landscape of Šibenik-Knin county and are the focus of the Krka National Park. Like the Plitvice Lakes (p164), the Krka waterfalls are a karstic phenomenon. The river water formed a deep canyon (up to 200m) through the limestone and brought with it

MARTIN MOOS

Boats moored at sunset, Šibenik (p180)

Carved stone heads outside the Cathedral
of St Jacob (p181)

MARTIN MOOS

MARTIN MOOS

A performance at the Cathedral of
St Jacob (p181)

Rock pools below the Skradinski Buk falls, Krka National Park (p184)

MARTIN MOOS

Diocletian's Palace at night, Split (p192)

Windsurfer in action off the
coast of Bol (p215)

Drumming up business in Trogir (p202)

Riding the waves off Brač Island (p211)

VLACHS – NOMADS OF THE BALKANS

The first settlers of the Krajina region north of Šibenik were a pastoral, nomadic people known as Vlachs or Morlachs. Darker skinned than their Slavic neighbours (Morlach is derived from Maurus, Latin for black), their origins are uncertain. They may have come from Serbia or Bosnia or they may have been Roman legionaries who were pushed into the Dalmatian interior by the 7th-century Slavs. By the time Austria invited them to settle the Vojna Krajina (Military Frontier) in the 16th century, most, although not all, belonged to the Orthodox Church.

Vlachs had little to do with their Austrian and Italian neighbours, preferring to live within their own unusual culture. The Catholic and Orthodox Vlachs detested each other and both viewed Venetians and Italianised coastal Dalmatia with contempt. As nomadic people, they were more comfortable with their livestock than with other people, whom they tended to avoid. The Venetians were horrified by their habit of sleeping with their animals and baffled by their refusal to eat frogs, which were considered a great delicacy. They were said to be violent people, who slept with a gun under their head and devoted more time to drunken festivals than working. Vlachs firmly believed in the existence of witches and fairies and were inclined to tear apart the dead body of anyone suspected of being a vampire.

Vlach marriages were especially peculiar. On her wedding day, the bride's parents would enumerate all her bad qualities to the groom who frequently responded by beating her. Upon marriage, the husband got the bed and the wife curled up on the ground. When she went to confession, the priest would deliver absolution by whacking her with a club.

The brutality inflicted upon Vlach women was probably not unusual in peasant cultures and, at least, the Vlachs allowed women to opt out of the system by entering into a same-sex marriage. Two women could swear oaths to each other in a church ceremony after which they were pronounced *posestre* (half-sisters). The 18th-century Italian writer Alberto Fortis witnessed a *posestre* ceremony between two women and commented upon the 'satisfaction that sparkled in their eyes when the ceremony was performed'.

The status of the Vlachs was a constant bone of contention between Austria and the Croatian *Sabor* (Parliament). For Austria, the Vlach soldiers were an essential bulwark against the Turks and well worth the exemption from serfdom they received in exchange for their military service. The Croatian Sabor was made up of noblemen who were profoundly threatened by the existence of free peasants, fearing that such a dangerous notion could radicalise their own serfs. It was not until the mid-19th century, when feudalism was in its death throes, that the issue faded away. At the same time, the Orthodox Vlach majority in the region began to identify themselves as Serbs and the terms Vlachs and Morlachs gradually disappeared.

calcium carbonate. Mosses and algae retain the calcium carbonate and encrust it in their roots. The material is called tufa and is formed by billions of plants that grow on top of one another. The growths create barriers in the river which produce waterfalls. Unlike Plitvice Lakes, the volume of water rushing through the canyon is much greater, averaging 55 cu metres of water per second at the last cascade, Skradinski Buk, making the spectacle even more dramatic.

Orientation

The main entries to the national park are located at the Skradin and Lozovac entrances, which lie on the western and eastern banks respectively.

Information

The **tourist office** (☎ 771 306; www.skradin.hr; Trg Male Gospe 3; ☟ 8am-9pm Jul & Aug, 9am-1pm & 5-8pm Sep-Jun) is along the harbour and organises bookings for private accommodation in and around Skradin for about 100KN per night per person. The **Krka National Park office** (☎ 217 720; www.npkrka.hr) has information and can arrange excursions.

Sights & Activities

The landscape of rocks, cliffs, caves and chasms is a remarkable sight, but the national park also contains several important cultural landmarks. Near its northernmost point there is an Orthodox monastery; it's sometimes called Arandjelovac (literally Holy Archangel), or often simply referred to as the **Krka monastery**. First mentioned in 1402 as the endowment of Jelena Šubić, the sister of Emperor Dušan of Serbia, it was built and rebuilt until the end of the 18th century. The monastery has a unique combination of Byzantine and Mediterranean architecture and had a valuable inventory dating back to the 14th century, some of which was destroyed during the recent war.

Below the monastery the river becomes a lake created by the **Roški Slap** barrier downstream and the valley narrows into a 150m gorge. Roški Slap is a 650m-long stretch that begins with shallow steps and continues in a series of branches and islets to become 27m-high cascades. On the eastern side of the falls you can see water mills that used to mill wheat.

The first kilometre of the lake is bordered by reeds and bulrushes sheltering marsh birds. Next downstream is the Medu Gredama gorge with cliffs 150m high cut into a variety of dramatic shapes. Then the gorge opens out into Lake Visovac with **Samostan Visovac**, its lovely island monastery. In the 14th century hermits built a small monastery and church which they abandoned under threat from the Turks in 1440. They were succeeded by Bosnian Franciscans in 1445, who remained throughout Turkish rule until 1699. The church on the island dates from the end of the 17th century and the bell tower was built in 1728. On the western bank is a forest of holm oak and on the eastern bank is a forest of white oaks.

Six kilometres downstream you come to the largest waterfall, **Skradinski Buk**, with an 800m-long cascade covering 17 steps and rising to almost 46m. As at Roški Slap, watermills used to grind wheat, mortars pounded felt and huge baskets held rugs and fabrics. The mills are deserted now but Venetians used to collect a small fortune in taxes from the Krka mills. Downstream from Skradinski Buk is less interesting due to the construction of the Jaruga power plant in 1904.

It takes about an hour to walk around Skradinski Buk and see the waterfalls. Bring a swimsuit because it is possible to swim in the lower lake.

Sleeping & Eating

There are several restaurants and grocery stores along the harbour. There are a few snack places and inexpensive restaurants at Skradinski Buk plus one renovated hotel in Skradin.

It's fairly standard issue in terms of decoration, but **Hotel Skradinski Buk** (☎ 771 771; www.skradinskibuk.hr; Burinovac bb; s/d 375/580KN; P 🅿 🖵) has rooms nicely outfitted with satellite TV and Internet access. Some of the rooms can be quite cramped.

Getting There & Away

Although several agencies sell excursions to the falls from Šibenik, Zadar and other cities, it is possible, and certainly more interesting, to visit the falls independently if you base yourself in Šibenik.

There are six daily buses from Šibenik which make the 30-minute run to Skradin. The bus drops you outside of the old town of Skradin. You pay the park admission fee (adult/concession 60/40KN in July and August, 50/35KN April, May, June, September and October and 20/10KN November to March) here, which allows you to board a boat to Skradinski Buk. If you take one of the five daily buses to Lozovac, you can take a bus to Skradinski Buk (also included in the park admission) but you miss out on the boat ride through the canyon which you can enjoy from Skradin.

From Skradinski Buk, there are three boats daily from April to October going to Visovac (adult/concession 70/40KN) and Roški Slap (adult/concession 100/60KN). From Roški Slap, there's a boat to the monastery (adult/concession 60/40KN). At other times of the year you should first call the Krka National Park office, or ask at the tourist office in Šibenik to find out the boat schedule.

KORNATI ISLANDS

On the last day of the Creation, God desired to crown His work, and thus created the Kornati Islands out of tears, stars and breath.

George Bernard Shaw

Composed of 147 mostly uninhabited islands, islets and reefs covering 69 sq km, the Kornati Islands are the largest and densest archipelago in the Adriatic. Typically karst terrain, the islands are riddled with cracks, caves, grottoes and rugged cliffs. Since there are no sources of fresh water on the islands, they are mostly barren, sometimes with a light covering of grass. The evergreens and holm oak that used to be found on some islands were long ago burned down in order to clear the land. Far from stripping the islands of their beauty, the deforestation has highlighted startling rock formations, whose stark whiteness against the deep blue Adriatic is an eerie and wonderful sight.

The Kornati Islands form themselves into four series running northwest to southeast. The first two series of islands lie closer to the mainland and are known locally as Gornji Kornat. The largest and most indented of these islands is **Žut**. The other two series of islands, facing the open sea, comprise the **Kornati National Park** (adult/child 50/25KN) and are the most dramatically indented. The island of **Kornat** is by far the largest island, extending 25km in length but only 2.5km in width.

Not only the land but also the sea is within the protection of the national park. Fishing is strictly limited now in order to allow the regeneration of fish shoals that had been severely overfished. Groper, bass, conger eel, sea bream, pickerel, sea scorpion, cuttlefish, squid, octopus and smelt are some of the fish trying to make a comeback in the region.

Human presence on the Kornati Islands appears to extend back to the Neolithic Age, and the remains of Illyrian settlements were found on the largest island, Kornat. Romans and early Christians inhabited Kornat Island, which has a small tower that was probably built in the 6th century AD.

The island of **Piškera** was also inhabited during the Middle Ages and served as a collection and storage point for fish. Until the 19th century the islands were owned by the aristocracy of Zadar, but about 100 years ago peasant ancestors of the residents of Murter and Dugi Otok bought the islands, built many kilometres of rock walls to divide their property and used the islands to raise sheep.

The islands remain privately owned, 90% belonging to Murter residents and the remainder to residents of Dugi Otok. Although there are no longer any permanent inhabitants on the islands, many owners have cottages and fields which they visit from time to time to tend the land. Olive trees account for about 80% of the land under cultivation, followed by vineyards, orchards and vegetable gardens. All told, there are about 300 buildings on the Kornati Islands, mostly clustered on the southwestern coast of Kornat.

For further information contact the **Kornati National Park office** (☎ 434 662; www.korn ati.hr; Butina 2, Murter).

Getting There & Away

The best way to visit the islands is by boat, especially your own. The largest marina is on the island of Piškera, on the southern part of the strait between Piškera and Lavsa. There's another large marina on the island of Žut and a number of small coves throughout the islands where boaters can dock.

Otherwise, you can book an excursion from Zadar, Šibenik, Split and other coastal cities or arrange for private accommodation from the island of Murter (see p184). There is no ferry transport between the Kornati Islands and the mainland.

Central
Dalmatia

CENTRAL DALMATIA

Roman ruins, spectacular beaches, old fishing ports, medieval and Renaissance architecture and unspoiled islands make Central Dalmatia the ideal region to combine hedonism with historical discovery.

The ruins in Solin and Diocletian's Palace in Split (a Unesco World Heritage site) recall the region's Latin heritage. Trogir, also a World Heritage site, provides many outstanding examples of medieval sculpture, and Hvar town is richly ornamented with Renaissance architecture.

Central Dalmatia runs from Trogir in the northwest to Ploče in the southeast and includes the large islands of Brač and Hvar as well as the smaller islands of Vis, Biševo and Šolta. The dramatic coastal scenery is due to the rugged Dinaric Range, which form a 1500m-high barrier separating Dalmatia from Bosnia and Hercegovina.

A warm current flowing north up the coast keeps the climate mild – dry in summer, damp in winter. Dalmatia is noticeably warmer than Istria or the Gulf of Kvarner, and it's possible to swim in the sea from the beginning of May right up until the end of September.

Beach buffs can choose the unusual Zlatni Rat beach on Brač, the long coastline of the Makarska Riviera or one of the countless secluded coves on Brač, Šolta, Vis and Hvar Islands. Boat transport efficiently links all the islands, especially in the summer, which makes it easy to see a lot in a short stay.

Split is the largest city in the region and a hub for bus and boat connections along the Adriatic coast. Hvar Island, which receives more hours of sunshine than anywhere else in Croatia, is Central Dalmatia's most popular destination, followed by Brač Island and the Makarska Riviera. The lovely Vis and Šolta Islands attract relatively few visitors, preserving a lazy Mediterranean ambience even at the height of the summer season.

CENTRAL DALMATIA

HIGHLIGHTS

- Imagining the Roman days in the ruins of **Solin** (p200)
- Boating through the Blue Grotto of **Biševo** (p210)
- Strolling the moonlit streets of Diocletian's Palace in **Split** (p190)
- Windsurfing in **Bol** (p215)
- Sipping cocktails at **Hvar town harbour** (p219)
- Navigating the medieval streets of **Trogir** (p202)

- TELEPHONE CODE: 021
- POSTCODE: 21000

SPLIT

pop 173,700

Split (Spalato in Italian), the second largest city in Croatia, is the heart of the Dalmatian coast. Sitting on the southern side of a high peninsula, it is a key jumping-off point for the many islands that protect it from the sea. The old town has a palm-lined harbour promenade and Diocletian's Palace, a Unesco World Heritage site. The entire western end of the peninsula is a vast wooded mountain park, while industry, shipyards, limestone quarries and the ugly commercial and military port are mercifully far enough away on the northern side of the peninsula. High coastal mountains set against the blue Adriatic provide a striking frame to the scene, which you'll appreciate on any ferry going to or from the city. Its unique setting and an exuberant nature makes Split one of the most fascinating cities in Europe. It's also the perfect base for excursions to many nearby attractions, so settle in for a few days.

History

Split achieved fame when the Roman emperor Diocletian (AD 245–313), noted for his persecution of early Christians, had his retirement palace built here from 295 to 305. After his death the great stone palace continued to be used as a retreat by Roman rulers. When the nearby colony of Salona was abandoned in the 7th century, many of the Romanised inhabitants fled to Split and barricaded themselves behind the high palace walls, where their descendants live to this day.

First the Byzantine Empire and then Croatia controlled the area, but from the 12th to the 14th centuries medieval Split enjoyed a large measure of autonomy which favoured its development. The western part of the old town around Narodni trg, which dates from this time, became the focus of municipal life, while the area within the palace walls continued as the ecclesiastical centre.

In 1420 the Venetians conquered Split, which led to a slow decline. During the 17th century, strong walls were built around the city as a defence against the Turks. In 1797 the Austrians arrived; they remained until 1918, with only a brief interruption during the Napoleonic Wars.

Orientation

The bus (Map p198), train (Map p198) and ferry (Map p198) terminals are adjacent on the eastern side of the harbour, a short walk from the old town. Obala hrvatskog narodnog preporoda, the waterfront promenade, is your best central reference point in Split. Most of the large hotels and the best restaurants, nightlife and beaches lie east of the harbour along Bačvice, Firule, Zenta and Trstenik Bays. The wooded Marjan Hill dominates the western tip of the city and has many beaches at its foothills.

Information

BOOKSHOPS

Algoritam (Map p198; Bajamontijeva 2) A good English-language bookshop.

International Bookshop (Map p198; Obala hrvatskog narodnog preporoda 21) Magazines and periodicals in a variety of languages.

Internet Games & Books (Map p198; ☎ 338 548; Obala Kneza Domagoja 3) Sells used books.

CULTURAL CENTRES

Alliance Française (Map p198; ☎ 347 290; Marmontova 3) The centre of French cultural life in Split.

INTERNET ACCESS

Internet Games & Books (Map p198; ☎ 338 548; Obala kneza Domagoja 3; per hr 25KN)

Mriža (Map p198; ☎ 321 320; Kružićeva 3; per hr 20KN)

LAUNDRY

Galeb (Map p198; ☎ 361 472; Kneza Višeslava 12; ☾ 6am-8pm Mon-Fri) It's not cheap but will wash your things.

TOP FIVE BEACHES

- **Zlatni Rat** (p215) – the famous beach finger that appears in nearly all Croatia's publicity
- **Brela** (p207) – a string of palm-fringed sandy coves
- **Pakleni Islands** (p222) – rocky islands near Hvar with clothing-optional coves
- **Šolta** (p200) – not far from noisy Split are these quiet, rocky coves
- **Milna** (p215) – Brač may be busy but the beaches here are usually deserted

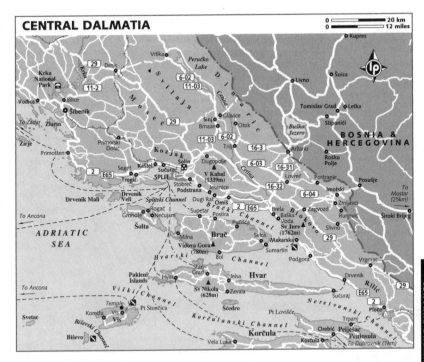

CENTRAL DALMATIA

LEFT LUGGAGE
Garderoba Bus station (Map p198; per day 10KN; 6am-10pm); Train station (Map p198; Domagoja 6; per day 10KN; 7am-9pm) The train station's left-luggage office is about 50m north of the station.
Internet Games & Books (Map p198; ☎ 338 548; Obala kneza Domagoja 3; per day 10KN)

MONEY
Change money at travel agencies or the post office. ATMs are around the bus and train stations.

POST
Main Post Office (Map p198; Šetalište Kralja Tomislava 9; 7am-9pm Mon-Sat)

TELEPHONE
There's a telephone centre at the main post office.

TOURIST INFORMATION
Croatian Youth Hostel Association (Map pp192-3; ☎ 396 031; fax 395 972; Domilijina 8) Has information about youth hostels all over Croatia.
Internet Games & Books (Map p198; ☎ 338 548;

Obala kneza Domagoja 3) Information for backpackers. Also has used books, Internet connection and luggage storage.
Splittours (☎ 346 100; Obala Lazareta 3)
Turist Biro (Map p198; ☎ /fax 342 142; turist-biro-split@st.htnet.hr; Obala hrvatskog narodnog preporoda 12) Arranges private accommodation; sells guidebooks and the Split Card (60KN), which offers free and discounted admissions to Split attractions.
Turistička Zajednica (Tourist Office; Map p198; ☎ /fax 342 606; www.visitsplit.com; Peristyle; 9am-8.30pm Mon-Sat, 8am-1pm Sun) It has information on Split and sells the Split Card.

TRAVEL AGENCIES
Atlas Travel Agency (Map p198; ☎ 343 055; Nepotova 4) It is also the American Express representative.
Jadrolinija stall (Map p198; ☎ 338 333, 355 399; Obala kneza Domagoja) Buy tickets for passenger ferries here.
SEM agency (Map p198; ☎ 338 292) In the ferry terminal, it handles tickets between Ancona, Split and Hvar.
SNAV (Map p198; ☎ 322 252) Also found in the ferry terminal; book here for a four-hour connection to Ancona and Pescara.
Touring (Map p198; ☎ 338 503; Obala Domagojeva 10) Near the bus station, it represents Deutsche Touring and sells tickets to German cities.

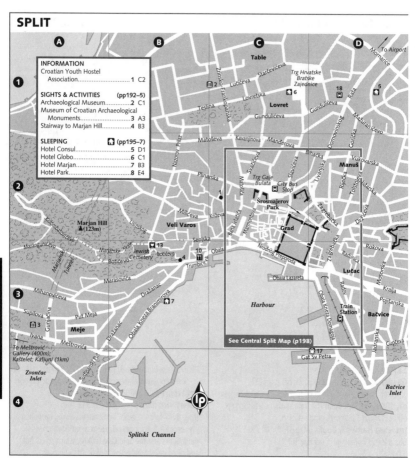

SPLIT

INFORMATION
Croatian Youth Hostel
Association.............................1 C2

SIGHTS & ACTIVITIES (pp192–5)
Archaeological Museum...............2 C1
Museum of Croatian Archaeological
Monuments.............................3 A3
Stairway to Marjan Hill..............4 B3

SLEEPING (pp195–7)
Hotel Consul.............................5 D1
Hotel Globo..............................6 C1
Hotel Marjan............................7 B3
Hotel Park...............................8 E4

To Airport

Table

Trg Hrvatske
Bratske
Zajednice

Lovret

Manuš

Veli Varos

Marjan Hill
▲(123m)

Jewish
Cemetery

Trg Gaje
Bulata   City Bus
          Stop

Srosmajerov
Park

Grad

Lučac

Obala Lazareta

Harbour

Train
Station

Bačvice

Meje

To Meštrović
Gallery (400m);
Kaštelet; Kašjuni (1km)

Zvončac
Inlet

Bačvice
Inlet

Gat Sv Petra

See Central Split Map (p198)

Splitski Channel

Sights

DIOCLETIAN'S PALACE

Facing onto the harbour, **Diocletian's Palace**
(Map p198) is one of the most imposing
Roman ruins in existence. Although the original structure was modified in the Middle
Ages, the alterations have only served to
increase the allure of this fascinating site.
Far from being a museum, the 220 buildings
within the palace boundaries are still home
to about 3000 people as well as housing
shops, cafés and restaurants.

The palace was built from lustrous white
stone from the island of Brač and construction lasted 10 years. Diocletian spared
no expense, importing marble from Italy
and Greece, and columns and sphinxes

from Egypt. A military fortress, imperial
residence and fortified town, the palace
measures 215m from east to west (including
the square corner towers) and 181m wide at
the southernmost point. The walls at their
highest point measure 26m and the entire
structure covers 31,000 sq metres.

There are fortified gates in the centre of
the eastern, northern and western walls,
as well as a smaller gate in the southern
wall, which led from the living quarters to
the sea. Each wall has a gate named after
metals: the northern gate is the Golden
Gate; the southern gate is the Bronze Gate;
the eastern gate is the Silver Gate; and
the western gate is the Iron Gate. From
the eastern to the western gate there's a

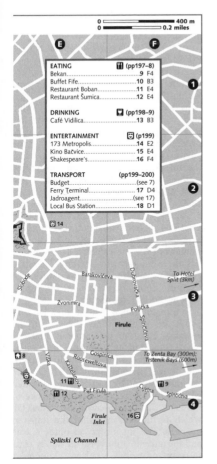

straight road (Krešimirova or Decumanus), which separates the imperial residence on the southern side, with its state rooms and temples, from the northern side which was intended for soldiers and servants. For a walking tour of the palace's main sights, see p194.

MUSEUMS & GALLERIES

Although it's north of the town centre, the **Archaeological Museum** (Map pp192–3; Arheološki Muzej; ☎ 318 720; Zrinsko-Frankopanska 25; adult/student 10/5KN; 🕑 9am-noon & 5-8pm Tue-Fri, 9am-noon Sat & Sun) is worth the walk. The emphasis is on the Roman and early Christian period, with exhibits devoted to burial sculpture and excavations at Salona. The quality of the

sculpture is high and there are interesting reliefs based on Illyrian mythical figures. There's also jewellery, ceramics and coins.

The **Museum of Croatian Archaeological Monuments** (Map pp192–3; Muzej Hrvatskih Arheološki; ☎ 358 420; Ivana Meštrovića bb; adult/student 10/5KN; 🕑 9am-8pm Mon-Fri), concentrates on medieval Croatian rulers, with inscribed stone fragments, parts of altars and furniture, late medieval tombstones, swords and jewellery. Captions are in Croatian, however, which makes it difficult to identify the exhibits.

In the centre of town is the mildly interesting **Ethnographic Museum** (Map p198; ☎ 343 108; Narodni trg 1; adult/student 10/5KN; 🕑 10am-1pm Tue-Fri Jun-Sep, 10am-4pm Tue-Fri, 10am-1pm Sat & Sun Oct-May), which has a collection of photos of old Split, traditional costumes and memorabilia of important citizens. Captions are in Croatian.

Split's finest art museum is the **Meštrović Gallery** (Map pp192–3; ☎ 358 719; Spomenika Šetalište Ivana Meštrovića 46; adult/student incl Kaštelet 15/10KN; 🕑 9am-9pm Tue-Sun Jun-Sep, 9am-4pm Tue-Sat & 10am-3pm Sun Oct-May, 10am-2pm Sun). You'll see a comprehensive, well-arranged collection of works by Ivan Meštrović, Croatia's premier modern sculptor, who built the gallery as a personal residence in 1931–39. Although Meštrović intended to retire here, he emigrated to the USA soon after WWII (for more on Meštrović, see p196).

Don't miss the nearby **Kaštelet** (Map pp192–3; ☎ 358 185; Spomenika Šetalisvte Ivana Meštrovića 39; admission by Meštrović Gallery ticket; 🕑 9am-9pm Tue-Sun Jun-Sep, 9am-4pm Tue-Sat & 10am-3pm Sun Oct-May), the fortress that Meštrović bought and restored to house his powerful *Life of Christ* cycle of wood reliefs.

Activities

From the Meštrović Gallery it's possible to hike straight up **Marjan Hill** (123m). Go up Ulica Tonća Petrasova Marovića on the western side of the gallery and continue straight up the stairway to Put Meja ulica. Turn left and walk west to Put Meja 76. The trail begins on the western side of this building. Marjan Hill offers trails through the forest, lookouts and old chapels.

The flourishing **beach life** gives Split its aura of insouciance in summer. The most popular beach is **Bačvice** on the eponymous inlet. The swimming is good and the ambience is lively. The other choice is to follow Šetašte Ivana Meštrovića west past the Meštrović studio to the quieter **Kašjuni cove**.

Walking Tour

DIOCLETIAN'S PALACE

Start: Gregorius of Nin statue
Finish: Basement Halls
Distance: 1km
Duration: 2hr

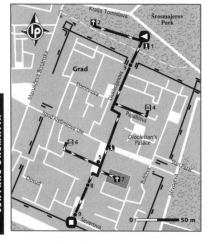

Begin the walk just outside the palace at the imposing statue of **Gregorius of Nin (1**; Grgur Ninski), the 10th-century Croatian bishop who fought for the right to use old Croatian in liturgical services. Sculpted by Ivan Meštrović, this powerful work is one of the defining images of Split. Notice that his left big toe has been polished to a shine. It's said that touching it brings good luck. To the west of the statue is the well-preserved corner tower of the palace. Between the statue and the tower is the remains of the pre-Romanesque church of St Benedict with the 15th-century **Chapel of Arnir (2)**. Peer through the protective glass and you'll see the altar slab and altar sarcophagus carved by the early Renaissance master Juraj Dalmatinac.

The statue is right outside the **Golden Gate (3**; Zlatna Vrata or Northern Palace Gate) which was once the starting point for the road to Solin. From the fragments that remain,

it's possible to visualise the statues, columns and arches that once decorated the gate. Turn left at Papalićeva ulica and at No 5 is **Papalić Palace (4)** with a courtyard, loggia and external staircase. Built by Juraj Dalmatinac for one of the many noblemen who lived within the palace in the Middle Ages, it is considered a fine example of late-Gothic style with an elaborately carved entrance gate that proclaimed the importance of its original inhabitants. The exterior of the palace is closer to its original state than the interior, which has been thoroughly restored to house the **Town Museum** (Gradski Muzej; ☎ 341 240; 5 Papalićeva ulica; adult/concession 10/5KN; 10am-noon Sat & Sun year-round, 9am-noon & 5-8pm Tue-Fri Jun-Sep, 10am-5pm Tue-Fri Oct-May). Captions are in Croatian but wall panels in a variety of languages provide a historical framework for the exhibits. The museum has three floors, with drawings, heraldic coats of arms, 17th-century weaponry, fine furniture, coins and documents from as far back as the 14th century.

Return to Dioklecijanova, turn left and you'll see the Peristyle, the ceremonial entrance court to the imperial quarters, measuring 35m by 13m and three steps below the level of the surrounding streets. The longer side is lined by six granite columns, linked by arches and decorated with a stone frieze. The southern side of the Peristyle is enclosed by the **Protiron (5)**, which is the entrance into the imperial quarters. The square has an outdoor café and the ancient stones provide handy seats to relax and people-watch in this popular meeting place.

Turn right (west) onto the narrow street of Kraj Sveti Ivana which leads to what used to be the ceremonial and devotional section of the palace. Although the two temples that once flanked the streets have long since disappeared, you can still see parts of columns and a few fragments. At the end of the street is the **Temple of Jupiter (6)**, later converted into a baptistry. The temple once had a porch supported by columns but the one column you see dates from the 5th century. The headless sphinx in black granite guarding the entrance was imported from Egypt at the time of the temple's construction in the 5th century. The walls of the temple support a barrel-vaulted ceiling and there's a decorative frieze around the other three walls. Below the temple is a crypt which was once used as a church.

Returning to the Peristyle, go up the eastern stairs to the **Cathedral of St Domnius** (**7**; Katedrala Svetog Duje; ☎ 342 589; Kraj Sveti Duje 5; ☽ 7am-noon & 4-7pm), originally built as Diocletian's mausoleum. The original octagonal form of the mausoleum, encircled by 24 columns, has been almost completely preserved. The domed interior is round with two rows of Corinthian columns and a frieze showing Emperor Diocletian and his wife, Prisca.

The oldest monuments in the cathedral are the remarkable scenes on the wooden entrance doors from the life of Christ. Carved by Andrija Buvina in the 13th century, the scenes are presented in 28 squares, 14 on each side, and recall the fashion of Romanesque miniatures of the time.

Notice the right altar carved by Bonino da Milano in 1427 and the vault above the altar decorated with mural paintings by Dujam Vušković. To the left is the altar of St Anastasius (Sveti Staš; 1448) by Juraj Dalmatinac, with a relief of *The Flagellation of Christ* that is one of the finest sculptural works of its time in Dalmatia. The main altar dates from the 13th century and the vault is ornamented with paintings by M Pončun.

The choir is furnished with 13th-century Romanesque seats that are the oldest in Dalmatia. Cross the altar and follow the signs to the **Treasury** (admission 5KN; ☽ 8am-noon Sun Jul & Aug, 10am-noon Sun Jun & Sep, 11am-noon Sun Oct-May), rich in reliquaries, icons, church robes, illuminated manuscripts and documents in Glagolitic script.

Part of the same structure, the Romanesque **belfry** (admission 5KN; ☽ 8am-noon Jun & Sep, 7am-noon Jul & Aug) was constructed between the 12th and 16th centuries and reconstructed in 1908 after it collapsed. Notice the two lion figures at the foot of the belfry and the Egyptian black-granite sphinx dating from the 15th century BC on the right wall. South of the mausoleum, there are remains of the Roman baths, a Roman building with a mosaic and the remains of the imperial dining hall in various stages of preservation.

Immediately to the left of the cathedral are the massive steps leading down through the Protiron into the **vestibule (8)**, which is the best-preserved part of the imperial residence. The circular ground floor is topped by a cupola once covered in mosaics and marble, although the centre of the dome has disappeared. Today, the cellars are filled with stands selling souvenirs and handicrafts. To the left is the entrance to the **basement halls** (**9**; adult/concession 6/3KN; ☽ 10am-6pm) of the palace. Although mostly empty, the rooms and corridors emit a haunting sense of timelessness that is well worth the price of the ticket. The cellars open onto the southern gate.

Tours
Atlas Travel Agency (Map p198; ☎ 343 055; Nepotova 4) runs excursions to Krka waterfalls (225KN) and Zlatni Rat beach on the island of Brač (140KN), as well as other day trips.

Festivals & Events
The traditional February **Carnival** has recently been revived. There's also the **Feast of St Dujo** (7 May), a **Flower Show** in May, and from June to September a variety of evening entertainment is presented in the old town, usually around the Peristyle. The four-day **Festival of Popular Music** is held around the end of June. The **Split Summer Festival** runs from mid-July to mid-August and features opera, drama, ballet and concerts on open-air stages. The summer concert season usually starts off with the **Split Jazz Festival** in late July.

Sleeping
The hotel situation in Split is slowly improving, but budget hotels of are still in short supply. Prices quoted here are for the high season – July and August – but they don't descend much (if at all) in the off-season.

BUDGET & MID-RANGE
There are no camping grounds in the immediate vicinity of Split; **Camping Galeb** (Map p198; ☎ 864 430; www.galeb.hr; Vukovarska bb, Omiš; per adult/site 28/38KN) at the northern end of Omiš town, about 20km east along the coast, is your closest option – it's not far from the beach.

Slavija (Map p198; ☎ 347 053; fax 344 062; Buvinova 3; r without/with bathroom 350/450KN) This 32-room hotel in the old town has the cheapest rooms, which may be why they are often

IVAN MEŠTROVIĆ

Croatia's greatest 20th-century sculptor was born in 1883 in the Sava valley and grew up in Otavice, a small village in the mountains northwest of Split. He received no formal education but his obvious artistic talent drew the attention of a stone-cutter in Split and, at the age of 15, he was invited to live in the stone-cutter's workshop as an apprentice. After only nine months, an Austrian mine-owner consented to pay for Meštrović to study at the Vienna Academy of Art.

In 1904 he married Ruza Klein, the daughter of a Jewish merchant, and in 1905 received his first major commission: *The Well of Life*, which stands outside the Croatian National Theatre in Zagreb. Its impressionism reflects the influence of the French sculptor August Rodin, whom Meštrović had befriended in Vienna. In 1910 he participated in the Viennese Secession exhibition where he attracted attention with his sculptures of south-Slavic heroes who had battled the Turks. His sculpture of the Serbian hero Kraljević Marko now stands in the Meštrović studio in Zagreb.

The choice of a Serbian hero reflected Meštrović's commitment to a union of the southern Slavs. His political activism against the Austro-Hungarian empire forced him to flee Split in 1914 and move to Rome, where he and two other Dalmatian activists organised the Yugoslav Committee on National Independence.

Fearful of the consequences of the Treaty of London, in which Dalmatia would be given to Italy as a reward for entering WWI, the group moved to London to agitate for independence. A Meštrović one-man show in the Victoria & Albert Museum in London helped publicise their cause and secure popular support in Britain for the post-war Kingdom of Serbs, Croats and Slovenes.

After WWI, Meštrović returned to Zagreb and built a studio. His work turned away from political themes and from 1919 to 1922 he executed the Racic Memorial Chapel in Cavtat for the dying daughter of a shipowner. In 1926 he produced the monument of Gregorius of Nin and gave it to Split.

His first marriage ended in divorce and in nearby Dubrovnik he met his second wife, Olga Kestercanek. In the 1930s, Meštrović built a summer home for his wife and new family in Split which, in accordance with his wishes, has now become a museum of his work. In his home town of Otavice, he built the Church of the Holy Redeemer, which was to serve as the family mausoleum.

When the quisling government of Ante Pavelić was installed in Zagreb in 1941, Meštrović was pressured to cooperate with the regime but he refused and was imprisoned for almost five months. Although highly unpopular because of his ties with the Yugoslav Committee, Meštrović's international reputation eventually forced Pavelić to release him. He sought safety in Rome but was soon forced to flee again to Switzerland for the duration of the war.

Although Tito implored Meštrović to return to postwar Yugoslavia, in 1946 the sculptor accepted a professorship at Syracuse University and sailed for the USA.

It was not his first visit. After a successful exhibition in 1924, he received a commission for the Chicago Indians series, which is his best known work in the USA.

Soon after his arrival in 1946, the Metropolitan Museum of New York staged an exhibition of his work, the first time in its history that a living artist was honoured with a one-person show. He became a US citizen in 1954 and in 1955 became Professor of Sculpture at the University of Notre Dame in Indiana. In addition to bestowing a number of his works on both Syracuse and Indiana campuses, Meštrović sent 59 statues from the USA to then-Yugoslavia.

Meštrović died in 1962 and was buried in the Church of the Holy Redeemer in Otavice, which now displays his work.

booked solid. Rooms are very basic and can be noisy but the location is excellent.

Hotel Adriana (Map p198; ☎ 340 000; info@hotel -adriana.com; Obala hrvatskog narodnog preporoda 9; s/d 550/750KN; 🖳) This new entry on the hotel scene has eight fresh new rooms, some of which have a sea view. All are sound-proofed. Prices stay the same all year.

Hotel Bellevue (Map p198; ☎ 347 499; www.hotel -bellevue-split.hr; Bana Josipa Jelačića 2; s/d 490/682KN) It's an old classic that has seen better days. Rooms on the street side can be noisy but the location is good and the old-fashioned rooms are well-tended. If you take a taxi from the port be ready for a long, meandering ride as the driver navigates the many one-way streets.

TOP END

Hotel Park (Map pp192-3; ☎ 406 400; www.hotelpark -split.hr; Hatzeov perivoj 3; s/d 795/1015KN; P ⋈ 🖳) Close to the centre, this hotel provides a resort experience with a large shady terrace and easy walk to the beach. Rooms are nicely decorated and comfortable although not large. Don't expect to be coddled by the rather aloof staff.

Hotel Globo (Map pp192-3; ☎ 481 111; info@hotel globo.com; Lovretska 18; s/d 710/920KN; P ⋈) With big rooms, bathrooms outfitted with hairdryers, air-con, TVs and minibars you'll be more than comfortable. The furnishings are plush and the lobby is impressive.

Hotel Consul (Map pp192-3; ☎ 340 130; www.hotel -consul.net; Trsćanska 34; s/d 565/830KN; P ⋈) You would hardly know that you're in the middle of a big metropolis, the rooms are so calm. Three rooms even have Jacuzzis and there are a few apartments available.

Hotel Split (Map pp192-3; ☎ 303 112; www.hotelsplit .hr; Put Trstenika 5; s/d 610/945KN; P ⋈ 🖳 ⋐) This is another luxury establishment, with an outdoor pool, a sauna and a beach. You need to have a car, however, since the hotel is far (east) from the town centre.

Hotel Marjan (Map pp192-3; ☎ 302 111; www.hotel -marjan.com; Obala Kneza Branimira 8; s/d 560/865KN; P ⋈) Near the marina about 1km west of the town centre, this was once the best hotel in town but has been outclassed by other more recent additions. The location is good and the rooms are adequate but hardly special.

PRIVATE ROOMS

In the summer, you may be deluged at the bus station by women offering *sobe* (rooms available). Make sure you are clear about the exact location of the room or you may find yourself several bus rides from the town centre. You could also book through the **Turist Biro** (Map p198; ☎/fax 342 142; turist-biro-split@ st.htnet.hr; Obala hrvatskog narodnog preporoda 12) or **Daluma Travel** (Map p198; ☎/fax 338 484; daluma-st@ st.htnet.hr; Obala Kneza Domagoja 1) but there is little available within the heart of the old town. Expect to pay about 100KN for a room where you will probably share the bathroom with the proprietor. If you have your own wheels and don't mind staying out of town, you will find a wealth of *pensions* along the main Split–Dubrovnik road just south of town.

Eating

TOWN CENTRE

Sarajevo (Map p198; ☎ 347 454; Domaldova 6; mains 45-65KN) This spacious restaurant in the heart of town specialises in traditional Dalmatian meat dishes such as *pastičada* (beef stuffed with lard, roasted in wine and spices). There are also several fish dishes on offer.

Galija (Map p198; Tončićeva; pizzas from 26KN) Hands down the best pizza in town, this perennial favourite still packs in a young, lively crowd.

Kod Joze (Map p198; ☎ 347 397; Sredmanuška 4; mains from 40KN) A die-hard faction of locals keeps this informal *konoba* (small, intimate dining spot) alive and kicking. It's Dalmatian all the way – ham, cheese and green tagliatelle with seafood.

Nostromo (Map p198; ☎ 091 405 66 66; Kraj Sv Marije 10; mains from 65KN) Marine creatures of all persuasions form a delightful menu in this sweetly decorated spot next to the fish market.

Buffet Fife (Map pp192-3; ☎ 345 223; Obala Ante Trumbía 11; mains around 30KN) Dragomir presides over a motley crew of sailors and misfits who drop in for the simple, savoury home cooking and his own brand of hospitality.

Burek Bar (Map p198; Domaldova 13) A spiffy place, just down from the main post office, Burek Bar serves a good breakfast or lunch of *burek* (a heavy pastry stuffed with meat or cheese) and yoghurt for about 12KN.

The vast **supermarket** (Map p198; Svačićeva 1) stocks a wide selection of meat and cheese for sandwiches and nearly everything else you might want for a picnic. Sit around the square and eat your goodies.

EAST OF CENTRE

Restaurant Boban (Map pp192-3; ☎ 510 142; Hektoro-vićeva 49; mains from 60KN) The décor may be sober and traditional but this family-owned restaurant devotes considerable effort to keeping its menu up to date. The ŗisotto is perfection and the angler wrapped in bacon mouth-watering.

Bekan (Map pp192-3; ☎ 525 870; Ivana Zajca 1; mains from 50KN) Bekan serves an array of fish pre-pared Dalmatian style. It's not cheap (unless you order the spaghetti with seafood for 52KN) but you can sample a savoury shrimp *buzara* (a sauce of tomatoes, white wine, onions and breadcrumbs) on an airy terrace overlooking the sea.

CENTRAL SPLIT

0 _____ 200 m
0 _____ 0.1 miles

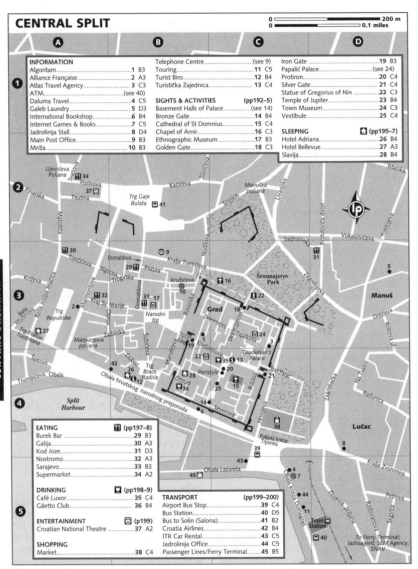

INFORMATION		
Algoritam.................................1	B3
Alliance Française......................2	A3
Atlas Travel Agency..................3	C3
ATM......................................(see 40)	
Daluma Travel..........................4	C5
Galeb Laundry..........................5	D3
International Bookshop...............6	B4
Internet Games & Books.............7	C5
Jadrolinija Stall........................8	D4
Main Post Office......................9	B3
Mriža...................................10	B3

Telephone Centre...................(see 9)	
Touring................................11	C5
Turist Biro.............................12	B4
Turistička Zajednica.................13	C4

SIGHTS & ACTIVITIES	(pp192–5)
Basement Halls of Palace........(see 14)	
Bronze Gate...........................14	B4
Cathedral of St Domnius............15	C4
Chapel of Arnir.......................16	C3
Ethnographic Museum...............17	B3
Golden Gate...........................18	C3

Iron Gate..............................19	B3
Papalić Palace.......................(see 24)	
Protiron................................20	C4
Silver Gate............................21	C4
Statue of Gregorius of Nin.........22	C3
Temple of Jupiter....................23	B4
Town Museum........................24	C3
Vestibule..............................25	C4

SLEEPING	(pp195–7)
Hotel Adriana.........................26	B4
Hotel Bellevue.......................27	A3
Slavija..................................28	B4

EATING	(pp197–8)
Burek Bar..............................29	B3
Galija...................................30	A3
Kod Joze...............................31	D3
Nostromo..............................32	A3
Sarajevo...............................33	B3
Supermarket..........................34	A2

DRINKING	(pp198–9)
Café Luxor............................35	C4
Gäetto Club...........................36	B4

ENTERTAINMENT	(p199)
Croatian National Theatre.........37	A2

SHOPPING	
Market.................................38	C4

TRANSPORT	(pp199–200)
Airport Bus Stop.....................39	C4
Bus Station............................40	D5
Bus to Solin (Salona)................41	B2
Croatia Airlines......................42	B4
ITR Car Rental.......................43	C5
Jadrolinija Office.....................44	C5
Passenger Lines/Ferry Terminal....45	B5

Restaurant Šumica (Map pp192–3; ☎ 515 911; Put Firula 6; mains from 65KN) For a splurge, you couldn't do better than this place. The pasta is home-made and is combined with salmon or other fish in imaginative sauces. The grilled scampi is perfection, but you pay a steep 320KN per kilogram. Before your meal you'll be served a dish of home-made fish pâté with bread to whet your appetite. Meals are served on an open-air terrace under pine trees with a view of the sea.

Drinking

The entertainment complex of Bačvice has a multitude of bars and clubs with a choice of Latin, Croatian or techno sounds.

Gäetto Club (Map p198; ☎ 346 879; Dosud) This secluded café is tucked into a tranquil courtyard. Relax in an overstuffed chair amid flower beds and a trickling fountain, sampling an exotic coffee – or join the party indoors.

Cafe Vidilica (Map pp192-3; ☎ 394 480; Nazorov prilaz 1) Any time of the day, you can come here to sip a coffee or cocktail and admire the view of Split from an outdoor terrace in front of the Jewish cemetery. There's no vehicle access but it's a nice walk.

Cafe Luxor (Map p198; Kralja Sv Ivana 11) In the heart of the Peristyle, this is everyone's favourite café, maybe because of the Hollywood references and posters or perhaps it's the magic of the sphinx, casting her spell over the terrace.

Entertainment

In summer everyone starts the evening at one of the cafés along Obala hrvatskog narodnog preporoda, on Ujevićeva Poljana or around the cathedral before heading to Bačvice and then a disco.

Croatian National Theatre (Map p198; ☎ 515 999; Trg Gaje Bulata) During winter, opera and ballet are presented here. The best seats cost about 60KN and tickets for the same night are usually available. Erected in 1891, the theatre was fully restored in 1979 in the original style; it's worth attending a performance for the architecture alone.

Kino Bačvice (Map pp192-3; ☎ 091 500 214; Bačvice bb) The after-dark entertainment zone of Bačvice is a perfect venue for the open-air cinema that runs nightly in summer.

DISCOS

173 Metropolis (Map pp192-3; ☎ 305 110; Koteks shopping centre; ☾ nightly Jun-Sep, Sat & Sun Oct-May) A popular dance spot, this place is in the huge white shopping complex 10 minutes' walk east of the old town.

Shakespeare's (Map pp192-3; ☎ 519 492; Uvala Zenta 3; ☾ nightly Jun-Sep) This open-air disco takes over summer nightlife and presents live concerts on Friday.

Shopping

Part of the palace basement halls (see p195), Diocletian's Cellars is a market for crafted jewellery, reproductions of Roman busts, silver cigarette cases, candlestick holders, wooden sailing ships, leather goods and other odds and ends. Prices aren't too steep and you might find the perfect lightweight item to fulfil back-from-a-trip, gift-giving obligations.

There's a daily market above Obala Lazerata where you can buy fruit, vegetables, shoes, confectionery, clothing, can openers, flowers, souvenirs and other products. If you can't find what you're looking for in this market, chances are it doesn't exist in Split.

Getting There & Away

AIR

Croatia Airlines (Map p198; Obala hrvatskog narodnog preporoda 8) operates one-hour flights to and from Zagreb up to four times a day and there's a daily flight to Dubrovnik. For international connections see p271.

BOAT

Jadrolinija (Map p198; ☎ 338 333, 355 399), in the large ferry terminal opposite the bus station, handles the coastal ferry line to Hvar Island and operates two to four times a week year-round, stopping in Stari Grad (74KN). However, the local car ferry is cheaper (32KN, 1½ hours), and there's a fast passenger boat to Hvar town (one hour) in July and August, as well as a passenger boat (24KN, two hours) that goes on to Vela Luka (35KN, 1¼ hours).

The schedules and tickets for all lines are available from **Jadroagent** (Map ppp192-3; ☎ 338 335), in the ferry terminal, which represents Adriatica Navigazione for its connections between Split and Ancona. For boats to Italy, see p275.

Car ferries and passenger lines leave from separate docks; the passenger lines leave from Obala Lazareta and car ferries leave from Sv Petra. You can buy tickets from either the main **Jadrolinija office** (Map p198; ☎ 338 333), in the large ferry terminal opposite the bus station, which handles all car ferry services that depart from the docks around the ferry terminal, or at one of the two stalls near the docks. In the summer it's usually necessary to reserve at least a day in advance for a car ferry and you are asked to appear several hours before departure. There is rarely a problem obtaining a ticket.

BUS

Advance bus tickets with seat reservations are recommended. There are buses from

CENTRAL DALMATIA

the main **bus station** (Map p198; ☎ 060 327 327; www.ak-split.hr in Croatian) beside the harbour to the following destinations, among others:

Destination	Cost	Duration	Frequency
Dubrovnik	72-111KN	4½hr	12 daily
Ljubljana	230KN	10hr	1 daily
Međugorje	54-89KN	3hr	4 daily
Mostar	54-65KN	2-4hr	4 daily
Pula	215-278KN	10hr	3 daily
Rijeka	161-231KN	8hr	14 daily
Sarajevo	93-128KN	7hr	11 daily
Zadar	66-89KN	3hr	26 daily

Bus No 37 to Solin, Split airport and Trogir leaves from a local bus station on Domovinskog, 1km northeast of the city centre.

CAR
If you want to rent a car try **ITR** (Map p198; ☎ 343 070; Obala Lazareta 2), **Budget** (Map pp192-3; ☎ 345 700) in the Hotel Marjan or **Avis** (Map pp192-3; ☎ 342 976), also in the Hotel Marjan.

TRAIN
There are three fast trains a day between Split **train station** (Map p198; ☎ 338 483; Obala knezza Domagoja 12) and Zagreb (138KN, six hours) and three overnight trains (8½ hours). From Monday to Saturday there are six trains a day between Šibenik and Split (33KN, two hours) and four trains on Sunday.

Getting Around
TO/FROM THE AIRPORT
The bus to Split airport (30KN) leaves from Obala Lazareta 3, about 90 minutes before flight times, or you can take bus No 37 from the bus station on Domovinskog (9.50KN for a two-zone ticket). A taxi will cost about 125KN.

BUS
Local buses run about every 20 minutes and connect the town centre and the harbour with outlying districts. A one-zone ticket costs 7KN for one trip in central Split if you buy it from the driver, but it costs 11KN for two trips and 55KN for 10 trips if you buy it from a kiosk. There's a kiosk that also distributes bus maps at the city bus stop.

AROUND SPLIT
Šolta
This lovely, wooded island is a popular getaway for Split inhabitants looking to escape the sultry summer heat. Only 59 sq km, the island's most accessible entry points from Split are Rogač and Nečujam on the northern coast. In Rogač the ferries from Split tie up in front of the **tourist office** (☎ /fax 654 491; www.solta.hr; ☻ 8am-7pm Mon-Sat July-Aug, 8am-3pm Mon-Fri Sep-Jun) and on the edge of a large bay. A shady path leads around the bay to smaller coves with rocky beaches and a small road leads uphill to a market. Nečujam is 7km from Rogač; set on a curving beach, it has a hotel, snack bar and outdoor shower.

Three to five daily car ferries run between Split and Rogač (19KN, one hour) and from June to September there are daily catamarans from Split to Rogač and Nečujam, and from Rogač to Nečujam. Ask at Atlas Travel Agency or the Turistička Zajednica (Tourist Office) in Split for information.

Solin (Salona)
The ruins of the ancient city of Solin (Roman Salona), among the vineyards at the foot of mountains just northeast of Split, are the most archaeologically important in Croatia.

Although Solin is today surrounded by noisy highways and industry, it was first mentioned in 119 BC as the centre of the Illyrian tribe. The Romans seized the site in 78 BC and under the rule of Augustus it became the administrative headquarters of the Roman Dalmatian province.

When Emperor Diocletian built his palace in Split at the end of the 3rd century AD, it was the proximity to Solin that attracted him. Solin was incorporated into the Eastern Roman Empire in the 6th century, but was levelled by the Slavs and Avars in 614. The inhabitants fled to Split and neighbouring islands, leaving Solin to decay.

SIGHTS
A good place to begin your visit to the city is at the main entrance near Caffe Bar Salona. There's a small **museum and information centre** (☎ 210 048; admission 10KN; ☻ 8am-3pm Mon-Fri) at the entrance. **Manastirine**, the fenced area behind the car park, was a burial place for early Christian martyrs prior to the

JON DAVISON

JON DAVISON

The island of Korčula (p245)

Old town of Dubrovnik with the dome of
the Cathedral of the Assumption of the
Virgin (p235)

Waterfront café at Cavtat (p241)

JON DAVISON

JON DAVISON

The walls of Dubrovnik (p229)

JON DAVISO

Anchored at Cavtat (p241)

Dubrovnik rooftops from the city walls (p229)

JAN STROMM

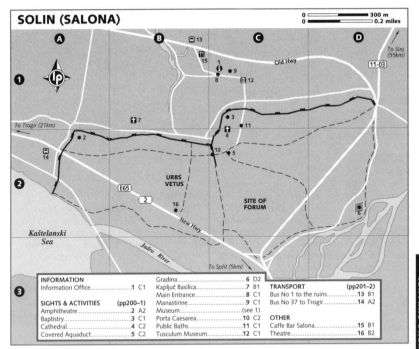

SOLIN (SALONA)

INFORMATION		Gradina	6	D2	
Information Office	1 C1	Kapljuč Basilica	7	B1	TRANSPORT (pp201–2)
		Main Entrance	8	C1	Bus No 1 to the ruins 13 B1
SIGHTS & ACTIVITIES (pp200–1)		Manastirine	9	C1	Bus No 37 to Trogir 14 A2
Amphitheatre	2 A2	Museum	(see 1)		
Baptistry	3 C1	Porta Caesarea	10	C2	OTHER
Cathedral	4 C2	Public Baths	11	C1	Caffe Bar Salona 15 B1
Covered Aquaduct	5 C2	Tusculum Museum	12	C1	Theatre 16 B2

legalisation of Christianity. The excavated remains of **Kapljuč Basilica** (cemetery) and the 5th-century **Kapjinc Basilica** inside it are highlights, although this area was outside the ancient city itself. Overlooking Manastirine is **Tusculum Museum**, an archaeological museum with interesting sculpture embedded in the walls and in the garden.

The Manastirine/Tusculum complex is part of an **archaeological reserve**. Pick up a brochure in the information office at the entrance to the reserve if it's open at the time of your visit.

A path bordered by cypresses runs south to the northern **city wall** of Solin. Notice the **covered aqueduct** located south of the wall. It was probably built around the 1st century AD and supplied Solin and Diocletian's Palace with water from the Jadro River. The ruins you see in front of you as you stand on the wall were an early Christian site; they include a three-aisled, 5th-century **cathedral** with an octagonal **baptistry**, and the remains of Bishop Honorius' Basilica with a ground plan in the form of a Greek cross. **Public baths** adjoin the cathedral on the east.

Southwest of the cathedral is the 1st-century eastern city gate, **Porta Caesarea**, later engulfed by the growth of Salona in all directions. Grooves in the stone road left by ancient wheels can still be seen at this gate. South of the city gate was the centre of town, the forum, with temples to Jupiter, Juno and Minerva, none of which are visible today.

At the western end of Solin is the huge 2nd-century **amphitheatre**, destroyed in the 17th century by the Venetians to prevent it from being used as a refuge by Turkish raiders. At one time it could accommodate 18,000 spectators, which gives an idea of the size and importance of this ancient city.

The southeastern corner of the complex contains the **Gradina**, a medieval fortress around the remains of a rectangular early Christian church.

GETTING THERE & AWAY

The ruins are easily accessible on Split city bus No 1, which goes directly to Caffe Bar Salona (look for the yellow bus shelter on the left) every half-hour from Trg Gaje Bulata.

CENTRAL DALMATIA

From the amphitheatre at Solin it's easy to continue on to Trogir by catching a westbound bus No 37 from the nearby stop on the adjacent new highway (buy a four-zone ticket in Split if you plan to do this). If, on the other hand, you want to return to Split, use the underpass to cross the highway and catch an eastbound bus No 37. Alternatively, you can catch most Sinj-bound buses (5KN, 10 daily) from the main bus station to take you to Solin.

TROGIR

pop 1600

Trogir (formerly Trau) is a jewel of a walled town with a wide waterfront promenade that encloses a maze of medieval streets. No other town in Dalmatia better encapsulates the cultural life that flourished along the coast in spite of a series of foreign rulers. The profusion of Romanesque and Renaissance architectural styles within 15th-century city walls, as well as the magnificent cathedral at the town centre, inspired Unesco to name the town a World Heritage site in 1997. Trogir is an easy day trip from Split and a relaxing place to spend a few days, taking a trip or two to nearby islands.

Backed by high hills in the north, the sea to the south and snug in its walls, Trogir (Tragurion to the Romans) proved an attractive place to settlers. The early Croats settled the old Illyrian town by the 7th century. Its defensive position allowed Trogir to maintain its autonomy throughout Croatian and Byzantine rule, while trade and nearby mines ensured its economic viability. In the 13th century sculpture and architecture flourished, reflecting a vibrant, dynamic culture. When Venice bought Dalmatia in 1409, Trogir refused to accept the new ruler and the Venetians were forced to bombard the town into submission. While the rest of Dalmatia stagnated under Venetian rule, Trogir continued to produce great artists who enhanced the beauty of the town.

Orientation

The old town of Trogir occupies a tiny island in the narrow channel between Čiovo Island and the mainland, just off the coastal highway. Many sights can be seen on a 15-minute walk around this island. The nearest beach is 4km west at the Hotel Medena.

The heart of the old town is divided from the mainland by a small channel and a few minutes' walk from the bus station. After crossing the small bridge near the station, go through the North Gate. Turn left (east) at the end of the square and you'll come to Trogir's main street, Ulica Kohl-Genscher (named jointly after the German chancellor and foreign minister who initially campaigned to recognise Croatia's independence in 1991). Trogir's finest sights are around Trg Ivana Pavla II, straight ahead. The old town is connected to Čiovo Island to the south by a drawbridge.

Information

There's no left-luggage office in Trogir bus station, so you'll end up toting your bags around town if you only visit on a stopover.

Atlas Travel Agency (☎ 881 374; www.atlas-trogir .hr; Obala kralja Zvonimira 10) It arranges private accommodation and runs excursions.

Čipiko Tourist Office (☎ 881 554; ☼ 9am-12.30pm & 2.30-5pm Mon-Fri Sep-Jun, 9am-8pm Mon-Sat Jul-Aug) This private tourist office opposite the cathedral sells a map of the area and arranges private accommodation.

Main Post Office (Ulica Kohl-Genscher) There's a telephone centre here.

Turistička Zajednica (☎ 881 412; Trg Ivana Pavla II Br 1; 8am-9pm daily Jun-Aug, 9am-2pm Mon-Fri Sep-May) It's another good source of information, although it doesn't arrange private accommodation.

Zagrebačka Banka (Gračška Vrata) There's an ATM outside.

Sights

There's a lot to see in Trogir, as the town has retained many intact buildings from its age of glory – between the 13th and 15th centuries. As you enter, notice the Renaissance **North Gate** with the statue of the town protector, St Ivan Orsini, hovering overhead. As you proceed down Ulica Kohl-Genscher you may wish to stop in the **Town Museum** (Gradski Muzej; ☎ 881 406; Ulica Kohl-Genscher 49; admission 10KN; ☼ 7am-3pm Mon-Fri Jul & Aug, by appointment only Sep-Jun) housed in the former Garanjin-Fanfogna palace. The five rooms exhibit books, documents, drawings and period costumes from Trogir's long history. Ask at one of the tourist offices for an appointment if you wish to visit outside of July and August.

The glory of the town is the three-naved Venetian **Cathedral of St Lovro** (☎ 881 426; Trg

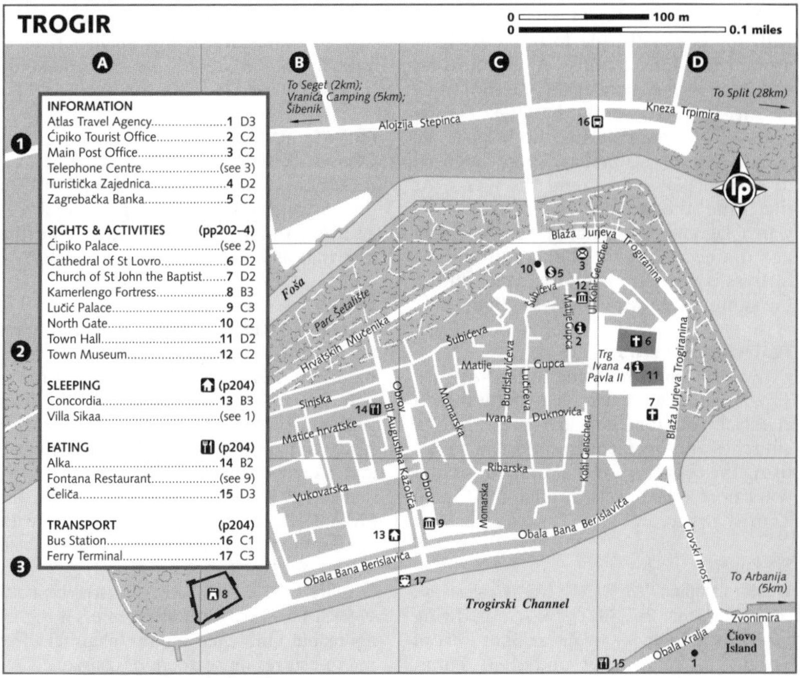
TROGIR
0 100 m
0 0.1 miles
A
B
C
D
1
2
3
INFORMATION
Atlas Travel Agency.....1 D3
Ćipiko Tourist Office.....2 C2
Main Post Office.....3 C2
Telephone Centre.....(see 3)
Turistička Zajednica.....4 D2
Zagrebačka Banka.....5 C2
SIGHTS & ACTIVITIES (pp202–4)
Ćipiko Palace.....(see 2)
Cathedral of St Lovro.....6 D2
Church of St John the Baptist.....7 D2
Kamerlengo Fortress.....8 B3
Lučić Palace.....9 C3
North Gate.....10 C2
Town Hall.....11 D2
Town Museum.....12 C2
SLEEPING (p204)
Concordia.....13 B3
Villa Sikaa.....(see 1)
EATING (p204)
Alka.....14 B2
Fontana Restaurant.....(see 9)
Čeliča.....15 D3
TRANSPORT (p204)
Bus Station.....16 C1
Ferry Terminal.....17 C3
To Seget (2km); Vranića Camping (5km); Šibenik
Alojzija Stepinca
Kneza Trpimira
To Split (28km)
Foša
Parc Šetalište
Hrvatskih Mučenika
Blaža Jurjeva Trogiranina
Šubićeva
Matije Gupca
Ul Kohl-Genscher
Trg Ivana Pavla II
Sinjska
Matice hrvatske
Obrov
Bl Augustina Kažotića
Momarska
Budislavićeva
Lučićeva
Ivana Duknovića
Kohl Genschera
Ribarska
Vukovarska
Obala Bana Berislavića
Čiovski most
To Arbanija (5km)
Trogirski Channel
Zvonimira
Obala Kralja
Čiovo Island

Ivana Pavla III; 8am-noon year-round & 4-7pm daily summer), built from the 13th to 15th centuries and one of the finest architectural works in Croatia. Note first the Romanesque portal (1240) by Master Radovan. The sides of the portal depict lion figures (the symbol of Venice) with Adam and Eve above them, the earliest example of the nude in Dalmatian sculpture. The outer pilasters show saints, the centre scenes represent the calendar months and the small posts feature hunting scenes. Overhead is the Nativity of Christ. At the end of the portico is another fine piece of sculpture – the baptistry sculpted in 1464 by Andrija Aleši. Enter the building through an obscure back door to see the richly decorated Renaissance Chapel of St Ivan, created by the masters Firentinac and Duknović from 1461 to 1497. Within the sacristy there are paintings of St Jerome and John the Baptist. Take a look at the treasury, which contains an ivory triptych and several medieval illuminated manuscripts.

A sign informs you that you must be 'decently dressed' to enter the cathedral, which means that men must wear tops (women too, of course) and shorts are a no-no. For a small fee, you can even climb the 47m cathedral tower (if it's open) for a delightful view. To be sure of visiting the cathedral, it's best to come in the morning. Its hours can be irregular and it is often closed in the afternoon.

Before leaving the square, look at the 15th-century **town hall** opposite the cathedral with a Gothic yard decorated with coats of arms and a stone head. Next to the cathedral, the Ćipiko Tourist Office occupies the **Ćipiko Palace**, with its stunning carved triforium, the work of Firentinac and Aleši.

Southeast of the cathedral, look at the magnificent carved portal on the **Church of St John the Baptist** (Pinakoteka) representing the mourning of Christ. Although closed for renovation when we visited, the church usually exhibits 14th- to 17th-century paintings and statues.

Walk along the waterfront and notice the portal and courtyard of the Renaissance **Lučić Palace**, next to the Fontana Restaurant. If you keep walking you'll come to the **Kamerlengo Fortress**, which looks exactly as a medieval fortress should. Once connected with the city walls, the fortress was built around the 15th century. At the furthest end, you'll see an elegant gazebo (now graffiti-covered) built by the French Marshal Marmont during the Napoleonic occupation of Dalmatia, where he used to sit and play cards amid the waves. At that time, the western end of the island was a lagoon; the malarial marshes were not drained until the 20th century. The fortress is now an open-air cinema during the summer, showing movies at 9pm.

Festivals & Events

Every year from mid-June to mid-August, Trogir hosts a **summer music festival** with classical and folk concerts presented in churches and open squares. Posters advertising the concerts are all around town and you can reserve tickets through the Ćipiko Tourist Office.

Sleeping

Vranića Camping (☎ 894 141; Seget Vranjica, Seget Donji; per adult/site 25/50KN; ⌚ mid-Apr–Oct) Lying just off the highway to Zadar 5km west of Trogir, this camping ground offers tennis, biking, windsurfing, water-skiing, sailing and horse riding. Take bus No 24 from the bus station right outside the town.

Seget (☎ /fax 880 394; Hrvatskih Žrtava 121, Seget Donji; per adult/site 25/50KN; ⌚ mid-Apr–Oct) Seget, 2km west of Trogir, is smaller than Vranića Camping but it offers the same range of activities.

Villa Sikaa (☎ 881 223; www.vila-sikaa-r.com; Obala kralja Zvonimira 10; s/d from 470/500KN; 🖵) Over the Atlas office, this hotel offers the best deal in town. The seven large rooms have double-glazed windows and satellite TV, and some have stunning views over the town. In an unusual touch, the owner offers Internet connection in each room for the price of a local phone call. There are more expensive rooms with a sauna and shower massage.

Villa Tina (☎ 888 305; www.vila-tina.hr; Arbanija; s/d 325/349KN; 🅿 🖵) About 5km east of Trogir is this delightful establishment which offers excellent value for money. It's right on the coast with swimming possibilities nearby. The rooms are impeccable and there are relaxing views from the terrace.

Concordia (☎ 885 400; www.concordia-hotel.htnet .hr; Obala Bana Berislavića 22; s/d 360/510KN; 🅿 🖵)

Concordia is in town right on the waterfront. The 14 rooms are slightly smaller than at Villa Sikaa, but are still pleasant and some have sea views.

PRIVATE ROOMS

Ćipiko Tourist Office and Atlas Travel Agency have private rooms from 170KN a double, studios for 230KN, and two-, three- and four-room apartments. Check out the offerings at www.trogir-online.com.

Eating

Fontana Restaurant (☎ 884 881; Obrov 1; mains around 55KN) When locals want to have a night out they usually head to the Fontana with its large waterfront terrace. You can get almost anything here, from inexpensive pizza and omelettes to pricier grilled fish and meat, but the speciality is fish.

Alka (☎ 881 856; Bl Augustina Kažotića 15; mains 65-85KN) Alka is another popular choice with similar prices to Fontana Restaurant; it also has an outdoor terrace.

Čeliča (☎ 882 344; Obala Kralja Zvonimira; mains 40-80KN) This boat-restaurant offers a highly agreeable ambience on the channel. The menu centres on seafood, of course.

Getting There & Away

Southbound buses from Zadar (130km) will drop you off in Trogir. Getting buses north can be more difficult, as they often arrive full from Split.

City bus No 37 runs between Trogir and Split (28km) every 20 minutes throughout the day, with a stop at Split airport en route. In Split, bus No 37 leaves from the local bus station. You can buy the four-zone ticket from the driver in either direction.

There's also a ferry once a week from Split that docks in front of the Concordia hotel.

AROUND TROGIR

Although there are beaches to the west of Trogir, it's a much better idea to head to the beaches on Drvenik Mali and Drvenik Veli Islands, an easy boat trip from town. Boats leave from the ferry terminal in front of the Concordia hotel. Both islands are sparsely inhabited and idyllic getaways. The smaller island, **Drvenik Mali**, has olive trees, a population of 56 and (finally) a sand beach that curves around the cove of Vela Rina.

Drvenik Veli also has secluded coves and olive trees plus a few cultural highlights to get you off the beach. The church of St George dates from the 16th century and houses baroque furniture and a Venetian altar piece. Outside Drvenik Veli village is the unfinished 18th-century church of St Nicholas, whose builder never quite got past the monumental front.

Unfortunately, the boat schedules are geared to islanders working in Trogir and not day trippers, but on Thursday and Saturday you can catch a 10am boat to the islands and spend a few hours there before catching the 6pm boat back from Drvenik Veli. If you're interested in spending more time on the islands, the tourist office in Trogir can find you private accommodation.

MAKARSKA
pop 15,000

This attractive town and port is the centrepiece of the 'Makarska Riviera', a 50km stretch of coast at the foot of the Biokovo range. The series of cliffs and ridges form an impressive backdrop to a string of beautiful pebble beaches. The foothills are protected from harsh winds and covered in lush Mediterranean greenery – pine forests, olive groves, figs and fruit trees.

With an abundance of hiking and swimming possibilities in such a spectacular natural setting, it's unsurprising that tourism has a long history in this region. The recent war in the former Yugoslavia severely disrupted the flow of visitors, however, and, outside a short summer season that runs for about six weeks in July and August, you should find the area relatively uncrowded.

Makarska is the largest town in the region and makes a good base for exploring both the coast and Mt Biokovo. Located on a large cove bordered by Cape Osejava in the southeast and the Sveti Petar Peninsula in the northwest, the landscape is dominated by Mt Biokovo looming over the town. The roads and trails that crisscross the limestone massif may be irresistible to hikers, but the less energetic can simply lie on the beach and watch the day-long play of light and shadow on the mountain's cracks and crevices.

Makarska owes its name to the Roman settlement of Muccurum, which probably existed in the village of Makar about 2km north of Makarska. Excavations on Sveti Petar Peninsula, however, reveal that there was another linked settlement, Inaronia, along the coast that served as a way station between Solin (Salona) and the important trading town of Narona down the coast. Both settlements were allegedly destroyed in 548 by Totila, king of the Eastern Goths.

History

The region was populated by migrating Slavs in the 7th century who eventually set up a booming piracy business that disrupted Venetian shipping. The Venetian warships that sailed into Makarska in 887 were severely trounced in battle and the Venetians were thereafter forced to pay for the right to sail past the settlement. In the 11th century, Makarska came under the rule of the Croatian-Hungarian kings, which lasted until 1324 when it fell to the Bosnian ruler Kotromanić. In 1499, the town was taken by the Ottoman Turks who were pushing against the Venetians for control of the Adriatic coast. During the 150 years that Makarska was under Turkish rule, it became an important port for the salt trade from Bosnia and Hercegovina. The Venetians took over the town in 1646 and held it until the end of their empire in 1797. Trade prospered and a new aristocracy built baroque mansions to the east and west of the town. After the fall of Venice, Makarska was then subject to Austrian, French and again Austrian rule before becoming part of the Kingdom of Yugoslavia.

Orientation

The bus station on Ante Starčevića is about 300m uphill from the centre of the old town, which opens like an amphitheatre onto the sea. Take Kralja Zvonimira from the bus station downhill to Obala Tomislava and you'll be on the main promenade of the old town with travel agencies, shops and restaurants.

There's a long pebble beach that stretches from the Sveti Petar park at the beginning of Obala Tomislava northwest along the bay, which is where you'll find most of the large hotels. The southeastern side of town is rockier, but you can still find plenty of places to stretch out on the rocks and take a swim.

Information

INTERNET ACCESS

Master (☎ 612 466; Jadranska 1; per hr 15KN) Behind Hotel Biokovo.

LEFT LUGAGE

Garderoba (per day 10KN; ☺ 6am-10pm) At the bus station.

MONEY

There are many banks and ATMs along Tomislava and you can change money at the travel agencies on the same street.
Zagrebačka Banka (Trg Tina Ujevića 1) It has an ATM.

POST

Post Office (Trg 4 Svibnja 533) You can change money, make phone calls or withdraw cash on MasterCard.

TOURIST INFORMATION

Biokovo Active Holidays (☎ 098-225 852; www .biokovo-active-holidays.fr; Tomislava bb) A font of information on Mt Biokovo, and organises hiking trips.
Turistička Zajednica (☎ /fax 612 002; www .makarska.com; Tomislava 16; ☺ 7am-9pm daily Jun-Sep, 7am-2pm Mon-Fri Oct-May) It publishes a useful guide to the city with a map that you can pick up here or at any travel agency.

TRAVEL AGENCIES

Atlas Travel Agency (☎ 617 038; fax 616 343; Kačićev trg 8) It is at the far end of town and finds private accommodation.
Mornar Tours (☎ 616 834; fax 616 836; Prvosvibanjska bb) In addition to money exchange and private accommodation services, it handles airline tickets for Croatia Airlines in case you need to change your ticket.
SB Tours (☎ 611 005; www.sb-tours.hr; Tomislava 15a) Changes money and finds private accommodation.
Turist Biro (☎ 611 688; www.turistbiro-makarska .com; Tomislava 2) Finds private accommodation and books excursions.

Sights

Makarska is more renowned for its natural beauty than its cultural highlights, but on a rainy day you could check out the **Town Museum** (☎ 612 302; Tomislava 17; adult/concession 5/3KN; ☺ 7am-3pm Mon-Fri, 9am-noon Sat), which traces the town's history in a less-than-gripping collection of photos and old stones.

More interesting is the **Franciscan monastery** (Franjevački Samostan; Franjevački Put 1; ☺ Mass only), built in 1400 and restored in 1540 and 1614.

The single-nave church is worth visiting for the **shell collection** (☎ 611 256; admission 10KN; ☺ 11am-noon) in the cloister and a painting of the Assumption by the Flemish artist Pieter de Coster (1760). The 18th-century **St Mark's Church** (Crkva Svetog Marka; ☎ 611 365; Kačićev trg; ☺ Mass only) features a baroque silver altar from 1818 and a marble altar from 18th-century Venice.

Activities

Mt Biokovo, rising behind the city, offers wonderful **hiking** opportunities. The Vošac peak (142m) is the nearest target for hikers, only 2.5km from the city. From St Mark's Church in Kačićev trg, you can walk or drive up Put Makra, following signs to the village of Makar, where a trail leads to Vošac (one to two hours). From Vošac a good marked trail leads to Sveti Jure, the highest peak at 1762m (two hours). Take plenty of water.

Another popular destination is the Botanical Garden (near the village of Kotišina), which can be reached by a marked trail from Makar that passes under a series of towering peaks. Although once a major regional highlight, the garden has fallen into decay since the recent death of its caretaker.

Biokovo Active Holidays (see left) is an excellent source of hiking and other information about Mt Biokovo. For scuba diving, try **More Sub** (☎ 611 727, 098 265 241; Hotel Dalmacija).

Tours

Biokovo Active Holidays offers guided walks and drives on Mt Biokovo for all levels of physical exertion. You can go part way up the mountain by minibus and then take a short hike to Sveti Jure peak, take a 5½-hour hike through black pine forests and fields of chamois and sheep, or enjoy an early drive to watch the sun rise over Makarska.

Sleeping

Baško Polje (☎ 612 329; per adult/tent 25/55KN; ☺ May-Oct) Between Makarska and Baška Voda, this is the closest autocamp to town and is on the beach.

Hotel Makarska (☎ /fax 616 622; www.makarska -hotel.com; Potok 17; s/d 280/430KN; P ⌘) This small, family-owned hotel in town is about 200m from the beach. The rooms are comfortable enough with satellite TV and minibars plus the service is attentive.

Hotel Biokovo (☎ 615 244; www.hotelbiokovo.hr; Tomislava; s/d 385/640KN; P ⊠) An attractive 50-room hotel right on the promenade, this place has double-glazed windows to keep out noise. There are a lot of business travellers, attracted by the well-outfitted rooms.

Hotel Dalmacija (☎ 615 777; www.hoteli-makarska .hr; Kralja Krešimira bb; s/d 375/685KN; P ⊠ ⌘) This towering structure of 190 rooms has an enclosed private beach and plenty of comforts.

Meteor (☎ 602 600; www.hoteli-makarska.hr; Šatalište Donja Luka 1; s/d 425/790KN; P ⊠ ⌘) This three-star hotel 400m west of the town centre on a pebble beach is the most luxurious. Each of the 280 rooms is air-conditioned and has a balcony with a sea view. There are indoor and outdoor swimming pools, shops and tennis courts. Don't expect much of a discount in room rates outside the high season.

PRIVATE ROOMS

All of the travel agencies listed on p206 can find private rooms. Count on spending from 200KN to 300KN for a double room. There are plenty available in the centre of town as well as the outskirts.

Eating

Riva (☎ 612 497; Tomislava 6; mains 27-52KN) On one of their rare nights dining out, local people usually head here for good quality at low prices. The menu is the usual range of dishes such as scampi, beef cutlet and squid, and you can sit under the trees on an outdoor terrace.

Pizzeria Lungo Mare (☎ 615 244; Tomislava; pizzas 30KN) Next to the Hotel Biokovo, this place serves hearty, freshly baked pizzas and there's a comfortable outdoor terrace.

Ivo (☎ 611 257; Starčevića 41; mains around 50KN) Because it's not near the beach, few tourists know about this place. Fish and meat dishes are cooked to perfection and expertly seasoned.

Picnickers can pick up supplies at the fruit and vegetable market next to St Mark's Church or at the **supermarket** (Tomislava 14).

Entertainment

Art Cafe (☎ 615 808; Don M Pavlinovića 1) A former disco, Art Cafe now holds a changing series of concerts, exhibits and events. It's one of the best hang-outs on the coast.

Otherwise, **Pjer** (Prvosvibanjska bb), along the harbour, is a popular bar for young people or there's **Opera** (☎ 616 838; Šetalište Fra Jure Radića), which, despite the name, is the town disco.

Getting There & Away

In summer there are three to five ferries a day between Makarska and Sumartin on Brač (23KN, 30 minutes), reduced to two a day in winter.

There are 10 buses daily from the **bus station** (☎ 612 333; Ante Starčevića 30) to Dubrovnik (92KN, three hours), 11 buses daily to Split (32KN, 1¼ hours), two buses daily to Rijeka (229KN, nine hours) and two buses daily to Zagreb (142KN, six hours). The **Jadrolinija stall** (☎ 338 333; Obala Kralja Tomislava) is near the Hotel Biokovo.

There's also a daily bus to Sarajevo (125KN, six hours).

AROUND MAKARSKA
Brela

The town of Brela, 14km northwest of Makarska, is surrounded by the longest and loveliest coastline in Dalmatia. Six kilometres of pebble beaches curve around coves thickly forested with pine trees, largely unmarred by ugly tourist developments. A shady promenade winds around the coves, the sea is crystal clear and there are convenient outdoor showers on some beaches.

ORIENTATION & INFORMATION

The bus stop (no left-luggage office) is behind Hotel Soline, a short walk downhill to Obala Kneza Domagoja, the harbour street and town centre. Beaches and coves are on both sides of the town but the longest stretch is the 4km coast west of the town centre. The best beach is **Punta Rata**, a stunning pebble beach about 300m southwest of the town centre.

Turistička Zajednica (☎ 618 455, 618 337; www .brela.hr; Trg Alojzija Stepinca bb; ⌚ 8am-9pm mid-Jun– mid-Sep, 8am-2pm Mon-Fri mid-Sep–mid-Jun) provides a town map and a cycling map for the region, and **Bonavia Travel Agency** (☎ 619 019; www.bonavia-agency.hr; Obala Kneza Domagoja 18) finds private accommodation, changes money and books excursions.

SLEEPING

The closest camping is available at Baško Polje (p206). For private accommodation you'll pay from 100/190KN a single/double.

There are no cheap hotels in Brela but much of the private accommodation on offer from the tourist office or travel agencies are really small *pensions*. The four large hotels are managed by **Brela Hotels** (☎ 603 190; www.brelahotels.com).

Hotel Marina (☎ 603 608; marina@hoteli-brela .htnet.hr; s/d 510/775KN; P ✗) The Marina is the least expensive hotel in town. A wall of pine trees separates this rather standard-issue hotel from a luxuriant beach.

Hotel Soline (☎ 603 207; soline@hoteli-brela.htnet .hr; s/d 550/835KN; P ✗ ✿) This well-turned-out establishment is the closest to town, on a beach, and sports an indoor swimming pool.

Hotel Berulia (☎ 603 599; berulia@hoteli-brela.htnet .hr; Frankopanska bb; s/d from 525/790KN; P ✗ ✿) About 300m east of the town centre, this hotel is a little more secluded than the others but also offers a full range of comforts.

GETTING THERE & AWAY

All buses between Makarska and Split stop at Brela, making it an easy day trip from either town.

VIS ISLAND

pop 4338

Ask a Croatian to name their top three islands and one of them is likely to be Vis. In addition to its unspoiled beauty, Vis has the allure of the forbidden. Used as a military base for the former Yugoslav army, it was off limits to the public until 1989 but is now becoming a top destination for international travellers looking to get away from it all. Rather than sprawling tourist resorts, the island has two small towns – Vis and Komiža – at the foot of two large bays and a rugged coast dotted with coves, caves and a couple of sand beaches.

The interior of the island is planted with vineyards producing Vis' well-known Vugava (white) and Plavac (red) wines. Fishing is the other cornerstone of the island's economy. The surrounding waters are rich in marine life and there's a sardine-canning plant near Komiža. Like many

islands, Vis has become dramatically de-populated in the years since WWII and sees tourism as its only chance for survival. In addition to the charms of sun and sea, the island's long history has produced an ar-chaeological treasure trove of amphorae, sculpture, jewellery and other remnants of antiquity that you can see in the Issa Mu-seum and around the town of Vis.

History

Inhabited first in Neolithic times, the island was settled by the ancient Illyrians who brought the Iron Age to Vis in the 1st millennium BC. In 390 BC a Greek colony was formed on the island, known then as Issa, from which the Greek ruler Dionysius the Elder controlled other Adri-atic possessions. The island eventually be-came a powerful city-state and established its own colonies on Korčula Island and at Trogir and Stobreč. Allying itself with Rome during the Illyrian wars, the island nonetheless lost its autonomy and became part of the Roman Empire in 47 BC. By the 10th century Vis had been settled by Slavic tribes and was sold to Venice along with other Dalmatian towns in 1420. Fleeing Dalmatian pirates, the population moved from the coast inland. With the fall of the Venetian Republic in 1797 the island fell under control of Austria, France, England, Austria again and then Italy during WWII as the Great Powers fought for control of this strategic Adriatic outpost. The island was an important military base for Tito's Partisans. He established his supreme headquarters in a cave in Hum Mountain, from which he coordinated military and diplomatic actions with Allied forces and allegedly made his famous statement, 'We will not have what is theirs but we will not give what is ours'.

Getting There & Around

Vis town is best reached by car ferry from Split but, like many small islands, the boat schedules are set to accommodate islanders working in town, not visitors popping out to the island. In July and August, however, there's a boat departing at 9.30am Friday, Saturday and Sunday from Split and a 5pm boat back from Vis, which makes a pleasant day trip. In the spring and autumn, there's a morning boat on Monday, Wednesday and Friday and in winter only on Monday and Friday – but there's no afternoon boat back in these seasons so you'll have to spend the night. The trip takes two hours and costs 30KN. There's an afternoon boat on Tuesday all year that also stops in Hvar town. In July and August SEM runs a catamaran between Vis and Split (26KN, 1½ hours). For connections to Italy see p275.

The only island bus transport connects Vis with Komiža. The bus meets the morning and afternoon Jadrolinija ferries at Vis town and leaves for Komiža at 3pm.

VIS TOWN
On the northeastern coast of the island, at the foot of a wide, horseshoe-shaped bay, lies the ancient town of Vis, the first settlement on the island. In only a short walk you can see the remains of a Greek cemetery, Roman baths and an English fortress. Regular ferry arrivals give spurts of activity to an otherwise peaceful town of coastal promenades and crumbling 17th-century buildings.

Orientation
The town is on the southern slope of Gradina hill and is a merger of two settlements: Luka on the northwestern part of the bay and Kut in the southeast. The ferry ties up at Luka and a harbour-side promenade runs from Luka to Kut. Most beaches are along this promenade while the ancient ruins and another beach in front of the Hotel Issa are a short walk north along the coast.

Information
You can change money at the bank, post office or any travel agency.

Ionios Travel Agency (☎ 711 532; fax 711 356; Obala Svetog Jurja 36) Finds private accommodation, changes money, rents bikes and scooters, and runs excursions.

Jadrolinija (☎ 711 032; Šetalište Stare Isse) Buy your boat tickets here.

Post Office (Obala Svetog Jurja 25)

Splitska Banka (Obala Svetog Jurja 34) There's an ATM.

Tourist Office (Turistička Zajednica; ☎ 711 017; www .tz-vis.hr; Šetalište Stare Isse 2; 🕑 8am-1pm & 6-8pm Jul-Aug, 8am-noon Mon-Fri Sep-Jun) It's right next to the Jadrolinija ferry dock.

Sights & Activities
The **Archaeological Museum** (Arheološki Muzej; ☎ 711 729; Baterija Fortress, Šetalis Viški boj 12; admission 10KN; 🕑 9am-1pm & 5-7pm Tue-Sun summer, 9am-1pm Tue-Sun winter) is a good introduction to the town's historical sights. Exhibits include Greek and Roman pottery, jewellery and sculpture, including an exquisite 4th-century bronze head of a Greek goddess that could be either Aphrodite or Artemis. A leaflet gives an overview of the exhibits, the history of Vis and a useful map showing the locations of the ruins around town.

Walk north from the dock about 100m and, behind the tennis court, you can see remains of a **Greek cemetery** next to remains of **Greek walls**. A few metres further along the coastal road you'll see remains of **Roman baths** behind a fence. During their four-year rule over the island through the Napoleonic Wars (1811–15), the British built several **fortresses** on hills around the bay; the one on the northern corner is the most prominent.

Scenic **coastal roads** with dramatic cliffs and hairpin turns make it worthwhile to rent your own wheels for a day. You can hire scooters for 170KN a day or mountain bikes for 60KN a day from Ionios Travel Agency (see left) in Vis town or Darlić & Darlić (p210) in Komiža.

Diving is excellent in the waters around Vis. Fish are plentiful and there's a wreck of an Italian ship dating from the 1866 naval battle between Austria and Italy. **Dodoro** (☎ 711 311; www.dodoro-diving.com; Kranjčevića 4) has an extensive diving programme. A full-day trip, including two boat dives and lunch, costs 420KN.

Tours
The island is best appreciated by boat and a trip that includes the Blue Grotto at Biševo (p210) is a must. You can book a boat trip around Biševo that includes a visit to the Blue Grotto for 100KN from Ionios Travel Agency.

Sleeping
There are no camping grounds in Vis and only a few hotels, but you should have no trouble finding private accommodation, either rooms or apartments. You'll have to rent through an agency however, since women offering *sobe* at the ferry landing are rare.

Hotel Paula (☎ 711 362; www.paula-hotel.htnet .hr; Petra Hektorovića; s/d 450/680; P X) By far the most original and welcoming of all the

CENTRAL DALMATIA

island's hotels, this little place has filled an important accommodation gap on Vis. Each room is different but all are imaginatively decorated and comfortably outfitted. Some even have kitchenettes. The hotel is in the Kuta or old part of Vis in the southeastern area of the bay. It also houses an excellent restaurant.

Hotel Tamaris (☎ 711 350; vis@st.htnet.hr; Svetog Jurja 30; s/d incl breakfast 410/648KN; **P**) For rooms that include phones and TVs in an attractive old building, this is a good deal. The hotel is only about 100m southeast of the ferry dock. Prices drop substantially outside the main July and August season.

Hotel Issa (☎ 711 164; vis@st.htnet.hr; Zanelle 5; s/d 410/648KN; **P**) Larger than the Hotel Tamaris, this place sits on a pebbly beach about 200m north of the town centre. Although the prices are the same, the Hotel Tamaris is in better condition. The only real reason to stay here is if the Hotel Tamaris is full.

PRIVATE ROOMS
The only agency that finds private accommodation is Ionios Travel Agency (p209). You'll pay about 100KN per person for a room with shared bathroom and 245KN for a small studio with a kitchenette and bathroom.

Eating

Restaurant Pojoda (☎ 711 574; Don Cvjetka Marasović 8; mains from 50KN) In the lush interior courtyard you can munch on an array of fresh Dalmatian dishes. Platters of meat, fish and seafood keep a devoted clientele happy.

Villa Kaliopa (☎ 711 755; V Nazora 32; mains from 60KN) No other place can match the extraordinary experience of eating here. The restaurant is in the exotic gardens of the 16th-century Gariboldi mansion. Palm trees, bamboo and classical statuary provide a romantic setting for a menu of Dalmatian specialities that are pricey but manageable if you choose carefully. This place is between Luka and Kut.

There are also a few pizzerias and a market in the square next to Hotel Tamaris.

KOMIŽA

On the western coast at the foot of Hum mountain, Komiža is a captivating small town on a bay, with sand and pebble beaches

on the eastern end. Narrow back streets lined with tawny 17th- and 18th-century houses twist uphill from the port, which has been used by fishermen at least since the 12th century. East of town is a 17th-century church on the site of a Benedictine monastery, and at the end of the main wharf is a Renaissance citadel dating from 1585.

Orientation & Information

The bus from Vis stops at the edge of town next to the post office and a few blocks away from the citadel. Walking all the way around the harbour you'll come to the municipal **Tourist Office** (☎ /fax 713 455; Riva 1; ☯ 8am-7pm Jul-Aug, 9am-noon Mon-Fri Sep-Jun). Next door to the tourist office, **Darlić & Darlić Travel Agency** (☎ 713 760; www.darlic-travel.hr; Riva Sveti Mikule 13) arranges excursions to the Blue Grotto for 100KN and a lunch-time fish picnic for 170KN.

Sleeping & Eating

Hotel Biševo (☎ 713 095; modra.spilja@st.htnet.hr; Ribarska 72; s/d from 370/610KN) Facilities are modest but the hotel is right near the beach. Try to get one of the renovated rooms.

Bako (☎ 713 008; Gundulićeva 1; mains from 50KN; ☯ dinner only Sep-Jun) Near the Hotel Biševo, this restaurant has a cool stone interior that contains a fish pond and a collection of Greek and Roman amphorae.

Konoba Jastožera (☎ 713 859; Gundulićeva 6; mains around 100KN) Lobster lovers, grab your pincers! The scaly delicacies are cooked to perfection here. Meat and fish dishes complete the menu in this unique restaurant where you eat on planks over the water.

PRIVATE ROOMS
Darlić & Darlić can find private accommodation for about the same prices as in Vis town.

AROUND KOMIŽA
Biševo

The tiny islet of Biševo has little other than vineyards, pine trees and a spectacular **Blue Grotto** (Modra Špilja). Between 11am and noon the sun's rays pass through an underwater opening in this coastal cave to bathe the interior in an unearthly blue light. Beneath the crystal-blue water, rocks glimmer in silver and pink to a depth of 16m. The only catch is that waters can be too choppy to enter the cave outside the summer months or when the *juga* (southern wind) is blowing. When the tourist season is at its peak in July and August, the cave can be woefully crowded and the line of boats waiting to get in discouragingly long. Outside of high season, you may be able to swim here. Unless you have your own boat you'll need to book an excursion either from a travel agency in Vis or Komiža or from one of the boats on the harbour. The price is the same.

BRAČ ISLAND

pop 13,824

As the largest island in Central Dalmatia, Brač offers two major resorts, several sleepy villages and a dramatic Mediterranean landscape of pines, maquis and steep cliffs sloping onto a rocky coast. The climate is sunny, hot and dry in the long summer and mild and rainy in winter. The island boasts over 2700 hours of sunshine a year, which is great for tourism but makes farming a challenge. In the interior you'll see piles of rocks, gathered by women throughout the ages to prepare the land for cultivation. With such backbreaking labour, the islanders have produced wine, olive oil, figs, almonds and sour cherries, but Brač's main export is stone. Diocletian's Palace in Split and the White House in Washington DC were built from Brač's lustrous white stone, which is still quarried and exported.

Breaking rocks for a living has its drawbacks, of course. Many islanders have emigrated, leaving villages in the dry interior nearly empty. The coastal villages of Supetar and Bol are now a magnet for sun-and-sea tourists, but the stone streets still evoke the intimacy of small-town life.

History

Remnants of a Neolithic settlement were found in Kopačina cave near Supetar but the first recorded inhabitants were the Illyrians, who built a fort in Škrip to protect against Greek invasion. The Romans arrived in 167 BC and promptly set to work exploiting the stone quarries near Škrip and building summer mansions around the island. Slavs settled the island in the 9th century, gathering in the interior to escape the notorious Dalmatian pirates. During the four centuries of Venetian rule (1420–1797), the interior villages were devastated by plague and the inhabitants moved to the 'healthier' settlements along the coast, revitalising the towns of Supetar, Bol, Sumartin and Milna. After a brief period under Napoleonic rule, the island passed into Austrian hands. Wine cultivation expanded until the phylloxera epidemic at the turn of the 20th century ravaged the island's vines and people began leaving for North and South America, especially Chile. The island endured a reign of terror during WWII when German and Italian troops looted and burned villages, imprisoning and murdering their inhabitants.

Although the tourism business took a hit in the mid-1990s, it has rebounded well and the island can be crowded in summer.

Getting There & Away

AIR

Brač's **airport** (☎ 631 370) is 14km northeast of Bol and 32km southeast of Supetar.

There are weekly flights from Zagreb to the Brač airport from April to October (414KN) and Atlas Travel Agency in Split sometimes runs minibuses between the airport and Bol (25KN), but there's no transport from the airport to Supetar so you'll need to take a taxi, which costs about 150KN.

BOAT

There are 13 car ferries a day between Split and Supetar in summer (22KN, one hour) and seven a day at other times of the year. The ferry drops you off in the centre of town, only steps from the bus station. Make bookings at **Jadrolinija** (☎ 631 357; Hrvatskih Vekikana bb, Supetar), about 50m east of the harbour.

Getting Around

Public transport to the island's highlights is sparse so you may wish to have your own wheels if you want to see a few sites in a short time. You can hire cars from travel agencies on the island or bring them from the mainland.

There's a daily fast boat in summer between Split and Bol (80KN, one hour) that goes on to Jelsa. There are also three to five car ferries per day between Makarska

BRAČ ISLAND

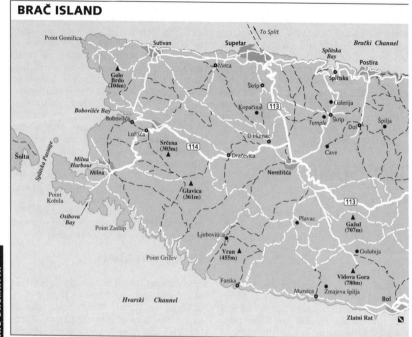

and Sumartin (23KN, 30 minutes) but you'll face a long wait for a bus to Supetar.

Supetar is the hub for bus transport around the island. There are five buses a day that connect Supetar with Bol (40 minutes) but not all of them connect with the ferries from Split. There are also five buses a day to Milna and three daily buses to Škrip.

SUPETAR

With regular year-round ferry connections to Split and buses to villages around the island, Supetar makes an excellent day trip from Split or jumping-off point for an island visit. The beaches are an easy stroll from the town centre and the cluster of Austrian-style buildings around the port lend the town an easy-going charm.

Orientation

Supetar is easy to navigate since most offices, shops and travel agencies are on the main road that radiates roughly east–west from the harbour. Called Porat at the harbour, the road becomes Hrvatskih Velikana in the east and Vlačica on to Put Vele Luke as it travels

west. There are five rocky beaches on the coast. Vrilo beach is about 100m east of the town centre. Walking west, you'll come first to Vlačica then Banj beach, lined with pine trees. Next is Bili Rat, site of the water-sports centre, then if you cut across St Nikolaus Cape you come to Vela Luka beach. The bus station is next to the Jadrolinija office (no left-luggage office).

Information

There's an ATM outside Privredna Banka Zagreb (at the dock) and another outside the Jadrolinija office.

Atlas Travel Agency (☎ /fax 631 105; Porat 10) It's near the harbour and holds mail for Amex clients.

Maestral (☎ 631 258; fax 631 461; Kovačića 3)

Main Post Office (Vlačica 13) You can change money or withdraw cash on MasterCard.

Supetar Travel (☎ 631 520; Bračka 2) It finds private accommodation, books hotels and changes money.

Tourist Office (☎ /fax 630 551; www.supetar.hr; Porat 1; ☼ 8am-10pm Jul-Aug, 8am-4pm Mon-Fri Sep-Jun) It's only a few steps east of the harbour and has a full array of brochures and leaflets on the activities and sights available in Supetar.

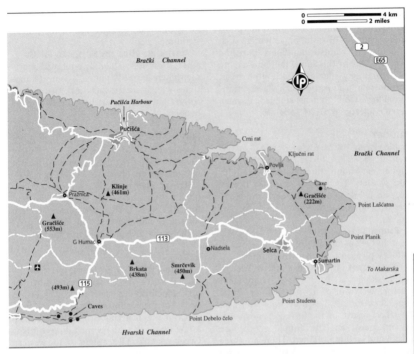

Sights & Activities

The baroque **Church of the Annunciation** (🕙 Mass only), west of the harbour, was built in 1733. Although the exterior is plain, except for the semicircular entrance staircase, the interior is painted in cool, minty pastels and contains an interesting set of altar paintings, particularly the altar painting of the Annunciation from the school of Giambattista Pittoni.

The cemetery is at the tip of St Nikolaus Cape and you can't miss the monumental **Mausoleum of the Petrinović family**. The sculptor Toma Rosandić from Split incorporated elements of Byzantine style into this impressive structure dominating the tip of the cape.

The best **diving** on the island is found off the southwestern coast between Bol and Milna, making Bol a better base for divers, but you can book dives, take a diving course and rent equipment at Hotel Kaktus in Supetar. One boat dive in a day costs 220KN, but this doesn't include equipment, which can cost up to 120KN a day.

Although the island is too big to circle around in one day, renting a boat to explore the various coves and inlets makes a wonderful outing. You can rent a motorboat from Jašić out of the **Konoba Vinotoka** (☎ 631 641; per hr/day 80/300KN).

Festivals & Events

Supetar Summer Cultural Festival lasts from June through to September. Folk music, dances and classical concerts are presented several times a week in public spaces and churches. Tickets to festival events are usually free or cost very little, and there are also frequent art exhibits around town.

Tours

Atlas runs full-day excursions rafting on the Cetina river for 520KN, a trip to the Blue Grotto for 435KN, a fish picnic for 195KN and an island tour for 170KN.

Sleeping

For such a small place, Supetar has a good range of accommodation options. Hotel Kaktus and its annexes Olea and Savia, together with Kaktus Apartments and Hotel Palma, are part of a tourist complex on the western edge of town that includes a sports centre, tennis school, two outdoor pools and a panoply of outdoor activities, such as diving and windsurfing. For a sprawling development of this kind, the landscaping is surprisingly pleasant, with pine trees, shrubbery and a nearby beach. Reservations for all these establishments are made through **Svpetrvs Agency** (☎ 631 066; fax 631 560).

BUDGET
Pansion Palute (☎ /fax 631 541; Put Pašika 16; s/d incl breakfast 195/340KN, half board per person 255/235KN) Open year-round, this is a small, family-run *pension*. The food is good, so it may be worthwhile to take half board and enjoy the occasional outdoor cook-outs for the guests.

Pansion Obačak (☎ 630 018; Šibnja 15; d 355KN) Just like Pansion Palute, this place also offers a pleasant, familial environment.

Pliva Complex (☎ 631 247; fax 630 011; Put Vele Luke; s/d 275/425KN) This is a tourist development further west out of town that offers basic but clean rooms. The hotel was built as a 'workers resort' by the former Yugoslavian government, but the simple rooms are clean and well maintained. There are three buildings in the complex; Vrilo and Vlačica are closest to the beach.

Camping Supetar (☎ 630 088; fax 630 022; per adult/site 30/40KN) A mid-sized autocamp about 300m east of town, which has access to a small rocky beach.

MID-RANGE & TOP END
Hotel Palma (☎ 631 133; fax 631 344; s/d from 340/515KN; 😣) The Palma offers simple rooms (no phone or TV). Your low expectations will be met.

Hotel-Restaurant Britanida (☎ 631 038; fax 630 017; Hrvatskih Velikana 26; s/d 415/500KN) This is a small hotel and restaurant on the eastern end of town across the street from the Autocamp Babura and a narrow, rocky beach. All rooms are pleasantly furnished in a Mediterranean style with phones and satellite TV. Try to get one of the rooms facing the sea for the view and the cool breeze.

Hotel Kaktus (☎ 631 133; fax 631 344; s/d from 430/640KN; 🅿 🖳) The hotel and its annexes are the most luxurious and expensive of the tourist complex's establishments. The more expensive rooms have balconies with sea views, satellite TV and minibars. Cheaper

rooms have simple furnishings and no view, but you still have use of the hotel's swimming pool.

Apartments Diana (☎ 631 133; fax 631 130; 4-person apt 670-770KN) The fully equipped apartments here have TV, phone, balcony (sometimes with barbecue facilities), two double rooms plus a pull-out bed for two more people.

PRIVATE ROOMS
During the summer, women often meet the ferries offering *sobe* at a good price but without the quality control of an agency.

Travel agencies can find you good-quality rooms, often with private bathroom, for 120KN to 211KN per person in high season. It can also find you private apartments for 340KN a night for a studio.

Eating
Vinotoka (☎ 630 969; Put Gustirne Luke; mains 50-90KN) A rustic tavern-style restaurant that serves shellfish in a variety of sauces. Fish is served by the portion rather than by weight, which makes ordering easier; there are also a few vegetarian plates including a crispy Greek salad. You'll see signs on the western edge of the harbour.

Jastog (☎ 631 486; Ulica Ive Lole Ribara 7; mains from 60KN) Near the Hotel Palma, Jastog offers somewhat more elegant dining than Vinotoka and an excellent selection of seafood and local dishes.

Bistro Palute (☎ 631 730; dishes 29-45KN) On the harbour next to Atlas Travel Agency, Bistro Palute specialises in grilled meat but fish dishes are also good. Dining is casual.

Entertainment
Fenix (Put Vele Luke 2) is the local disco on the western edge of town and **Hotel Kaktus** (☎ 631 133) has a nightclub and small disco.

AROUND SUPETAR
One of the more interesting sites is the village of **Škrip**, the oldest settlement on the island, about 8km south of Supetar. Formerly a refuge of the ancient Illyrians, the Romans took over the fort in the 2nd century BC, followed by inhabitants of Solin fleeing 7th-century barbarians and eventually early Slavs. Remains of the Illyrian wall are visible around the citadel in the southeastern corner. The most intact

Roman monument on the island is the mausoleum at the base of Radojkovic's tower, a fortification built during the Venetian-Turkish wars; the tower is now a museum. Sarcophagi from the early Christian period are near Cerinics citadel, with a nearby quarry containing a relief of Hercules from the 3rd or 4th century. You can catch an early-morning bus here from Supetar and an early afternoon bus back.

The port of **Milna**, 20km southwest of Supetar, is the kind of lovely, intact fishing village that, in any other part of the world, would have been long ago commandeered by package tourists. The 17th-century town is set at the foot of a deep natural harbour that was used by Emperor Diocletian on the way to Split. Paths and walks take you around the harbour which is studded with coves and rocky beaches that are usually deserted. Besides the picture-perfect setting, there's the 18th-century Church of Our Lady of the Annunciation with a baroque front and early-18th-century altar paintings. Milna is an easy day trip from Supetar, with a morning bus to the town and an afternoon bus back to Supetar. During the summer, the early evening hydrofoil from Bol stops at Milna before going on to Split.

The new **Illyrian Resort** (☎ /fax 636 566; www .illyrian-resort.hr; Milna; apt 830KN; P ✖ ☀) right on Milna beach provides an extraordinary level of modernity, style and comfort. There are plenty of water sports on offer if lazing around by the pool becomes too soporific.

BOL
pop 1480

Bol is an example of how to maximise tourism without wrecking the landscape. Virtually all hotels are in a pine forest west of town within easy reach of Zlatni Rat beach. A coastal promenade shaded by pine trees connects the town centre with the hotels, preserving the rustic tranquillity of the beaches and coves. The old town is attractive, but the real highlight is Zlatni Rat, the protruding sliver of beach that appears in almost all Croatian tourist brochures.

Orientation

The town centre is a pedestrian area that stretches east from the bus station. Zlatni Rat beach is 2km west of town and in between are Borak and Potočine beaches. Behind them are several hotel complexes including Hotel Riu Borak, Elaphusa and Bretanide.

Information

There's an ATM outside both banks. There are also many moneychangers in the port area and you can get cash advances on MasterCard and change money at the post office.

Atlas Travel Agency (☎ 635 233; fax 635 707; Rudina 12) Here you can rent a boat, a scooter or a bike.
Boltours (☎ 635 693; www.boltours.com; Vladimira Nazora 18) It books excursions and finds private accommodation.
Post Office (Uz Pjacu 5) You can make phone calls here.
Splitska Banka (Riva Frane Radića)
Tourist Office (☎ 635 638; www.bol.hr; Porat Boskih Pomoraca; ✹ 8.30am-10pm daily Jul & Aug, 8.30am-2pm & 5-8pm Mon-Sat & 9am-noon Sun Sep-Jun) It's a good source of information on town events. You can check your email here during opening hours.
Zagrebačka Banka (Uz Pjacu 4)

Sights

Most people come to Bol for the unusual **Zlatni Rat** beach, which extends like a tongue into the sea for about 500m from the western end of town. Made up of smooth white pebbles, the tip of the beach changes shape according to the wind and waves. Pine trees provide shade and rocky cliffs rise sharply behind the beach, making the setting one of the loveliest in Dalmatia.

East of the town centre on the Glavica Peninsula is the **Dominican monastery** (Samostan Dominikanaca; ☎ 635 132; Rabadana 4; ✹ Mass only) and the **Church of Our Lady of Mercy** (Crkva Gospe od Milosti; ☎ 635 132; Rabadana 4; ✹ Mass only). The monastery and church were built in 1475 on the site of a 12th-century episcopal palace. The late-Gothic church is notable for a late-16th-century altar screen, as well as ceiling paintings by the Croatian baroque painter Tripo Kikolija. The church is partly paved with tombstones, some of which have initials of various monastic orders or inscriptions in Glagolitic script.

Nearby is the **Monastery Museum** (☎ 635 132; Andelka Rabadana 4; admission 10KN; ✹ 9am-noon & 5-9pm Apr-Oct), presenting prehistoric items excavated from the Kopačina cave, a collection of ancient coins, amphorae and church vestments. The highlight of the

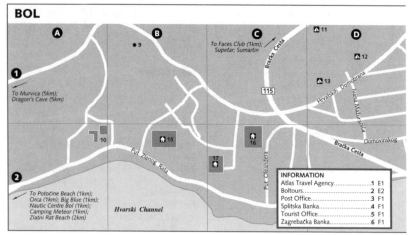

collection is the altar painting *Madonna with Child and Saints* attributed to Tintoretto, for which the museum retains the original invoice of 270 Venetian ducats.

You can go by foot to **Dragon's Cave**, an extremely unusual set of reliefs believed to have been carved by an imaginative 15th-century friar. Carved angels, animals and a gaping dragon decorate the walls of this strange cave in a blend of Christian and Croat pagan symbols. First you walk 5km to Murvica, and from there it's a one-hour walk to the cave. The cave is closed to the public but the tourist office occasionally organises guided excursions at a cost of 100KN.

Activities

Bol is undoubtedly the **windsurfing** capital of Croatia and most of the action takes place at Potočine beach, west of town. Although the *maestral* (strong, steady westerly wind) blows from April to October, the best time to windsurf is at the end of May and the beginning of June, and at the end of July and the beginning of August. The wind generally reaches its peak in the early afternoon and then dies down at the end of the day.

There are two major equipment rental places along Potočine beach: **Orca** (www.orca-sport.com) and **Big Blue** (☎ /fax 635 614; www.big-blue-sport.hr). Prices are roughly the same, so pick your spot according to where the wind is whipping up. A half-day 'funboard' rental costs 260KN; a school board costs 75KN an hour; and an eight-hour beginners' course starts at 750KN.

There are professional-quality clay tennis courts at the **Tennis Centre** (☎ 635 222; Zlatni Rat; per hr 40-60KN) along the road to Murvica. Depending on time of day, a tennis pro will help you work on your serve (or whatever) for 90/130KN per hour for one/two people. Rackets and balls can be rented.

You can **scuba dive** with Big Blue. There are no wrecks to dive but there are some coral reefs at 40m and a large cave. Big Blue's office adjoins the Hotel Riu Borak and boats go out regularly during the season.

You can rent motorboats from the **Nautic Center Bol** (☎ 098 361 651; Potočine Beach; per day/hr 400/100KN), which is opposite the Bretanide hotel. In the evening the same stall is located in the harbour.

Big Blue rents mountain bikes for 75KN per half-day and also runs sightseeing mountain bike excursions around the island.

Tours

Most of the excursions are run by Atlas Travel Agency (p215). You can go to the Blue Grotto at Biševo for 320KN, the Krka waterfalls for 420KN and rafting on the Cetina River for 420KN.

Festivals & Events

There's a **Summer Cultural Festival** in Bol at which dancers and musicians from around

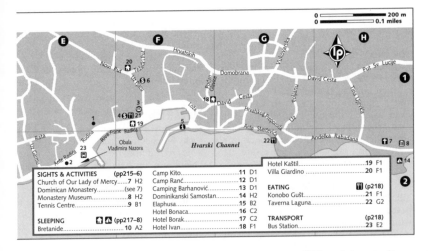

the country perform in churches and open spaces. The festival is held in July and August.

The patron saint of Bol is Our Lady of Carmel; on her feast day (5 August) there's a procession with residents dressed up in traditional costumes as well as music and feasting on the streets.

Sleeping

The camping grounds are near town and are relatively small. As elsewhere along the coast, there are few small hotels but several large tourist complexes. The hill between the town and the coast has been almost entirely given over to the Hotel Riu Borak, Elaphusa and Bretanide resorts; the area remains appealing, though, as the development blends in well with the landscape. Several hotels are 'all-inclusive'. Reservations for most hotels are handled by **Zlatni Rat Marketing** (☎ 306 206; www.zlatni-rat.hr).

BUDGET

West of town and near the big hotels you'll find **Camping Meteor** (☎ 635 630; Hrvatskih Domobrana; per adult/site 32/25KN; ☼ May–Oct), **Camp Ranč** (☎ 635 635; Hrvatskih Domobrana; per adult/site 31/22KN; ☼ May–Oct) – which is behind a restaurant of the same name – and **Camp Kito** (☎ 635 551; Bračka Cesta; per adult/site 40/28KN; ☼ mid-Apr–mid-Sep). They are all well kept and placed in scenic spots.

Another camping ground, **Dominikanski Samostan** (☎ 635 132; Šetalište Andeleka Rabadana;

per adult/site 32/38KN; ☼ May–Oct), is east of town near the Dominican monastery.

MID-RANGE

Villa Giardino (☎ 635 286; Novi Put 2; s/d 560/650KN; Ⓟ) An iron gate opens onto a luxuriant garden at the end of which is this old, white house. The tastefully restored rooms are furnished with antiques and some overlook the garden. It's an oasis of peace.

Hotel Riu Borak (☎ 306 202; zlatni-rat@bol.hr; Zlatni Rat; s/d 765/1140KN; Ⓟ ☒ ☒) This is the best deal for active holiday-makers since it is central for nearly all sporting activities. You'll have a comfortable place to relax after your windsurfing, diving or whatever. Rooms are renovated to the nth degree and deserve their four-star status.

Hotel Bonaca (☎ 306 269; zlatni-rat@bol.hr; Zlatni Rat; per person 685-835KN; Ⓟ ☒) This is an all-you-can-eat-and-do hotel that is perfect for active families. All meals and drinks are included plus tennis, biking, windsurfing and a range of kid-oriented programmes. Rooms have ceiling fans but no air-con and children under 14 are free.

Hotel Kaštil (☎ 635 995; www.kastil.hr; Riva Frane Radiča 1; s/d 610/880KN; Ⓟ ☒) If you prefer the town centre, this is an excellent alternative. Rooms have been beautifully renovated and some overlook the sea.

Elaphusa (☎ 306 200; zlatni-rat@bol.hr; Zlatni Rat; s/d from 650/990KN; Ⓟ ☒ ☐ ☒) Indoor swimming pool, plush, handsomely equipped rooms, an on-site gym and Internet café

CENTRAL DALMATIA

make this the kind of place you never have to leave – or want to.

TOP END

Hotel Ivan (☎ 640 888; www.hotel-ivan.com; David cesta 11a; s/d 575/1060KN; P ☒ ☐ ☒) In a spruced-up stone building lie sleek, modern doubles, and a number of suites with balconies. Even nicer is the full panoply of health treatments offered by the hotel including aromatherapy, a quit-smoking programme, a slimming programme, acupressure etc. They cost extra of course.

Bretanide (☎ 740 140; www.bretanide.com; Zlatni Rat; s/d from 840/1260KN; P ☒ ☒) Sitting on the hill, Bretanide is the closest to Zlatni Rat beach and also offers an all-inclusive deal with a comprehensive sport and wellness programme. Excluded are certain beauty and wellness extras but the attractiveness of the hotel and its rooms make this an excellent deal.

PRIVATE ROOMS

Boltours (p215) finds private accommodation from 110/165KN a single/double. A four-person equipped apartment costs 600KN in high season and there are other sizes available.

Eating

It would be hard to find a definitively bad meal in Bol as the restaurant scene is so competitive. Fish is always fresh; the only difference is in the subtlety of the sauces and the chef's ability and style.

Konobo Gušt (☎ 635 911; Riva Frane Radića 14; mains 48-70KN) This restaurant offers good, informal tavern-style dining in a setting of burnished wood, old photos and knick-knacks. The fish and meat dishes are prepared simply but well and you can get a plate of fried calamari with vegetables and potatoes for 65KN.

Taverna Laguna (☎ 635 692; Ante Starčevića 9; mains from 65KN) This place is in a romantic spot next to a quiet lagoon that would make the restaurant a stand-out even if the food was mediocre. The pasta and seafood dishes are far better than average.

Entertainment

Faces Club (☎ 635 410; Bračke Ceste; ☾ nightly Jun-Sep, Sat & Sun Oct-May) After strolling the harbourside promenade or the marble road to Zlatni

Rat, night owls usually head to this 2000-person disco on the road to Gorni Humac, about 1km out of town.

There are also small nightclubs at the Elaphusa and Bretanide hotels, and live entertainment on the patio of the Hotel Riu Borak.

SUMARTIN

Sumartin is a quiet, pretty port with a few rocky beaches and little to do, but it makes a nice retreat from the busier tourist centres of Bol and Supetar. The bus station is in the centre of town next to the ferry, and the tourist office, **Turističko Društo** (☎ 648 209), located right on the dock, will help you to find private accommodation if you decide to stay.

Sumartin is the entry point on Brač if you're coming from Makarska. There are two to five daily car ferries from Makarska to Sumartin and back, depending on the season. You can book at the Jadrolinija offices. Buses go from Sumartin to Supetar but only very early in the morning and late afternoon.

HVAR ISLAND

pop 11,459

Rapidly becoming the island of choice for a swanky international crowd, Hvar deserves the honour for it is the sunniest and greenest of Croatian islands. Called the 'Croatian Madeira', Hvar receives 2724 hours of sunshine each year – more than anywhere else in the country. Yet the island is luxuriantly green, with brilliant patches of lavender, rosemary and heather. The fine weather is so reliable that hotels give a discount on cloudy days and a free stay if you should ever see snow. Between the cruise ships, yachts and package tourists, the town centre can become frenzied in July and August, but there's so much to explore around the island that you won't mind escaping the town for a breather.

Part of Hvar's scenic splendour is Sveti Nikola, the crest that stretches across the middle of the island, 628m at the highest peak. The northern part of the island is defined by the fertile Velo Polje plain and a highly indented coastline dotted with coves and inlets. Most of the interior villages developed around Velo Polje, which produces grapes, olives, figs and fruit. Lavender is cultivated on the slopes of the nearby hills. Most of the original forests were cleared, leaving small groves of fir and holm oak interspersed by low shrubs and *macchia* (an oily Mediterranean brush that catches fire easily).

History

The island was first settled by the Illyrians, who fought numerous battles with Greek colonisers in the 4th century BC. The Greeks won and established the colony of Faros on the site of present-day Stari Grad. The Romans conquered the island in 219 BC but it was not an important outpost for the Romans and there are few remains from that period. With the collapse of the Roman Empire, Hvar came under Byzantine rule.

In the 7th and 8th centuries Slavic tribes settled the island, and in the 11th century it became part of Croatia under King Petar Krešimir. After several centuries in which Venice, Byzantium and Croatian-Hungarian kings ruled the island, in 1331 it opted for the most powerful of the lot – Venice – as protection against the notorious pirates of Omiš. The island staged several serious rebellions that were ruthlessly crushed by Venice's superior forces.

Getting There & Away

The Jadrolinija ferries that operate between Rijeka and Dubrovnik call at Hvar twice a week during winter and four times a week from June to early September, stopping in Stari Grad before continuing on to Korčula. The **Jadrolinija agency** (☎ 741 132; Riva) beside the landing sells tickets.

The local car ferry from Split calls at Stari Grad (32KN, 1½ hours) three times a day (five times a day in July and August). Besides the local ferries that run from Split to Stari Grad, there are connections to Italy (see p275).

There's a daily passenger boat connecting Hvar town with Split (23KN, one hour) and travelling on to Vela Luka. The boat leaves Split in the afternoon, however, making a day trip impossible.

It's possible to visit Hvar on a (hectic) day trip from Split by catching the morning Jadrolinija ferry to Stari Grad, a bus to Hvar

town, then the last ferry from Stari Grad directly back to Split.

Getting Around

Buses meet most ferries that dock at Stari Grad and go to Hvar town and Jelsa. There are six buses a day between Stari Grad and Hvar town in the summer months but services are reduced on Sunday and in low season.

If you're driving from Stari Grad to Hvar town, be aware that there are two routes: the scenic route, which is a narrow road winding through the interior mountains; and the direct route, which is a modern roadway (2960) that gets you to town rapidly.

HVAR TOWN

Within the 13th-century walls of medieval Hvar lie beautifully ornamented Gothic palaces and traffic-free marble streets. A long seaside promenade, dotted with small, rocky beaches, stretches around the harbour. A few tasteful bars and cafés along the harbour are relaxing spots for people-watching. For more activity, hop a launch to the Pakleni islands, famous for nude sunbathing.

Orientation

Hvar is such a small, easily manageable town that it doesn't even have street names. The main commercial street is the wide promenade that runs along the harbour which is where you'll find most sights. Trg Sveti Stjepana is the town square. On the northern slope above the square and within the old ramparts are the remains of some palaces that belonged to the Hvar aristocracy. Some hotels are along this stretch, while others are northwest of the town centre. From the bus station to the harbour, the town is closed to traffic; this preserves the medieval tranquillity.

Information

There's an ATM outside the Jadrolinija office.

Atlas Travel Agency (☎ 741 670) On the western side of the harbour.

Garderoba (⏱ 7am-midnight) In the bathroom next to the bus station.

Hotel Slavija (☎ 741 820; fax 741 147; Riva; per hr 20KN) You can use the Internet at this hotel.

Mengola Travel (☎ /fax 742 099; www.mengola.hr)

HVAR ISLAND

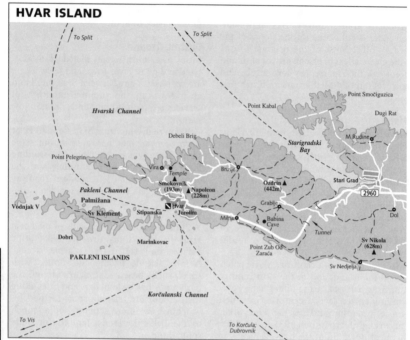

Post Office (Riva) You can make phone calls here.
Privedna Banka (Fabrika)
Splitska Banka (Riva) It changes money.
Tourist Office (☎ /fax 742 977; www.hvar.hr; ☯ 8am-1pm & 5-9pm Mon-Sat, 9am-noon Sun Jun-Sep, 8am-2pm Mon-Sat Oct-May) It's in the arsenal building on the corner of Trg Sveti Stjepana.

Sights

Don't organise your stay around the opening hours of the museums and churches as they tend to be highly irregular.

Begin your tour around town at the main square, **Trg Sveti Stjepana**, which was formed by filling in an inlet that once stretched out from the bay. At 4500 sq m, it's one of the largest old squares in Dalmatia. The town first developed in the 13th century to the north of the square and later spread south of the square in the 15th century. Notice the well at the northern end of the square which was built in 1520 and has a wrought-iron grill dating from 1780.

On the southern side of the square is the **Arsenal**, built in 1611 to replace a previous building destroyed by the Turks.

Mentioned in Venetian documents as 'the most beautiful and the most useful building in the whole of Dalmatia', the Arsenal once served as a repair and re-fitting station for war galleons. Although the 10m span of the arches now curves over souvenir shops, try to visualise the immense interior of this structure. The northern side of the building was used to store food, and in 1612 a **Renaissance theatre** was built that is reported to be the first theatre in Europe open to plebeians and aristocrats alike. The theatre remained a regional or cultural centre throughout the centuries, and plays are still staged here for small audiences only – the old building is too unstable to support crowds.

It can be entered from the adjoining **Gallery of Contemporary Croatian Art** (☎ 741 009; Arsenal; admission 10KN; ☯ 10am-noon & 7-11pm Jun-Sep, Christmas week & Holy Week, 10am-noon rest of year). The gallery has changing exhibitions of regional artists.

Another landmark building in Hvar town is the **Cathedral of St Stjepan** (Katedrala Sveti Stjepan; Trg Sveti Stjepana; ☯ twice daily, half

an hour before Mass), which forms a stunning backdrop to the square. The bell tower rises four levels, each more elaborate than the last. The cathedral was built in the 16th and 17th centuries at the height of the Dalmatian Renaissance on the site of a previous cathedral destroyed by the Turks. Parts of the older cathedral are visible in the nave and in the carved 15th-century choir stalls, but most of the interior dates from the 16th and 17th centuries.

The **Bishop's Treasury** (Riznica; ☎ 741 269; admission 10KN; ◷ 9am-noon, 5-7pm Jul & Aug, plus Christmas week & Holy Week, 10am-noon off-season), behind the tower and adjoining the cathedral, houses the cathedral treasury of silver vessels, embroidered Mass robes, numerous Madonnas, a couple of 13th-century icons and an elaborately carved sarcophagus.

Northwest of the square, you'll come first to the unfinished Gothic **Hektorović Mansion**. Go up a few stairs to the **Benedictine monastery** (☎ 741052; admission 10KN; ◷ 10am-1pm & 4-6pm Jul & Aug Christmas week & Holy Week, closed rest of year), which has a re-creation of a Renaissance house and a collection of lace

painstakingly woven by the nuns from dried agave leaves.

Next you'll see the 16th-century **loggia** in front of the Palace Hotel. In front of it is an 18th-century column **Štandarac**, from which governmental decisions used to be announced. The same road will take you to the remains of the Dominican **Church of St Marko**, which was destroyed by the Turks in the 16th century. In the apse there is a small **Archaeological Museum** (☎ 741 009; admission 10KN; ◷ 10am-noon Jun-Sep, closed rest of year), which has some Neolithic weapons and ceramics on display.

Return to the **Main Town Gate** and you'll find yourself in a network of tiny streets with small palaces, churches and old houses. Climb up through a park to the **Fortress Španjol** citadel, built on the site of a medieval castle to defend the town from the Turks. It was strengthened in 1557 and then again in the 19th century by the Austrians, who added barracks. Inside is a tiny collection of ancient amphorae recovered from the sea bed, and the view over the harbour is magnificent.

Returning to town, proceed south along the harbour to the 15th-century **Franciscan monastery and museum** (☎ 741 193; admission 10KN; ◷ 10am-noon & 5-7pm daily Jun-Sep, Christmas week & Holy Week, closed rest of year), which overlooks a shady cove. The elegant bell tower was built in the 16th century by a well-known family of stonemasons from Korčula. The Renaissance cloister leads to a refectory containing lace, coins, nautical charts and valuable documents, such as an edition of Ptolemy's *Atlas*, printed in 1524. Your eye will immediately be struck by *The Last Supper*, an 8m by 2.5m work by the Venetian Matteo Ingoli dating from the end of the 16th century. The cypress in the cloister garden is said to be more than 300 years old. The adjoining church, named Our Lady of Charity, contains more fine paintings such as the three polyptychs created by Francesco da Santacroce in 1583, which represent the summit of this painter's work, and the *Cruxifixion* by Leandro Bassano on the altar. Below the altar is the tomb of Hannibal Lucić, 16th-century author of *Female Slave*, the first nonreligious drama in Croatia. The Renaissance relief over the portal, *Madonna with Child*, is a small gem created by Nikola Firentinac in 1470.

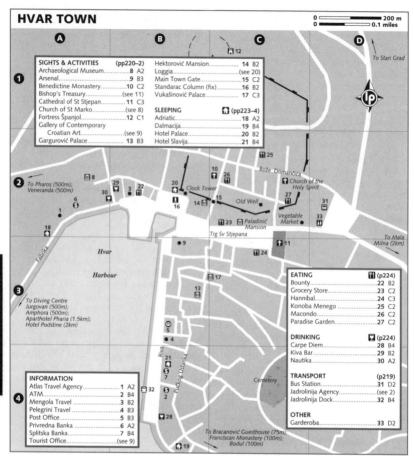

HVAR TOWN

0   200 m
0   0.1 miles

SIGHTS & ACTIVITIES (pp220–2)
Archaeological Museum.............**8** A2
Arsenal..............................**9** B3
Benedictine Monastery.........**10** C2
Bishop's Treasury................(see 11)
Cathedral of St Stjepan.........**11** C3
Church of St Marko...............(see 8)
Fortress Španjol.................**12** C1
Gallery of Contemporary
   Croatian Art....................(see 9)
Gargurović Palace................**13** B3

Hektorović Mansion................**14** B2
Loggia.............................(see 20)
Main Town Gate...................**15** C2
Standarac Column (fix)...........**16** B2
Vukašinović Palace...............**17** C3

SLEEPING   (pp223–4)
Adriatic...........................**18** A2
Dalmacija.........................**19** B4
Hotel Palace.....................**20** B2
Hotel Slavija....................**21** B4

EATING   (p224)
Bounty..............................**22** B2
Grocery Store.....................**23** C2
Hannibal...........................**24** C3
Konoba Menego...................**25** C2
Macondo...........................**26** C2
Paradise Garden..................**27** C2

DRINKING   (p224)
Carpe Diem........................**28** B4
Kiva Bar............................**29** B2
Nautika............................**30** A2

TRANSPORT   (p219)
Bus Station........................**31** D2
Jadrolinija Agency...............(see 2)
Jadrolinija Dock..................**32** B4

OTHER
Garderoba.........................**33** D2

INFORMATION
Atlas Travel Agency...............**1** A2
ATM.................................**2** B4
Mengola Travel **3** B2
Pelegrini Travel **4** B3
Post Office.........................**5** B3
Privredna Banka...................**6** A2
Splitska Banka....................**7** B4
Tourist Office....................(see 9)

To Stari Grad

Bože Domančića

Church of the
Holy Spirit

Clock Tower

Old Well

Vegetable
Market

Paladinić
Mansion

Trg Sv Stjepana

To Mala
Milna (2km)

Hvar

Harbour

To Pharos (500m);
Veneranda (500m)

To Diving Centre
Jurgovan (500m);
Amphora (500m);
Aparthotel Pharia (1.5km);
Hotel Podstine (2km)

Riva

Pučka Ulica

Fabrika

Cemetery

To Bracanović Guesthouse (75m);
Franciscan Monastery (100m);
Bodul (100m)

As you return north, stroll through the old streets and notice the **Vukašinović Palace** with its seven balconies and monumental entrance, and the 15th-century **Gargurović Palace**.

Activities

In front of the Hotel Amphora, **Diving Centar Jurgovan** (☎ 742 490; www.divecenter-hvar.com) is a large operation that offers a certification course, dives (from 190KN) and all sorts of water sports (banana boating, snorkelling, water-skiing), as well as hotel packages. It also offers mountain bikes for 55KN a day or 250KN a week. You can also rent bikes at Mengola Travel for 60KN per day or a motorboat for 350KN per day.

There are coves around the Amphora and the Dalmacija Hotels for **swimming**, but most people head to the **Pakleni Islands** (Pakleni Otoci) which got their name from Paklina, the resin that once coated boats and ships. Taxi boats leave regularly during the high season from in front of the Arsenal to the islands of Jerolim and Stipanska, which are popular naturist islands (although nudity is not mandatory) and then continue on to Zdrilca and Palmižana. The cost is 15KN.

Tours

Atlas Travel Agency organises a city tour for 105KN, Biševo–Vis Island hydrofoils for 385KN, a fish picnic for 240KN and an island tour for 170KN. It also runs an 8km walking tour (280KN) that involves a bus to Veliko Grablje, a walk to Malo Grablje and then on to Milna for lunch.

Sleeping

As one of the Adriatic's most popular resorts, don't expect any bargains in the summer. You'll be lucky to get a room at all. The prices below are based upon a one-night stay from mid-July to August. Since the town centre is closed to traffic, you must either carry your luggage yourself or telephone in advance to arrange for a porter. Most hotels are closed from October to May, but usually either the Palace Hotel or the Slavija remains open all year. The hotels listed here are owned by the **Sunčani Hvar company** (☎ 741 956; www.suncanihvar.hr). Mala Milna is the only camping ground near town. If it's full, head to Jelsa.

BUDGET

Jagoda & Ante Bracanović Guesthouse (☎ 741 416, 091 520 3796; virgilye@yahoo.com; Poviše Škole; s 100-120KN; d 190-220KN) The Bracanović family has turned a traditional stone building into a small *pension*. Rooms come with balconies, private bathrooms and access to a kitchen, and the family goes out of their way for guests. The *pension* is hard to find, but Jagoda or Ante will meet you wherever you are if you call.

Mala Milna (☎ 745 027; per adult/site 28/35KN; May-Sep) The closest camping ground to town is this site, 2km southeast of town, which is small but beautifully situated on Milna Bay. It's best if you have your own wheels as there are few buses.

MID-RANGE

Aparthotel Pharia (☎ 778 080; www.orvas-hotels .com; Majerovica bb; s/d 385/610KN, apt from 830KN; P) This new complex is only 50m from the water in a quiet neighbourhood slightly west of the town centre. All the rooms and apartments have balconies, some with views over the water. For a small hotel, you couldn't do better.

Hotel Slavija (☎ 741 820; fax 741 147; Riva; s/d 533/840KN;) The great thing here is that you step off the passenger boat from Split and into hotel reception. Rooms are perfectly acceptable without being exceptional in any way and the terrace-restaurant is great for people-watching on balmy summer nights.

Dalmacija (☎ /fax 741 120; s/d 445/670KN) On a quiet cove near the harbour, this place has simple rooms, some overlooking the sea.

Pharos (☎ /fax 741 028; s/d 533/840KN; P) Overlooking the town, Pharos is above the disco Veneranda (think about that), but it does have an outdoor swimming pool.

Bodul (☎ /fax 741 744; s/d 513/800KN) This unattractive hotel is another package-tour favourite, but with 300 beds, it may have space when other hotels are full.

TOP END

Hotel Palace (☎ 741 966; fax 742 420; s/d from 565/915KN;) Prices here depend on size and location of room. With more character than any of the modern hotels, this hotel was built at the turn of the 20th century on the site of the Ducal Palace and is behind an elegant 16th-century loggia. Its luxuries include a heated indoor swimming pool and a sauna, but no air-con.

Amphora (☎ 741 202; fax 741 711; s/d from 560/845KN; P) Located around the cove, this is the best-equipped hotel in Hvar. There's an indoor swimming pool, sauna, private beach and gym, but the architecture and décor are less than captivating.

Hotel Podstine (☎ 741 118; www.podstine.com; s/d 659/1147KN;) Just 2km southwest of the town centre on the secluded Podstine cove lies this beautifully restored and romantic hotel with its own private beach. The landscaping and décor are stylish and you can rent a bike, scooter or motorboat to facilitate your trips back and forth to town.

Adriatic (☎ /fax 741 024; s/d 745/1245KN; P) The Adriatic is well located on the western side of the harbour near swimming areas and has adequate rooms, some of which overlook the sea. An all-inclusive arrangement is mandatory from June to September. The rest of the year, prices are about 50% less and you can still take advantage of the heated indoor swimming pool.

PRIVATE ROOMS

Accommodation in Hvar is extremely tight in July and August. A reservation is highly recommended. For private accommodation, try **Mengola Travel** (☎ /fax 742 099; www .mengola.hr) or **Pelegrini Travel** (☎ /fax 742 250; kuzma.novak@st.htnet.hr). Expect to pay from 160/280KN per single/double with private bathroom in the town centre. Outside the high season you can negotiate a much better price.

Eating

The pizzerias along the harbour offer the most predictable inexpensive eating. The following restaurants are open for lunch and dinner, but not in between.

Bounty (☎ 742 565; mains from 40KN) For a step up try this place next to Mengola Travel, which has good-quality fish, pasta and grilled meat at prices that won't dent your budget.

Konoba Menego (☎ 742 036; mains from 40KN) On the stairway above the Church of the Holy Spirit on a steep street, this is also a wonderful choice. Marinated meats, cheeses and vegetables are prepared the old-fashioned Dalmatian way and the menu is rounded out by aromatic fisherman's platters.

Hannibal (☎ 098-231 808; Trg Sveti Stjepana; mains from 55KN) Hannibal has a good selection of pasta cooked with shrimp, lobster, fish or mushrooms and also does grilled meat and fish dishes. You can either eat at a table on the square or in the spacious interior.

Paradise Garden (☎ 741 310; mains 55-75KN) This eatery, up some stairs on the northern side of the cathedral, serves up a memorable spaghetti with seafood, as well as the usual excellent assortment of grilled or fried fish. You will dine outdoors on an enclosed patio.

Macondo (☎ 741 851; mains from 80KN) In a narrow alley over the main square, this is slightly more expensive than the other restaurants but slightly better. The cold mixed plate offers two fish pâtés, octopus salad and salted anchovies which make a tasty opening to the main meal (fish specialities) or a good light meal.

The **grocery store** (Trg Sveti Stjepana) is your best alternative to a restaurant, and there are benches in front of the harbour just made for picnics, or you can pick up snack supplies at the vegetable market.

Drinking

Hvar has some of the best nightlife on the Adriatic coast, mostly centred around the harbour.

Carpe Diem (☎ 742 369; Riva) From a groggy breakfast to late-night cocktails, there is no time of day when this swanky place is dull. The music is smooth, the drinks fruity and expensive and the sofas cushiony.

Nautika (Fabrika) With cocktails called 'Sex on the Beach' and nonstop dance music – ranging from techno to hip-hop – this place is ground zero for Hvar's explosive nightlife.

Kiva Bar (Fabrika) Just up the street, this is the place to chill out and talk between dance numbers.

Entertainment

On summer evenings there's live music and dancing on **Hotel Slavija's** (☎ 741 820; Riva) terrace.

A former fortress on the slope above Hotel Delfin, **Veneranda** (☉ cinema 9.30pm) becomes an open-air cinema in summer and then a disco later on. Raves are sometimes organised.

Shopping

Lavender, lavender and more lavender is sold in small bottles, large bottles, flasks or made into sachets. Depending on the time of year, there will be anywhere from one to 50 stalls along the harbour selling the substance, its odour saturating the air. Various herbal oils, potions, skin creams and salves are also hawked. Prices run anywhere from 10KN to 50KN depending on the size of the bottle.

STARI GRAD

Stari Grad (Old Town), on the island's northern coast, is older than Hvar town and is certainly attractive, though it can't compete with the stylish architecture and stunning setting of its more fashionable sister.

Although most ferries connecting the island to the mainland list Stari Grad as their port of call, in fact the town is a couple of kilometres northeast of the ferry dock and, since buses connect the ferries to Hvar town and Jelsa, Stari Grad can easily be bypassed. There are some worthwhile sights in the town however, and when Hvar town is wall-to-wall with vacationers, Stari Grad provides a little more breathing room.

Road signs around Stari Grad note a secondary name – 'Faros' – a reference to the Greek colony that was founded here in 385 BC. The local population resisted Greek rule but the Greek navy from Issa (present-day Vis) defeated the islanders in one of the oldest historically confirmed naval battles.

The Romans ousted the Greeks in 219 BC, and razed the town. Later, Slavs settled it and it became the political and cultural capital of the island until 1278, when the bishopric moved to Hvar town.

The town occupied itself with navigation and shipbuilding, and in the 16th century the poet Petar Hektorović built a mansion here which has become the highlight of a visit to Stari Grad.

Orientation & Information

Stari Grad lies along a horseshoe-shaped bay with the old quarter on the southern side of the horseshoe. The bus station (no left-luggage office) is at the foot of the bay and the northern side is taken up by residences, a small pine wood and the sprawling Helios hotel complex.

The **Tourist Office** (☎ /fax 765 763; tzg-stari -grad@st.htnet.hr; Obala Zrinskhi Frankopana; ☾ 8am-10pm mid-Jun–mid-Sep, 8am-2pm Mon-Fri mid-Sep–mid-Jun) distributes a good map, the **post office** (Trg Tvrdalj) is on the main square and there are ATMs at **Splitska Banka** (Riva 12) and outside the tourist office.

Sights

Tvrdalj (☎ 765 068; Trg Tvrdalj; admission 10KN; ☾ 10am-noon Jun-Sep) is Petar Hektorović's 16th-century fortified castle. The leafy fish pond reflects the poet's love for fish and fishermen. His poem *Fishing and Fishermen's Chat* (1555) paints an enticing portrait of his favourite pastime. The castle also contains quotes from the poet's work inscribed on the walls in Latin and Croatian.

Another highlight of Stari Grad is the old **Dominican monastery** (Dominikanski Samostan; admission 10KN; ☾ 10am-noon & 6-8pm Jun-Sep), which was founded in 1482, damaged by the Turks in 1571 and later fortified with a tower. In addition to the library and archaeological findings in the monastery museum, there is a 19th-century church with *The Interment of Christ* attributed to Tintoretto, and two paintings by Gianbattista Crespi.

Sleeping

Helios (☎ 765 555; fax 765 128; s/d 385/520KN; ℗) This modern hotel is part of a complex that has commandeered the northern wing of

the town. Other hotels in the complex are the Arkada and the Adriatic.

Kamp Jurjevac (☎ 765 843; Predraga Bogdanica; per adult/site 30/52KN; ☾ Jun-Sep) This is near swimming coves off the harbour just east of the old town.

The only agency finding private accommodation is **Mistraltours** (☎ /fax 765 281; Grofa Vranjicanija 2), near the bus station, which will find singles/doubles with private facilities for 130/220KN in July and August.

JELSA

Jelsa is a small town, port and resort 27km east of Hvar town surrounded by thick pine forests and high poplars. Although it lacks the Renaissance buildings of Hvar, the intimate streets and squares are still pleasant and the town is within easy reach of swimming coves and sand beaches. Hotel accommodation is cheaper than in Hvar town and there are two camping grounds outside town.

Jelsa emerged in the 14th century as a port for the inland village of Pitve and spread around the churches of Sts Fabian and Sebastian and St John in the Field. In the 16th century a fort was erected over the town to protect it from the Turks and by the 19th century Jelsa had grown into a prosperous fishing village.

In the middle of the 19th century the marshes around the coast were drained and the town gradually spread out. In 1868 the public library became the first public reading room in the Dalmatian islands, and in 1881 it became the centre of Matica Hrvatska, a celebrated Croatian literary circle.

Like most coastal villages, fishing has now given way to tourism, and the town has become a popular alternative to Hvar.

Orientation & Information

Jelsa is wrapped around a bay with several large hotels on each side and the old town at the foot of the harbour. A promenade stretches from the west end of the bay and rises up the hill on the eastern side leading to a sandy cove. The bus station is on the edge of the main road leading into town (no-one bothers with street names). As you proceed into town you'll come to the post office.

You can change money at any travel agency and there's an ATM at Privredna

Banka on the main square. **Splitska Banka** (Trg Tome Gamulina) is on the eastern side of the harbour. At the harbour you'll find **Atlas Travel Agency** (☎ 761 038; Obala bb). **Turistička Zajednica** (☎ /fax 761 017; www.jelsa-online.com; Obala bb. ⏰ 7.30am-noon & 6.30-8.30pm Mon-Sat, 9am-noon Sun) is across the street from Atlas and along the quay.

Sights & Activities

If you get to the **Church of Sts Fabian and Sebastian** (Crkva Sv Fabijana i Sebastijana; ⏰ Mass only) 30 minutes before the service, you can see a 17th-century baroque altar by wood carver Antonio Porri and a wooden statue of the Virgin Mary brought by refugees from the village of Čitluk, near Sinj, who were fleeing the Turks in the 16th century.

In addition to the sand beach near the Hotel Mina, there is a daily taxi boat to the naturist beaches of Zečevo and Glavice (25KN), or you can rent wheels and head across the hill to the coves surrounding the village of Zavala. The hair-raising road is superbly scenic and takes you through the tiny village of Pitve, before descending to a number of isolated coves.

The **Island Tours agency** (☎ 761 404) on the road to Mina rents scooters for 240KN a day and motorcycles for 300KN a day.

For scuba diving, the place to go to is **Dive Centre Jelsa** (☎ /fax 761 822; Hotel Jadran; 1/2 boat dives excl equipment 122/245KN).

Tours

Atlas Travel Agency offers more or less the same programme as in Hvar town but the prices sometimes differ.

Sleeping

Grebišće (☎ 761 191; Uvala Grebišće; per adult/site 42/32KN; ⏰ Apr-Sep) A camping ground 5km east of the Hotel Mina, Grebišće has access to a beach.

Hotel Mina Campground (☎ /fax 761 210; Gradine; per adult/site 28/26KN; ⏰ Apr-Sep) This is another camping ground near Hotel Mina with access to a beach.

Pansion Murvica (☎ /fax 761 405; pansion-murvica@ st.htnet.hr; per person without/with breakfast 120/175KN) This lovely little *pension* is on a side street that runs parallel to the main road leading into town. The comfortable studios are attractively decorated and the shady terrace restaurant serves up delicious meals.

Hotel Jadran (☎ 761 026; s/d incl breakfast 325/550KN) This is one of three bland hotel-resorts around Jelsa, all of which have the same prices and similar rather basic facilities. Of the three, this is closest to the town centre.

Book through **Hoteli Jelsa** (☎ 761 182; www .hoteli-jelsa.hr) for the Hotel Jadran, the Hotel Fontana (further north with a swimming pool), and the Hotel Mina (east of town with both indoor and outdoor swimming pools).

Atlas Travel Agency finds private rooms for 100KN per person in high season.

Southern Dalmatia

The southeastern tip of Croatia is a lush region of coves, forested islands and, its crowning jewel, the walled city of Dubrovnik. Off the rocky shores lies the large island of Korčula and a flurry of smaller islands, including the idyllic national park on Mljet Island. Together with the mountainous Pelješac Peninsula, the entire area comprises Dubrovnik–Neretva county. Steeped in sunshine and bathed in mild Mediterranean breezes, the coastal belt stretches from Ploče in the north to the Montenegrin border, and is separated from Bosnia and Hercegovina by the Dinaric Range. With the exception of Korčula Island, the county largely follows the borders of the former independent Republic of Ragusa (Dubrovnik).

Refreshingly free of heavy industry, the inhabitants rely on agriculture and tourism. The region is famous for its wines, especially the Postup and Dingač red wines of Pelješac, and the Posip and Grk white wines of Korčula. The seafood of Ston is legendary throughout Croatia. Even with its wine, olive oil and seafood production, tourism is becoming the main focus of economic activity, spearheaded by the international appeal of Dubrovnik.

The lure of Dubrovnik has given a boost to the entire region as hotels spread outward from the walled city, creating a 'Dubrovnik Riviera'. Unlike other parts of the Adriatic coast, however, there are no mega-resorts here and no sprawling tourist settlements – which has discouraged mass tourism but makes individual travel especially rewarding.

SOUTHERN DALMATIA

HIGHLIGHTS

- Examining the roofs of **Dubrovnik** (p229) from a walk around its walls
- Sipping a cappuccino at a café on **Dubrovnik's Placa** (p229)
- Biking around the lakes of **Mljet Island** (p242)
- Watching the moreška sword dance in **Korčula** (p247)
- Lazing on the beaches of **Orebić** (p253)
- Taking an island tour of **Korčula** (p247)
- Sampling seafood in **Ston** (p254)

- TELEPHONE CODE: 020
- POSTCODE: 20000

DUBROVNIK

pop 45,800

Only a handful of the world's cities can claim to represent an ideal larger than themselves and Dubrovnik is one of them. The thick stone walls, which have protected the city for seven centuries against assault, proclaim invincibility in the face of aggression. The wide marble street, Placa, lined with businesses, cafés, churches and palaces, encourages the fusion of commerce, pleasure and faith into a vibrant community life. The profusion of fine sculpture and architectural detail on public buildings and monuments underscores a common artistic heritage available to anyone who cares to look. The way in which the towering walls both define and blend into the landscape of sea, sky and hills is an argument for a human presence that enhances rather than spoils the environment.

Although the shelling of Dubrovnik in 1991 shocked the world, the city has bounced back vigourously from those dark days. The blasted-apart streets and damaged buildings were patiently mended while international funds poured in to start the painstaking work of re-sculpting its fine monuments. Replacing the distinctive honey-coloured roofs with matching tiles was extremely problematic however, and you'll notice a patchwork of colours as you walk around the city walls (see Dubrovnik: Destruction & Reconstruction on p234). The tourism industry which declined precipitously in the early 1990s is now booming, especially in the summer months when cruise ships deposit thousands of passengers at the city gates. Now Dubrovnik faces another challenge: how to retain a sense of itself as a living community and avoid becoming an Adriatic theme park. With centuries of experience protecting its commercial and political interests, Dubrovnik has so far managed to welcome tourists and maintain its unique cultural and spiritual heritage.

History

The story of Dubrovnik begins with the 7th-century onslaught of barbarians that wiped out the Roman city of Epidaurum (site of present-day Cavtat). The residents fled to the safest place they could find, which was a rocky islet separated from the mainland by a narrow channel.

Recent excavations reveal that the islet was probably inhabited at the time but the new settlers increased the population and named their new sanctuary Laus, Greek for 'rock'. Eventually it became known as Rausa, Ragusa and Ragusium. This inaccessible settlement was located around the southern walls of present-day Dubrovnik.

Building walls was a matter of pressing urgency at the time, when barbarian invasions were a constant threat; it appears that the city was well fortified by the 9th century when it resisted a Saracen siege for 15 months.

The town had help in the form of the powerful Byzantine Empire, however, under whose protection Ragusa remained from the 7th to the 12th century. Meanwhile, another settlement emerged on the mainland, stretching from Zaton in the north to Cavtat in the south. This settlement became known as Dubrovnik, named after the *dubrava* (holm-oak) that carpeted the region. The two settlements merged in the 12th century, and the channel that separated them was paved over to become Placa.

By the end of the 12th century Dubrovnik had become an important trading centre on the coast, providing an important link between the Mediterranean and Balkan states. From the hinterlands, cattle and dairy products, wax, honey, timber, coal, silver, lead, copper and slaves were exported, along with Dubrovnik products such as salt, cloth, wine, oil and fish.

As the city grew increasingly prosperous it posed a threat to the other major commercial interest in the Adriatic – Venice. Dubrovnik came under Venetian authority in 1205 and remained under its control for 150 years. Despite accepting governance from Venice, the city continued to establish its own independent commercial relations and finally broke away from Venetian control in 1358. Although the city thereafter acknowledged the authority of the Croatian-Hungarian kings and paid them tribute, it was largely left alone to do what it did best – make money.

By the 15th century 'Respublica Ragusina' (the Republic of Ragusa) had extended its borders to include the entire coastal belt from Ston to Cavtat, having previously acquired Lastovo Island, the Pelješac Peninsula and Mljet Island. It was now a

SOUTHERN DALMATIA

SOUTHERN DALMATIA

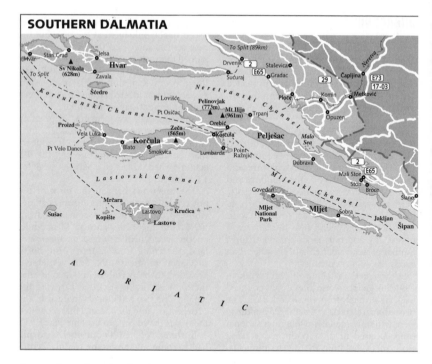

force to be reckoned with. The city turned towards sea trade and established a fleet of its own ships which were dispatched to Egypt, Syria, Sicily, Spain, France and later Turkey. Through canny diplomacy the city maintained good relations with everyone – even the Ottoman Empire, to which Dubrovnik began paying tribute in the 16th century.

Centuries of peace and prosperity allowed art, science and literature to flourish. Marin Držić (1508–67) was a towering figure in Renaissance literature, best known for his comic play *Dundo Maroje*. Ivan Gundulić (1589–1639) was another Dubrovnik poet/dramatist whose greatest work was the epic *Osman*. To the world of science, Dubrovnik gave Ruđer Bošković (1711–87), who produced a seminal work in the field of theoretical physics as well as numerous tomes on optics, geography, trigonometry and astronomy. Composers, poets, philosophers and painters turned Dubrovnik into a major cultural centre on the Adriatic.

Tragically, most of Dubrovnik's Renaissance art and architecture were destroyed in the earthquake of 1667 which killed 5000 people and left the city in ruins. Only the Sponza Palace and the Rector's Palace survived to give an idea of what Renaissance Dubrovnik must have looked like. The city was rebuilt in a uniform baroque style with modest dwellings in rows and shops on the ground floor. The earthquake also marked the beginning of the economic decline of the town, accentuated by the opening of new trade routes to the east and the emergence of rival naval powers in Western Europe.

The final *coup de grace* was dealt by Napoleon whose troops entered Dubrovnik in 1806 and announced the end of the republic. The Vienna Congress of 1815 ceded Dubrovnik to Austria, where the city maintained its shipping but succumbed to social disintegration. It remained a part of the Austro-Hungarian empire until 1918 and then slowly began to develop its tourist industry.

Like Venice, Dubrovnik's fortunes now depend upon tourism. Stari Grad, the perfectly preserved old town, is unique for its marble-paved squares, steep cobbled

streets, tall houses, convents, churches, palaces, fountains and museums, all cut from the same light-coloured stone. The intact city walls keep motorists at bay and Dubrovnik's renowned Summer Festival has re-established the city's position as a coastal cultural centre.

Orientation

The city extends about 6km from the mouth of the Rijeka River in the west to the cape of Sveti Jakov in the east and includes the promontory of Lapad. This leafy residential suburb with rocky beaches contains the hostel and most of the town's hotels. The old walled town lies southeast of Lapad at the foot of Srd Hill halfway between Gruž Harbour and the cape of Sveti Jakov. The entire old town is closed to cars and is divided nearly in half by the wide street Placa, also referred to as Stradun. There are no hotels in the old town but plenty of restaurants.

Pile Gate is the western entrance to the old town and the last stop for local buses from Lapad and Gruž. The eastern gate is Ploče, which leads to several luxury hotels along Frana Supila. The Jadrolinija ferry terminal and the bus station are a few hundred metres apart at Gruž, which is about 2km northwest of the old town. To get to the old town from the bus station, go down Put Republike to Dr. Ante Starčevića and follow it to Pile Gate. Take any bus except No 7.

The city boundaries also include the Elafiti Islands (Šipan, Lopud, Koločep, Olipe, Tajan and Jakljan).

Information

BOOKSHOPS
Algoritam (Map p236; Placa) Has a good selection of English-language books, including guidebooks.

INTERNET ACCESS
Dubrovnik Internet Centar (Map pp232-3; ☎ 311 017; Starčevića 7; per hr 20KN; ☾ 9am-9pm)
DU Club Net (Map pp232-3; ☎ 356 894; Put Republike 7; per hr 20KN; ☾ 10am-10pm)

LEFT LUGGAGE
Garderoba (Map pp232-3; ☾ 5.30am-9pm) At the bus station.

MONEY
You can change money at any travel agency or post office. There are numerous ATMs in town and near the ferry terminal.
Dubrovačka Banka (Map pp232-3; Put Republike 9) It's the closest ATM to the bus station.

POST
Branch Post Office (Map pp232-3; Ante Starčevića 2)
Lapad Post Office & Telephone Centre (Map pp232-3; Krajla Zvonimira 21)
Main Post Office (Map p236; cnr Široka & Od Puča) In the old town.

TOURIST INFORMATION
Atlantagent (Map pp232-3; ☎ 419 044; Stjepana Radića 26; ☾ 10am-4pm) Tickets for boats to Mljet and Elafiti Islands.
Tourist Information Centar (Map p236; ☎ 323 350; fax 323 351; Placa 1) Located across from the Franciscan monastery in the old town, it's privately run and moderately helpful.
Turistička Zajednica (www.tzdubrovnik.hr); Harbour (Map pp232-3; ☎ 417 983; Gruška obala bb); Old town (Map pp232-3; ☎ 323 587; Miha Pracata bb); Pile Gate (Map p236; ☎ 427 591; Starčevića 7; ☾ 8am-8pm Mon-Sat, 9am-noon Sun Jun-Sep, 9am-7pm Mon-Fri, 9am-1pm Sat Oct-May)

DUBROVNIK

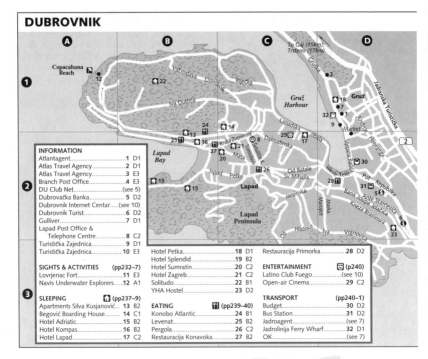

INFORMATION
Atlantagent.................................**1** D1	
Atlas Travel Agency..................**2** D1	
Atlas Travel Agency..................**3** E3	
Branch Post Office....................**4** E3	
DU Club Net...........................(see 5)	
Dubrovačka Banka....................**5** D2	
Dubrovnik Internet Centar.....(see 10)	
Dubrovnik Turist.......................**6** D2	
Gulliver.....................................**7** D1	
Lapad Post Office &	
Telephone Centre.................**8** C2	
Turistička Zajednica..................**9** D1	
Turistička Zajednica................**10** E3	

SIGHTS & ACTIVITIES (pp232–7)
Lovrjenac Fort.........................**11** E3
Navis Underwater Explorers.....**12** A1

SLEEPING (pp237–9)
Apartments Silva Kusjanović....**13** B2
Begović Boarding House..........**14** C1
Hotel Adriatic..........................**15** B2
Hotel Kompas..........................**16** B2
Hotel Lapad............................**17** C2

Hotel Petka.............................**18** D1
Hotel Splendid.........................**19** B2
Hotel Sumratin........................**20** C2
Hotel Zagreb...........................**21** C2
Solitudo..................................**22** A1
YHA Hostel.............................**23** D2

EATING (pp239–40)
Konobo Atlantic......................**24** B1
Levenat...................................**25** B2
Pergola...................................**26** C2
Restauracija Konavoka.............**27** B2

Restauracija Primorka..............**28** D2

ENTERTAINMENT (p240)
Latino Club Fuego..................(see 10)
Open-air Cinema......................**29** C2

TRANSPORT (pp240–1)
Budget....................................**30** D2
Bus Station..............................**31** D2
Jadroagent..............................(see 7)
Jadrolinija Ferry Wharf.............**32** D1
OK...(see 7)

TRAVEL AGENCIES

Atlas Travel Agency Sv Đurđa 1 (Map pp232-3; ☎ 442 574); Lučarica 1 (Map p236; ☎ 323 609); Gruška obala (Map pp232-3; ☎ 418 001) In convenient locations at the harbour, in the old town and outside Pile Gate, Atlas is extremely helpful for general information as well as finding private accommodation. All excursions are run by Atlas.

Dubrovnik Turist (Map pp232-3; ☎ 356 959; dubrovnikturist@net.hr; Put Republike 7) Closest to the bus station, it finds private accommodation, rents cars etc.

Gulliver (Map pp232-3; ☎ 313 300; fax 419 119; Radića 32) Near the Jadrolinija dock, it finds private accommodation, changes money and rents cars and scooters.

Sights

You'll probably begin your visit at the city bus stop outside **Pile Gate** (Map p236) which dates from 1537. Notice the statue of St Blaise, the city's patron saint, set in a niche over the Renaissance arch. Originally, the drawbridge at the gate's entrance was lifted every evening, the gate was closed and the key handed to the prince.

As you pass through the outer gate you come to an inner gate dating from 1460, and then Placa, Dubrovnik's wonderful pedestrian promenade. In front of you is the **Onofrio Fountain** (Map p236), one of Dubrovnik's most famous landmarks. It was built in 1438 as part of a water-supply system that involved bringing water from a well 12km away. Originally the fountain was adorned with sculpture but it was heavily damaged in the 1667 earthquake and only 16 carved masks remain with water jets gushing from their mouths into a drainage pool.

On the left is lovely **St Saviour Church** (Map p236; Crkva Sveti Spasa; Placa; ♥ for occasional exhibitions & concerts), which was built between 1520 and 1528 and was one of the few buildings to have survived the earthquake of 1667.

Next to St Saviour Church is the **Franciscan monastery and museum** (Map p236; Muzej Franjevačkog Samostana; ☎ 426 345; Placa 2; adult/concession 10/5KN; ♥ 9am-6pm). Over the door of the monastery church is a remarkable *Pietà* sculpted by the local masters, Petar and Leonard Andrijić, in 1498. Unfortunately, the portal is all that remains of the richly decorated church that was destroyed in the 1667 earthquake.

Inside the monastery complex is the mid-14th century **cloister**, one of the most

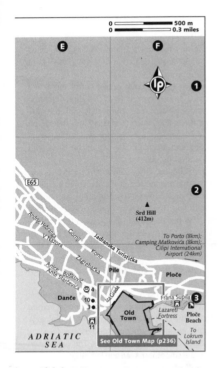

0 — 500 m
0 — 0.3 miles

E **F**

1

2

E65

▲ Srd Hill (412m)

To Porto (8km);
Camping Matkovića (8km);
Čilipi International
Airport (24km)

Andre Hebranga
Gornji
V. Nazora
Jadranska Turistička
Komo
Zagrebačka
Anice Bošković
Ante Starčevića
Pile
Ploče
Frana Supila **3**

Danče 10
3
11

Stradun
Lazareti
Fortress
Old Town
Lazareti
Ploče
Beach
To Lokrum Island

*ADRIATIC
SEA*

See Old Town Map (p236)

---

beautiful late-Romanesque structures in Dalmatia. Notice how each capital over the dual columns is topped by a different figure, portraying human heads, animals and floral arrangements.

Further inside you'll find the third-oldest functioning pharmacy in Europe, which has been in business since 1391. The pharmacy may well be the first pharmacy in Europe open to the general public. Before leaving, visit the monastery museum with its collection of relics, liturgical objects, paintings, gold work and pharmacy items such as laboratory gear and medical books. The **church** (Map p236; ☑ 7am-7pm) has recently undergone a long and expensive restoration to startling effect.

As you proceed down Placa you may wish to make a detour up Nikole Božidarevića to Od Puča, site of a **Serbian Orthodox Church** (Map p236; Muzej Pravoslavne Crkve; ☎ 426 260; Od Puča 8; adult/concession 10/5KN; ☑ 9am-1pm Mon-Sat) dating from 1877, which contains a fascinating collection of icons dating from the 15th to the 19th century. In addition to portraits of the biblical family originating in Crete, Italy, Russia and

Slovenia there are several portraits by the illustrious Croatian painter Vlaho Bukovac.

Proceed up to Žudioska to visit the city's 15th-century **synagogue** (Map p236; Sinagoga; ☎ 412 219; Žudioska 5; admission free; ☑ 9am-1pm Mon-Fri), which is the oldest Sephardic and the second-oldest synagogue in Europe.

At its eastern end Placa widens into Luža Sq, formerly used as a market place. The **Orlando Column** (Roland's Column; Map p236) is a popular meeting place and used to be the place where edicts, festivities and public verdicts were announced. Carved in 1417, the forearm of this medieval knight was the official linear measure of the Republic – the ell of Dubrovnik, which measures 51.1cm.

The **Clock Tower** (Map p236) dominates the square and makes an elegant punctuation point at the end of Placa. First built in 1444, it was restored many times, most recently in 1929, and is notable for the two bronze figures in the bell tower that ring out the hours.

Across the square is the 16th-century **Sponza Palace** (Map p236) which was originally a Customs House, then a minting house, a State treasury and a bank. Now it houses the **State Archives** (Državni Arhiv u Dubrovniku; ☎ 321 032; admission free; ☑ 8am-3pm Mon-Fri, 8am-1pm Sat) which contains a priceless collection of manuscripts dating back nearly a thousand years. This superb structure is a mixture of Gothic and Renaissance styles beginning with an exquisite Renaissance portico resting on six columns. The 1st floor has late-Gothic windows and the 2nd-floor windows are in a Renaissance style, with an alcove containing a statue of St Vlaho. The interior follows a complex, harmonious plan but cannot be visited.

Crossing the square you'll pass **Little Onofrio's Fountain** (Map p236), part of the same water project as its larger cousin to the west but built to supply water to the market place on Luža Square. In front of you is the imposing **St Blaise's Church** (Map p236; Crkva Sveti Vlaha; Luža Square; ☑ morning & late-afternoon Mass Mon-Sat), built in 1715 to replace an earlier church destroyed in the earthquake. Built in a baroque style following the church of St Mauritius in Venice, the ornate exterior contrasts strongly with the sober residences surrounding it. The interior is notable for its marble altars and a 15th-century silver

DUBROVNIK: DESTRUCTION & RECONSTRUCTION

Caught in the cross hairs of the civil war that ravaged former Yugoslavia, Dubrovnik was pummelled with some 2000 shells in 1991 and 1992. When the smoke finally cleared in June 1992, the extent of the damage was severe.

Shells struck 68% of the 824 buildings in the old town, leaving holes in two out of three tiled roofs. Building façades and the paving stones of streets and squares suffered 314 direct hits and there were 111 direct hits on the great wall. Nine historic palaces were completely gutted by fire while the Sponza Palace, Rector's Palace, St Blaise's Church, Franciscan monastery and the carved fountains, Amerling and Onofrio, sustained serious damage. The total damage was estimated at US$10 million. It was quickly decided that the repairs and reconstruction would be done with traditional techniques, using traditional materials whenever feasible.

One of the first and most urgent problems was repairing the city's tiled roofs in order to prevent water damage from rainfall. The rosy terracotta tiles that had topped all of Dubrovnik's buildings were originally produced in a tile factory in Kupari, south of Dubrovnik, that had long since closed. Replacements of the same colour proved impossible to find. The city first turned to Agen, France for 200,000 tiles, then Slovenia, before finally settling on Bedekovčina in the Krapina River valley. Though the red and ochre colours of the new tiles blends badly with the more subdued shade of the old Kupari tiles, the older tiles are gradually being replaced, building by building.

The restorers faced a similar problem in finding a source of the fine white limestone used to build the city. The original stone came from nearby Vrnik, off the island of Korčula, but the quarries have since fallen into disuse and are only capable of producing small amounts of stone.

The island of Brač has a long tradition of stonemasonry and a ready supply of high-quality stone; even with this stone, though, restorers worried that the obvious differences in colour and texture would only magnify over time. The solution was to use the Brač stone in places that had already used the stone or where it would not be readily visible, such as in drainage gutters.

To the casual observer, Dubrovnik has regained most of its original grandeur. The great town walls are once again intact, the gleaming marble streets are smoothly paved and famous monuments such as the 15th-century Onofrio Fountain and the Clock Tower have been lovingly restored. Damage to the Sponza Palace, the Rector's Palace, St Blaise's Church, the cathedral and various 17th-century residences has been repaired with the help of an international brigade of specially trained stoneworkers.

With the restoration work largely completed, architects have turned their attention to fortifying the structures to withstand the earthquakes that have periodically ripped through the region, most severely in 1667 when much of the old town was flattened. A milder quake that damaged 45 houses in September 1995 again reminded the inhabitants of the precariousness of their city. The original desire for total authenticity in materials and workmanship has been tempered by the need to reinforce the buildings and monuments in accordance with modern safety standards. Buildings and monuments are now being continually monitored for their structural integrity. Located in a zone that is seismic both geologically and politically, Dubrovnik's citizens have become more · determined than ever to protect their fragile, wondrous town.

gilt statue of St Blaise who is holding a scale model of pre-earthquake Dubrovnik.

Continuing along the broad street beside St Blaise is the Gothic-Renaissance **Rector's Palace** (Map p236; ☎ 426 469; Pred Dvorom 3; adult/student 15/7KN; ☾ 9am-5pm), built in the late 15th century with outstanding sculptural ornamentation. Although rebuilt many times, it retains a striking compositional unity. Notice the finely carved capitals and the ornate staircase in the atrium which is

often used for concerts during the Summer Festival. Also in the atrium is a statue of Miho Pracat, who bequeathed his wealth to the Republic and was the only commoner in the one thousand years of the Republic's existence to be honoured with a statue (1638). We may assume that the bequest was considerable.

The palace was built for the rector who governed Dubrovnik and contains the rector's office, his private chambers, public halls and administrative offices. Interestingly, the elected rector was not permitted to leave the building during his one-month term without the permission of the senate. Today the palace has been turned into a museum with artfully restored rooms, portraits, coats of arms and coins, which try to evoke the glorious history of Dubrovnik.

Across the square from the Rector's Palace is the **Cathedral of the Assumption of the Virgin** (Map p236; Stolna Crkva Velike Gospe; Poljana M Držića; morning & late-afternoon Mass). The church was built on the site of a 7th-century basilica that was enlarged in the 12th century, supposedly as the result of a gift from England's King Richard I, the Lionheart, who was saved from a shipwreck in the nearby island of Lokrum.

Soon after the earlier cathedral was destroyed in the 1667 earthquake, work began on this new cathedral which was finished in 1713 in a purely baroque style. The cathedral is notable for its fine altars, especially the altar of St John Nepomuk made of violet marble. The cathedral **treasury** (Riznica; ☎ 411 715; adult/child 7/4KN; 8am-5.30pm Mon-Sat, 11am-5.30pm Sun) contains relics of St Blaise as well as 138 gold and silver reliquaries largely made in the workshops of Dubrovnik's goldsmiths between the 11th and 17th centuries. Among a number of religious paintings, the most striking is the polyptych of the Assumption of the Virgin, made in Titian's workshop.

From the cathedral, walk down Androvića to the **St Ignatius Church** (Map p236; Crkva Sveti Ignacija; Uz Jezuite; late-evening Mass), built in the same style as the cathedral and completed in 1725. Inside are frescoes displaying scenes from the life of St Ignatius, founder of the Jesuit society. Abutting the church is the **Jesuit College** at the top of a broad flight of stairs leading down to Gundulićeva Poljana, a bustling morning market. The monument in the centre is of Dubrovnik's famous poet, Ivan Gundulić. The reliefs on the pedestal depict scenes from his epic poem, *Osman*.

Return to the cathedral and take Od Pustijerne to the **aquarium** (Map p236; ☎ 427 937; St John Fort at Kneza Damjana Jude 2; adult/child 20/10KN; 9am-8pm). Fed by fresh sea water, there are tanks with electric rays, sting rays, conger eels, scorpion fish and spotted dogfish, sea breams, groper, poisonous snake-like

morays and seahorses. Smaller glass tanks display colourful sponges, sea anemones, sea stars, shells, snails, urchins and an eight-footed octopus that varies its shape and colour as it swims. The aquarium is a great favourite with kids.

Return to the Sponza Palace and follow the road to the Ploče Gate. On your left, you'll see the **Dominican monastery and museum** (Map p236; Muzej Dominikanskog Samostana; ☎ 426 472; off Svetog Dominika 4; adult/child 15/7KN; 9am-5pm), another architectural highlight in a transitional Gothic-Renaissance style with a rich trove of paintings. Built at the same time as the city walls in the 14th century, the stark exterior resembles a fortress more than a religious complex.

The interior contains a graceful 15th-century cloister constructed by local artisans after the designs of the Florentine architect Massa di Bartolomeo, and a large, single-naved church with an altarpiece by Vlaho Bukovac. The eastern wing contains the monastery's impressive art collection which includes paintings from Dubrovnik's finest 15th- and 16th-century artists. Notice the works of Božidarević, Dobričević and Hamzić.

By this time you'll be ready for a leisurely walk around the **city walls** (Map p236; Gradske Zidine; adult/child 30/10KN; 9am-6.30pm daily Apr-Oct & 9am-6.30pm Tue-Sun Nov-Mar) themselves. Built between the 13th and 16th centuries and still intact today, these powerful walls are the finest in the world and Dubrovnik's main claim to fame.

The first set of walls to enclose the city were built in the 13th century. In the middle of the 14th century the 1.5m-thick walls were fortified with 15 square forts. The threat of attacks from the Turks in the 15th century prompted the city to strengthen the existing forts and add new ones so that the entire old town is now contained within a curtain of stone over 2km long and up to 25m high. The walls are thicker on the land side – up to 6m – but run 1.5m to 3m on the sea side. The round **Minčeta Tower** (Map p236) protects the northern edge of the city from land invasion, while the western end is protected from land and sea invasion by the detached **Lovrjenac Fort** (Map pp232-3). The Pile Gate is protected by the **Bokar Tower** (Map p236) and the **Revelin Fort** (Map p236) protects the eastern entrance.

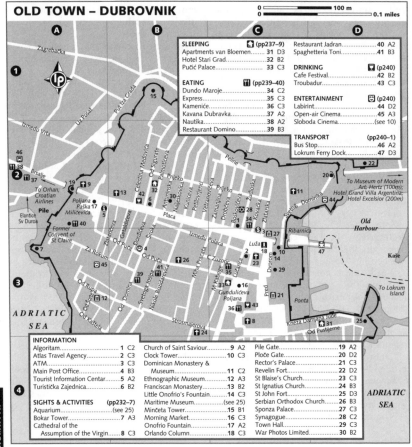

OLD TOWN – DUBROVNIK

0 _____ 100 m
0 _____ 0.1 miles

SLEEPING (pp237–9)
Apartments van Bloemen........31 D3
Hotel Stari Grad........................32 B2
Pučić Palace............................33 C3

EATING (pp239–40)
Dundo Maroje..........................34 C2
Express.....................................35 C3
Kamenice..................................36 C3
Kavana Dubravka......................37 A2
Nautika....................................38 A2
Restaurant Domino....................39 B3

Restaurant Jadran....................40 A2
Spaghetteria Toni......................41 B3

DRINKING (p240)
Cafe Festival............................42 B2
Troubadur................................43 C3

ENTERTAINMENT (p240)
Labirint....................................44 D2
Open-air Cinema.......................45 A3
Sloboda Cinema...................(see 10)

TRANSPORT (pp240–1)
Bus Stop..................................46 A2
Lokrum Ferry Dock....................47 D3

To Museum of Modern
Art; Hertz (100m);
Hotel Grand Villa Argentina;
Hotel Excelsior (200m)

Old Harbour

Kaše

To Lokrum
Island

ADRIATIC SEA

ADRIATIC SEA

INFORMATION
Algoritam.....................................1 C2
Atlas Travel Agency......................2 C3
ATM...3 C3
Main Post Office...........................4 B3
Tourist Information Centar............5 A2
Turistička Zajednica.....................6 B2

SIGHTS & ACTIVITIES (pp232–7)
Aquarium.............................(see 25)
Bokar Tower.................................7 A3
Cathedral of the
Assumption of the Virgin.......8 C3

Church of Saint Saviour...............9 A2
Clock Tower...............................10 C3
Dominican Monastery &
Museum...............................11 C2
Ethnographic Museum...............12 A3
Franciscan Monastery................13 B2
Little Onofrio's Fountain............14 C3
Maritime Museum...............(see 25)
Minčeta Tower..........................15 B1
Morning Market........................16 C3
Onofrio Fountain.......................17 A2
Orlando Column........................18 C3

Pile Gate..................................19 A2
Ploče Gate................................20 D2
Rector's Palace..........................21 C3
Revelin Fort..............................22 D2
St Blaise's Church......................23 C3
St Ignatius Church.....................24 B3
St John Fort..............................25 C3
Serbian Orthodox Church..........26 B3
Sponza Palace...........................27 C3
Synagogue...............................28 C2
Town Hall.................................29 C3
War Photos Limited...................30 B2

The views over the town and sea are great, so be sure to make this walk the high point of your visit. The entrance to the walls is immediately to the left of Pile Gate when you enter the city. You can enjoy Shakespeare's plays which are staged on the Lovrjenac fortress terrace during the Summer Festival.

In addition to a profusion of old churches that can be visited before or after Mass, Dubrovnik has other attractions. The **Ethnographic Museum** (Map p236; ☎ 412 545; Od Rupa; adult/student 15/7KN; 9am-2pm Sun-Fri), in the 16th-century Rupe Granary, contains exhibits relating to agriculture. There's also a **Maritime Museum** (☎ 426 465; St John Fort; adult/child 15/7KN; 9am-5pm) in **St John Fort** (Map

p236) that traces the history of navigation in Dubrovnik with ship models, navigational objects and paintings. Art lovers may wish to head up to the **Museum of Modern Art** (Map p236; ☎ 426 590; Frana Supila 23; admission free; 10am-7pm Tue-Sun) for a look at contemporary Croatian artists, particularly the local painter Vlaho Bukovac.

For a change from the ancient and the artsy, try the excellent **War Photos Limited** (Map p236; ☎ 326 166; Antuninska 6; admission 25KN; 9am-9pm May-Oct, 9am-4pm Mon-Fri, 9am-2pm Sat Nov-Dec, Mar-Apr) managed by former photojournalist Wade Goddard. The award-winning photos on display here concentrate on the subtleties of human violence rather than on its carnage. The permanent exhibition focuses on the Balkan wars but temporary exhibits will include other wars.

There is a colourful **market** (Map pp232-3; Gundulićeva Poljana; ☎ 6am-1pm daily) displaying local products every morning .

Activities

The waters around Dubrovnik offer excellent scuba diving opportunities. **Navis Underwater Explorers** (Map pp232-3; ☎ 099 502 773; fax 356 501; Copacabana Beach; single dives 240KN, 6-dive package 1200KN) offers a full range of dives, courses and diving services. Dives to the Roman wreck (see p244) cost extra as it involves obtaining special permission papers.

The closest beach to the old city is just beyond the 17th-century Lazareti (former quarantine station) outside Ploče Gate. There are also 'managed' hotel beaches on the Lapad Peninsula that you're free to use at no charge.

An even better option is to take the ferry which shuttles hourly in the summer to **Lokrum Island** (35KN return), a luxuriantly wooded island with a rocky naturist beach, a botanical garden and the ruins of a medieval Benedictine monastery.

Tours

Atlas (p232) offers full-day tours to Mostar (240KN), Međugorje (220KN), the Elafiti Islands (240KN) and Mljet (360KN), among other destinations. Its tour to Montenegro (310KN) is a good alternative to taking the morning bus since the schedules make a day trip there impractical.

Festivals & Events

Dubrovnik's Summer Festival (☎ 323 400; www .dubrovnik-festival.hr; Od Sigurate 1), from mid-July to mid-August, is the most prestigious summer festival in Croatia and has taken place every year since 1950. For five weeks in July and August, a programme of theatre, concerts and dance are presented on open-air stages throughout the city. The opening ceremony takes place on Luža Square and usually includes fireworks and a band.

In addition to attracting the best national artists and regional folklore ensembles, the programme usually includes one or two big-name international artists. Theatre productions feature the plays of Marin Držić, Shakespeare, Moliére and the Greek tragedians. Tickets range from 50KN to 250KN and are available from the festival office on Placa or on site one hour before the beginning of each performance. You can also reserve and buy them online.

The **Feast of St Blaise** (3 February) is another city-wide bash marked by pageants and processions. Carnival festivities heralding the arrival of Lent in February are also popular.

Sleeping

Most of Dubrovnik's hotels are gathered in the Lapad and Ploče areas, with the more expensive resort hotels located east of town.

OLD TOWN

Hotel Stari Grad (Map p236; ☎ 321 373; hotelstarigrad@ yahoo.com; Palmoticeva; s/d 725/1040KN; 🔀) Staying in the heart of the old town in a lovingly restored stone building is an unmatchable experience. There are only eight rooms, each one furnished with taste and a sense of comfort. From the rooftop terrace, you have a marvellous view over the town. Prices stay the same all year.

Pucić Palace (Map p236; ☎ 324 111; www.thepucic palace.com; Od Puća 1; s/d 2200/4000KN; P 🔀) Right in the heart of the old town these palatial digs have been designed and decorated to the cutting edge of fashion. Warm and cosy it's not, but the countesses and moguls that stay here probably don't care.

LAPAD

Most of the less expensive hotels are in Lapad as well as a few more luxurious establishments. On the whole, the suburb is not a bad place to stay. Since it's a mixed residential and 'tourist' neighbourhood, you don't get the feeling that you've been banished to some faraway tourist ghetto. The main road is Šetalište Kralja Tomislava while the pedestrian tree-lined Krajla Zvonimira makes a pleasant stroll past stalls and outdoor cafés. A walk along the coast past the Hotel Kompas leads to lots of spots for stretching out along the rocks and taking a swim. After about 1km you'll come to the Hotel Neptune and a series of package-tour hotels. Buses No 1A, No 1B and No 6 run between Pile Gate and the bus stop in Lapad near the post office.

Budget

YHA hostel (Map pp232-3; ☎ 423 241; dubrovnik@hfhs.hr; Vinka Sagrestana 3; per person B&B/half board 95/140KN)

It's not exactly restful but you'll have a lot of fun. To get here head up Vinka Sagrestana from Bana Josipa Jelačića 17. This hostel was refurbished in 1996. Dinner can also be arranged, but as Bana Josipa Jelačića is one of the liveliest streets in Lapad, full of bars, cafés and pizzerias, you may prefer to grab something there.

Solitudo (Map pp232-3; ☎ 448 686; Iva Dulčića 39; per person/site 32/60KN; mid-May–mid-Oct) This pretty and renovated site is on Lapad promontory and within walking distance of the beach.

Porto (Map pp232-3; ☎ 487 078; Mlini; per adult/site 28/50KN; ☼ May-Oct) This is a small camping ground near a quiet cove, 8km south of Dubrovnik. It's best to call first. Take buses No 10 or 16 to Srebeno.

Camping Matkovića (Map pp232-3; ☎ 486 096; Mlini; per adult/site 28/50KN; ☼ May-Oct) It's next to Porto, 8km south of Dubrovnik. Call first. Bus No 10 or 16 to Srebeno leaves you nearly at its gate.

Gaj (Map pp232-3; ☎ 891 215; Zaton; per adult/site 32/25KN; ☼ May-Oct) It's much larger than Porto and Camping Matkovića and unlike them its opening times are reliable. It's located about 15km northwest of the city in Zaton.

Trsteno (Map pp232-3; ☎ 751 060; Potok 4, Trsteno; per adult/site 25/50KN; ☼ Apr–mid-Oct) A few kilometres west of Zaton, this is a small, private camping ground.

Mid-Range

Hotel Sumratin (Map pp232-3; ☎ 436 333; hot-sumratin@ du.htnet.hr; Kralja Zvonimira 31; s/d 355/600KN; Ⓟ) No-one would accuse this hotel of being over-decorated but the rooms are quite adequate and the hotel is well located near the shops of Lapad, the beach and the Hotel Kompas.

Hotel Zagreb (Map pp232-3; ☎ 436 146; hot-sumratin@ du.htnet.hr; Šetalište Kralja Zvonimira 27; s/d 385/655KN) This is under the same ownership as Hotel Sumratin, but Hotel Zagreb is in a restored 19th-century building with more character than you usually find along the coast. The ceilings are high and the hotel is behind a shady garden.

Hotel Lapad (Map pp232-3; ☎ 432 922; www.hotel -lapad.hr; Lapadska Obala 37; s/d from 600/775KN; Ⓧ Ⓐ) The hotel is a solid old limestone structure, with simple but neat and cheerful rooms. There are more expensive rooms available with air-con. There's no beach access but the hotel runs a daily boat to a remote beach near Zaton for a small charge.

Hotel Adriatic (Map pp232-3; ☎ 437 302; www.hoteli maestral.com; Masarykov Put 9; s/d from 520/670KN) This large hotel has simple but serviceable rooms and is close to the beach. Front rooms are more expensive and overlook the sea but could be noisy.

Top End

Hotel Splendid (Map pp232-3; ☎ 437 304; www.hoteli maestral.hr; Masarykov Put 10; s/d 900/1280KN; Ⓟ Ⓧ) This resort hotel has 59 comfortable rooms with terraces overlooking the sea. It's convenient to public transport and only a few steps from the beach.

Hotel Kompas (Map pp232-3; ☎ 352 000; www.hotel -kompas.hr; Šetalište Kralja Zvonimira 56; s/d from 825/ 910KN; Ⓟ Ⓧ Ⓐ Ⓓ) This sprawling complex, along the coast, has an indoor and outdoor swimming pool, a sauna and an Internet café. It's so close to the beach you can practically roll out of bed and into the water in a single movement.

GRUŽ

Hotel Petka (Map pp232-3; ☎ 410 500; fax 410 127; Obala Stjepana Radića 38; s/d from 520/700KN; Ⓟ Ⓧ) This renovated hotel, opposite the Jadrolinija ferry dock, has 104 rooms, each with TV, phone and minibar. It's all business but the location is good if you need to catch an early-morning ferry.

PLOČE

The best luxury establishments are east of the old town along Frana Supila within walking distance of the city centre.

Hotel Grand Villa Argentina (Map p236; ☎ 440 555; www.hoteli-argentina.hr; Frana Supila 14; s/d from 1160/1540KN; Ⓟ Ⓧ Ⓐ) This reliable accommodation option was overhauled to offer luxury suites as well as sleek, well-serviced modern rooms, some of which overlook the sea. There's an indoor and outdoor swimming pool but the swimming is excellent from the rocks next to the hotel. You also have access to a sauna and a fitness room. The Villa Orsula part of the complex has the more characterful rooms.

Hotel Excelsior (Map p236; ☎ 353 353; www.hotel -excelsior.hr; Frana Supila 12; s/d from 1280/1590KN; Ⓟ Ⓧ Ⓐ) With two restaurants, a piano bar, hairdresser, conference room and business centre, indoor and outdoor swimming pools and a full 'wellness programme' the Excelsior well deserves its five-star status.

PRIVATE ROOMS

Private accommodation is generally the best option in Dubrovnik but beware of the scramble of private owners at the bus station or Jadrolinija wharf. Some offer what they say they offer, others are scamming. Try to pin down the location in advance or you could wind up staying a considerable distance from town. Be aware that most accomodation in the old town involves sharing the flat with the owner's family. The establishments listed here are reputable and can often refer you to other places if they are full. All will meet you at the station if you call in advance. Otherwise head to any of the travel agencies or the Turistička Zajednica.

Expect to pay about 200KN to 220KN for a room in high season. Officially, there are no single rooms but during the off-season you may be able to knock 20% off the price of a double room. There are also apartments available starting at about 380KN for a studio.

Apartments van Bloemen (Map p236; ☎ 323 433, 091 33 24 106; www.karmendu.tk; Bandureva 1; apt 750KN; 🏿) This is the most personal and original accommodation, with a great location in the old town. All four apartments are beautifully decorated with original art. Three sleep three people comfortably.

Begović Boarding House (Map pp232-3; ☎ 435 191; fax 452 752; Primorska 17; per person 110KN) A long-time favourite with our readers, this friendly place in Lapad has three rooms with shared bathroom and three apartments. There's a terrace out the back with a good view. Breakfast is an additional 30KN.

Apartments Silva Kusjanović (Map pp232-3; ☎ 435 071, 098 244 639; antonia_du@hotmail.com; Kardinala Stepinća 62; per person 100KN) Sweet Silva has four large apartments that can hold four to eight beds. All have terraces with gorgeous views and it's possible to barbecue.

Eating

OLD TOWN

You can get a decent meal at one of the touristy seafood or pasta places along Prijeko, a narrow street parallel to Placa.

Kavana Dubravka (Map p236; ☎ 426 319; Brsalje 1; snacks 25KN; 🏿) Try this place located right outside Pile Gate for a quick snack of pastries, small pizzas or sandwiches. There is an outdoor terrace behind the comfortable, air-con interior.

Express (Map p236; ☎ 323 994; M Kaboge 1; mains from 16KN) It's self-service but soups, salads, vegetables and desserts are freshly prepared and vegetarians will have an easy time assembling a meal.

Kamenice (Map p236; ☎ 421 499; Gundulićeva Poljana 8; dishes from 40KN) Portions are huge at this convivial hang-out known for its mussels. Plus, its outdoor terrace is on one of Dubrovnik's more scenic squares.

Orhan (Map p236; ☎ 414 183; Od Tabakarijeje 1; mains from 50KN) Beautifully located on a rocky cove, you get excellent value for money here with a full menu of fresh seafood dishes.

Spaghetteria Toni (Map p236; ☎ 323 134; Božidarevića 14; pizzas from 30KN) Pizza, pasta, pasta, pizza. There are a million joints in town which serve pizza and pasta but this is the best. Vegetarians will find good veggie pizzas.

Dundo Maroje (Map p236; ☎ 321 445; Kovačka; mains from 55KN) Nothing too startling, but everything is cooked exactly as it should be. The menu is wide ranging with an accent on seafood.

Restaurant Jadran (Map p236; ☎ 323 405; Former Convent of St Claire; mains from 35KN, set menu 80KN) It may be touristy but the ambience here in the convent's atrium is great and prices are reasonable.

Restaurant Domino (Map p236; ☎ 432 832; Od Domina 6; mains from 100KN) Head here for a meat fix. The restaurant offers a selection of cow cuttings as well as other meat dishes and an assortment of grilled fish at about the same prices as Nautika.

Nautika (Map p236; ☎ 442 573; Brsalje 3; mains around 100KN) This elegant restaurant offers good but expensive dining and a spectacular view over the sea. It's class all the way with an emphasis on dressed-up seafood dishes. If the prices make you wince, at least enjoy a drink in the downstairs coffee shop with an outdoor terrace.

LAPAD

Levenat (Map pp232-3; ☎ 435 352; Šetalište Nikai Meda Pucića 15; mains 45-120KN) The interior is classic and the outdoor terrace has a smashing view. The food is superb and there's even a vegetarian plate. There's no better address in Lapad.

Restauracija Primorka (Map pp232-3; ☎ 356 176; Nikole Tesle 7, Gruž; mains from 30KN) It's just west of the department store and offers a good selection of seafood and national dishes at medium prices. In the summer months you dine below the trees on a lamp-lit terrace.

Restauracija Konavoka (Map pp232-3; ☎ 435 105; 38 Kralja Zvonimira; seafood mains 45-75KN) Near the Hotel Sumratin, this restaurant has an upstairs roof terrace attractively decorated with potted plants, making it a pleasant place to hang out or enjoy a seafood meal, cheap pizza or vegetarian platter.

Konobo Atlantic (Map pp232-3; ☎ 098 185 96 25; Kardinala Stepinca 42; mains around 40KN) It's not terribly atmospheric at the outdoor tables since it's next to a bus stop, however install yourself indoors, and you can sample superb home-made pasta like vegetarian lasagne (35KN) and tagliatelle with assorted seafood sauces.

Pergola (Map pp232-3; ☎ 436 848; Šetalište Kralja Tomislava 1; mains 60-90KN) On a busy corner in Lapad, the outdoor terrace is an oasis of calm in which to enjoy delicious fish and meat dishes accompanied by local wine.

Drinking

The crowd that used to go to Jelačića in Lapad has now turned to Bunićeva Poljana on mild nights. Beery refreshment is in one of the cafés along the square while, out-doors, the strummers, pluckers, crooners and blowers entertain their fans.

Troubadur (Map p236; ☎ 412 154; Bunićeva 2) This place has been the hippest bar in Dubrovnik for years. Marko, the owner is a jazz lover and musician. If he's not on with his group, there's sure to be a guest group to keep this sizzling.

Café Festival (Map p236; ☎ 321 148; Placa) Placa is one of the world's most beautiful streets and this café is the best place to kick back and enjoy the view. The interior is also inviting if the weather outside isn't.

Entertainment

FOLK MUSIC

St Blaise's Church (Map p236; Luža Sq) Open-air folklore shows are conducted in front of the church at 11am on Sundays through May, June and September.

CLASSICAL MUSIC

Dubrovnik Orchestra (Map p236; ☎ 417 101) The orchestra regularly gives concerts in the atrium of the Rector's Palace and various other sites around town.

Dubrovnik String Quartet (St Saviour Church, Placa) The quartet gives concerts throughout

autumn on Monday night in St Saviour Church. Look for posters around town or ask at the tourist office.

CINEMAS

Sloboda Cinema (Map p236; ☎ 321 425; Clock Tower) This is the most centrally located cinema. Posters outside advertise the nightly showings.

Open-air cinema (Za Rokum, old town; Kumičića, Lapad) In two locations, it is open nightly in July and August with screening starting after sundown (9pm or 9.30pm); ask at Sloboda Cinema for the schedule.

DISCOS

Latino Club Fuego (Map pp232-3; Ante Starčevića 2) Despite the name, you'll find a gamut of dance music that includes techno and pop at this disco. The atmosphere is relaxed with no glowering bouncer and no rigid dress code.

Labirint (Map p236; ☎ 322 222; Svetog Dominika 2) This is a vast restaurant, nightclub, disco and cabaret complex that caters to high rollers. It can chew through your wallet pretty quickly unless you just come for a romantic cocktail on the roof terrace.

Getting There & Away

AIR

Daily flights to/from Zagreb are operated by **Croatia Airlines** (☎ 413 777; Brsalje 9). The one-way fare is about 400KN but can run higher in peak season. There are also nonstop flights to Rome, London and Manchester from April to October.

BUS

Daily buses from Dubrovnik:

Destination	Cost	Duration	Frequency
Korčula	80KN	3hr	1 daily
Mostar	77KN	3hr	2 daily
Orebić	80KN	2½hr	1 daily
Rijeka	295-309KN	12hr	4 daily
Sarajevo	160KN	5hr	1 daily
Split	72-111KN	4½hr	14 daily
Zadar	160-190KN	8hr	7 daily
Zagreb	165-199KN	11hr	8 daily

There's a daily 11am bus to the Montenegrin border, from where a bus takes you to Merceg-Novi (60KN, two hours) and on to

Kotor (100KN, 2½ hours) and Bar (130KN, three hours). For international buses, see p274. In a busy summer season and on weekends, buses out of Dubrovnik **bus station** (☎ 357 088) can be crowded, so book a ticket well before the scheduled departure time.

BOAT

In addition to the **Jadrolinija** (Map p236; ☎ 418 000; Gruž) coastal ferry north to Hvar, Split, Zadar and Rijeka, there's a local ferry that leaves Dubrovnik for Sobra on Mljet Island (26KN to 32KN, 2½ hours) throughout the year. In summer there are two ferries a day. There are several ferries a day year-round to the outlying islands of Šipanska, Sugjuraj, Lopud and Kološep.

Jadroagent (Map p232-3; ☎ 419 000; Radića 32) books ferry tickets and has information. For information on international connections see p275.

Getting Around
TO/FROM THE AIRPORT

Čilipi international airport is 24km southeast of Dubrovnik. The Croatia Airlines airport buses (30KN) leave from the main bus terminal on Put Republike 1½ hours before flight times. A taxi costs about 220KN.

CAR RENTAL

Car rental companies:
Budget (Map p232-3; ☎ 091 201 46 38; S Radića 24)
Gulliver (Map p232-3; ☎ 448 296; S Radića 31)
Hertz (Map p236; ☎ 425 000, F Supila 5)
OK (Map p232-3; ☎ 418 950; S Radića 32)

BUS

Dubrovnik's buses run frequently and generally on time. The fare is 10KN if you buy from the driver but only 8KN if you buy a ticket at a kiosk.

AROUND DUBROVNIK
Elafiti Islands

A day trip to one of the islands in this archipelago northwest of Dubrovnik makes a perfect escape from the summer crowds. The most popular islands are Kološep, Lopud and Šipan, which are easily accessible during the summer by a morning boat from Dubrovnik (off-season there are only afternoon boats). Atlantagent (p232) in Dubrovnik also runs

a fast boat to Kološep (20 minutes) and Lopud (35 minutes) on Saturday mornings or you can take one of the tours offered by Atlas (p232).

Kološep is the nearest island (25 minutes from Dubrovnik) and has several sand-and-pebble beaches as well as centuries-old pine forests, olive groves and orange and lemon orchards.

Lopud is 25 minutes further and has a number of interesting churches and monasteries dating from the 16th century, when the inhabitants' seafaring exploits were legendary. The village is composed of stone houses surrounded by exotic gardens and there's a beach nearby. No cars are allowed on the island.

Šipan is the largest of the islands (1¾ hours from Dubrovnik) and was a favourite with the Dubrovnik aristocracy, who built houses there in the 15th century. The boat lands in Šipanska Luka in the northwest of the island which has the remains of a Roman villa and a 15th-century Gothic duke's palace.

Cavtat
pop 1930

Cavtat is a small town that curves around an attractive harbour bordered by beaches. Although not as interesting as Dubrovnik, it makes a good alternative place to stay if Dubrovnik is fully booked or the summer crowds become overwhelming. If you do stay in Dubrovnik, Cavtat's close proximity means that you can easily visit in a day. You could do a little sightseeing in the morning, relax on a beach in the afternoon and still get back to Dubrovnik in time for dinner.

Originally a Greek settlement called Epidauros, it became a Roman colony around 228 BC and was later destroyed during the 7th-century Slavic invasions. Throughout most of the Middle Ages it was part of the Dubrovnik republic and shared the cultural and economic life of the capital city. It's most famous personage was the painter Vlaho Bukovac (1855–1922), one of the foremost exponents of Croatian modernism.

ORIENTATION

The old town is by the harbour and several gargantuan tourist complexes lie on the eastern edge, along the town's best beach.

INFORMATION

Adriatica (☎ 478 713; Trumbićev put 3) This place changes money, book excursions and finds private accommodation.

Atlas Travel Agency (☎ 479 031; Trumbićev put 2) For excursions and private accommodation.

Post Office (Kneza Domagoja 4) Near the bus station.

Tourist Office (Turistička Zajednica; ☎ 479 025; www .tzcavtat-konavle.hr; Tiha 3; 8am-3pm Mon-Fri & 9am-noon Sat & Sun Sep-Jun, 8am-6pm daily Jul & Aug)

SIGHTS

Several sights make the city well worth a stop. The Renaissance **Rector's Palace** (☎ 478 556; Obala Ante Starčevića 18; adult/student 10/5KN; ◷ 9am-1pm Mon-Fri), near the bus station, houses a rich library (which belonged to 19th-century lawyer and historian Balthazar Bogišić) as well as lithographs and a small archaeological collection. Next door is the baroque **St Nicholas Church** (Crkva Sveti Nikole; Obala Ante Starčevića; admission 5KN; ◷ 10am-1pm) with wooden altars.

The **birth house of Vlaho Bukovac** (☎ 478 646; Bukovac 5; admission 20KN; ◷ 10am-1pm, 4-8pm Tue-Sun), Cavtat's most famous son, is at the northern end of Obala Ante Starčevića and has recently been renovated and opened to the public. The early-19th-century archi-tecture provides a fitting backdrop to the mementos and paintings of Croatia's most renowned painter. Next door is the **Monas-tery of Our Lady of the Snow** (Samostan Snježne Gospe; Bukovac), which is worth a look for some notable early-Renaissance paintings.

A path leads uphill from the monastery to the cemetery which contains the **mauso-leum** (admission 5KN; ◷ 10am-noon) of the Račić family, built by Ivan Meštrović. The elabor-ately sculpted monument reflects the sculptor's preoccupation with religious and spiritual concerns.

SLEEPING & EATING

For private accommodation try Atlas, Adriatica or one of the other agencies around the town centre. Top-end rooms in the high season cost from 185KN to 335KN.

Hotel Supetar (☎ 478 833; hotel.supetar@hoteli -croatia.hr; Obala Ante Starčevića 27; s/d 550/575; ✖) The cheapest hotel in town, it has fairly basic rooms but some overlook the water and you're not far from the hotel's own beach. It is in an attractive old stone building that belies the modern rooms within.

Hotel Cavtat (☎ 478 246; www.iberostar.com; Ulica Tiha bb; s/d 640/910KN; Ⓟ ✖) The Cavtat has 94 rooms in the town centre overlooking the beach. The warmly decorated rooms are in very good condition and are equipped with satellite TV.

Hotel Croatia (☎ 475 555; www.hoteli-croatia.hr; Frankopanska 10; s/d from 1200/1260KN; Ⓟ ✖ ⚲) It's a major resort complex with a bit too much concrete for some tastes but still a five-star wonder. There's an indoor and outdoor pool, sauna, gym and private beach. It's a few hundred metres south of the town centre and occupies a good portion of the little cape that surrounds it.

Restaurant Kolona (☎ 478 269; Put Tihe 2; mains 45-65KN) Overlooking the bus stop, this has a verdant terrace and the freshest fish in town, which is evident when you order the mussels *bouzara* (a sauce of tomatoes, onions, herbs, white wine and breadcrumbs). Grilled fish, squid and an assortment of risottos are excellently prepared.

GETTING THERE & AWAY

Bus No 10 runs hourly to Cavtat from Dubrovnik's bus station (15KN, 45 min-utes), or you can take a boat from the Lokrum boat dock (60KN return, three times daily), near Ploče Gate.

MLJET ISLAND

pop 1237

Of all the Adriatic islands, Mljet (mil-yet) may be the most seductive. Over 72% of the island is covered by forests and the rest is dotted by fields, vineyards and small villages. The western half of the island has been named a national park where the lush vegetation and gentle coves are unmarred by development schemes, large resorts or nearly any other trappings of tourism. You may pay more or have to go to more trouble to stay here, but you'll be rewarded by an unspoilt oasis of tranquillity that, ac-cording to legend, captivated Odysseus for seven years. We're sure he didn't regret a moment.

Ancient Greeks called the island 'Melita' or 'honey' for the many bees humming in the forests. It appears that Greek sailors came to the island for refuge against storms, to gather fresh water from the springs and probably to unwind a little. At that time the island was populated by Illyrians who erected hill forts and traded with the mainland. They were conquered by the Romans in 35 BC who expanded the settlement around Polače by building a palace, baths and servants quarters.

The island fell under the control of the Byzantine Empire in the 6th century and was later subject to the 7th-century invasions of Slavs and Avars which pushed inhabitants of neighbouring regions to flee to the island. After several centuries of regional rule from the mainland it was given to the Benedictine order in the 13th century, who constructed a monastery in the middle of Veliko Jezero, one of two lakes on the island's western end. Dubrovnik was extending its influence in the region at the time and formally annexed the island in 1410.

Although Mljet's fortunes were thereafter tied to those of Dubrovnik, the inhabitants maintained their traditional activities of farming, viticulture, livestock rearing and seafaring. Except for seafaring, the traditional activities are still the foundation of the economy. The island's inhabitants produce wine and olive oil, cultivate medicinal herbs and fish. Establishing the national park in 1960 helped bring tourism to Mljet, but the islanders are deeply ambivalent about the many depredations that tourism often entails and seem content to keep visitors down to manageable levels. Priorities here are peace and quiet, even if it means foregoing needed cash.

Orientation & Information

The island is 37km long, and has an average width of about 3km. Fifty-four sq km on the island's northwestern end are set aside as a national park. The main points of entry are Pomena and Polače, two tiny towns about 5km apart. Tour boats from Korčula arrive at Pomena wharf just outside the national park's western end and site of the island's only hotel, the Hotel Odisej. There's a good map of the island posted at the wharf.

Jadrolinija ferries arrive at Sobra on the eastern end and they are met by a local bus for the 1½-hour ride to Pomena and Polače. The **tourist office** (☎ 744 186; np-mljet@np-mljet.hr; ☻ 8am-1pm & 5-8pm Mon-Fri Oct-May, 8am-8pm Mon-Sat & 8am-1pm Sun Jun-Sep) is in Polače and the only ATM on the island is at the Hotel Odisej in Pomena. The admission price for the national park is 65/45KN adult/

concession during July and August and 45/30KN from September to June. The price includes a bus and boat transfer to the Benedictine monastery and there is no park admission price if you stay overnight on the island.

The administrative centre of the island is at Babino Polje, 18km east of Polače, where there is another **tourist office** (☎ /fax 745 125) and a post office.

Sights & Activities

The highlights of the island are **Malo Jezero** and **Veliko Jezero**, the two lakes on the island's western end connected by a channel. Veliko Jezero is connected with the sea by the Soline Canal, which makes the lakes subject to tidal flows.

In the middle of Veliko Jezero is an islet with a **Benedictine monastery**; it was originally built in the 12th century but has been rebuilt several times, adding Renaissance and baroque features to the Romanesque structure. The monastery contains the **Church of St Mary** (Crkva Svete Marija), which was built around the same time. In addition to building the monastery, the Benedictine monks deepened and widened the passage between the two lakes, taking advantage of the rush of sea water into the valley to build a mill at the entrance to Veliko Jezero. The monastery was abandoned in 1869 and the structure housed the government's forest-management offices for the island until 1941. It was then converted into a hotel that was trashed during the 1990s war. Now it contains a pricey but atmospheric restaurant.

There's a boat from Mali Most (about 1.5km from Pomena) on Malo Jezero that leaves for the island monastery four times a day (price included in the national park entry fee, see left). It's not possible to walk right around the larger lake as there's no bridge over the channel connecting the lakes to the sea. If you decide to swim, keep in mind that the current can be strong.

Polače features a number of remains dating from the 1st to 6th centuries. Most impressive is the **Roman palace**, probably dating from the 5th century. The floor plan was rectangular and on the front corners are two polygonal towers separated by a pier. On a hill over the town you can see the remains of a late-antique fortification

MLJET ISLAND

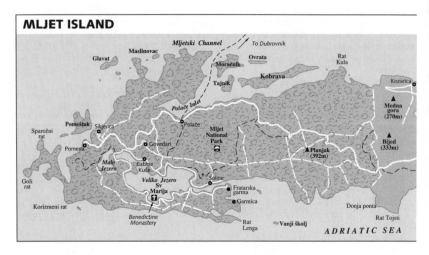

and northwest of the village are the remains of an early Christian basilica and a 5th-century church.

Renting a bicycle is an excellent way to explore the national park. You can rent from a **private operator** (☎ 098 428 074) on Mali Most, at the Hotel Odisej in Pomeno or along the harbour in Polače. The price is 15/90KN per hour/day. If you plan to cycle the 5km between Pomena and Polače be aware that the two towns are separated by a steep mountain. The bike path along the lake is an easier and very scenic pedal but it doesn't link the two towns.

The island offers some unusual opportunities for **diving**. There's a Roman wreck dating from the 3rd century in relatively shallow water. The remains of the ship, including amphorae, have calcified over the centuries and this has protected them from pillaging. There's also a German torpedo boat from WWII and several walls to dive. Contact **Kronmar diving** (☎ 744 022; Hotel Odisej).

Tours

See p240 and p250 for agencies offering excursions to Mljet. Tours last from about 8.30am to 6pm and include the park entry fee. The boat trip from Korčula to Pomena takes at least two hours, less by hydrofoil. From Dubrovnik it takes longer. Lunch isn't included in the tour price and the opportunities for self-catering are limited. From Pomena it's a 15-minute walk to a jetty on Veliko Jezero, the larger of the two

lakes. Here the groups board a boat to the Benedictine monastery islet. Those who don't want to spend the rest of the afternoon swimming and sunbathing on the monastery islet can catch an early boat back to the main island, and spend a couple of hours walking along the lakeshore before catching the late-afternoon excursion boat back to Korčula.

Sleeping

The Polače tourist office (p243) arranges private accommodation for 200KN per double room, but it is essential to make arrangements before arrival in peak season. There are more *sobe* (rooms available) signs around Pomena than Polače but practically none at all in Sobra. A number of the restaurants listed rent out rooms as well (220KN to 240KN).

Hotel Odisej (☎ 744 022; www.hotelodisej.hr; Pomena; d from 335KN; 🛁) The only hotel option available on the island is this modern structure in Pomena which has decent enough rooms and offers a range of activities.

There's no camping permitted inside the national park but there are two sites outside it.

Marina (☎ 745 071; Ropa; per person/site 25/25KN; ❂ Jun-Sep) It's a small camping ground in Ropa, about 1km from the park.

Camping Mungos (☎ 745 300; Babino Polje; per person/site 30/47KN; ❂ May-Sep) Not very shady but well located, this new camping ground is not far from the beach and the lovely grotto of Odysseus (Odisejeva).

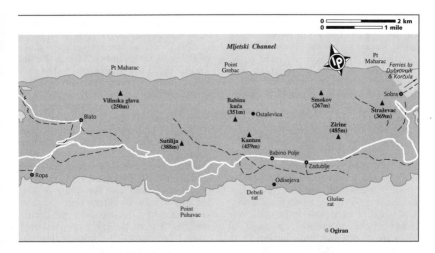

Ogigija (☎ 744 090; Polače) The rooms at this place (which also serves food) are a good deal.

Eating

The restaurants on Mljet serve good-quality food at prices that are somewhat higher than in Dubrovnik. The emphasis is on seafood and fresh fish costs about 320KN per kilogram.

Ogigija (☎ 744 090; Polače) With its big terrace and a parade of fresh, local dishes, this place is always busy.

Galija (☎ 744 028; Pomena; mains from 75KN) Overlooking the sea and opposite Hotel Odisej in Pomena, Galija serves decent enough food.

Stella Maris (☎ 744 059; Polače; mains from 80KN) The Stella Maris, on the main road, overlooks the sea and turns out perfectly fragrant seafood.

Nine (☎ 744 037; Pomena; mains from 80KN) The Nine, also opposite Hotel Odisej, is by the sea and, though touristy in high season, turns out succulent seafood.

Getting There & Away

Most people take a day trip to Mljet from Korčula but there's a regular ferry Monday to Saturday (32KN, two hours), which leaves from Dubrovnik at 2pm and docks in Sobra on the northern coast, about 7km east of Babino Polje. The return ferry leaves from Sobra at 6am which means a very early morning departure by local bus from

the national park. There are additional ferries in both directions in July and August and a connection from Sobra to Lopud (1½ hours) that goes on to Dubrovnik.

The big Jadrolinija coastal ferries also stop at Sobra once a week in summer which means that you can get to Sobra from Korčula town (95KN, two hours). Local buses meet the ferry in Sobra and stop in Babino Polje, Ropa, Goveđari, Polače and Pomena.

The *Nikolina* is a small boat that makes a 2¾-hour run to from Dubrovnik to Polače three times a week, leaving in the morning and returning in the late afternoon (45KN). Tickets are sold in Dubrovnik at **Turistička Zajednica** (☎ 417 983; Gruška obala bb), in Gruž at **Atlantagent** (☎ 419 044; Stjepana Radića 26; ⊗ 10am-4pm) or on board, but it's advised to buy in advance as the boat fills up quickly.

SEM agency (☎ 021-338 292) in Split makes a run three times a day from June to September connecting Polače with Trstenik (40KN, 1½ hours) on the Pelješac Peninsula.

KORČULA ISLAND & PELJEŠAC PENINSULA

pop 17,038

Separated from the Pelješac Peninsula by a narrow channel, Korčula (Curzola in Italian) is the sixth-largest Adriatic island, reaching nearly 47km in length and 5km to

8km in width. Besides the dense woods that led the original Greek settlers to call the island Korkyra Melaina (Black Korčula), the island is graced with indented coves, rolling hills and a walled old town that resembles a miniature Dubrovnik.

The island's interior is rich in vineyards, olive groves, small villages and hamlets. The steep southern coast is dotted with quiet coves and small beaches while the northern shore is flatter and has several natural harbours. Traditional culture flourishes on the island. The devout population keeps alive age-old religious ceremonies and an influx of tourism ensures that folk dances and music always have an eager audience.

A Neolithic cave (Vela Špilja) near Vela Luka on the island's western end points to the existence of a prehistoric settlement on the island but it was Greeks who first began spreading over the island in the 6th century BC. Their most important settlement was in the area of today's Lumbarda around the 3rd century BC. Romans conquered the island in the 1st century, giving way to the Slavs in the 7th century. The island was conquered by Venice in AD 1000 and then passed under Hungarian rule. It was briefly part of the Republic of Dubrovnik before again falling under Venetian rule in 1420, where it remained until 1797. Under Venetian rule, the island became known for its stone which was quarried and cut for export by skilled local artisans. Shipbuilding also flourished despite Venetian attempts to restrict competition with its own shipyards. After the Napoleonic conquest of Dalmatia in 1797, Korčula's fortunes followed those of Dalmatia which changed hands among the French, Austro-Hungarians and English before finally becoming a part of Yugoslavia in 1921.

Besides tourism, the most important economic activity on the island is agriculture. Although islanders produce cereals, vegetables and citrus fruit, the most important product is olive oil from the many olive groves. Unfortunately a ferocious fire in the summer of 1998 decimated a huge portion of the olive trees and the future of that industry remains uncertain. Korčula is also known for its wine, especially the dessert wine made from the *grk* grape cultivated around Lumbarda. The shipbuilding tradition continues on a lesser scale in a shipyard near Vela Luka.

Getting There & Around
BOAT

The island has two major entry ports – Korčula town and Vela Luka. All the Jadrolinija ferries between Split and Dubrovnik stop in Korčula town. Jadrolinija runs a passenger boat daily year-round from Split to Vela Luka (27KN, two hours), stopping at Hvar. There's also a summer fast boat running from Split to Korčula (55KN, 2¾ hours) that leaves three to five times a week between June and September, stopping at Hvar. It also leaves

KORČULA ISLAND & PELJEŠAC PENINSULA

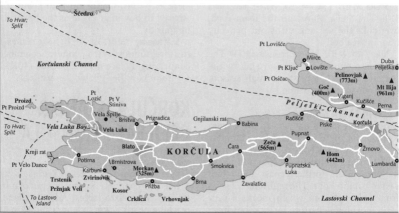

SOUTHERN DALMATIA

from Prigradica, near Blato. For further information, contact Marko Polo tours (see p248) in Korčula or **Splittours** (☎ 346 100; Obala Lazareta 3) in Split.

There's a regular afternoon car ferry between Split and Vela Luka (35KN, three hours) on the island's western end that stops at Hvar most days (although cars may not disembark at Hvar). Six daily buses link Korčula town to Vela Luka (24KN, one hour) but services from Vela Luka are reduced on the weekend.

From Orebić, look out for the passenger launch (15KN, 15 minutes, at least four times daily year-round), which will drop you off near Hotel Korčula right below the old town's towers. There is also a car ferry to Dominče (10KN, 15 minutes) which stops near the hotel Bon Repos where you can pick up the bus from Lumbarda or take a water taxi to town (10KN). The car ferry is the only alternative on weekends. On Saturday, it connects with the bus from Lumbarda but on Sunday there's only one bus in the morning from Korčula to Orebić and one late-afternoon bus coming back.

For information on international connections see p271.

BUS

Transport connections to Korčula are good. There's one bus every day to Dubrovnik (80KN, 3 hours) and Zagreb and one a week to Sarajevo (152KN, eight hours).

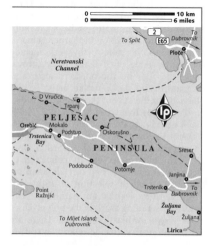

KORČULA
pop 3000

The town of Korčula at the northeastern tip of the island hugs a small, hilly peninsula jutting into the Adriatic. With its round defensive towers and compact cluster of red-roofed houses, Korčula is a typical medieval Dalmatian town. It's a peaceful little place with grey-stone houses nestling between the deep green hills and gunmetal-blue sea. There are rustling palms all around and lots to see and do, so it's worth planning a relaxed four-night stay to avoid the 30% surcharge on private rooms. Day trips are possible to Lumbarda and Vela Luka, to Orebić on the Pelješac Peninsula, and to the islands of Badija and Mljet.

Although documents indicate that a walled city existed on this site in the 13th century, it wasn't until the 15th century that the current city was built. Construction of the city coincided with the apogee of stone-carving skills on the island, lending the buildings and streets a distinctive style. The town's layout was cleverly designed to ensure the comfort and safety of its inhabitants. Streets running west are straight in order to open the city to the refreshing *maestral* (strong, steady westerly wind), while streets running east are slightly curved to minimise the force of the *bura* (cold northeasterly wind). Streets fan out towards the north, allowing the city's defenders to easily reach the towers and walls, especially the critical northern portion facing the Pelješki Channel.

In the 16th century, carvers added decorative flourishes such as ornate columns and coats of arms on building façades which gave a Renaissance look to the original Gothic core. People began building houses south of the old town in the 17th and 18th centuries as the threat of invasion diminished and they no longer needed to protect themselves behind walls. The narrow streets and stone houses in the 'new' suburb attracted merchants and artisans and, even today, this is where you'll find most commercial activity.

Orientation

The big Jadrolinija car ferry usually drops you off below the walls of the old town of Korčula in the eastern harbour unless there's too much wind, in which case the

SOUTHERN DALMATIA

ferry ties up in the western harbour in front of the Hotel Korčula and the tourist office. The passenger launches to Orebić also tie up in the western harbour. The bus station (no left-luggage office) is south of town past the marina on the way to the large hotels.

Most people head to the beaches of Orebić but the waters around town are clean enough to swim from any point. There's a small cove next to the large Governor's Gate, and rocky beaches around the hotels and around the Sveti Nikole promenade southwest of the old town.

Information
INTERNET ACCESS
Tino's Internet (☎ 091 509 1182; Ul Tri Sulara; per hr 25KN) Tino has another outlet at the ACI Marina, both of which are open long hours.

MONEY
There are ATMs in town at Splitska Banka and Dubrovačka Banka. You can change money there, at the post office or any of the travel agencies.

POST
Post Office (☑ 7.30am-7pm Mon-Fri, 8am-noon Sat) Hidden next to the stairway up to the old town, there are telephones here.

TOURIST INFORMATION
Jadrolinija office (☎ 715 410) About 25m up from the west harbour.
Tourist Office (☎ 715 701; www.korcula.net; Obala Franje Tuđana bb; ☑ 8am-3pm & 5-9pm Mon-Sat, 8am-3pm Sun Jun-Sep, 8am-1pm & 5-9pm Mon-Sat Oct-May) On the west harbour; an excellent source of information.

TRAVEL AGENCIES
Atlas Travel Agency (☎ 711 231) There a couple of these agencies in town, and they use the same phone number. It represents American Express, runs excursions and finds private accommodation.
Marko Polo Tours (☎ 715 400; marko-polo-tours@ du.htnet.hr; east harbour) Finds private accommodation and organises excursions.

Sights
Take a closer look at the remaining walls and towers that make a sea approach to the town particularly striking. On the western harbour the **Tower of the West Sea Gate** has an inscription in Latin from 1592 stating that Korčula was founded after the fall of

Troy. Nearby are the conical **Large Governor's Tower** (1483) and the **Small Governor's Tower** (1449), which protected the harbour and the Governor's Palace which used to stand next to the town hall.

The entrance to the old city is through the **Veliki Revelin Tower** southern land gate. Built in the 14th century and later extended, the tower is adorned with coats of arms of the Venetian doge and Korčulan governors. There was originally a wooden drawbridge here but it was replaced in the 18th century by the wide stone steps that give a sense of grandeur to the entrance. The only remaining part of the town walls stretch west of this tower.

Other sightseeing is centred on **Cathedral Square** (Trg Sv Marka Statuta 1214), dominated by the magnificent **St Mark's Cathedral** (Katedrala Svetog Marka; Trg Sv Marka Statuta 1214; ☑ 10am-noon, 5-7pm Jul & Aug, Mass only off-season). This 15th-century cathedral was built from Korčula limestone in a Gothic-Renaissance style by Italian and local artisans. Over the solemn portal, the triangular gable cornice is decorated with a two-tailed mermaid, an elephant, and other sculptures. The bell tower that rises from the cathedral over the town is topped by a balustrade and ornate cupola, beautifully carved by the Korčulan, Marko Andrijić.

The interior of the cathedral features modern sculptures in the baptistry, including a *Pietà* by Ivan Meštrović. The ciborium was also carved by Andrijić and behind it is the altarpiece painting *Three Saints* by Tintoretto. Another painting attributed to Tintoretto or his workshop, *The Annunciation*, is on the baroque altar of St Antony. Other noteworthy works include a bronze statue of St Blaise by Meštrović near the altar on the northern aisle, and a painting by the Venetian artist Jacopo Bassano in the apse of the southern aisle.

The **Abbey Treasury of St Mark** (☎ 711 049; Trg Sv Marka Statuta; admission 10KN; ☑ 9am-7pm daily Jun-Aug) in the 14th-century Abbey Palace next to the cathedral is also worth a look. Past the anteroom with its collection of icons, you enter the hall of Dalmatian art with an excellent selection of 15th- and 16th-century Dalmatian paintings. The most outstanding work is the polyptych of *The Virgin* by Blaž Trogiranin. There are also liturgical items, jewellery, furniture

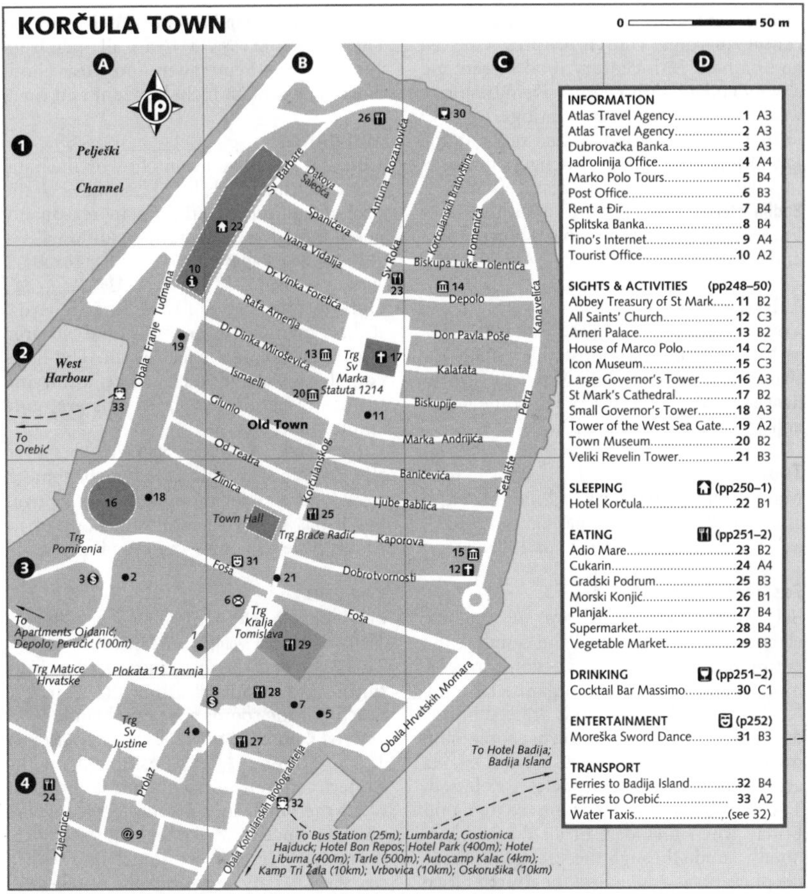
KORČULA TOWN
0
50 m
A
B
C
D
1
2
3
4
Pelješki
Channel
West
Harbour
To
Orebić
To
Apartments Ojdanić;
Depolo; Peručić (100m)
Trg
Pomirenja
Trg Matice
Hrvatske
Plokata 19 Travnja
Trg
Sv
Justine
Prolaz
Zajednice
Obala Franje Tuđmana
Sv Barbare
Đakova
Šalecića
Španićeva
Ivana Vidalija
Antuna Rozanovića
Korčulanskih Bratovština
Pomenića
Sv Roka
Biskupa Luke Tolentića
Dr Vinka Foretića
Rafa Arnerija
Dr Dinka Miroševića
Ismaelli
Giunio
Old Town
Od Teatra
Žlinica
Town Hall
Korčulanskog
Trg
Sv
Marka
Statuta 1214
Depolo
Don Pavla Poše
Kalafata
Biskupije
Marka Andrijića
Baničevića
Ljube Bablića
Kaporova
Dobrotvornosti
Trg Braće Radić
Foša
Trg
Kralja
Tomislava
Kanavelića
Petra
Šetalište
Obala Hrvatskih Mornara
Obala Korčulanskih Brodograditelja
To Hotel Badija;
Badija Island
To Bus Station (25m); Lumbarda; Gostionica
Hajduck; Hotel Bon Repos; Hotel Park (400m); Hotel
Liburna (400m); Tarle (500m); Autocamp Kalac (4km);
Kamp Tri Žala (10km); Vrbovica (10km); Oskorušika (10km)
INFORMATION
Atlas Travel Agency....1 A3
Atlas Travel Agency....2 A3
Dubrovačka Banka....3 A3
Jadrolinija Office....4 A4
Marko Polo Tours....5 B4
Post Office....6 B3
Rent a Đir....7 B4
Splitska Banka....8 B4
Tino's Internet....9 A4
Tourist Office....10 A2
SIGHTS & ACTIVITIES (pp248–50)
Abbey Treasury of St Mark....11 B2
All Saints' Church....12 C3
Arneri Palace....13 B2
House of Marco Polo....14 C2
Icon Museum....15 C3
Large Governor's Tower....16 A3
St Mark's Cathedral....17 B2
Small Governor's Tower....18 A3
Tower of the West Sea Gate....19 A2
Town Museum....20 B2
Veliki Revelin Tower....21 B3
SLEEPING (pp250–1)
Hotel Korčula....22 B1
EATING (pp251–2)
Adio Mare....23 B2
Cukarin....24 A4
Gradski Podrum....25 B3
Morski Konjić....26 B1
Planjak....27 B4
Supermarket....28 B4
Vegetable Market....29 B3
DRINKING (pp251–2)
Cocktail Bar Massimo....30 C1
ENTERTAINMENT (p252)
Moreška Sword Dance....31 B3
TRANSPORT
Ferries to Badija Island....32 B4
Ferries to Orebić....33 A2
Water Taxis....(see 32)

and ancient documents relating to the history of Korčula.

The **Town Museum** (Gradski Muzej; ☎ 711 420; Trg Sv Marka Statuta; admission 10KN; 9am-1.30pm Mon-Sat Jun-Aug) is in the 16th-century Gabriellis Palace opposite the treasury. It traces the history and culture of Korčula throughout the ages beginning with a tablet recording the Greek presence on the island in the 3rd century BC. The stone-carving collection follows the development of that craft with sculptures and stonemason tools, and the shipbuilding hall displays tools and models of local ships. There's also an archaeology collection with prehistoric objects, and an art collection with furniture, textiles and portraits. Explanations are in English.

Before leaving the square, notice the elegantly ornamented **Arneri Palace** (Rafa Arnerija) next door to the museum and extending west down the narrow street of the same name.

It's said that Marco Polo was born in Korčula in 1254 and for a small fee, you can climb the **tower** (Depolo; admission 5KN; 10am-1pm & 5-7pm Mon-Sat Jul & Aug) of the house that is supposed to have been his. There's also an **Icon Museum** (Trg Svih Svetih; admission 8KN; 10am-noon & 5-7pm Mon-Sat). It isn't much of a museum, but it has some interesting Byzantine icons painted on wood on gold backgrounds, and 17th- and 18th-century ritual objects. Visitors are let into the beautiful old **All Saints' Church** (Crkva Svij

Svetij) next door as a bonus. This 18th-century baroque church features a carved and painted 15th-century rood screen and a wooden late-18th-century *Pietà* besides a wealth of local religious paintings.

In the high season, water taxis at the Jadrolinija port collect passengers for visits to various points on the island as well as **Badija Island**, which features a 15th-century Franciscan monastery (now a dormitory) and a naturist beach.

Activities

You can rent a bike at **Hotel Park** (☎ 726 473; per hr/day 15/60KN) or a motorcycle (90KN for two hours) or boat (460KN per day) from **Rent a Đir** (☎ 711 908; Biline 5). For some beach activity, head to Orebić (p253).

Tours

Marko Polo offers tours to Mljet (220KN) and guided tours of Korčula Island (220KN), as well as a half-day cruise for 125KN.

Festivals & Events

Holy Week celebrations are particularly elaborate. Beginning on Palm Sunday, the entire week before Easter is devoted to ceremonies and processions organised by the local religious brotherhoods dressed in traditional costumes. The townspeople sing medieval songs and hymns, Biblical events are re-enacted and the city gates are blessed. The most solemn processions are on Good Friday when members of all the brotherhoods parade through the streets. A schedule of events is available at the tourist office but keep in mind that these are religious events and spectators are expected to be discreet about photos.

Sleeping

BUDGET

There's one large and several small camping grounds. There are other camping grounds near Vela Luka and in Orebić.

Autocamp Kalac (☎ 711182; fax 711 146; per person/site 40/50KN; ◷ Jun-Sep) The largest camping ground, this attractive site is behind Hotel Bon Repos in a dense pine grove near the beach.

About 10km southwest of town near Račišće are three small camping grounds that offer more privacy and access to uncrowded beaches. **Kamp Tri Žala** (☎ 721 244;

trizala@vip.hr), **Kamp Vrbovica** (☎ 721 311) and **Kamp Oskorušica** (☎ 710 747) are all open from June to mid-September and cost about 50KN per person, including tent and car.

MID-RANGE

Cute and quaint you won't find on the hotel scene, but the hotels listed here have all the proper equipment and are in reasonably good, though hardly mint, condition.

Hotel Bon Repos (☎ 711 102; htp-korcula@du.htnet.hr; s/d 535/755KN; 4-person apt 1365KN; P ☀) Outside town on the road to Lumbarda, it has manicured grounds and a large pool overlooking a small beach. The hotel complex is so large you could get lost trying to find reception but the rooms are quite comfortable.

Hotel Park (☎ 726 004; htp-korcula@du.htnet.hr; s/d 640/910KN; P) This concrete behemoth would never win any architectural prizes but it has its own beach and many of its rooms have balconies and sea views.

TOP END

Hotel Liburna (☎ 726 006; htp-korcula@du.htnet.hr; Obala Hrvatskih Mornara; s/d 745/1065KN; P ☀) There's a pool, tennis courts and opportunities to windsurf from the concrete beach but the rooms are fairly bland.

Hotel Korčula (☎ 711 078; htp-korcula@du.htnet.hr; s/d 745/1065KN; P ☒) Positioned on the western harbour, it has the most character of all the hotels and a wide terrace where you can linger over coffee. The mediocre rooms vary in size; try to get one with a sea view. Many are absurdly overpriced. There's no elevator and you'll have to carry your bags to your room.

PRIVATE ROOMS

The big hotels in Korčula are overpriced but there are a wealth of guesthouses that offer clean, attractive rooms and friendly service. Atlas and Marko Polo Tours arrange private rooms, charging from 200KN to 220KN for a room with a private bathroom and apartments starting at about 400KN. Or, you could try one of the following:

Tarle (☎ 711 712; fax 711 146; Stalište Frana Kršinića; d with/without kitchen 270/210KN) Next to the Hotel Marko Polo, about 500m southeast of the bus station, this place has a pretty enclosed garden and attractive rooms with balconies.

MARCO POLO – FIRST SON OF KORČULA

Adventurer, merchant and author of the world's first travel book, Marco Polo had a controversial, action-packed life. He spent 17 years in China as a close personal friend of Kublai Khan and then, while in a Genoese prison, dictated a fantastical account of his experience to a fellow inmate who happened to be a popular romance writer. Although rich in detail about 13th-century China, mainland Asia and even Japan and Zanzibar, his tales were widely discounted at the time. Yet, it got Western Europeans thinking about the Far East and, for 700 years, his book remained an essential source on Mongol China. Modern researchers are now questioning whether he ever visited China or only rehashed accounts from Arab and Persian sources. How did he miss Chinese women's bound feet, the popularity of tea or the Great Wall of China?

Korčulans are untroubled by such piddling details. They claim that he was born in Korčula in 1254, went to Venice with his family in 1269, wandered the world, returned to Venice and was captured in the great Venice-Genoa naval battle of 1296 which landed him in the Genoese prison. The house in which he was allegedly born is being turned into a small museum in honour of his voyages. Korčulans celebrated the 700th anniversary of his birth in 1954, the 700th anniversary of his return from China in 1995 and recently celebrated the 700th anniversary of the Venice-Genoa naval battle that took place near Korčula. Plans are afoot for a Marco Polo Information Centre.

Evidence for the claim that Marco Polo was born in Korčula is sketchy. Korčulans point to the Depolo family that has evidently been based in Korčula for many centuries, at least as far back as Marco Polo's birth. Records indicate that the house on Depolo, considered to be his birthplace, was given to the Depolo family in 1400, 76 years after Marco Polo's death. Perhaps they reclaimed it?

The claim that Marco Polo came from a Dalmatian family is somewhat more strongly supported. A number of early Italian chroniclers theorise that his family was Dalmatian and a more recent writer, HH Hart, in his book *Venetian Adventurer: Marco Polo*, propounded the view that Marco Polo's family came from Šibenik. Under this theory, his name was originally Pile, which means 'chicken' in Croatian, and over time became Polo – 'chicken' in early Italian.

Wherever Marco Polo was born, it is the Korčulans who are now the most devoted to him. He deserves to be remembered even if it turns out that his travel book was written about a place he never visited (which could never happen today, rest assured). Over the centuries he has come to symbolise the unquenchable human need to explore faraway lands, to boldly go where no-one has gone before, and then produce an 'as-told-to' bestseller about it all.

Depolo (☎/fax 711 621; tereza.depolo@du.htnet.hr; d with/without sea view 240/200KN; 🐶) Closer to the old town in the residential neighbourhood of Sveti Nikola and 100m west of the bus station, this guesthouse has attractive and modern rooms.

Other guesthouses nearby for about the same price include **Peručić** (☎/fax 711 458), with great balconies, and the homy **Ojdanić** (☎/fax 711 708; roko-taxi@du.htnet.hr). The owner, Ratko Ojdanić, also has a water taxi and lots of experience with fishing trips around the island.

Eating & Drinking

You can pick up picnic and other basic supplies at the supermarket.

Adio Mare (☎ 711 253; Ulica Sveti Roka; mains around 80KN) Just around the corner from Marco Polo's house, this restaurant has a charming maritime décor and serves a variety of fresh-fish dishes. On summer nights you may have a long wait to get in, but the fresh fish and mussels are worth it.

Morski Konjic (☎ 711 878; Šetalište Petra Kanavelica; mains around 75KN) Also known as the Sea Horse, this is another good seafood place and dishes cost about the same price as Adio Mare.

Gradski Podrum (☎ 711 222; Kaporova; mains from 70KN) Situated just inside the southern gate, it's a little less expensive than the Sea Horse and also serves fish Korčula style – boiled with potatoes and topped with tomato sauce – for 70KN. Pasta and seafood dishes are also reasonable.

Planjak (☎ 711 015; Plokata 19 Travnja; mains from 50KN) This restaurant-grill, between the supermarket and the Jadrolinija office in town is popular with a local crowd who

---

SWORD DANCES

One of the island's most colourful traditions is the Moreška Sword Dance, performed in Korčula since the 15th century. Although probably of Spanish origin, Korčula is now the only place in which it is performed. The dance tells the story of two kings – the White King (dressed in red) and the Black King – who fight for a princess abducted by the Black King. In the spoken introduction the princess declares her love for the White King and the Black King refuses to relinquish her. The two armies draw swords and 'fight' in an intricate dance accompanied by a band. Enthusiastic townspeople perform the dance which takes place outside the southern gate. Although traditionally performed only on Korčula's town day, 29 July, the dance now takes place every Monday and Thursday evening in July and August (sometimes in June and September).

There are also Kumpanija dances around the island regularly in Pupnat, Smokvica, Blato and Čara. This dance also involves a 'fight' between rival armies and culminates in the unfurling of a huge flag. It is accompanied by the local instrument, the *mišnice* – a sort of bagpipe – and drums.

---

appreciate the fresh, Dalmatian dishes as much as the low prices.

Gostionica Hajduk (☎ 711 267; Kalac; mains from 55KN) It's worth the 20-minute walk outside town along the road to Lumbarda to this other local favourite, which serves delicious home-cooked food in a spot with a laid-back ambience. Rooms are also available here.

Cukarin (☎ 711 055; Zajednice) The Cukarin serves up scrumptious local pastries such as *cukarini*, which is a sweet biscuit, *klajun*, a pastry stuffed with walnuts, and *amareta*, a round, rich cake with almonds.

Cocktail Bar Massimo (Šetalište Petra Karnevelića) It's original, you have to grant them that. Lodged in a turret and accessible only by ladder, the drinks are brought up by pulley. You also get a lovely view of the cathedral.

Entertainment

Every visitor who happens to be in Korčula from June to September inevitably winds up at the Moreška Sword Dance (see Sword

Dances, left) held 9pm Monday and Thursday in July and August by the old-town gate. Tickets cost 60KN and can be purchased on the spot or from any travel agency. If you can work out the transportation, the Kumpanija dances in Pupnat, Smokvica, Blato and Čara make a fun night out but, as yet, there's no bus that makes the run.

LUMBARDA

Surrounded by vineyards and coves, Lumbarda is a laid-back village around a harbour on the southeastern end of Korčula island. The sandy soil is perfect for the cultivation of grapes, and wine from the *grk* grape is Lumbarda's most famous product. Greeks were the first to settle the island followed by Romans. In the 16th century, aristocrats from Korčula built summer houses around Lumbarda, and it remains a bucolic retreat from the more urbanised Korčula town. The town beaches are small but sandy. A good ocean beach (Plaza Pržina) is on the other side of the vineyards beyond the supermarket.

Information

Lovor (☎ /fax 712 023; lovor@du.htnet.hr) Arranges hotels and private accommodation.

Post Office It's next door to the tourist office.

Turistička Zajednica (☎ /fax 712 005; tz-lumbarda@ du.htnet.hr; ☒ 9am-9pm Jul & Aug, 8.30am-2pm Mon-Fri Sep-Jun) It's up the street from the bus stop.

Sleeping & Eating

There are several small, inexpensive camping grounds up the hill from the bus stop.

Bebić (☎ 712 505; info@korculainfo.com; d 300KN, studios 350KN, d with half board per person 300KN; Ⓟ ☒) This *pension*-cum-restaurant has a breathtaking view over the coast and serves delicious food. Located on a cove across from town, the *pension* has a small beach for swimming. Even if you're staying elsewhere, try to grab a meal at Bebić's place. Breakfast costs 30KN.

Pansion Marinka (☎ 712 007, 098 344 712; marinka .milina-bire@du.htnet.hr; per person not inc breakfast 75KN) This is a working farm and winery in a beautiful setting within walking distance of the beach. The owners turn out excellent wines and liqueurs, catch and smoke their own fish and are happy to explain the processes to their guests who are invited to participate if they like. They bill their farm as a 'place where you can forget all your problems', which is surely correct.

Hotel Borik (☎ 712 433; lovor@du.htnet.hr; s/d 225/325KN) It is set back from the road on a small hill in the centre of town and is definitely quiet. Rooms are simple.

Getting There & Away

In Korčula town, water taxis wait around the Jadrolinija port for passengers to Lumbarda. You'll only pay about 45KN depending on the number of passengers. Buses to Lumbarda (9KN, 15 minutes) run about hourly until mid-afternoon, but there's no service on Sunday. The bus stops in the town centre.

VELA LUKA

Vela Luka, at the western end of Korčula, is a simple, sober port town, with only an embryonic tourist industry. Surrounded by hills covered with olive trees, most of the town is engaged in the production and marketing of Korčula's famous olive oil. Others are involved in the fishing industry which thrives because of its large sheltered harbour. Although tourists used to rush through and catch the next bus to Korčula, it's now becoming a good alternative place to stay. Although there are no beaches around town, small boats take you to the idyllic offshore islands of Proizd and Osjak.

Orientation & Information

Most of the town and nearly all commercial activity is clustered around the harbour. Note that the numbers in the addresses refer to the number *of* the street, not the number *on* the street.

On the quay and near the bus station, **Atlas Travel Agency** (☎ 812 078; tur-agen-atlas@du.htnet.hr; Obala 3) finds private accommodation.

Coming from Korčula, the **Turist Biro** (☎ / fax 813 619; tzo-vela-luka@du.htnet.hr; ulica 41) is at the entrance to town.

Sights & Activities

There isn't a lot to see at Vela Luka but if you have some time to kill, take a look at the Neolithic **Vela Špilje Cave** (admission 5KN; ☺ variable) which is spacious enough to make cave-dwelling seem like a viable accommodation option. Signs from town direct you to the cave which overlooks the town and harbour.

For a total veg-out at the beach, nothing beats the offshore islands of **Proizd** and **Osjak**. The clear, blue water and white stones of Proizd are dazzling, while Osjak, the larger island, is known for its forest. Bring plenty of sunscreen as there is little shade. There are inexpensive eating options on both islands. Several small boats leave each morning in July and August and pick you up in the afternoon.

The bay of **Gradina**, 5km northwest of Vela Luka, is another lovely, peaceful spot graced with a few beaches. You'll need your own wheels though.

Sleeping & Eating

Camping Mindel (☎ 813 600; 6km northwest of Vela Luka; per adult/site 45/20KN; ☺ May-Sep) There's no bus service to the camping ground so you'll need your own transport.

Hotel Dalmatia (☎ /fax 812 022; www.humhotels .hr; Obala bb; s/d with breakfast 420/565KN) This is one of several hotels in Vela Luka managed by Hum Hotels. Rooms are adequate, if underdecorated, but at least it's on the waterfront. Considering the prices elsewhere on the island, this is more than reasonable.

Pod Bore (☎ 813 069; Obala 5; mains from 40KN) This spacious restaurant with an outdoor terrace offers a pleasant view over the harbour, and the food isn't bad either.

OREBIĆ
pop 1489

Orebić, on the southern coast of the Pelješac Peninsula between Korčula and Ploče, has the best beaches in Southern Dalmatia – wide, sandy coves bordered by groves of tamarisk and pine. Only 2.5km across the water from Korčula, Orebić is a perfect day trip from Korčula or an alternative place to stay.

After enough lazing on the beach, you can take advantage of some excellent hiking up and around Mt Ilija (961m) or poke around in a couple of churches and museums. Mt Ilija protects the town from harsh northern winds, allowing Mediterranean vegetation to flourish. The temperature is usually a few degrees warmer than Korčula; spring arrives earlier and summer leaves later.

Orebić and the Pelješac Peninsula became part of Dubrovnik in 1333 when it was purchased from Serbia and remained in the Republic until 1806. Until the 16th century, the town was known as Trstenica (the name of its eastern bay) and was an important maritime centre. In fact, the town is named after a family of sea captains who, in 1658, built a citadel as a defence against the Turks. Many of the houses and exotic gardens built by prosperous sea captains still grace Orebić and its surroundings. The height of Orebić seafaring occurred in the 18th and 19th centuries when it was the seat of one of the largest companies of the day – the Associazione Marittima di Sabioncello. With the decline of shipping, Orebić has reverted to the classic fallback position of all struggling local economies – tourism.

Orientation & Information

The ferry from Korčula ties up in the town centre, just steps from the tourist office. The bus station (no left-luggage office) is at the end of the ferry dock and the main commercial street, bana Josipa Jelačića, runs parallel to the port. There's a beach west of the dock, but the best beach is the long stretch at Trstenica cove about 500m east of the dock along Šetalište Kneza Domagoja.

The **tourist office** (☎ /fax 713 718; www.tz-orebic .com; Trg Mimbeli; ☺ 8am-8pm Jul & Aug, 8am-1pm & 5-8pm Mon-Fri Sep-Jun) finds private accommodation, changes money and dispenses information. The post office is next door. **Orebić Tours** (☎ 713 367; www.orebic-tours.hr; bana Josipa Jelačića 84a) also finds private accommodation, changes money and books excursions.

Sights & Activities

The **Maritime Museum** (☎ 713 009; Obala Pomoraca; admission 10KN; ☺ 10am-noon & 6-9pm Mon-Fri, 6-9pm Sat), next to the tourist office, is interesting, although not a must-see. There are paintings of boats, boating memorabilia, navigational aids and prehistoric finds from archaeological excavations in nearby Majsan. Explanations are in English.

Orebić is great for **hiking** so pick up a map of the hiking trails from the tourist office. A trail through pine woods leads from Hotel Bellevue to a 15th-century **Franciscan monastery** (admission 5KN; ☺ 8am-noon & 5-7pm) on a ridge 152m above the sea. From their vantage point, Dubrovnik patrols could keep an eye on the Venetian ships moored on Korčula and notify the

authorities of any suspicious movements. The village of Karmen near the monastery is the starting point for walks to picturesque upper villages and the more daring climb to the top of **Mt Ilija**, the bare, grey massif that hangs above Orebić. Your reward is a sweeping view of the entire coast. On a hill east of the monastery is the **Lady of Karmen Church** (Gospa Od Karmena), next to several huge cypresses as well as a baroque **loggia** and the **ruins** of a duke's castle.

Sleeping & Eating

The tourist office or Orebić Tours finds private rooms from 100KN per person as well as studios and apartments.

All the modern resort complexes are west of town and there's one good camping ground.

Glavna Plaža (☎ 713 399; Trstenica; per adult/site 25/50KN; ☺ Apr-Sep) This family-run camping ground overlooks the long, sandy Trstenica beach.

Hotel Bellevue (☎ /fax 713 148; Sveti Križa 104; s/d 310/420KN; P ☒) On a rocky beach, it's the closest resort to town. Facilities include tennis courts and water sports on the hotel beach.

Restoran Amfora (☎ 713 719; Kneza Domagoja 6; mains from 40KN) This family-run restaurant is a local favourite for its fantastic seafood dishes.

Getting There & Away

If you're coming from the coast, there are three daily ferries (seven in summer) from Ploče to Trpanj which connect with a bus to Orebić. Korčula buses to Dubrovnik, Zagreb and Sarajevo stop at Orebić. For more bus and ferry information, see p246.

STON & MALI STON
pop 740

The two settlements of Ston and Mali Ston are 59km northwest of Dubrovnik on an isthmus that connects the Pelješac Peninsula with the mainland. Formerly part of the Republic of Dubrovnik, Ston was and is an important salt-producing town. Its economic importance to the Republic of Dubrovnik led to the construction of a 5.5km wall in 1333; the longest fortification in Europe. The walls are still standing, sheltering an appealing cluster of medieval buildings in the town centre. Mali Ston, a little village and harbour situated about 1km northeast of Ston, was built along with the wall as part of the defensive system and now is known for the oyster beds along its bay. Both Ston and Mali Ston are major gastronomic highlights, turning out the best seafood in Croatia.

Orientation & Information

The bus stop is located in the centre of Ston, near the tourist office, bank and post office.

The **tourist office** (Turistička Zajednica; ☎ /fax 754 452; Peljestki put 1; ⏲ 7am-1pm & 5-7pm Mon-Fri, 7am-1pm Sat Jul & Aug, 7am-3pm Mon-Fri Sep-Jun) has a small selection of brochures and can arrange private accommodation.

Sights & Activities

The major sight in Ston is the 14th-century **walls** (admission free; ⏲ 10am-dusk) which stretch from the town far up the hill. The clear Pelješac air allows for magnificent views over the peninsula.

There are no beaches in town but it's an easy walk to the Camping Prapratno, 4km southwest of town, where there's a cove and a pebble beach.

Sleeping & Eating

Each of the hotels listed here has an excellent restaurant, but there are also a few other possibilities for sampling the superb seafood.

Camping Prapratno (☎ 754 000; fax 754 344; 4km southwest of Ston; per adult/site 28/42KN; 🏊) This camping ground is right on Prapratno Bay and offers tennis and basketball courts as well as swimming facilities.

Vila Koruna (☎ 754 359; www.vila-koruna.hr; s/d 445/595KN; Ⓟ 🎱) In an old house on the harbour of Mali Ston, this six-room hotel provides warm, personal service and comfortable rooms with TV and phone.

Ostrea (☎ 754 555; www.ostrea.hr; s/d with half board 740/1115KN; Ⓟ 🎱 🖳) Rooms are on a grander scale in this harbourside hotel in Mali Ston, containing modern bathrooms, computer terminals and minibars.

Kapetanova Kuća (☎ 754 452; mains from 65KN) Near the Ostrea hotel, this is one of the most venerable seafood restaurants in the region. The oysters and mussels are to die for.

Bella Vista (☎ 753 110; mains from 65KN) On a cliff overlooking Prapratno Bay, this friendly restaurant serves up delicious seafood platters and has a marvellous view of the bay.

Getting There & Away

There are three daily buses from Dubrovnik to Orebić (44KN, 1½ hours) and one to Korčula (49KN, two hours); all services travel via Mali Ston and Ston.

Directory

DIRECTORY

CONTENTS

ACCOMMODATION

In this book, budget accommodation includes camping grounds, hostels and some guesthouses and costs around 100KN to 200KN per night per person. Mid-range accommodation costs about 400KN to 700KN a double, while top-end can reach as high as 2000KN per double.

Along the coast, accommodation is priced according to four seasons, which vary from place to place. November to March are the cheapest months. There may only be one or two hotels open in a coastal resort but you'll get great rates – often no more than 350KN for a double in a good three-star hotel and 250KN in a lesser establishment. Generally, April,

May and October are the next cheapest months and June and September are the shoulder season, but in July and August count on paying top price, especially in the peak period, which starts in mid-July and lasts until mid- or late August.

Prices quoted in this book are for the peak period based upon a four-night stay. Deduct about 25% from the prices in this book if you come in June, the beginning of July, or September, about 35% for May and October and about 50% for all other times. Prices for most accommodation in Zagreb, Rijeka and Split are constant all year. Some large, and nearly all small, hotels and guesthouses charge a 30% surcharge for stays less than four nights and include 'residence tax', which varies from 4KN to 7.50KN per person per day, depending on the season and the classification of the town. Accommodation is generally cheaper in Dalmatia than in Kvarner or Istria, but in July and August you should make arrangements in advance wherever you go.

This book provides the phone numbers of most accommodation facilities. Once you know your itinerary it pays to buy a phonecard and start calling around to check prices and availability. Most receptionists speak English.

As Croatia heats up as a star destination, it's becoming harder to get a confirmed reservation without a deposit, particularly in high season. Very few hotels, and no guesthouses, are equipped to reserve accommodation using a credit-card number. Most are now asking for a SWIFT wire transfer (your bank wires directly to their bank). Unfortunately, banks charge fees for the transaction, usually in the range of US$15.

Camping

Nearly 100 camping grounds are scattered along the Croatian coast. Most operate from mid-April to mid-September only, although a few are open March to October. In spring and autumn, it's best to call ahead to make sure that the camping ground is open before beginning the long trek out. Don't go by the opening and closing dates you read in travel brochures or even this

- Electrical supply is 220V, 50Hz AC. Croatia uses the standard European round-pronged plugs.

- Widely read newspapers include *Vecernji List, Vjesnik, Jutarnji list, Slobodna Dalmacija* and the *Feral Tribune*. The most popular weeklies are *Nacional* and *Globus*.

- The radio station HR2 broadcasts traffic reports in English every hour on the hour from July to mid-September.

- Bills include a service charge, but it's common to round up the bill.

- Croatia uses the metric system (see conversion chart on the inside front cover).

- Mobile phones are GSM 900/1800, which is compatible with the rest of Europe and Australia, but not with the North American GSM 1900.

- The video system is PAL.

book, as these can change. Even local tourist offices can be wrong.

Many camping grounds, especially in Istria, are gigantic 'autocamps' with restaurants, shops and row upon row of caravans. Expect to pay up to 100KN for the site at some of the larger establishments. Most camping grounds charge from 30KN to 50KN per person per night. The tent charge is sometimes included in the price, but occasionally it's an extra 10KN to 15KN. The auto charge is sometimes included; it may be an extra 10KN to 50KN. If you bring a caravan you'll pay about 30% more for a site, then there's an electricity charge that may be included or may cost an extra 15KN per night. The residence tax costs about an extra 7KN per person per night, depending on the season and the region. Prices in this book are per adult and site, which includes a tent and car.

Although small, family-owned camping grounds are starting to pop up, most grounds are still autocamps. If you want a more intimate environment, the town tourist office should be able to refer you to smaller camping grounds, but you may have to insist upon it. Naturist camping grounds (marked FKK) are among the best

because their secluded locations ensure peace and quiet. However, bear in mind that freelance camping is officially prohibited. A good website for camping information and links is www.camping.hr.

Hostels

The **Croatian YHA** (☎ 01-48 47 472; www.hfhs.hr; Dežmanova 9, Zagreb) operates youth hostels in Dubrovnik, Punat, Zadar, Zagreb and Pula. Nonmembers pay an additional 10KN per person per day for a stamp on a welcome card; six stamps entitles you to membership. Prices given in this book are for the high season, July and August; prices fall the rest of the year. The Croatian YHA can also provide information about private youth hostels in Krk, Zadar, Dubrovnik and Zagreb.

Hotels

Tourism really started to take off in Croatia (then part of Yugoslavia) in the 1970s and 1980s, which was when most of the hotels along the coast were built. At the time, the idea was to market the coast to package tourists and then send them to 'tourist settlements', usually far from town and along a stretch of beach. Since they were all state-owned and built at the same time with the same idea, it's unsurprising that they all look alike. There is nothing particularly Istrian or even Croatian in an Istrian hotel complex to distinguish it from a Dalmatian or Spanish hotel complex.

The advantage of this approach is that it left the historic old towns more or less alone, free of a lot of the tourist trappings that would have been present if tourists had commandeered the towns for the summer. From a visitor's point of view, the disadvantage is the lack of small family-owned hotels where the owner's taste and personality is reflected in the rooms. For a more personal experience, you have to stay in private accommodation. As Croatia heads towards a privatised economy, many family-run establishments that used to rent rooms through the local travel agency are proclaiming themselves *pensions*. Since the owners usually have decades of experience in catering to travellers, these private *pensions* offer excellent value. Some *pensions* are included in this book, but as more and more pop up each season, it pays to ask the local tourist office about them. Don't go by the printed brochures as these often cover only the larger hotels.

Zagreb and other big cities have at least one grand old hotel built in the 19th century, when the railway came through. Opatija was a popular resort in the Austro-Hungarian empire and has a conglomeration of elegant, European-style hotels that retain a certain faded splendour.

Private entrepreneurs have recently begun changing the top end of the hotel scene in Croatia. There are more and more completely overhauled hotels along the coast that offer a high standard of amenities and service. Although not cheap (figure on 900KN to 1200KN for a double), the rooms are spiffy and there are often saunas, gyms, massage facilities and other healthy extras.

Croatian hotels may not charm you, but they are clean, serviceable and fairly efficient. Double rooms, if not singles, are a good size, and nearly all rooms in Croatian hotels have private bathrooms. The vast majority of hotels in Croatia fall into the moderate range – around 650KN for a double in the summer along the coast, dropping to around 350KN in late spring or early autumn. At that price you can get a pleasant, clean but unexceptional room equipped with a private bathroom, a telephone and sometimes a TV with a satellite hook-up. Since there's usually no surcharge for a short stay, hotels can be a better deal than private accommodation if you're only staying a night or two.

Most hotels offer the option of half board. In a 'tourist settlement' far from town, half board may be the only dining possibility within reach. Sometimes half board is only a marginal increase over the B&B rate, making it worth considering even if you only plan to take a few meals at the hotel. Except in luxury establishments, the meals centre on cheaper cuts of meat, although some hotels are starting to offer a vegetarian menu.

Croatian hotels are rated according to a star system that is largely meaningless. One-star hotels offer hostel-like accommodation and five-star hotels offer clearly superior rooms and facilities (gym, sauna, swimming pool), but otherwise the stars are awarded too inconsistently to provide much indication as to the quality of the establishment. The distinction between two- and three-star hotels seems particularly whimsical.

Private Rooms

The best accommodation in Croatia is a private room in a local home – the equivalent of small private guesthouses in other countries. Not only is a private room cheaper than a hotel, the service is likely to be friendlier and more efficient, and the food better. Such rooms can be arranged by travel agencies, but they add taxes and commission to your bill, so you'll almost always do better dealing directly with proprietors you meet on the street or by knocking on the doors of houses with *sobe* (rooms available) or *zimmer* (rooms available) signs. This way you avoid the residence tax and possibly the four-night minimum stay (unless it's high season). You also, however, forgo the agency's quality control.

Language barriers can make negotiation difficult, since proprietors are likely to speak only Croatian, German or Italian. If you choose the knocking-on-doors approach, start early in the day since proprietors may be out on errands in the afternoon. You'll be more comfortable and in a better position to negotiate a price if you leave your luggage in a *garderoba* (left-luggage office) before trudging around town.

Proprietors will sometimes look for potential customers at coastal bus stations and ferry terminals, so if you're struggling to find a room you may find something at these places. Try to pin the proprietor down on the location of the accommodation, or you could get stuck way out of town. Cafés are also a good source of accommodation leads, but remember to exercise the usual caution.

If the price asked is too high, bargain. Be sure to clarify whether the price agreed upon is per person or per room. Tell the proprietor in advance how long you plan to stay, or they may try to add a surprise 'supplement' when you leave after a night or two. In high season along the coast it may be impossible to find a proprietor willing to rent you a room for one night only. At the agencies, single rooms are expensive and scarce, but on the street, *sobe* prices are usually per person, which favours the single traveller. Showers are always included but often breakfast is not, so ask about the breakfast charge.

If possible, it may be worthwhile to take a half-board option and stay with a family. Most families on the coast have a garden, a vineyard and access to the sea. You could find yourself beginning your evenings with a home-made aperitif before progressing on to garden-fresh salad, home-grown potatoes and grilled fresh fish, all washed down with your host's very own wine.

Although renting an unofficial room is common practice along the Adriatic coast, be discreet, as technically you're breaking the law by not registering with the police. Don't brag to travel agencies about the low rate you got, for example.

If you stay less than four nights, the agencies will add a 30% surcharge. Often there is a one-time 'registration tax' to register you with the police.

Travel agencies classify private rooms according to a star system. The most expensive rooms are three-star and include a private bathroom. In a two-star room, the bathroom is shared with one other room, and in a one-star room, the bathroom is shared with two other rooms or with the owner. Studios with cooking facilities can be a good deal, costing little more than a double room, but remember that self-catered meals are not cheap in Croatia. If you're travelling in a small group, it may be worthwhile to get an apartment. In no event will private accommodation include TV or telephone.

Accommodation rates are usually fixed by the local tourist association and don't vary from agency to agency, although some agencies may not handle rooms in the cheapest category. The prices quoted in the Sleeping sections of this book assume a four-night stay in high season. Prices fall dramatically outside July and August.

ACTIVITIES
Hiking
The steep gorges and beech forests of Paklenica National Park, 40km northeast of Zadar, offer excellent hiking. Starigrad, the main access town for the park, is well connected by hourly buses from Zadar. Hotels, private accommodation and a camping ground are available in Starigrad.

Risnjak National Park at Crni Lug, 12km west of Delnice between Zagreb and Rijeka, is a good hiking area in summer. Due to the likelihood of heavy snowfalls, hiking is advisable only from late spring to early autumn. It's a 9km, 2½-hour climb from the park entrance at Bijela Vodica to Veliki Risnjak (1528m).

For a great view of the barren coastal mountains, climb Mt Ilija (961m) above Orebić, opposite Korčula, or Sveti Jure (1762m) from Makarska.

Kayaking
There are countless possibilities for anyone carrying a folding sea kayak, especially among the Elafiti Islands (take the daily ferry from Dubrovnik to Lopud) and the Kornati Islands (take the ferry from Zadar to Sali). For information on sailing and kayaking tours, see p279.

Rock Climbing
The karstic stone of Croatia's coast provides excellent climbing opportunities. Paklenica National Park (p167) has the widest range of routes – nearly 400 – for all levels of experience. Spring, summer and autumn are good seasons to climb, but in winter you'll be fighting the fierce *bura* (cold northeasterly wind). Other popular climbing spots include the rocks surrounding Baška on Krk Island (p113), which can be climbed year-round (although if you come in summer, you can combine climbing with a beach holiday). Brela on the Makarska Riviera (p207) also allows climbing and beach-bumming, but in winter there's a strong *bura*. Also on the Makarska Riviera is the wall from Baška Voda to Makarska on Mt Biokovo (p206), with 200m to 400m routes. For more information, contact the **Croatian Mountaineering Association** (☎ /fax 01-48 24 142; www.hps.inet.hr; Kozaričeva 22, 10000 Zagreb).

Scuba Diving
The varied underwater topography of the Croatian coast has spurred a growing diving industry. From Istria to Dubrovnik, nearly every coastal resort has a dive centre, usually German-owned. Although there's a little bit of everything along the coast, the primary attractions are shipwrecks and caves. The porous karstic stone that forms the coastal mountains has created an astonishing variety of underwater caves all along the coast, but especially in the Kornati Islands (p186). Shipwrecks are

---

DIVING WEBSITES

For information on diving in Croatia, check out these websites:

■ **Diving Croatia** www.diving.hr

■ **Croatian Diving Federation**
www.diving-hrs.hr

■ **Croatia** www.croatia.hr

---

also a common sight, most notoriously the *Baron Gautsch* wreck near Rovinj (p142). Remains of Roman wrecks with 1st-century amphorae can be found within reach of Dubrovnik (p229), but special permission is necessary since they are protected cultural monuments. Diving from Lošinj Island (p105) offers a good mixture of sights – sea walls, caves and wrecks.

The marine life is not as rich as the Red Sea or the Caribbean, for example, but you'll regularly see gropers, eels, sardines and snails. Sponges and sea fans are common sea flora, but coral reefs tend to lie in deep water – around 40m – since the shallower coral has already been plundered. The waters around Vis Island (p208) are richest in marine life because the island was an off-limits military base for many years and the sea was not overfished.

Windsurfing

Although most coastal resorts offer windsurfing courses and board rentals, serious windsurfers gravitate to the town of Bol on Brač Island. The *maestral* (strong, steady westerly wind) blows from April to October, and the wide bay catches the wind perfectly. The best windsurfing is in late May, early June, late July and early August. The wind generally reaches its peak in early afternoon and then dies down at the end of the day.

Another good spot to windsurf is Viganj on the Peljesac Peninsula, not far from Orebić (p253) which has windsurfing schools and is the site of various windsurfing championships.

Yachting

There's no better way to appreciate the Croatian Adriatic than by boat. The long, rugged islands off Croatia's mountainous coast all the way from Istria to Dubrovnik make this a yachting paradise. Fine, deep channels with abundant anchorage and steady winds attract yachties from around the world. Throughout the region there are quaint little ports where you can get provisions, and yachts can tie up right in the middle of everything.

There are 40 marinas along the coast, some with more facilities than others. Every coastal town mentioned in this book has a marina, from little Sali on Dugi Otok to the large marinas in Opatija, Zadar, Split and Dubrovnik. Most marinas are open throughout the year but it's best to check first. A good source of information is **Udruženje Nautičkog Tourism** (Association of Nautical Tourism; ☎ 051-209 147; fax 051-216 033; Bulevar Oslobođenja 23, 51000 Rijeka), which represents all Croatian marinas. You could also try the **Adriatic Croatia International** (ACI; ☎ 051-271 288; www.aci-club.hr; M Tita 51, Opatija), which represents about half the marinas.

Although you can row, motor or sail any vessel up to 3m long without authorisation, for larger boats you'll need to get authorisation from the harbour master at your port of entry, which will be at any harbour open to international traffic. Come equipped with a boat certificate, documents proving your sailing qualifications, insurance documents and money.

Yachting enthusiasts may wish to charter their own boat. Experienced sailors can charter a yacht on a 'bareboat' basis or you can pay for the services of a local captain for a 'skippered' boat. **Sunsail** (UK ☎ 0870 777 0313, USA ☎ 888 350 3568; www.sunsail.com) is an international operator with offices in the UK and the USA. It offers bareboat and skippered charters from Pula and Rogoznica near Trogir. In the UK, you could also try **Cosmos Yachting** (☎ 0800 376 9070; www.cosmos yachting.com), which offers charters out of Dubrovnik, Pula, Rovinj, Split, Trogir and Zadar, or **Nautilus Yachting** (☎ 01732-867 445; www.nautilus-yachting.com), which offers rentals from Pula and Split. The price depends upon the size of the boat, the number of berths and the season.

BUSINESS HOURS

Official office hours are from 8am to 4pm Monday to Friday. Banking and post office hours are 7.30am to 7pm on weekdays and 8am to noon on Saturday. Many shops are open 8am to 7pm on weekdays and until

2pm on Saturday. Croats are early risers; by 7am there will be lots of people on the street and many places already open. Along the coast life is more relaxed; shops and offices frequently close around noon for an afternoon break and reopen at about 4pm.

Restaurants are open long hours, often from noon to midnight, with Sunday closings out of peak season. Cafés are usually open daily from 10am to midnight, and bars are open from 9pm to 2am. In Zagreb and Split, discos and nightclubs are open year-round, but many places along the coast are only open in summer. Cybercafés are also open long hours – usually seven days a week.

CHILDREN

Successful travel with young children requires planning and effort. Don't try to overdo things by packing too much into the time available. Involve the kids in the planning, and balance that visit to the art museum with a trip to the zoo or time spent on a playground. Lonely Planet's *Travel with Children* by Cathy Lanigan offers a wealth of tips and tricks to make travelling with tots child's play.

In Croatia, children's discounts are widely available for everything from museum admissions to hotel accommodation. The cut-off age is often nine. Hotels may have children's cots, but numbers are limited.

For greater comfort, look into renting an apartment. There's much more space for the same price as a hotel room, and a kitchen can be handy for preparing kids' meals.

Disposable nappies are easy to find, particularly American Pampers and German Linostar. Look for supermarkets such as Konzum, and the pharmacy DM. Very few restaurants or public restrooms have nappy-changing facilities. For more on where to buy baby formula see p44. Keep in mind that electric sterilisers are expensive and hard to find. Breast-feeding in public is uncommon, but generally accepted if done discreetly.

Kids love the beach, but choose your sites carefully, as many 'beaches' are rocky with steep drop-offs. Sandy beaches are more kid-friendly. Try Baška on Krk Island, Brela along the Makarska coast, the beaches surrounding Orebić and the narrow stretch of shingle beach on Crveni Otok near Rovinj. The beach near the Hotel Kompas in Dubrovnik is also kid-friendly.

CLIMATE CHARTS

The climate varies from Mediterranean along the Adriatic coast, to continental inland. The sunny coastal areas experience hot, dry summers and mild, rainy winters, while the interior regions are warm in summer and cold in winter. Wind patterns

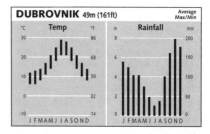

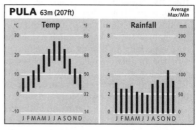

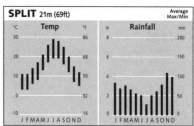

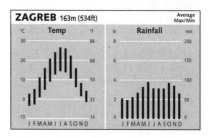

cool the coast with refreshing breezes in the summer, but high mountains shield the coast from bitter winter weather. The sea stores heat in the summer and radiates the heat onto the land in the winter, warming the surrounding air.

In spring and early summer, the *maestral* keeps the temperature down along the coast. It generally starts blowing at around 9am, increases until early afternoon and dies down in late afternoon. This strong, steady wind makes good sailing weather.

Winter weather is defined by two winds. The southeasterly *široko* from the Sahara Desert brings warm, moist air to the mainland and can produce a heavy cloud cover. This wind also has the steady strength that sailors love. The northeasterly *bura* blows from the interior to the coast in powerful gusts, bringing dry air and blowing away clouds.

Sun-lovers should note that the island of Hvar gets 2715 hours of sun a year, followed by Split with 2697 hours, Vela Luka on Korčula Island with 2671 hours and Dubrovnik with 2584 hours. The lack of rainfall along the coast, especially on islands further removed from the mainland, has produced severe water shortages in Dalmatia throughout its history. Summer dry periods can last up to 100 days, nearly as long as Sicily and Greece. Before pipelines to the Cetina and Neretva Rivers were laid, islanders often had to collect rainwater in cisterns. For more climate information, see p9.

CUSTOMS

Travellers can bring their personal effects into the country, along with 1L of liquor, 1L of wine, 500g of coffee, 200 cigarettes and 50mL of perfume. The import or export of kuna is limited to 15,000KN per person. Camping gear, boats and electronic equipment should be declared upon entering the country. There is no quarantine period for animals brought into the country, but you should have a recent vaccination certificate from your veterinarian. Otherwise, the animal is subject to inspection by a local veterinarian who, needless to say, may not be immediately available.

Taxes & Refunds

Travellers who spend more than 500KN in one store are entitled to a refund of the value-added tax (VAT), which is equivalent to 22% of the purchase price. In order to claim the refund, the merchant must fill out the *Poreski ček* (required form), which you must present to the customs office upon leaving the country. Mail a stamped copy to the store, which will then credit your credit card with the appropriate sum. There is also a service called Global Refund System, which will give you your refund in cash at the airport or at participating post offices. Post offices in Zagreb, Osijek, Dubrovnik, Split, Korčula and a few dozen other towns participate in the system. For a complete list, see www.posta.hr. Both the VAT and the refund system are newfangled notions in Croatia, so don't be surprised if merchants don't always have the necessary forms.

DANGERS & ANNOYANCES

Personal security, including theft, is not a problem in Croatia, but the former confrontation line between Croat and federal forces was heavily mined in the early 1990s. Over a million mines were laid in eastern Slavonia, around Karlovac in the hinterlands north of Zadar. The hills behind Dubrovnik also contain some mines. Although the government has invested heavily in de-mining operations, it's a slow job. In general, the mined areas are well signposted with skull-and-crossbones symbols and yellow tape, but don't go wandering off on your own in sensitive regions before checking with a local. Never go poking around an obviously abandoned and ruined house.

Croatia is not unduly burdened with biting or stinging creatures but mosquitoes do abound in Eastern Slavonia, and sea urchins are nearly everywhere along the coast.

DISABLED TRAVELLERS

Due to the number of wounded war veterans, more attention is being paid to the needs of disabled travellers in Croatia. Public toilets at bus stations, train stations, airports and large public venues are usually wheelchair accessible. Large hotels are wheelchair accessible, but very little private accommodation is. Bus and train stations in Zagreb, Zadar, Rijeka, Split and Dubrovnik are wheelchair accessible but the local Jadrolinija ferries are not. For further information, get in touch with **Savez Organizacija Invalida Hrvatske** (☎ /fax 01-48 29 394; Savska cesta 3, 10000 Zagreb).

DISCOUNT CARDS
Camping Card International

The Camping Card International (CCI; formerly the Camping Carnet) is a camping ground ID that can be used instead of a passport when checking into a camping ground; it includes third-party insurance. As a result, many camping grounds offer a small discount (5% to 10%) if you sign in with one. CCIs are issued by automobile associations and camping federations. In the UK, the AA issues them to its members for £6.35, and in the USA the AAA issues them for US$15.

Student & Youth Cards

Most museums, galleries, theatres and festivals in Croatia offer student discounts of up to 50%. Although any proof of attendance at an educational institution is acceptable, most people get an International Student Identity Card (ISIC), which is the best international proof of your student status.

To get an ISIC card, you must be enrolled in full- or part-time study. The application must include proof of student registration (eg transcript or bursar's receipt), a US$22 registration fee and one passport-size photo. The card comes with a handbook listing discounts for cardholders.

People under the age of 26 who are not students qualify for the International Youth Travel Card (IYTC). Applicants must present proof of age (a copy of your birth certificate, passport or driving licence), a US$22 fee, and one passport-size photo. The card, valid one year from the date of issue, also comes with a travel handbook.

Both the ISIC and IYTC cards carry basic accident and sickness insurance coverage, and cardholders have access to a worldwide hotline for help in medical, legal or financial emergencies.

Croatia is a member of the **European Youth Card Association** (www.euro26.hr), which offers reductions in shops, restaurants and libraries in participating countries. All Youth Card holders (€26) can use their cards at around 1400 places of interest in Croatia.

STA Travel (www.statravel.com), an international company specialising in youth travel,

offers all of the cards discussed here. In Croatia, contact **Dali Travel** (☎ 01-48 47 472; travel section@hfhs.hr; Dežmanova 9, 10000 Zagreb).

EMBASSIES & CONSULATES
Croatian Embassies & Consulates

Croatian embassies and consulates abroad:
Australia (☎ 02-6286 6988; 14 Jindalee Cres, O'Malley, ACT 2601)
Canada (☎ 613-562 7820; 229 Chapel St, Ottawa, Ontario K1N 7Y6)
France (☎ 01 5370 0287; 2 rue de Lubeck, Paris)
Germany (Berlin ☎ 030-219 15 514; Ahornstrasse 4, 10787; Bonn ☎ 022-895 29 20; Rolandstraße 52, 53179)
Ireland (☎ 1 4767 181; Adelaide Chambers, Peter St, Dublin)
Netherlands (☎ 70 362 36 38; Amaliastraat 16, The Hague)
New Zealand (☎ 09-836 5581; 131 Lincoln Rd, Henderson, Auckland)
South Africa (☎ 012-342 1206; 1160 Church St, 0083 Colbyn, Pretoria)
UK (☎ 020-7387 2022; 21 Conway St, London W1P 5HL)
USA (☎ 202-588 5899; www.croatiaemb.org; 2343 Massachusetts Ave NW, Washington, DC 20008)

Embassies & Consulates in Croatia

The following addresses are in Zagreb (area code ☎ 01) unless otherwise noted:
Albania (Map pp60-1; ☎ 48 10 679; Jurišićeva 2a)
Australia (Map pp60-1; ☎ 48 91 200; www.auembassy.hr; Kaptol Centar, Nova Ves 11)
Bosnia and Hercegovina (Map pp60-1; ☎ 46 83 761; Torbarova 9)
Bulgaria (Map pp60-1; ☎ 48 23 336; Novi Goljak 25)
Canada (Map pp60-1; ☎ 48 81 200; zagreb@dfait-maeci .gc.ca; Prilaz Gjure Deželića 4)
Czech Republic (☎ 61 77 239; Savska 41)
France (Map pp60-1; ☎ 48 93 680; consulat@ambafrance .hr; Hebrangova 2)
Germany (☎ 61 58 105; www.deutschebotschaft -zagreb.hr; avenija grada Vukovara 64)
Hungary (Map pp60-1; ☎ 48 22 051; Pantovčak 128/I)
Ireland (☎ 48 77 900; Zrinskog 5)
Netherlands (☎ 46 84 880; nlgovzag@zg.htnet.hr; Medvešćak 56)
New Zealand (Map pp60-1; ☎ 65 20 888; avenija Dubrovnik 15)
Poland (Map pp60-1; ☎ 48 99 444; Krležin Gvozd 3)
Romania (Map pp60-1; ☎ 45 77 550; roamb@zg.tel.hr; Mlinarska ul 43)
Serbia and Montenegro (Map pp60-1; ☎ 01 45 79 067; Pantovčak 245)
Slovakia (Map pp60-1; ☎ 48 48 941; Prilaz Gjure Deželića 10)
Slovenia (Map pp60-1; ☎ 63 11 000; Savska 41)

UK (Map pp60-1; ☎ 60 09 100; I Lučića 4)
USA (Map pp60-1; ☎ 66 12 200; www.usembassy.hr; Ul Thomasa Jeffersona 2)

FESTIVALS & EVENTS

FEBRUARY
Carnival Banned in former Yugoslavia, pre-Lent celebrations have taken Croatia by storm since independence. For the best costumes, dancing, and general revelry, join the parties in Rijeka, Samobor or Zadar.

MARCH
Days of Croatian Film The Film Artists Association of Croatia arranges showings of short features, animated films and videos in theatres throughout Zagreb, followed by awards.
Vukovar Puppet Spring Festival In the last week of March, Vukovar becomes a puppet town with workshops, demonstrations and performances.

APRIL
Biennial of Contemporary Music In odd-numbered years, Zagreb hosts this prestigious musical event. By 'contemporary', do not read 'pop'.
Queer Zagreb FM Festival (www.queerzagreb.org) During the last week of April, gays come out of the closet and celebrate their lifestyle with a host of gay-themed films and music.

MAY
Dance Week Festival (www.danceincroatia.com) Held the last week of May. Avant-garde and experimental dance companies from around the world are showcased in Zagreb.

JUNE
Festival of Animated Films (www.animafest.com) In even-numbered years, Zagreb hosts this festival where animated films (don't call them cartoons) are honoured.
International Children's Festival Introducing the young 'uns to the artistic life is the goal of this festival in Šibenik, which presents puppets, theatre troupes, performances and workshops all geared to the kiddies.
International Festival of New Films (www.split filmfestival.hr) Films, videos, installations, workshops and discussions attract experimental film makers from around the world.

JULY
Dubrovnik Summer Festival (www.dubrovnik-festival .hr) From mid-July to mid-August, Dubrovnik showcases the finest local and national classical musicians in concerts throughout the city.
International Folklore Festival Zagreb becomes a whirlwind of colour and music as costumed fiddlers and dancers descend on the capital from all over the world.

Motovun Film Festival (www.motovunfilmfestival .com) This relatively new festival is attracting increasingly well-known independent films, and is probably Croatia's most glamorous film festival.
Poreč Annale The oldest and most prestigious international art event in Croatia, this month-long series of exhibits showcases the finest young Croatian artists.

SEPTEMBER
Baroque Evenings of Varaždin Baroque music in the baroque city of Varaždin.

FOOD
Restaurants offer excellent value for money in Croatia. From budget to top end, you can get a plate of pasta or a risotto for 40KN to 70KN, which means that you can eat almost anywhere for very much the same price if you confine yourself to a few dishes. The difference is in the main courses. Budget restaurants have a greater variety of inexpensive, usually meat-based, main courses that cost about 50KN. Mid-range restaurants will have more elaborately prepared dishes and better cuts of meat at prices that range from 70KN to 100KN. The wine list is also more sophisticated and more expensive. The few top-end places in Croatia offer a fine-dining experience for over 100KN for a main course, and wine that can cost that much just for a bottle. Fish and seafood are expensive everywhere, from 300KN to 320KN a kilo. The cheapest bet is calamari; about 60KN a portion whether grilled or fried.

Groceries are not cheap in Croatia, which is worth keeping in mind if you'll be self-catering. There are good deals on fresh produce but anything in a bottle or a can is no cheaper than anywhere else in Western Europe. Special and tasty local ham, sausage, cold cuts and cheese can be pricey indeed. You can get good deals on fish out of season, but during the summer the best fish goes directly to the restaurants.

For the full lowdown on Croatian cuisine, see p42.

GAY & LESBIAN TRAVELLERS
Homosexuality has been legal in Croatia since 1977 and is tolerated, but not welcomed with open arms. Public displays of affection between members of the same sex may be met with hostility, especially outside major cities. Exclusively gay clubs are a rarity outside Zagreb, but many of the large

discos attract a mixed crowd. Raves are also a good way for gays to meet.

On the coast, gays gravitate to Rovinj, Hvar, Split and Dubrovnik and tend to frequent naturist beaches. In Zagreb, the last Saturday in June is Gay Pride Zagreb day, an excellent opportunity to connect with the local gay scene. Venues that are gay-friendly are listed throughout this book.

Most Croatian websites devoted to the gay scene are in Croatian only, but a good starting point is www.touristinfo.gay.hr. Otherwise, there's **Iskorak** (www.iskorak.hr), the LGBT rights organisation, **LORI** (www.lori.hr), the lesbian organisation based in Rijeka, and **Crol-Lesbians** (www.cro-lesbians.com), the lesbian information centre.

HOLIDAYS

Croats take their holidays very seriously. Stores and museums are shut and boat services are reduced. On religious holidays, the churches are full; it can be a good time to check out the artwork in a church that is usually closed. Holidays falling in the milder months are often marked by street spectacles that include dancing and bands. Easter and Holy Week are especially good times to catch local celebrations. In and around Dubrovnik, palm or olive twigs are decorated with flowers, blessed and placed in homes on Palm Sunday. Holy Week preceding Easter is celebrated with processions on Hvar, Brač and Koročula Islands. Central Croatia celebrates Holy Week with *krijes* (bonfires), and painted eggs are given as Easter gifts.

Croatian public holidays are as follows:

New Year's Day 1 January
Epiphany 6 January
Easter Monday March/April
Labour Day 1 May
Corpus Christi 10 June
Day of Antifascist Resistance 22 June – marks the outbreak of resistance in 1941
Statehood Day 25 June
Victory Day & National Thanksgiving Day 5 August
Feast of the Assumption 15 August
Independence Day 8 October
All Saints' Day 1 November
Christmas 25 & 26 December

INSURANCE

A travel insurance policy to cover theft, loss and medical problems is a good idea. You should check your existing insurance policies at home before purchasing travel insurance, as some may already provide worldwide coverage. Some credit cards also offer limited accident insurance.

A good travel agent should be able to guide you in choosing the right policy. There's a variety of policies available, so check the small print. Some policies specifically exclude 'dangerous activities', which can include scuba diving, motorcycling and even trekking. A locally acquired motorcycle licence is not valid under some policies.

You may prefer a policy that pays doctors or hospitals directly rather than you having to pay on the spot and claim later. If you have to claim later, make sure you keep all documentation. Some policies ask you to call (reverse charges) a centre in your home country where an immediate assessment of your problem is made. Check that your policy covers ambulances and an emergency flight home.

For additional insurance information, see Health (p280) and Transport (p271).

INTERNET ACCESS

Cybercafés are listed under Information in the specific regional chapters of this guide, but many come and go with startling speed. The local tourist office should have the latest on the scene. In smaller towns, the tourist office may let you quickly check your email on their computer if you ask nicely. Public libraries usually have Internet access but their hours can be limited. Most travellers make constant use of Internet cafés and free Web-based email such as **Yahoo** (www.yahoo.com) or **Hotmail** (www.hotmail.com). If you need to access another non-Web-based account, you'll need to know your incoming (POP or IMAP) mail-server name, your account name and your password.

If you're travelling with a notebook or hand-held computer, be aware that your modem may not work once you leave your home country. The safest option is to buy a reputable 'global' modem before you leave home, or a local PC-card modem if you're spending extended time in any one country. For more information on travelling with a portable computer, see www.teleadapt.com.

LEGAL MATTERS

Although it is highly unlikely that you'll be hassled by the police, you should keep

DIRECTORY

identification with you at all times as the police have the right to stop you and demand ID. By international treaty, you have the right to notify your consular official if arrested. Consulates can normally refer you to English-speaking lawyers, although they will not pay for one.

MAPS

Freytag & Berndt publishes a series of country, regional and city maps. Its 1:600,000 map of Croatia, Slovenia and Bosnia and Hercegovina is particularly useful if you'll be travelling in the region. Other good maps include *Croatia, Slovenia* (1:800,000) by GeoCenter and *Hrvatska, Slovenija, Bosna i Hercegovina* (1:600,000) by Naklada Naprijed in Zagreb. Regional tourist offices often publish good regional driving maps showing the latest roads. Except for Zagreb, Split, Zadar, Rijeka and Dubrovnik, there are few top-quality city maps. Local tourist offices usually publish helpful maps.

MONEY

In May 1994 the Croatian dinar was replaced by the kuna. Commonly circulated banknotes come in denominations of 500, 200, 100, 50, 20, 10 and five kuna, bearing images of Croat heroes such as Stjepan Radić and Ban Josip Jelačić. Each kuna is divided into 100 lipa. You'll find silver-coloured 50- and 20-lipa coins, and bronze-coloured 10-lipa coins.

The kuna has a fixed exchange rate tied to the euro. To amass hard currency, the government makes the kuna more expensive in summer when tourists visit. You'll get the best exchange rate from mid-September to mid-June. Otherwise, the rate varies little from year to year. Accommodation and international boat fares are priced in euros, not kuna, although you pay in kuna. In this book, we list prices for hotels, camping and private accommodation in kuna. For more information about expenses, see p9; for exchange rates see the Quick Reference on the inside front cover.

ATMs

Automatic teller machines are prevalent nearly everywhere in Croatia and can be a convenient way of changing money. Most are tied in with Cirrus, Plus, Diners Club and Maestro. Privredna Banka usually has

---

STREET NAMES

Particularly in Zagreb and Split, you may notice a discrepancy between the names used in this book and the names you'll actually see on the street. In Croatian, a street name can be rendered either in the nominative or possessive case. The difference is apparent in the name's ending. Thus, Ulica Ljedevita Gaja (street of Ljudevita Gaja) becomes Gajeva ulica (Gaja's street). The latter version is the one most commonly seen on the street sign and used in everyday conversation. The same principle applies to a *trg* (square), which can be rendered as Trg Petra Preradovića or Preradovićev trg. Some of the more common names are Trg svetog Marka (Markov trg), Trg Josipa Jurja Strossmayera (Strossmayerov trg), Ulica Andrije Hebranga (Hebrangova), Ulica Pavla Radića (Radićeva), Ulica Augusta Šenoe (Šenoina), Ulica Nikole Tesle (Teslina) and Ulica Ivana Tkalčića (Tkalčićeva). Be aware also that Trg Nikole Sća Zrinjskog is almost always called Zrinjevac.

ATMs for cash withdrawals using American Express cards. Most other ATMs also allow you to withdraw money using a credit card, but you'll start paying interest on the amount immediately, in addition to paying the withdrawal fee. All post offices will allow you to make a cash withdrawal on MasterCard or Cirrus, and a growing number work with Diners Club as well.

Cash

There are numerous places to change money in Croatia, all offering similar rates; ask at any travel agency for the location of the nearest exchange. Post offices change money and keep long hours. Most places deduct a commission of 1% to 1.5% to change cash, but some banks do not. Travellers cheques may be exchanged only in banks. Kuna can be converted into hard currency only at a bank and only if you submit a receipt of a previous transaction. Hungarian currency (the forint) is difficult to change in Croatia. Make sure you have a four-digit personal identification number (PIN). If you can't get to an exchange operation, you can pay for a meal or small services in euros, but the rate is not as good.

Credit Cards

Credit cards (Visa, MasterCard, Diners Club, American Express) are widely accepted in hotels but rarely accepted in any kind of private accommodation. Many smaller restaurants and shops do not accept credit cards.

Amex card holders can contact Atlas travel agencies in Dubrovnik, Opatija, Pula, Poreč, Split, Zadar and Zagreb for the full range of Amex services, including cashing personal cheques and holding clients' mail. Privredna Banka is a chain of banks that handles many services for Amex clients.

Listed below is the contact information for the major credit-card companies. All addresses are in Zagreb (area code ☎ 01):

American Express (☎ 61 24 422; www.american express.hr; Lastovska 23)

Diners Club (☎ 48 02 222; www.diners.hr; Praška 5)

Eurocard/Mastercard (☎ 37 89 620; www.zaba.hr; Zagrebačka banka, Samoborska 145)

Visa (☎ 46 47 133; www.splitskabanka.hr; Splitska banka, Tuškanova 28)

PHOTOGRAPHY

Colour-print film produced by Kodak and Fuji is widely available in photo stores and tourist shops. It's fairly expensive in Croatia compared to a lot of other countries so stock up ahead of time. If you choose to develop your photos in Croatia, remember that the standard size for prints is only 9cm x 13cm. Digital-imaging techniques are available in Zagreb and other large cities, but few places develop APS film. One-hour developing is not widely available. Slide film is widely available in major cities and tourist centres but can be scarce in out-of-the-way places.

If you're shooting in one of Croatia's steamy summer months, remember that film should be kept cool and dry after exposure. The intense summer light can wash out colour between mid-morning and late afternoon, and the overcast skies of winter may dictate the use of a fairly fast film.

As in any country, politeness goes a long way when taking photos or filming; ask permission before photographing people. Military installations may not be photographed, and you may have a lot of angry, naked people after you if you try to take pictures in a naturist resort.

POST

HPT Hrvatska, recognised by its red, white and blue sign, offers a wide variety of services, from selling stamps and phonecards to sending faxes. If you want to avoid a trip to the post office and just want to send a few postcards, you can buy *pismo* (stamps) at any *tisak* (newsstand) and drop your mail into any of the yellow postboxes on the street. It takes anywhere from five days (Europe) to two weeks (North America and Australia) for a card or letter to arrive at its destination.

Domestic mail costs 2.80KN for up to 20g, and 5KN for up to 100g. Postcards are 1.80KN. For international mail, the base rate is 3.50KN for a postcard, 5KN for a letter up to 20g, and 15KN for a letter up to 100g. Then, add on the airmail charge for every 10g: 1KN for Europe, 1.50KN for North America, 1.60KN for Africa and Asia, and 2KN for Australia.

If you have an Amex card or are travelling with Amex travellers cheques, you can have your mail addressed to branches of Atlas travel agencies in Dubrovnik, Opatija, Poreč, Pula, Split, Zadar and Zagreb; mail will be held at the office for up to two months.

SHOPPING

The finest artisans' product from Croatia is the intricate lace from Pag Island, part of a centuries-old tradition that is still going strong. Although you'll sometimes see it in handicraft shops in Zagreb and Dubrovnik, it's more fun to take a trip out to Pag where you can buy the patches of lace directly from the women who make them.

Embroidered fabrics are also featured in many souvenir shops. Croatian embroidery is distinguished by the cheerful red geometric patterns set against a white background, which you'll see on tablecloths, pillowcases and blouses.

Lavender and other fragrant herbs made into scented sachets or transmuted into oils make popular and inexpensive gifts. You can find them on most Central Dalmatian islands, but especially on Hvar Island, known for its lavender fields.

Brač Island is known for its lustrous stone. Ashtrays, vases, candlestick holders and other small but heavy items carved from Brač stone are on sale throughout the island.

Samples of local food, wine and spirits can also make great gifts or souvenirs. If you're in Samobor, pick up some mustard or Bermet liquor. In Pag you can buy savoury home-made cheese, but be aware that customs regulations in many countries forbid the importation of unwrapped cheese. *Cukarini* pastries from Korčula Island keep for a while if they are wrapped in cellophane. Local brandies, often with herbs inside the bottle, can conjure up the scents and flavours of each region, since it seems that almost every town produces its own special brandy.

A recent addition to the Croatian shopping scene is the jewellery stores that are cropping up in cities and towns. They are usually run by immigrants from Kosovo who have a centuries-old tradition in silver working. Although the shops also sell gold, the workmanship on silver filigree earrings, bracelets and *objets d'art* is often of astonishingly high quality.

SOLO TRAVELLERS

The joy of travelling solo is that it is a compromise-free trip. You do what you want when you want to do it, but you will pay for the privilege. Very few hotels, guesthouses or private rooms have special rates for singles, although you may be able to knock a few kuna off the double-room price if you visit out of season.

If you want to meet other travellers and sample the local life, it's best to stay away from large resort-style hotels, as they tend to be frequented by families and couples. They are also isolated from community life. It's much better to stay in guesthouses that have a few rooms where you can meet other travellers. To mix with the locals, try to find a place in the centre of town where you can go out to cafés and bars. Cybercafés are also good places to meet both travellers and locals. The staff at cybercafés often speak excellent English.

If you find that dining out alone is a forlorn experience, make lunch the main meal of your day, when the dining room is more likely to contain solo business-or-pleasure diners. Solo diners can often get short shrift, but if you take out a notebook and start writing you might be mistaken for a restaurant critic; your treatment will improve dramatically.

TELEPHONE

To call Croatia from abroad, dial your international access code, then ☎ 385 (the country code for Croatia), then the area code (without the initial zero) and the local number. To call within Croatia, start with the area code (with the initial zero). Phone numbers with the prefix ☎ 060 are free and phone numbers that begin with ☎ 09 are mobile (cellular) phone numbers, which are billed at a much higher rate than regular numbers (figure on about 2KN per minute).

There are few coin-operated phones, so you'll need a phonecard to use public telephones. Phonecards are sold according to *impulsa* (units), and you can buy cards of 25 (15KN), 50 (30KN), 100 (50KN) and 200 (100KN) units. These can be purchased at any post office and most tobacco shops and newspaper kiosks. Many new phone boxes are equipped with a button on the upper left with a flag symbol. Press the button and you get instructions in English. If you don't have a phonecard you can call from a post office.

Remember that calls placed from hotel rooms are much more expensive. For local and national calls, the mark-up is negligible from cheaper hotels but significantly more from four-star establishments. Private accommodation never includes a private telephone, although you may be able to use the owner's for local calls.

A three-minute call from Croatia using a phonecard will be around 12KN to the UK and Europe and 15KN to the USA or Australia. Local calls cost 0.80KN whatever the time of day although owners of a fixed line get cheaper rates from 7pm to 7am.

The international access code is ☎ 00. Some other useful numbers are ☎ 92 for the police, ☎ 93 for the fire department, ☎ 94 for emergency medical assistance and ☎ 901 to place an operator-assisted call.

Mobile Phones

Croatia uses GSM 900/1800, which is compatible with the rest of Europe and Australia but not with the North American GSM 1900 system or the totally different system in Japan (though some North Americans have GSM 1900/900 phones that do work there). If you have a GSM phone, check with your service provider before you leave about using it in Croatia, and beware of calls being routed internationally (it will be very expensive for a 'local' call). If you have a GSM phone, you can buy a SIM card for about 300KN, which includes 30 minutes of connection time. If you don't have a GSM phone and want the convenience of a mobile phone, you can buy a packet (mobile and phonecard) at any telecom shop for about 800KN, which includes 30 minutes of connection time. Renting a phone costs about 40KN per day.

TIME
Croatia is on Central European Time (GMT/UTC plus one hour). Daylight saving comes into effect at the end of March, when clocks are turned forward an hour. At the end of September they're turned back an hour.

TOURIST INFORMATION
The **Croatian National Tourist Board** (☎ 01-45 56 455; www.htz.hr; Iblerov trg 10, Importanne Gallerija, 10000 Zagreb) is a good source of information. There are regional tourist offices that supervise tourist development, and municipal tourist offices that have free brochures and good information on local events. Some arrange private accommodation. Contact information for local tourist offices is listed in the regional chapters.

Following is contact information for regional tourist offices:

Dubrovnik-Neretva County (☎ 020-324 222; www .visitdubrovnik.hr; Cvijete Zuzorić 1/l, 20000 Dubrovnik)

Istria County (☎ 052-452 797; www.istra.com; Pionirska 1a, 52440 Poreč)

Krapina-Zagorje County (☎ 049-233 653; tzkzz@ kr.htnet.hr; Zagrebačka 6, 49217 Krapinske Toplice)

Osijek-Baranja County (☎ 031-675 897; www.osjecko -baranjska-zupanija.hr; Sunčana 39, 31222 Bizovac)

Primorje-Gorski Kotar (Kvarner) County (☎ 051- 272 988; www.kvarner.hr; N Tesle 251410 Opatija)

Split-Dalmatia County (☎ 021-490 032; www .dalmacija.net; Prilaz Braće Kaliterna 10/l, 21000 Split)

Šibenik-Knin County (☎ 022-219 072; www.sibenik -knin.com; Fra N Ružića bb, 22000 Šibenik)

Zadar County (☎ 023-315 107; www.zadar.hr; Š Leopolda B Mandića 1, 23000 Zadar)

Zagreb County (☎ 01-48 73 665; www.tzzz.hr; Preradovićeva 42, 10000 Zagreb)

Tourist information is also dispensed by commercial travel agencies such as **Atlas**

(www.atlas-croatia.com), Croatia Express, Generalturist and Kompas, which also arrange private rooms, sightseeing tours etc. Ask for the schedule for coastal ferries.

Croatian tourist offices abroad:

Austria (☎ 01-585 3884; office@kroatien.at; Kroatische Zentrale für Tourismus, Am Hof 13 1010 Vienna)

Czech Republic (☎ 02-2221 1812; infohtz@iol.cz; Hrvatska turistiška zajednica OS, Krakovská 25, 11000 Prague)

France (☎ 01 45 00 99 55; croatie.ot@wanadoo.fr; 48 avenue Victor Hugo, 75016 Paris)

Germany Frankfurt (☎ 069-238 5350; kroatien-info@ gmx.de; Kroatische Zentrale für Tourismus, Kaiserstrasse 23, D-60311); Munich (☎ 089-223 344; kroatien -tourismus@t-online.de; Kroatische Zentrale für Tourismus, Rumfordstrasse 7, D-80469)

Hungary (☎ 01-266 6505; www.horvatinfo@axelro .hu; Horvát Idegenforgalmi Közösség Magyar u. 36, 1053 Budapest)

Italy Milan (☎ 02-86 45 44 97; info@enteturismocroato .it; Ente nazionale Croato per il turismo, Piazzete Pattari 1/3, 20123); Rome (☎ 06 32 11 0396; officeroma@ enteturismocroato.it; Via dell' Oca 48 00186)

Netherlands (☎ 31182 670 244; info@brouwerbetist .nl; Kroatische Centrale voor Tourisme, Hoge Gouwe 93, 2800 Ag Goude)

UK (☎ 020-8563 7979; info@cnto.freeserve.co.uk; Croatian National Tourist Office, 2 Lanchesters, 162-64 Fulham Palace Rd, London W6 9ER)

USA (☎ 212-279 8672; cntony@earthlink.net; Croatian National Tourist Office, Suite 4003, 350 Fifth Ave, New York, NY 10118)

VISAS
Citizens of the EU, USA, Canada, Australia, New Zealand, Israel, Ireland, Singapore and the UK do not need a visa for stays of up to 90 days. South Africans must apply for a 90-day visa in Pretoria. Contact any Croatian embassy, consulate or travel agency abroad for information.

If you want to stay in Croatia longer than three months, the easiest thing to do is cross the border into Italy or Austria and return.

Croatian authorities require foreigners to register with local police when they arrive in a new area of the country, but this is a routine matter normally handled by the hotel, hostel, camping ground or agency securing private accommodation. That's why they need to take your passport away for the night.

If you're staying elsewhere (eg with relatives or friends), your host should take care of it for you. See p271 for information about passports and entering the country.

WOMEN TRAVELLERS

Women face no special danger in Croatia. Women on their own, however, may occasionally be harassed and followed in large coastal cities, and some of the local bars and cafés can seem like private men's clubs – a woman alone is likely to be greeted with sudden silence and cold stares. It's important to be careful about being alone with an unfamiliar man, since claims of 'date rape' are not likely to be taken very seriously.

Croatian women place a high priority on good grooming and try to buy the most fashionable clothes they can afford. Topless sunbathing is considered acceptable, and, judging from the ubiquitous photos of topless women in tourist brochures, it seems almost obligatory.

Transport

THINGS CHANGE...

The information in this chapter is particularly vulnerable to change. Check directly with the airline or a travel agent to make sure you understand how a fare (and ticket you may buy) works and be aware of the security requirements for international travel. Shop carefully. The details given in this chapter should be regarded as pointers and are not a substitute for your own careful, up-to-date research.

GETTING THERE & AWAY

ENTERING THE COUNTRY
Passport

A valid passport is necessary to enter Croatia. To avoid problems, it's best to ensure that your passport will remain valid for the entire course of your stay. Always make a photocopy of your passport and keep the photocopy in a separate place. In case your passport is lost or stolen, producing a photocopy of the original at your embassy or consulate will greatly facilitate its replacement. If your passport disappears right before your departure, take your airline tickets to your embassy or consulate and you will normally get a temporary passport enabling you to at least re-enter your home country. See p269 for information about visas.

AIR
Airports & Airlines

Major airports in Croatia:

Dubrovnik (airport code DBV; ☎ 020-773 377; www
.airport-dubrovnik.hr)
Pula (airport code PUY; ☎ 052-530 105; www.airport
-pula.com)
Rijeka (airport code RJK; ☎ 051-842 132)
Split (airport code SPU; ☎ 021-203 506; www.split
-airport.hr)
Zadar (airport code ZAD; ☎ 023-313 311; www.zadar
-airport.hr)
Zagreb (airport code ZAG; ☎ 01-62 65 222; www.zagreb
-airport.hr)

In addition to domestic connections to Zagreb, Rijeka has a direct flight to London (Heathrow), Pula has a direct flight to Manchester, and Split has direct flights to Manchester, London (Gatwick), Prague and Rome (Fiumicino). These flights normally function in summer only.

Dubrovnik has direct flights to Manchester, London (Gatwick), Glasgow and Vienna, as well as flights to Zagreb and Split.

Zagreb is connected domestically to Dubrovnik, Split, Pula, Rijeka and Zadar and internationally to all European capitals plus Munich, Frankfurt, Istanbul and Damascus.

Zadar receives domestic flights from Zagreb only.

The following are the major airlines flying into the country:
Adria Airways (☎ 01-48 10 011; www.adria-airways
.com; hub Ljubliana)
Air Canada (☎ 01-48 22 033; www.aircanada.ca;
hub Toronto)
Air France (☎ 01-48 37 100; www.airfrance.com;
hub Paris)
Aeroflot (☎ 01-48 72 055; www.aeroflot.ru;
hub Moscow)
Alitalia (☎ 01-48 10 413; www.alitalia.it; hub Milan)
Austrian Airlines (☎ 062 65 900; www.aua.com)

Croatia Airlines (☎ 01-48 19 633; www.croatiaairlines .hr; Zrinjevac 17, Zagreb; hub Zagreb)
ČSA (☎ 01-48 73 301; www.csa.cz; hub Prague)
Delta Airlines (☎ 01-48 78 760; www.delta.com; hub Atlanta)
KLM-Northwest (☎ 01-48 78 601; www.klm.com; hub Amsterdam)
Lot (☎ 01-48 37 500; www.lot.com; hub Warsaw)
Lufthansa (☎ 01-48 73 121; www.lufthansa.com; hub Frankfurt)
MALEV Hungarian Airlines (☎ 01-48 36 935; www .malev.hu; hub Budapest)
Turkish Airlines (☎ 01-49 21 854; www.turkishairlines .com; hub Istanbul)

Tickets

With a bit of research – ringing around travel agencies, checking Internet sites, perusing the travel ads in newspapers – you can often get yourself a good travel deal. Start early, as some of the cheapest tickets need to be bought well in advance and popular flights can sell out.

Full-time students and people under 26 years (under 30 in some countries) have access to better deals than other travellers. You have to show a document proving your date of birth or a valid International Student Identity Card (ISIC) when buying your ticket and boarding the plane.

The best prices are generally found by booking on the Internet. Many airlines, full-service and no-frills, offer some excellent fares to Web surfers. They may sell seats by auction or simply cut prices to reflect the reduced cost of electronic selling.

Many travel agencies around the world have websites, which can make the Internet a quick and easy way to compare prices. There is also an increasing number of online agents which operate only on the Internet.

Online ticket sales work well if you are doing a simple one-way or return trip on specified dates. Online superfast fare generators, however, are no substitute for a travel agent who knows all about special deals, has strategies for avoiding layovers and can offer advice on everything from which airline has the best vegetarian food, to the best travel insurance.

You may find that the cheapest flights are advertised by obscure agencies. Such firms are usually honest and solvent, but there are some rogue fly-by-night outfits around. Paying by credit card generally

offers protection, as most card issuers provide refunds if you can prove you didn't get what you paid for. Similar protection can be obtained by buying a ticket from a bonded agent, such as one covered by the Air Travel Organiser's Licence (ATOL; www.atol.org.uk) scheme in the UK. Agents who accept only cash should hand over the tickets straight away and not tell you to 'come back tomorrow'. After you've made a booking or paid your deposit, call the airline and confirm that the booking was made. It's generally not advisable to send money (even cheques) through the post unless the agent is very well established – some travellers have reported being ripped off by fly-by-night mail-order ticket agencies.

If you purchase a ticket and later want to make changes to your route or get a refund, you need to contact the original travel agent. Airlines issue refunds only to the purchaser of a ticket – usually the travel agent who bought the ticket on your behalf. Many travellers change their routes halfway through their trips, so think carefully before you buy a ticket which is not easily refunded.

Asia

Although most Asian countries are now offering fairly competitive airfare deals, Bangkok, Singapore and Hong Kong are still the best places to shop around for discount tickets. A one-way fare from Bangkok to Zagreb is around US$586. Hong Kong's travel market can be unpredictable, but some excellent bargains are available if you are lucky.

The reliable STA Travel (www.statravel.com) has branches in Hong Kong, Tokyo, Singapore, Bangkok and Kuala Lumpur; check the website for contact details.

Australia

Two well-known agencies for cheap fares are STA Travel (www.statravel.com) and Flight Centre (☎ 133 133; www.flightcentre.com.au). STA Travel has offices in all major cities and on many university campuses. Flight Centre also has dozens of offices throughout Australia.

Flights from Sydney or Melbourne will be via another European city such as London, Rome or Frankfurt. Return fares begin at around A$1600 in low season and A$2200 in high season.

Canada

Canada's main student travel organisation is **Travel Cuts** (Voyages Campus in Québec; ☎ 1-866-246-9762; www.travelcuts.com), with offices in Toronto and Montreal.

Return fares from Toronto to Zagreb are around C$1200 in low season and C$1400 in the high season.

Continental Europe

Though London is the travel discount capital of Europe, there are several other cities in which you will find a range of good deals to Zagreb.

In Amsterdam, try **NBBS Reizen** (☎ 900 10 20 300; www.nbbs.nl; 66 Rokin, Amsterdam) and **Malibu Travel** (☎ 020-626 32 30; Prinsengracht 230). Expect to pay around €400 for a return flight from Amsterdam.

In Paris, recommended travel agencies include **OTU Voyages** (☎ 08 20 81 78 17; www.otu.fr) and **Nouvelles Frontières** (☎ 08 25 00 08 25; www.nouvelles-frontieres.fr; 87 blvd de Grenelle). On the Internet, there's **Lastminute** (☎ 08 92 70 50 00; www.lastminute.com). Return fares to Zagreb start from around €325 with Croatia Airlines.

In Italy, a recommended travel agency in Rome is **CTS Viaggi** (☎ 06-462 0431; www.cts.it). A return fare from Rome to Zagreb costs around €250.

A recommended agency in Germany is **STA Travel** (☎ 030-310 0040; www.statravel.de; Hardenbergstrasse, Berlin).

New Zealand

A good place to start price shopping is the travel section of the *New Zealand Herald*, which carries adverts from travel agencies.

Flight Centre (☎ 0800 243 544; www.flightcentre.co.nz; cnr Queen & Darby Sts) has a large central office in Auckland at National Bank Towers and many branches throughout the country. **STA Travel** (☎ 0508 782 872; www.statravel.co.nz) has offices throughout New Zealand.

The cheapest fares to Europe are generally routed through the USA. Otherwise, you can fly from Auckland to pick up a connecting flight in Melbourne or Sydney. Online, look at www.travel.co.nz. A return flight from New Zealand would cost around NZ$1800.

UK

London is one of the best centres in the world for discounted air tickets.

For students or travellers under 26 years, popular travel agencies in the UK include **STA Travel** (☎ 0870 160 0599; www.statravel.co.uk) and **Trailfinders** (☎ 020-7628 7628; www.trailfinder.com; 215 Kensington High St, London). Trailfinders produces a lavishly illustrated brochure that includes airfare details.

The weekend editions of national newspapers sometimes have information on cheap fares. In London, also try the *Evening Standard*, *Time Out* and *TNT*, a free weekly magazine ostensibly for antipodeans. Fare checking on Internet travel sites can turn up some good deals. Try the following:

Cheapest Flights (www.cheapestflights.co.uk)
Online Travel (www.onlinetravel.com) Good deals on flights from more than a dozen British cities.

A standard return flight from London would cost around £250.

USA

Discount travel agencies in the USA are known as consolidators (although you won't see a sign on the door saying Consolidator). San Francisco is the ticket consolidator capital of America, although some good deals can be found in Los Angeles, New York and other big cities. Try the following websites:

Cheap Tickets (www.cheaptickets.com)
Expedia (www.expedia.msn.com) Microsoft's travel site.
Flight Centre International (www.flightcentre.com)
Orbitz (www.orbitz.com)
STA Travel (☎ 800-777 0112; www.statravel.com)
Ticket Planet (www.ticketplanet.com)
Travelocity (www.travelocity.com)

Travellers with Special Needs

If they're warned early enough, airlines can often make special arrangements for travellers with special needs, such as wheelchair assistance at airports or vegetarian meals on the flight. Children under two years travel for 10% of the standard fare (or free on some airlines) as long as they don't occupy a seat. They don't get a baggage allowance. 'Skycots', baby food and nappies should be provided by the airline if requested in advance. Children aged between two and 12 can usually occupy a seat for half to two-thirds of the full fare, and do get a baggage allowance.

The disability-friendly website www.everybody.co.uk has an airline directory that provides information on the facilities offered by various airlines.

LAND
Car & Motorcycle

The main highway entry and exit points between Croatia and Hungary are Goričan (between Nagykanizsa and Varaždin), Gola (23km east of Koprivnica), Terezino Polje (opposite Barcs) and Donji Miholjac (7km south of Harkány). There are 29 crossing points to and from Slovenia – too many to list here. There are dozens of border crossings into Bosnia and Hercegovina and into Serbia and Montenegro, including the main Zagreb-to-Belgrade highway. Major destinations in Bosnia and Hercegovina, such as Sarajevo, Mostar and Međugorje, are all accessible from Zagreb, Split, Osijek and Dubrovnik.

Austria
BUS

Eurolines (www.eurolines.com) runs buses from Vienna to Zagreb (€32, six hours, two daily), Rijeka (€47, 8¼ hours), Split (€51, 15 hours) and Zadar (€43, 13 hours).

TRAIN

The *Ljubljana* express travels daily from Vienna to Rijeka (€65.50, 11½ hours, two daily) through Ljubljana and the EuroCity *Croatia* from Vienna to Zagreb (€60.50, 6½ hours). Both travel via Maribor, Slovenia.

Belgium
BUS

Eurolines operates a twice-weekly service all year from Brussels to Zagreb (€103, 22 hours), and another weekly bus to Split (€112, 28 hours), stopping at Rijeka.

Bosnia and Hercegovina
BUS

There are daily connections from Sarajevo (€22, five hours, daily) and Mostar (€10.65, three hours) to Dubrovnik; from Sarajevo to Split (€14 to €16, seven hours, five daily), which stop at Mostar; and from Sarajevo to Zagreb (€28, eight hours) and Rijeka (€34).

TRAIN

There's a daily train service to Zagreb from Sarajevo each morning (9½ hours), a daily train to Osijek (8½ hours) and two daily

trains from Sarajevo to Ploče (4½ to 5½ hours).

Germany
BUS

As Croatia is a prime destination for Germans on vacation and Germany is a prime destination for Croatian workers, the bus services between the two countries are good. All buses are handled by **Deutsche Touring GmbH** (☎ 069-79 03 50; www.deutsche-touring.com; Am Romerhof 17, Frankfurt) and fares are cheaper than the train. There are no Deutsche Touring offices in Croatia, but numerous travel agencies and bus stations sell its tickets. There are buses between Zagreb and Berlin, Cologne, Dortmund, Frankfurt, Main, Mannheim, Munich, Nuremberg and Stuttgart; buses depart four times a week from Berlin, and daily from the others. There's a weekly bus to Istria from Frankfurt and two buses a week from Munich.

The Dalmatian coast is also served by daily buses from German cities and there's a twice weekly bus direct from Berlin to Rijeka and on to Split.

TRAIN

There are three trains daily from Munich to Zagreb (€76, nine hours) via Salzburg and Ljubljana. Reservations are required southbound but not northbound.

Hungary
BUS

Hungary is well connected to Varaždin, with two daily buses from Nagykanizsa (three hours). Nagykanizsa is more convenient if you're travelling to or from Budapest. From Pećs (Hungary), there are two daily buses to Osijek (2½ hours) via Mohaćs (1½ hours).

TRAIN

The four daily trains from Zagreb to Budapest (€30, 6½ hours) also stop in Nagykanizsa, the first main junction inside Hungary (€11). The price is the same for one way and return.

Italy
BUS

Trieste is well connected with the Istrian coast. There are around six buses a day to

Rijeka (€7.50, two to three hours), plus buses to Rovinj (€10.50, 3½ hours, three daily), Poreč (€8.50, 2¼ hours, three daily) and Pula (€14, 3¾ hours, four daily). There are fewer buses on Sunday. To Dalmatia there's a daily bus that leaves at 5.30pm and stops at Rijeka, Zadar (€32, 7½ hours), Split (€35.60, 10½ hours) and Dubrovnik (€64, 15 hours). There are also two daily buses from Trieste to Varaždin (six hours).

There's also a bus from Venice, Monday to Saturday, that stops in Poreč (2½ hours), Rovinj (three hours) and Pula (€24, 3¼ hours). For schedules, see www.saf.ud.it. There's a weekly bus in the summer from Milan to Poreč, Rovinj and Pula (€49, 8½ hours).

TRAIN
Between Venice and Zagreb (€41, eight hours), there's a daily connection via Ljubljana.

Slovenia
BUS
Slovenia is also well connected with the Istrian coast. There is one weekday bus between Rovinj and Koper (€11, three hours) and Poreč and Portorož (€5.50, 1½ hours), as well as a daily bus in summer from Rovinj to Ljubljana (5050SIT, 5½ hours) and Piran (2020SIT, 2½ hours).

TRAIN
There are up to eleven trains daily between Zagreb and Ljubljana (€23, 2¼ hours) and four between Rijeka and Ljubljana (€25, three hours).

Serbia and Montenegro
BUS
There's one bus each morning from Zagreb to Belgrade (€25.50, six hours). At Bajakovo on the border, a Yugoslav bus takes you on to Belgrade. The border between Serbia and Montenegro and Croatia is open to visitors, allowing Americans, Australians, Canadians and Brits to enter visa-free. There's a daily bus from Kotor to Dubrovnik (100KN, 2½ hours, daily) that starts at Bar and stops at Herceg-Novi.

TRAIN
Five daily trains connect Zagreb with Belgrade (€17.50, six hours).

SEA
Regular boats from several companies connect Croatia with Italy and Slovenia. Prices quoted refer to deck passage in the summer season. Prices are about 10% less in the off-season and taking a car costs about an additional €40 on the Ancona–Split line. A couchette on an overnight boat costs about an extra €15 and an inside cabin with two berths and a toilet is about twice the price. Passengers in cabin class have breakfast included, otherwise the price is about €3.50. There is no port tax if you are leaving Croatia by boat. All of the boat-company offices in Split are located inside the ferry terminal.

> **DEPARTURE TAX**
>
> There is an embarkment tax of €3 from Italian ports.

Adriatica Navigazione (Venice ☎ 041-781 611, Ancona ☎ 071-20 74 334; www.adriatica.it) Connects Ancona and Split and runs between Trieste and Rovinj (€15.49, 3½ hours) and Poreč (€14.89, 2½ hours).
Archibugi Ravenna (☎ 0544- 422 682; archibugi@tin .it; Via Magazzini anteriori 27); Rijeka (☎ 051- 325 540; travel.rijeka@transagent.hr; Verdijeva 6) Runs a daily ferry from July to mid-September connecting Ravenna to Rijeka (€40, eight hours).
Jadrolinija (Rijeka ☎ 51-211 444, Ancona ☎ 071-20 71 465, Bari ☎ 080-52 75 439; www.jadrolinija.hr) Croatia's national boat line, it runs car ferries from Ancona to Split (€44, 10 hours) and Zadar (€41, seven hours) stopping at Stari Grad (Hvar) and Korčula for about the same price. There's also a year-round service from Bari (Italy) to Dubrovnik (€49, eight hours).
Lošinjska Plovidba (☎ 51-352 200; www.losinjska -plovidba.hr; Rijeka) Runs boats connecting Koper, Slovenia with Pula (€9, 4½ hours), Mali Lošinj (€12, eight hours) and Zadar (€23, 13½ hours).
Miatours (Zadar ☎ 023-211 005, Ancona ☎ 071204 282; www.miatours.hr) In summer, Miatours runs passenger boats connecting Ancona and Pescara with Zadar (€60, four hours) Božava (€60,1½ hours), Bol (€100, 6½ hours) and Hvar (€100, five hours).
SEM (Split ☎ 21-338 292, Ancona ☎ 071-20 40 90; www.sem-marina.hr) Runs the Blue Line car ferries connecting Ancona with Zadar and Split, and continuing on to Stari Grad (Hvar) for the same price as Jadrolinija. Also connects Ancona with Vis in the summer.
SNAV (Ancona ☎ 071-20 76 116, Naples ☎ 081-76 12 348, Split ☎ 21 322 252; www.snav.com) Has a fast car

ferry that links Pescara and Ancona with Split (€73, 4½ hours) and Pescara with Hvar (€80, 3½ hours), as well as a passenger boat that connects Civitanova and Ancona with Zadar (€70, 3¼ hours) and Ancona and Civitanova with Mali Lošinj (€60, three hours).

Venezia Lines (☎ 041-52 22 568; www.venezialines .com; Santa Croce 518/A, Venice 30135) Runs weekly and twice-weekly passenger boats from Venice to Pula (€45, three hours), Rovinj (€45, 3¾ hours) and Poreč (€45, 2½ hours), as well as from Trieste to Rovinj(€45, 2¼ hours) and Poreč (€45, 1¼ hours).

In Croatia, contact **Jadroagent** (☎ 211 276; Trg Ivana Koblera 2) in Pula and **Istra Line** (☎ 52-451 067; Partizansko 2) in Poreč for information and tickets on boats between Italy and Croatia.

GETTING AROUND

AIR

Croatia Airlines (☎ 062 77 77 77, 01-48 72 727; www .croatiaairlines.hr; Zrinjevac 17, Zagreb) is the one-and-only carrier for flights within Croatia. The price of flights depends on the season and you get better deals if you book ahead. Seniors, children under 12 and people aged under 26 get discounts. There are daily flights between Zagreb and Dubrovnik (549KN, one hour), Pula (170KN, 45 minutes), Split (207KN, 45 minutes) and Zadar (341KN, 40 minutes). Note that all batteries must be removed from checked luggage when leaving from any airport in Croatia.

BICYCLE

Cycling can be a great way to explore the islands, and bicycles are easy to rent along the coast and on the islands. Relatively flat islands such as Mljet and Mali Lošinj offer the most relaxed biking but the winding, hilly roads on other islands offer spectacular views. Some tourist offices, especially in the Kvarner and Istria regions, have maps of suggested routes. Cycling along the coast or on the mainland warrants special caution, as most roads are busy two-lane highways without bicycle lanes.

BOAT
Coastal Ferries

Year-round, Jadrolinija car ferries operate along the Bari–Rijeka–Dubrovnik coastal route, stopping at Zadar, Split, and the islands Hvar, Korčula and Mljet. Services

are less frequent in winter. The most scenic section is Split to Dubrovnik, which all Jadrolinija ferries cover during the day. Ferries are a lot more comfortable than buses, though somewhat more expensive. From Rijeka to Dubrovnik the deck fare is €21/25 in low/high season, with high season running from about the end of June to the end of August, and there's a 20% reduction on the return portion of a return ticket. With a through ticket, deck passengers can stop at any port for up to a week, provided they notify the purser beforehand and have their ticket validated. This is much cheaper than buying individual sector tickets but is only good for one stopover. Cabins should be booked a week ahead, but deck space is usually available on all sailings.

Deck passage on Jadrolinija is just that: *poltrone* (reclining seats) are about €4 extra and four-berth cabins (if available) begin at €37/44 in low/high season (Rijeka to Dubrovnik). Cabins can be arranged at the reservation counter aboard ship, but advance bookings are recommended if you want to be sure of a place. You must buy tickets in advance at an agency or a Jadrolinija office, since they are not sold on board. Bringing a car means checking in two hours in advance.

Meals in the restaurants aboard Jadrolinija ships are about 100KN for a fixed-price menu of somewhat mediocre food. All the cafeteria offers is ham-and-cheese sandwiches for 30KN. Coffee is cheap in the cafeteria, but wine and spirits tend to be expensive. Breakfast in the restaurant costs about 30KN but is included in the price of a cabin ticket. Do as the Croatians do: bring some food and drink with you.

Local Ferries

Local ferries connect the bigger offshore islands with each other and with the mainland. On most lines, service is less frequent between October and April. Passenger and car tickets must be bought in advance, as there are no ticket sales on board.

Taking a bicycle on these services incurs a small charge and taking a vehicle aboard obviously incurs a larger charge. The car charge is calculated according to the size of your vehicle and begins at about four times the price of a passenger ticket. In summer, ferries to the islands fill up fast, so you should reserve as far in advance as possible if you're bringing your car. Some of the ferries operate only a couple of times a day and, once the vehicular capacity is reached, the remaining motorists must wait for the next available service. Even with the reservation, you will have to show up several hours before boarding. On some of the shorter routes such as Jablanac to Mišnjak or Drvenik to Sućuraj, the ferries run non-stop in the summer and an advance reservation is unnecessary. If there's no Jadrolinija office in town, you can buy the ticket at a stall near the ferry stop that usually opens 30 minutes before departure. In summer you'll be told to arrive one to two hours in advance for ferries to the more popular islands even if you've already bought your ticket. Foot passengers and cyclists should have no problem getting on.

Extra passenger boats are added in the summer and are usually faster, more comfortable and more expensive than the car ferries. Companies connecting Split and Zadar with Italy usually make stops on the islands of Hvar, Brač or Vis. See p271 for more information.

BUS

Bus services are excellent and relatively inexpensive. There are often a number of different companies handling each route so prices can vary substantially, but the prices in this book should give you an idea of costs (unless otherwise noted, all bus prices are for one-way fares). Luggage stowed in the baggage compartment under the bus costs extra (7KN a piece, including insurance). Following are some prices for the most popular routes, but it's generally best to call or visit the bus station to get the complete schedule and compare prices.

Route	Cost	Duration	Frequency
Zagreb–Dubrovnik	164KN	11hr	7 daily
Zagreb–Korčula	195KN	12hr	1 daily
Zagreb–Pula	121-147KN	7hr	13 daily
Zagreb–Split	113-137KN	9hr	27 daily
Dubrovnik–Rijeka	300-309KN	12hr	4 daily
Dubrovnik–Split	100-111KN	4½hr	14 daily
Dubrovnik–Zadar	160-190KN	8hr	7 daily

Phone numbers and websites (if they exist) to book services are listed in the regional chapters, but the companies listed below are among the largest:

Autotrans (☎ 051-66 03 60; www.autotrans.hr) Based in Rijeka with connections to Istria, Zagreb, Varaždin, Kvarner.

Brioni Pula (☎ 052-502 997; www.brioni.hr) Based in Pula with connections to Istria, Trieste, Padua, Split, Zagreb.

Contus (☎ 023-315 315; www.contus.hr) Based in Zadar with connections to Split and Zagreb.

Croatiabus (☎ 01 2331 566; www.croatiabus.hr) Connecting Zagreb with towns in the Zagorje and Istria.

At large stations, bus tickets must be purchased at the office, not from drivers; try to book ahead to be sure of a seat, especially in the summer. Departure lists above the various windows at bus stations tell you which window sells tickets for your bus. On Croatian bus schedules, *vozi svaki dan* means 'every day' and *ne vozi nedjeljom ni praznikom* means 'no service Sunday and public holidays'.

Some buses travel overnight, saving you a night's accommodation, but don't expect to get much sleep, as the inside lights will be on and music will be blasting the whole night. Don't complain – it keeps the driver awake. Take care not to be left behind at meal or rest stops, which usually occur about every two hours.

CAR & MOTORCYCLE

Croatia has recently made a major investment in infrastructure, the highlight of which is a new and badly needed motorway connecting Zagreb with Split. As matters stand, its completion date is projected around the end of 2005. Zagreb and Rijeka are now connected by motorway and an Istrian motorway has shortened the travel time to Italy considerably. Although the new roads are in excellent condition, service stations and facilities are not yet up and running.

Along the coast, the spectacular Adriatic highway from Italy to Albania hugs the steep slopes of the coastal range, with abrupt drops to the sea and a curve a minute. You can drive as far south as Vitaljina, 56km southeast of Dubrovnik, and then cross the border into Montenegro. (See the table on p278 for the road distances between major towns.)

Any valid driving licence is sufficient to drive legally and rent a car; an international

ROAD DISTANCES (KM)

	Dubrovnik	Osijek	Rijeka	Split	Zadar	Zagreb
Dubrovnik	---					
Osijek	495	---				
Rijeka	601	459	---			
Split	216	494	345	---		
Zadar	340	566	224	139	---	
Zagreb	572	280	182	365	288	---

driving licence is not necessary. **Hrvatski Autoklub** (HAK; Croatian Auto Club; ☎ 01-66 11 999) offers help and advice. You can also contact the nationwide **HAK road assistance** (Vučna Služba; ☎ 987).

Petrol stations are generally open from 7am to 7pm and often until 10pm in summer. Petrol is Eurosuper 95, Super 98, normal or diesel. See www.ina.hr for up-to-date fuel prices.

You have to pay tolls on the motorways around Zagreb, to use the Učka tunnel between Rijeka and Istria, the bridge to Krk Island, as well as the road from Rijeka to Delnice. In 2005, the long-awaited motorway connecting Zagreb and Split is scheduled to open which will cut the travel time to the coast to about five hours. For general news on Croatia's motorways and tolls, see www.hac.hr.

Hire

In order to rent a car, you must be 21 and have a major credit card. Independent local companies are often much cheaper than the international chains, but the big companies have the advantage of offering one-way rentals that allow you to drop the car off at any one of their many stations in Croatia free of charge.

Major car-rental companies:

Avis Autotehna (☎ 01-48 36 006; www.avis.hr)
Budget Rent-a-Car (☎ 01-45 54 943; www.budget.hr)
Hertz (☎ 01-48 46 777; www.hertz.hr)
Mack (☎ 01-36 94 555; www.mack-concord.hr)

Sometimes you can get a lower car-rental rate by booking the car from abroad. Tour companies in Western Europe often have fly-drive packages that include a flight to Croatia and a car (two-person minimum).

Third-party public liability insurance is included by law, but make sure your quoted price includes full collision insurance, known as a collision damage waiver (CDW). Otherwise, your responsibility for damage done to the vehicle is usually determined as a percentage of the car's value beginning at around 2000KN.

Road Rules

Unless otherwise posted, the speed limits for cars and motorcycles are 50km/h in the built-up areas, 80km/h on main highways and 130km/h on motorways. On any of Croatia's winding two-lane highways, it's illegal to pass long military convoys or a line of cars caught behind a slow-moving truck. In a desperate measure to get a handle on the country's high accident rate, the government passed a 'zero tolerance' law, making it illegal to drive with any alcohol whatsoever in the blood. At the time of research, an outcry from the bar and restaurant brigade was looking successful in overturning the law. Drive defensively, as some local drivers lack discipline, to put it mildly.

HITCHING

Hitching is never entirely safe in any country in the world, and we don't recommend it. Travellers who decide to hitch should understand that they are taking a small but potentially serious risk. People who do choose to hitch will be safer if they travel in pairs and let someone know where they are planning to go.

Hitching in Croatia is a gamble. You'll have better luck on the islands but in the interior you'll notice that cars are small and usually full. Tourists never stop. Unfortunately, the image many Croats have of hitching is based on violent movies such as *Hitchhiker*.

LOCAL TRANSPORT

Zagreb and Osijek have a well-developed tram system as well as local buses, but in the rest of the country you'll only find buses. Buses in major cities such as Dubrovnik, Rijeka, Split and Zadar run about once every

20 minutes, less on Sunday. A ride is usually around 7KN, with a small discount if you buy tickets at a *tisak* (newsstand). Small medieval towns along the coast are generally closed to traffic and have infrequent links to outlying suburbs. Bus transportation within the islands is also infrequent since most people have their own cars. Whatever transportation exists is scheduled for the workday needs of the inhabitants, not the holiday needs of tourists. To get out and see the islands, you'll need to rent a bike, boat, motorcycle or car.

TOURS

Atlas Travel Agency (☎ 20-442 222; www.atlas -croatia.com; Čira Carića 3, Dubrovnik) Offers a wide variety of bus tours, fly-drive packages and 'adventure' tours, which feature bird-watching, canoeing, caving, cycling, diving, fishing, hiking, riding, sailing, sea kayaking and white-water rafting, in both Croatia and Slovenia.

Inselhüpfen (☎ 7531-942 3630; www.island-hopping .de) A German company which combines boating and biking and takes an international crowd through southern Dalmatia, Istria or the Kvarner Islands, stopping every day for a bike ride.

Katarina Line (☎ 051-272 110; www.katarina-line.hr; Maršala Tita 75, 51410 Opatija) Offers week-long cruises from Opatija to Split, Mljet, Dubrovnik, Hvar, Brač, Korčula, Zadar and the Kornati Islands on an attractive wooden ship.

TRAIN

Zagreb is the hub for Croatia's less-than-extensive train system. You'll notice that no trains run along the coast and only a few coastal cities are connected with Zagreb. For travellers, the main lines of interest run from Zagreb to Rijeka and Pula; Zagreb to Zadar, Šibenik and Split; Zagreb to Varaždin and Koprivnica; and Zagreb to Osijek. The big news on the train scene is the new high-speed 'tilting train' connection between Zagreb and Split, which has cut travel time by a third.

Trains are less frequent than buses but more comfortable. Domestic trains are either 'express' or 'passenger' (local). Express trains have smoking and nonsmoking as well as 1st- and 2nd-class cars. A reservation is advisable and they are more expensive than passenger trains which offer only unreserved 2nd-class seating. Prices in this book are for unreserved 2nd-class seating.

There are no couchettes available on any domestic services but there are sleeping cars on the overnight trains between Zagreb and Split. Baggage is free on trains and most train stations have left-luggage offices charging about 10KN apiece per day (passport required).

EU residents who hold an InterRail pass can use it in Croatia for free travel, but it is unlikely that you would take enough trains in the country to justify the cost.

For information about schedules, prices and services, contact **Croatian Railways** (Hrvatske Željeznice; ☎ 060 33 34 44; www.hznet.hr).

On posted timetables at train stations, the word for 'arrivals' is *dolazak*, and for 'departures' it's *odlazak* or *polazak*. Other terms you may encounter include *poslovni* (executive train), *brzi* or *ubrazni* (fast train), *putnički* (local train), *rezerviranje mjesta obvezatno* (compulsory seat reservation), *presjedanje* (change of trains), *ne vozi nedjeljom i blagdanom* (no service Sunday and holidays) and *svako-dnevno* (daily).

TRANSPORT

Health

CONTENTS

Travel health depends on your predeparture preparations, your daily health care while travelling and how you handle any medical problem that does develop. The standard of medical care in Croatia is high, and all foreigners are entitled to emergency medical aid at the very least.

BEFORE YOU GO

Prevention is the key to staying healthy while abroad. A little planning before departure, particularly for pre-existing illnesses, will save trouble later: see your dentist before a long trip, carry a spare pair of contact lenses and glasses, and take your optical prescription with you. Bring medications

It's usually a good idea to consult your government's travel health website before departure, if one is available:
Australia www.dfat.gov.au/travel
Canada www.travelhealth.gc.ca
United Kingdom www.dh.gov.uk
United States www.cdc.gov/travel

in their original, clearly labelled, containers. A signed and dated letter from your physician describing your medical conditions and medications, including generic names, is also a good idea. If you are carrying syringes or needles, be sure to have a physician's letter with you documenting their medical necessity.

INSURANCE

If you're an EU citizen, an E111 form, available from health centres in Europe or post offices in the UK, covers you for most medical care. E111 will not cover you for non-emergencies or emergency repatriation home. Citizens from other countries should find out if there is a reciprocal arrangement for free medical care between their country and the country visited. If you do need health insurance, strongly consider a policy that covers you for the worst possible scenario, such as an accident requiring an emergency flight home. Find out in advance if your insurance plan will make payments directly to providers or if it will reimburse you later for any overseas health expenditures. The former option is generally preferable, as it doesn't require you to pay out of pocket in a foreign country.

RECOMMENDED VACCINATIONS

The World Health Organization (WHO) recommends that all travellers should be covered for diphtheria, tetanus, measles, mumps, rubella and polio, regardless of their destination. Since most vaccines don't produce immunity until at least two weeks after they're given, visit a physician at least six weeks before departure.

INTERNET RESOURCES

The WHO's publication *International Travel and Health* is revised annually and is available online at www.who.int/ith/. Other useful websites include www.mdtravelhealth.com (travel health recommendations for every country; updated daily), www.fitfortravel.scot.nhs.uk (general travel advice for the layperson), www.ageconcern.org.uk (advice on travel for the elderly) and www.mariestopes.org.uk (information on contraception and women's health).

FURTHER READING

'Health Advice for Travellers' (currently called the 'T6' leaflet) is a leaflet which is updated annually by the Department of Health in the UK, and available free in post offices. It contains some general information, reciprocal health agreements, an E111 application form and lists the legally required and recommended vaccines for different countries. Lonely Planet's *Travel with Children* includes advice on travel health for younger children. Other recommended references include *Traveller's Health* by Dr Richard Dawood and *The Traveller's Good Health Guide* by Ted Lankester.

IN TRANSIT

DEEP VEIN THROMBOSIS (DVT)

Blood clots may form in the legs during plane flights, chiefly because of prolonged immobility. The longer the flight, the greater the risk. The chief symptom of DVT is swelling or pain of the foot, ankle, or calf, and is usually, but not always, on just one side. When a blood clot travels to the lungs, it may cause chest pain and breathing difficulties. Travellers with any of these symptoms should immediately seek medical attention.

To prevent the development of DVT on long flights you should walk about the cabin, contract the leg muscles while sitting, drink plenty of fluids and avoid alcohol and tobacco.

JET LAG & MOTION SICKNESS

To avoid jet lag (which is common when crossing more than five time zones) try drinking plenty of nonalchoholic fluids and eating light meals. Upon arrival, get exposure to natural sunlight and readjust your schedule (for meals, sleep and so on) as soon as possible.

Antihistamines such as dimenhydrinate (Dramamine) and meclizine (Antivert, Bonine) are usually the first choice for treating motion sickness. A herbal alternative is ginger.

IN CROATIA

AVAILABILITY & COST OF HEALTH CARE

Good health care is readily available and for minor illnesses pharmacists can give valuable advice and sell over-the-counter medication. They can also advise when more specialised help is required and point you in the right direction. The standard of dental care is usually good, however it is sensible to have a dental check-up before a long trip.

INFECTIOUS DISEASES

Tickborne encephalitis is spread by tick bites. It is a serious infection of the brain and vaccination is advised for those in risk areas who are unable to avoid tick bites (such as campers, forestry workers and walkers). Two doses of vaccine will give a year's protection, three doses up to three years'.

TRAVELLER'S DIARRHOEA

If you develop diarrhoea, be sure to drink plenty of fluids, preferably an oral rehydration solution (eg dioralyte). A few loose stools don't require treatment, but if you start having more than four or five stools a day, you should start taking an antibiotic (usually a quinolone drug) and an antidiarrhoeal agent (such as loperamide). If diarrhoea is bloody, persists for more than 72 hours or is accompanied by fever, shaking, chills or severe abdominal pain you should seek medical attention.

ENVIRONMENTAL HAZARDS
Heat Exhaustion & Heat Stroke

Heat exhaustion occurs following excessive fluid loss with inadequate replacement of fluids and salt. Symptoms include headache, dizziness and tiredness. Dehydration is already happening by the time you feel thirsty – aim to drink sufficient water to produce pale, diluted urine. To treat heat exhaustion, replace lost fluids by drinking water and/or fruit juice, and cool the body with cold water and fans. Treat salt loss with salty fluids such as soup or Bovril, or add a little more table salt to foods than usual.

Heat stroke is much more serious, resulting in irrational and hyperactive behaviour and eventually loss of consciousness and death. Rapid cooling by spraying the body with water and fanning is ideal. Emergency fluid and electrolyte replacement by intravenous drip is recommended.

Insect Bites & Stings

Mosquitoes are found in most parts of Europe. They may not carry malaria but can cause irritation and infected bites. Use a DEET-based insect repellent.

Bees and wasps cause real problems only to those with a severe allergy (anaphylaxis). If you have a severe allergy to bee or wasp stings carry an 'epipen' or similar adrenaline injection.

Bed bugs lead to very itchy, lumpy bites. Spraying the mattress with crawling insect killer after changing bedding will get rid of them.

Scabies are tiny mites that live in the skin, particularly between the fingers. They cause an intensely itchy rash. Scabies is easily treated with lotion from a pharmacy; other members of the household also need treating to avoid spreading scabies between asymptomatic carriers.

Sea Urchins

Watch out for sea urchins around rocky beaches; if you get some of their needles embedded in your skin, olive oil will help to loosen them. If they are not removed they could become infected. Wear rubber shoes while walking on the rocks or bathing, as a precaution.

Snake Bites

Avoid getting bitten – do not walk barefoot or stick your hand into holes or cracks. Half of those bitten by venomous snakes are not actually injected with poison (envenomed). If bitten by a snake, do not panic. Immobilise the bitten limb with a splint (eg a stick) and apply a bandage over the site firmly, similar to a bandage over a sprain. Do not apply a tourniquet, or cut or suck the bite. Get medical help as soon as possible so that antivenin can be given if necessary.

TRAVELLING WITH CHILDREN

All travellers with children should know how to treat minor ailments and when to seek medical treatment. Make sure the children are up to date with routine vaccinations, and discuss possible travel vaccines

well before departure, as some vaccines are not suitable for children under a year.

In hot moist climates any wound or break in the skin is likely to let in infection. The area should be cleaned and kept dry.

Remember to avoid contaminated food and water. If your child has vomiting or diarrhoea, lost fluid and salts must be replaced. It may be helpful to take rehydration powders for reconstituting with boiled water.

Children should be encouraged to avoid and mistrust any dogs or other mammals because of the risk of rabies and other diseases. Any bite, scratch or lick from a warm blooded, furry animal should immediately be thoroughly cleaned. If there is any possibility that the animal is infected with rabies, immediate medical assistance should be sought.

WOMEN'S HEALTH

Emotional stress, exhaustion and travelling through different time zones can all contribute to an upset in the menstrual pattern. If using oral contraceptives, remember that some antibiotics, diarrhoea and vomiting can stop the pill from working and lead to the risk of pregnancy – remember to take condoms with you just in case. Time zones, gastrointestinal upsets and antibiotics do not affect injectable contraception.

Travelling during pregnancy is usually possible but there are important things to consider. Always seek a medical check-up before planning your trip. The most risky times for travel are during the first 12 weeks of pregnancy and after 30 weeks. Antenatal facilities vary greatly between countries and you should think carefully before travelling to a country with poor medical facilities or where there are major cultural and language differences from home. Illness during pregnancy can be more severe, so take special care to avoid contaminated food and water and insect and animal bites. A general rule is to only use vaccines, like other medications, if the risk of infection is substantial. Remember that the baby could be at serious risk if you were to contract infections such as typhoid or hepatitis. Some vaccines are best avoided (eg those that contain live organisms). However, there is very little evidence that damage has been caused to an unborn child when vaccines have been given to a woman very early in pregnancy, before the pregnancy was suspected. Take written records of the pregnancy with you. Ensure your insurance policy covers pregnancy delivery and postnatal care, but remember insurance policies are only as good as the facilities available.

SEXUAL HEALTH

Emergency contraception is most effective if taken within 24 hours after unprotected sex. The **International Planned Parenthood Federation** (www.ippf.org) can advise about the availability of contraception in different countries.

When buying condoms, look for a European CE mark, which means that they have been rigorously tested, and then make sure you keep them in a cool dry place or they may perish.

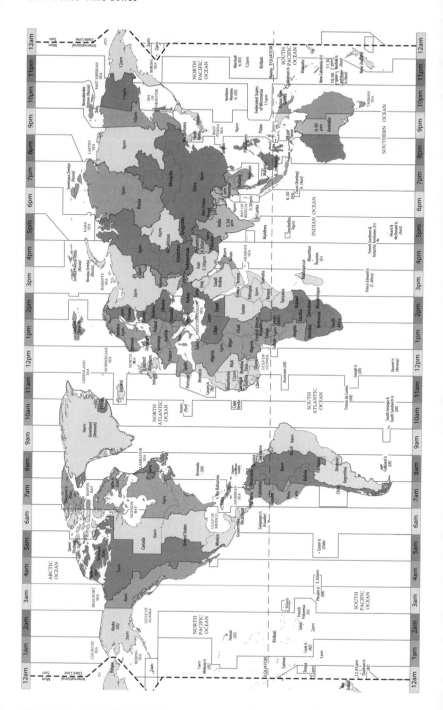

Language

CONTENTS

Croatian is a southern variant within the Slavonic language family. Other languages in this group include Serbian, Bosnian and Slovene.

The strife of recent times, which led Croatia to break away from the former Yugoslavia in 1992, has had an impact on the language. Though it's now referred to as 'Croatian', it's not actually a separate language from Serbian or Bosnian. Politics aside, the three languages are so similar in linguistic terms that they are dialects of the one language.

For words and phrases to help you when eating out, check out p44.

PRONUNCIATION

The Croatian writing system is phonetically consistent, meaning that every letter is pronounced and its sound will not vary from word to word. With regard to the position of stress, only one rule can be given: the last syllable of a word is never stressed. In most cases the accent falls on the first vowel in the word.

Croatian is written in the Roman alphabet (unlike Serbian, which uses both the Cyrillic and Roman alphabets) and many letters are pronounced as in English. The following outlines some pronunciations that are specific to Croatian.

c	ts	as the 'ts' in 'cats'
ć	ch	as the 'tu' in 'future'
č	ch	as the 'ch' in 'chop'
đ	j	as the 'j' in 'jury'
dž	j	as the 'dj' in 'adjust'
j	y	as the 'y' in 'young'
lj	ly	as the 'lli' in 'million'
nj	ny	as the 'ny' in 'canyon'
š	sh	as the 'sh' in 'hush'
ž	zh	as the 's' in 'pleasure'

ACCOMMODATION

I'm looking for a ...
Tražim ... tra·zheem ...
 camping ground
 kamp kamp
 guesthouse
 privatni smještaj za pree·vat·nee smyesh·tai za
  najam nai·am
 hotel
 hotel haw·tel
 youth hostel
 prenoćište za mladež pre·naw·cheesh·te za mla·dezh

Where's a (cheap) hotel?
Gdje se nalazi (jeftin) hotel?
gdye se na·la·zee (yef·teen) haw·tel
What's the address?
Koja je adresa?
koy·a ye a·dre·sa

MAKING A RESERVATION
(for written and phone inquiries)

To ...	do	do
From ...	od	od
Date	datum	da·toom
credit card	kreditna karta	kre·deet·na kar·ta
number	broj	broy
expiry date	rok važenja	rok va·zhen·ya

I'd like to book ...
 Želim rezervirati ...
 zhe·leem re·zer·vee·ra·tee ...
In the name of ...
 na ime ...
 na ee·me ...
Please confirm availability and price.
 Molim potvrdite ima li slobodnih soba i cijenu.
 mo·leem pot·vr·dee·te ee·ma lee slo·bohd·nih
  saw·ba ee tsye·noo

Could you write it down, please?
Možete li to napisati?
maw-zhe-te lee to na-*pee*-sa-tee

Do you have any rooms available?
Imate li slobodnih soba.
ee-ma-te lee *slaw*-bawd-nih *saw*-bah

I'd like (a) ...
Želio/Željela bih ...
zhe-lee-aw/*zhe*-lye-la bee ...

   bed
   krevet (m)
   kre-vet
   single room
   jednokrevetnu sobu
   yed-naw-*kre*-vetnoo *saw*-boo
   double/twin bedroom
   dvokrevetnu
   dvo-kre-*vet*-noo *sobu saw*-boo
   room with a bathroom
   sobu sa ku-paonicom
   saw-boo sa koo-pa-*aw*-nee-tsom
   to share a dorm
   krevet u student-skom domu
   kre-vet oo stoo-*dent*-skom *do*-moo

How much is it ...?
Koliko stoji ...?
kaw-*lee*-kaw *stoy*-ee ...
   per night
   za noć
   za nawch
   per person
   po osobi
   paw *aw*-saw-bee

May I see it?
Mogu li je vidjeti?
maw-goo lee ye *vee*-dye-tee

Where is the bathroom?
Gdje je kupaonica?
gdye ye koo-pa-*aw*-nee-tsa

Where is the toilet?
Gdje je toalet?
gdye ye to-a-*let*

I'm leaving today.
Ja odlazim danas.
ya *awd*-la-zeem da-nas

We're leaving today.
Mi odlazimo danas.
mee *awd*-la-zee-mo da-nas

CONVERSATION & ESSENTIALS

Hello.	*Zdravo./Bog.*	zdra-vaw/bawg
Goodbye.	*Doviđenja.*	daw-vee-*je*-nya
Yes.	*Da.*	da

No.	*Ne.*	ne
Please.	*Molim.*	*maw*-leem
Thank you.	*Hvala vamti.*	hva-la *vam*-tee
You're welcome.	*Nema na čemu.*	ne-ma na *che*-moo
Excuse me.	*Oprostite.*	aw-*praw*-stee-te
Sorry.	*Žao mi je.*	zha-aw mee ye
Just a minute.	*Trenutak.*	tre-*noo*-tak

Where are you from?
Odakle ste/si? (pol/inf)   aw-*da*-kle ste/see?

What's your name?
Kako se zovete/   *ka*-kaw se *zaw*-ve-te/
zoveš? (pol/inf)   *zaw*-vesh

My name is ...
Zovem se ...   *zaw*-vem se ...

I'm from ...
Ja sam iz ...   ya sam eez ...

I (don't) like ...
Ja (ne) volim ...   ya (ne) *vaw*-leem ...

DIRECTIONS

Where is ...?
Gdje je ...?   gdye ye ...?

Go straight ahead.
Idite ravno naprijed.   ee-dee-te *rav*-naw na-*pree*-yed

Turn left.
Skrenite lijevo.   skre-nee-te lee-*ye*-vaw

Turn right.
Skrenite desno.   skre-nee-te *de*-snaw

at the corner
na uglu   na *oo*-gloo

at the traffic lights
na semaforu   na *se*-ma-faw-roo

behind	*iza*	ee-za
in front of	*ispred*	ee-spred
far (from)	*daleko (od)*	da-le-kaw (awd)
near	*blizu*	blee-zoo
next to	*pored*	paw-red
opposite	*nasuprot*	na-soo-prawt
beach	*plaža*	pla-zha
bridge	*most*	mawst

SIGNS		
Entrance	*Ulaz*	oo-laz
Exit	*Izlaz*	eez-laz
Open	*Otvoreno*	ot-vo-re-no
Closed	*Zatvoreno*	zat-vo-re-no
Prohibited	*Zabranjeno*	zab-ra-nye-no
Toilets/WC	*Zahodi*	za-haw-dee
Men	*Muškarci*	moosh-*kar*-tsee
Women	*Žene*	zhe-ne

LANGUAGE

castle	zamak	za·mak
cathedral	katedrala	ka·te·dra·la
church	crkva	tsr·kva
island	otok a	w·tok
lake	jezero	ye·ze·ro
main square	glavni trg	glav·nee trg
old city (town)	stari grad	sta·ree grad
palace	palača	pa·la·cha
quay	kej	kay
riverbank	riječna obala	ree·yech·na aw·ba·la
ruins	ruše vine	roo·shee vee·ne
sea	more	maw·re
square	trg	trg
tower	kula	koo·la

EMERGENCIES

Help!
Upomoć!
o·paw·mawch
There's been an accident!
Desila se nezgoda!
de·see·la se nez·gaw·da!
I'm lost.
Izgubio/Izgubilasam se. (m/f)
eez·goo·bee·aw/eez·goo·bee·la·sam se
Leave me alone.
Ostavite me na miru.
aw·sta·vee·te me na mee·ru
Call a doctor!
Zovite liječnika.
zaw·vee·te le·yech·nee·ka
Call the police!
Nazovite policiju.
na·zaw·vee·te paw·lee·tsee·yoo

HEALTH

I'm ill.
Ja sam bolestan/   ya sam baw·le·stan/
bolesna. (m/f)   baw·le·sna
It hurts here.
Boli me ovdje.   baw·lee me awv·dye

I'm ...
Ja imam ...   ya ee·mam ...

asthmatic	astmu	ast·moo
diabetic	dijabetes	dee·ja·be·tes
epileptic	epilepsiju	e·pee·lep·see·ju

I'm allergic to ...
Ja sam alergičan/alergična na ... (m/f)
ya sam a·ler·gee·chan/a·ler·geech·na na ...

antibiotics	antibiotike	an·tee·bee·aw·tee·ke
aspirin	aspirin	a·spee·reen
penicillin	penicilin	pe·nee·tsee·leen
bees	pčele	pche·le
nuts	razne orahe	raz·ne aw·ra·he
peanuts	kikiriki	kee·kee·ree·kee

antiseptic	antiseptik (m)	an·tee·sep·teek
aspirin	aspirin	as·pee·reen
condoms	kondomi	kon·daw·mee
contraceptive	sredstva za	sreds·tva za
	kontracepciju	kon·tra·tsep·tsee·yu
diarrhoea	proljev (m)	pro·lyev
medicine	lijek	lee·yek
nausea	mučnina (f)	mooch·nee·na
sunscreen	krema za	kre·ma za
	sunčanje	soon·cha·nye
tampons	tamponi	tam·paw·nee

LANGUAGE DIFFICULTIES
Do you speak (English)?
Govorite/Govoriš li (engleski)? (pol/inf)
gaw·vaw·ree·te/gaw·vaw·reesh lee (en·gle·skee)
Does anyone here speak (English)?
Da li itko govori engleski?
da lee eet·kaw gaw·vaw·ree en·gle·skee
How do you say ... in Croatian?
Kako se kaže ... na hrvatskom?
ka·kaw se ka·zhe ... na hr·vat·skom
What does ... mean?
Što znači ...?
shtaw zna·chee ...
I (don't) understand.
Ja (ne) razumijem.
ya (ne) ra·zoo·mee·yem
Could you write it down, please?
Možeš li molim te to napisati? (inf)
maw·zhesh lee maw·leem te taw na·pee·sa·tee
Can you show me (on the map)?
Možete li mi to pokazati (na karti)?
maw·zhe·te lee mee taw paw·ka·za·tee (na kar·tee)

NUMBERS

0	nula	noo·la
1	jedan/jedna/	ye·dan/yed·na/
	jedno (m/f/n)	yed·naw
2	dva/dvije (m&n/f)	dva/dvee·ye
3	tri	tree
4	četiri	che·tee·ree
5	pet	pet
6	šest	shest
7	sedam	se·dam
8	osam	aw·sam
9	devet	de·vet
10	deset	de·set

11	jedanaest	ye·da·na·est
12	dvanaest	dva·na·est
13	trinaest	tree·na·est
14	četrnaest	che·tr·na·est
15	petnaest	pet·na·est
16	šesnaest	shes·na·est
17	sedamnaest	se·dam·na·est
18	osamnaest	aw·sam·na·est
19	devetnaest	de·vet·na·est
20	dvadeset	dva·de·set
21	dvadesetjedan (m)/	dva·de·set·ye·dan/
	dvadesetjedna (f)/	dva·de·set·yed·na/
	dvadesetjedno (n)	dva·de·set·yed·naw
22	dvadesetdva (m&n)/	dva·de·set·dva/
	dvadesetdvije (f)	dva·de·set·dvee·ye
30	trideset	tree·de·set
40	četrdeset	che·tr·de·set
50	pedeset	pe·de·set
60	šezdeset	shez·de·set
70	sedamdeset	se·dam·de·set
80	osamdeset	aw·sam·de·set
90	devedeset	de·ve·de·set
100	sto	staw
1000	tisuću	tee·soo·choo

PAPERWORK

name	ime	ee·me
nationality	nacionalost	na·tsee·awn·na·lost
date of birth	datum rođenja	da·toom ro·je·nya
place of birth	mjesto rođenja	mye·sto ro·je·nya
sex/gender	spol	spawl
passport	putovnica	poo·tov·nee·tsa
visa	viza	vee·za

QUESTION WORDS

Who?	Tko?	tkaw
What?	Što?	shtaw
What is it?	Što je?	shtaw ye
When?	Kada?	ka·da
Where?	Gdje?	gdye
Which?	Koji/Koja/	koy·ee/koy·a/
	Koje? (m/f/n)	koy·e
Why?	Zašto?	za·shtaw
How?	Kako?	ka·kaw

SHOPPING & SERVICES

I'm just looking.
Ja samo razgledam.
ya sa·maw raz·gle·da
I'd like to buy (an adaptor plug).
Želim kupiti (utikač za konverter).
zhe·leem koo·pee·tee (oo·tee·kach za kon·ver·ter)
May I look at it?
Mogu li to pogledati?
maw·goo lee taw paw·gle·da·tee

How much is it?	Koliko stoji?	kaw·lee·kaw stoy·ee
It's cheap.	To je jeftino.	taw ye yef·tee·no
It's too dear.	To je preskupo.	taw ye pre·skoo·paw
I like it.	Sviđa mi se.	svee·ja mee se
I'll take it.	Uzeću ovo.	oo·ze·choo aw·vo

Do you	Da li	da lee
accept ...?	prihvaćate ...?	pree·hva·cha·te ...
credit cards	kreditne	kre·deet·ne
	kartice	kar·tee·tse
travellers	putničke	poot·neech·ke
cheques	čekove	che·kaw·ve

more	više	vee·she
less	manje	man·ye
smaller	manji/manja/	man·yee/man·ya/
	manje (m/f/n)	man·ye
bigger	veći/veća/	ve·chee/ve·cha/
	veće (m/f/n)	ve·che

Where's ...	Gdje je ...?	gdye ye ...
a bank	banka	ban·ka
the church	crkva	tsrk·va
the city centre	centar grada	tsen·tar gra·da
the ... embassy	... ambasada	... am·ba·sa·da
the hospital	bolnica	bawl·nee·tsa
the market	pijaca	pee·ya·tsa
the museum	muzej	moo·zay
the police	policija	paw·lee·tsee·ya
the post office	pošta	pawsh·ta
a public phone	javni telefon	yav·nee te·le·fon
a public toilet	javni zahod	yav·nee za·hawd
the telephone	telefonska	te·le·fon·ska
centre	centrala	tsen·tra·la
the tourist	turistički	too·rees·teech·kee
office	biro	bee·ro

TIME & DATES

What time is it?	Koliko je sati?	kaw·lee·kaw ye sa·tee
It's (one) o'clock.	(Jedan) je sat.	(ye·dan) ye sat
It's (10) o'clock.	(Deset) je sati.	(de·set) ye sa·tee

in the morning	ujutro (n)	oo·yoo·traw
in the afternoon	poslijepodne (n)	paw·slee·ye·pawd·ne
in the evening	navečer (f)	na·ve·cher
today	danas	da·nas
tomorrow	sutra	soo·tra
yesterday	jučer	yoo·cher

Monday	ponedjeljak (m)	paw·ne·dye·lyak
Tuesday	utorak (m)	oo·taw·rak
Wednesday	srijeda (f)	sree·ye·da
Thursday	četvrtak (m)	chet·vr·tak
Friday	petak (m)	pe·tak
Saturday	subota (f)	soo·baw·ta
Sunday	nedjelja (f)	ne·dye·lya

January	*siječanj* (m)	see-ye-chan'
February	*veljača* (f)	ve-lya-cha
March	*ožujak* (m)	aw-zhoo-yak
April	*travanj* (m)	tra-van'
May	*svibanj* (m)	svee-ban'
June	*lipanj* (m)	lee-pan'
July	*srpanj* (m)	sr-pan'
August	*kolovoz* (m)	kaw-law-vawz
September	*rujan* (m)	roo-yan'
October	*listopad* (m)	lee-staw-pad
November	*studeni* (m)	stoo-de-nee
December	*prosinac* (m)	praw-see-nats

TRANSPORT
Public Transport

What time does the ... leave/ arrive?	*U koliko sati kreće/stiže ...?*	oo ko-lee-ko sa-tee kre-che/stee-je ...?
boat	*brod*	brawd
bus	*autobus*	a-oo-to-boos
plane	*avion*	a-vee-awn
train	*vlak*	vlak
tram	*tramvaj*	tram-vai

I'd like a ... ticket.	*Želio/Željela* (m/f) *jednu ... kartu.*	zhe-lee-aw/zhe-lye-la yed-noo ... kar-too
one-way	*jednosmjernu*	yed-naw-smyer-noo
return	*povratnu*	paw-vrat-noo
1st class	*prvorazrednu*	pr-vaw-raz-red-noo
2nd class	*drugorazrednu*	droo-go-raz-red-noo

I want to go to ...
Želim da idem u ...   zhe-leem da ee-dem oo ...
The train has been delayed.
Vlak kasni.   vlak kas-nee
The train has been cancelled.
Vlak je otkazan.   vlak je awt-ka-zan

the first	*prvi*	pr-vee
the last	*posljednji*	paws-lyed-nyee
platform number	*broj perona*	broy pe-ro-na
ticket office	*blagajna*	bla-gai-na
timetable	*red vožnje*	red vawzh-nye
train station	*željeznička postaja*	zhe-lyez-neech-ka paws-ta-ya

Private Transport
I'd like to hire a/an ...
Želio/Željela bih iznajmiti ... (m/f)
zhe-lee-aw/zhe-lye-la beeh eez-nai-mee-tee ...

bicycle
bicikl
bee-*tsee*-kl

car
automobil
a-oo-to-*mo*-bee
4WD
automobil sa pogonom na sva četiri kotača
a-oo-to-mo-beel sa po-go-nom na sva che-tee-ree kaw-ta-cha
motorbike
motocikl
maw-to-*tsee*-kl

ROAD SIGNS

Danger	
Opasno	o-pas-no
Detour	
Obilaznica	o-bee-laz-nee-tsa
Entry	
Ulaz	oo-laz
Exit	
Izlaz	eez-laz
Give Way	
Ustupite Pravo	oo-stoo-pee-te pra-vaw
Prednosti	pred-naw-stee
No Entry	
Ulaz Zabranjen	oo-laz za-bra-nyen
No Overtaking	
Zabranjeno	za-bra-nye-no
Preticanje	pre-tee-tsa-nye
No Parking	
Zabranjeno Parkiranje	za-bra-nye-no par-kee-ra-nye
One Way	
Jedan Pravac	ye-dan pra-vats
Slow Down	
Uspori	oo-spaw-ree
Toll	
Putarina	poo-ta-ree-na

Is this the road to ...?
Je li ovo cesta za ...?
ye lee aw-vaw tse-sta za ...?
Where's a service station?
Gdje je benzinska stanica?
gdye ye ben-zeen-ska sta-nee-tsa
Please fill it up.
Pun rezervoar molim.
poon re-zer-vaw-ar maw-leem
I'd like ... litres.
Trebam ... litara.
tre-bam ... lee-ta-ra

diesel	*dizel gorivo* n	dee-zel gaw-ree-vaw
leaded petrol	*olovni benzin* (m)	aw-lov-nee ben-zeen
unleaded petrol	*bezolovni benzin* (m)	be-zaw-lawv-nee ben-zeen

(How long) Can I park here?
(Koliko dugo) Mogu ovdje parkirati?
(ko·*lee*·kaw *doo*·go) *maw*·goo *awv*·dye par·*kee*·ra·tee
Where do I pay?
Gdje se plaća?
Gdye se *pla*·cha?
I need a mechanic.
Trebam automehaničara.
tre·bam *a*·oo·to·me·*ha*·nee·cha·ra
The car/motorbike has broken down (at ...)
Automobil/Motocikl se pokvario (u ...)
a·oo·to·*maw*·beel/mo·to·*tsee*·kl se pawk·*va*·ree·aw (oo ...)
The car/motorbike won't start.
Automobil/Motocikl neće upaliti.
a·oo·to·*maw*·beel/mo·to·*tsee*·kl *ne*·che oo·*pa*·lee·tee
I have a flat tyre.
Imam probušenu gumu.
ee·mam *praw*·boo·she·noo *goo*·moo
I've run out of petrol.
Nestalo mi je benzina.
ne·sta·law mee ye ben·*zee*·na
I've had an accident.
Imao/Imala sam prometnu nezgodu. (m/f)
ee·ma·aw/ee·*ma*·la sam *praw*·met·noo *nez*·gaw·doo

TRAVEL WITH CHILDREN
Do you mind if I breast-feed here?
Da li vam smeta ako ovdje dojim?
da lee vam *sme*·ta *a*·kaw *awv*·dye *doy*·eem
Are children allowed?
Da li je dozvoljen pristup djeci?
da lee ye *dawz*·vaw·lyen *pree*·stoop *dye*·tsee?

formula	*formula*	*for*·moo·la
highchair	*visoka stolica*	vee·saw·ka *staw*·lee·tsa
	za bebe (sg)	za *be*·be
potty	*tuta* (sg)	*too*·ta
pusher/stroller	*dječja*	*dyech*·ya
	hodalica (sg)	*haw*·da·lee·tsa

Is there a/an ...?
Imate li ...?
ee·ma·te lee ...
I need a ...
Treba/Trebaju mi ... (sg/pl)
tre·ba mee/tre·bai·oo mee ...
  baby change room
  sobu za previjanjebeba
  saw·boo za pre·*vee*·ya·nye *be*·ba
  car baby seat
  sjedalo za dijete (sg)
  sye·da·law za dee·*ye*·te
  child-minding service
  usluge čuvanja djece
  oo·sloo·ge *choo*·va·nya *dye*·tse
  children's menu
  dječji jelovnik
  dyech·yee ye·*lawv*·neek
  (disposable) nappies/diapers
  pelene (za jednokratnu upotrebu)
  pe·le·ne (za yed·*naw*·krat·noo oo·paw·tre·boo)
  (English-speaking) babysitter
  dadilja (koja govori engleski) (sg)
  da·dee·lya (koy·a *gaw*·vaw·ree *en*·gle·skee)

Croatian

Also available from Lonely Planet:
Croatian Phrasebook

Glossary

For food and drink terms, see Eat Your Words on p44.

ACI Club – Adriatic Croatia International Club, an association of Croatian marinas
amphora (s), **amphorae** (pl) – large, two-handled vase in which wine or water is kept
apse – altar area of a church
autobusni kolodvor – bus station
Avars – Eastern European people that waged war against Byzantium from the 6th to 9th centuries

balkon – balcony
ban – viceroy or governor
basilica – early Christian church
benzin – petrol
bermet – liquor
bife – snack bar
breks – Istrian truffle-hunting dogs
brijeg – hill
britva – razor
brod – boat
brzi – fast train, also *ubrazni*
bura – cold northeasterly wind

cesta – road
ciborium – permanent arched canopy over an altar
cijena – price
citura – zither
crkva – church

dnevna karta – day ticket
dolazak – arrivals
dom – dormitory, mountain cottage or lodge
doručak – breakfast
drmeš – accelerated polka danced by couples in small groups
dubrava – holm-oak

fortica – fortress
fumaioli – exterior chimneys

galerija – gallery
garderoba – left-luggage office
Glagolitic – ancient Slavonic language put into writing by Greek missionaries Cyril and Methodius
gora – mountain
gostionica – family-run restaurant, sometimes with a few rooms to rent
grad – city

HAK – Croatian Automobile Association

HDZ – Hrvatska Demokratska Zajednica, the former ruling party
HPT – Croatian post and telecommunications system
hrid – rock

Illyrians – ancient inhabitants of the Adriatic coast, defeated by the Romans in the 2nd century BC
impulsa – units (phonecards)
izlaz – exit

jezero – lake
juga – southern wind
Jugoslavenstvo – south-Slavic unity

Kajkavski – local dialect of the Hrvatsko-Zagorje region named after their word for 'what?' *(kaj?)*
karst – porous limestone marked by underground rivers, gorges and caves
karta – ticket
kasa – cash register
kava – coffee
kavana – café
kazalište – theatre
kino – cinema
Klapa – an outgrowth of church-choir singing
kniza – books
knjižara – bookshop
kolo – Slavic circle dance often accompanied by a *tamburitza*
kolodvor – train station
konoba – traditional term for a small, intimate dining spot, often located in a cellar, now applies to a wide variety of restaurants
körperkultu movement – German physical culture
krajina – frontier
krijes – bonfires

ljekarna – pharmacy
lože – lodge
luka – harbour, port

macchia – shrubs
maestral – strong, steady westerly wind
malo – little
maquis – a dense growth of mostly evergreen shrubs and small trees
mišnice – a sort of bagpipe
mjenjačnica – exchange office
morčići – traditional symbol of the city of Rijeka. The image of a black person topped with a colourful turban is made into ceramic brooches and earrings.

moretto – historical term for *morčići*
most – bridge
muški – men (toilet)
muzej – museum

nave – central part of a church flanked by two aisles
NDH – Independent State of Croatia
ne vozi nedjeljom i blagdanom – no service Sunday and holidays

obala – waterfront
odlazak – departures, also *polazak*
opatija – abbey
otok (s), **otoci** (pl) – island
otvoreno – open

parket – orchestra
Partisans – WWII antifascist liberation organisation lead by Maršal Tito
Paška Robinja – traditional folk play, literally 'The Slave Girl of Pag'
pećina – cave
pismo – stamps
pivnica – pub, beer hall
plaža – beach
pleter – plaited ornamentation often found in churches
plovidba – navigation
polazak – see *odlazak*
polje – collapsed limestone area often under cultivation
poltrone – reclining seats
poreski ček – required form
posestre – half-sisters
poskočica – dance featuring couples creating various patterns
poslovni – express train
potok – stream
presjedanje – change of trains
put – path, trail
putnički – local train

restoran/restauracija – restaurant
rezerviranje mjesta obvezatno – compulsory seat reservation

rat – cape, promontory
rijeka – river
ris – lynx
ručak – lunch

Sabor – Parliament
samoposluzivanje – self-service restaurant
Šetalište – walkway
široko – southeasterly wind bringing warm, moist air
sobe – rooms available
stanica – stop (bus or tram)
svako-dnevno – daily
sveti/svetog – saint

tamburitza – a three- or five-string mandolin, also *tamburica*
tisak – newsstand
toplice – spa
trajekt – ferry
travertine – tufa
trg – square
Turbofolk – version of Serbian music
turistički ured – tourist office
turistički zajednica – tourist association

ulaz – entrance
ulica – street
uskoks – a community of pirates in Senj in the 16th century
uvala – bay

večera – dinner
velik – large
vlak – train
vozni red – timetable
vrh – summit, peak

zatvoreno – closed
ZET – Zagreb tram system
zemlja – soil
ženski – women (toilet)
zimmer – rooms available
zvijezda – star

Behind the Scenes

THIS BOOK

Jeanne Oliver has written all three editions of Lonely Planet's *Croatia*.

The Health chapter was adapted from material written by Dr Caroline Evans.

THANKS FROM THE AUTHOR

Innumerable people in Croatia went out of their way to make my stay enjoyable and my work smoother. Among them were Andrea Petrov of the National Tourist Board, Mark van Bloeman and the Begovićs in Dubrovnik, Tomislav Vukusić in Opatija, Stanka Kraljević and Aljoša Milat in Korčula and Radenko Sloković in Pazin. At home, I'd like to thank David and Ginna Zoellner for looking after Raymond, and John and Cédric Enée for their love and support during the course of this project.

CREDITS

This title was commissioned by Imogen Franks and Fiona Christie. Cartography for this guide was developed by Mark Griffiths.

Coordinating the production for Lonely Planet were Jack Garvan (cartography), Tamsin Wilson (cover design), Quentin Frayne (language) and Andrew Weatherill (project management), with cartography assistance from Kelly Stanhope, Adrian Persoglia, Jacqueline Ngugen and Wayne Murphy.

Coordinating the production for Palmer Higgs Pty Ltd were Celia Purdey (editorial), Sandra Goodes (layout design), Andrew Seymour (layout design and photo researcher), Selina Brendish (project management) and John Simkin (indexer),

with assistance from Danielle De Maio (editorial), Tony Davidson (editorial), Jane Fitzpatrick (editorial) and Simon Longstaff (editorial production support).

THANKS FROM LONELY PLANET

Many thanks to the travellers who used the last edition and wrote to us with helpful hints, useful advice and interesting anecdotes:

A K Arlen, Elizabeth Ashford **B** Arnold Bake, Miriam Baxter, Biljana Bedzovska, Ralph Bennett, Daniel M Berry, Mijke Bolsius, Jesper Borglund, Graeme Brock, Janelle Burrows **C** Bridget Calzaretta, Roy Camp, Jacqueline Catherall, Luke Cavanagh, Jemetha Clark, Laura Coates, Robert Cosgrove, Jim Crawford, Ivan Crozier **D** Matthew D'Arcy, Michel De Bona, Katrijn De Ronde, Josie Dean, Angela Diggle, Geri D'Souza **E** Nigel Eacock, Hans Elander, Sylvia Emory **F** Rob Ferrara, Robert Foster **G** Srecko Gnjidic, Katja Goertz, Marinko Golik, Jack Gore, Meahan Grande, Mariana Grubelic, Martin Guerin **H** Paul Hagman, Chloe Harding, Claire Harding, Maximillian Hartmuth, Neal Hattersley, Terje Hensrud, Julie Hirschler, Hagay Hochman, Filip Horvat, Tineke Houthuyzen, Denis Hughes, Jackie Hughes, Marc Hutchinson **J** Judy Jennings, Nels Johnson **K** Minte Kamphuis, Janet Kehelly, Ciaran Kissane, Mark Koltun, Bronwen Koolik, Ben Kurrein **L** Emily Lake, Charlotte Ledoux, David Lessnau, Jacky Levy, John Lines, Deby Linsell-Fraser, Christian Loepfe, Chris Louie, Barb Lyle **M** Damir Madunic, Jelena Marelj, Kristina Maskarin, Martin Mayer, Shawn McKee, Jody McMiles, Brian Michaels, Alan Millward, Mark Mocicka, Maura Moralic, Jamie Morrison, Elaine Muir, Robert Mumford **N** Nadja Nickol **O** Franziska Ohnsorge **P** Steve Paul, AJ Peile, Noa Perez, Stjepan Perkovic, Magnus Perlestam, Pavla Peterova, Alan Petschack, Mirjana Plazonic, Michael & John Patrick Plunkett, Jared Pruch, Kathy Prunty, Borko Pusic **R** Doug

THE LONELY PLANET STORY

The story begins with a classic travel adventure: Tony and Maureen Wheeler's 1972 journey across Europe and Asia to Australia. There was no useful information about the overland trail then, so Tony and Maureen published the first Lonely Planet guidebook to meet a growing need.

From a kitchen table, Lonely Planet has grown to become the largest independent travel publisher in the world, with offices in Melbourne (Australia), Oakland (USA) and London (UK).

Today Lonely Planet guidebooks cover the globe. There is an ever-growing list of books and information in a variety of media. Some things haven't changed. The main aim is still to make it possible for adventurous travellers to get out there – to explore and better understand the world.

At Lonely Planet we believe travellers can make a positive contribution to the countries they visit – if they respect their host communities and spend their money wisely.

Rand, Paul Rebich, Ronald Reinds, Tamsen Resor, Louise Robert, Roger Rooney, Tim Rooth **S** Marie-Zelie Sainz, CT Sartain, Liisa Satukangas, Matthias Schmidt, Christa Schroder, Larry Schwarz, Said Shafa, Jelena Smoljan, Paul Spaas, Branimir Sprajcer, Martin Stanley, Ruth Stanley, Richard Szmola **T** Greer Taylor, Paul Tiebosch, Alessio Tixi, Mrs A Turnbull **V** Rob Van Mierlo, Niel Van Staden, Tineke Vaningelgem, Rik Verdellen, Nele Verhaeghe, Agnès Visser-de Matteïs, Jeff Vize **W** Peter Waitt, Katy Wall, E-J Walsh, Peter Weller, Jonathan Wheatley, Monica Widman Elander, Alan Williams, Lise Winters, Alec Wohlgroth, Keith Wood **Z** Saskia Zegelaar, Aco Zrnic

SEND US YOUR FEEDBACK

We love to hear from travellers – your comments keep us on our toes and help make our books better. Our well-travelled team reads every word on what you loved or loathed about this book. Although we cannot reply individually to postal submissions, we always guarantee that your feedback goes straight to the appropriate authors, in time for the next edition. Each person who sends us information is thanked in the next edition – and the most useful submissions are rewarded with a free book.

To send us your updates – and find out about LP events, newsletters and travel news – visit our award-winning website: **www.lonelyplanet.com**.

Note: We may edit, reproduce and incorporate your comments in Lonely Planet products such as guidebooks, websites and digital products, so let us know if you don't want your comments reproduced or your name acknowledged. For a copy of our privacy policy visit www.lonelyplanet.com/privacy.

Index

INDEX

INDEX

INDEX

MAP LEGEND

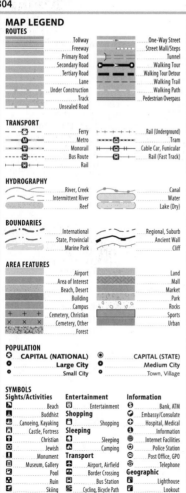

ROUTES

Tollway	One-Way Street
Freeway	Street Mall/Steps
Primary Road	Tunnel
Secondary Road	Walking Tour
Tertiary Road	Walking Tour Detour
Lane	Walking Trail
Under Construction	Walking Path
Track	Pedestrian Overpass
Unsealed Road	

TRANSPORT

Ferry	Rail (Underground)
Metro	Tram
Monorail	Cable Car, Funicular
Bus Route	Rail (Fast Track)
Rail	

HYDROGRAPHY

River, Creek	Canal
Intermittent River	Water
Reef	Lake (Dry)

BOUNDARIES

International	Regional, Suburb
State, Provincial	Ancient Wall
Marine Park	Cliff

AREA FEATURES

Airport	Land
Area of Interest	Mall
Beach, Desert	Market
Building	Park
Campus	Rocks
Cemetery, Christian	Sports
Cemetery, Other	Urban
Forest	

POPULATION

⊛ **CAPITAL (NATIONAL)**	◉ CAPITAL (STATE)
● **Large City**	◉ Medium City
● Small City	○ Town, Village

SYMBOLS

Sights/Activities	Entertainment	Information
Beach	Entertainment	Bank, ATM
Buddhist	**Shopping**	Embassy/Consulate
Canoeing, Kayaking	Shopping	Hospital, Medical
Castle, Fortress	**Sleeping**	Information
Christian	Sleeping	Internet Facilities
Jewish	Camping	Police Station
Monument	**Transport**	Post Office, GPO
Museum, Gallery	Airport, Airfield	Telephone
Pool	Border Crossing	**Geographic**
Ruin	Bus Station	Lighthouse
Skiing	Cycling, Bicycle Path	Lookout
Zoo, Bird Sanctuary	General Transport	Mountain
Eating	Taxi Rank	National Park
Eating	**Other**	Pass, Canyon
Drinking	Other Site	River Flow
Drinking	Parking Area	Shelter, Hut
Café	Toilets	Waterfall

LONELY PLANET OFFICES

Australia
Head Office
Locked Bag 1, Footscray, Victoria 3011
☎ 03 8379 8000, fax 03 8379 8111
talk2us@lonelyplanet.com.au

USA
150 Linden St, Oakland, CA 94607
☎ 510 893 8555, toll free 800 275 8555
fax 510 893 8572, info@lonelyplanet.com

UK
72–82 Rosebery Ave,
Clerkenwell, London EC1R 4RW
☎ 020 7841 9000, fax 020 7841 9001
go@lonelyplanet.co.uk

Published by Lonely Planet Publications Pty Ltd
ABN 36 005 607 983

© Lonely Planet 2005

© photographers as indicated 2005

Cover photographs: Primošten Croatia, Sime/eStock Photo (front);
Stair rail in Vela Luka old town, Wayne Walton/Lonely Planet Images
(back). Many of the images in this guide are available for licensing
from Lonely Planet Images: www.lonelyplanetimages.com.

Printed through Colourcraft Ltd, Hong Kong
Printed in China